Saint-Simon

Make way for the King!

Saint-Simon

THE MEMOIRS

OF LOUIS DE ROUVROY
DUC DE SAINT-SIMON
COVERING THE YEARS
1691-1723

SELECTED TRANSLATED & EDITED BY
DESMOND FLOWER

THE HERITAGE PRESS

NEW YORK

ACKNOWLEDGEMENT

More than twenty years ago, Mr. Ralph Wright was commissioned to translate and edit a text for a new edition of the *Memoirs of Saint-Simon*. Because of the war, work on the book was abandoned. Mr. Wright had, however, already completed the translation of a substantial fragment, largely centred round the *lit de justice,* and I have been able to use this as the basis of the version which I offer here. I would like to acknowledge the work which Mr. Wright did so long ago; but I must add that all failings and shortcomings in the whole of the version here presented are entirely mine.   D. F.

TABLE OF CONTENTS

THE ILLUSTRATIONS
by Pierre Brissaud

THE INTRODUCTION
by Desmond Flower

LOUIS DE ROUVROY DUC DE SAINT-SIMON was born during the night of the 15–16 January, 1675, the only child of Charlotte de l'Aubespine, the second wife of Claude Rouvroy, first Duc de Saint-Simon.

Saint-Simon's mother considered that her husband, already sixty-nine years of age, was unlikely to live long enough to exert any suitable paternal influence over her son, so she made herself responsible for his upbringing and instilled in him a strict sense of values to arm him against the temptations of glittering court life. But in fact the old Duke lived for a further eighteen years and had a very marked effect upon his son's life and conduct. In early life the first Duke had been a favourite of Louis XIII, at first a page and then successively Master of the Wolfhounds, First Gentleman of the Bedchamber, First Equerry and Governor of Blaye—an important post, since this fortified town on the Gironde was a key position in the defences of Bordeaux. He was created a Duke and Peer in 1635; two years later Richelieu drove him from the court. Claude Rouvroy believed that Louis XIII was the greatest King whom God had ever been pleased to place upon the throne of France. 'My father never got over the death of Louis XIII,' Saint-Simon wrote, 'and never spoke of him without tears in his eyes; he never failed to go to Saint-Denis on 14 May, the anniversary of the King's death, and if he found himself at Blaye he had a solemn mass said.' Next, the old gentleman believed that to be a Duke and a Peer of France was the greatest piece of good fortune which a man could enjoy. He was intensely proud of his lineage, which he traced back to Charlemagne. Further, he never forgot the injustices of which he considered himself to have been the victim, and he never forgave Anne of Austria, who he thought had deprived him of the chance to be Master of the Horse, or her ministers Chavigny and Mazarin. All these views he firmly implanted in his son. Saint-Simon in consequence never liked Louis XIV, but all his life wore on his finger a miniature of Louis XIII set in diamonds; he was always jealous of the standing and privileges of the Peerage, and he was touchy and resentful of any slight, real or imaginary.

For his mother Saint-Simon always retained a deep respect. Even when he was fifty and a member of the Regency Council he bowed to her will when she wanted her granddaughter to marry the Prince de

Chimay; he and his wife were against the match but, he said, 'My mother wishes it and she is accustomed to make decisions.'

Saint-Simon's life falls into four parts. The first is his youth until his presentation at court in 1691; during these years he was absorbing his father's ideas and even his language, as the memoirs show. During the second period, which ended with the death of Louis XIV in 1715, he was a typical courtier, except that instead of wasting his time in complete idleness he watched and observed everything which went on around him. From 1715 until the death of the Regent in 1723 he was one of the most prominent figures in French and European politics; this was the most important period of his life. After 1723 he retired to his estates and devoted himself to writing his memoirs, which he finished in 1751. He died at his country house, La Ferté, in 1755.

Saint-Simon was presented to Louis XIV by his father in 1691. The King was then fifty-three years old and his reign had already passed the peak of its glory. He had succeeded to the throne at the age of five under the regency of his mother, Anne of Austria, who, dominated by Mazarin, grossly neglected him. The civil wars of the Fronde made him the poverty-stricken victim of the warring nobles and a wanderer in his own realm—a hard experience which he never forgot. When Mazarin died in 1661 Louis uttered his famous dictum, 'L'État, c'est moi,' and decided not only to rule alone, but to reduce the nobility to such dependence upon him that they never again could cause any civil disturbance. The construction of the vast château of Versailles served not only to indulge the love of luxury for which he had been so starved as a child, but provided a whole world of its own at which the constant attendance of the nobility was demanded so that the King could keep an eye on them.

With Colbert as Controller General and Louvois as Secretary of State for War, the affairs of France were put in such good order that Louis could afford to embark upon the wars which brought such glory to France and to himself. 'The character of a conqueror,' he wrote, 'is regarded as the noblest and highest of titles.' He reached the height of his power with the treaties of Nijmegen, 1678–9, which consolidated his conquests and added the Franche-Comté to his realm, and with the capture of Luxembourg in 1684. His first mistake was made the following year, when he revoked the Edict of Nantes and drove out of the country between two and three hundred thousand Huguenot business men, technicians, soldiers, and sailors whom France was soon to need badly. When James II lost the throne of England in 1688, Louis espoused his cause and found himself involved in another war which only ended in 1697 with the peace of Ryswick, leaving France

xiv

intact but exhausted. To his chagrin, Louis was forced to acknowledge William of Orange as King of England.

When Saint-Simon came to court, then, he was presented to a King in the full vigour of middle age, proud and over-sure of himself—but as gracious and polite as ever. Although he disliked his King personally, Saint-Simon never denied that Louis was the most regal person imaginable and upheld his mighty office with the greatest possible dignity.'There was no one to compare with him,' Saint-Simon wrote, 'at reviews, fêtes, and every occasion at which the presence of ladies gave a tone of gallantry, a gallantry always majestic. Sometimes there was gaiety, but never untimely or indiscreet. His slightest gesture, his bearing, his countenance, all were measured, noble, and majestic but quite natural. One had to get used to him to overcome one's embarrassment when speaking to him. His replies were always brief and to the point, but rarely without some pleasant or even flattering remark fitting the occasion. His presence imposed silence and even fear upon everyone.' In his personal life, too, the King was quietening down. Long since gone were the sweet and lovely Louise de la Vallière, the brilliant and rapacious Montespan. Instead the court had become respectable under the influence of the quiet, pious, and wise Madame de Maintenon, and Louis, who had married her secretly in 1685, spent his evenings in her apartments discussing affairs of state with his ministers, while the courtiers tried to amuse themselves with gossip and cards in the long succession of public rooms centered round the Galerie des Glaces. Saint-Simon was never one to disguise or moderate his likes or dislikes, and his portrait of Madame de Maintenon is one of the most biased in the memoirs; he frankly loathed her, rejoiced in any discomfort she suffered, and was totally blind to her merits. She for her part treated him with frigid dignity.

The young Saint-Simon was enrolled by the King's command in the Grey Musketeers, and for the next few years his life was no different from that of any man of birth and breeding of his time and of his years. He fought with the army in the summer and spent the winter at Versailles. He says that he badgered his father into presenting him so that he might bear arms, since the great friend of his youth, the Duc de Chartres, had already seen action. This friendship was of immense importance in Saint-Simon's life, for the Duc de Chartres succeeded his father as Duc d'Orléans and on the death of Louis XIV became Regent. The close relations of these two men later account for Saint-Simon's sudden rise to political prominence—which helped to assuage the deep resentment he felt because Louis XIV never gave him any employment.

Saint-Simon was in action for the first time at the siege of Namur in 1692; in the following year the King permitted him to buy a company in the Royal Roussillon Regiment, and Saint-Simon commanded this company at the battle of Nerwinden, where the Maréchal de Luxembourg defeated the Dutch. Back at court that winter, the youthful officer bought a cavalry regiment, but what was more important in his own life was the fact that he got mixed up in his first quarrel over precedence and standing. There was an action between the Dukes and Peers and the Maréchal de Luxembourg, which the latter won. When spring came it was for this reason undesirable that Saint-Simon should rejoin the army of Flanders under Luxembourg, and he was sent instead with his regiment to the army of the Duc de Lorges on the Rhine. There, in 1694, at the age of nineteen, and at a place he calls Guinsheim (which was probably Kingersheim), he began to write his memoirs. He had always been interested in history, he said, and decided to compile a description of his own age which he hoped might be comparable with the memoirs of the ancients which he had so much enjoyed. The following year he married the elder daughter of his commander-in-chief. The Lorges were not an old family, and the alliance called forth some derision from the snobs, but in fact the marriage was an unusually happy one. His wife proved to be a woman of great common sense who supported him nobly and who extricated him from many scrapes into which his impetuosity and bias were to lead him.

At the turn of the century there was a new political crisis. In March, France signed a treaty with England and Holland in London. In one clause of this treaty the French renounced any claim to the throne of Spain. In October of the same year Charles II of Spain died, naming as his sole heir Louis's second grandson the Duc d'Anjou providing that the two thrones were never united. The combination of these two powerful countries under one monarch was a threat to Europe, for the claims of the Bourbons were well founded. Louis XIV himself was half Spanish, for his mother, despite her name of Anne of Austria, was the daughter of Philip IV. Louis after some hesitation accepted the proviso, and the Duc d'Anjou was generally recognized as Philip V. During the next few months, however, Louis changed his mind; he guaranteed the eventual right of Philip V to the throne of France; he suddenly occupied various fortified towns on the Dutch border; and when James II of England died at Saint-Germain Louis alienated William III by recognizing the Old Pretender as James III, rightful King of England. By September 1701 he found arrayed against him the Alliance of the Hague, comprising England, Holland, most of the German princes,

and the Emperor; the War of the Spanish Succession had begun;
France was fighting to all intents the rest of Europe.

To begin with, things went well; the Maréchal de Villars beat the
Germans at Friedlingen in 1702 and again at Hochstädt in 1703. Saint-
Simon was to take no part in this war, for he resigned his commission
in 1702. A list of promotions to general rank was published, and as his
name was not included he wrote to the King asking permission to leave
the service on the grounds of ill health. The King, he reports, was
highly annoyed and for a long time did not speak to him or take any
notice of him.

In 1704 the tide turned once and for all against France: Marlborough
and Prince Eugène won the battle of Blenheim. In 1706 the Maréchal
de Villeroy was crushed at Ramillies by Marlborough, losing the
Netherlands, while the Duc de la Feuillade was chased out of Piedmont by Prince Eugène. Two years later the Duc de Bourgogne, ig-
noring the advice of the great Duc de Vendôme, was defeated at
Oudenarde. The allied troops entered France. Conditions at home deteriorated with increasing rapidity. When famine spread through the
land in 1709, Louis swallowed his pride and asked for peace, but the
terms laid down were so stiff that he broke off negotiations. The
French army and people responded magnificently to their King's call
for one more effort; the Maréchal de Villars fought Marlborough and
Eugène to a standstill at Malplaquet, inflicting 23,000 casualties, and
the Duc de Vendôme won a resounding victory in Spain. But Prince
Eugène, working his way forward on the northern flank, prepared
to march on Paris, and only a brilliant coup by Villars, who in
1712 surprised the Austrians at Denain, succeeded in creating the favourable atmosphere for negotiations which the King so desperately
needed.

The war was ended by two treaties, the first signed at Utrecht in
1713 and the other at Rastadt in 1714. Philip V kept his throne but
renounced all claims to France. England kept Gibraltar, Newfound-
land, and the lands marching with the mouth of the St. Lawrence river.
France gained nothing, barely saved her face, and was so exhausted
physically, financially, and morally that her whole future was precarious. The King, for long separated from his people by his own pomp
and vainglory, finally lost their sympathy. When he died the following
year at the age of seventy-seven there were few who mourned him.
His great gifts, his past glory were forgotten; only the ashes of his
reign remained for all to see.

During these increasingly unhappy years Saint-Simon lived at Versailles. For some time after he had resigned his commission he lived

xvii

in the apartment of his brother-in-law the Duc de Lorges, who had inherited it from his father the Marshal and was able to let Saint-Simon have it because he himself lodged with his father-in-law Chamillart, Controller General and Secretary of State for War. Since the presence of every noble was required constantly by the King, there was great competition to get a room or rooms in the Château, because otherwise it meant a wearisome drive in the small hours to one's home or lodging where one would arrive more or less in time to turn round and go back for the King's *lever*.

When Chamillart was dismissed in 1709, the Duc de Lorges moved back into his own apartment and Saint-Simon was in difficulties; he was saved by Pontchartrain, the Chancellor, who offered him one room in his own apartment. It was not until his wife was appointed a Lady-in-Waiting to the Duchesse de Berry in 1710 that they became entitled to an apartment of their own. Once they had moved in, they remained there until the death of Louis XIV and were seldom away from Versailles for anything more than visits to friends and courtesy calls on the few members of the royal family who had their own homes. Once Saint-Simon went to Rouen to sue the Duc de Brissac; after ten days he received a letter from Pontchartrain saying that the King had noticed his absence and wanted to know why and for how long he would be away.

During these years Saint-Simon saw everything and watched the court deteriorate into a sad, quiet place of constant mourning. There is a wonderful vignette of the courtiers crowding to the windows at night when they heard the clatter of a despatch rider arriving in the court below, their faces pressed to the glass like children, their chatter stilled in fear that the news would be as bad as ever. He meticulously described the long religious quarrels which resulted from the King's resumption of faith under Madame de Maintenon: Louis could do nothing by halves, and he tried by force to press into the orthodox mould every heretic or variant—Huguenot, Jansenist or Quietist—and merely left a simmering stew of unresolved problems for his successors. Saint-Simon saw, too, the death of almost all the royal relations and those whom the King knew so well and was accustomed to see around him. The most crushing blows fell within twelve months from Easter 1711 to the early spring of 1712. First the King's son died of smallpox, in turn his son—the hope of France—became Dauphin but died with his wife in the following February. Then early in March Louis's two little grandchildren also became desperately ill; the elder, aged five, died, while the younger—the little Duc d'Anjou who was not yet weaned—survived and became the new Dauphin. So Louis had only Madame de

Maintenon remaining near to him, and a tiny child as his heir whom on
his death-bed he embraced and warned against the pitfalls into which
he himself had fallen—too much building and too many wars. He left
800 million livres of debts, the revenue already absorbed, and a budget
deficit of 77 million. And he left a will.

Louis XV was five when he succeeded his great-grandfather; the
Duc d'Orléans was forty-one and Saint-Simon forty. The great question was who should conduct the affairs of France during the King's
minority. The death of the much respected Duc de Bourgogne in 1712
had left the Duc d'Orléans as the senior member of the family. This
horrified Louis XIV, for he had never really liked his nephew, whose
licentious habits revolted him in his later, more religious years. The
old King had steadily entrenched his own bastards; as early as 1694
he had placed the Duc du Maine and the Comte de Toulouse directly
after the Princes of the Blood in the order of precedence, and above
the Dukes and Peers—much to the everlasting fury of Saint-Simon.
In 1714 he further ordained that the children of the Duc du Maine
should enjoy the same honours as their father, and later the same year
declared that in default of a legitimate heir a child of the legitimized
bastards might inherit the throne. He also drew up a will in which he
expressed a wish that during his great-grandson's minority, power
should be exercised by a Council of fourteen which included the Duc
du Maine, Comte de Toulouse, Duc d'Orléans, and the Maréchaux
Villeroy and Villars. There was no mention of a Regent. The Duc du
Maine was to command the Household Troops and to have charge of
the young King's education with the Maréchal de Villeroy as tutor.

Three days after the old King's death, on 4 September 1715, the
Duc d'Orléans summoned a meeting of all three Chambers of the
Parlement of Paris to hear the reading of the will, which was followed
on 12 September by a *lit de justice*. Since these two political instruments play a particularly prominent part during the Regency, a word
must be said about them.

The *Parlement* had no relation to what we know today as a Parliament (for that reason I have kept the French word throughout) but
was in fact the supreme Court of Justice. An offshoot of earlier legal
machinery, it was established by Philippe le Bel in the late thirteenth
century. It had two functions, judicial and political. Its judicial work
was to hear appeals from lower courts. Its political duty was to register
the decisions of the King—in the turbulent Middle Ages this served to
place these decisions on record and to lend them added weight against
the opposition of warring barons. By tradition the *Parlement* also
claimed the privilege of tabling its remonstrance against any decision

xix

of the King which it considered contrary to the public interest. As legal business increased during the centuries the *Parlement* of Paris was divided into three Chambers: the *Chambre des Enquêtes,* dealing with appeals; the *Chambre des Requêtes,* dealing with points of law; and a third Chamber devoted entirely to criminal cases. In addition twelve provincial *Parlements* were instituted, but the political duties remained confined to the original Court in Paris.

During the civil wars of the Fronde the *Parlement* had come out on the side of the rebels, and in consequence Louis, as soon as he had the power, very quickly clipped their wings by vetoing their rights of remonstrance; he confined them to their judicial duties and had no more trouble with them.

But apart from the ruthless autocracy of Louis XIV there was a traditional method by which the King could override a remonstrance tabled by *Parlement*, which was the holding of a *lit de justice*. This was a solemn ritualistic session at which the King summoned the *Parlement* before him in the presence of all the Princes of the Blood, Peers temporal and spiritual, the Marshal of France, and all officers of the crown. It was called a *lit* because the King sat on a throne on a dais supported by five cushions—one for his head and one for each arm and leg. The ritual was traditional and if one minute detail was omitted or wrongly performed all the business transacted was automatically null and void. The earliest recorded *lits de justice* seem to have been merely judicial assemblies which the King honoured with his presence, but the first to assume importance was in 1369 when Charles I formally accused the Black Prince of felony. Thereafter they became occasions which by their solemnity and ritual could lend public gravity to the King's wishes on matters of prime importance, and thence developed into the proper form for overruling the intransigence of *Parlement* when it made too fertile a use of its remonstrance. The last stage, which we find in the Regency, was the use of the *lit de justice* as the setting for a *coup d'état*.

As a preliminary to the meeting on 4 September 1715 the Duc d'Orléans promised to restore to the *Parlement* the right of remonstrance which his uncle had removed nearly fifty years before, so that he could count on their support. The Bastards arrived at the meeting in high spirits, for they knew the contents of the old King's will; but to their intense chagrin the Duc d'Orléans was unanimously declared Regent before the will was even opened. To complete their discomfort, the Regent was given absolute power to select the Council, which was to have advisory powers only. All of this was confirmed at the *lit de justice* a week later, and the old King's will had been deliberately

set aside within less than a fortnight of his death. But the newly appointed Regent, either confident that he had done enough or lacking
the temerity to achieve more, left two things alone which were later to
cause him infinite trouble: the precedence of the Bastards was allowed
to stand, and the Duc du Maine was left with the Household Troops
and the King's education in his hands.

The new Regent was Saint-Simon's oldest and closest friend. They
were close in age and had been brought up together. For him always
Saint-Simon had felt the warmest personal allegiance, and through all
the vicissitudes and vicious accusations to which the Duc d'Orléans
had been subjected he gave him his strongest and most vocal support.
Of the Duke his own mother said that the fairies at his birth had each
given him a talent, but one who was not asked prophesied that he
would possess every talent except the ability to use them. He was
handsome, genial, generous, and intelligent. He was a brave soldier
and a good general when his uncle gave him a chance—which was
seldom, and indeed Louis's refusal to allow him any responsibility led
to the development of the other side of his nature. He could work
hard and ably when he chose, but lack of opportunity led to a dissolution of his character until, when power came to him, it was too late
for him to reform. In his private life he was a drunken womanizer with
a foul tongue, who preferred the most degraded and disgraceful company. He was impious and cynical, all morality and principles having
been carefully educated out of him by the evil genius who had been
his tutor, the Abbé Dubois. Mindful of the humiliations he had suffered at his uncle's hands in Versailles, which consequently he loathed,
he had long resided in the Palais Royal where his debauchery developed into one of the greatest scandals of French history. When he became Regent there can be no doubt that it suited him that the child
King should move to Paris so that he could continue his own way of
life in the Palais Royal, and for seven years Versailles was left empty.

One of the first people whom the Regent appointed to the Council
was Saint-Simon, who now entered upon the most important phase
of his career. He not only enjoyed the confidence of the Duc d'Orléans
but, although the junior by almost two years, had always given him
advice, whether asked for or not. During the years of the Regency he
lectured the Duke unceasingly, and, while some of the advice which
he gave sprang from his own prejudices, without question much of it
was extremely good.

One of the first moves to which he persuaded the Duke was the
setting up of seven councils to control the various departments of
state business, instead of all decisions being made by the King closeted

xxi

with the responsible minister; the Presidents of these Councils sat on the Regency Council. This was part of the design to take absolute power from the hands of the King and to increase the influence of the nobility, but it was not an improvement and was abolished in 1718.

Further problems which had to be faced were the growing power of the Duc du Maine, a weakling with an ambitious wife, the *Parlement,* and the financial chaos. After his first friendly relations, the Regent found that the *Parlement* became more and more difficult, demanding the right to veto legislation; an extremely insubordinate atmosphere quickly spread throughout the country. This was dealt with at a *lit de justice,* and the *Parlement* reduced once more to a purely judicial role. At the great *lit de justice* of 1718 also the Bastards were reduced to their proper rank, and the King's education was taken out of the hands of the Duc du Maine. This was Saint-Simon's finest hour, and he dwells upon it at tremendous length. Other contemporary accounts give a different version of what actually happened, but Saint-Simon's description is a fascinating story of a well-planned and executed coup. I have included a great deal of this description in my selection, indeed it preponderates over every other subject, not only because Saint-Simon was so prominent in it but because it gives such an insight into the way the minds of these people—the Regent and his immediate advisors— worked. The height of the crisis was the Cellamare conspiracy. Although Philip V of Spain had renounced the throne of France he thought that he should be Regent, and in this he was egged on by the Duchesse du Maine, who would do anything to revenge herself on those who had slighted her husband by tearing up the old King's will. Alberoni, the all-powerful minister in Madrid, conceived the idea of kidnapping the Regent and putting Philip V in his place; the French end of the conspiracy was the Duchesse du Maine and the go-between was Cellamare, the Spanish Ambassador in Paris. The Marquis d'Argenson, the able Lieutenant General of Police who had just been made Keeper of the Seals and later became Secretary of State, got to know of the affair without undue difficulty, gave Cellamare enough rope to hang himself, and then arrested his couriers with incriminating letters upon them. The outcome was the arrest of the Duc and Duchesse du Maine, who were banished separately to remote castles in the country, and the Regent had reasserted his authority.

In some ways the most extraordinary event of all during the Regency was the attempt—so nearly successful—to find a way out of the financial chaos. The Finance Council, over which the pusillanimous Duc de Noailles presided, attempted first to recover monies from the Government contractors and also consulted the Banks. The result of

their efforts was infinitesimal; the national income was declining
rapidly and industry was dying for lack of capital. At this point John
Law appeared upon the scene.

Law was the son of a wealthy Edinburgh goldsmith and he enjoyed
a tempestuous life. After racketing around London for some time, he
was condemned to death for duelling and, getting his sentence commuted with some difficulty, he escaped from prison and fled the
country. In 1700 he turned up again in Scotland and tried to persuade
the Parliament to adopt his financial system; failing, he went to France
and appeared as one of the most prodigious gamblers in Paris. His
play and his debts were so high that he was expelled by the police,
and then wandered round Europe trying to sell his theories to a
multitude of princes. A month after the death of Louis XIV he returned to Paris and gained the confidence of the Regent; he was
forty-four years of age at the time.

Law postulated that since industry needed capital, the State should
use its credit and provide the money. The basic principle of his system
was the issue of paper money by the State Bank which would enable
the wheels of industry and commerce to turn once more without recourse to costly loans at a high rate of interest. Since the Regent's
confidence in Law was not at first generally shared, he was only permitted to set up a private bank with the right to issue paper money,
but within two years things were going so well that his organization
was transformed into a State Bank and its notes became legal tender.
If matters had stayed there, Law would probably have pulled the
country out of its troubles and the whole history of France might well
have been different. But he had other ambitious schemes involving
the development and colonization of France's overseas territories. To
this end the Mississippi Company was formed and the new idea caught
the imagination of the people and the cupidity of those who saw a
quick way to fortune. Speculation in the Company's shares became a
craze: they mounted and mounted, with more and more paper being
issued to cover the enormous amount of money changing hands. The
spiral of inflation set in and one day, like the spectacular crash of 1929,
the pipe dream was over and for no specific reason the bubble burst.
The canny had made fortunes on the way up; suicide and ruin overwhelmed many on the way down. The sudden unloading of shares in
the Company took the Bank with it into ruin. That Law was an adventurer the facts of his life testify, that he was also a genius cannot be
gainsaid; all that he advocated is today current financial practice, and
his visions of colonization showed a statesman's foresight a hundred
years ahead of his time. The tragedy was that his theories were so new

that no one could think what action to take when the wind began to blow. Law fled to Venice, where he died in 1729.

There was one further matter in which the Regent encountered difficulties, and that was religion. He himself was a cynical disbeliever but he wished to do his best, which took the form of a moderate religious toleration when he first assumed office. However, when closer relations with the Vatican were necessary as a payment for the Abbé Dubois's Cardinal's hat, in 1717 he suddenly veered and advocated complete submission to the Papal claim to authority as expressed in the controversial bull *Unigenitus* from which stemmed the problem of the 'Constitution.' The Regent's defalcation—for so it was regarded by many—knocked one more prop away from the foundations upholding his authority.

The Regent's stock dropped steadily during the eight years he was in office. Partly there was a general sense of disappointment that the most enlightened prince living had been able to achieve so little after the disastrous autocracy of Louis XIV's later years; partly, it seems too much was expected. Perhaps the people, without being able to put their finger on it, knew that France was to be saved now or never— and saw their hopes fade before their eyes. But I must qualify that by one statement: it has often been said that the Regent's shortcomings made the revolution inevitable: this is untrue. The Regent had a chance to put the affairs of France in order: he tried hard and failed; others had many a chance after him and failed equally. The last person who had the power to save his country was Louis XV's minister Choiseul, and he too—for all his great ability—found the task beyond him, for reasons which lie outside the scope of this work.

Saint-Simon was never reluctant in offering his advice to the Regent, and showed without question his hurt feelings when his views were not adopted. It is hardly surprising that the Regent—a man of honour and conscience, hopelessly distracted by good and bad advice, befuddled by his own intemperate habits—should have come to resent the constant whisperings of this tight-lipped busybody. After the great *lit de justice* Saint-Simon became gradually estranged from his master, who preferred to go down hill his own way. If Saint-Simon had been a little less of a prig, if the Regent could have taken a little good advice, who knows what might have happened? And, too, if the Duke could have been strong enough to dismiss the Abbé Dubois, a debauched and evil-minded prelate, instead of promoting him to Prime Minister and actively campaigning for his hat—again who knows? The Regency is one of the critical periods when France hung in the balance. It was not the fault of the people that the scales tipped the wrong way:

xxiv

it was not even the fault of her rulers—they tried their best but they failed.

Saint-Simon had seen the writing on the wall as far back as the great *lit de justice* of 1718. He fought tooth and nail to prevent the Duc de Bourgogne from assuming the powers lately in the hands of the Duc du Maine because he could see endless trouble for the future. He was right—as, for all his tetchy, narrow views, he so often was. The Duc d'Orléans, no longer Regent but confirmed as Prime Minister, lost his popularity and drank himself into his grave at the age of forty-four. The King, of age and crowned, could summon no one to assume office as Prime Minister but the Duc de Bourbon, an incompetent descendant of the Grand Condé—a situation which Saint-Simon had foreseen and fought against when the Duc du Maine had been deprived of his position in charge of the King's education.

Saint-Simon was overwhelmed by the death of the Duc d'Orléans, and he had every right to be. It was the end of his political life. When the Duc de Bourbon took office as Prime Minister, Saint-Simon sat in his apartment awaiting a summons, but none came. He knew that he was out: France, which for all its shortcomings he deeply loved, would be driven on without his advice being offered to the helmsman. He did the only thing a discarded statesman can do in such circumstances: he retired to his estates and began the vast labour of setting his memoirs in order.

The task was finished four years before the end of his long life, and the result, which was published piece by piece over many years, constitutes the biggest memoirs ever written: in their complete form they comprise forty volumes.

Saint-Simon was a snob with a small mind fixed on matters many of which seem to us supremely unimportant; he was both prejudiced and belligerent. It is not at all surprising that Louis XIV, whose failings cannot deny or overshadow his greatness, should have declined to employ him. He was a bad enemy but a good friend. In spite of his shortcomings, he had a mind like a camera and the divine gift of catching on paper the essence of the incredible events of which he was the witness. His memoirs fall into two halves: his description of the years before he came to court, which is second-hand gossip of no importance, and his account of the events which he witnessed between 1691 and 1723—prejudiced, biased, sometimes inaccurate, often highly coloured in his own favour, but so vivid that one can hear, smell, and nearly touch the Sun King and his unfortunate successors. As Lytton Strachey wrote:

'A happy stroke of fortune placed him in the one position where he

XXV

Introduction
by
Desmond Flower could exercise to the full his extraordinary powers: never, before or since, has there been so much to observe; never, before or since, so miraculous an observer.'

No selection from these vast memoirs can be any more than a succession of fragments; and whatever one may offer, there is as much and more which would be equally exciting. What I have done is to present the great *lit de justice* of 1718 at length: not only because it was the one supreme occasion when Saint-Simon held the future of France in his hand, but because the backstairs discussions which culminated in this *coup d'état* present one of the most dramatic and clear-cut pictures of the way the minds of these statesmen—if they may be so called —worked in the early eighteenth century. This great event dominates the book. The rest can be no more than selections which illustrate the life of a court which revolved about the aging King and his brilliant but debauched nephew.

I must perhaps add one word about Saint-Simon's style. It is an extraordinary mixture of formality and slang. In what I have translated here the reader will sometimes find himself shocked by an expression which will seem quite out of keeping with its sober surroundings. But that is the way Saint-Simon wrote, and the sudden flashes of unexpected slang are in keeping with his extraordinary perception which will illumine at any moment, however unexpected, some description of ritual or etiquette.

I hope that this selection will give to those who read it a picture of France at the end of her greatest age. It is centred very much round Versailles because it was the avowed intention of the old King to make his vast new palace the centre of the universe. Whether he succeeded or not those who read these pages and feast their eyes upon the lovely illustrations of Monsieur Brissaud must judge for themselves. And whether they like Saint-Simon, or the monarch and Regent whom he served so well according to his lights, I hope that these pages will at least give them pleasure and make them feel that the ills and troubles from which we suffer today are not, after all, either so bad or so new as we would like to think.

DESMOND FLOWER

Tignals
  Headley
    Hampshire

1958

NOTES ON THE MOST IMPORTANT
PEOPLE FOUND IN THESE MEMOIRS

BEAUVILLIERS, Paul, Duc de Saint-Aignan, and Duc de. Died 1714. First intended for the Church, he gave up his benefices on the death of his elder brother and became chairman of the Finance Council 1685, Governor of Havre, Surveyor General of France, Governor of the Duc de Bourgogne 1689, the Duc d'Anjou 1690 and the Duc de Berry 1693. Minister of State 1691. He was sagacious, far-sighted, and utterly upright, one of the few really fine characters of his age. He and Saint-Simon were close friends, and he was also devoted to Fénelon, the Archbishop of Cambrai and famous author. His family name is found spelled both with and without a final *s*.

BERRY, Duc et Duchesse de. The Duke was the third son of Louis, the Grand Dauphin, and his wife Marie-Christine de Bavière; born 31 August 1686, died following a fall from a horse at Marly 4 May 1714. He married in 1710 Marie-Louise-Elizabeth d'Orléans, elder daughter of the Duc d'Orléans. She was born 20 August 1695 and died 21 July 1719. Within a matter of days after her marriage she took a lover from among her staff, and this was typical of her life. The premature death of her husband and her father's office as Regent placed her in a privileged position of which she took the fullest advantage. Her debauchery, her irreligion and filthy language caused a major scandal even in an age of low morals. There seems little doubt that she was her father's mistress, and among her disagreeable habits was that of drinking herself into such a state of intoxication that she vomited over her guests. She died after a long and painful illness which it must be said she endured with great fortitude.

CHAMILLART, Michel de (1651–1721). Intendant of Normandy, Maître des Requêtes, Intendant of Finance 1690, Comptroller General 1699, Minister of State 1700, Secretary of State for War 1701, Grand Treasurer of the Orders 1706. He reached his high position through the favour of Madame de Maintenon,

but he had little ability beyond an infinite devotion to his work. Louis XIV was very fond of him and finally relieved him of his offices with great reluctance when the affairs of the country were in a critical state.

CHARTRES, Duc de. Title of the eldest sons of the Ducs d'Orléans. At the beginning of these memoirs the Duc de Chartres was Philippe, later to be Regent and Saint-Simon's close friend; he succeeded his father, the younger son of Louis XIII and Anne of Austria, as Duc d'Orléans in 1701. His son in turn was born at Versailles on 4 August 1703 and died at Paris on 4 February 1752. He was an upright and studious man and would have nothing to do with Saint-Simon, who consequently writes of him almost with contempt. On the death of his wife in 1742 he was attacked by melancholia and retired to a religious foundation to study theology.

DUBOIS, Guillaume, Abbé and later Cardinal. Born at Brives-la-Gaillarde (Corrèze) 6 September 1656, died at Versailles 10 August 1723. When he first came to Paris he was preceptor in various religious houses until he was chosen to become tutor to the young Duc de Chartres; instead of developing the great talents of his charge he introduced him to debauchery and religious cynicism. For his part in promoting the marriage of the Duke with Mlle de Blois he was awarded the Abbey of Saint-Just. His charge, now Duc d'Orléans, on assuming the Regency appointed him to the Council of State and he became Secretary of State for Foreign Affairs, in which capacity he negotiated the Triple Alliance of France, England, and Holland against Spain in 1717. In spite of his notorious way of life he was appointed Archbishop of Cambrai, which necessitated his taking all the various holy orders in one day. He then spent an immense amount of time and trouble to get his hat, which was granted to him by Innocent XIII in July 1721. Appointed Prime Minister on 23 August 1722, he died a year later. His utter lack of principles or morals made him generally reviled, but for all his lack of scruples he had a sharp and cunning mind.

LA VALLIÈRE, Françoise-Louise de la Baume-le-Blanc, Duchesse de. The first mistress of the King, she does not come into the part of the Memoirs with which this book is concerned, but must be mentioned because of her children. She was the daughter of an army officer, and was born at Tours on 6 August 1644. She became Maid of Honour to Henrietta of England, the wife of Philippe d'Orléans, Louis XIV's brother. When Louis and Henrietta fell in love it was decided that, to avoid a scandal, the young King ought to take a mistress; and the lovely and innocent Maid of Honour was selected. The result, unexpectedly, was a passionate love affair. She was succeeded by Mme de Montespan and finally left the Court in 1674, entered the Carmelite house in the Faubourg Saint-Jacques, Paris, and the following year took her vows under the name of Sister Louise. She died there on 6 June 1710.

LOUIS XIV. King of France and Navarre. Son of Louis XIII and Anne of Austria; born at Saint-Germain-en-Laye on 5 October 1639, died at Versailles 1 September 1715. His reign was the longest in the French monarchy, as he succeeded to the throne on his father's death on 14 May 1643. In 1660 he married the Infanta Marie-Thérèse of Spain, by whom he had two sons and three daughters: 1. Louis, called Monseigneur or the Grand Dauphin, b. 1 November 1661, d. 14 April 1711; 2. Philippe, Duc d'Anjou, b. 2 August 1668, d. 18 July 1671; 3. Anne-Elizabeth, b. 18 November 1662, d. 30 December same year; 4. Marie-Anne, b. 16 November 1664, d. 26 December same year; 5. Marie-Thérèse, b. 2 July 1667, d. 1 March 1672. His illegitimate children were numerous. By Louise, Duchesse de la Vallière: 1. Louis de Bourbon, Comte de Vermandois, Admiral of France, b. 2 October 1667, d. 18 November 1683; 2. Marie-Anne de Bourbon, called Mlle de Blois, b. 2 October 1666, married 16 January 1680 to the Prince de Condé, d. 3 May 1739. By Athénaïs, Marquise de Montespan: 1. Louis-Auguste de Bourbon, Duc du Maine, b. 31 March 1670, d. 14 May 1736; 2. Louis-César de Bourbon, Comte de Vexin, b. 20 June 1672, d. 10 January 1683; 3. Louise-Françoise de Bourbon, called Mlle de Nantes, b. 1673, married 1685 to Louis, Duc

de Bourbon, d. 16 June 1743; 4. Louis-Alexandre de Bourbon, Comte de Toulouse, b. 6 June 1678, d. 1 December 1737; 5. Louise-Marie de Bourbon, called Mlle de Tours, b. 1675, d. 15 September 1681; 6. Françoise-Marie de Bourbon, called Mlle de Blois, b. May 1677, married 1692 Philippe, Duc d'Orléans, d. 1 February 1749; two further children died in infancy. The Duchesse de Fontanges also bore the King a son who died in infancy.

LOUIS XV. King of France and Navarre, called *Bien Aimé*. Third son of Louis, Duc de Bourbon, grandson of Louis XIV, and his wife Marie-Adelaïde de Savoie. Born 15 February 1710; succeeded his great-grandfather 1 September 1715; died at Versailles 10 May 1774. The will of Louis XIV was broken and Philippe, Duc d'Orléans, appointed Regent. Saint-Simon's memoirs cover only the young King's minority, his coming of age, his engagement to the young Infanta of Spain which was eventually broken off, and his coronation.

'MADAME.' Charlotte-Elisabeth de Bavière, Princesse Palatine, the second wife of 'Monsieur' (*q.v.*). Born at Heidelberg 27 May 1652, the daughter of Charles-Louis, Count Palatine. She was virtuous, short-tempered, and ugly. She was devoted to her son, the Duc de Chartres (later Duc d'Orléans and Regent) and her Protestant soul revolted at his forced marriage with Louis XIV's illegitimate daughter, Mlle de Blois. During her son's Regency she remained an indulgent, yet perspicacious and critical, mother. She died at Saint-Cloud on 8 December 1722.

MAINE, Duc and Duchesse du. Louis-Auguste de Bourbon, Duc du Maine, was the son of Louis XIV and Mme de Montespan, born at Versailles 31 March 1670. He was a weak and incompetent character, loaded with honours far beyond his capacity by his doting father. He was appointed Colonel General of the Swiss Guards in 1674, Sovereign Prince of Dombes in 1680, Governor of the Languedoc in 1682, General of the Galleys in 1688, Lieutenant General in 1690, Master Gunner in 1694. In 1714 Louis elevated him and his brother, the Comte de Toulouse, to the rank of Princes of the Blood and declared them both in succession to the throne in the absence of a legitimate heir; and in the King's will he was entrusted with the education and safety of the young King and command of all the Household Troops. The day after the death of Louis XIV the will was broken and the Duc d'Orléans became Regent. Later he was stripped of his offices and in consequence allowed his wife to drag him into the Cellamare conspiracy. Both of them were arrested and imprisoned separately in the provinces; after a year he was released, and, recovering part of his lost honours, spent the remainder of his days in decent obscurity. He died at his château at Sceaux on 14 May 1736. On 13 March 1710 he had married Anne-Louise-Bénédictine de Bourbon, daughter of the Prince de Condé and Anne de Bavière. She was a tiny woman of great energy and overweening ambition. She was born on 8 November 1676. In the last years of Louis XIV and the first of the Regency she turned her house at Sceaux into a centre of political intrigue, designed to advance her husband and culminating in the Cellamare conspiracy. After fifteen months she was released and retired to Sceaux, where she was hostess to the most notable men of letters of the day. She died there on 23 January 1753.

MAINTENON, Françoise d'Aubigné, Marquise de. Born 27 November 1635 in prison at Niort, where her father was confined as a Huguenot malcontent accused of treason. When her father was released the family emigrated to Martinique; Françoise was brought back to France on her father's death in 1645 and given a very strict upbringing by an aunt. In 1657 she married the crippled poet Scarron, to whom she was more a nurse than a wife; he died in 1660. Scarron's pension was confirmed on his widow first by the Queen Mother and then by Mme de Montespan, who put her in charge of the children which she had borne the King. In 1678 the King decided to have his children at Court and their nurse came with them; in the same year she bought out of her savings the Maintenon estate, which the King elevated to a Marquisate. Despite every difficulty placed in the way by Mme de Montespan, Mme de Maintenon became the King's mistress. The Queen said that the years when Mme de Maintenon was in favour were the only ones during which she was treated decently, and she died in the reigning favourite's arms. At some time during 1685 or 1686 it is generally accepted that Louis was married to Mme de Maintenon by Harlay, the Archbishop of Paris, but no public announcement was ever made. In spite of her difficult past, Mme de Maintenon was most upright—indeed straight-laced. Once she was in ascendancy the Court of the aging King became dull compared with the years before. She played a considerable part in politics; everything was talked over with her by the Ministers before it was put to the King, and they were usually received by Louis during the evening in her apartments. She was a born teacher and founded a home for poor girls at Rueil; this was moved first to Noisy and then, richly endowed by the King in 1683, to Saint-Cyr, where she herself died on 15 April 1719. Saint-Simon was completely blind to her merits, and missed no opportunity of recording in his memoirs any gossip which could be construed to show her in an unfavourable light.

'MONSEIGNEUR.' The title given during the reign of Louis XIV to the Dauphin, the King's eldest son Louis, who was born 1 November 1661 and died on 14 April 1711. This is the only use in this connection of this courtesy title in French history.

'MONSIEUR.' Philippe, Duc d'Orléans, younger brother of Louis XIV and father of the future Regent. Born 27 September 1640, died suddenly at Saint-Cloud on 9 June 1701. He first married in 1661 Henrietta, sister of Charles II of England, with whom Louis fell in love; the marriage was not a success, as he was dominated completely by his favourite, the Chevalier de Lorraine. Henrietta died in 1670 and in the following year he married the Princesse Palatine, Charlotte-Elisabeth de Bavière. By his first wife he had Marie-Louise d'Orléans, who married Charles II of Spain, and Anne-Marie d'Orléans, who married Victor Amédée II of Sardinia; by his second wife Philippe, later Regent, and Elisabeth-Charlotte, who married Charles, Duc de Lorraine. In the 1670's he spent some time in the field and commanded the army in Flanders with such success that Louis, in a fit of jealousy, recalled him and never allowed him t o command again

MONSIEUR LE DUC. Louis-Henri de. Condé, Duc de Bourbon (1692–1740). His branch of the Bourbon family was descended from the younger brother of Antoine de Bourbon, father of Henry IV; he was the great-grandson of the Grand Condé. On the death of Louis XIV, after the great mortality of the last few years, he found himself the second senior surviving Bourbon aside from the boy King Louis XV; the Duc d'Orléans was of course the first. He made a fortune out of speculating in Law's shares, and his country home was the famous Château de Chantilly. He was a tiresome young man, but the Regent was forced in 1718 to enlist his aid in the struggle with the Duc du Maine and the *Parlement*. On the death of the Duc d'Orléans in 1723 he was appointed Prime Minister, *faute de mieux*, and Saint-Simon expected to be called by him to political office, but no call came and Saint-Simon retired to the country for life. Monsieur le Duc displayed a total incapacity for high office and Louis XV, who disliked him, replaced him in 1729 by Cardinal Fleury. He then withdrew to Chantilly to study chemistry and natural history.

'MONSIEUR LE PRINCE.' Henri-Jules de Bourbon, Prince de Condé. Son of the Great Condé, and Premier Prince of the Blood Royal. Born in Paris on 29 July 1643, died 1 April 1709. In his youth he fought in several of his father's most famous victories. He was a mentally unstable character who alienated everyone. He married in 1663 the second daughter of Edward of Bavaria, Prince Palatine, and had ten children of whom Anne-Louise-Bénédictine, Duchesse du Maine, was the eighth.

MONTESPAN, Françoise-Athénaïs de Rochechouart, Marquise de. Born 1641 at the Château de Tonnay-Charente, died at Bourbon-l'Archambault on 28 May 1707. Daughter of Gabriel de Rochechouart, Duc de Mortemart, she married in 1663 Henri-Louis de Pardaillan de Gondrin, Marquis de Montespan; soon she was appointed Dame du Palais to the Queen. She became the King's mistress in 1668. She does not come into these memoirs but is mentioned because of the nine children which she bore the King. They will be found enumerated under *Louis XIV*, and one particularly—the Duc du Maine—vitally affects our narrative. She was given her congé in 1683 when Madame de Maintenon came into favour. Aristocratic, lovely to look at, luxurious and rapacious, she reigned over the Court during all the years of its great glory and she was the friend of Corneille, Racine, and La Fontaine, the patron of artists and architects. When she finally lost the King, she tried to draw him back to her by magic; her last few years at Court were distracted until in 1691 she retired

to a religious house where she lived in great state and dignity.

ORLÉANS, Duc de. *See* CHARTRES and 'MONSIEUR.'

PONTCHARTRAIN, Louis Phélypeaux, Comte de (1643–1727). First President of the *Parlement* of Rennes, then Intendant of Finance 1667. He became Comptroller General of Finance in 1689; he showed little capacity and was succeeded ten years later by Chamillart; in addition he became Secretary of State for the Navy and Comptroller of the Royal Household in 1690. He was appointed Chancellor of France in 1699. In 1714 he resigned his offices and retired to the Oratory. His only son, Jérôme (1674–1747), in 1693 became Assistant Secretary of State to his father, whom he succeeded when the latter became Chancellor. He was forced to resign in 1715 and was succeeded in turn by his own son, the Comte de Maurepas.

ROCHEFOUCAULD, François, Duc de la, and Prince de Marcillac. Son of the famous author of the *Maxims,* he was born 15 June 1634 and died at Paris on 12 June 1714. He was loaded with honours by Louis XIV, to whom he was of assistance in various love affairs. He was Master of the Hounds, Master of the Robes, Governor of Berry, and Chancellor of the Royal Orders.

TORCY, Jean-Baptiste Colbert, Marquis de (1665–1746). Nephew of the famous Minister Colbert. Envoy extraordinary to Portugal 1684, Denmark 1685 and England 1687; Minister and Assistant Secretary of State for Foreign Affairs 1689, Secretary 1696. He was largely responsible for Louis XIV's accepting the will of Charles II of Spain. During the Regency he was a member of the Council, and he retired from public life when Louis XV reached his majority. He was an upright and firm man who inspired respect.

TOULOUSE, Louis-Alexandre de Bourbon, Comte de (1678–1737). Third son of Louis XIV and Madame de Maintenon. Created Grand Admiral of France at the age of five. Governor of Guyenne 1689. He was wounded at the Siege of Namur in 1691. He was a very good sailor, and in 1704 commanded a French fleet which fought a glorious action against greatly superior Anglo-Dutch forces off Málaga. Two years later ill health forced him to leave the service. He was a man of the utmost probity, universally respected, and would have nothing to do with the constant intrigues of his elder brother, the Duc du Maine.

VENDÔME, Louis-Joseph, Duc de. Great-grandson of King Henri IV and Gabrielle d'Estrées. The greatest French general between Turenne and Napoleon. Born 1 July 1654 at Paris, died 15 June 1712 at Viñaroz, Valencia. His early career as a soldier was brilliant, and Louis XIV, in spite of a personal dislike, gave him an army in 1695. For the next two years he fought victoriously in Spain. In the War of the Spanish Succession he succeeded Villeroy in command in Italy (1702) and for four years defied the imperial forces under Prince Eugène. In July 1708 he was recalled from Italy to re-establish the fortunes of the army in Flanders which had been driven from the field by Marlborough after Ramillies; he shared the command with the Duc de Bourgogne, and since no love was lost between them the operations were a failure and the French forces were again defeated at Oudenarde. In the following year Vendôme was not employed, but in 1710 he was sent back to Spain, where he conducted a brilliant campaign culminating in the victory of Villaviciosa, which secured the throne of Philip V, grandson of Louis XIV. Vendôme was a man of the filthiest and most degrading personal habits, which with his unabashed cynicism horrified the King and revolted many others, such as the Duc de Bourgogne. He was a bad administrator, so that his army always suffered from bad health and bad logistics. But he was a brilliant strategist and tactician who must rank among France's greatest soldiers. Saint-Simon disliked him because he was descended from a bastard royal line, and hence dwells at length on his personal habits without being able to recognize his real ability.

VILLARS, Claude-Louis-Hector, Duc de. Marshal (1653–1734). The last of Louis XIV's generals and one of the best. In 1686 he was sent as Minister Plenipotentiary to Vienna, where he showed great ability. As a Lieutenant General he distinguished himself in the armies of Flanders and the Rhine in the war which ended in the Peace of Ryswick in 1697, after which he was again sent to Vienna. On the outbreak of the War of the Spanish Succession

he was given command of the army destined to effect a junction with the Elector of Bavaria; his victory at Friedlingen (1702) won him his Marshal's baton. By taking Kehl and Kissingen he met the Elector, but they could not get on together and Villars returned to France and resigned his command. Louis XIV then charged him with the pacification of the Cévennes uprising, in which he was successful (1704). In 1705 he was given the Army of the Moselle and succeeded in containing Marlborough, who was threatening to invade France. After spending 1708 in fighting against the Duke of Savoy, he succeeded Vendôme in command of the Army of Flanders which in 1709 was in a parlous state. He spent some months on the defensive, reorganizing his forces, but in September, having been given permission to assume the offensive, he engaged Marlborough and Prince Eugène at Malplaquet. Although driven from the field, the French crippled the Allies by inflicting 20,000 casualties against a loss of 7000 men suffered by themselves. Villars was badly wounded in the knee, and handed over command to the Maréchal de Boufflers, who made a perfect withdrawal. Villars, created a peer, returned to his army in 1710 and remained on the defensive. By 1712 France was reduced to one army which Villars commanded with the task of holding Prince Eugène's invasion; he succeeded so well that he got across his opponent's lines of communications, captured his stores, and forced his withdrawal to Brussels, which made it possible for Louis to negotiate peace terms. He was loaded with honours of every kind. During the Regency he was a member of the Council. Saint-Simon says that he enjoyed the most complete and constant good fortune of any man in the reign of Louis XIV, but his glory was tarnished by his avidity and his atrocious pillaging.

VILLEROY, François de Neufville, Duc de. Born 7 April 1644 at Paris, and died there 18 July 1730. His advancement in the service was rapid; Lieutenant General in 1677, he was made a Marshal in 1693. In 1695 he succeeded the Duc de Luxembourg as commander in chief of the army in Flanders, which he led with singular incompetence. But he enjoyed the complete confidence of Louis XIV and Mme de Maintenon and in consequence was given the Army of Italy on the outbreak of the War of the Spanish Succession; in this campaign his chief contribution was to get himself captured at Cremona, after which his troops, relieved of his presence, drove the enemy from the field. After ten months of captivity he was released and again assumed command of the Army of Flanders; here his endless mistakes culminated in the crushing defeat of Ramillies, after which his stock was so low that the King no longer dared employ him at the front.

Nevertheless in his will Louis XIV asked that he be tutor to the young King, and he continued in this office, which he discharged with his usual incompetence, for some years. His overbearing manner and habitual insolence moved the Regent to have him arrested on 13 August 1722 and rusticated to his estates at Villeroy.

The Memoirs

Presentation to the King

1691

MY FIRST MEETING WITH THE KING

✤✤✤✤✤ N 1691 I was studying philosophy and learning to ride at the
✤ *I* ✤ Academy of MM. Mesmont and Rochefort, and being anx-
✤ ✤ ious to enter the service, I was rapidly tiring of both lessons
✤✤✤✤✤ and teachers. The siege of Mons, begun by the King in person during the early Spring, had attracted nearly all the young men of
my age for their first campaign, and, what irritated me more than anything, the Duc de Chartres had gone to see active service for the first
time. I had been practically brought up with him, being his junior by
eight months, and, if I may be allowed to use the expression of two so
young and so widely separated in station, a strong friendship bound
us to one another. I determined therefore to put my childhood behind
me.

I need not go into all the tricks by which I tried to get my way. First
I went to my mother, but I quickly saw that she was not going to take
me seriously. So I went to my father and convinced him that the King,
having undertaken one major siege this year, would be sure to rest
during the following year. So I deceived my mother, who did not discover what I was up to until my father had finally made up his mind.

The King had made a rule, to which Princes of the Blood and the
royal Bastards were the only permitted exceptions, that every young
man had to spend a year in one of his two companies of musketeers
and then, in order to learn to take orders, either command a troop of
cavalry, or go into his own regiment of foot as a subaltern, before being allowed to purchase a regiment. So my father took me to Versailles,
where he had not been since he had returned from Blaye after his serious illness.[1] He was still terribly ill when my mother brought him
back to Paris in a coach, and up to now had not been well enough to go
to see the King. On the feast of St. Simon and St. Jude, at half-past
twelve, he paid his respects as the King was coming out of the Council,
and presented me as wishing to become a musketeer.

His Majesty did my father the honour of embracing him three times;
then, seeing that I was rather small and looked delicate, he said that I
was still very young, to which my father replied that I would be able to

---

[1] A fortified port on the Gironde of which the Duke had been governor since 1630.
He had been so ill that news of his death actually circulated.

1691 serve all the longer. The King then asked in which of the two companies my father wanted me enlisted, and father chose the first because it was commanded by a very old friend, Maupertuis. Beside thinking of my own well-being, he knew very well how carefully the King inquired of the two captains, and especially of Maupertuis, how young officers under their command were getting on, and that their reports weighed a great deal with the King and could have far-reaching effects on a young man's future. My father was right, and I undoubtedly owe to Maupertuis's kindness the first good impression which the King formed of me.

1692

TWO ROYAL MARRIAGES

✤✤✤✤✤ HE King, bent on raising still further the standing of his
✤ $\mathcal{F}$ ✤ Bastards, which he improved almost daily, had married two
✤ ✤ of them to Princes of the Blood. Mme la Princesse de Conti,
✤✤✤✤✤ the only daughter of Mme de la Vallière,[1] was a childless widow; the other, his elder daughter by Mme de Montespan, had married
M. le Duc.[2] For a long time Mme de Maintenon, even more than the
King, thought of nothing but raising these children higher and higher,
and they both wanted to marry Mlle de Blois, second daughter of the
King by Mme de Montespan, to the Duc de Chartres. The Duke was
the King's only nephew, and ranked far above the Princes of the Blood
because of his position as Grandson of France and because of the separate court of Monsieur, his father. The two marriages which I have
just mentioned shocked everybody. The King knew this, and he was
well aware how much greater the effect of another even more startling
marriage would be. For four years he had been turning the matter
over in his mind, and had taken the first steps towards bringing it
about. There were great difficulties. Monsieur was very sensitive about
anything touching his own position. Madame came from a country
where bastardy and any form of *mésalliance* are abhorred, and her character was such that there was no hope of her willingly accepting the
match for her son.

To overcome the obstacles the King first tackled Monsieur le
Grand,[3] who had always enjoyed the royal confidence, in order to get
the support of his brother, the Chevalier de Lorraine,[4] who had complete influence over Monsieur. The Chevalier's features had been beautiful: Monsieur made no secret of the fact that he did not like women,

---

[1] Marie-Anne de Bourbon (1661–1739) was legitimized in 1667. She married the
Prince de Conti in 1680.

[2] Louis, Duc de Bourbon, son of Henri-Jules, Prince de Condé; always known as
'M. le Duc.'

[3] The Grand Equerry was always known as 'Monsieur le Grand'; he presided over the
Great Stable at Versailles, in which the saddle horses were kept. The harness horses and
the carriages were kept in the Small Stable, under the supervision of the First Equerry,
known as 'Monsieur le Premier.'

[4] Philippe de Lorraine (1643–1702), called 'Chevalier,' because he had been destined
for the celibate order of the Knights of Malta, later known as Prince Philippe. He and
his elder brother, Monsieur le Grand, were sons of the celebrated Comte d'Harcourt.

1692 and in consequence the Chevalier de Lorraine had established a life-long ascendancy over him. The two brothers asked for nothing better than to assist the King in so delicate a matter, and, like all clever people, to do themselves a good turn in passing. The first move was made in the summer of 1688. At that time the Order[1] was reduced to about a dozen Knights, and it was obvious that there would soon have to be some fresh creations. The two brothers wanted to be included in the Order, and further demanded that they should have precedence over all dukes at the ceremony of installation. Because of their ambitions, the King had never given the Order to any member of the house of Lorraine, and he was most unwilling to do so now; but the two brothers insisted, and they got their way. The Chevalier de Lorraine, thus paid in advance, guaranteed to obtain Monsieur's consent to the marriage and to find a means of persuading Madame and the Duc de Chartres.

Early one afternoon, as I was passing along the upper gallery, I saw the Duc de Chartres, looking downcast and worried, come out from his apartments by a side door, attended only by one adjutant of Monsieur's guards. I asked him where he was off to so fast at that hour of the day; he replied abruptly in a cross tone that the King had sent for him. I did not think it proper to accompany him, and, turning to my tutor, I remarked that I smelt a marriage in the offing and we might expect an announcement soon. Rumours had been flying for the last few days, and, since I thought there would be squalls, I kept my eyes and ears open.

The Duc de Chartres found the King in his study, alone with Monsieur, whom he had not expected. The King received him kindly, and said that he wanted to see him settled in life; that the war spreading on all sides ruled out many princesses who would otherwise have made a suitable match; that there was no Princess of the Blood of the right age; and that he could not show his affection more clearly than by offering his own daughter, whose two sisters had married Princes of the Blood, thus making the bridegroom son-in-law as well as nephew; but, he added, however much he himself might desire this marriage, he would not insist, and he left the matter open. This speech, delivered with all the awe-inspiring majesty which came so naturally to the King, and made at a timid young prince who had had no chance to think of a

[1] Order of the Saint-Esprit. In 1686 it had run down to four princes of the royal house, four bishops, three foreign knights, and thirteen French knights—mostly very old men; there were sixty-seven vacancies, but the King was always chary of creating a fresh knight because of the backbiting and jealousy which would inevitably follow.

6

reply, threw the latter into complete confusion. He tried to play for time by passing the responsibility to Monsieur and Madame; he stammered that of course the King was master, but his own wishes must accord with those of his parents. 'Very proper,' replied the King, 'but if you consent, your father and mother will not offer any opposition.' And turning to Monsieur, he asked, 'Is that not so, my brother?' Monsieur again agreed, having already done so in private; then the King said that there now only remained Madame, and he sent for her at once. While they were waiting the two of them talked together without taking the slightest notice of the Duc de Chartres's evident alarm and despondency.

Madame arrived, and the King said at once that he trusted she would not be opposed to a matter which Monsieur wished and to which M. de Chartres had consented—that is to say, the marriage between her son and Mlle de Blois, which he himself strongly desired; and he briefly repeated what he had just said to M. de Chartres—all with an imposing air as if he expected that Madame was bound to be delighted, although he knew perfectly well what her feelings actually were. Madame, who had relied upon her son's refusing as he had promised her—a promise which he had done his best to keep by his embarrassed and conditional reply—found herself caught with nothing to say. She darted a furious look at Monsieur and M. de Chartres, and remarked that if they were happy she had nothing to add; then she made a very slight bow, and withdrew to her own apartments. Her son followed her immediately, and she, without giving him a chance to explain what had happened, went for him in floods of tears and chased him out of the room.

Shortly afterwards Monsieur left the King and went to her apartments, but, except that he was not actually driven out, he fared no better—so that after a few minutes he left without having been able to get a word in edgeways. All this was over by four o'clock, and there was to be an *appartement* that evening—in winter they were held three times a week; on the other three weekday nights a comedy was played, and on Sundays nothing.

An *appartement* was a gathering of the whole court between seven and ten o'clock, when the King sat down to supper; it took place in the suite of rooms which runs from the Galerie des Glaces to the gallery of the chapel. First there was music; then tables were set up for games; there was one for lansquenet, at which Monseigneur and Monsieur always played, and a billiard table. Anyone was at liberty to make up his own party, and to send for more tables if none was free. Beyond the billiard room there was a room set aside for refreshments; the whole was brilliantly lit. When the *appartements* were first begun the King used to appear and play for a while; but he had long since given this up—although he liked people to attend regularly, and they, of course, did so, being anxious to please him. He spent the time in Mme de Maintenon's apartments, working with various of his Ministers.

This evening, soon after the music had finished, the King sent for Monseigneur and Monsieur, who had already sat down to lansquenet; for Madame, who was idly watching a game of ombre; for the Duc de Chartres, who was rather gloomily playing chess; and for Mlle de Blois, who had only just come out, but on this occasion was wearing all her jewels. She had no idea what was going on and, being naturally timid and absolutely terrified of the King, she thought she was going to be scolded for something; she came into the room in such a complete state of prostration that Madame de Maintenon made her sit on her lap, where she remained, though scarcely reassured. As soon as it was known that these royal personages had been summoned to Mme de Maintenon's room, and that Mlle de Blois was with them, a rumour of the engagement flashed through the gathering, at the very moment when the King was formally making it known to his own circle. The whole thing only lasted a few minutes, and when they all returned to the *appartement* a public announcement was made. I came in just at that moment. I found the whole company split up into little groups, and astonishment on every face. I soon heard the news, but I must say that after what I had seen in the afternoon I was hardly surprised.

Madame walked up and down the Gallery with her favourite, a most worthy one, Mme de Châteautiers.[1] She was walking very fast, her handkerchief in her hand, crying openly, shouting and gesticulating. She looked like Ceres after the rape of her daughter Proserpine, searching for her and imploring Jupiter to give her back. Out of respect, everyone left her to herself, and only went past her if they had to get through to one of the other rooms. Monseigneur and Monsieur had gone back to their lansquenet. The former looked quite unmoved; but I never saw anyone more shamefaced than Monsieur, and he did not get back to normal for more than a month afterwards.

The Duc de Chartres seemed desperate and his future bride was in an extremity of sadness and embarrassment. Young as she was, and splendid as the marriage was for her, she could not help being aware of the feelings about her, and she was understandably apprehensive

---

[1] Anne, daughter of the Comte de Châteautiers (1662–1741). Highly regarded by the King, she was accorded the honour of sometimes riding in his carriage. Madame said that she was the only really disinterested person she had met in forty years.

for the future. With very few exceptions, there was general consternation. Only the Lorraines were triumphant: they had rendered a signal service to the cause of sodomy and double adultery and had been richly rewarded, so they had every cause to feel pleased with themselves, and, being quite shameless, showed it openly.

It might seem as if the intrusion of politics would have made this *appartement* dull, but in fact it was full of life and interest and I found that it ended all too soon. Eventually the King sat down to supper, and I took care to miss nothing of what went on. The King himself seemed just the same as ever. The Duc de Chartres sat beside Madame, who took not the slightest notice either of him or of Monsieur. Her eyes were filled with tears, which brimmed over from time to time, and as she wiped them away she looked round as if she wanted to see what everyone was thinking. Her son's eyes also looked red and swollen, and neither of them ate much. I noticed that the King offered Madame every dish which was set before him, but she brusquely refused them all. This made no difference to the attention and politeness which the King continued to show to her to the very end of the meal.

It was also noticed that at the end of supper, with his circle still about him, the King bowed unusually low to Madame, and while he was doing so she turned away so abruptly that when he rose again he saw nothing but her back making for the door.

The next day the whole court visited Monsieur, Madame, and the Duc de Chartres, but not a word was spoken: everyone just paid his respects in silence. After that we all went to the usual rising of the Council in the Galerie des Glaces and to the royal Mass. Madame was there too. When her son approached her to kiss her hand in the customary manner, she smacked his face so hard that the sound of it echoed— in the presence of the whole court; the poor prince was covered with confusion, and all of us were astonished. The same day the immense dowry was announced,[1] and on the following day the King paid a visit to Monsieur and Madame, which was a pretty gloomy affair. After that no one thought of anything except the preparations for the wedding.

On Sunday, 17 February, there was a court ball, opened with a branle.[2] That morning I went to call on Madame, who could not resist

[1] The King gave his daughter 2 million livres, a pension of 150,000 livres a year, and jewels valued at 600,000 livres. Monsieur was given the Palais-Royal to live in, and on his death the Duc de Chartres was promised a further pension of 200,000 livres in addition to the 150,000 a year he already had.

[2] A form of round dance, as opposed to the formal dances of the period in which the participants faced one another or advanced in line.

remarking tartly that apparently I was looking forward to all these balls, which was all very well at my age, but she, having grown old, would be glad when they were over. The Duc de Bourgogne[1] danced at this ball for the first time, and led the branle with Mademoiselle.[2] This was also the first time I had attended a court ball; I danced with Mlle de Sourches,[3] a very good dancer. Everyone was superbly dressed.

The betrothal and signing of the marriage contract took place soon after in the King's study, with the whole court present. The same day the household of the future Duchesse de Chartres was announced; the King allowed her a Gentleman of Honour and a Lady-in-Waiting, privileges hitherto reserved for Daughters of France, and, in keeping with the strangeness of this innovation, she was also to have a Lady of Honour. The Duc de Villars was appointed Gentleman of Honour, the Maréchale de Rochefort Lady of Honour, the Comtesse de Mailly Lady-in-Waiting, and the Comte de Fontaine-Martel Equerry. . . .

On the Monday before Lent (18 February 1692) the bride and bridegroom with all the royal wedding party, magnificently dressed, assembled a little before noon in the King's study, and thence made their way to the chapel. The congregation was assembled in its normal order except that between the royal *prie-dieu* and the altar there were two seats for the bridal pair, so that they had their backs to the King. The Cardinal de Bouillon in all his vestments emerged from the vestry and performed the ceremony; afterwards he celebrated Mass. From the chapel everyone went straight to the dinner-table, which was arranged in the shape of a horseshoe: the Princes and Princesses of the Blood being placed on the right and the left according to their rank, ending with the two royal Bastards, and (included for the first time) the Duchesse de Verneuil: so that the Duc de Verneuil, the bastard of Henri IV, became recognized as a Prince of the Blood long after his death. The Duc d'Uzès found it so amusing that he walked in front of her crying 'Make way, make way for Mme Charlotte Séguier!'[4]

After dinner the King and Queen of England[5] came to Versailles with their court. There was much music and much card-playing. The

---

[1] Louis de France, Duc de Bourgogne, grandson of Louis XIV. Born 1682, he became heir to the throne on the death of his father in 1711, but died a year later.

[2] Elisabeth-Charlotte d'Orléans (1676–1744), sister of the Duc de Chartres, being the daughter of Monsieur by his second wife, Elizabeth-Charlotte de Bavière.

[3] Daughter of the Marquis de Sourches (1645–1716), Grand Provost of France.

[4] Catherine-Henriette de Balzac, Duchesse de Verneuil, became the mistress of Henri IV after the death of Gabrielle d'Estrées in 1599. By the King she had one son, Gaston-Henri (1601–82), who became Archbishop of Metz, but later gave up holy orders and married Charlotte, daughter of the Chancellor Séguier. She lived on until 1704.

[5] The exiled James II.

Montbron's son invites ridicule

King was present throughout, superbly dressed and in great humour, wearing his blue riband over his coat in the old-fashioned way. Supper was in the same style as dinner; the King of England had the Queen his wife on his right and our King on his left, each with his cadenas[1] before him. Afterwards the bride and groom were conducted to the bridal apartments; the Queen of England handed the new Duchesse de Chartres her nightdress, and the King of England did the same for the Duke—though at first he had refused, saying that he was too unlucky. The bed was blessed by the Cardinal de Bouillon.

On Shrove Tuesday the Duchesse de Chartres received at her toilette, and the King and Queen of England as well as our King and the whole court were present; after which the King's Mass was celebrated, and then dinner as the day before. During the morning, however, Mme de Verneuil was packed off back to Paris as she had already had enough attention. After dinner our King withdrew with the King and Queen of England, and then another great ball followed. Except that this time the new Duchesse de Chartres was partnered by the Duc de Bourgogne, everyone wore the same costume and danced with the same partners as the time before.

I cannot resist telling about one perfectly ridiculous thing which happened to the same person at both balls—the son of Montbron,[2] who was no more competent to dance at a court ball than his father was to be a member of the Order (to which, however, he was promoted in 1688). This young man, who had hardly ever appeared at court before, partnered Mlle de Moreuil (of a bastard branch of the great house of Moreuil), daughter of the Lady of Honour of Mme la Duchesse, and no more worthy of such an honour than he. On being asked if he danced well, he had replied with such self-confidence that everyone hoped he would prove to be no good. They were satisfied. At the very first bow he lost his nerve, and he got out of step in the first movement. He tried to recover himself and to hide his mistakes with languishing airs and exaggerated movements with his arm. This only made him more ridiculous; there were smiles, then laughter, and finally, in spite of the presence of the King, real barracking.

The next day, instead of going away or keeping quiet, he went about saying that the King's presence had put him off and promising marvels

---

[1] A metal box containing knife, fork, spoon, and toothpicks. They were locked before use in order to prevent any attempts on a prince's life by poisoning the implements.

[2] The father, Alexandre du Puy, Marquis de St. André et de Montbron (1600–73), began his military career in the religious wars of Louis XIII's reign. Later he served under Gustavus Adolphus, and then went to Venice, where he became Captain General of the Armies of the Republic.

for the next ball. He was a friend of mine and I really felt for him. In fact I would have warned him had I not thought that my own success would have made anything I said seem ungracious.[1] At the second ball, as soon as he took the floor everyone stood up to watch, and those at the back climbed on anything there was to climb on; there were derisive cheers and even applause. Everyone, including the King, was sick with laughter, and I don't suppose anything like it had ever happened to anyone before. Young Montbron disappeared immediately afterwards and did not come back for a long time. He later commanded the Dauphin's infantry regiment and died young, a bachelor. It was a great pity, for he was a man of honour and courage. He was the last of the spurious branch of the Montbrons—or rather his father, who survived him, was.

Ash Wednesday put an end to these rather sad rejoicings-to-order, and no one talked of anything except what was going to happen next.

The Duc du Maine wished to get married. The King tried to dissuade him and pointed out that people in his position ought not to have issue. But Mme de Maintenon, who had brought M. du Maine up and felt all the affection of a nurse towards him, pressed the King, who yielded and decided at least to gain for him the powerful support of the house of Condé by marrying him to a daughter of Monsieur le Prince. Monsieur le Prince expressed himself as delighted; he saw grow day by day the rank, standing, and connections of the Bastards; but this marriage, coming immediately after that of the Duc de Chartres, was nothing new for him and merely bound him doubly close to the King. Madame was also relieved: she had a horrible suspicion that the King, having taken away her son, was now casting eyes on her daughter, and the marriage instead to M. le Prince's girl came as a merciful deliverance.

There were three daughters to choose from. The second, being the tallest by an inch, was chosen. All three of them were tiny. The eldest was good-looking and witty, but the incredible strain under which all around M. le Prince laboured[2] proved heart-breaking for her—she bore it with constancy, wisdom, and restraint, and was admired by all. But she paid heavily for her self-control and eventually her health was affected.

The King, agreeing with the choice, went to Versailles to request the agreement of Madame la Princesse; and shortly afterwards, at the end of Lent, the betrothal took place in the King's study. Immediately

---

[1] Saint-Simon very much fancied himself as a dancer.
[2] He was subject to periodic fits of insanity.

afterwards the court moved to the Trianon, where there was an *appartement* and a grand supper for eighty ladies at four tables presided over by the King, Monseigneur, Monsieur, Madame, and the new Duchesse de Chartres. The next day, Wednesday, 19 March, the marriage was celebrated at the royal Mass by the Cardinal de Bouillon. The dinner was the same, also the supper. The King of England handed the nightshirt to the Duc du Maine. Mme de Montespan[1] did not appear at all, or sign either of the marriage contracts.

---

[1] The Duke's mother.

1693

THE DEATH OF LA VAUGUYON

✣✣✣✣✣N Sunday, 29 November, the King, returning from Divine
✣O✣Service, was told by the Baron de Beauvais that La Vauguyon
✣✣had committed suicide that morning: he had sent his serv-
✣✣ants to Mass and then, lying on his bed, shot himself twice
✣✣✣✣✣
in the throat.

La Vauguyon was one of the most socially undistinguished and the
poorest men in France. His name was Bétoulat, and he also bore that
of Fromenteau. He had a superb figure, but was very dark and Spanish-
looking; he was graceful, with a charming voice, and could accompany himself well on the lute or the guitar. Also he was witty and was
liked by the ladies.

With these talents, and other accomplishments of a more private
nature, he insinuated himself into the good graces of Madame de Beauvais, first Lady of the Bedchamber of the Queen Mother and her intimate confidante. She was courted by everyone because she had the
King's ear and is reputed to have been his first love. I have seen her attending the toilette of Madame la Dauphine de Bavière, old, rheumy,
and blind in one eye; she always had a long conversation alone with
the King, who retained a high regard for her. Her son, who had assumed the title of Baron de Beauvais, was captain of the territories
surrounding Paris. He had been brought up with the King, took part
in his ballets and amusements; and, being gallant, enterprising, and
good-looking, he had made a niche for himself in the innermost court
circle and was treated by the King with a distinction which caused him
to be both feared and flattered. He was a shrewd man about the court
and very spoiled, but he was always willing to put in a good word with
the King for a friend or a bad word for an enemy. Altogether he was a
man of honour, and always knew his place with the great. He was always, too, a man of fashion.

Fromenteau insinuated himself into Mme de Beauvais's good
graces, and she introduced him to all her guests who, to please her,
were nice to the young popinjay. Little by little she brought him to the
notice, first of the Queen Mother, and then of the King, and under the
former's patronage he became a courtier. He seemed to have some
talent and he was brave in action; in due course he was employed at
the courts of several German Princes. Bit by bit he grew till he was ap-

pointed Ambassador in Denmark, and then in Spain. Wherever he went he was accepted with pleasure; the King gave him one of the military seats on the Council of State and then in 1688, to everyone's surprise, promoted him to the Order. Twenty years before he had married the daughter of Saint-Maigrin, a remarkably ugly widow with one son. By this marriage Fromenteau became ennobled and called himself Comte de la Vauguyon. So long as his embassies lasted and his stepson was young, he could manage, but when his wife had to pay her son an allowance they found themselves in straitened circumstances. La Vauguyon, loaded with honours beyond his wildest dreams, often spoke to the King of the miserable state of his affairs but very seldom got even the most trifling help. His constant poverty little by little unbalanced him, though it was a long time before anyone noticed it. One of his first outbursts was at the house of Mme Pellot,[1] widow of the First President of the Rouen Parliament, who every evening gave a small card party for her friends. She asked only the best people, and La Vauguyon was almost always there. Playing brelan she antied and he would not follow. She joked about it and said she was glad to learn that he was a coward at heart. La Vauguyon did not answer; but when the game was done he waited until everyone else had gone home, then locked the door and shoved her up against the fire-place, seizing her head in his two hands and shouting that he could not imagine what stopped him from bashing her to a pulp for calling him a coward. The terrified woman bobbed up and down in his arms as best she could, curtsying and flattering him, while he shouted and swore. Finally he dropped her, more dead than alive, and left. She was a good, kind person and, although she instructed her staff never to leave her alone with him again, she said nothing about it until after his death, and continued to receive him as if nothing had happened—and he continued to come as if nothing had happened.

Some time afterwards, in one of the dark corridors at Fontainebleau at two in the afternoon, he drew his sword on the Prince de Courtenay and forced him to defend himself—despite the latter's insistence that there was no quarrel and that the place was unseemly. When they heard the noise, those who were in the grand salon came at the double and separated them, calling for the Swiss Guard, of whom there were always a few on duty at the doors of the Queen Mother's old apartments near by. La Vauguyon, already a Chevalier

---

[1] Madeleine Colbert, daughter of the King's secretary and a relation of the great Colbert. As her second husband she married in 1674 Pellot, the son of an extremely rich Lyons silk merchant.

de l'Ordre, struggled free and ran to the King's study, wrenched open the door, pushed past the usher, and threw himself at the King's feet, crying that he had come to offer his head. The King, who never relished the unexpected and who never received anyone except when he summoned them, got to his feet and asked him with some feeling what was the reason for his intrusion. La Vauguyon, on his knees, said that he had drawn his sword in the royal house, insulted by M. de Courtenay, and that his concern for his honour had outstripped his sense of duty. The King had a job getting rid of him and said he would look into it; a few minutes later both men were arrested by the Grand Provost and confined to their rooms. Two coaches were then brought, and the adjutants who had arrested them took the two of them to Paris, to the Bastille, one in each coach. They remained there for seven or eight months, with permission after the first few weeks to receive their friends; both were treated exactly alike. The fuss occasioned by such an affair can be imagined: no one could understand it. The Prince de Courtenay was a fine, brave man, but he was of a kindly disposition and had never quarrelled with anyone in his life. He insisted that there was nothing between him and La Vauguyon, but that he had been attacked and forced to draw in self-defence. On the other hand no one yet suspected La Vauguyon's mental condition, and, as he also protested that he had been attacked and insulted, no one knew whom to believe or what to think. Finally, in the absence of any explanation, when their misdemeanour had been sufficiently punished, both were released and shortly afterwards reappeared at court.

Some time later a fresh incident threw more light on the matter. On his way to Versailles, La Vauguyon met a groom in the livery of M. le Prince, leading a saddle-horse on the Sèvres road. La Vauguyon stopped, and asked the groom whose horse he was leading. The groom replied that it was from the stables of M. le Prince. La Vauguyon said he was sure that M. le Prince would not mind his riding it, and jumped into the saddle. The astonished groom did not know what to say to a man who he saw had the blue riband across his coat, so he just followed. La Vauguyon cantered in through the Porte de la Conférence, turned along the ramparts and dismounted at the Bastille, where he gave the groom a tip and sent him away. He went up to the Governor's office and said that, having been unfortunate enough to displease the King, could he please have a room. The surprised Governor asked to see the King's committal order, and was even more surprised when he was told that there was none; he refused this voluntary prisoner, but agreed finally to allow him to stay until instructions could be obtained from Pontchartrain, to whom an express messenger was sent. Pontchartrain reported the matter to the King, who could not imagine what it was all about; an order was sent that La Vauguyon was not to be taken in, but in spite of that the Governor had the utmost difficulty in getting him off the premises. This business and the borrowing of M. le Prince's horse caused a considerable stir and made the affair with M. de Courtenay more understandable. Meanwhile the King intimated to La Vauguyon that he might reappear at court, but everyone was afraid of him and avoided him; only the King, out of the goodness of his heart, was at pains to be kind to him.

It can be imagined that these occurrences in public were not the only incidents: there were other domestic upheavals which were kept as quiet as possible. But the situation became so intolerable for his poor wife, much older than he and of a retiring nature, that she left Paris for her country estate. She was not there long, for she died in October of that year (1693). This was the final blow required to send her husband off his head: with his wife, he lost his income; he had no means of his own, and received but little from the King. He only survived his wife for a month. He was sixty-four, nearly twenty years younger than she was, and they had no children. It came out that for the past two years he had carried a pair of loaded pistols in his carriage and often flourished them at his coachman and postilion when he was coming to or leaving Versailles. It is certain that if it had not been for the Baron de Beauvais, who took care of him and gave him money, he would after the death of his wife have been completely destitute. Beauvais often spoke to the King about it, and it seems inconceivable that the King, having raised the man to a position of such eminence and always shown him such particular goodwill, could just let him die of hunger and go mad with misery.

1696

THE KING'S ANTHRAX

The War which eventually ended at the Peace of Ryswyck in 1697 marks the beginning of the decline of Louis XIV's reign. Louis's constant endeavour to extend France's territory to the Maas and the Rhine for defensive reasons wore out both the French people and himself—he tired as his people did before the never-ending task. It is therefore small wonder that as the war degenerated his health showed signs for the first time of a decline.

✠✠✠✠ HE King had an anthrax on his neck, which at first was thought to be a boil but which soon grew so much worse that it caused some alarm. He was feverish, and it became necessary to cut the thing open several times. He made a point of being seen every day and went on with his work sitting up in bed. All Europe watched the progress of an illness which was not without its dangers. He sent a most friendly message to the Duc de la Rochefoucauld, who was spending a month at his lovely home at Verteuil, telling of his illness and saying that he would like to see him. The Duke left for Versailles at once and seemed to be more in favour than ever.

Since very little was happening in Flanders, and little looked like happening, the King asked the Maréchaux de Villeroy and de Boufflers to send the Princes home—particularly since the Prince of Orange had left his own army—and they arrived a few days later.

It was during this illness that the King ratified the Peace of Savoy,[1] made up his mind about the treatment of the Princesse de Savoie, and named the two hostages who were to be handed over from our side until the territorial clauses of the treaty were carried out. M. de Savoie, who was extremely astute in matters concerning the courts of Europe, thought that the Ducs de Foix and de Choiseul would be easy meat. The former was concerned with nothing but his own pleasure, while the latter thought only of his poverty and bad luck. Both were very second-rate, with no sense of duty, easily led, quickly satisfied, and yet

[1] Victor-Amédée II of Savoy, in spite of having joined the League of Augsburg (a defensive alliance of most of western Europe against France) and suffered several defeats, managed to negotiate a favourable peace with Louis in 1696. It was arranged that his daughter, Marie-Adelaïde, should marry Louis, Duc de Bourgogne, grandson of Louis XIV. This took place in 1697.

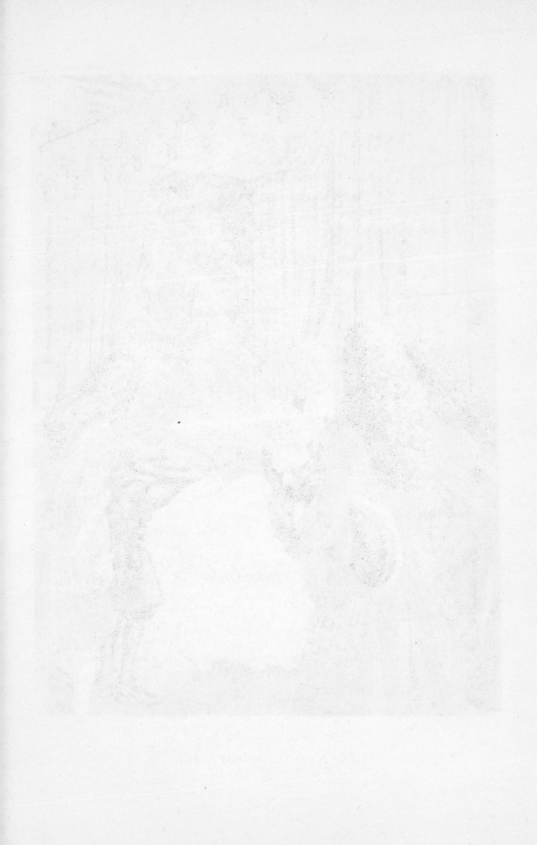

The King is confined to bed

of the highest birth and Knights of the Order—which was precisely the combination of characteristics which best suited M. de Savoie. He thought that they would be just what he wanted during this diplomatic crisis, so he asked the King if they could be named as the hostages, and they were—each with an equipment allowance of 12,000 livres and 1,000 écus a month.

The Comte de Brionne, Knight of the Order and Master of the Horse, was nominated to go to meet the Princess at Pont-Beauvoisin, together with Desgranges, one of the chief clerks of Pontchartrain and Master of Ceremonies, who was in charge of the arrangements for the Princess's journey.

It took longer to appoint her household. For some time there had been neither Queen nor Dauphine:[1] every lady of standing was jockeying for position: anonymous letters, tittle-tattle, and false accusations were rampant. In fact, everything was arranged privately by the King and Mme de Maintenon, who never left his bedside and was alone with him throughout his illness except when the court was allowed into the room. She had made up her mind to bring up the Princess herself,[2] and so to attach the girl to her own person that, while being an amusement to the King, she would not become a menace when she reached a more advanced age. She also expected by this means to be able to establish a hold one day over the Duc de Bourgogne—the more so since, as we have seen, her relations with the Duchesses de Chevreuse and de Beauvilliers were strained—indeed she saw to it that both of them were barred from the office of Lady of Honour which either would have filled so well. Mme de Maintenon was thus determined to surround the Princess entirely with persons of her own party, or with those who were so witless that they could do no harm.

On Saturday morning between twelve and one, the day before the household appointments were announced, the King, who was still confined to his bed, was talking alone with Monsieur. Monsieur, always curious, was trying to draw the King out on the subject of the Lady of Honour; and while they were talking he saw through the window the Duchesse de Lude in her chair, returning across the courtyard from Mass. 'There is someone,' he said to the King, 'who would like the position and thinks she has a good chance of getting it.' 'Yes,' replied the King, 'she would be the best choice in the world for teaching the Princess to put on patches and paint,' and went on to express his personal dislike of her; this was because he was more deeply re-

---

[1] The Queen died in 1683, the Dauphine in 1690.
[2] The bride was twelve and the bridegroom fifteen

ligious than ever at that time and such things shocked him. Monsieur, who was not really interested in the Duchess and had mentioned her merely out of curiosity, let the King run on and went off to dinner convinced that the Duchess was out of the hunt.

The next day, at the same hour, Monsieur was sitting alone in his study when an usher came in and told him that the Duchesse de Lude had received the appointment. Monsieur laughed and replied that that was a good one; the usher insisted, and, thinking that Monsieur was just making fun of him, went out and shut the door. A few minutes later M. de Châtillon came in with the same news, and Monsieur still would not take it seriously. Châtillon asked why he would not believe it and assured him again that it was true. While they were still arguing, others came into the room and confirmed the news, so that there could no longer be any doubt. Then Monsieur appeared so surprised that everyone wondered and asked him why. Keeping a secret had never been Monsieur's strong point, and he told them all that the King had said no more than twenty-four hours before. The whole business came out and excited so much curiosity that in the end the reason for the sudden change became known. The Duchesse de Lude knew that among the aspirants to the position there was one before whom she could not hope to be preferred, so she had recourse to backstairs lobbying. Mme de Maintenon had kept on one old woman who had been her only servant in the days of her poverty when, as the widow of Scarron, she had no income beyond a small pension from the parish of St. Eustache. This old woman enjoyed quite a position because of the great consideration shown her by Mme de Maintenon, who still called her Nanon—though to everyone else she was Mlle Balien. Nanon kept herself to herself as much as her mistress, dressed and did her hair in the same way, imitated her affectations, her way of speaking, her mannerisms, and her piety. She was a witch-like creature, to whom the Princesses were glad to have a chance of speaking even though they were the King's daughters, and to whom those Ministers who came on business to Mme de Maintenon's apartments always bowed low. Inaccessible as she was, Nanon still kept a few intimate friends from her old days with whom she occasionally hobnobbed, and one of them was an old woman who had brought up the Duchesse de Lude and still loved her passionately. The Duchesse attacked through these two old crones, and in the end 20,000 crowns settled the matter the very evening of the Saturday on which the King had expressed his dislike of her so openly to Monsieur. Such is court life! A woman like Nanon can sell the most important and most brilliant offices, and a Duchess, rich and of high birth both in her own right and by marriage, childless, free, independ-

20

ent, and without ties of any kind, is so foolish as to buy herself at great cost into servitude! Her joy was extreme, but she managed not to show it too much; and her way of life and her vast number of friends and acquaintances both in town and at court assured that her appointment was applauded by the majority.

The Duchesse d'Arpajon and the Maréchale de Rochefort were livid. The latter complained bitterly and indiscreetly that the promise, on the strength of which she had consented to become Lady of Honour to the Duchesse de Chartres, had been broken; she neatly confused the position of Lady of Honour and Lady-in-Waiting in order to lend more colour to her complaint—it was the latter post she had held with Mme la Dauphine and which she had been promised [with the future Duchesse de Bourgogne]. Mme de Maintenon, who despised her, was roused by this because it was she who had caused the post to be given to the Duchesse de Lude. She told the Maréchale that she had brought it on herself by standing up for her own daughter, who otherwise ought long ago to have been banished from court. In a rage the Maréchale swallowed this and abandoned her daughter, who was rusticated to Paris with orders not to reappear at court. This daughter was very rich. By her first husband, with whom she had been on very bad terms, she was the mother of Nangis and she undoubtedly ruined him. Later she became pregnant by Blanzac,[1] who was brought back from the army to marry her; she gave birth to Mme de Tonnerre on her wedding-night. No one could be cleverer than she was, no one seemed milder, could convey a hint more delicately, possessed a keener wit, or could so perfectly match her conversation to the company in which she found herself. At the same time there never was a woman more mischievous, wicked, dangerous, artificial, false through and through, who could tell tales with such a convincing air of simplicity that even those who knew there was not a word of truth in them were convinced. For all that, she was an enchanting siren from whom there was no safety save in flight, even for those who knew her for what she was. Her conversation was delightful, and no one succeeded so easily, so amusingly, and so cruelly in making people look ridiculous, even when they were really not ridiculous at all. So long as she remained beautiful she attracted a constant succession of lovers; as time went on she became less and less discriminating, and she ended by picking up the lowest type of servants. For all her vices, she was eagerly sought after both at court and in the city; her drawing-room was always filled with the most brilliant company, drawn thither either by fear or by her

****

[1] Charles de la Rochefoucauld de Roye, Comte de Blanzac (1665–1732).

1696 magic, and she had a host of friends, both men and women. The King's three daughters were rivals for her affection, but owing to her mother's appointment she was closer to the Duchesse de Chartres than to the others, and she completely dominated her. The jealousies and bickerings which arose over this attachment earned her the detestation of Monsieur and the Duc de Chartres and she was sent away. In time the tears and the wiles of the Duchesse de Chartres secured her recall. She came back to Marly and was admitted to several intimate parties with the King, whom she amused so much that he could talk about nothing else. Mme de Maintenon was thoroughly alarmed and set about first keeping her away from the King—which she accomplished with considerable skill—and then having her rusticated again, and this incident which I have just described was used as an opportunity of getting her own way. The mother became a laughing-stock for her stupidity in being party to such an affair for the sake of an appointment which she would not have had anyway, but the daughter was forced to stay in Paris for a long time.[1]

[1] She lived in Paris for at least eight years.

1697

MME DE MAINTENON'S BROTHER

✠✠✠✠✠ESPITE her remarkable rise from the lowliest beginnings, ✠ 𝔇 ✠ even Mme de Maintenon was not without her tribulations, ✠ ✠ and among them the continual follies of her brother were by ✠✠✠✠✠ no means the least. He was called the Comte d'Aubigné. He had risen no higher than captain in an infantry regiment, but he never stopped talking about the engagements in which he had taken part, and, in his opinion, it was a piece of gross injustice that he had not long since been made a Marshal of France—though sometimes he jokingly remarked that he had compounded his baton for money.[1] He was always going on at Mme de Maintenon because she had not had him created a duke and peer, and because he had never been given anything except the governorships of Belfort, then Aigues-Mortes, then Cognac (which he retained with that of Berry), and the riband of the Order. He was always chasing women in the Tuileries garden and elsewhere; he usually kept several of them at the same time and lived on the most familiar terms with them and their brood—a most expensive pastime. He was a spendthrift, mad enough to be put away, but pleasant and amusing, with a gift for unexpected sallies. But for all his shortcomings, he was a good and honest man, well mannered and without any of that intolerable vanity which his sister's elevated position might well have inspired in him. He was a great talker, and it was most amusing to listen to him holding forth about the old days of Scarron and the hôtel d'Albret, or of even earlier times and of his sister's various adventures and liaisons, frequently comparing them with her new piety and high position, and marvelling at so prodigious a change of fortune. Though it was amusing, this could be extremely embarrassing, for once he started it was impossible to stop him; nor did he talk thus only among friends—but at table, in front of anyone, on a seat in the Tuileries, and even more freely in the Great Gallery at Versailles, where he never stopped joking and normally referred to 'my brother-in-law' when he meant the King. I have often listened to him, particularly at my father's house, to which he came more often than he was welcome, and often laughed to myself at the acute

---

[1] Though only a captain, he held two governorships in Holland out of which he made a considerable profit in addition to those mentioned by Saint-Simon below.

embarrassment of my parents who did not know which way to look.

A man of this kind, incapable of self-restraint, with so sharp a wit and with so little fear of ridicule or of any serious consequences which might befall him, was a great trial to Mme de Maintenon. Nor was she much better off with her sister-in-law. This woman was the daughter of a small doctor named Piètre who was *procureur du Roi* at Paris, and d'Aubigné married her in 1678 at the time when his sister was looking after Mme de Montespan's children; he had some hopes of making his fortune by the marriage. She was an obscure creature—more obscure even than the insignificance of her forbears demanded: modest and virtuous—as she well needed to be with such a husband—unbelievably stupid, undistinguished in appearance, and with no idea of how to dress. She was a source of embarrassment to Mme de Maintenon, who could do nothing with her and finally received her only in private. She never saw anyone fashionable and lived in squalor with a few cronies. Complaints were constantly being made about her husband to Mme de Maintenon, who, queen of everyone else about her, could no nothing with him—and indeed was often herself roughly handled by him.

At last, weary of so extravagant a brother, she persuaded him—since he did everything on an impulse and was always short of money—to give up his debauchery, his independence, and his domestic up-heavals, and go into a sort of retreat for gentlemen set up by a M. Doyen in the shadow of St. Sulpice, where she paid all his expenses and gave him plenty of spending money. Mme d'Aubigné, for the sake of peace and quiet (and because Mme de Maintenon insisted), also went into retreat, telling her friends at the same time that it was very hard and she did so against her will. M. d'Aubigné also told everyone that his sister was laughing at him by pretending that he had become de-vout, that he was plagued by priests, and that he was being driven into his grave at M. Doyen's establishment. In no time at all he was back . with the women in the Tuileries and anywhere else he could find them; but they picked him up again and put him in the charge of the dullest priest at St. Sulpice, who followed him about like a shadow and wore the heart out of him. Anyone worth anything would never have taken on such a job, but this Father Madot had nothing better to do and hadn't even the wits to be bored. He had to put up with constant in-sults, but he was paid for it—and certainly no one else could have earned his money with such assiduity.

M. d'Aubigné had an only daughter, who lived in Mme de Main-tenon's apartments and was brought up by her as though she were her own.

1698

SAINCTOT AND COURT ETIQUETTE

✤✤✤✤✤AINCTOT, Gentleman Usher of the Ambassadors, did an
✤ S ✤extremely stupid thing which might have had the most em-
✤ ✤barrassing consequences for the Duchesse de Lude. The
✤✤✤✤✤Savoy Ambassador Ferreiro, Chevalier de l'Annonciade,
was going to have a ceremonial audience of the Duchesse de Bourgogne when Sainctot told the Duchesse de Lude that she should receive him in the antechamber with all the Ladies of the Palace. They,
always anxious to escape being under the Lady of Honour's charge,
did not wish to go. The Duchesse de Lude said she had never seen
the other Ladies of Honour nor the Dauphine go to receive ambassadors, but Sainctot insisted and made her do it. The King found it quite
wrong and reprimanded Sainctot the same day; but the embarrassing
thing was that every ambassador subsequently expected to be received in audience with the same honour. It was an extremely difficult
matter to explain to them that this procedure resulted solely from ignorance on the part of an official and could not be taken as a precedent,
and it was only after long discussions, and much coming and going of
couriers, that they were satisfied with a document signed by Torcy
certifying that this honour had never been accorded to any ambassador
and that what happened with Ferreiro had arisen out of ignorance and
would not be allowed to recur. After this certificate had been issued
audience went on in the usual way, with the Duchesse de Lude standing beside and slightly behind the Duchesse de Bourgogne.

Not very long after, Sainctot blundered again. The Dutch Ambassador, Heemskirk, brought his wife and daughter to court. This wife
was received publicly by the Duchesse de Bourgogne in the midst of
her circle, with the Duchesse de Lude on the left, all of them seated on
their stools as is customary. When the Ambassadress arrived, she was
received at the door by the Lady of Honour and led up to the Duchess,
the hem of whose skirt she kissed, and by whom she was then kissed
in the usual manner accorded to all ladies of title. Then the Ambassadress presented her daughter who had been led forward by Sainctot.
The girl kissed the Duchess's skirt and then put up her cheek to be
kissed. The Duchesse de Bourgogne, taken by surprise, hesitated; the
Duchesse de Lude shook her head; but Sainctot, pushing the girl forward, said 'Kiss her, Madame, it is her due.' The Duchess, young, in-

experienced, and not wishing to upset anyone, deferred to Sainctot's
dangerous advice and kissed her. Everyone present murmured out
loud—the seated ladies and the women behind, as well as the courtiers.
The King, who always looked in at these receptions in order to honour
the Ambassadors' wives without receiving them himself, could not see
what was happening for the crowd.

From there the Ambassadress went to wait upon Madame. There
was the same ceremony and the same forward attempt by the daughter.
When Madame, who had been accustomed to ceremonial all her life,
saw this cheek being put up towards her, she recoiled sharply. Sainctot
said that the Duchesse de Bourgogne had done the young thing the
honour of kissing her. 'That is too bad,' replied Madame; 'it is a piece
of stupidity that you have led her into, which I have no intention of following.' There was a considerable sensation, and it was not long before the King heard of it. He sent for Sainctot at once and, threatening
to relieve the man of his office on the spot, was much more angry than
he usually allowed himself to be. But the Ambassadors could not make
anything out of this: their standing, which is shared by their wives,
since husband and wife are one, does not extend to their children, so
that they could not presume on the blunder.

This Sainctot was a man who did what he liked and favoured whom
he pleased—even at the risk of being severely reprimanded: which in
fact seldom happened, partly through ignorance and partly because of
the few occasions which occurred when full ceremonial was called for.[1]

THE ENGLISH AMBASSADOR

MADAME, who wept for deceased members of her family in direct relation to their degree of propinquity, as others govern their mourning,
was much upset by the death of the wife of the Elector of Hanover. He
had married Sophia, a daughter of Elizabeth, sister of the unfortunate
King Charles I of England, and the Elector Palatine who became King
of Bohemia, lost his lands, and died in exile. Even though Madame had
hardly ever seen her aunt, she had faithfully written volumes to her
twice or three times a week ever since she came to France. The King
waited upon her when he heard of her aunt's death.

The King of England was extremely satisfied that he had at last been

---

[1] A number of contemporary writers commented upon the fact that the French court
was remarkable for its lack of ceremonial, compared with the other courts of Europe,
and there appears to have been little protocol.

The wedding of the Duc de Bourgogne

recognized by our King[1] and was settled peacefully on his throne; but a usurper can never really feel happy, and he was annoyed because the legitimate King and his family remained at Saint-Germain—which was too near our court and too near England for safety. He did everything he could, in the Ryswyck conference as well as through the discussions between the Earl of Portland[2] and the Maréchal de Boufflers, to get them sent out of the Kingdom, or at least banished from court— but he found our King inflexible. He determined to make one more big effort, and thought that by overwhelming the King with praise and respects he might in passing get what he wanted. With this in mind he sent the Duke of St. Albans, K.G., to compliment the King on the marriage of the Duc de Bourgogne. The King could not have chosen anyone more eminent for so simple a task, but many were surprised that the Duke accepted it, since he is a bastard son of Charles II [by Nell Gwynne], the elder brother of James II. He wished to receive special marks of honour, but with polite firmness he was treated as no more than any other English envoy: the Dukes of that country have no more standing here than ours have in England. The King had made the Duchess of Portsmouth and her son the Duke of Richmond Duke and Duchess by licence,[3] and also gave an honorary stool to her friend the Duchess of Cleveland.[4] The Duchesse de la Force,[5] who went to England for religious reasons, and before her the Duchesse de Mazarin,[6] who fled to England to escape her husband, both attained

---

[1] Louis recognized William III as King of England and Anne as heir to the throne in the Peace of Ryswyck, 1697.

[2] William Bentinck, Earl and later Duke of Portland (1649–1709). A close friend of William of Orange and accompanied him to England when he ascended the throne. Earl, and Groom of the Stole 1689. His informal negotiations with the Maréchal de Boufflers in Hull during the summer of 1697 materially forwarded the Treaty of Ryswyck, concluded that September. In the following year he undertook the ambassadorial mission to France, here described, and with the Maréchal de Tallard worked out the general lines of the Partition Treaties designed to settle the Spanish succession. In 1699 he resigned his offices because he found himself supplanted in William's favour by Arnold van Keppel, Earl of Albemarle.

[3] Louise-Renée de Keroval (1649–1734). She came of a Breton family, and first appeared at the English court as Lady-in-Waiting to the Queen in 1670. She bore Charles II a son, Charles Lennox, later Duke of Richmond, in 1672. For her services to France, and at the request of Charles II, Louise was given the lands of the Duchy of d'Aubigny-sur-Nère in 1673.

[4] Barbara Villiers, Duchess of Castlemaine, mistress of Charles II in 1661; she was created Duchess of Cleveland, and came to France frequently. The most senior ladies at court were permitted to be seated on a stool in the royal presence; it was an extraordinary privilege for this to be accorded to a foreigner.

[5] The Duchesse de la Force was persecuted for her religion until the death of her husband in 1699, when she retired to England and died there in 1731.

[6] Hortense Mancini (1643–99) was one of the nieces of Cardinal Mazarin. She had an adventurous life, including a period as the mistress of Charles II.

27

1698 to the rank of Duchess in that country; but all these were special cases.

The Duke of St. Albans took his leave on the arrival of the Duke of Portland, than whom there could not have been a more distinguished Ambassador. His suite was numerous and superb; he kept a magnificent table, and his horses, his footmen, equipages, furnishings, clothes, and plate were of an exquisite refinement and delicacy. His whole train arrived together, for he came from Calais and took his time on the way, receiving military and civil honours *en route*. It was while he was on the road that fire practically destroyed Whitehall, the biggest and most shabby palace in Europe: it has not been rebuilt, and consequently at present the King is somewhat uncomfortably housed in St. James's Palace. Portland had his first private audience of the King on 4 February, and remained four months in France. He arrived before Tallard[1] or any other representative of the King had left for London. Portland had a personal distinction, a polish, gallantry, and courtly air which surprised everyone. At the same time he was extremely dignified, even haughty—but with discernment and judgement. The French, who love any novelty and enjoy a magnificent display, were charmed. He captivated everyone, but he showed a knowledge of our court and was careful to seek only the best and most distinguished company. It soon became the fashion to call upon him, to entertain him, and to attend his parties. The most extraordinary thing was that the King, who was still angry with King William, himself paid more attention to this Ambassador than he ever had to any other: possibly the King thought that in this way he could recompense him for the fact that his mission was doomed to failure from the start. The very first time the Duke saw Torcy,[2] before going to Versailles, he asked about the possibility of sending King James and his family away from Saint-Germain. Torcy wisely spoke quite frankly: he said that the whole subject had been thrashed out in Portland's previous discussions with the Maréchal de Boufflers and had been rejected in various forms at the Ryswyck conference—in fact it had been rejected all round and must now be regarded as closed; he knew that the King not only would not change his mind, but would be very put out if the subject were brought up again. He added that the King was quite prepared to enjoy friendly relations

---

[1] Camille d'Hostun, Comte de Tallard (1652–1728), was head of the missions which went to London in 1698 and 1700 to negotiate treaties regulating the Spanish monarchy. Later he fought in Flanders and was created a Marshal, and Duc d'Hostun. He commanded the French army at Blenheim. Louis XIV named him in his will as a member of the Council, but he was not summoned when the Regent took charge.

[2] Jean Baptiste Colbert, Marquis de Torcy (1665–1746), at this time Secretary of State for Foreign Affairs.

with the King of England and wished to receive well the Ambassador himself, but one word about Saint-Germain would upset everything and make Portland's time in France most unpleasant, and that his own personal advice was never to refer to the matter. Portland believed him and accepted his views, but not without some annoyance; the King highly approved of Torcy's action in closing the subject firmly. Great care was taken to see that none of the English from the court at Saint-Germain should bump into any of the Ambassador's suite either at Versailles or in Paris, and these instructions were most carefully carried out.

Portland frequently used to ride to Monseigneur's hounds; twice he went from Paris to Meudon for a wolf-hunt, and on both occasions Monseigneur asked him to stay to supper. At one *coucher* the King handed him the candlestick, a mark of His Majesty's especial esteem. Ambassadors rarely achieved such standing that they were allowed to pay their court at that hour at all, and such an honour had almost never before been accorded to any of them. Portland took his leave on 20 May, covered with honours and fêted in every possible way. The Maréchal de Villeroy was directed by the King to show him Marly and to do the honours. He wanted to see everything, and he was especially charmed with Fontainebleu, which he liked best of the royal residences. Although he had taken his official leave, Portland was accorded the very great honour of having yet another interview with the King, who was being dosed. To crown it all, the King invited him within the railing about his bed, an honour never before accorded to any foreigner, whomsoever it might be, except sometimes to Ambassadors at their first official reception. On leaving, Portland went to join Monseigneur out hunting, and for the third time was invited to supper at Meudon. The Grand Prior[1] deliberately took precedence over him, which, even though he had taken his leave, annoyed the Ambassador considerably so that the next morning he went back to the King again and said proudly that if His Majesty had accorded the rank of Princes of the Blood to MM. de Vendôme he could not dispute it, but if not he thought that the Grand Prior should pay him the respect due to him. The King replied that he had accorded no such rank to the Vendôme brothers, and he would send a message to Monseigneur, who was still at Meudon, to see that such a thing did not occur again.

Monsieur wished to show the Ambassador Saint-Cloud[2] himself;

---

[1] Of the Order of the Knights of Malta. Philippe, Chevalier de Vendôme, younger brother of the Duc de Vendôme.

[2] Monsieur's own home.

1698 Madame deliberately did not go. Monsieur gave a large banquet, and the company present included Monseigneur—also in itself a great honour.

But among so many bouquets there were some thorns too—occasioned by the continued presence in France of the legitimate King of England. On one occasion Portland was pulling on his boots for a hunt at Meudon when Monseigneur was warned that the King of England was at the meet. At once he sent a message to Portland and begged him to postpone his hunting to another day. There was nothing for him to do but take his boots off again and return to Paris. He was a great rider to hounds, and, being most anxious to follow the King's pack, he was surprised that he received nothing more than a polite bow whenever he met the Duc de la Rochefoucauld, the Master of the Hounds. He expressed his wish so often that he could not believe the Duke did not know about it. As nothing happened, he went straight up to the Master of the Hounds one morning as they were both leaving the King's *lever* and put his request to him direct. Not in the least embarrassed, Rochefoucauld replied that although he had the honour of being Master of the Hounds, he did not make the arrangements for the hunt, which were in the hands of the King of England, who rode frequently to hounds, but one never knew till the last moment whether he was going to be at the meet or not: and with that he bowed and left Portland furious but with no come-back. M. de la Rochefoucauld was the only great dignitary of the court who did not pay service to Portland, and this was purely out of generosity towards the King of England. In fact the English King, although he had a great say in the management of the royal pack, did not by any means follow every hunt, and it would not have been difficult for M. de la Rochefoucauld to tell Portland when he could attend without fear of embarrassment. But, annoyed by the lack of respect shown for the court of Saint-Germain even in their very presence, he could not help mortifying in this one respect the triumphant Ambassador of the usurper who had captivated everyone, even up to M. de Lauzun,[1] in spite of this nobleman's old attachment and appointment to the King and Queen of England.

At last Portland, full of honours, took his departure. The rising favour of the Duke of Albemarle[2] disturbed him and caused him to

[1] Antonin Nompar de Caumont, Comte (later Duc) de Lauzun (1633–1723). Being in England in 1688, he was entrusted by James II with the task of conveying the Queen and the Prince of Wales to France. He was made a Duke in 1690 after commanding the French forces in James II's unsuccessful campaign in Ireland.

[2] Arnold-Juste van Keppel (1670–1718), scion of an old Dutch family, was page to William of Orange, and then successively Gentleman of the Bedchamber, Master of the Robes, and a Knight of the Garter.

hurry home. Monsieur le Prince asked him to stop at Chantilly on the way, and gave a magnificent banquet marked by that exquisite taste so typical of everything the Condés do. Thence Portland went on through Flanders. Not only had he the King's permission to see whatever he liked, but engineers were instructed to accompany him and explain anything he wanted to know. He was received everywhere with great honour, and was accompanied always by a captain and fifty horse. At the end of so brilliant a journey he found himself supplanted at home by a young rival, with nothing left but the memory of the confidence he had once enjoyed and regrets at so prolonged an absence. When he left Paris he said that so long as King James remained at Saint-Germain he would see that the Queen was not paid the pension which had been agreed at the Peace of Ryswyck, and he kept his word.

MORE WEDDINGS

IN March 1698 old Seissac married the youngest daughter of the Duc de Chevreuse by his second wife; she was young and pretty, and, having no money, she was willing because she hoped soon to become a widow with great expectations. He was an intelligent man of good qualities, and had been Master of the Robes; he was very rich, a real Gascon, a great gambler, and a frequenter of the best society, but he was not much liked and his success at cards was regarded with some suspicion. At that time the King liked to play for high stakes, and brelan[1] was the fashionable game. One evening the King was playing at the same table with Seissac when the Duc de Lorges[2] whispered in his ear and called him away. The King gave his cards to M. de Lorges, asking him to play on until he could get back, and went into his study with M. de Louvois.[3] Meanwhile Seissac made a play against M. de Lorges, contrary to the principles of the game, which was nevertheless highly successful and won a great deal of money. M. de Lorges thought it his duty to tell the King what had happened. The King had both the page responsible for issuing the cards and the card-maker quietly apprehended, and the pack was found to be marked. The card-maker then confessed that Seissac had ordered them, promising him a cut of

---

[1] A game for three players, each drawing three cards and betting against one another.

[2] Saint-Simon's father-in-law, Gui-Aldonce de Durfort, Marquis de Lorges (1630–1702), Marshal of France; a nephew of Turenne, and a fine soldier.

[3] François Michel le Tellier, Marquis de Louvois (1639–91), most able Secretary of State for War. Saint-Simon is obviously recounting an early anecdote here, before Louvois's death.

the profits. The following morning Seissac was ordered to resign his office and remove himself from the palace. A few years later he was granted permission to go to England, where he played for a few years and made a great deal of money. When he came back he was allowed to go where he liked, short of appearing in the royal presence: he set up house in Paris, where he continued to make money. Later Monsieur, who always liked gambling, asked the King if Seissac might play with him in Paris and at Saint-Cloud. Monseigneur, at Monsieur's suggestion, obtained the same permission for Meudon; between them they so arranged it that he was finally able to get back to Versailles and then to Marly. He was an extraordinary man, who cared nothing for the dislike in which he knew he was held. Also he never wore mourning for anyone—he said it was useless and he found it upsetting; he never respected the death of even his nearest relatives—and his relations returned the compliment, for neither M. de Chevreuse nor any of his family recognized his death in any way.

Another marriage was more brilliant and the parties more suitably matched in their ages: it was that of the Comte d'Ayen[1] and Mlle d'Aubigné.[2] The King very much wanted her to marry the Prince de Marcillac, grandson of the Duc de la Rochefoucauld. M. de la Rochefoucauld had never been on good terms with Mme de Maintenon; he had always been close to Mme de Montespan, and above all to Mme de Thianges, whose children he was still fond of. The King was well aware of this, and he wanted to improve their relations. Since there had never been any open breach between the two, it was very difficult to find any basis on which to bring them together. When the King mentioned the subject, M. de la Rochefoucauld consented to a *rapprochement* only out of respect and to oblige; on the other hand, Mme de Maintenon, who had reasons of her own for following a different course, gave a very dusty answer. Such a frigid response from both sides rebuffed the King, who returned rather half-heartedly to the attack by asking Mme de Maintenon where she could find a better match for birth, wealth, and prospects than the Prince de Marcillac. She suggested the Comte d'Ayen. The King, in turn, did not respond as Mme de Maintenon hoped: he disliked the Duchesse de Noailles,[3]

---

[1] Adrien-Maurice, Comte d'Ayen, later Duc de Noailles (1678–1766), Marshal of France, who spent much of his life soldiering. Later a great favourite of Louis XV. Commanded the French Army at the battle of Dettingen in 1743, renowned in English history as the last engagement at which an English monarch was present.

[2] Niece of Mme de Maintenon.

[3] Françoise de Bournonville, Duchesse de Noailles, mother of the Comte d'Ayen She was a highly intelligent woman, who bore her husband no fewer than twenty-one children and died in 1748 at the age of ninety-four.

who was too clever, too forthcoming, and too much of an intriguer for him, and such a marriage would admit her into his most intimate circle, which he dreaded. Mme de Maintenon, however, was most anxious to be on good terms with M. de Paris[1] and, with the support of M. de Cambrai,[2] to worm her way into Church affairs, and more particularly the bestowal of benefices, which Père de la Chaise[3] had always prevented her from doing. Since the King liked M. de Noailles, she worked on him to such an extent, with a solemn promise to keep Mme de Noailles at arm's length, that finally he agreed to the marriage. Mme de Maintenon promised the bride 600,000 livres; and the King gave her 300,000 livres in cash, 500,000 livres on the hôtel de ville,[4] 100,000 livres' worth of precious stones, the reversion of M. de Noailles's governorship, 38,000 livres of rents, and above all the position of Lady of the Palace. The engagement was announced on 11 March. The next day Mme de Maintenon on leaving table lay on her bed and her doors were thrown open formally to the whole court. The Duchesse de Bourgogne, in formal dress, spent the whole day there with Mlle d'Aubigné, and doing the honours like any ordinary person. On the last Thursday in March the engagement was solemnized in the chapel, with the Duchesse de Bourgogne and the whole court in the gallery and the bridal pair below. On the following day, late in the forenoon, Mme de Maintenon and everyone concerned with the wedding went to the parish church of Versailles, where M. de Paris celebrated Mass and performed the marriage ceremony. After that the Duc de Noailles entertained the whole company at dinner in the apartments of the Comte de Toulouse, which had been lent for the occasion.[5] After dinner Mme de Maintenon on one bed and the Comtesse d'Ayen on another in the next room received the whole court.[6] That evening there was a supper in Mme de Maintenon's rooms, with the ladies in one room and the men in another, and after supper the bridal pair were put to bed in the same apartment. The King handed the nightshirt to M. d'Ayen, and Mme de Bourgogne gave the nightdress

---

[1] Louis-Antoine de Noailles, Archbishop of Paris, created Cardinal in 1700. Uncle of the Comte d'Ayen.

[2] François de Salignac de la Mothe-Fénelon, the celebrated writer, Archbishop of Cambrai.

[3] Her confessor.

[4] Bonds issued by the hôtel de ville and met out of imposts sanctioned by the King; a method of raising money begun during the wars of Louis's reign.

[5] These were the *appartements du Bain*, originally laid out for Mme de Montespan, later occupied by the Duc du Maine.

[6] The habit of receiving complimentary visits while lying on one's bed was well established; it apparently obviated certain awkward questions of precedence.

to the bride. The King attended throughout the ceremony; he himself drew the curtains of the bed, and as a good-night present he said he would give them each an allowance of 8,000 livres. At the same time the King paid the debts of M. de la Rochefoucauld, which had got out of hand.

The Duc de la Rochefoucauld's pleasure was somewhat marred by the loss of his brother the Abbé de Marcillac [after a long illness]: I say 'somewhat' because, although there had been no open quarrel, they were not on very good terms. Those who knew them both say that the Abbé de Marcillac was very like his brother. As soon as he was dead his livings were given to the Abbé de la Rochefoucauld, the paternal uncle of the Duke and of about the same age. He was a man who loved hunting so much that he was familiarly known as the 'Abbé View-Halloo.' When M. de la Rochefoucauld had been in need, his uncle had kept him going, and in consequence the Duke was extremely fond of him and was always his host whenever he came to court. He was a fine man, though as simple as they come, and only remarkable for his constantly perfect health. Neither he nor the Abbé de Marcillac was in holy orders.

About this time the Prince de Conti lost his little four-year-old son, the Prince de Roche-sur-Yon. The King went into black mourning.[1] Usually he wore no mourning for children under seven—even his own children; but he had done M. du Maine the honour of mourning one of his children, and after that did not feel that he should omit the same honour for Princes of the Blood. He went to pay his respects to M. le Prince, Mme la Princesse, and Mme la Princesse de Conti; the Princes of the Blood found him there and escorted him back as far as the apartments of Mme de Maintenon.

MANŒUVRES AT COMPIÈGNE

Now that peace had been signed, the King wished to impress Europe with a display of his strength, which was generally thought to have been exhausted by the long war, and at the same time to arrange, in the name of the Duc de Bourgogne, a superb spectacle for Madame de Maintenon. He decided to give the young Duke as realistic an impression of war as was possible in peace-time and to give him his first

---

[1] The King of France went into full mourning (purple) for crowned heads, their children, and relations up to first cousins inclusive. Half mourning, for Princes of the Blood and Princes of foreign houses, was black.

The King bends to Madame de Maintenon

lessons in the technique of military leadership by ordering full-scale manœuvres at Compiègne, which were to be directed by the Maréchal de Boufflers[1] under the titular leadership of the young Duke himself. The units to take part and the generals who were to have commands were named, and the King announced when he himself proposed to be there—adding that he expected a large attendance from the court.

Soon everyone was talking of nothing but Compiègne, where 60,000 troops were concentrating under canvas. The King let it be known that he expected the troops to be well turned out and that he hoped there would be a genuine spirit of competition between units; this was enough to touch off a rivalry which in the end could lead to nothing but regrets. Not only was the turn-out so universally excellent that it was quite impossible to consider one corps as better than another, but the commanders did everything they could to add to the splendid appearance of men, horses, and equipment, and in addition officers of all ranks ruined themselves by ordering superb uniforms which would have done duty at a *fête*.

Colonels and officers down to Captains kept splendid tables; the six Lieutenant Generals and fourteen Brigadiers distinguished themselves by the lavishness of their entertainment. But everyone was put in the shade by the Maréchal de Boufflers, whose outlay, whose superb display of tasteful abundance was so staggering throughout the manœuvres, twenty-four hours a day, that it even gave a lesson in entertainment to the King himself, and even to Monsieur, whose taste in such matters was unsurpassed. There was never a spectacle so brilliant, so astonishing, and yet one which, I must admit, was rather frightening. No one appeared less involved than the General himself, who oversaw every little detail while outwardly appearing to be concerned solely with the conduct of the manœuvres. There were innumerable tables, always freshly laid and ready at all times for the entertainment of any officers, courtiers, or spectators who might drop in—the merest sightseer was made welcome and served with courteous promptitude by his innumerable staff. There was every sort of drink, hot and cold, that you can think of—French wines, foreign wines, and the rarest liqueurs flowed in

---

[1] Louis-Francois de Boufflers, Duc de Boufflers (1644–1711). As Comte de Cagny he distinguished himself in the war of the League of Augsburg, commanding first the army of the Moselle, then that of the Meuse. He was created a Marshal and governor of Flanders. His heroic defence of Namur in 1695, which he only surrendered after a siege of 67 days, earned him a dukedom. In the War of the Spanish Succession he gained further successes. He was besieged in Lille in 1703 and though again forced to capitulate he showed such heroism that he was made a peer of France. After the defeat at Malplaquet in 1709 he commanded the retreat and saved the army from annihilation.

abundance. There was every sort of game and venison, and the most unusual sea food was brought from Normandy, Holland, England, Brittany, and the Mediterranean fresh several times a day by means of a prodigious number of couriers. Even the water, since the local supply was inadequate, was brought from Sainte-Reine, the Seine, and the best springs. It is impossible to think of anything which had not been provided for everyone from the highest to the lowest; wooden buildings decorated as sumptuously as any Paris salon had been built specially, and the staff—the cooks and the innumerable staff required to keep up a twenty-four-hour service—were housed in a vast number of huge marquees which in themselves made up a camp of no mean size.

On Thursday, 28 August, the court left for Compiègne; the King went via Saint-Cloud, spent the night at Chantilly, remained there the following day, and arrived at Compiègne on Saturday. The headquarters was in the village of Condun. The King, taking the Duc and the Duchesse de Bourgogne with him, was served on his arrival with so magnificent a dinner that he said afterwards to Livry[1] that nothing set up for his household in the field could compare with what he had just had, and that when his grandson arrived he should eat at the Maréchal de Boufflers's table. The King loved watching the troops concentrating, and showing them off to the ladies; he was interested in every detail of the troops' arrival—the convoys, their marching, the rations, their quarters, and their drill. The Duchesse de Bourgogne and the Princesses often dined with the Marshal, where the Maréchale de Boufflers did the honours. Monseigneur dined there sometimes, and the King took the King of England, who spent three or four days watching the exercises. It was many years since the King had paid anyone such a compliment, and the fuss over entertaining two kings together was considerable.

The King wished every side of war to be represented. So Compiègne was besieged, although the business—the digging of trenches, saps, and batteries—was speeded up; Crenan defended the place. There was an old rampart round the château from which there was a splendid view of the open country; and this was only a step from the King's quarters. Saturday, 13 September, was the day set for the assault on the town; in the most lovely weather the King, followed by all the ladies, went out on the rampart, whence the whole countryside and the disposition of the troops could be seen. I was in the semicircle a few paces behind the King, with no one between us. It was a wonderful sight— the vast army, cavalry and infantry, deployed, and the game of attack-

[1] The King's major-domo.

ing and defending the city. But what struck me most, and remains as clear in my mind today after forty years, was the King on that rampart in supreme command over the whole army and that vast mass of myrmidons around him, crowded on the rampart and spread over the plain.

Madame de Maintenon was there at the edge of the plain in her sedan-chair with glass on three sides; her porters withdrew. On the left shaft was perched the Duchesse de Bourgogne; on the same side, standing in the semicircle just behind, was the Duchesse d'Orléans, the Princesse de Conti, and the other ladies, with the men behind them. The King stood by the right-hand window, with the most distinguished men grouped in a semicircle behind him. The King remained uncovered most of the time and frequently bent down to talk to Madame de Maintenon through the window and to explain to her what was going on. Each time he bent down she opened the window four or five inches, but never as much as half-way—I know that, for I watched carefully, and I must confess I watched this business more closely than I watched the troops. Sometimes she opened the window to ask the King something; but generally it was he who spoke first, and sometimes he had to knock on the glass when he wanted to tell her something. He spoke to no one else, except to give a few abrupt orders or to make an occasional remark to the Duchesse de Bourgogne.

When the moment for the capitulation of the town arrived Madame de Maintenon apparently asked permission to go to the scene of action; the King shouted 'Madame's bearers'; they came and bore her away. Less than a quarter of an hour later the King withdrew, followed by the Duchesse de Bourgogne and the rest. Everyone was talking about it, even the private soldiers—and before long the story of the King bending down talking through the window of that sedan-chair spread throughout Europe, and was as much a subject of gossip as the splendour and magnificence of those manœuvres.

THE PAINTER INRI

THE Marquis de Gesvres, who considered himself well read and used to store little scraps of information to work into his conversation, was chatting one day in the King's studies and admiring the magnificent pictures on the walls, among which were several of the crucifixion by various eminent masters. He said was it not odd that the same man should have painted the same subject so often. Everyone laughed and pointed out that the pictures were by different hands, as one could readily see from their styles.

'Of course not,' cried the Marquis, 'they are all one man's work, the painter who called himself INRI. Can't you see he's signed them all?'

THE UNFORTUNATE TAILOR'S HOUSE

THE King had Charnacé[1] arrested, being already severely displeased over his conduct in Anjou. Charnacé had gone off to live at his house in the country there, and was thence removed to Montauban accused of various misdemeanours including forgery. He was a man of considerable intelligence, who had been a Page and had held a commission in the Household Troops; subsequently he retired to his estates where he was always up to mischief, although he was always excused and protected by the King. One of his exploits in particular was extremely funny.

Leading up to his house in Anjou[2] was a long avenue of very great beauty in the middle of which was a cottage, with a small garden, belonging to a peasant family which apparently had been there before the avenue was planted. Neither Charnacé nor his father had ever been able to persuade any of them to sell, whatever they offered. Charnacé was at a loss as to what to do next, and had left the thing alone for some time. Finally, bored with this little building which completely spoiled his enjoyment of his own avenue, he thought of a way through.

He sent for the tailor, who was a bachelor—the last of the line—living alone, and said that, having been summoned to court to take up an important appointment, he needed a new uniform in a hurry. They agreed on the terms, but Charnacé stipulated that, since he could not allow any delay whatever, the tailor must come to the château, eat and sleep there, and not leave until the job was finished. The tailor agreed and started work.

While the suit was being cut out, Charnacé had the tailor's house, garden, and possessions meticulously measured and noted, even down to the exact position of the smallest kitchen utensil. Then he had the house pulled down and re-erected stone by stone about half a mile away, with everything put back in its exact position and a new garden planted round it; then the gap in the trees of the avenue was filled up.

All this was achieved and completed before the new uniform was

---

[1] Jacques-Philippe de Girard, Baron de Vaux (1640–1720). In recognition of the services which his family had given to the State he was permitted in 1673 to revive and assume the title of Marquis de Charnacé. He obtained various sinecures, and was usually in hot water of one kind or another.
[2] At Linière.

made, and during the operation the tailor was kept well out of sight so that there could be no leakage. Finally both tasks were completed, and Charnacé kept his guest amused until night—a particularly dark one—had fallen, then paid him and sent him happy on his way.

The tailor eventually reached the avenue, which seemed to him to be surprisingly long; at long last he came to the trees—and nothing more. He got to the far end and then carefully made his way back again; he counted up and back, but still could not find his house, and could not understand it. He spent the rest of the night on his feet, until dawn was light enough for him to find his house; but still he could not see it. He rubbed his eyes and looked around for recognizable landmarks. Finally he came to the reluctant conclusion that the devil had taken his house away. As he walked up and down in bewilderment he saw a house in the middle distance which looked uncommonly like his own; he didn't think that it could be, but curiosity drew him across to this site on which he had never seen a house before. The nearer he got the more it looked like his own home. He put his key in the lock and the door opened; he went in and everything was just as he had left it. He nearly fainted and remained convinced that the whole affair was sorcery. Before the day was far advanced the laughter at the château and the gossip in the village made him realize what had happened, and he was furious; he wanted to go to law, he demanded justice. The King heard about it and was very amused; so Charnacé was in the clear, and if he had never done worse he would have kept both his reputation and his liberty.

1699

THE DEATH OF RACINE

✣ ✣ ✣ ✣ ✣ N April we lost Racine, so well known for his plays. No one
✣ ✤ ✣ had a sharper wit; there was nothing of the poet in his man-
✣ ✣ ner; he was always modest, well bred, and—latterly—most
✣ ✣ ✣ ✣ ✣ virtuous. He numbered among his friends the most illustrious figures at court, as well as men of letters, and it is they who can
speak for him far better than I. For the pleasure of the King and Mme
de Maintenon, and for performance by the girls of Saint-Cyr, he wrote
two masterpieces, *Esther* and *Athalie*—his task being made more difficult by the fact that there could be no love-story, and, being religious
tragedies, the plot as set out in the Bible could not be altered in any detail. The Comtesse d'Ayen and Mme de Caylus[1] were far and away the
best in acting these plays before the King, and the company invited to
Mme de Maintenon's apartments for the performance was most select.

Racine was charged with writing the history of the King's reign with
his friend Boileau. This task, together with the writing of the plays I
have just mentioned, gained him some degree of intimacy with the
King. The King used to receive his Ministers during the evening in
Mme de Maintenon's apartments, but occasionally, particularly on
Fridays, he had no work to do, and then, if the weather was bad or the
winter evenings long, they often sent for Racine to amuse them. Unfortunately the dramatist was prone to fits of absent-mindedness. One
evening the conversation turned to the Paris theatres, and when they
had talked about the opera, the subject of comedy came up. The King
asked about both actors and plays and why it was that the standards of
comedy had, as he had been told, fallen far below what they had been
previously. Racine produced several reasons and concluded by saying
that in his opinion the real cause was that, in the absence of any fresh
authors and new plays, the comedians were driven to reviving old pro-
ductions, among them those of Scarron which were quite worthless
and drove audiences away. At this the poor widow blushed, not because the literary reputation of her unfortunate cripple was maligned,
but at the mention of his name before his successor; the King was embarrassed. The ensuing silence awoke Racine to the enormity of his

---

[1] Marthe-Marguerite de Villette de Murçay, Marquise de Caylus (1673–1729), cousin
of Mme de Maintenon.

40

gaffe; realizing the pitfall into which his absent-mindedness had led him, he was the most embarrassed of the three, and did not dare raise his eyes. The silence lasted for several minutes, then the King sent Racine away, saying that he had to work. After that neither the King nor Mme de Maintenon spoke to Racine or took any notice of him. He was so distressed that he fell into a decline and died two years later. He was buried at Port-Royal, with the illustrious inmates of which he had been intimate in his youth—an intimacy which his life of poetry had hardly interrupted, even though they could scarcely approve of it.

TWO DARING THEFTS

THERE was a particularly daring theft while the King was in residence at Versailles on the night of 3–4 June: all the saddles and saddle-cloths, worth about 50,000 crowns, were taken from the Great Stables. The thieves laid their plans so well that, even on that short summer night, no one in a huge house inhabited by a positive multitude saw any trace of them. Monsieur le Grand, with all his subalterns, arrived in a fury; search-parties were sent out in every conceivable direction without result. Which reminds me of another extraordinary thing which happened just before I began to compile these memoirs.[1] The grand apartments from the gallery to the tribune were done up in crimson velvet with gilt trimmings, and one day it was found that all the gilt had been cut off—a most extraordinary thing to happen in a place so full of people by day, so completely closed at night, and so carefully guarded at all times. Bontemps[2] in despair ordered a thorough search, completely without success. Five or six days later I attended the King's supper, and on this occasion there was only d'Aquin, the royal doctor, between me and the King, and no one in front of me. As the *entremets* were being brought in, I saw a large black object sail through the air and land on the end of the table to the left of the King, where Monsieur and Madame (who happened to be in Paris) usually sat with their backs to the great courtyard. The thing landed with a crash, and the weight of it nearly broke the table, making all the plates jump. The King half turned his head and, quite unmoved, remarked, 'I think that must be my fringes.'

The parcel was about as wide as the brim of a priest's hat and about

---

[1] That is to say, in 1694.
[2] Alexandre Bontemps, *premier valet de chambre* to the King, and steward of Versailles and Marly.

41

two feet high, shaped like a rather untidy pyramid. It came from somewhere behind me, midway between the doors of the two antechambers, and as it went through the air a little bit of fringe fell out and landed on top of the King's wig, whence Livry,[1] who was on his left, removed it. Livry then went down to the end of the table and opened the parcel, which everyone saw did in fact contain the fringes all screwed up; there was a note attached to them, which he took out, and then left the parcel on the table. The King held out his hand for the note and said, 'Let me see.' But Livry very properly would not but, stepping back, first read it to himself, and then passed it behind the King to d'Aquin, over whose shoulder I read it. In a disguised female hand it said: 'Take back your fringes, Bontemps, they are more trouble than they are worth. My respects to the King'; it was folded but not sealed. The King again tried to get hold of it, but d'Aquin stepped back, first smelled it and rubbed it in his fingers, turning it over and over, and finally held it up for the King to read without letting him touch it. 'That is a piece of insolence,' said the King quietly and quite impersonally; then he ordered the packet to be removed, but it was so heavy that Livry could hardly lift it. The King made no further reference to the matter and no one else dared mention it; supper went on as if nothing had happened.

Quite apart from the impertinence of the whole thing, it is extraordinary that whoever did it should have run such a risk. How on earth could anyone throw so large and so heavy an object at the King's supper, where the crowd was so great that it was almost impossible to move, unless he had been surrounded by accomplices? And even with accomplices, how could the movement required to throw the parcel escape notice? The Duc de Gesvres was on duty: neither he nor anyone else thought of shutting the doors until some time after the King had left the table, so that those who were responsible had about three-quarters of an hour in which to leave the room. When the doors finally were shut there was only one person present whom no one knew, so he was arrested. He said he was a gentleman from Saintonge and known to the Duc d'Uzès, Governor of that province. The Duke happened to be at Versailles and was sent for just as he was going to bed; he said that he knew and could vouch for the man, who was thereupon released with apologies. No one ever found out who stole the fringes, nor who was responsible for the extraordinary way they were returned.

[1] The King's major-domo.

The return of the golden fringes

THE PROPHETIC BLACKSMITH

A T this time a blacksmith suddenly arrived at Versailles; he came from the little village of Salon, in Provence, and said to Brissac, major of the royal bodyguard, that he must speak to the King privately. He would not take 'No' for an answer; finally the King heard about it and sent a message that he didn't see anyone just like that. The blacksmith still insisted and said that, if he could have an audience, he would disclose secrets known only to the King himself, which would be proof that he had a mission and had matters of importance to disclose; he asked that at least he might see a Minister of State. The King sent a message for him to see Barbezieux.[1] It was a complete surprise to everyone when the blacksmith, who had never before been out of his own village nor interested himself in anything except his profession, flatly refused to see Barbezieux and stated that he had asked to see a Minister of State, that he would only speak to a Minister of State, and that Barbezieux was not one. At that the King nominated Pomponne, who went to see the man without more ado.[2] The blacksmith's story was as follows: he had been on his way home one evening when he had found himself surrounded by a great light beside a tree just outside the village, and he saw there a fair and shining figure, in royal robes, who called him by his name and spoke to him for half an hour. She said she was the Queen, who had been married to the King,[3] and she bid him go to court to speak of those things which she had told him—one of which was a secret which would be known only to the King himself and which would prove the truth of all the other things which he was to recount. If he could not get to the King, he was to see a Minister of State, but part of her message was still to be reserved for the ears of the King himself. She bade him carry out his mission with promptitude, diligence, and boldness —on pain of death. The blacksmith promised to do what he was told and the Queen disappeared, leaving him in darkness under the tree, where he fell asleep. The next day he thought the whole thing had been an illusion and he did not tell anyone about it. But two days later he had the same vision again; this time the Queen reprimanded him for his doubts and again threatened him with what would happen if he did not do what he was told—finally ordering him to see the Governor

---

[1] Louis-François-Marie le Tellier, Marquis de Barbezieux (1668–1701). Fifth child of Louvois, he was chosen by Louis to succeed his father as Secretary of State for War in 1691 in spite of his extreme youth.

[2] Simon Arnauld, Marquis de Pomponne (1618–99), Marshal of France and Secretary of State.

[3] She had died in 1683.

of the Province who would arrange for him to get to Versailles and would give him money for the journey. This time the blacksmith was convinced, but, torn between fear of the threats and the difficulty of the mission, he had no idea how to start; so he kept it to himself for a week while he thought it over. He had pretty well made up his mind not to do anything when, passing by the same tree, he saw the vision for a third time, and this time he decided to leave at once.

Two days later he was in Aix and saw the Governor, who urged him on his way and gave him the money to take a coach. He had three long interviews with Pomponne, each lasting two hours. M. de Pomponne reported privately to the King, who told him to give a complete account of what had been said to the Council of State. The Council meeting was long, though some of the time may have been spent on other matters. As a result the King decided to see the blacksmith; he had the man brought up the small staircase from the marble court— the way he himself used when he went out hunting or for a walk—and saw him in one of the studies. A few days later he saw him again, and each time talked for more than an hour, making sure that no one was within earshot. The morning after the first talk, the King was coming down the same small staircase to go hunting when he met M. Duras, who had the baton,[1] and who was on terms of familiarity with his royal master. Duras started to run down the blacksmith, and quoted the bad saying that either the man was crazy or the King was ignoble. When he said this, the King stopped and turned towards him—something which he normally never did when he was walking—and said: 'If that is so, then I am ignoble, for I have listened to him at some length and he has talked a great deal of good sense; I can assure you that he is not crazy.' The last words were spoken with a considered gravity which made a great impression on all who heard them. After the second interview the King was convinced that the blacksmith had described something which had happened over twenty years before and which he had told no one about; he added that it was a ghost which he had seen in the forest of Saint-Germain and never mentioned to anyone. He kept talking about him for some time after he had gone home, and saw to it that all his expenses were paid, and also instructed the Governor to make sure that, without elevating him beyond his profession and station in life, he should want for nothing for the rest of his days.

It was a remarkable thing that none of the Ministers ever wanted to talk about the matter; their closest friends cross-questioned them

[1] Symbol of rank of the captain of the in-lying company of guards.

without finding out a thing, for they always deliberately changed the subject. I myself sounded out the Duc de Beauvilliers and M. de Pontchartrain, and I know that their most intimate friends had no more success than I had; the same was true of Pomponne and Torcy.

The blacksmith was a man of about fifty; he had a family and was well known in his own district. He showed himself to be a most level-headed fellow in his simplicity, disinterestedness, and modesty. He considered himself excessively well rewarded for what he had done, and once having seen the King and M. de Pomponne he never showed any ambition to have another audience, for, as he said, having completed his mission he had nothing to see them about. Those who were charged with looking after his interests tried to pump him, but they were completely unsuccessful, for he would not swallow any bait and merely put an end to the conversation by saying 'my lips are sealed.' When he got home he never referred to the court again, and did not change his way of life at all; when he was asked if he had seen the King he replied simply 'Yes,' without enlarging on how or where.

1700

FESTIVITIES FOR THE
DUCHESSE DE BOURGOGNE

❧❧❧❧❧ HIS year from Candlemas till Lent there was a succession ❧ 𝓕 ❧ of balls and festivities at court. The King gave a whole ❧ ❧ series of masquerades, receptions, and fêtes—really for his ❧❧❧❧❧ own amusement, but under the pretext of entertaining the Duchesse de Bourgogne.[1] There were music and comedies in Mme de Maintenon's apartments. Monseigneur also gave several balls in honour of the Duchesse de Bourgogne. Monsieur le Prince managed to surprise the whole court by giving in his constricted apartments, made up of a few small rooms, the most fashionable and successful party of the whole lot. He gave a formal masked ball, with a reception, and a fair made up of stalls showing novelties from different countries, a supper with charming decorations; everyone was there—no one was turned away, yet he managed to arrange the whole thing without the rooms being uncomfortably crowded.

At this party a lady who later became a close friend of mine had an embarrassing experience. She was quite young, but was beginning to make her mark at court and would have undoubtedly risen to a position of eminence if smallpox had not carried her off a few years later. She had fallen in love with the Comte d'Évreux,[2] but few people as yet had noticed it. About half-way through the ball a man came in wearing a mask made up of four faces of well-known court figures: they were made of wax and were very good likenesses, and the Comte d'Évreux was one of them.[3] This man wore a long cloak beneath which was concealed a simple mechanism by which he could bring any one of the four masks in front of his face whenever he wished. He attracted a great

---

[1] She was now fifteen years old. When the festivities ended on 23 February she said she had enjoyed herself so much that she intended to begin again in October and keep it up until the following St. Germain's fair, on 1,000 pistoles which the king had given her. Neither pyorrhoea nor colic was allowed to interfere, but she had such a time that the Cardinal de Noailles finally took matters in hand and directed that festivities in 1701 would be rather less hectic.

[2] Henri-Louis de la Tour-d'Auvergne (1679-1753), younger brother of the Duc d'Albret.

[3] These masks of living people were very popular at this time; they were made by a man named Ducreux, who appeared himself at a ball at Marly wearing a mask in the likeness of a notorious drunkard named Bapaume.

deal of attention, and soon he took the floor in a minuet, turning his faces round the whole time to everyone's amusement. Next, being an absolute devil, he bowed to this poor woman and asked her to dance— turning to the front the face of the Comte d'Évreux. Even worse, he was a superb dancer, and he manœuvred himself so well that every time he faced the lady he was dancing with he had this same most embarrassing mask turned towards her. She went absolutely scarlet, but she did not know how to stop him without losing face. The second time round she gave him her hand (as a sign that she wished to stop): the man in the mask seemed as if he was going to take it, then just touched her fingers and went on for another round. She hoped to stop him the next time, but not a bit of it—just the same touch of the fingers, and the same mask embarrassingly staring at her. You can imagine how it attracted everyone's attention: people crowded round the floor, and those behind climbed up on the chairs to see better, but there was no barracking because she came from a high-born family which was respected everywhere. In this way the poor soul was forced to go on through a minuet three times longer than the normal. The masked man stayed long enough, then discreetly disappeared. About this time the lady's husband arrived, masked: one of his friends met him at the door, said the floor was terribly crowded, and suggested that the two of them should take a turn in the Galerie des Princes. Finally the husband got tired of this and insisted on going into the ballroom, where he saw the man with the four masks, and however upset he may have been, he showed nothing at all; at least he had been spared the minuet which by then was finished. There was a great deal of talk, but in spite of it the inevitable happened and lasted for a long time.[1] What was most unusual was that neither before nor afterwards was any other name linked with hers, although she had one of the most beautiful faces at court: she was so quiet and dignified that in any gathering she put all other women in the shade.

Another ridiculous situation arose at one of the balls at Marly. I will give the names of the people concerned, because everything that occurred was public knowledge. The Duc and Duchesse de Luxembourg were at Marly; there was a shortage of dancers, which was why Mme de Luxembourg was asked, for otherwise her way of life was such that no one wanted to meet her if he could help it. In those days debauchery had to be kept within reasonable bounds; unfortunately

---

[1] The description fits the Duchesse de Villeroy who died of smallpox in 1711, though it is known also that in 1700 the Comte d'Évreux began a liaison with the Duchesse de Lesdiguières which lasted until her death in 1747.

nowadays people are not so squeamish.[1] M. de Luxembourg was probably the only person in France who had no idea of what his wife was up to: she was so nice to him that he never suspected her. As there were so few dancers, the King pressed people to join in who were really past it—among them M. de Luxembourg.[2] It was to be a masked ball. M. de Luxembourg was very friendly with Monsieur le Duc, the Prince de Conti, and Monsieur le Prince, and there was no doubt that the last-named was the leading authority on anything to do with parties, masquerades, and festivities in general, and so the Duc de Luxembourg went to him for advice as to what he should wear. Monsieur le Prince, who was as malicious as any man who ever lived and who never felt warmly towards anyone, promised that he would do so—seeing a good chance to have some fun himself and amuse the whole court; he said that M. de Luxembourg should have supper with him and afterwards he would dress him suitably for the ball.

These balls at Marly, whether formal or masked, were the same as those at Versailles, with the dancers drawn up in two lines—at one end there was a chair for the King, or three if the King and Queen of England were going to be present, as they often were. And on either side the royal family was assembled in a straight line, as far as and including the Grandsons of France. Sometimes in the middle of the ball Mme la Duchesse and Mme la Princesse de Conti would move in, pretending they were talking to someone, and tack themselves on to the end of the line. Down the sides of the room, right and left of the King, were the ladies, the senior members of the nobility, and then the rest; in front of the King were the Princes of the Blood and the dancers, and those Princes who were not dancing. When it was a masked ball everyone formed up with his face uncovered and his mask in his hand; but sometime after the ball had begun there were new arrivals, and some of those who had been there already went out to change their clothes, so that when they came back masked, no one knew who was who.

I had just arrived at the ball and sat down when I saw in front of me a figure draped in some sort of muslin, light and floating, surmounted by a fantastic head-dress including a pair of enormous stag's horns which went up so high that they got caught in one of the chandeliers. Everyone wondered who it could be, and then when he turned round and we saw that it was the Duc de Luxembourg there was an absolutely outrageous burst of laughter. A few minutes later he came and sat down between the Comte de Toulouse and myself, and the Count

[1] He was writing in his old age, in 1740.
[2] He was then thirty-eight.

48

asked what had put the idea for such a costume into his head—but the victim was not sharp enough to detect the edge in the question: in fact he was not very bright altogether, and looked about him benignly, regarding the raucous laughter as a tribute to the originality of his get-up. He told all and sundry that he had supped with Monsieur le Prince who had designed his costume for him, and he bowed to right and left so that his head-dress could the better be admired. Then the ladies entered, and immediately after them the King. There was renewed laughter, and M. de Luxembourg went the rounds presenting himself to the company with a ravishing self-assurance. His wife, although she knew quite well that her way of life was common knowledge, blushed deeply; and the whole court laughed at the pair of them. Monsieur le Prince, who stood just behind the King's chair, was delighted by the success of his malicious joke. The applause went on throughout the ball, and even the King, who rarely allowed himself to show any feelings in public, laughed heartily. This very cruel joke provided a subject for conversation throughout the evening and for several days afterwards.

Hardly a night passed without a ball. A particularly brilliant one was given by the Chancellor's wife at the Chancellery. At ten in the evening the Chancellor received Monseigneur, his three sons, and the Duchesse de Bourgogne at the entrance, and then he himself went to bed. There were different rooms prepared for the formal ball, the masks, and a superb supper, and the stalls where goods from all over the world were offered for sale—but no money was accepted, all the articles on display having been presents to the Duchesse de Bourgogne and her ladies; there was excellent music too, and a comedy. Everything was superb and most beautifully arranged, and the Chancellor's wife moved about among her guests with politeness, elegance, and freedom as if she had no responsibilities. Everybody enjoyed himself enormously and we all went home at eight o'clock in the morning. Mme de Saint-Simon went everywhere with the Duchesse de Bourgogne, which was a mark of great favour; she and I did not see the light of day for three weeks. At these balls it was not done for anyone to leave before the Duchesse de Bourgogne, and once at Marly when I and several others were trying to escape quietly she had us stopped at the door. I was delighted when Ash Wednesday came, and for several days after that I was dead to the world, and my wife was actually not able to last out through Shrove Tuesday.

During this time the King used to play cards in Mme de Mainte-non's apartments with a group of chosen ladies on those evenings when he had no ministers waiting on him or if their work did not take long.

They played brelan, primero,[1] and occasionally reversi.[2] These amusements were continued a little while into Lent.

THE DEATH OF LE NÔTRE

André Le Nôtre was the son of a gardener at the Tuileries who had acquired a great deal of landed property in Paris, largely along the Faubourg Saint-Honoré; he was born in 1613. He first worked under his father at the Tuileries, then became gardener to Monsieur, and finally in 1643 was put in charge of the King's buildings and gardens. He and his friend Mansard, the celebrated architect, were both made Knights of the Order of Saint Michael.

LE NÔTRE died in full possession of all his faculties after having enjoyed eighty-eight years of perfect health. He had become famous for the beautiful gardens which he had designed in France and which so eclipsed the great reputation of the Italians in this art that the leading men came from that country to France to learn from him. Le Nôtre had an honesty and integrity and an attention to detail which earned him everyone's esteem and admiration. He never took liberties above his station and was always perfectly disinterested; he gave the same service to private clients as he did to the King, always trying to make the best of the natural advantages of the site on which he was working at the lowest possible cost. He had a *naïveté* and straightforwardness which charmed everyone. Once the Pope asked the King if he might borrow him for a few months. When he entered the Pope's study, instead of falling on his knees, he went up and kissed the Pontiff on both cheeks, saying 'Good morning, Reverend Father, how well you look. I am delighted to see you in such good health!' The Pope, who was Clement X Altieri, laughed; he was delighted by such an unusual entrance and was very kind to Le Nôtre.

When he returned to France the King took him into the gardens at Versailles to see what had been done in his absence. When he saw the new colonnade he did not say a word; when the King pressed him to say what he thought of it, he replied: 'Well, Sir, what do you want me to say? You have turned a stone-mason into a gardener (it was Mansard) and he has certainly given you a basin-full of his trade.' The

---

[1] A game in which each player was given four cards; *primero* consisted in having each card of a different colour, and *grand primero* if their pips totalled over thirty.

[2] A game for four, introduced from Savoy, in which the object was to take the fewest tricks.

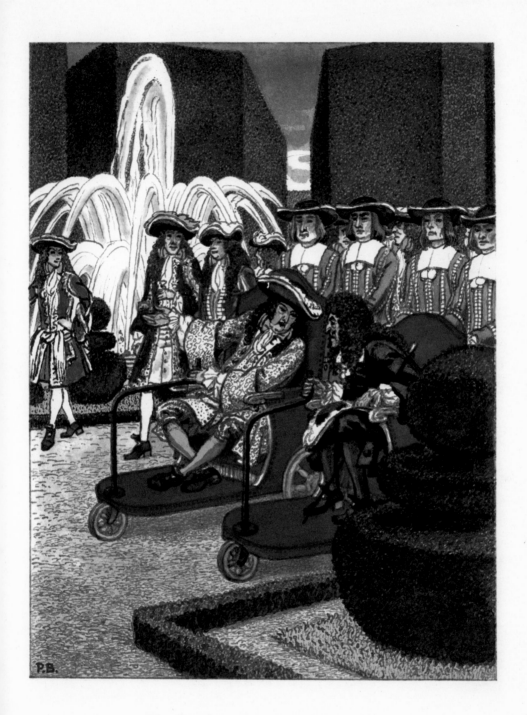

The King and Le Nôtre at Versailles

King did not say anything, and everyone smiled, for it was quite true
that all that masonry, which was really supposed to be nothing more
than a fountain, was really quite out of place in a garden.

Only a month before his death the King, who liked to see him and
enjoyed talking to him, took him round the gardens, and, because of
his great age, had him wheeled in a chair; Le Nôtre said: 'Ah, my dear
father, my joy would be complete if you could be here to see your son,
a poor gardener, being wheeled along beside the greatest king in the
world!'

He was inspector of buildings, and he lived in the Tuileries, where
he had charge of the palace as well as the garden which he had designed
himself. Everything which he designed is infinitely superior to anything which has been done since, although everyone has tried to copy
his style. He used to say that the flower-beds at Versailles were of no
use to anyone except nurses who could not leave the children in their
charge and needed something to look at out of the second-floor windows. Nevertheless he arranged them just as well as he did every other
feature in a garden, but he never liked them—and he was quite right,
for no one ever walks in that part of the garden.

1701

INDIGESTION OF MONSEIGNEUR

✤✤✤✤✤s the King was saying his prayers before going to bed on
✤ 𝒜 ✤ Saturday, 19 March, the eve of Palm Sunday, he heard a dis-
✤ ✤ turbance in the next room, which was full of courtiers, and
✤✤✤✤✤calls for Fagon and Félix.[1] Monseigneur had been taken extremely ill. He had spent the day at Meudon, where he had only had
a light lunch, and then, supping with the King, he absolutely stuffed
himself full of fish—he was a great eater like the King, and like his
mother and grandmother. He did not appear after supper. Later he
came down from the King's study, and, as was his habit also, said his
prayers before undressing. Then when he sat down to get undressed,
he lost consciousness. His horrified servants and several courtiers who
were present for his *coucher* ran to the King's room to find the royal
doctor and surgeon with the resulting fuss I have just mentioned.

The King, with his clothes all undone, got up at once from his pray-
er-stool and went down to Monseigneur's rooms by a tiny back staircase which went straight down from one corner of his room to the
'cellar,' which was a very small dark room, looking into the small
court, with just sufficient space for a bed, in which Monseigneur slept
in cold weather, though it was so small that he undressed in and generally used the larger room next door. The Duchesse de Bourgogne arrived at the same time as the King, and in a matter of minutes the main
bedroom, which was vast, was packed. They found Monseigneur, half
naked, being walked, or rather dragged, round the room. He did not
recognize anyone, not even the King, and he struggled against Félix,
who was trying to bleed him on the spot, and finally succeeded. As he
gradually recovered consciousness he asked for a confessor: the King
had already sent for the curé. Then they gave him a strong emetic,
which took some time to work, but at the end of two hours produced a
prodigious evacuation at both ends. After two and a half hours there
did not seem to be any further danger and the King, who had been in
tears, went back to bed, leaving orders that he was to be told if anything happened. By five o'clock all the effects had worn off and the
doctors left their patient to rest, ordering everyone out of the room.
He was confined to his room for eight or ten days, and when he was

[1] First doctor and first surgeon to the household.

better, played cards or watched others playing all day long; the King came to see him twice a day. After that he was more careful about his health and took care not to abuse his digestive system. If he had been taken ill a quarter of an hour later his first valet, who slept in the room, would have found him dead in his bed.

Monseigneur was very popular in Paris, probably because he went often to the opera. The herring-mongers in the market decided to make their mark: they chose four of their number as representatives to go and ask after the patient's health. Monseigneur asked the women to come in; one of them put her arm round his neck and kissed him on both cheeks, while the others kissed his hand. They were very well received; Bontemps showed them round the apartments and then entertained them at dinner, Monseigneur sent them a present of money, and so did the King. They were delighted; they ordered a *Te Deum* at St. Eustache and had a feast afterwards.

QUARRELS BETWEEN THE KING
AND HIS BROTHER

THE army in Flanders was put under command of the Maréchal de Boufflers, and the army in Germany was given to the Maréchal de Villeroy. The Duc de Bourgogne was to have commanded the latter, but plans were changed because Monsieur was so furious that the Duc de Chartres was not allowed to serve. The King was agreeable to his going on the campaign in the hope that Monsieur would refuse out of pique because his son had not been given an army.

But the Duc de Chartres felt that since he had taken every opportunity to go on active service he could not, at his age, be refused a command the following year, and in consequence both he and his father were agreed in the present instance. This question of a future command was the very reason why the King did not want his nephew to go on active service, and, surprised to find father and son in agreement, felt—if one may be allowed to use the phrase—that he had been had. But he would not give in and he then refused his consent with an abruptness which he hoped would close the subject—but here he was wrong again. M. de Chartres was mixed up in a number of rather imprudent incidents, quite understandable at his age, but which annoyed the King and embarrassed him even further. The King did not know what to do with his nephew whom he had compelled to become his son-in-law, and for whom he had done nothing except the bare minimum that was agreed in writing in the marriage contract. This refusal to allow the Duke to take the field, which put off still further any chance of a command, opened all over again the sore wound caused by the matter of the Brittany Governorship,[1] and gave Madame a fresh opportunity for jeering at her husband for being so feeble in the first place as to consent to the marriage of her son, of which he had been one of the first to repent. The Duc de Chartres now began planning all sorts of crazy expeditions with friends of his own age, some to Spain and some to England. Monsieur knew all about it, but realizing that his son was unlikely to embark on any of these scatter-brained ideas, said nothing to the King even when the latter became rather worried. The King took the matter up with Monsieur and, when he got rather a cold reception, accused his brother of having no authority over his own son. Monsieur then lost his temper and asked the King what a boy of his age was expected to do when he had been shoved into a marriage against his will and condemned to do nothing but walk up and down the corridors at Versailles while he saw his brother-in-law loaded with honours and appointments without rhyme or reason. He said his son was worse off than any young man in France, for everyone else was allowed to take the field and earn his promotion. He added that idleness was the father of vice, and it made him sad to see his only son sinking into debauchery, bad company, and ridicule; but it was unfair to blame a young man suffering under such a sense of disappointment—the fault lay with the man who had brought him out and then refused to give him a chance.

If anyone was ever disconcerted by such plain speaking, it was the King. Monsieur had never been within a thousand miles of using words like that before, and it was the more shaming because his arguments were irrefutable. In the embarrassed moments of surprise which followed, the King was sufficiently master of himself to reply, not as a monarch, but as a brother: he said he could forgive Monsieur's paternal affection, he caressed him, and did all that he could to appease him by gentleness and kindness. But the crux of the matter was still the question of field service which Monsieur hoped would lead to command, and which the King was determined should do no such thing. So the conversation was long and heated, with Monsieur on his high horse and the King apologetic. In the end they parted, with Monsieur furious but not daring to lose his temper completely, and

---

[1] The King promised the Duc de Chartres, at the time of his marriage, the first available governorship, but when the rich appointment in Brittany fell vacant it was given to the King's bastard, the Comte de Toulouse.

the King angry but not wishing to alienate his brother or to have their disagreement noticed by anyone else.

Monsieur usually spent the summer at Saint-Cloud with a large party, and he went there now, to await a reconciliation; occasionally he came over to dine with the King, but less frequently than usual, and such conversation as they had was usually rather sharp—but they tried to show no outward signs of their feelings, although those who saw them constantly noticed the unaccustomed attentiveness of the King and Monsieur's unusual coldness in reply. In time Monsieur came to see that he was not going to get what he wanted; he realized, on the advice of the Maréchal de Villeroy, the Chevalier de Lorraine, and the Marquis d'Éffiat, that it would be unwise to push the King too far, and that it was high time he stopped his son's adventures. He did this bit by bit, but he remained very sour about the whole thing. . . .

THE DEATH OF THE KING'S BROTHER

THE King of England came back from Bourbon without any improvement in his health, and Monsieur was still at Saint-Cloud sulking as I have already described. This situation completely upset him; for he had always been subservient to and on good terms with the King. The King constantly allowed him the privileges of a brother in private and in public treated him with the kindness and affection due to so close a relation—taking care, however, that he should not get ideas above himself. If he or Madame had so much as an ache in their little finger, he went to see them, and continued to visit them until they were well again. But at this time Madame had had a recurring fever for some weeks, which she treated in her own German way without having a doctor. But the King did not go to see her, because besides his annoyance over the Duc de Chartres he was angry with her about something else—as we shall see. Monsieur did not know of the King's private displeasure, and took this lack of attention as a public rebuke, and, as he was both proud and sensitive, this was the last straw.

He had reasons also for considerable mental disquiet. For some time he had had a confessor who, although a Jesuit, was very strict with him: he was a man of good Breton family, named Père du Trévou. His confessor not only forbade him his peculiar pleasures but, as a penance for his past life, forbade him other more normal forms of entertainment. He often told Monsieur he was old, worn out, fat, short in the neck, and from all appearances would probably die of apoplexy in the near future. These were strong words for one of the most voluptuous princes alive who had long since sunk into complete idleness and was quite incapable of any form of self-discipline, application, or even serious reading. He was mortally afraid of the devil, and remembered that his previous confessor, who had not wanted to die in such employment, had before his death warned him in very similar terms. These words had enough impression on him to make him mend his ways for a short time and to exercise what passed for self-restraint. He said his prayers often, obliged his confessor and had some regard for his homilies on gambling and such matters, bearing his frequent strictures with patience and occasionally reflecting on them. He became sad, subdued, and talked less than usual—that is to say, not more than about enough for three or four women; everyone noticed the difference.

On Wednesday, 8 June, Monsieur came from Saint-Cloud to dine with the King at Marly and walked in, as usual, just as the Council of State was rising. He found the King very incensed by the way M. de Chartres was treating his daughter. The Duke was in love with Mlle de Séay, Maid of Honour to Madame, and he was prosecuting the affair with considerable diligence. The King used this as a starting-point for his remarks and heaped reproaches on Monsieur for the conduct of his son. Monsieur, who was already in a touchy state, replied tartly that fathers who had led a certain kind of life were hardly in a position to reprove their children? The King, who felt the force of what his brother said, took cover behind the patience of his daughter, and said that at least intrigues ought to be kept out of his sight. Monsieur now thoroughly lost his temper and reminded the King forcibly of the way he had made the Queen suffer for his mistresses, even to publicly riding with them in his own carriage. The King, nettled, answered him back, and the two of them began to shout at one another.

At Marly the four great apartments downstairs were all alike. The salon was small and at this time of day was full of courtiers waiting to see the King go through to dinner, and, by one of those differences of custom which are difficult to explain, at Marly the door from it into the royal study always stayed open once the Council was finished, while in every other royal palace it was always closed; there was merely a curtain across it which an usher drew back when anyone wished to enter. When this official heard the noise, he came in and told the King that every word could be heard by the courtiers waiting in the next room. There was another small room opening out of this one, curtained off for the King's *chaise-percée*, and there were always *valets de chambre* in there, who heard the whole of the conversation and repeated it word for word to me afterwards. The usher's warning made

them lower their voices, but could not stop Monsieur's recriminations
—beside himself with fury, he said that when the Duc de Chartres was married the King had promised him the earth but had done not one thing about it—not even to the extent of a single governorship; that he himself had desperately wanted his son to go on active service to keep him away from women, and that his son too had begged to be allowed to go; and since he had met with nothing but a blank refusal, it was small wonder if he consoled himself where he could. Monsieur added that he had no intention of interfering with his son's amusements, and he now saw only too clearly what others had long predicted—that this wretched marriage would bring nothing but shame and dishonour, without a penny of profit. The King, whose temper was rising rapidly, retorted that the war was costing a great deal and that, since Monsieur was so little disposed to do as he was asked, economies would start in his household rather than in the King's own. At that point the King was told that dinner was served. A moment later they came out together. Monsieur's eyes were gleaming with rage and he had a high colour; in fact many people present remarked that he looked as if he needed bleeding. They had been saying the same at Saint-Cloud and he even admitted it himself. In spite of their disagreements the King also begged him to have it done; but since Tancrède, his surgeon, was old and did not bleed well, Monsieur did not want to be bled by him, and yet not wishing to offend the old man would not have it done by anyone else. The King spoke to him about it again; and said he had a good mind to take him into the next room and have him done on the spot. Dinner passed off without further incident, and Monsieur ate enormously as he always did at his two meals a day—not to mention his chocolate in the morning, and the fruit, pastries, and sweets which he was always stuffing: his desk drawer and his pockets were full of them. When they rose from table, the King by himself, Monseigneur with the Princesse de Conti, the Duc de Bourgogne by himself, and the Duchesse de Bourgogne with her ladies, all went off to see the King and Queen of England at Saint-Germain. Monsieur, who had brought the Duchesse de Chartres with him from Saint-Cloud to dine with the King, took her on with him, and they were just leaving Saint-Germain together when the King himself arrived.

That evening after supper, when the King was in his study with Monseigneur and the Princesses, Saint-Pierre arrived from Saint-Cloud and said that he had a message for the King from the Duc de Chartres. He was told to come in, and reported that Monsieur had been taken ill during supper, that he had been bled and seemed a little better, and that he had been given an emetic. The facts are that he had

had supper as usual with the ladies at Saint-Cloud; as they were bringing in the *entremets*, he was just pouring a glass of wine for Mme de Bouillon when he started to stammer and make signs with his hand. As he used sometimes to talk Spanish, some of the ladies asked him to repeat what he had said; but others cried out in alarm. It all happened in a minute, and he fell back in an apoplexy into the arms of the Duc de Chartres. He was taken to his room, walked up and down, bled freely and given an emetic, but he showed little sign of life.

When he heard this news the King, who used to hurry over to Monsieur on the slightest pretext, went up to Mme de Maintenon's rooms, woke her up, and talked to her for a quarter of an hour. Then he came down and went to his own room; he ordered his carriage to be kept in readiness, and he sent the Marquis de Gesvres over to Saint-Cloud with orders to come back and wake him if Monsieur got any worse; then he went to bed. I think that he thought Monsieur was putting it on in the hope of ending their quarrel, that it was this aspect of the situation which he talked over with Mme de Maintenon, and that he decided that he would rather appear uncharitable than be made a fool of. Mme de Maintenon did not like Monsieur; she was afraid of him; he paid her little respect; and for all his timidity and his attitude of deference, he let fall from time to time in front of the King remarks which showed his dislike of her and his shame at public opinion [because of the union of his brother with Mme de Maintenon]. She was not particularly anxious, therefore, that the King should travel at night and lose his sleep to visit a sick-bed, and she hoped that if events moved with satisfactory speed he might be spared the trouble of going at all. Soon after the King had got into bed a page arrived to say that Monsieur was better, and to get some Schaffhausen water (good for apoplexy) from the Prince de Conti. An hour and a half later Longueville, sent by the Duc de Chartres, woke the King and told him that the emetic had had no effect and Monsieur was extremely ill. The King dressed and left; on the way he met M. de Gesvres, who was also on the way to him with the bad news. You can imagine what a night of chaos and rumour it was at Marly, and what horror reigned at Saint-Cloud, that palace of delights. Everyone who was at Marly hurried to Saint-Cloud as fast as he could, piling into the available carriages without any regard for sex or rank. The King arrived just before three in the morning. Monsieur had been unconscious from the moment he was taken ill; he had just a ray of semi-consciousness when Father du Trévou said Mass after midnight, and that was all. Even the most horrible spectacles often have their funny side, and some of the less moved round the bedside started to giggle when Father du Trévou came back

Monseigneur and the herring-mongers

and stood over the unconscious figure saying over and over again,
'Monsieur, don't you know your confessor? Don't you know your good little Father du Trévou when he speaks to you?'

When the King came in his face was bathed in tears, for he always cried easily; he was really extremely fond of his brother, and, in spite of all their quarrels over the last two months, all that fondness now came back. Perhaps he felt that their scene that morning had precipitated his brother's death. Monsieur was two years the younger, and his constitution had always seemed as good, if not better, than the King's.

The King heard Mass at Saint-Cloud, and then at eight o'clock, since there was no hope for Monsieur, he got back into his carriage with Mme de Maintenon and the Duchesse de Bourgogne. Just before leaving he had a few words with M. de Chartres, both of them in tears, and the young Prince, taking his chance quickly, knelt, clutching the King around the knees, and cried: 'Ah! Sire, what ever will become of me? I am losing Monsieur, and I know that you don't like me.' The King, surprised and touched, embraced him and said all the kind things that he could.

When he got back to Marly the King went to Mme de Maintenon's rooms with the Duchesse de Bourgogne. Three hours later M. Fagon appeared; he had been ordered to remain at the bedside until Monsieur was either dead or recovered, though it was recognized that the latter would have been a miracle. When the King saw him he said: 'Well, Monsieur Fagon, my brother is dead?' 'Yes, Sire,' the doctor replied, 'there was no remedy that could help him.' The King wept for some time. They urged him to have a quiet snack with Mme de Maintenon, but he insisted on dining in the normal way with the ladies. The tears streamed down his face during the meal, which was kept short, and as soon as it was over he went back to Mme de Maintenon's apartment. There he stayed, working with Chamillart and Pontchartrain on the ceremonial for Monsieur's funeral and giving instructions to Desgranges, the Master of Ceremonies—since the Grand Master, Dreux, was away with the army in Italy. At seven he went for a short walk in the garden; he had supper an hour earlier than usual and went to bed soon after.

As soon as the King had left, the crowd gradually drifted away from Saint-Cloud, so that the dying man, laid out on a day-bed in his study,[1] was left in full view of the servants who, whether from

---

[1] He had been moved there from his proper bed to make it easier for the doctors to work on him.

affection or self-interest, were in a state of great distress. Those officers of the household who were losing their appointments and the salaries that went with them filled the air with their cries, and the women of Saint-Cloud, seeing the end of their high standing and of all their amusement, were running about screaming and dishevelled like a lot of Bacchantes. The Duchesse de Ferté, whose part-worn and ageing daughter had married one of Monsieur's favourites, came in and, looking down at the still breathing body, remarked: 'Well now, it's a fine marriage my daughter has got herself into!' Châtillon, who was himself losing everything, said: 'Madam, we have much more to worry about today than whether your daughter is well or badly settled.'

All this time Madame, who neither liked nor respected Monsieur, but who was worried about her own downfall, stayed in her room, crying, 'Not a convent! Don't mention convents! I won't go into a convent!' The Princess had not gone out of her mind: she remembered clearly that her marriage contract gave her the option, if she were widowed, of retiring either to a convent or to the Château de Montargis, and, knowing that she had much to fear from the King (though in fact she did not yet realize how much), she thought she could escape from the latter easier than the former.[1] As soon as the last breath had left Monsieur's body, she got into her carriage with her ladies and went to Versailles, followed by the Duc and Duchesse de Chartres and their entourage.

On the following morning, the Friday, the Duc de Chartres went to see the King, who was still in bed and who greeted him most affectionately. The King said that henceforth the Duc must look upon him as a father, that he would look after his position and his interests, and that he trusted they could both now let bygones be bygones. It will surprise no one that M. de Chartres knew how to reply suitably.

After such terrible scenes and so many tears, no one had any doubt but that the three remaining days at Marly would be extremely gloomy. But that very next day after Monsieur's death, when the ladies of the palace went at noon to Mme de Maintenon's apartments, where the King and the Duchesse de Bourgogne were, they heard her in the next room singing songs from the current opera. A little later the King, seeing the Duchesse de Bourgogne sitting disconsolate in

---

[1] Saint-Simon was wrong; the marriage contract stipulated only retirement to Montargis with a pension. He must have been thinking of an earlier recorded conversation between the King and Duchesse de Ventadour in which were discussed various possible courses for Madame in the event of Monsieur's death, among them retirement to a convent where her aunt was abbess.

a corner, asked Mme de Maintenon what on earth was the matter with her; he tried to cheer her up himself and sent for several of the court ladies so that the two of them could make up a game. This, of course, happened in private, but it was not all. After dinner, barely twenty-four hours after Monsieur's death, the Duc de Bourgogne asked the Duc de Montfort to play brelan.

'Brelan!' cried Montfort, 'you can't realize what you are saying, with Monsieur not yet cold.'

'I am sorry,' replied the Prince; 'I realize quite well what I am saying. But the King does not want anyone at Marly to be bored and he has told me to see that everyone plays cards. So that no one shall be embarrassed about starting, he has told me to begin first.'

So the two of them started to make up a brelan, and in a short time the salon was full of card-tables.

Such was the measure of the King's distress at the death of his brother. As for Mme de Maintenon, Monsieur's death came as a deliverance and she could hardly restrain her joy. She saw that the King was already consoled; it was a sympathetic rôle for her to see that his sadness was distracted, and it was most convenient to have everything return to normal as quickly as possible, so that no one would think about Monsieur any more, or grieve at his departure. She did not care about appearances; but for all that, the whole thing was scandalous and everyone said so privately.

Monseigneur had always seemed to be very fond of Monsieur, who had been kind to him and gave balls in his honour—yet the very next day he went wolf-hunting, and when he returned, finding the salon full of card-players, he sat down at one of the tables and joined in. The Duc de Bourgogne and the Duc de Berry had never seen Monsieur except on public occasions, so they could hardly be expected to feel his death much. But the Duchesse de Bourgogne was very upset: he was her grandfather, and she adored her mother who was very fond of Monsieur, and furthermore he had always been very sweet to her and had put on a great many entertainments for her. Although she did not love many people, she loved Monsieur, and it was a great strain on her to have to hide her grief which lasted for a long time. We have already seen how upset Madame was. As for the Duc de Chartres, his grief was extreme. Father and son had loved one another dearly; Monsieur was the kindest man in the world, and he had never stood in the way of his son in anything—furthermore, he had been a buffer between his son and the King, whose wrath would now fall unimpeded on the young man. And the whole position and future of the Duc would now depend upon the King's goodwill

1701 —also he would have drastically to alter his conduct towards his wife if he was to get anywhere.

Mme de Chartres, although always well treated by Monsieur, was delighted that this obstacle between her and the King—an obstacle which had permitted her husband to behave towards her as he liked— was now removed. Also she had found it irksome to attend Monsieur's court, whether in Paris or Saint-Cloud, which was full of strangers with whom she had nothing in common. From now on she hoped she would be able to stay at court, without having anything more to do with Monsieur's *ménage*, and that Madame and the Duc de Chartres would in future be forced to show a little more regard for her than they had in the past.

Most of the court missed Monsieur; it was he who had been responsible for all the fun, and when he was away everything was lifeless and nothing happened. He had a liking for princes, and he was interested in rank, precedence, and distinctions: he saw to it that order in such matters was maintained, and he himself set a most scrupulous example. He liked society, and his affability and straightforwardness endeared him to everyone; he also knew to a nicety the amount of time and attention to give to every single person according to his rank. When he received people he weighed up perfectly their birth, dignity, age, and merit, and acted towards them with an ease and a natural dignity which delighted them. His familiarity was charming, but he kept his natural dignity and no one ever attempted to take any liberties with him. In his own home he allowed everyone perfect freedom without allowing any diminution of dignity. He had learnt the art of holding a court from his mother—and he liked it to be well attended, which it always was. There was always a crowd at the Palais-Royal. At Saint-Cloud, where all his numerous household assembled, there were always a number of ladies who, one must admit, would hardly have been received anywhere else, though several of them were of high rank; there was also a large number of gamblers. Every kind of game, the extreme beauty of the palace, the thousand calèches always ready to take lazy guests for a drive, the music and the good cheer gave the place great grandeur and magnificence and made it a constant delight. Madame contributed very little; she dined and supped with Monsieur and the ladies, went out occasionally in a calèche with one of them, was often sulky in public,[1] and made herself

[1] Not altogether surprising. Gambling was almost the sole occupation at Saint-Cloud; Madame did not like cards, had not got enough money to risk the habitually high stakes, and was not allowed to watch while Monsieur was playing.

feared by her ferocious ill humour and her tart remarks. She spent her days in a study which she had chosen, with windows more than ten feet above the ground, gazing at the portraits of various German Princes with which the walls were hung, and writing voluminous letters all day and every day in her own hand and carefully keeping copies. Monsieur could not prevail upon her to be more sociable, so he left her to it; he lived on quite good terms with her without being in the least interested, and he almost never saw her alone.

At Saint-Cloud Monsieur received after dinner many people who came to pay court both from Paris and Versailles—Princes of the Blood, the nobility, Ministers of the Crown, and many ordinary people. It was important to make the journey specially, and not to look in on one's way from Paris to Versailles or vice versa, for he always asked, and showed what he thought of such flying visits so unmistakably that no one dared do it.

Monsieur was extremely brave, and won the battle of Cassel in 1677; he showed a real flair at all the sieges in which he had taken part; but there was nevertheless a bad feminine streak in his character. He had no gifts except wit, he never read a book, he knew nothing about anything except family histories and births and marriages, and he was quite incapable of any kind of positive action. There never was a man so flabby in mind and body, so feeble, so timid, so often deceived, and so easily led. He was ruled by his favourites and was frequently given extremely bad advice by them—which he always took. He was a mischief-maker, and he could not keep a secret. He was suspicious and mistrustful, and he liked to start quarrels among those around him to split up cliques, to find things out, or sometimes just to amuse himself. To so many faults and so few virtues he added one abominable trait which was a public scandal: he lavished gifts on his numerous favourites on a scale without equal even at that time; they could get anything out of him, and in return often treated him with the greatest insolence. On top of this, he was always having to sort out their quarrels and horrible jealousies; and since every one of these gentry had his own following, Monsieur's small court was a constant storm-centre—with a large number of worthless women adding to the endless disturbance. All of this Monsieur thoroughly enjoyed. The Chevaliers de Lorraine and de Châtillon had both made a fortune out of Monsieur's passion for their good looks. The latter, who started with neither material nor mental gifts, did particularly well in dragging himself up to the top. The former was a typical Guise who was capable of doing anything without so much as a blush; he rode Monsieur with a tight rein all his life, and was loaded with riches and

honours; he was shameless, too, in displaying his command over
Monsieur and in his open nepotism towards his own family. Everything he did had in it all the pride and artful calculation of the Guises,
by which he managed to insinuate himself between the King and
Monsieur so cleverly that he was feared by both of them, and was
shown as marked a consideration by the one as by the other.

It would be difficult to be more timid or more submissive towards
the King than Monsieur was—even to the extent of flattering the
Ministers of the Crown and his royal mistresses; yet he still somehow
managed to preserve the easy familiarity of a brother, although he
did it with great respect. When they were alone, he would pull up an
arm-chair without being told to sit down; and after supper with the
King no one else was seated—not even Monseigneur. But in waiting
on the King, on entering or leaving the room he never failed to show
the greatest respect, and he adorned everything he did with a natural
grace and dignity. Occasionally he got rather irritated with the King,
but it never lasted long—since his gambling, Saint-Cloud, and his
favourites were most costly, the money which the King gave him was
a great soothing agent. He never got on well with Mme de Maintenon, and could not resist an occasional dig at the King or a sly reference to her in public. It was not that he minded her being in favour,
but the idea of Scarron's widow being his sister-in-law was more
than he could stomach.

He was extremely proud, but not arrogant; he was very conscious
of his due. The Princes of the Blood had become more and more
haughty in their behaviour as a result of all the honours accorded to
the royal Bastards, not so much the Prince de Conti as Monsieur le
Prince—and above all Monsieur le Duc, who bit by bit avoided doing
any service for Monsieur: this was not difficult, but he was silly
enough to boast that he would never serve him. Since the world is
full of people who enjoy paying their court at the expense of others,
Monsieur soon heard about it, and promptly went to the King in a
rage. The King told Monsieur that it was not worth getting worked up
about, and that what he should do was to find some occasion when the
Duke could not avoid serving, and if he refused then he could be
firmly snubbed. Assured of the King's support, Monsieur bided his
time. One morning he was looking out of his window at Marly, where
he was using one of the downstairs rooms, when he saw the Duke in
the garden. He called out to him, and the Duke came. Monsieur re-
treated from the French window so that the Duke had to follow him
into the room. And, keeping the conversation going as he walked
backwards, Monsieur suddenly took off his dressing-gown. At a sign

from the First Gentleman of the Bedchamber, the *valet de chambre* presented the shirt to the Duke, who, caught on the wrong foot, had no option but to take it and offer it to Monsieur. As soon as Monsieur had put the shirt on he burst out laughing and said: 'Good-bye, dear cousin; off you go—I won't keep you any longer.' Monsieur le Duc was furious, the more so because Monsieur afterwards treated the incident with the utmost hauteur.

Monsieur was a little man with a big stomach, trotting on high heels. He was always as carefully dressed as a woman, his hands covered in rings, his wrists in bracelets and his clothes in precious stones. He wore a black powdered wig, combed forward—ribands everywhere, drenched in perfume, and yet a picture of neatness. People said he used rouge. His nose was long, his face full but long; his mouth and his eyes were splendid. All his portraits were very like him. It used to annoy me to see how much he resembled Louis XIII, for, apart from physical courage, he had nothing in common with that great King.

THE DEATH OF JAMES II

THE King of England's taking the waters did him little good, and he passed into a decline. After the middle of August his health grew rapidly worse, and on about 8 September he was overtaken by paralysis and all hope of his recovery was abandoned. The King, Mme de Maintenon, and all the royal family visited him often. He received the last sacrament with the same dignified piety which had marked his whole life, and there was nothing more to do than to wait for the end. Expecting this, the King made a decision more worthy of the generosity of Louis XII and François I than it was notable for its wisdom. He went over from Marly to Saint-Germain on Tuesday, 13 September. The King of England was so ill that when our King was announced he barely opened his eyes. Our King said he had come to assure the sick man that he could die in peace because his son, the Prince of Wales, should be recognized as King of England, Scotland, and Ireland. The few English people who were present sank to their knees, but their King himself showed hardly a sign of life. The Prince of Wales was sent for and told; the gratitude of both mother and son can be imagined. When he got back to Marly the King told the whole court what he had done; his announcement was received with applause and nothing but praise.

It was easy to applaud at the time, but sharp criticism soon followed

—even if it was not expressed in public. The King hoped all along that the moderation of his policy in Flanders, the return of the Dutch garrisons,[1] the deliberate inactivity of his armies at a time when they could have overrun the whole country would dissuade Holland (a free agent) and England from coming out on the side of the House of Austria. It was a far-fetched aspiration, but the King still clung to it, and hoped by this means to have a free hand to wind up the war in Italy and settle the whole question of the succession to the Spanish throne and its vast dependencies, over which the Emperor would never have been able to fight by himself.[2]

Nothing could be more prejudicial to these hopes than the action which the King had just taken or to the solemn undertaking which he had given at the Peace of Ryswyck to recognize the Prince of Orange as King of England—an undertaking which up till then he had scrupulously observed. It was an offence to William, through him to the whole of the English people, and to Holland as well. So far as the Prince of Wales was concerned, this pronouncement gave him no solid advantage, while it revived the jealousy of his opponents in England and strengthened their determination to secure the Protestant succession to the utter detriment of the Stuart and Catholic interests. It made the English more bitter than ever against France which presumed to decide for them who should wear their crown: yet the King had no more power to put the Prince of Wales back on his throne than he had been able to restore James II even after a long war, or to secure the Spanish succession for his own grandson.

The King of England in his short intervals of lucidity appeared to appreciate what the King had done, and he made him promise that there should be no ceremony after his death. The end came at three

---

[1] By the Peace of Ryswyck Dutch troops were allowed to garrison certain fortifications along the frontier of the Spanish Netherlands.

[2] Charles II of Spain had one sister married to Louis XIV and another to the Emperor Leopold I; he himself had no children. In the event of his death, therefore, France and the Empire would be in direct competition for succession to the extremely rich Spanish throne. To avoid hostilities Louis XIV and William III made two agreements (1698 and 1700) to partition the Spanish Empire between the claimants. Charles II, however, made a will leaving all his Dominions to Philippe, Duc d'Anjou, second son of the French Dauphin. When the Spanish King died in November 1700 Louis repudiated the partition and accepted Charles's will; his action destroyed William's policy and found much support, even in England and Holland. Louis's recognition of the Old Pretender, however, hardened opinion in Britain, and by the time that William died in February 1702 he had regained his people's confidence and had been able to press on with preparations for war. Hostilities broke out almost immediately thereafter, and the War of the Spanish Succession, in which Marlborough so distinguished himself, raged from 1702 to 1710.

A rebuke from the Duchesse de Gesvres

in the afternoon of 16 September 1701. The Prince de Conti had spent
the whole of the last days at Saint-Germain because he and the Queen
of England were first cousins, their mothers being the Martinozzi
sisters who were nieces of Cardinal Mazarin. The Papal Nuncio stayed
too, and by order of the Pope he recognized the Prince of Wales as
King of England. The Queen of England spent that night at the Filles
de Sainte-Marie de Chaillot (a house of retreat set up by the widow
of Charles I in 1651), of which she was very fond. The next day at
seven in the evening the body of the King of England, with a small
cortège and the English colony from Saint-Germain in carriages, was
conveyed to Paris and buried in the chapel of the English Benedictines, in the rue St. Jacques. There it was to await the day, apparently
still remote, when it could be taken back to England. The heart was
taken separately and buried in the Filles de Sainte-Marie de Chaillot.

This Prince was well known throughout the world as Duke of
York and King of England, so that there is no need for me here to
give an account of his life. He was renowned for his valour and his
goodness, and distinguished by the constant magnanimity with which
he bore his misfortune, and by his saintly nature.

On 20 September the King went to Saint-Germain and was received in the same way as he had been by the new King's father the
first time he went there. The new King wore a formal violet cloak,
but his wife wore no cloak and was anxious to avoid all ceremony.
The whole of the royal family and the Princes of the Blood in undress
paid a visit while our King was there—he himself was the last to
leave, and remained standing all the time he was there. On the following day the King of England in his violet cloak came to Versailles
to call upon the King, who received him as he had received his father,
and as he himself had been received. The King placed his visitor
always on his right hand, and for some time they sat together in arm-
chairs. The Duchesse de Bourgogne also received him and accompanied him to the door of her room, as she herself had been received
by him. He did not see Monseigneur nor his sons, for they had left
for Fontainebleau early that morning. As soon as his visitor had left,
the King went to Sceaux for the night with the Duchesse de Bourgogne, and then on to Fontainebleau. Soon afterwards the new King
of England was recognized by the King of Spain.

The Earl of Manchester, the English Ambassador, did not appear
at Versailles once the Prince of Wales had been recognized as King
of England, and a few days after our King had gone to Fontainebleau
he departed without taking his leave. King William was dining with
some German Princes and other notabilities in his house at Loo when

he heard the news of James II's death, and the recognition of his son. He did not say a word, but went red in the face and pulled his hat down over his eyes. He sent orders to London for Poussin to be sent packing —Poussin was representing the King in the absence of both Ambassador and Envoy, and he arrived at Calais in no time at all. This rupture was quickly followed by the formation of the Grand Alliance, in which the Emperor, England, and Holland (joined later by other Powers) were pledged to joint action, both offensive and defensive, against France. This caused the King to call further troops to the colours.

1702

THE DEATH OF
THE DUC DE COISLIN

N September the Duc de Coislin died, to the great grief of his brother the Cardinal and the general distress of all. He was a rather small, unprepossessing man, but he was honour, virtue, probity, and valour personified. He was intelligent, with a prodigious memory; but his most marked characteristic was his excessive politeness, which drove everyone to distraction—although with it he never lost his dignity. He was a Lieutenant General with a good reputation and Quartermaster General of the cavalry in succession to Bussy-Rabutin, from whose disgrace he did not wish to benefit by acquiring the post at an arbitrary price;[1] afterwards he quarrelled with the Marquis de Louvois, sold the office again, and left the service. For all his good qualities, which earned him general respect and the King's favour, he was so odd that I feel I must say something about him.

On one occasion a German Rhinegrave taken prisoner was confined to the Duke's charge after the battle and his 'host' offered him the use of his bed—a mattress on the floor. The two of them stood over it saying 'After you, Sir,' for so long that finally both slept on the floor, one on one side of the mattress and one on the other. After the campaign was over the Rhinegrave came to call upon the Duke in Paris; when the time came for him to leave, there was such an exchange of compliments that the German could bear it no longer and fled from the room, locking the door behind him. M. de Coislin was not to be outdone; as his rooms were only a few feet above ground-level, he opened the window, jumped out, and was standing by the coach door by the time the now thoroughly rattled Rhinegrave got to it. In his trip through the window the Duke put his thumb out, and Félix, the King's surgeon, had to be sent for to put it back. Several days later Félix returned and found that his patient's thumb was now happily mended. When he had finished his visit the surgeon went to let himself out, but the Duke beat him to it and the two of them stood wrestling each other for the door-handle. The upshot was that the

---

[1] On 5 December 1665 Bussy-Rabutin was clapped into the Bastille and forced to sell his office to Coislin for 252,000 livres, which was 18,000 less than he had given for it.

Duke dislocated his thumb all over again, and Félix had to go back to work on the spot.

My wife and I found the Duke one night with the Bishop of Metz, his son, trudging through Ponthierry on their way to Fontainebleau after his coach had broken down. We sent to ask them to ride back with us, but the message was subjected to so many complimentary interruptions that I finally had to climb down into the mud myself and go and ask him. M. de Metz by now had had more than enough and made up his father's mind for him. But when he was just about committed, the Duke started to go over the whole thing again and said that he could not possibly turn 'these ladies' out. I told him that 'these ladies' were two of our maids who could quite well wait in his coach until it was repaired and come on later. M. de Metz and I were finally made to promise that one at least of the girls should ride back with us. When we finally got to the carriage, both maids got down in a welter of compliments (all of which took time). Under cover of the discussion I told the footman to slam the door the second I was in, and to tell the coachman to drive off at once as fast as he could go. But as soon as we got under way the Duke shouted that he would throw himself out if we left the one young lady behind; he was hanging so far out of the window, with me holding on to the top of his pants, that I had to order the coach to stop. He sat down at last, puffing and swearing that he would have done as he threatened. The maid was called back, and when she arrived, having had to struggle through a dung-heap to get to the coach, she covered us with filth and stank the place out.

Once on a visit which the King paid to Nancy[1] two adventures befell the Duke. The Duc de Créquy, who was not holding office that year, did not like the quarters assigned to him when the entourage reached the city. He was tough, and accustomed to being treated well because of the air of favour and authority which he seemed to have about the court. He went round looking for something better and picked on the Duc de Coislin's rooms—in no time at all he had footmen and baggage out on the pavement. When the Duke came back and found all his things in the street, he could say nothing since Créquy was his senior, but he searched until he found the Maréchal de Créquy, the Duke's younger brother, and had his things out in less time than it takes to tell. The Maréchal, a choleric regular soldier, made a bee-line for Cavoye, and so on—there was general post all through the night.

_____

[1] The capital of the sovereign Duchy of Lorraine.

The Duc de Coislin had never grown out of the old children's game
of tag, and if anyone touched him could not resist running after him
and touching that person back. On this same visit to Nancy, M. de
Longueville tipped off two of his pages who were torch-bearers; as
they were leaving the King's *coucher* one of them touched Coislin,
said 'You're it,' and made off at the double, with the Duke after him.
Taking a short cut, M. de Longueville watched the hunt pass him and
then went home quietly to bed—while the pages in full flight led M. de
Coislin round the entire town. He finally gave up and went home
exhausted, in a muck sweat; afterwards he laughed about it, but he
was not really very pleased.

There was another incident in which he showed himself to be a
man of quick wits in a difficult situation. The second son of M. de
Bouillon (heir to his father's dukedom through the death of his elder
brother, and meantime known as the Duc d'Albret), being in holy
orders, was to read a thesis before the whole gathering of the Sor-
bonne. In those days Princes of the Blood used to attend any university
ceremonies in which distinguished persons were taking part. On this
occasion Monsieur le Prince, Monsieur le Duc (later Prince de Condé),
and MM. the two young brothers of the Prince de Conti were all
present. The Duc de Coislin came in just after them, and, being junior
in rank, left several chairs vacant between himself and the eminent
persons who had preceded him.

The next person to come in was Norion, First President, with a
group of the *présidents à mortier*. Norion made his obeisance to the
Princes of the Blood, and then slipped into the first vacant chair next
to them. M. de Coislin was astonished by such a piece of effrontery;
after looking round, he picked his chair up and planted it in front of
the First President. There was a general murmur, but the Duke was
clever enough to jam his chair right up against the First President's
legs so that he could not move. The Cardinal de Bouillon tried to
intervene, but the Duke said that he was seated where he should be
because the First President had forgotten his proper place. The President himself was furious, but there was nothing he could say; the
présidents à mortier muttered among themselves. Finally the Cardinal
and his brothers went to Monsieur le Prince to ask him to put an end
to this scene, which was completely holding up the proceedings.
Monsieur went over to the Duke, who begged to be excused from
rising, as to do so would release his prisoner. Monsieur criticized the
First President to his face, and then invited the Duke to rise and so
allow the First President to release himself and leave the room. The
Duke wanted to stay where he was until the thesis was over. But at

last, prevailed upon by Monsieur le Prince and the Bouillons, he gave way on condition that Monsieur himself promised that the President would leave the room at once without further skullduggery. Norion, stammering, said that he promised, but the Duke said that he despised the man too much to accept his word and it was Monsieur who must promise: Monsieur promised. So at last the Duc de Coislin got up, moved his chair, and said 'Off you go, Sir, off you go!'—and the President left the place and took to his carriage. Then the Duke picked up his chair, went back to where he had started from, and sat down again. Monsieur le Prince and the three Princes of the Blood came across to compliment him, and everyone of any consequence followed their example. I forgot to say that MM. de Bouillon first tried to solve the problem by sending a message to the Duke to say that he was wanted on most important business outside the door, to which he sent a reply that 'No business was as important as teaching the First President his place, and anyway there was nothing in the world which could get him out of the room unless the President went first.' The Duke remained throughout the whole proceedings and then went home. The four Princes of the Blood went to call on him later in the day and were followed by pretty well everyone who had witnessed or heard about what had happened, so that his house was thronged till late that night.

The next day he went to the *lever* of the King, who had heard from those coming back from Paris after the thesis what had happened. As soon as he saw the Duke the King complimented him on what he had done, and reproved the First President as an impertinent man who had got above himself—words far stronger than those which the King normally used. When the *lever* was finished the King went into his study and made the Duke not only describe what had happened but act it. Then the King sent for the President, tore a huge strip off him,[1] and asked him what gave him the idea that he could take precedence over a Duke except in the *Parlement*; furthermore, he directed that the President should go to see the Duke to apologize— and really see him, not just ask for him at the front door and then go away. Norion's shame and rage can be understood, after what he had already been through; he asked the Duc de Gesvres and others to speak for him to such good effect that after forty-eight hours the Duc de Coislin, satisfied with the sharp lesson he had administered, let his victim off and when the call was made, in spite of the King's instructions, said he was not at home, so that the President was able to go

---

[1] Saint-Simon says that Louis 'lava sa tête.'

away feeling slightly better. The King complimented the Duke on his tact.

The Duc de Coislin was the soul of probity itself. He was one of my father's best friends; he always received me most kindly and spoke freely in my presence. I have often heard him tell this story about the First President, and describe many other curious incidents. He was so sensitive that his brother, the Cardinal, got the reversion of the office of Grand Almoner for the Abbé de Coislin, his second son, without telling him, because if the office had been refused he would have felt it so bitterly. For the same reason the Cardinal got the King to promise never to refuse his brother an entry if he put his name down for Marly —a privilege of which the Duke never took improper advantage. He was not very old, but crippled with gout which attacked his eyes, nose, and tongue. But even when he was in this state his rooms were always filled with the best society from both court and city, and so long as he could walk he was welcome everywhere, for he was generally respected. He was poor, for his rich mother outlived him. He left two sons and one daughter, the Duchesse de Sully.

THE DEATH OF
THE DUCHESSE DE GESVRES;
THE PRINCESSE D'HARCOURT

ABOUT this time the Duchesse de Gesvres died—separated from a husband who was the plague of the whole family and who had spent millions of her money. Her name was du Val, and she was the only daughter of the Marquis de Fontenay-Mareuil, French Ambassador in Rome at the time of the Duc de Guise's affair in Naples.[1] She was a tall, thin, witch-like creature, and walked like one of those big birds that are called the ladies of Numidia.[2]

She seldom came to court, but, in spite of the odd famished look which her husband's excesses had given her, she still had about her a certain spirit and dignity. I remember one summer that the King was going often to the Trianon in the evenings, and he invited the whole court, both men and women, to accompany him. There was

[1] He put himself at the head of the Neapolitans when they revolted against Spanish rule in 1648; he was taken prisoner and kept in Spain until 1652. In 1654 he made a second fruitless attempt at an insurrection in Naples.

[2] Storks.

usually a big supper for his daughters, the Princesses, who asked all their own friends. The Duchesse de Gesvres took it into her head one day to go to the Trianon and attend the supper. Her age, her infrequent appearances at court, her odd clothes, and her looks set the Princesses off making fun of her to their friends in an undertone. She noticed it and, without the least embarrassment, told them exactly what she thought of them so straight that they shut up and looked away. Nor was that all: after supper she was so amusing at their expense that they got frightened and begged her pardon. Mme de Gesvres said that she would grant it, provided they minded their manners in future. After that they never dared look her in the face.

These evenings at the Trianon were unbelievably splendid. All the flowers in the beds the whole length of the terraces were completely changed every day, and I have seen the King and the court forced to go indoors because of the perfume of the mass of tuberoses—it was so strong that no one could stand it, in spite of the fact that the garden is enormous and lies along one arm of the canal.

After an absence from the royal presence of seventeen years, the Prince d'Harcourt was given permission to pay his respects. He had accompanied the King on all the successful campaigns in the Low Countries and the Franche-Comté, but he had been little to court since his visit to Spain, whither he and his wife accompanied the daughter of Monsieur when she married Charles II. Afterwards he took service with the Venetians; he distinguished himself in the Morea, and he did not return until the Republic made peace with the Turks. He was a huge, well-built man, intelligent and dignified—in spite of which he looked like any actor in a provincial stock company. He was a born liar, a libertine, extravagant in a big way, an outrageous cheat, with a taste for really low debauchery which ruined his life.[1] After hanging about Paris for a bit after his return, and finding that he could not stand his wife (one of the few occasions on which he showed good taste), he moved to Lyons. There he himself set up with a vast cellar, a succession of mistresses picked up off the streets and a household to match, a pack of hounds, and a gambling-table to help him make his expenses off any fools, drunks, or sons of wealthy merchants whom he could draw into his clutches. After some years he tired of this life and returned to Paris. The King, who despised him, left him alone but refused to see him, and it was only after two

---

[1] The only good thing that anyone seems able to say of him is that he loved horses and introduced horse-racing into France from England.

months' constant petitioning by the whole of the Lorraine family that he allowed the man into his presence.

His wife was a great favourite of Mme de Maintenon for unpleasant reasons[1] and she went everywhere with the court. She wanted to get her husband invited to Marly, to which husbands generally went automatically when their wives were received. She stayed away in the hope that Mme de Maintenon would miss her enough to obtain the royal permission for the pair of them. But she was wrong: Mme de Maintenon, while making a duty of looking after her, was often embarrassed, and got on very well without her. Fearing that Mme de Maintenon would learn to do without her altogether, she went back to Marly by herself. But the King took good care to see that her husband was never allowed in: this made the Prince somewhat disgruntled with court life and, having lost his taste for the provinces, he finally made for Lorraine.

It is worth describing the Princesse d'Harcourt because her character throws light on the nature of the court at which she was received. She had once been beautiful and very free with her favours,[2] but now, although she was not old, her grace and beauty had gone to seed. She had become a big, fat creature, always in a bustle, with a muddy complexion, thick ugly lips, and tow-coloured hair which was always coming undone and untidy like her dirty, squalid clothes—always intriguing, pretentious, pushing, quarrelling; either in a fit of deepest dejection or high as the sky according to the state of her latest affair. She was a blonde fury—indeed, a harpy: she was shameless, ill-natured, and deceitful; violent, avaricious, and greedy. She was a glutton and gorged herself without scruple; she was the despair of those with whom she went to dine because she made such a beast of herself that often she was taken short at the table, and, failing to leave the room in time, left a filthy trail across the carpet to the door. The servants of Mme du Maine and Monsieur le Grand used to dread her coming. She was not in the least embarrassed on these occasions, but picked up her skirts, and later came back, blandly remarking that she had been taken ill. Everyone got used to it in the end. She was always mixed up in the most peculiar deals, and worked just as hard for a hundred francs as she would for a hundred thousand. The Controllers General were hard put to keep away from her, and whenever she could she put a fast one over on the business men with whom she dealt. Her effrontery in cheating at cards was inconceivable, and she made no bones

---

[1] Her father, M. de Brancas, had been an intimate friend of Mme de Maintenon.
[2] Her father is said to have tried to sell her to the King in 1665.

about it. If she was caught, she begged pardon and got away with it; it came to be regarded as a natural hazard of playing at court. She even tried her tricks at Marly, while playing lansquenet with Monseigneur and Madame la Duchesse de Bourgogne. At other games, such as hombre, people did their best to avoid making up a table with her, but it was not always possible. And at the end of an evening's play, when she had pocketed everything she could lay her hands on, she always said that she was perfectly willing to give up anything she had won which could be called into the slightest question, provided that everyone else round the table did the same—and she took very good care to see that no one took her up on it. She always did this because she made a great play of religion, and always wanted to have her conscience clear because, as she said, 'one can always make mistakes.' She went constantly to church and was a regular communicant —always trying to receive the sacrament after gambling, whatever the hour, even if it were four o'clock in the morning.

One day when there was a fête at Fontainebleau and the Maréchal de Villeroy was on duty, she went to see the Maréchale between Vespers and Evensong. Out of pure malice, Mme la Maréchale suggested a hand at cards so that her guest would miss Evensong. The Princess demurred and said she could not miss the service because Mme de Maintenon would be there. The other insisted, saying that it was ridiculous to suppose that Mme de Maintenon would notice who was in chapel and who was not. So they played. And after the service Mme de Maintenon, who normally never went to see anyone, took it into her head to visit the Maréchale de Villeroy, since she was passing the very door of her apartments. The door opened and the distinguished visitor was announced in a loud voice, to the complete discomfort of the Princesse d'Harcourt. 'I am lost,' she screamed at the top of her voice, 'for she will see me playing cards instead of having gone to Evensong!' She threw her hand on the table, and herself into a chair, quite overcome. The Maréchale laughed happily because what she wanted had succeeded so well. Mme de Maintenon came in slowly and found five or six of them at the table. The Maréchale de Villeroy, who was full of character, said how honoured they were that she should visit them and apologized for their informality, apologizing particularly for the Princesse d'Harcourt's state of disarray. Mme de Maintenon smiled with an air of majestic goodness, and addressed herself to the Princesse d'Harcourt, saying: 'So I see, Madam, that this is the way you have celebrated Evensong today.' The Princesse d'Harcourt jumped up, half in a swoon, saying that was just the sort of way people went on, that she was constantly persecuted, and she had no doubt at all that the Maréchale de Villeroy knew all along that Mme de Maintenon was coming, and that was why she had pressed on with the gambling so that they would all miss Evensong. 'Persecuted!' said the Maréchale, 'why, I thought that I could hardly suggest anything you would enjoy so much as a game of cards. It is true that you felt a twinge of conscience when the time for Evensong came round, but your love of playing quickly won. That,' she said, turning to Mme de Maintenon, 'is all I have done wrong.' At that everyone laughed all the harder. Mme de Maintenon, in order to put an end to the quarrel, told them to go on playing; the Princesse, grumbling as usual and completely distracted, had no idea what she was doing and her fury caused her to throw her hands away. The whole thing provided gossip for the court for several days, since the Princess was feared, unpopular, and mistrusted.

Monseigneur and the Duchesse de Bourgogne were always perpetrating practical jokes on her. One day they had firecrackers laid out all along the path from Marly to the Perspective where she lived. She was very nervous, and two footmen were always on duty to carry her home in her chair when she was ready to go. On this occasion everyone crowded to the windows to watch the fun, and when she got about half-way the crackers began to go off; she screamed at the top of her voice, while the footmen put down the chair and fled. She thrashed about so much that she turned the whole thing over and was trapped inside, screaming her head off. The assembled company ran out to enjoy a closer view and to hear her shouting abuse at everyone who came near, from Monseigneur and the Duchess downwards. Another time Monseigneur tied a cracker under her chair when she was playing picquet; but just as he was about to set it off, some kindly soul warned him that the explosion might seriously maim her, so he desisted. Sometimes they formed up a procession of twenty or so Swiss Guards with a band at their head and marched into her bedroom, waking her up abruptly with a horrible din.

These practical jokes usually took place at Marly. On another occasion in midwinter, freezing cold with snow on the ground, when she was staying in the château itself, in a suite near the guardroom, everyone waited until she had gone to bed and was fast asleep. Then, led by the Duchesse de Bourgogne, they went out on to the terrace and made a lot of snowballs, turning out the guard to carry more ammunition for them. With a pass-key they slipped quietly in, and, flinging back the curtains of her bed, pelted her. The sight of this dirty creature in bed, rudely awakened, dishevelled, and covered in snow, wriggling like an eel, and crying, kept them amused for quite half an hour—by which time the snow had all melted, soaked through the bed, and swamped the floor. The next day she sulked, and that provoked more merriment.

She had fits of the sulks when the jokes at her expense went too far, or when the Grand Equerry had been telling her what he thought of her. This official felt that no one bearing the name of Lorraine should allow herself to be the butt of such buffoonery, and, having a brutal tongue, he would often express himself in minute detail across the dinner-table, whereupon the Princess would first burst into tears, then storm, and finally sulk. Then for fun the Duchesse de Bourgogne would pretend to sulk too. The victim could never keep it up long; she would cringe to the Duchess, tearfully ask pardon for having sulked, and beg them to make all the fun of her they wanted. When they had reduced her to a snivelling mess, the Duchess would allow herself to be moved: and things went on worse than ever. In the eyes of the King and Mme de Maintenon the young Duchess could do no wrong, and there was no one to whom the Princesse d'Harcourt could turn for help—nor dared she quarrel with any of those who helped the Duchess torment her: although otherwise it was inadvisable to offend her.

She paid her servants badly, or never paid them at all. So one day, by arrangement, her coach stopped suddenly on the Pont Neuf. The driver and the footmen got down, giving her a piece of their mind through the window; her equerry and her lady's maid, who were riding with her, got down, and all of them went off together, leaving her to get along as best she could. She started haranguing the crowd that quickly gathered, and was lucky to find a hackney-coachman who got up on the box and drove her home. Another time Mme de Saint-Simon, coming back in her coach to Versailles from Mass at the Recollects, met the Princesse d'Harcourt standing by the roadside in full dress with her train over her arm: it was the same story—her servants had just left her there.

She used to beat her staff, for she was very strong and violent; and she changed her servants every day. Once she engaged a lady's maid who was very tough and well built; from the first day she started to knock her about. The lady's maid said not a word; but after five or six days, when there were no wages owing to her, she told the others what she was going to do, arranged for them to make themselves scarce, and sent off her luggage. In the morning when she went into the bedroom the Princess rounded on her as usual, but at the first blow she went for her mistress and beat her from head to foot. Then she left her Princess screaming on the floor, locked the door, and walked out of the house. Every day there were fights and some new incident. Her neighbours used to say it was impossible to sleep at Marly for the constant disturbance which went on. Such was the favourite of Mme de Maintenon—insolent and impossible to everyone, who was always shown favour and preference, grew rich on the families she had ruined, and made herself dreaded by the whole court up to the Princesses and even the King's Ministers.

1704

THE DUCHESSE DE BOURGOGNE'S
ADMIRERS

SUPPOSE that I would be wiser not to tell this story—but I must say that, having seen it all happen at close quarters, I find it extremely interesting. And I am inclined to tell it because the whole thing was no secret, although the details were not generally known at the time—and anyway the histories of any courts in any age are full of similar tales.

Well, at our court we had a sweet Princess[1] who had captivated the hearts of the King, Mme de Maintenon, and the Duc de Bourgogne by her charming ways. Their well-founded displeasure with her father, the Duc de Savoie, made no difference to their fondness for her. The King kept no secrets from her, and if she came into the room while he was working with his Ministers he would carry on, only being careful to make no reference to her father. When they were alone she used to sit on the King's knee, put her arms round his neck, and tease him; she ruffled his papers and opened his letters, even when he really did not want her to. She was just the same with Mme de Maintenon. In spite of her familiarity she never said anything spiteful—on the contrary, indeed, whenever she had a chance she always put in a good word for anyone she could. She was considerate to the King's servants, down to the lowest, and she was a good mistress to her own staff. She treated her ladies, both young and old, as friends and allowed them absolute freedom. She was the life and soul of the court and everyone adored her. Everyone was anxious to please her. When she was there everything went well, and the court was very dull in her absence. The great favour which she enjoyed with the King gave her a position of importance, and her charm conquered every heart. In a position of such brilliance, her own heart did not remain whole.

Nangis, who is nowadays just a very dull Marshall, was then the finest flower among the youth at court.[2] He was good looking and well built, though not brilliantly handsome. He had been initiated into the ins and outs of intrigue and love-affairs by his grandmother, the

---

[1] The Duchesse de Bourgogne.

[2] Louis-Armand de Buchanteau, Marquis de Nangis (1682–1742). Lieutenant General 1718, Director General of Infantry 1721, Marshal of France 1741.

Maréchale de Rochefort, and his mother, Madame de Blanzac—both past mistresses of such matters. When he was still quite young he had been introduced into the best circles. He had no particular talent— except that of making himself agreeable to women; he attracted a number of the most charming ladies, and he kept his mouth shut about his conquests with an old-fashioned courtesy rare in one so young. Although he was a most fashionable young man, in the field he had shown himself an excellent and most courageous officer, which further endeared him to the opposite sex. At the court of the Duc de Bourgogne, who was about his own age, he was one of the leaders. The Duke was not so handsome as Nangis, but he was particularly fond of his wife, and the Princess seemed to return his love so entirely that to the day he died he never imagined that she had ever so much as looked at another man. But she did look—she looked at Nangis, and before long her eyes were cast too often in his direction. Nangis was not unmoved, but he feared that if anything happened it would end in disaster, and anyway he had already given his heart to Mme de la Vrillière.

Although not really beautiful, Mme de la Vrillière was very pretty and as graceful as Aphrodite. She was the daughter of Madame de Mailly, Lady-in-Waiting to the Duchesse de Bourgogne. She was in everything at court, and it was not long before she knew what was going on and got jealous. She was not in the least inclined to give up her man to the Duchess, and joined battle with her. This rivalry embarrassed Nangis intensely; he was afraid that his mistress would one day create a terrible scene, though in truth she pretended to be nearer bursting-point than she really was. To add to it, he loved her and realized that a scandal would ruin him. On the other hand, there was no future for him if he brushed off a Princess who, already powerful, would one day be omnipotent and who was in no mood to suffer a rival, much less take second place. This deadlock was fascinating to anyone who knew what was going on.

At this time I was frequently a visitor at the house of Mme de Blanzac in Paris, and to the rooms of the Maréchale de Rochefort at Versailles. I also knew several of the Ladies of the Palace very well; they knew everything; and kept no secrets from me. In addition I enjoyed the confidence of the Duchesse de Villeroy, who got all the news from two ladies who were deeply and intimately concerned in what was going on—Madame d'O and the Maréchale de Cœuvres. My sister-in-law, the Maréchale de Lorges, also knew about it and every evening kept me posted as to the day's events. From all these sources I was very well informed. Besides being most amusing, the affair might have most serious consequences in the future and it was essential for anyone with any personal ambition to keep abreast of the latest developments. Finally everyone at court knew about it, but, either from love for or fear of the Princess, the secret was kept—discussed in whispers, but never allowed out into the open. This situation continued for some time: Madame de la Vrillière losing her temper with the Princess and bordering on insolence, the Princess showing her dislike in extreme coldness.

Whether the Princess thought that Nangis needed the prick of jealousy to spur him on or whether it came about naturally I do not know, but before long he realized that he had a rival. Maulévrier, a nephew of Colbert who had nearly died of disappointment at not being made a Marshal at the same time as Villeroy, was married to a daughter of the Maréchal de Tessé. He hardly seemed to have been designed by nature for love-affairs; he was quite plain and altogether very average-looking. He was clever, especially at any sort of back-stairs intrigue, a little crazy, and consumed by boundless ambition. His wife was pretty but dumb; she loved making mischief, and in spite of looking as if butter would not melt in her mouth she could be infinitely spiteful. The Duchesse de Bourgogne prided herself on showing her gratitude to Tessé because he had arranged her marriage treaty, and, since she was his daughter, Madame de Maulévrier was gradually admitted to the inner circle of her court.

Maulévrier was one of the first to realize what was up between the Princess and Nangis. Through his father-in-law he made opportunities of getting to know the Princess better, paid court assiduously and finally, emboldened by Nangis's example, dared to hint at his passion. Since she would not listen to him, he took to writing her notes which, it is said, Madame Cantin used to take, thinking that they were from her great friend Tessé, and of no particular consequence. It is thought that replies were sent through the same channel, addressed to Tessé but intended for his son-in-law. There were other things too which were generally believed but over which I shall draw a veil. Whether these things were true or not, they spread round the court and were treated with the same discreet silence. Using her friendship as an excuse, the Princess went several times to Madame de Maulévrier's rooms when they were all at Marly, to have a quiet cry with her on the imminent departure of the latter's husband to the army in the field; sometimes Mme de Maintenon went with her. The whole court laughed, and no one was sure whether the tears were really for Maulévrier or Nangis—but they served their purpose of stirring Nangis up, and Madame de la Vrillière gave way more and more to her temper.

His imminent departure seemed to Maulévrier to be the end of all his hopes. To what length will a man not go when he is driven by love or ambition! He let it be known that he was consumptive, put himself on a milk diet, and pretended that he had lost his voice—he did it so well that for a whole year he never spoke above a whisper. By this means he got out of going on active service and stayed at court. He was unwise enough to tell his secret to the Duc de Lorges, who told me at the time. Having, as he pretended, to speak in whispers, he took every chance he could get of talking like that to the Duchesse de Bourgogne without anyone realizing that there were secrets between them. In this way he could say anything he liked to her every day, and he worked it so that into much of what he said, to which she replied out loud, he slipped in a few personal asides which she answered briefly without anyone noticing. Most people got so used to it that no one paid any attention, and they were only sorry for his affliction: but those who had much to do with the Duchess realized only too well what was going on and always moved away when Maulévrier came to speak to her. This went on for over a year. Maulévrier used to chide the Princess about Nangis, but a lover can seldom make headway by this sort of reproach. He realized that Madame de la Vrillière was furious, and it worried him: he imagined from it that Nangis was in favour, and the thought was unbearable. Beside himself with rage and jealousy, he finally behaved like a fool.

One day as Mass was ending he went to the tribune and offered his hand to the Duchesse de Bourgogne as she came out, to conduct her to her rooms. He had carefully chosen a day when he knew that Dangeau, her Chevalier d'Honneur, was away, and on such occasions the equerries, who were under his father-in-law as First Equerry, usually left the privilege to him so that he could talk to the Princess; out of respect they fell back out of hearing. Her ladies also followed at a distance, so that although the rooms were crowded Maulévrier enjoyed a *tête-à-tête* with the Princess all the way to her own rooms. This time he reproached her furiously over Nangis, called her all the names he could think of, threatened to tell the King, Madame de Maintenon, and the Prince, and as he talked he crushed her fingers till he nearly broke them. When they got to her rooms, the Princess was trembling and nearly in a faint. She retired at once to her dressing-room and sent for Madame de Nogaret, whom she called her dear nurse and to whom she always turned when she was in trouble. She told her what had happened, saying she had nearly died from fright and could not think how she had managed to get back to her own rooms. Madame de Nogaret had never seen her in such a state; she told Madame de Saint-Simon and myself about it the same day—of course in the strictest confidence. She advised the Princess not to have an open breach with a man who was obviously unbalanced, but to keep out of his way, and above all avoid anything which would give him a hold over her.

The trouble was that Maulévrier went about muttering about Nangis, saying he had been grossly insulted and swearing he would call his rival out as soon as he could get at him. It was obvious what the insult was intended to be, although he never specified it. The terror hanging over the Princess, and the state of Madame de la Vrillière and Nangis can be imagined. Nangis was brave enough—there was not a man living he was afraid of—but shrank from the idea of fighting over an affair like this; he saw visions of his own future, and that of a number of others, being dragged down into ruin by a lunatic. All he could do was to take care never to run into Maulévrier, and to keep quiet.

For six weeks the Duchess lived in a state of terror and had to take constant avoiding action, but she got out of it in the end with nothing worse than a severe fright. I don't know how Tessé came to hear of it, but he was warned somehow, and he acted with great perspicacity. He told his son-in-law that his fortune could be made in Spain and persuaded him that they should go there together. He talked it over with Fagon, an honourable and worthy man, who from the fastness of the King's study had kept a wary eye on the whole proceedings. Fagon appreciated the situation and, since every other course had failed to mend Maulévrier's lungs, prescribed a warm climate as the only remedy to save him from death in the cold of the coming French winter. So Maulévrier's health was given out as a good reason for sending him to Spain; the King and Madame de Maintenon believed every word that Fagon said. Tessé did not waste a minute in removing his son-in-law from the court to put a stop to his lunatic goings-on and to quickly stifle public comment at a man in Maulévrier's condition undertaking so long a journey. It was early in October when Tessé took his leave of the King at Fontainebleau and set off with his son-in-law for Spain.

PUYSIEUX MADE
CHEVALIER DE L'ORDRE

ABOUT this time Puysieux[1] came home on leave from Switzerland, where he was Ambassador and most successful. His grandfather had been Chancellor and his father Secretary of State; his grandmother was an Estampes, sister of M. de Valençay, who was created Chevalier de l'Ordre in 1619. Her husband died in 1640, but she lived on till 1677, when she was eighty. She was very intimate with the Queen Regent;[2] during their childhood the King and Monsieur were always at her house; and the King treated her with consideration to the end of her life. She was tremendously extravagant and dissipated the fortunes of herself and her children.

At that time it was fashionable for ladies to wear a great deal of Genoese lace, which was extremely expensive. In one year Madame de Puysieux got through 100,000 crowns' worth by chewing the swathes of it that she wore round her head and shoulders. M. de Sillery, her eldest son, married a daughter of M. de la Rochefoucauld, famous for his wit and the prominent part which he played during the minority of Louis XIV. Sillery had no money and saw little service with the army; his brother-in-law extended his hospitality at Liancourt to him and his wife and they remained there until the end of their lives. They had several children, and the Puysieux of whom I am speaking was the eldest.

He was short and fat, most cheerful and amusing, polite, respectful, and a very good man. He had very good taste, and was extremely well informed although always modest about it; he was very good company, with an inexhaustible fund of stories. Everyone liked him. He served with the army as long as he could, but resigned when M. de Louvois took a dislike to him and saw to it that he got no further promotion. He stood well with the King, who had kind memories of his grandmother. The Duc de la Rochefoucauld got him the post of Ambassador in Switzerland, and through influence and his own friendly relations with the King he obtained the privilege, never granted to any other Ambassador, of having a private audience whenever he came home on leave or to report. I may add that Torcy was the only Minister with whom M. de la Rochefoucauld was on close terms.

---

[1] Roger Brulart, Marquis de Puysieux et de Sillery (1640–1719), Ambassador to Switzerland, 1697–1708.

[2] Anne of Austria, mother of Louis XIV.

1704 Puysieux came back from Switzerland just after the court had re-turned from Fontainebleau; at his private audience he was most graciously received. As he knew the King well and could be most amusing, he suddenly made up his mind to take advantage of the opportunity. The King in a most friendly way said that he was very pleased with the conduct of affairs in Switzerland. Puysieux then asked if the King was really pleased, or just saying it; the King assured him he meant what he said. So Puysieux jovially remarked that that was as may be, but he himself was not nearly so pleased with His Majesty. 'Why not, Puysieux?' asked the King. 'Well, Sir,' Puysieux replied, 'because although you are the most honourable man in the Kingdom, for more than fifty years now you have failed to keep a promise to me.' 'How is that?' 'Your Majesty has a good memory,' said Puysieux, 'and you surely cannot have forgotten that day when I had the honour of playing blind-man's-buff with you at my grand-mother's house. In order to disguise yourself better you took off your blue riband and put it round my neck; when the game was over I handed it back and you promised that when you were your own master you would give me one of my own. Well, you have certainly been your own master for long enough now, and I still don't see any sign of that riband.'

The King remembered the occasion perfectly; he laughed, and said Puysieux was quite right. Then he said he would convene the Chapter of the Order so that Puysieux might receive his riband on New Year's Day. Directions were given at once for the Chapter and the name of the recipient was made known. Hardly an important story—but an unusual one in the life of so serious and important a monarch as Louis XIV.

1705

THE DEATH OF NINON DE LENCLOS

✣✣✣✣ INON, the famous courtesan, who since she gave up her
✣ 𝒩 ✣ profession was known as Mlle de Lenclos, was another ex-
✣ ✣ ample of the triumph of vice—joined with wit, and touched
✣✣✣✣ with some virtues. The scandal which she occasioned and,
even more, the debauchery into which she led the most distinguished
and most brilliant young men overcame the indulgence which the
Queen Mother usually showed towards anyone gallantly inclined,
and an order was sent for her to retire to a religious home. The *lettre
de cachet* was taken to her by an adjutant; she opened and read it, then
said: 'Monsieur, since the Queen in her great goodness has left to me
the choice of the religious house to which I must retire, will you be
good enough to tell her that I choose the monastery of the Franciscan
monks in Paris,' and with a bow she handed the letter back to him.
The adjutant, stupefied by such unparalleled effrontery, left without
uttering a word, and the Queen was so amused that she let the matter
drop.

Ninon had a host of admirers, but never more than one lover at a
time, and when she was tired of him she said so frankly and took
another. There was no use the discarded lover grumbling or arguing:
it was an order; and so great was the empire which this woman had
built for herself that he would never think of picking a quarrel with
his successor—he was only too pleased to be allowed into the house
as a friend. Sometimes if she was very pleased with her lover she would
remain faithful to him throughout his absence on a campaign. When
he was leaving to join the army Le Castre begged to be one of these
lucky few, but Ninon was rather evasive and he pressed her to give
him her promise in writing. She did, and he carried her note about
with him, boasting. But the note was not honoured, and every time
she gave herself to a man she cried, 'Ah! what a wonderful chit Le
Castre has!' One of her lovers[1] finally asked her why she said that.
She told him, and the story was repeated so that Le Castre became a
joke—it even reached the troops serving under him.

Ninon had many illustrious friends and was clever enough to hold
them all and to keep the peace between them—at least to the extent

[1] Whom she used to call her 'whims.'

of avoiding any open quarrels. In her own house there was a respect for the decencies which the highest Princess finds it hard to keep if she has any weakness in her. Because of this she had friends in the highest court circles—so much so that it was fashionable to be seen at her house, and it was a useful means of meeting the right people. She allowed no gambling, coarse laughter, arguments, or discussion of religion or politics. The conversation was brilliant, and there was always the latest gossip—though she never allowed it to degenerate into back-biting. The tone was light and discreet, and she kept it going with her own wit and knowledge of the world.

It was a strange thing that she attracted a circle of friends as numerous as it was distinguished long after her physical charms had faded, and was treated with every respect and consideration. She knew the details of every intrigue, whether serious or frivolous, which had taken place from Louis XIII's reign right up to the present. Her conversation was charming, disinterested, faithful, discreet, and she could be trusted with any secret; apart from her one weakness, she was a woman of virtue and probity. She often helped her friends with money or, by using her influence, acted for them in many important matters, and zealously guarded large sums of money and dangerous secrets which were confided to her. These characteristics earned her a great reputation and enormous respect.

All the time that Madame de Maintenon lived in Paris they had been friends. Madame de Maintenon did not like her to be mentioned in conversation, but she never disavowed her, and she sent friendly letters from time to time until Ninon's death. Lenclos—a name which Ninon only took when she finally at a a quite advanced age gave up her profession—was not so reserved over her own friends, and whenever she wanted something very badly or wished particularly to help someone she had no hesitation in writing to Madame de Maintenon, who did what she wanted with alacrity. But once Madame de Maintenon had gone up in the world they only met two or three times, and then always in secret.

Lenclos had an admirable gift for repartee. Two remarks which she made to the last Maréchal de Choiseul are still remembered with pleasure: one was a well-earned rebuke, while the other held up a very true mirror to nature. Choiseul, one of her old friends, had once been a handsome, gay spark. He was on bad terms with M. de Louvois, and this was a great worry to him. When the King, in face of his Minister's opposition, included him in the batch of promotions to the Order in 1688, he had not expected that he would get it, in spite of his high birth and his rank as one of the most senior (as well as one of the best)

88

Lieutenant Generals. He was completely overjoyed, and used to preen himself in front of the mirror, fingering the riband. Lenclos saw him doing it two or three times and finally said impatiently: 'M. le Comte, if I catch you at that again I will remind you of some of the other people who have the Order.' Some of them indeed were enough to make a man weep at having his name inscribed on the same list—but even they were giants compared to the successful candidates of 1724 and later. The Marshal was very worthy, but a bit heavy handed. At the end of one of his long visits Lenclos yawned, looked at him for a moment, and said: 'Lord, how many are the virtues that you make me hate!' which is a line from some play or other.[1] Everyone laughed at this sally when it became known, but it did not cause a breach between them.

Lenclos was over eighty when she died, still highly intelligent, still receiving, and still highly thought of. Her last years she gave up to God.

THE ABBÉ DE POLIGNAC

BEFORE finishing with the year 1705 I must mention the beginning of a story which ends later. The Abbé de Polignac,[2] after his adventures in Poland and the exile which followed, had at last got his head above water. He was a tall, well-built man with a handsome face; very intelligent, well mannered, and well informed. He had an enchanting voice, manly, persuasive, charming, with striking expressions peculiar to himself. No one knew more about literature, no one could better explain the most abstruse matters simply, no one told stories better, or had a wider superficial grasp of every art and profession. But the one profession about which he knew nothing was his own—the priesthood. He was always trying to make himself agreeable—as readily to a valet or a lady's maid as to their master and mistress. He tried always to appeal to the heart, the intelligence, and the eyes of his listeners. He managed to make his audience feel very intelligent. For all that, he had no interest in anyone but himself, possessed no friends, and was completely devoid of gratitude. False, dissipated, unscrupulous, respecting neither God nor man, he yet spoke with such delicate restraint that most people

---

[1] The last line of Act III of Corneille's *Pompée*.

[2] Melchior de Polignac (1661–1741). Latin poet. Ambassador to Poland, 1695; endeavoured to bring about the election of the Prince de Conti as king and was subsequently exiled until 1702. Member of the Academy 1704. Cardinal 1710. After further exile, he was Ambassador in Rome 1721–30.

were taken in. He was always involved in some affair, not because he really liked debauchery, but either because the opportunity was thrown at his feet or because it suited his ambition. His heart was false, his soul debauched, his judgement non-existent, his common sense deficient, and any plans which he made were ill conceived—with the result that any matters of importance with which he was entrusted died on him.

To a handsome face and considerable talent he added the virtue of good birth, but he was saved from the envy of his friends by the fact that his share of the world's goods was not up to the same high standards. He had won the hearts of the most agreeable ladies at court and the most distinguished men. From the beginning he had his eye firmly fixed on a Cardinal's hat. Twice he started studying for a university degree, and twice gave it up. Schoolbooks, forms, the seminary, and all the study for the episcopacy were absolutely anathema to him.[1] He was interested only in affairs of the moment and intrigues on the grand scale. The business of the Cardinal de Bouillon, to whom he had attached himself at one time, nearly proved his undoing.[2] But Torcy, with whom he had particularly made friends, got him out of several scrapes and was always a good friend to him. And after his most recent return to court he was constantly the centre of the most brilliant circles. Even the King had become reconciled to him, through the good offices of the Duc du Maine, with whose wife the Abbé was on the closest terms. He was invited to Marly every time the court moved there, where he worked hard to assert his charm. In spite of watching himself, he once let fall a miserable flattery which is still remembered with amusement. He was following the King one day in the gardens of Marly when it began to rain. The King made a friendly remark to him about his coat, which was ill suited to withstand the elements. 'It is nothing, Sire,' he replied; 'the rain at Marly is never wet.' Everyone laughed out loud.

In such an agreeable situation he looked around and began to envy the permanent good fortune of Nangis and the temporary inroads of Maulévrier in the same field; he thought that he could do likewise,

[1] In fairness it must be added that the Marquis d'Argenson, a fair-minded man, had a completely contrary view: he said that Polignac's student career was excellent, and his theses were perfect—so much so that on one occasion he swept the board by winning every prize for which he was eligible at the Collège d'Harcourt.

[2] Emmanuel-Théodore de la Tour-d'Auvergne, Cardinal de Bouillon (1644–1715), Grand Almoner of France, was disgraced for his continual impertinence. In 1694 he tried unsuccessfully to get himself appointed Prince-Bishop of Liége. Instead he was sent as Ambassador to Rome, where he disobeyed his instructions so flagrantly that he was recalled, but refused to return in 1700. In 1701 he was relieved of his office as Grand Almoner, but only returned to France when his source of income was withdrawn.

and he began his campaign along the same lines. He made friends with
Madame d'O and the Maréchale de Cœuvres, and they soon listened
to what he wished to say to them. Soon he was taking advantage of
the lovely nights in the gardens of Marly, in spite of the danger from
the Swiss Guards. Nangis grew pale with anger, and Maulévrier, although by now well out of the running, was equally furious.[1]

The Abbé's activities shared the fate of everyone else's: everyone
knew perfectly well what was going on, but there were whispers in
private and public silence. To enjoy such a triumph while still so
young was not enough: he wanted to see tangible results. His knowledge of the arts and sciences, and the various affairs of State which he
had handled successfully made him feel that he might gain admittance
to the Duc de Bourgogne's private study, and once there he saw no
end to what he might achieve. To get in he needed to gain the confidence of the man who held the key: the Duc de Beauvilliers who,
after their schooldays, continued to enjoy the complete confidence of
the young Prince. The Duke's official duties took up the whole of
his time, and he was not much of a one for either the arts or sciences,
nor did the Abbé know any of his personal friends, so there was little
possibility of a direct approach. But the Duc de Chevreuse (Beauvilliers's brother-in-law), who seemed less busy (I shall explain later
what I mean by 'seemed'),[2] seemed rather more accessible. He was interested in intellectual matters, and once his attention had been caught
it was easy—he became the Abbé's line of attack. First a few words by
chance at the King's audiences, then the postulating of some interesting problem exciting the curiosity, then long conversations walking
up and down in the big gallery—thus the Abbé insinuated himself into
his victim's rooms which would normally have been closed to him.
In no time at all he had charmed M. de Chevreuse, in whose rooms he
had the good fortune to meet M. de Beauvilliers, to whom he gave
an impression of being discreet, reserved, and elusive. Little by little
he became an agreeable relaxation for them in what moments of
leisure they had. Both of them were alike, and when he pleased one
he pleased both. Both of them were absorbed in, I might say sub-
merged by, their duties, and their position at court was so senior that
they practically lived like hermits, oblivious of everything which went
on around them. Charmed by the Abbé, and quite ignorant of any
implications, they thought that it would be a good deed to bring anyone so intelligent and so amusing into the presence of Monseigneur

[1] In fact Polignac was not received at Marly until after the death of Maulévrier.
[2] Chevreuse was Minister of State *incognito*.

le Duc de Bourgogne, who enjoyed much the same talents himself. We shall see later how far things were to go with this young Prince; meanwhile we must go back for a little.

I saw every move in the game between Polignac and the Duc de Chevreuse. Unfortunately I was not capable of keeping my mouth shut as the two Dukes did. One evening I went to Marly, as I did almost every day, to have a private talk with the Duc de Beauvilliers. By now he treated me with a confidence which was greater than my years normally warranted, and I could talk to him about anything— even himself. On this occasion I gave him my views on what I had noticed concerning the Abbé de Polignac and the Duc de Chevreuse. I said that there were no two men at the court who had less in common, and that with the exception of Torcy there was no one in the Abbé's circle whom the two Dukes could stand, that I had watched the whole thing grow, and that M. de Chevreuse was being fooled by the Abbé and being used merely as a stepping-stone to Beauvilliers himself—whom when the time came he would likewise charm with his conversation—and that the object of the whole exercise was to gain admittance to the private study of Monseigneur the Duc de Bourgogne. I was too late, for I found that Beauvilliers was sold already but had not yet had much to do with Polignac and had not yet made up his mind to introduce him to the young Prince.

'Well,' he said, 'what does all this add up to? What do you make of it?'

'What do I make of it?' I replied, 'I don't think either of you realize the kind of man you are up against. Both of you will be taken in; you will introduce him to Monseigneur the Duc de Bourgogne, and then you will find that is all the use he has for you——'

Interrupting me, he said: 'How will that be taking us in? If his conversation is useful and agreeable to Monseigneur the Duc de Bourgogne, what could be better than bringing them together?'

'All right,' I answered, 'you interrupted me and you can have it your own way. But I warn you, and I know what I am talking about, that you and he have less in common than any two people you can think of at court. The time will come when he will find you in his way. Once you have introduced him to the Duke, he will charm your pupil like a siren, and you will find yourself completely dispossessed.'

When I said this the Duke's whole expression changed; he looked annoyed and told me coldly that he did not want to hear any more about it, that I went too far, and anyway I never had a good word to say for anyone, that he was quite sure that no such idea had ever entered the Abbé's mind nor even entered the bounds of possibility, and, as he did not wish to pursue the matter any further, would I please shut up.

By now I was angry too, and I said: 'Monsieur, I will do as you say, but you will see that I am right in the end. I promise that I will never mention the subject again.'

He sat for a few minutes in concentrated thought. I talked about other matters—he seized the opportunity, and soon our conversation was back to normal.[1]

---

[1] Within a matter of months Torcy had got the Abbé nominated as *auditeur du roi*— a considerable step forward.

1706

THE DUC DE VENDÔME

Although, as we shall see, he was a man of idle habits and lax morals, the Duc de Vendôme—the King's bastard second cousin—was nevertheless the best soldier of France in the latter years of Louis XIV's reign. In the 1690's he was invincible in the Low Countries; at the end of the century he held his own against the Spanish and English armies in Catalonia. He was posted to the Italian command in 1702, and by 1705 had cleared that great soldier, Prince Eugène, right out of Italy. In 1708 he fought an unsuccessful campaign against Marlborough, starting at a disadvantage by having to share command with the young Duc de Bourgogne who loathed him. But in 1710 he was sent back to Spain, where his spectacular victories ensured the succession of Louis XIV's grandson to the Spanish throne as Philip V. He seldom came to Versailles, but when he did the event created such a stir that it is worth considering the astonishing portrait which Saint-Simon painted of him. Editors of Saint-Simon have pointed out that this portrait, with all its merits and despite its flagrantly unfavourable bias, dominates every interpretation of Vendôme's character to this day.

At this time the court and Paris witnessed a prodigious spectacle. The Duc de Vendôme had not left Italy since he took over from the Maréchal de Villeroy after the nonsense at Cremona.[1] The battles which he had won (such as they were), the towns he had taken, the power which had come to him, the reputation which he had usurped, and his incomprehensible success in worming his way into the King's good books all made him feel that he wanted to come home and play a brilliant rôle at court—which, in the event, surpassed even his most sanguine expectations. But before we describe the arrival of a man whose rise had been so incredible and whom I have so far only mentioned in passing, it would be as well to describe him in all his extraordinary detail.

He was of medium height, rather stout, but strong, active, and vigorous; his features were handsome and his mien was proud; his bearing was graceful and his voice was good—he spoke easily with a natural frankness which gradually lapsed into the most outspoken

---

[1] On 1 February 1702 Villeroy was completely surprised in Cremona by Prince Eugène; he himself was taken prisoner, but after his removal from the scene the French garrison succeeded in fighting off the Imperial forces.

effrontery. He had a great knowledge of the world, the court, and all the personalities who came there, and under a superficially happy-go-lucky air had a very good eye for the main chance. He was a polished courtier, and he knew how to slip his most abominable excesses past under cover of the King's great respect for his own ancestry.[1] He was carefully and deliberately polished, but he could be unbearably insolent when he thought his position was impregnable. At the same time he got on well and was popular with the lower classes—an affectation which nourished his vanity and brought out the vulgarity in him. At bottom, it was pride which governed everything that he did, said, or felt. As he was promoted and his standing increased, his pride, his lack of self-control, and his confidence in his own opinions gradually made him impervious to anyone else's views, so that he would not even listen to anyone outside a very small circle of intimates, and to his servants. Eventually flattery, admiration, and finally adoration were the only means by which one could approach this demi-god, who could put forward the most ridiculous ideas without any of those around him even daring to disagree, much less contradict.

Better than any man he understood the weaknesses in the French character and took advantage of them. Little by little he got the junior officers in his army, and then all ranks, to call him 'Monseigneur' and 'Votre Altesse.' In the absence of any opposition, this gangrene spread right up to Lieutenant Generals and the most distinguished people; they were all like sheep, and not one of the lot of them dared fail to use these improper terms of address. With time it became a habit, and woe betide anyone who did not address him in the manner which he had laid down.

What seems so extraordinary is that the real filth of his personal life never seemed to upset the King, who, although he had himself been very free with women, had an absolute horror of unnatural vice —and there can be no doubt that the King knew all about it. Vendôme himself was quite open about it, but always behaved as anyone would behave who was enjoying the lightest and most normal affair. Scandals surrounded him throughout his life—at court, at Anet,[2] or in the field. His servants and junior officers satisfied his perverted tastes and were notorious for it, so that those about the Marshal curried favour with them in the hope of gaining personal preferment.

---

[1] As the genealogical tree shows, they shared a common grandfather of great eminence in Henry IV; and Vendôme's mother, the famous Gabrielle d'Estrées, was much respected.

[2] The lovely home built by Henri II for Diane de Poitiers which later became the country estate of the Ducs de Vendôme.

1706 I have described before with what audacious effrontery he publicly retired to take the great cure,[1] being the first person who ever dared formally to take his leave of the King for the purpose, and how his health became a topic of conversation at court—the King himself setting the example by condoning conduct which he would never have tolerated in a Son of France.

M. de Vendôme's idleness was quite inconceivable. More than once he was nearly taken prisoner because he would not leave a headquarters situated too far away from his troops to be practicable, but which he found comfortable; and often he risked the whole success of a campaign, letting the initiative pass to the enemy, because he did not move out of a camp where he had settled down at his ease. When in the field he saw little for himself, he relied on those about him, and then frequently disbelieved them. This was because he disliked any interference with the normal routine of his daily life. He was very dirty in his person, and proud of it—the more foolish hangers-on used to say he was just a man of simple habits. In bed he was always surrounded by dogs, and sometimes bitches produced their litters by his side. He never restrained himself in his physical needs, wherever he might be. One of his theories was that everyone was just as dirty in their habits as he was, but most people would not admit it. He let this idea off one day on the Princesse de Conti, the most scrupulously clean and most refined person in the world.

In the field he used to get up rather late, and would sit down at once on his *chaise-percée*. In this curious position he dealt with his correspondence and dictated the day's orders. If any of his divisional commanders or distinguished visitors wanted to see him, this was the time when it was easiest to talk to him. The whole army had got used to this routine. Still sitting there, he would then eat an enormous breakfast with two or three friends, eating, talking, and giving orders, with a large audience watching. The unpleasant details which follow are necessary to an understanding of this extraordinary man's character. He evacuated mightily, and when the pot was full it was carried out in front of the entire assembled company. On the days when he was shaved, the same pot did duty. According to him, these were simple habits, without any frills, worthy of the ancient Romans. When all this was over, he got dressed and had a game of ombre or piquet; if it was absolutely essential for him to make a mounted reconnaissance, this was when he did it. Once he had turned back for his headquarters, nothing would get him out again.

---

[1] Mercury treatment for syphilis.

He would consume a huge supper with a few intimate friends; he was a great eater, with a passion for fish—particularly when it had gone off. They used to sit on at table arguing and discussing, then going on to flattery and homage. He never forgave anyone who criticized him; he wished to be considered the greatest soldier of his age, and spoke most slightingly of Prince Eugène and every other general; to contradict him was a crime. Private soldiers and N.C.O.'s adored him for his familiarity with them and the general licence which he deliberately permitted in order to gain their confidence—which he counteracted by the stiff-necked attitude which he adopted towards anyone of rank or birth. In Italy he treated the most important people in the same way.

This was what made the fortunes of the famous Alberoni.[1] The Duke of Parma, having to treat with M. de Vendôme, sent as envoy the Bishop of Parma, who was horrified at being received by the Marshal on his *chaise-percée*, and more distressed still when his host got up, turned his back, and wiped himself. He turned around and went back to Parma without delay, saying that nothing on earth would induce him to have anything more to do with such a horror. Alberoni was the son of a gardener, and, conscious of his own ability, had taken minor orders in order to gain an entrée into circles which could accept an abbé's soutane when they would hardly accept workman's overalls. He was a buffoon: the Duke of Parma was amused by him and thought that there was enough wit in him to make him a not inadequate diplomat. The Duke thought that the sight of the Duc de Vendôme on his *chaise-percée* would not be likely to upset him, and charged him with going and finishing the work which the Bishop in his flight had left undone. Alberoni had nothing to lose and, knowing what Vendôme was like, was determined to make himself agreeable at all costs and so advance himself in the eyes of his master. He was received by M. de Vendôme in the usual way, and enlivened his discussion of his affairs with a suitable leaven of flattery and a few jokes which made the General laugh. Vendôme behaved exactly as he had with the Bishop: he got up and wiped himself. When Alberoni saw the exposed portions of Vendôme's anatomy turned towards him, he cried '*O culo di angelo!*' and kissed them! Nothing ever did him more good than this infamous piece of buffoonery. M. de Parme, who was constantly in negotiation with M. de Vendôme, realized what a

---

[1] Giulio, Cardinal Alberoni (1664–1752), an adventurous Italian who, from a modest beginning, rose to be Prime Minister of Spain 1715–19 and a candidate for the Papacy in 1724.

good start Alberoni had made and went on to employ him regularly. Alberoni took the trouble to make friends with Vendôme's servants and to stay on as long as possible. To tickle M. de Vendôme's love of strange dishes, he made him cheese soups and odd ragouts which went down very well. Alberoni was invited to share the General's table and so ingratiated himself that he eventually changed masters—while making it perfectly clear what an enormous future he had given up by deserting the Duke of Parma. Without abandoning his role of professional funny man, or as a chef composing a wide range of attractive dishes, he soon got his hands on Vendôme's correspondence, and became principal secretary dealing with the most private and confidential matters. This upset all the other secretaries, and jealousy increased to such a point that one of them (Magnani) on one occasion drove Alberoni along in front of him for the best part of a mile in full view of the whole army, belabouring him with a stick. M. de Vendôme was not very pleased, but that was all; and Alberoni, who was not the man to be turned aside by any insults from the course he had set himself, managed to make the incident seem almost a good point in the eyes of his master, into whose confidence and innermost circle he wormed his way more and more securely.

Since his positions in Italy were firm and Prince Eugène for the time being had gone back to Vienna, M. de Vendôme thought this would be a good opportunity to return home and gather some of the fruits of his labours. He applied for and was granted permission to do a tour of duty at court, leaving his army under the command of Maldévy, the senior Lieutenant General. Vendôme came straight to Marly, arriving on 12 February. There was a tremendous coming and going; everyone—pages, chair porters, and servants—dropped everything and crowded round his post-chaise. No sooner had he gone up to his room than there was a queue, headed by the Princes of the Blood—the very people who had been in such a fury at his being given a command. Everyone, Ministers and all, ran to pay their respects, so that there was no one left in the public rooms at the palace but women. M. de Beauvilliers was at Vaucresson, and, for my part, I was content to remain a spectator without going out of my way to pay court to the general hero. The King and Monseigneur sent for him. As soon as he could get dressed in the midst of all this mob, he went down to the salon, borne along by the crowd. Monseigneur stopped the music when he saw him come in, and embraced him. Then the King, who was working with Chamillart in Mme de Maintenon's rooms, sent for him to come up; he came out from the small study and greeted the General in the big room, embraced him, spent some

The Duc de Vendôme at home

minutes in conversation, and then said that he would like to see him again on the following day when they could talk at leisure. In fact the interview in Mme de Maintenon's rooms the following day lasted, I am told, over two hours.

Chamillart, saying that they had much work to do and it could be done better at their leisure, gave a superb fête for him at l'Étang which went on for two days. Following his example, Pontchartrain, Torcy, and all the most distinguished figures at court did the same. Vendôme, sought after by everyone, could not accept all the invitations showered upon him. Everyone was falling over each other to lay on fêtes for him, and to scrounge invitations to his parties. There was never such a triumph; each step he took seemed to bring fresh honours to him. It seemed as though everyone—Princes of the Blood, courtiers, noblemen, and Ministers—faded into insignificance in comparison with him, even to the extent that the King only seemed to be King for the purpose of honouring this hero. The people at Versailles and Paris were the same and his carriage was followed by cheering crowds through the streets. If it was known that he was going to the opera, the house sold out at double prices like a first night.

Vendôme took all this in his stride, but even he was surprised by the general excitement and, although he was determined to keep his stay short, he was afraid that the enthusiasm could hardly last until his departure. In order to make his public appearances less frequent he asked permission to retire to Anet between his two visits to Marly; he was only two days at Versailles, and he squeezed in one night at Meudon to please Monseigneur. No sooner had Vendôme got to Anet with a few friends than the court was deserted and the house and the village of Anet were bulging at the seams—Monseigneur, the Princes of the Blood, and the Ministers all went chasing out there. The King, who normally loathed being left alone, rather enjoyed the quietness at Versailles while everyone was at Anet, and he used to ask people if they had been or if they were going.

It was obvious that it was part of a deliberate policy to make a hero out of Vendôme, and he was not slow to realize it: he decided to make something out of it himself. He renewed his demand to be named Commander of all the Marshals of France. How could they refuse such a thing to a man who had been worshipped even as the god of war himself? His commission as Marshal General was drawn up on the same lines as that of Turenne,[1] which hitherto had been unique. It

---

[1] Henri de la Tour d'Auvergne, Vicomte de Turenne (1611–75), one of the greatest soldiers in French history. He took command of Louis's small army in 1651 and by 1659,

99

had been drawn up thus in an effort to avoid the King's having to refuse something he had no intention of granting, but it did not satisfy either M. de Vendôme or M. du Maine. They both wanted the seniority over the whole body of Marshals to be based on claims of birth alone, and M. de Vendôme suggested that a specific clause to this effect should be written into the commission.

I do not know how the Maréchal de Villeroy got wind of this, but he did, and in time to go to the King with the most vigorous protests. At that time he was at the height of his favour and he won the day; Vendôme was told that not a line was to be written into his commission, which was to conform exactly to that of Turenne. He was furious and refused it point blank. His refusal was a bold move, but he knew the man he was dealing with and the strength of his own support. Not long before he had been stubbornly refused seniority even over such Marshals as were junior to him in Army command. From that situation to the commission now being offered to him, which gave him seniority over all the Marshals, was a much greater step up than the additional one he was asking for—that such seniority should be by virtue of birth. He felt sure that if he held out he would get what he wanted, and we shall see later in this same year that he was right.

His brother, who was not on very good terms with him, was one of the many visitors to Anet and hoped that the hero could get him back into the King's good books. Vendôme offered to present him to the King and get him an allowance of 10,000 écus. But the insolent Grand Prior was not interested in anything less than the command of an Army in Italy, and he left Anet in a huff; when his brother returned to court, he moved off to give vent to his rage at Clichy.

This Grand Prior was equally as debauched as his brother (though without the same perversions) and drowned himself in self-indulgence with even greater imagination;[1] he also had one advantage over his brother in that every night without fail for the past thirty years he had been put to bed dead drunk—an agreeable habit which he kept up to the end of his life. There was not one spark of military talent in him; his cowardice was notorious, though he tried to hide it beneath a blustering air. He was more proud even than his brother, and be-

---

when the triumphant Peace of the Pyrenees was signed, had driven all the King's enemies off French soil. He was then offered the honour of *Maréchal Général des camps* if he would give up his Protestant faith, but he did not do so until 1668, two years after the death of his wife. He continued his victorious career until he was killed in action at Salzbach.

[1] A broad rendering of the now obsolete and almost untranslatable seventeenth-century phrase *d'être au poil et à la plume*.

cause of this none of the officers of his Order would have anything to do with him except a few very obscure juniors. He was a liar, a swindler, a cheat, and a thief—dishonest to the very marrow in his bones, if he had any left after the ravages of disease; supremely conceited, yet toadying to anyone he could get something out of, and ready to do anything or suffer any indignity for money—for he was the most unmanageable spendthrift in existence. He was witty,[1] and in his youth had had a fine figure and really beautiful features. But now he had become the vilest, the most contemptible, and at the same time the most dangerous creature it is possible to imagine.

THE END OF MAULÉVRIER

MAULÉVRIER came back from Spain and arrived at Marly just when the Princesse des Ursins was enjoying her most brilliant triumph, and she was closeted constantly with Mme de Maintenon, who was anxious to start her off back to Madrid as soon as possible; he brought with him various despatches from the Queen of Spain and Tessé. He took advantage of his old closeness with Mme des Ursins,[2] whom he had served well; he ran after her, and was careful to see that she knew of the standing which he had achieved with the Duchesse de Bourgogne, and that the Duke also had received him and found him amusing. And he had no hesitation in playing up his own importance in the eyes of his friend, to whom he had told such important secrets at Toulouse that she readily believed there was more in what he told her than met the eye. Even though she was leaving many friends behind when she went back to Spain, she still thought it worth while to cultivate Maulévrier and bind him to her with the closest possible ties. She was well aware how important a part such secret influences could play in court matters and their ultimate success. Maulévrier made use of her to gain admission to Mme de Maintenon, who was so anxious to find out what was going on in Spain, hoping to extend her own influence there through Mme des Ursins, and could not refuse to receive her protégé. He was therefore received in private; these conversations became more and more frequent, and sometimes lasted as long as three hours;

[1] La Fontaine said that sometimes the Grand Prior could be the most amusing man he had ever met.

[2] Anne-Marie de la Trémoïlle, Princesse des Ursins (1641–1722). Twice widowed by 1701, she played an important part in engineering the marriage of Philip V of Spain and Marie-Louise de Savoie, after which she was all-important at the court in Madrid and exercised an influence which was largely instrumental in saving Philip's crown for him.

he was careful to drive home the points he made with a deluge of letters and memoranda. Mme de Maintenon always enjoyed new acquaintances, and she recommended Maulévrier to the King.

Maulévrier, who had been down and out when he came back from Spain, suddenly found himself returned to favour and he became positively airborne;[1] he began to treat the Ministers of the Crown with contempt and consistently disregarded the advice sent to him by his father-in-law. The affairs with which he was concerned and the secret correspondence which he kept up with Spain gave him many opportunities for private talks with both the Duc and the Duchesse de Bourgogne—so that his aspirations were rekindled. Both Nangis and the Abbé de Polignac drove him to distraction. He tried to make every sort of sacrifice, without receiving any return. His wife, who was furious with him, began to make advances to Nangis who, the better to cover up his own affairs, seemed to respond. Maulévrier noticed it, and it was more than he could bear. He knew his wife's malicious disposition only too well, and was afraid of what she would get up to. So many violent and conflicting emotions quite turned his head. One day he was in his rooms when the Maréchale de Cœuvres came to see him, apparently to make up some disagreement: he shut the door in her face, barricaded it, and for a whole hour shouted at her exactly what he thought of her—and she had the patience to stand there and listen.

After that he came very seldom to court and spent most of his time in Paris. He used to go out at the strangest hours, hire a coach, and drive off to all sorts of remote places, such as the back of the Carthusian monastery. There he would get out, walk on by himself, and whistle: sometimes an old man would shuffle out from a corner and hand him a package, sometimes a parcel would be dropped down to him from a window, and once he picked up from behind a milestone a box which was apparently full of despatches. I was told of these peculiar goings-on by people whom, in his indiscretion and vanity, he allowed to witness them. Then he would write to Mme de Maintenon and the Duchesse de Bourgogne—as time went on, nearly always to the latter, through Mme Quantin. I know people, the Duc de Lorges among them, to whom Maulévrier showed bundles of these letters and his replies, and read out, among others, one from Mme Quantin in which she tried to calm him down over the Duchesse de Bourgogne and said in the frankest terms that he could always count on her.

───

[1] *commença à perdre terre.*

He went once more to Versailles, when he saw the Duchess pri- vately and they had a most bitter quarrel. On the same day he had dinner with Torcy, with whom he remained on apparently good terms, and was foolish enough to tell the whole story of his rage and what had happened to the Abbé de Caumartin, who was there and who promptly told me. Then he went back to Paris, and his mind, tormented by every form of love, ambition, and jealousy, gave way. Doctors were called in, and it was necessary to keep everyone out except essential visitors, and they were only allowed in at times when he was fairly quiet. A hundred strange visions raced through his head. Sometimes he was away in Spain, sometimes he raved about the Duchesse de Bourgogne and Nangis, whom he sometimes wanted to kill in a duel and sometimes have violently assassinated. Sometimes, filled with remorse over the friendship of the Duc de Bourgogne which he had so little deserved, he uttered reflections so strange that they were unbearable and everyone left the room. At other times, gentle and removed from the follies of the world, he would hark back to his early education in the Church and could talk only of penance and retreat. Then he would send for a confessor to comfort him in his despair of God's mercy. Sometimes he thought himself desperately ill and at death's door.

But everyone, even his nearest relations, thought that all this was merely make-believe. In order to put an end to it, they told him that he was generally considered to be quite mad, and if he did not want people to think so he had better get up and show himself. This was the last straw which was his ruin. Realizing that if people thought this of him it would be the downfall of all his desperate ambitions, he abandoned himself to hopeless despair. Although he was most carefully watched by his wife, a few intimate friends, and the staff, he managed to give all of them the slip at eight o'clock on Good Friday morning and, running down a passage behind his room, flung himself out of the window into the courtyard, smashing his skull on the pavement.

VILLEROY RELIEVED OF
HIS COMMAND IN FLANDERS

Louis was anxious to bring the War of the Spanish Succession to an end, but he needed a victory as a basis for negotiation. He urged his favourite, the Maréchal de Villeroy, to bring his enemies to battle in Flanders—but expressly forbade him to fight until very substantial reinforcements had arrived from the Rhine. Villeroy, a proud and stupid man, thought he knew better and faced up to Marlborough in an impossible position at Ramillies. After this shattering defeat, the King removed Villeroy gently but firmly from his command, believing that the only remedy was to bring Vendôme from Italy to hold the victorious English general.

VENDÔME arrived at Versailles on the last Saturday in July. He made his obeisance to the King as he got down from his carriage; he was greeted as the hero who would put everything to rights. He followed the King to Mme de Maintenon's apartments, where they remained closeted with Chamillart. He boasted of the perfect state in which he had left everything in Italy, and assured the King that there was no hope of Prince Eugène relieving Turin.[1] On the Sunday he went to see Monseigneur at Meudon and worked for hours with Chamillart. On Monday, 2 August, M. de Vendôme had a long interview with the King in his study, alone. From the King's hand he received a letter giving him seniority over all the Marshals of France, and directing all of them wheresoever they might be to take his orders. That was what he and M. du Maine had so long striven for, and had achieved against the King's better judgement. By this means, without any further commission and without any mention of his birth, M. de Vendôme was raised to equal status with the Princes of the Blood. He took his leave then, and spent the night at Clichy; the next day he set out for Valenciennes. The Maréchal de Villeroy, who was hanging about at Saint-Amand, was recalled; he did not meet M. de Vendôme.

Villeroy's return was different from what had happened in previous years. He arrived at Versailles on Friday, 6 August, and saw the King in Mme de Maintenon's apartments: he got a short and frigid reception. It was his turn for duty as Captain of the Guard, but he had little difficulty in obtaining a few days' leave on the grounds that his baggage had not arrived and he had private affairs to attend to. He

---

[1] In fact the enemies of France under Prince Eugène's able leadership were rapidly gaining in strength.

promptly went back to Paris, ostentatiously failed to call on Chamillart, and did himself a great deal of harm by complaining about him loud and long. The time for bombast was over; the royal favour which for so long had held him up had evaporated. Chamillart was not responsible for his deliberately disobeying the orders given to him to wait for reinforcements, nor had any part in the choice of terrain which had resulted not only in a defeat but in a subsequent panic which lost the whole of Flanders. No one listened to him except a few personal friends; no one wished to risk a quarrel with Chamillart for the sake of a general who had had his time.

Villeroy, deprived of his favour at court and his army command, lost all his brilliance. His grand airs and rodomontade gave way to a hang-dog look and perpetual embarrassment. His tour of duty was most unpleasant: the King never spoke to him except to give him an order. He felt terribly that the King found him in the way, and, what is more, that everyone noticed it; he never opened his mouth, for no one wanted to hear what he had to say; he knew the dice were loaded against him. His humiliation showed in his face, which was like a wrinkled bladder out of which all the air has drained. As soon as his tour of duty was finished he went back to Paris, and to Villeroy, and stayed there until he was duty officer again. He very rarely appeared at court, and when he did the King took no notice of him. Mme de Maintenon was sorry for him; occasionally she received him, and this small honour kept him from total extinction.

THE DUC D'ORLÉANS IN THE FIELD

After the Duc de Vendôme had been recalled to take command of the Army in Flanders, the King was hard put to it to choose a new commander to face Prince Eugène in Italy. His choice eventually fell on the Duc d'Orléans, who had for so long wanted a command in the field; but the appointment was somewhat spoiled by the King making the Duke promise that he would not make any move whatever without the consent of the Maréchal de Marsin, the senior military commander on the spot. The army lay south-east of Turin, covering the approaches to the city.

THE Duc d'Orléans—left on his own by M. de Vendôme, or rather, what was worse, under the tutelage of the Maréchal de Marsin—left one corps under Médavy to guard his supply route, and concentrated all the rest of his forces, including one cavalry corps which he had to ask La Feuillade[1] for twice and had great difficulty in getting. After watching the enemy for several days, he decided to take up a position between Alessandria and Valenza which would either bring the enemy to battle or deny him the passage of the Tanaro. This crossing was the only one which would enable the enemy to make any appreciable penetration—if he did not attempt it he must perforce give up any idea of relieving Turin, and if he did try to force the river line he would be engaged. The Duke put his plan to the Maréchal, but failed to convince him. I can't tell you why not, because Marsin himself could not produce any arguments against it which made any sense—he was too influenced by La Feuillade, who wanted the main body to fall back on him. And Marsin had no idea in his head except pleasing the son-in-law of a powerful Minister.[2] Neither of them could see that preventing any relief of Turin was not only essential for the success of the campaign, but also to the maintenance of their own miserable reputations. While the Duke and the Marshal were still arguing the point, a packet of despatches were brought in: they had been taken off a captured courier going from Prince Eugène to the Emperor. The Duke went through all the keys he had, but found that he could not break the cipher; it was sent on to Vaudémont, who also failed, and there was nothing for it but to send them to the King, who would undoubtedly be able to have them deciphered. They arrived at Versailles and were duly dealt with— but when? On the very day of the battle of Turin. The despatches in clear were rushed back: they contained an appreciation of the situation which Prince Eugène was sending to the Emperor—which in fact precisely echoed the views which the Duke had tried so vainly to impress on Marsin, and ended by saying that if the Duke took up the positions which he, as opposed to Marsin, wanted to adopt, it would be impracticable—that was the exact phrase used—to force the passage of the Tanaro, and in consequence the relief of Turin would be impossible. Such was the praise which Prince Eugène himself sent in a most secret despatch to the Emperor, which the King and his ministers saw with their own eyes. What must have been the feelings of the King and his Minister at having placed in leading strings—and such bad ones at that—a prince who was in so little need of them!

Since Marsin refused to be persuaded, the Duke was forced to fall back slowly on Turin and effect a junction with the besieging forces. He arrived on the evening of 28 August. As La Feuillade now

[1] Louis, Vicomte d'Aubusson, Duc de Roannais et de la Feuillade (1673-1725). Created a Marshal in 1724.
[2] La Feuillade was the son-in-law of Chamillart.

had two superior officers present, one would have thought he might
have become more tractable; but on the contrary, having risen so
meteorically to the command of so important an army, he was not
inclined to yield an inch to anyone. He knew that the Duke was not
allowed to make a move without Marsin's consent, and he set to work
to establish such an ascendancy over the Marshal that, whatever
orders the Duke might give, what was actually done depended on the
whims of La Feuillade—with disastrous results for his country.

The object of the campaign was the capture of Turin, but the
method whereby this could best be achieved was the subject of endless
discussion. The Duke was rightly furious with La Feuillade for having
countermanded all the orders he had given when he had inspected
the siege-works previously;[1] he insisted on their being carried out,
since he felt sure that otherwise the place would never be taken.
Indeed, the siege was making little progress; the covered way[2] had
been lost and La Feuillade had also given up all the *contre-gardes*[3] and
other defences which he had taken—suffering heavy casualties among
his sappers and his infantry in the process. Not only was no progress
being made but, what was worse, no one had any idea what to do
next; and lack of success had put La Feuillade in such a bad temper
that he was quite intractable. The Duc d'Orléans inspected the lines
again, and also had a good look at the only lines of approach open to
Prince Eugène: he was extremely unhappy about everything he saw.
He found everything wrong with the siege: he thought the trenches
were badly laid out and badly dug, too long and inadequately
manned.[4]

Meanwhile the latest information was that Prince Eugène was advancing; the Duke wished to go forward to meet him on the line of
the Doria—a position less readily defensible than that of the Tanaro,
but at least better than waiting to be attacked in a badly designed and
worse constructed defensive position which it would be quite im-

---

[1] The Duc d'Orléans paid a very quick visit for a conference with the Duc de Vendôme
before succeeding him. He inspected the siege-works and was magnificently received by
La Feuillade; but he was most critical, and said that the main effort was being directed
from the wrong flank—in which Vauban, who had actually designed the defences of the
city himself, agreed with him.

[2] A covered communication trench built into the forward parapet of the moat which
enabled the defender to move round the outer defences.

[3] Small defended posts built out from major earthworks to give a good field of fire.

[4] In view of the fact that the Duke, who had never before commanded in the field,
seems to have been laying about him, it is only fair to add that an impartial military
observer records that in his opinion the Duke had a miraculous eye for ground and was
a genius at appreciating a situation from the map.

possible to hold. To this suggestion he met with the same opposition as he had to his idea of holding the Tanaro line. Marsin's objection was based on the fact that the garrison of Turin was short of powder and that if the siege was in any way relaxed it would be possible for the enemy to supply them: several skins of powder had already been found drifting down the river in the hope that the current would carry them in to the enemy. It was obvious that to deny the relief of the city would bring about its fall, but whether it could be done on a purely defensive basis was a matter for considerable speculation: Marsin at any rate could not be got to agree to any more constructive plan.

Since Prince Eugène had for some time been marching through country which had been ravaged, there was no hope of his being able to support his army on it for any time at all—in fact, if he failed to get into the city of Turin with all its reserves of food he would be lost. From the French point of view all that was needed was to engage him and hold him in a favourable position; for if the enemy made no progress he would be in trouble. If Prince Eugène were beaten he would be forced to withdraw through French-dominated territory, and give up any idea of relieving Turin which would then be bound to fall. If the Imperial army brought the matter to the test, the action at least would be fought on ground of French choosing, with consequent advantages. And if they were beaten they would have to take a long way round and withdraw through French-dominated Savoy.

But Marsin, under the influence of La Feuillade, replied that the Duke's proposals made a great deal of sense, but could not be carried out without reinforcements from the 46 battalions which Albergotti had on the Capuchin heights—and if these were withdrawn it would enable the enemy to supply the place. This was to some extent true, but it was also true to say that nothing was sillier than to base one's plan on various tenuous possibilities open to the enemy. But the Marshal remained adamant. The argument grew so heated that finally Marsin consented to a council of war at which every officer from Lieutenant General upwards should be present. But when it came to the point the majority took care to vote with La Feuillade and Marsin, only d'Estaing speaking his own mind frankly. Albergotti, being a cunning Italian, saw what was coming and said his headquarters were too far away for him to attend the meeting. The Duke protested against the servile attitude of the meeting and, saying that since he had no say in the conduct of the campaign there was no reason why he should accept responsibility for the set-back the country was bound to suffer, ordered his coach. Marsin, La Feuillade and the most senior of the council of war did everything they could to make him stay. Having made his point as strongly as he could, the Duke consented to remain, but he refused point blank to accept any responsibility and would not even give out the password—referring anyone who came for orders to Marsin, La Feuillade, or any other senior general under whose authority the matter fell. The basis of La Feuillade's foolish opposition was the vain hope that Prince Eugène would not dare to attack the lines and that, when he had withdrawn, Turin would fall—not through any military action, or any victory which the Duke might win, but through the siege which he himself had planned, so that he would claim the entire credit. Such was the burning pride of youth which overwhelmed Marsin and inflicted a terrible wound on France. This disastrous stalemate persisted throughout the last three disastrous days of the siege. The Duke spent half his time in his headquarters and half in walking—he wrote a very outspoken letter to the King, telling him exactly what had happened; this he showed to Marsin and requested him to send it to Versailles by the next courier since, having resigned his command, he did not think it proper to send it off himself.

During the night of the 6th–7th—the day of battle—although he disclaimed all responsibility, he was awoken and given a message from a partisan which told him that Prince Eugène had attacked the Castello di Pianezza as a preliminary to making an assault crossing of the Doria. In spite of his intention to have no part of it, the Duke got up and dressed hurriedly. He went to Marsin, who was sleeping soundly, woke him and showed him the message. He suggested that they should attack at once and catch the enemy on the wrong foot while he was in the act of crossing the river, which was a tricky job. A simple calculation showed that the factors of time and distance were on the French side. Saint-Nectaire, a senior member of the Order and an experienced soldier, arrived at that moment outside Marsin's headquarters and confirmed the message which the Duke had received. But it was written in the shape of things to come that France should be beaten that day: the Marshal was immovable; he was certain that the Duke had been misinformed, and advised him to go back to bed; he did not give a single order to meet any emergency which might arise. No sooner had the Duke gone back to his bed than information came in that Prince Eugène was in fact advancing along the whole front—but he was past caring. D'Estaing and a group of senior officers then arrived and forced him to get dressed again and call for his horse, but he could not bring himself to do more than ride slowly round the whole of the positions; the discussions of the past three days had not gone unnoticed, and rumours had spread right down to the private soldiers. His rank, the rightness of what he wanted to do, which was not lost on the senior soldiers (who are by no means bad judges of such matters), and the fact that there were some there who remembered his service at Leuze, Steinkerque, and Nerwinden, started murmurs as to who did command the army. As he was riding along the forward positions a soldier in the Piedmont Regiment called out to him by name and asked if he was going to refuse to fight with them. This had more effect than all the persuasion of the generals; the Duke replied to the soldier that he asked something which could not be refused, and made up his mind at once to put all argument behind him and help Marsin and La Feuillade in spite of themselves.

But it was no longer possible to go forward and catch the enemy at a disadvantage since his forward elements were already visible. Marsin, more dead than alive and seeing that all his hopes had been in vain, lost his head completely and was quite incapable of giving a coherent order. There were great gaps in the line: to fill them the Duke sent for the 46 battalions of Albergotti, which were too thin on the ground to hold the Capuchin heights and too far away to bother Prince Eugène; but La Feuillade of course thought otherwise and had forbidden them to move. A second order from the Duke arrived at the same time as an order for La Feuillade for them to stand fast. Meanwhile the Duke, believing that these battalions would soon arrive, plugged the gaps in his front line with dismounted squadrons of cavalry drawn from his own second line. Then he ordered a few more troops up, across a small bridge—but La Feuillade, driven by God knows what demon of perversity, stood on the bridge himself and ordered them back. The disobedience reached such a pitch that when the Duke gave a direct order to a squadron commander to move, he refused; the Duke cut him across the face with his sword and subsequently reported him to the King.

The attack came in at ten in the morning and was pressed home with great vigour. Langallerie,[1] who had served Prince Eugène very well on the approach march, was equally good in action: he was the first to break in through one of the weak spots which our thinness on the ground inevitably left. Prince Eugène reinforced the success, and before long our line gave way. In the middle of the battle Marsin was hit in the stomach and, immediately taken prisoner, was evacuated some distance to the rear. La Feuillade was rushing about tearing his

---

[1] Marquis de Langallerie (1656–1717), a French adventurer in the service of the Emperor.

hair and making no sense at all. The Duke was in complete command, but he was still badly obeyed. He did miracles, being everywhere under the hottest fire, driving on the officers and men by his own example; he was hit twice—a flesh-wound in the buttock, and a very painful wound in the wrist—but he would not weaken. As things began to break up, he called on the officers by their first names, and shouted to the men, leading squadron after squadron and battalion after battalion into the attack himself. Beaten at last by intense pain and loss of blood, he allowed himself to go for a few minutes to a First Aid Post. But as soon as he had had his wounds dressed he went back to where the action was hottest; but that day everything— terrain, order of battle, and discipline—seemed to be against the French. Three times Le Guerchoys with his battalion of the Vieille-Marine threw back the enemy with great loss, spiked their guns, and restored the front; at last, weakened by casualties among both officers and men, he asked the Brigade commander on his right to advance in order to conform with his own line and help him meet a fourth heavy attack which was just forming up. The Brigadier, whose name is better left in decent obscurity, flatly refused. That was the last chance: once it had been thrown away nothing but confusion, disaster, and flight remained. The most horrible part is that the senior officers, more particularly the generals, with very few exceptions thought more about saving their baggage and the loot they had accumulated than rallying their men, and were worse than useless.

The Duke, finally convinced that there was no hope of saving the day, turned to retrieving what he could. He got his light artillery out, and saved his ammunition and all the stores which were in the forward siege works. Then, gathering round him all the general officers he could find, he told them firmly but shortly that there was nothing for it but to withdraw into Italy—by which means they would remain masters of the field, leaving the army which had just won so resound-ing a victory at Turin mouldering in a belt of completely scorched earth: while the army of the King, keeping its supply lines open, could live on the fat of the land and build up its strength at its leisure. This was the last straw as far as the officers of the army were con-cerned, for the only consolation the disaster had for them was to be able to get back to France as soon as possible with all their ill-gotten loot. La Feuillade, who had every reason for keeping his mouth shut, started to argue as usual, but the Duke was having no more of it and told him to keep quiet so that the others could speak. D'Estaing again was the only one who spoke up for the Italian plan. The argument began to get as disorderly as the whole day had been; finally the Duke said that there was no time for protracted arguments, and that, tired of being right and never listened to, he was now going to have his own way, and he gave the order to cross the bridge into Italy. He was completely worn out physically and mentally, and after marching for some distance he threw himself into his post-chaise and went on his way thus, crossing the Po by the bridge, and with the generals openly muttering as they followed behind him. The muttering became so loud that the Duke finally lost his temper; he put his head out of the coach and went for one of them, shouting out the name of his mistress and saying that for all the good he was to the army he might as well have stayed with her. This quietened them all.

But it was decreed that the spirit of stupidity and blunder should fall upon the French forces and save our enemies. As they were emerging on the far side of the bridge Major General d'Arène galloped up from Albergotti's corps and presented an officer to the Duke; this officer said that the enemy lay astride the route they had to take. Questioned by the Duke, he swore that the enemy was well dug in, and that he had recognized the flags of the White Cross regiment, and had even seen the Duc de Savoie in person. In spite of the circumstantial detail the Duke was suspicious of the report and said that he would go on—turning back only if he found his way barred by forces which he could not disperse. But the generals had no intention of going to Italy; the road to the French Alps was open, and they sent all the ammunition and rations that way. After half a day's march they told the Duke that there was not much point in his going to Italy, since the ammunition and rations had gone to France, and if he went on he would only be cut off from his supplies by the enemy. Worn out by pain and loss of blood, in a paroxysm of rage and despair at a further exhibition of such criminal insubordination, he flung himself back in his coach and said they could go where they liked— he could not be bothered to argue about it any more.

Such is the story of the disaster in Italy. It was found out afterwards that the story about the route being cut was entirely without foundation. Furthermore, if he had only gone on, the victory won two days later by Médavy would have made him master of Lombardy and rendered Prince Eugène's situation extremely critical. All this reduced the Duke to the depths of depression when he reached Oulx, in the middle of the Alps, where the seriousness of his wounds confined him to his quarters.

Saint-Léger, one of the Duke's *premiers valets de chambre,* was sent to bring this bad news to the King; he got to Versailles on 14 September before the *lever* and said that Nancré would follow with the details.

In its turned-about withdrawal the army was marching back-to-front. This reversal of the march-table meant that a large number of vehicles loaded with stores which should have been on ahead found themselves in the rear-guard, where they were set upon and pillaged during the night in the mountain passes. Albergotti, who as we have seen was not committed during the battle, was in command of the rear-guard, and considering the darkness, the length of the column, and the general confusion on the narrow roads it must be admitted that he did very well. There was no trouble from the enemy: they were quite content to rest on their unexpected victory. Their army was exhausted and was in no state to harass our retreat. As I have already said, our guns, ammunition, and most important stores were got off the field in good order. It was known afterwards that Prince Eugène had made up his mind to break off the engagement if de Guerchoy's men had stood up to his fourth attack, and only the cowardice of the Brigadier on his flank had prevented him from standing fast. It was known also that Turin had a few days' powder left. For all that, we were in the depths and the enemy had his tail right up. . . .

Marsin, when he arrived at the post to which he was taken in the enemy's rear, asked at once if the Duc d'Orléans had been killed. He was brought in with an aide-de-camp and two or three servants; he asked at once for a confessor, put his affairs in order, and handed over the letter of criticism which the Duke had written to the King and which he had read and was determined to forward; after that he wished only to commune with God and he died during the night. Among his papers was found a mountain of minor matters, a mass of extraordinary vows which he had undertaken, utter disorder, and debts equal to six times the value of his estate. . . .

During such a difficult retreat it is not surprising that to add to the other difficulties there was a shortage of bread. The Duke himself, even though wounded, was the only person who made the least effort to grapple with the multitudinous problems. He halted for the tail of the column to catch up and to be issued with rations. Then he detached Vilbraye with a strong independent force with which he was to seize the Château de Bar, thus keeping open the only route by which the army could be got back into Italy. La Feuillade was responsible for the force; he delayed their departure for forty-eight hours and then set off without any rations, so that on the second day they had to halt and wait for supplies to come up. The despair of the Duke, confined to his bed, can hardly be imagined when he heard that this column which he imagined was well on its way had barely got out of sight. The rations were sent and the force moved on, only to find that the enemy had beaten them to their objective by eight hours. It was entirely due to La Feuillade's negligence that this final ignominious reverse overtook the army; all he could do was to turn tail and go back.

When La Feuillade got to Oulx the Duke was in a serious condition, for he had grossly overtaxed himself in billeting and rationing his troops, with the greatest care and considerable expense, in order to get them fit as quickly as possible for the march into Italy. When La Feuillade came into the Duke's room he found Albergotti there, amongst others; the Duke, furious at the failure of the column which had just returned, rounded on both of them for their disobedience in staying on the Capuchin heights during the recent battle. Both of them started to reply, but the Duke, feeling that he had put up with too much to be able to trust his self-control much further, told them to keep quiet. Sassenage[1] and a few others standing round the bed got them both to withdraw, grumbling louder and louder as they got near the door. They had hardly reached the far end of the room before Albergotti roundly declared that any criticism from the Duke should rest solely on La Feuillade's shoulders, since he himself was under the latter's orders; this La Feuillade hotly denied and laid his hand on his sword. Albergotti, scarlet with rage, stepped back; the others quickly stepped between them and hustled them out of the room—asking if they realized where they were, or if they had completely taken leave of their senses. The Duke, behind the curtains of his bed, either did not hear or did not choose to listen.

La Feuillade, frightened by his own foolishness, sent a despatch to his father-in-law Chamillart, resigning his position as governor of the Dauphiné, saying that he was unworthy of any further consideration or of the King's favour, or even of further life. He said that on the following day he intended to ask the Duke's permission to go to Antibes where the construction of new defences offered an excuse for his presence; there he could put himself under Médavy and hope to expiate his faults. But Chamillart, still admiring him, returned his letter of resignation and sent him a note of encouragement.

At the same time the Duke received despatches from the King approving of his intention of marching again into Italy. ... Although still far from well, he went round the troops' quarters as often as he could, and distributed a good deal of money among them. He was still anxious to get back into Italy, and he sent Bezons back to Versailles to explain the difficulties and ask for the King's views. The outcome was that it was decided that a fresh invasion of Italy could not be attempted before the Spring, and the army was ordered into winter quarters. The Duke returned to Versailles where he arrived at two thirty on 8 November: the King was taking his dinner in bed, as was

[1] Commander of the Duke's guards.

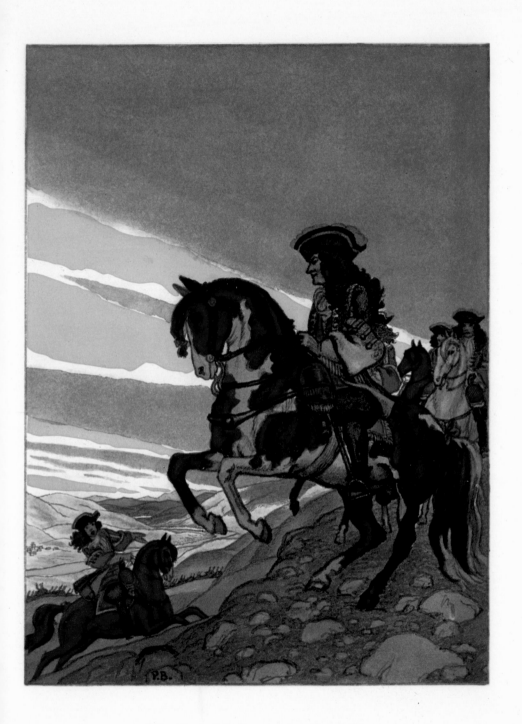

The Duc d'Orléans takes the field

his custom when he had been dosed. No one could have been better received; he then went to call upon Monseigneur at Meudon, and then returned to have supper with the King.

When he spoke to me, the Duke said that he gathered from what the King had said that La Feuillade had had his time. He added that he had done his best to gloss over the wretched man's shortcomings, terrible as they were; he had left La Feuillade in the Dauphiné, and Chamillart (who did not dare speak to the King himself) had begged him to ask the King that he might be allowed to remain there, but after what had been said he did not dare, and he felt sure that La Feuillade would be recalled.

A few days later the order for his recall was sent, and Gévaudan was appointed in his place. Although he had no hope of being able to stay in Grenoble, his recall was such a bitter pill that La Feuillade procrastinated for over a fortnight, sending off despatch after despatch to his father-in-law. The King was furious at such insubordination and Chamillart was in a most difficult position. Finally a peremptory order was sent for him to start back at once, to the great satisfaction of everyone locally. No sooner had he arrived than he quarrelled with Cardinal de Camus, who was only prevented by the King's direct request from excommunicating him on the spot for a particularly filthy masquerade which he gave. He stayed several days in Paris without daring to come near Versailles. Chamillart finally obtained permission for him to pay his respects—in Mme de Maintenon's rooms, so as to avoid the embarrassment of a public scene. On 13 December Chamillart, going to work with the King in Mme de Maintenon's room, took him with him. As soon as the King saw him come in, he rose and went to the door. Before La Feuillade could open his mouth, the King said, 'Monsieur, we are both of us most unfortunate,' and with that turned his back. La Feuillade, left by the door, could not come in and had no chance to utter a word. The King never spoke to him again. It was a long time before permission was given for Monseigneur to receive him at Meudon, or before he was allowed to appear at Marly on account of his wife's standing. It was noticed by everyone that if the King ever set eyes on the man, he deliberately looked away. Such was the downfall of this Phaëton. Realizing that there was no more hope for him he sold his equipment and, forgetting that he had wanted to join Médavy, gave out that having once commanded an army, he could not bring himself to serve under a Lieutenant General—and, being in such disgrace, there was obviously nothing that he could do right and no depths to which he might not fall. He went about complaining of his fate and explaining away what had happened, but nobody cared enough to listen to him.

1707

CHAMILLART'S BURDEN OF OFFICE

✤✤✤✤✤ ROUND down under the burden of his two offices—the
✤ **G** ✤ Ministries of War and Finance—Chamillart had no time
✤ ✤ either to sleep or eat. Every campaign saw fresh armies
✤✤✤✤✤ rendered unfit for battle after a series of defeats, and our
immense frontiers shrank constantly through the ineptitude of our
commanders in the field: thus our resources of both man-power and
finance were whittled away. At his wits' end in trying to fill the constant deficiencies, the Minister had on numerous occasions told the
King that the burden of two such offices, which in normal times were
considered full-time jobs for two men, was quite beyond him in the
present crisis. But the King, who had given him both offices to avoid
the wearing disputes which had raged in the days when Colbert and
Louvois had Finance and War respectively, could not bring himself
to relieve Chamillart of the responsibility for the nation's finances.[1]
Chamillart gave everything he had got, but in the end the machine
just collapsed. He had attacks of giddiness, he could not keep any
food down, and he grew thinner day by day. But the wheels had to
turn and he was the only man who could keep them turning. He wrote
a pitiful letter to the King asking to be allowed to resign: he spoke
frankly of the critical situation with which, he said, he could scarcely
grapple even if he were given the time and blessed with good health.
He reminded the King that matters of State business poured in to him
which required long and careful thought, but the weight of affairs
forced him to dismiss them in a matter of minutes. He ended by saying that it would be a poor reward for all the goodness which the
King had shown him if he did not speak his mind—which was that
the whole State would go down into disaster if the situation were not
remedied. He always wrote his notes to the King on sheets which
were folded down the middle, leaving one half blank on which the
King might add his comments and return them. Chamillart showed
me this note after he had received it back: all that the King had
written in the margin was: 'All right. We will go down together.'

---

[1] There is extant a letter from Chamillart, dated 1707, in which he writes of the financial
state of the country: 'I am now entering the realms of the impossible. May God inspire me
to find some solution!'

Chamillart was overwhelmed by the King's showing so much confidence in him, but at the same time he was in despair; and such confidence did not give him any more physical strength, which was what he most needed for his task. He began to skip the Council meetings, particularly those at which despatches were tabled, so that he might avoid having to make a report; and if there was a meeting at which his presence was essential, the King allowed him to state his views and then withdraw. The main reason was that only Princes or Dukes might be seated during a Council, and he was now quite incapable of standing that long.

THE CAPTURE OF BERINGHEN

ON 7 March a most extraordinary event caused the King a great deal of trouble and had the court and the town by the ears. On that day Beringhen, First Equerry, after accompanying the King to Marly, went back to his rooms at Versailles and then set out alone for Paris. He travelled in a carriage from the royal stable, with two footmen mounted behind and a groom on the leading horse bearing a torch. He was abducted in the Billancourt plain, between a farm near the Sèvres bridge and an inn called the Point-du-Jour. Fifteen or sixteen horsemen bore him off. Then the coachman turned back to Versailles as fast as he could and gave the alarm; as soon as he got there the King was informed, and he sent instructions to the four Secretaries of State to have all routes watched by which an enemy group could have penetrated into and might return from Artois.

No one could bring himself to believe that the First Equerry could have been carried off by an enemy detachment, which would have had to come from the Duke of Marlborough's army in the Netherlands. But since the victim himself had no enemies of any kind who would or could do such a thing and there was no one who could possibly extract a worthwhile ransom for him, there was no other explanation.

In fact he had been captured by an enemy raiding party. A man named Guethem, who had been a prisoner of the Elector of Bavaria since the previous war, declared his willingness to take up arms against France and was in consequence given a command. He quickly showed himself to be a bold and intrepid raider and was promoted to Colonel. Talking with his friends one evening, he said that he thought he could capture a senior member of the King's household somewhere between Versailles and Paris. He picked a group of thirty horsemen, mostly officers. They crossed the various rivers before them as merchants, which enabled them to plant post-horses at strategic points for the execution of their plan. They split up into groups and spent several days at Sèvres, Saint-Cloud, and Boulogne; a few of them were bold enough to come right in and attend the King's supper at Versailles.[1]

One of them was picked up the following day, and was pretty insolent when he was questioned by Chamillart; a second was found by one of M. le Prince's men in the Chantilly Forest—from the latter it was discovered that the first part of the plan was to put the prisoner in a carriage at La Marlaye, but that in fact the party had already got over the Oise.

The great mistake they made was in not taking Beringhen on in the coach in which they found him—in the first place they could have gone on through the night without anyone being any the wiser, so giving themselves a much greater margin of safety—and also they would not have exhausted their prisoner, who quickly tired when made to trot, canter, and gallop on a horse for hours on end.

They let the Chancellor go by because it was daylight, and missed the Duc d'Orléans because he was unexpectedly riding in an ordinary post-chaise. Their situation was getting serious, for they could not remain much longer in hiding, when this coach from the royal stable appeared. And when they surrounded it they saw inside a man wearing the riband of the Order over his coat—as only the best people did —so they thought they had really got something. It did not take Beringhen long to establish his identity, and Guethem assured him of his personal respects and of a desire to cause him the least possible inconvenience. Indeed he treated his prisoner with such respect that it led to his downfall: they allowed him to rest twice, and also to ride in a post-chaise, which led to considerable delay because one set of horses was not ready. Besides the warning of the frontier posts, all garrisons along the road had been alerted, various detachments of the Royal Guards had set out and the whole of the Small Stables—where the First Equerry was very popular—fanned out for the hunt. But in spite of all precautions, they—three of them with three French officers who had given their parole—got across the Somme and were within four leagues of Ham before they were intercepted; the first to make contact with them was a sergeant-major from the Livry

---

[1] The group is said to have been made up of one captain (Guethem), six lieutenants, and two sergeant-majors: they must have had some troopers with them, to look after their spare horses, if nothing more. They came in through Courtray, and split up into three groups, riding through Chantilly, Saint-Ouen, and Sèvres.

Regiment, shortly followed by two detachments from the same unit.
Seeing that resistance was useless, Guethem and his two companions
surrendered. The First Equerry, delighted at his rescue and pleased
at the kindly treatment he had received, led the party on to Ham,
stayed there a day, and entertained his prisoners as well as he in turn
had been looked after. He despatched a message both to his wife and
to Chamillart; the King, much relieved, heard the news from him
at supper. Beringhen arrived back at Versailles at 8 P.M. on the 29th
and went straight to Mme de Maintenon's rooms, where the King
received him and made him tell the whole story of his adventures.
Although the King was very fond of Beringhen, he was not at all
pleased to learn that the Small Stables were *en fête* in honour of their
master's return, and he sent a message forbidding the projected fire-
work display or any special marks of rejoicing: occasionally he had
these fits of jealousy, and thought that every mark of distinction
should be reserved for himself and himself alone.

The First Equerry was well received on all sides, which made up
for the strain of his experience. He sent Guethem and the two other
officers to his house in Paris, where they were treated as if they were
in their own homes, and told to await the King's pleasure. Beringhen
obtained permission for Guethem to attend the King's review at
Marly. Furthermore, he also presented Guethem privately to the
King, who remarked upon the good treatment which he had shown
the First Equerry and added that one should always make war like a
gentleman. Guethem, who had his wits about him, replied that he
was overwhelmed to find himself in the presence of the greatest King
in the world who was going so far as actually to speak to him personally, and that he could find no words with which to reply. He
stayed in Paris about ten days as the First Equerry's guest, seeing the
sights and going to the Opera and the Comedy—where he himself
was the centre of attraction. Wherever he went he was greeted with
applause for his daring. The First Equerry, in addition to putting
him up, placed a coach at his disposal as well as a guide to take him
wherever he wanted to go, and as much spending money as he could
use. In the end he went on parole to Rheims to join his comrades who
had the run of the town while awaiting exchange: but in fact most
of them had already escaped. This project, which had originally been
planned as the capture of Monseigneur or one of his sons, led to very
strict regulations being imposed on the frontiers which made business
difficult and led to a large number of arrests.

SPYING ON THE
DUCHESSE DE BOURGOGNE

THE Duchesse de Bourgogne was on such terms of playful familiarity with the King and Mme de Maintenon that she used to go through their papers when they were there, and even open their letters. One day she began running through the papers on the desk; Mme de Maintenon, who was sitting on the other side of the room and was the only person present, told her more seriously than usual to stop it. That was enough to make the Princess thoroughly curious, and, laughing, she went on—until suddenly she came across a letter about herself. Surprised, she read a bit, then turned over and saw that it was signed by Mme d'Épinay. Shocked by what she had seen and by the signature on the letter, she blushed and fell silent. Mme de Maintenon could have stopped her reading it if she had really wanted to, and it is possible she was not altogether sorry that the young Duchess had seen the letter.

Looking up, she said: 'What is it, my sweet? You are in a state! What have you found?'

The Princess looked even more embarrassed; Mme de Maintenon went across to see what she was looking at, and the Princess pointed to the signature.

'Well,' said Mme de Maintenon, 'it's a letter from Mme d'Épinay, and that is what comes of being too inquisitive; sometimes people come across things they would rather not see.' Then, in a different tone, she went on: 'Since you have read part of it, Madame, you had better read the whole, and I hope that it will teach you a lesson,' and she made her read every word of it.

The letter was a detailed report of everything the Duchess had said or done for the last four or five days, set down in the most intimate detail as if Mme d'Épinay, who in fact saw her but seldom, had in fact never let her out of her sight. Even more surprising than the letter itself was the fact that Mme d'Épinay should have put her name to it, and that Mme de Maintenon, having received it, should not at once have destroyed it or locked it away.

The poor Duchess was so embarrassed she blushed furiously and almost fainted. Mme de Maintenon took the opportunity of giving her a good scolding, and said that a lot of things which may seem to have been quite secret were in fact known to everyone at court. She pointed out what the consequences of her conduct would be, and finished by saying that when she had remonstrated in the past it was

on information received from Mme d'Épinay and several other ladies
of the court who had been instructed to report on the young Duchess's
conduct.

When the interview was over, the Duchess fled to her own room.
She sent at once for Mme de Nogaret, whom she called her nurse and
who was her confidante. She recounted the whole thing, in floods of
tears and full of resentment against Mme d'Épinay. Mme de Nogaret
let the storm blow over, and then said what she thought about such
a letter and the kind of person who would write it. But she added
most strongly that the Duchess should not let Mme d'Épinay see that
anything had happened, for she would be lost if she showed the
woman anything less than the usual courtesies. It was good advice,
but easier said than done. But still the Duchess, who respected Mme
de Nogaret and her knowledge of the world, did her best and Mme
d'Épinay never discovered that her secret was out. The following day
Mme de Nogaret, who was a friend of ours, told Mme de Saint-Simon
what had happened.

THE DEATH OF
MME DE MONTESPAN

ON 27 May the Marquise de Montespan died suddenly at Bourbon,
aged sixty-six.

I will not speak of the days when she was in favour, for it was before my time. But there is one story which is worth telling because it
is not generally known. It was more her husband's fault than her own
that she yielded to the King. She warned her husband and told him
that an entertainment which the King was giving was primarily for
her, and she begged him to take her away to their country house in
Guyenne until the whole thing had blown over and the King's roving
eye had been attracted elsewhere. It was to no purpose—Montespan
would not listen, and soon had good reason to repent his obtuseness.
What was worse was that he loved her till the day she died, though he
refused ever to see her again after the trouble began.

I will not describe how it was fear of hellfire which finally, after
various backslidings, separated her from the court. It was Monsieur du
Maine[1] who undertook the task of telling her she had had her time
when, to the King's intense embarrassment, no one else would do it;

[1] Her own son by Louis XIV.

and it was the Bishop of Meaux[1] who rounded the job off. She left in tears and a fury and never forgave M. du Maine, though he won Mme de Maintenon's support for the rest of her life by the part he played.

Mme de Montespan retired to the Convent of St. Joseph, which she herself had built, but it took her a long time to adapt herself to her new way of life. She spent much of her enforced and unwelcome leisure at Bourbon, Fontevrault, and at d'Antin's[2] country place—and it took her several years to settle down. But at last God reached her heart. Even in her sinful life she had never lost her faith; she would often leave the King suddenly to go and pray in her own room, and nothing would induce her to break a day of abstinence, nor did she ever neglect the demands of Lent. She gave freely to charity, respected good church-goers, and never said anything approaching scepticism or impiety. But she was imperious, haughty, and most sarcastic, and she had the defects of a woman who had climbed to her position through her own beauty.

She finally made up her mind to make some use of the leisure which she had not invited. And after consideration she placed herself in the hands of Père de la Tour, the General of the Oratory, well known as a preacher and a spiritual director. From then until her death she went from strength to strength. First she had to put away from her heart those last lingerings of a taste for court life which still remained there, and then she had to give up hopes which she had always harboured, however much they lacked foundation. She had always flattered herself that it was only a fear of hell which had forced the King to give her up; she knew that Mme de Maintenon was getting on in years and, she persuaded herself, enjoyed bad health. She thought that her successor might die and then the King, being a widower, would be susceptible to the charms of his old flame. Then, she thought, with all religious scruples satisfied, he might take her back again for the sake of their children.

Her children shared her hopes, and she was passionately fond of them—except the Duc du Maine whom she hardly ever saw. . . .

As time passed, she gave most of her riches to the poor. For several hours every day she used to make shirts for the poor, and any visitors were made to help. In marked contrast to the rich table she used to

[1] Bossuet, the great preacher. Although he had been the young King's instructor and was very fond of him, he held himself apart from the court until Mme de Montespan was dismissed.

[2] The Marquis d'Antin, who later succeeded Mansard as Master of Works, was Mme de Montespan's only legitimate child.

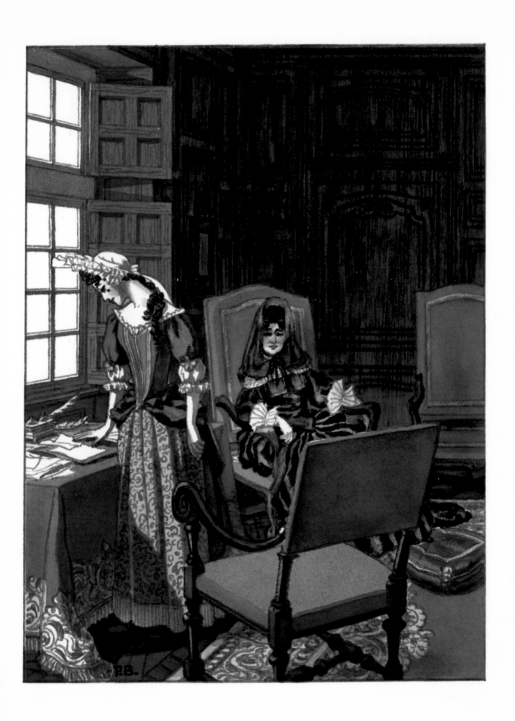

The Duchesse de Bourgogne learns a lesson

keep, she was now most frugal. She fasted frequently; and cards for
low stakes, her only relaxation, were often interrupted by calls to
prayer. Whatever she was doing she would leave to go and pray in
her own room. She paid frequent penances and wore shifts of the
coarsest material, although she hid them under richer garments of
normal material. She always wore a belt and wrist- and ankle-bands
of iron with spikes, which frequently chafed her skin into ugly sores.
Her tongue, once so formidable, was now gentle. The thought of
death frightened her so much that she paid several women to sit in
her room at night with candles lit and the curtains drawn so that if
she woke up she could be reassured by seeing them playing cards or
eating.

In spite of her changed way of life, she never gave up the attributes
of royalty which she had seized in her days of power, and to which
no one any longer took exception. Her arm-chair stood at the foot of
her bed, and it was the only one in the room: none of her children or
even the Duchesse d'Orléans was allowed one. Monsieur and la
Grande Mademoiselle had always been fond of her and went to see
her from time to time, and for them arm-chairs were brought in; but
she never got up to welcome them or conducted them to the door.
Madame did not appreciate being treated in this way and in consequence hardly ever went there. It is not hard to imagine the way in
which she received lesser lights who came to see her. . . .

Everyone of any importance used to go to see her: I don't know
how it came about, but it was really considered part of one's duty to
go there from time to time. Ladies of the court went out of respect
for her daughters; there were fewer men, and they went either for
specific reasons or on ceremonial occasions. When she addressed anyone it was in the most regal manner, as though she were doing them
a favour. No one, whatever his standing, approached her without
making the deepest reverence. She never went out except to see
Monsieur, Madame, la Grande Mademoiselle, or to the Hôtel de
Condé. There was an air of distinction about her house which was
quite unmistakable, and there was always a throng of coaches before
her door.

To the end of her life she was lovely. And although she was a
hypochondriac, in fact she hardly ever suffered a day's illness. Worrying about her health was the main reason why she kept travelling, and
she always took about eight ladies with her. She was brilliant company; her charm made people overlook her haughty airs, and generally made her even more attractive. Her conversation was unique:
it was an incomparable blend of wit, grace, and eloquence. She had a

way so entirely her own of putting things and such a genius for the *mot juste* that she seemed to speak a different language. . . .

One night Mme de Montespan was taken so ill that the ladies sitting up with her had to call for help. One of the first to arrive was the Maréchale de Cœuvres; finding Mme de Montespan nearly suffocated and wandering in her mind, she administered an emetic—but the effects were so violent that they lost their nerve and stopped it, and that probably cost the sick woman her life. In a few minutes of lucidity and comparative comfort, Mme de Montespan received the sacrament and took leave of her servants. . . . D'Antin arrived just before the end. She gazed at him and said that things were very different from when she had last seen him at Bellegarde. As soon as she expired, d'Antin went back to Paris and made arrangements for the funeral.

One might suppose that the removal of a former royal mistress whom she had supplanted and driven from court would have been some relief to Mme de Maintenon. But it was not so; when she heard the news, Mme de Maintenon was overcome with grief. She could not keep back her tears, and, to hide them, she retired to her close-stool. The Duchesse de Bourgogne followed her and was as surprised by her intense grief as she was by the King's complete insensibility. She could not keep from saying something to him about it; and he replied that when he parted from Mme de Montespan he never expected to see her again and so far as he was concerned she had been dead from that day. From this it may be presumed that he was not very well pleased by the grief which her children showed, but, although they were all very much afraid of him, they did not allow anything to interfere with their mourning. The whole court went to pay its respect to them without saying a word—a most curious performance.

1708

THE KING'S SELFISHNESS

✤✤✤✤✤HE Duchesse de Bourgogne was pregnant and far from well.
✤ *T* ✤ The King had announced that, contrary to his usual custom,
✤ ✤ he intended to go to Fontainebleau as soon as the good
✤✤✤✤✤weather came, and meantime he wanted to pay his customary
visit to Marly. He could not do without the company of his granddaughter, who amused him, but in her condition so much travelling
was not good for her. Mme de Maintenon was worried about it and
Fagon discreetly let it be known that he was against it. This annoyed
the King, who was used to being indulged in every whim, and had
been spoiled by his mistresses, who travelled anywhere when he
wanted them to whether pregnant or only just arisen from childbed.
The remarks about Marly rubbed him up the wrong way without
shaking him in his resolution. The only concession he made was to
put off his departure from Low Sunday to the middle of the following
week, defying every effort, first to dissuade him, and then to get him
to allow the Duchess to remain at Versailles.

The following Saturday the King was walking on the terrace after
Mass, amusing himself feeding the carp, when he saw the Duchesse de
Lude coming towards him alone—without there being any ladies in
attendance on her, which was unusual in the morning. The King
realized that she had something urgent to tell him; he went to meet
her, and everyone else fell back so that they could talk in private. Their
conversation was not long. She left, and the King walked back
towards us, beside the carp pool, without saying a word. Everyone
realized what had happened, but no one wanted to say anything.
Finally the King turned and looked at the senior individuals present
and, without addressing anyone in particular, said in an irritated tone,
'The Duchesse de Bourgogne has had a miscarriage.'

The Duc de la Rochefoucauld, M. de Bouillon, the Duc de Tresmes, and the Maréchal de Boufflers all expressed their deep regret.
M. de la Rochefoucauld then added that it was such a pity as it had
happened before, and everyone hoped it would not recur.[1] 'Well,
what of it?' interrupted the King with a sudden burst of rage, 'what

[1] In 1703 the Duchess's miscarriage caused the King to put off his departure for Marly
for a whole week.

do I care? Hasn't she got a son already? And if he dies, there's the Duc de Berry who is old enough to marry and have children. They're all my grandchildren, I don't care which of them succeeds me.' Then he burst out: 'Thank God, if she had to have a miscarriage, she's got it over with, and I shan't have my arrangements upset any more by nattering doctors and old women. I shall go and come as I please, and be left in peace.'

Silence followed at these words, and you could have heard a pin drop. Everyone lowered his eyes and scarcely dared to breathe. Every-one was stupefied—even the builders and gardeners who were within earshot. Silence reigned for fully a quarter of an hour. The King broke it by leaning on the balustrade and remarking on the size of one of the carp; no one replied. Then he addressed some remark about the fish to the workmen, but they had nothing to say either. The silence hung heavy, and finally the King walked away.

Once he had gone, our eyes met and spoke volumes, and for a few minutes we all felt the same. Astonishment, distress, and shrugging of shoulders—as long as time lasts, I shall never forget that moment. M. de la Rochefoucauld was seething with rage—for once, rightly. The First Equerry was faint with terror. I kept my eyes and ears open, watching them all, and I was not altogether displeased because I had long made up my mind that the King had no interest in anyone except himself, and had no regard for anyone else's feelings except his own.

MADAME DE THIANGES

IT was about this time that Monsieur de Vaudémont obtained control of Commercy; at the same time he was given the very small but con-venient apartment at Versailles left vacant by the death of Thianges.

Thianges came from the ancient house of Damas; he was very brave, a man of intelligence, honourable and upright, but so odd that he lived always in a world of his own and made nothing out of the fact that he was the son of Madame de Montespan's sister, and at that a sister who was herself so distinguished and stood so well with the King as long as she lived. She did not die until 1693, in her mag-nificent apartments on the ground floor next to those of Monseigneur where the children whom her sister had borne the King used to visit her, in mixed feelings of love and fear, together with every other person of any distinction at Court. Monsieur called upon her fre-quently, and there was no Minister of the Crown who did not come to pay his compliments. Young as I was, she received me kindly be-

cause of the kinship and friendship between her and my mother. I
remember that she always sat at the far end of her room which she
would never leave for anyone, and seldom rose. Her eyes were
rheumy; she wore a green shade and a linen bib, which was a necessity since she dribbled constantly. Even in these circumstances she
looked and acted like a queen. Every evening, shade and bib and all,
she was carried in her chair to the head of the King's private staircase
and remained with him and his family, seated in an arm-chair, from
after supper until the King went to bed. Some said that she was even
more intelligent than Madame de Montespan and more malicious.
She used to lead the conversation and argue bitterly with the King,
who loved to egg her on. She was unbelievably imperious and
splendid on even the most pleasant subject. She was always boasting
to the King about her family, which was indeed very ancient, and the
King to annoy her was always running it down. Sometimes when she
lost her temper she insulted him, and the more the King laughed the
angrier she became. One day the King said that for all its greatness,
her family could not compare with the house of Montmorency with
its Constables and Grand Masters.

'That's very amusing!' she replied. 'The fact of the matter is that
those people round Paris were quite content to serve you Kings,
while we, kings in our own Province, had our own officers as grand
as they and our own gentlemen about us.'

She was never at a loss for a reply and she was never embarrassed;
on the contrary she very frequently embarrassed everyone present.
She seldom left Versailles except to see Madame de Montespan. Her
one real friend was the Duc de la Rochefoucauld. Mademoiselle was
also close to her, and both of them were very fastidious over their
food. The King used to amuse himself by putting hairs in their butter
and their bread, and similar pleasantries; they would scream and
throw up, while he howled with laughter. Madame de Thianges would
get up to leave, rant at him and threaten to throw the food he had
polluted at him. She was at every party and on every trip whenever
she felt like it, and the King even pressed her to come when her health
had really made her take things more quietly. She spoke to her sister's
children in a tone and with an authority which went beyond that of an
aunt, and they for their part treated her with the greatest deference
and respect. She had once been good looking, but not so lovely as
her sisters. She was the mother of the Duchesse de Nevers, the
Duchesse Sforze and of the Marquis de Thianges for whom she never
had much time. He was in Monseigneur's personal suite, was a
Lieutenant General and a most upright man.

THE DUC D'ORLÉANS IN SPAIN

The King, tiring, decided once more to give a command to the nephew whom he disliked and distrusted, yet who could, he knew, have become one of his great generals. He sent the Duc d'Orléans to Spain, and several victories followed, but the general result of the campaign was disappointing. The Duke returned to France while the army was in winter quarters, but he was sent back to Spain in the early months of the following year.

WHEN the Duc d'Orléans arrived in Spain he found it necessary to stay there much longer than he had intended; he found that nothing had been done and stores of every sort were incomplete; he was forced to undertake the acquisition of supplies himself, which was by no means easy. This obviously took time, but ill-natured tongues in Paris spread rumours that he was staying in Madrid because he was in love with the Queen of Spain. Monsieur le Duc, infuriated at his own enforced idleness and the growing reputation of the Duc d'Orléans, and Madame la Duchesse were the chief promoters of this rumour which spread from the Court to the city, from the city to the provinces, but gained no credence in Spain since it was entirely without foundation.

In Madrid the Duc d'Orléans had more serious matters to attend to; would to God that he had taken the difficulties seriously and that his worries had not led to his losing control of his tongue! One evening, after working from morning to night as he had done daily since his return in his endeavours to overcome the appalling negligence which was prejudicing any possibility of opening the campaign, he sat down to supper with several important Spaniards and some Frenchmen of his own suite. Worried as he was, his mind settled upon the Princesse des Ursins[1] who had all Spain in her hand and had done absolutely nothing to make the necessary preparations which would have enabled the army to get on the march.

The supper warmed up, perhaps rather too much so. The Duc d'Orléans, who was high,[2] raised his glass, looked round the assembled company and said, 'Gentlemen, I give you the frigging Cap-

---

[1] Anne-Marie de la Trémoïlle, Princesse des Ursins (1641–1722). She spent many years in Spain as Lady-in-Waiting to the Queen. Her energy and sense of diplomacy did much to save Philip V's throne for him, but the antagonism between her and the Duc d'Orléans naturally biased Saint-Simon against her.

[2] He was one of those unfortunate people who could take very little alcohol without being affected by it; an occasion has been recorded when he even felt the effect of eating a handful of over-ripe grapes.

tain and the frigging Lieutenant.' The guests enjoyed the toast. None of them, not even the Prince, offered any explanation, but they all laughed and the joke was stronger than any political discretion. Although the exact words were not mentioned, the subject of the toast became known, and within half an hour the Princesse des Ursins had been told. She realized without a shadow of a doubt that she was meant as the Lieutenant and Madame de Maintenon as the Captain. She was beside herself with rage and made her views known to Madame de Maintenon, who in turn was equally furious. *Inde irae.* Neither of them ever forgave the Duke and we shall see how they brought about his downfall in that theatre. Up till then Madame de Maintenon had neither liked nor disliked him, and the Princesse des Ursins missed no chance of pleasing him. That was what annoyed her most: that after all the trouble she had taken, one single cruel joke could ridicule her political aspirations. From that moment they swore to destroy him, and it is fair to say that they very nearly succeeded. But although he escaped, for the rest of the King's life and up to her death he had good reason to realize what an implacable enemy he had made in Madame de Maintenon.

At long last the Duc d'Orléans managed to begin his campaign, though he never had more than fourteen days' stores and ammunition in hand. Early in June he took Gandesa, whence he sent Lieutenant General Gaëtano with three thousand infantry and eight hundred horse to fall upon twelve hundred infantry, four hundred horse and a thousand irregulars encamped at Falceto, five leagues away; the enemy was taken by surprise and tried to disperse into the mountains, but they were pursued so hotly that their cavalry fled, about five hundred were killed and the same number taken prisoner, as well as a number of officers, all their baggage train and ammunition. Don José Vallejo, sent at the same time down the Tortosa-Tarragona road, routed the guards set over the herds of cattle which had been assembled there, fought his way through the irregulars who opposed his withdrawal, and drove back a thousand beef and six thousand mutton on the hoof which the Duc d'Orléans distributed to the troops. A number of small positions were also taken, yielding a considerable number of prisoners.

The Duke closed in on Tortosa, captured five ships carrying in flour and salt meat, and laid siege to the town on 12 June. He threw two bridges across the Ebro, one above and one below the place, which was garrisoned by nine battalions, two squadrons of horse and two thousand irregulars. The main sap was opened on the night of 21–22 June, about half musket range from the walls; the ground was almost all rock and very difficult to work. Asfeld,[1] who much later was created a Marshal of France, performed wonders on the supply side, and I often said afterwards to the Duc d'Orléans that he was lucky to have with him the best administrative officer in the French army without whom the siege might never have been successful. The engineers and the gunners, on the other hand, were extremely inefficient and the Duke took command of these two essential services himself; they caused him endless trouble. One of the bridges broke and there was a general shortage of stores: no reserve boats, planks, or rope. Quite apart from the loss of time and the attendant uncertainty, the repair of this bridge cost the Duke an infinity of trouble, but he succeeded in the end. By the night of 9–10 July the covered way was creeping forward; the garrison put up a spirited defence and made one major sortie which was beaten back. The next day they surrendered, and four days later were marched out to Barcelona. They lost about half the garrison; the Duc d'Orléans had some six hundred casualties, but fortunately only one well-known officer— Monchamp, a Major General. The Marquis de Lambert was sent by the Duke to bring news of the victory to the King, who was delighted that his nephew had surmounted all the difficulties in his way. On no other front in Spain was much happening, and the Duc d'Orléans, weak as his forces were, had the honour and glory of driving Starhemberg back and back throughout the campaign. But the writing was on the wall and each succeeding year was fatal to Spain which, like an old tree, lost branch after branch in the cruel winds which blew upon it.

In spite of the success which the Duc d'Orléans achieved, the war did not go well. Sardinia was lost, and Minorca, which with Gibraltar enabled the English to dominate the Mediterranean. The Duke had a few more months of mock war, for he and Lord Stanhope, who was commanding the English forces in Spain, were old friends and took every opportunity of calling a truce so that they could spend the evening together. Then he returned to France where, largely through the influence of the Princesse des Ursins, he fell unjustifiably under a cloud.

---

[1] Claude-François Bidal, Chevalier and later Marquis d'Asfeld (1673–1743), later Inspector of the Fortifications of France.

The King teases Madame de Thianges

OUDENARDE

Faced by the implacable alliance of Marlborough and Prince Eugène in Flanders, the King decided upon a demonstration of force. A considerable army was assembled, and the titular command was given to his own grandson, although Vendôme was to be the military brains. Unfortunately the austere and upright Duc de Bourgogne could not stomach the filthy habits and morals of the Duc de Vendôme; the antipathy was mutual, which boded ill for the forthcoming campaign.

On his way to join the army the Duc de Bourgogne passed through Cambrai, where he stopped to dine at the post-house; among others the Archbishop[1] waited upon him and he embraced his old tutor and expressed several times his great obligation to him. He hardly spoke to anyone else and his looks betrayed all the feelings which, owing to religious differences, the King had forbidden him to express.

The Duke's forces consisted of two hundred and six squadrons of cavalry, one hundred and thirty-one battalions of infantry in fifty-six brigades. Included were Household Troops, Gendarmerie, Carabiniers and Guards; eighteen Lieutenant Generals and a variety of Marshals. The army was complete in all respects, in good shape and ready for action; no force ever took the field better equipped with stores and artillery. All those officers who were to join hastened to do so as soon as the Princes[2] left for the field. Nothing remained but to get on the move, but the Duc de Vendôme took root very easily wherever he was comfortable and showed no signs of wanting to budge. He was the only person who did not advocate an immediate advance, but he expressed himself with such authority that he got his own way.

The army finally moved and both Ghent and Bruges were taken without a shot being fired in the first week of July, and there was great, though short-lived, rejoicing at the French Court.

Prince Eugène marched from the Moselle into Flanders and his move drove a wedge between the two elements of the Elector Palatine's forces. What the Elector retained under his own hand consisted of forty-two battalions and seventy-three squadrons; the Duke

---

[1] Fénelon.

[2] In addition to the Commander, the Duc de Bourgogne, the Duc de Berry was present and also the English King under the title of the Chevalier de Saint-George—he commanded the English troops fighting under the French flag.

of Berwick was detached to take thirty-four battalions and sixty-five squadrons into Flanders.

It appeared a simple matter to take advantage of our two easy victories by crossing the Escaut and burning Oudenarde, thus putting the enemy in a very difficult supply position while we remained in an impregnable fortified camp with all our requirements coming in by water. The Duc de Vendôme admitted the wisdom of this, but the main point was that to carry out the plan meant moving—and this was just what the Duke, in his usual state of sloth, had no desire to do. The Duc de Bourgogne, supported by the whole army and even Vendôme's old cronies, pointed out that if, as was agreed by all, the movement was the right one, the sooner it was carried out the better so as to avoid being surprised by the enemy, which even Vendôme admitted might be a little irritating. Vendôme did not relish the thought of an approach march and having to change his headquarters —it interfered with his personal comfort—and in the ensuing argument he won the day.

Marlborough realized that this was the movement which Vendôme should make and that he himself would have little answer to it. Marlborough decided to move first; he had to march through a wide arc of some twenty-five leagues, while Vendôme, to anticipate him, needed only to march some six leagues across the chord of that arc. The enemy move fast and secretly, and they had already made three forced marches before Vendôme became aware of the danger—even though the armies were in close proximity to one another. When finally he was told he discounted the information as usual, but in the end accepted it and said he would march the next morning. The Duc de Bourgogne begged him without success to march that night, and anyone else who dared to said the same, but it was useless; the general negligence was such that no one had even thought of bridging a stream which lay on the line of march hardly outside the bivouac area, and the sappers had to spend most of the night on the job.

Biron, who is now a Duke and Peer and doyen of the Marshals of France, had expected to be given a post about the person of the Duc de Bourgogne on this campaign. He was a Lieutenant General and actually commanded one of the two reserve forces some distance from the main camp which lay to one flank with another detached corps at some distance on the other. That evening he was ordered to pull in the other corps and bring them both to join the main body. As he was nearing the camp he received a fresh order to advance to the Escaut, towards which the main body would be moving to effect a crossing. When he reached the intermediate stream the bridges were not finished, which surprised him—even though he was used to the Duc de Vendôme's way of going on. However, he got his troops over somehow and closed up to the Escaut, where again he effected a crossing on unfinished bridges and gained the high ground beyond. He was in position by about 2 P.M. on 11 July, and as soon as he made a reconnaissance he saw the main body of the enemy on the move with the heads of their columns well beyond Oudenarde and in a fair way to attacking him. He sent an aide-de-camp to the Princes and the Duc de Vendôme putting them in the picture and asking for orders. The aide found Headquarters dismounted and having a snack. Vendôme, furious at finding his predictions so completely reversed, said that the information could not possibly be correct. A second messenger from Biron merely annoyed him more; and it was not until a third officer arrived with the same story that he condescended to rise from the table and get on his horse, grumbling that the devil must have been behind the enemy because to have got there so soon wasn't human. The first officer he sent back to Biron, ordering him to attack and promising reinforcements. He told the Princes to follow slowly with the main body while he would go on and feed Biron with the minimum the situation needed. Biron meanwhile deployed as best he could in very broken ground, occupying a village, various hedge-rows, and an escarpment; once that was completed he went over to his right flank and found that the enemy was pretty nearly on top of him. He would very much have liked to have carried out the order to attack, not because such a manœuvre had the slightest chance of success but because he knew only too well that the soldier under whom he was serving was liable to order an ugly *post mortem* after the battle from which he could only emerge the loser. While he was in this unhappy frame of mind Puységur arrived and, having rapidly weighed up the situation, told Biron to stay where he was. A few minutes later the Maréchal de Matignon rode up and took the same view. While this talk was going on, Biron heard heavy fire on his left, around the village. He went over and found that the enemy infantry had engaged; he did what he could, but the enemy continued to make ground round his left flank. To his front the ravine held them up and thus gave time for the reinforcements promised by the Duc de Vendôme to arrive; unfortunately these were handled very unimaginatively and went into action in column against an enemy advancing in line so that the balance of fire power which could be brought to bear was very much against us. In any case these troops arrived piecemeal and so exhausted that, roughly handled as soon as they appeared, some of them gave way and became entangled with other units coming up behind them. Considerable confusion resulted. At this point the intervals of time between the arriving units proved an embarrassment, because they kept pouring in just too quickly for any order to be restored among the existing chaos, and yet there was not sufficient time between them to pull any single unit out and reform it. The Cavalry and the Household Troops got inextricably mixed with the Infantry, and none of them knew whether he was coming or going. This gave the enemy a break during which he managed to fill the ravine with fascines and thus he was able to infiltrate as well round our right flank, which so far had held solid. Our troops here folded practically on sight and swept over to the left, taking with them the Princes who had been watching the battle from a windmill; fortunately when they got there they pulled themselves together and deployed in a soldierly manner against an enemy who was still being more or less contained. In fact they deployed so smartly that the Prince's non-combatant servants found themselves out in front in uncomfortable proximity to the enemy.

The rough ground over which the enemy's left had to advance against our right gave us a little breathing space and for a while we were able to hold them. But our men were tired and the action soon got out of hand. The Household Troops were saved by a fluke: an enemy despatch rider, seeing their red uniforms, took them for his own side and rode into their midst; the despatches which he had on him warned them that they were about to be outflanked, and they then knew that if they wanted to move, they had better move fast. They at once withdrew in disorder, and so, for that matter, did everyone else. The chaos mounted from hour to hour: cavalry, dragoons, infantry—everyone was on the way out, not by battalions or squadrons, but every man for himself and all inextricably mixed. At dusk the day had been lost without more than half our troops having been committed; the situation was so unpleasant that the Princes consulted the Duc de Vendôme, and he, whose temper had landed the army in a losing position, was in a rage again.

The Duc de Bourgogne wished to speak, but the Duc de Vendôme, full of fury and self-esteem, shut him up and reminded him that he had only been allowed to join the army on condition that he was unconditionally under his, Vendôme's, command. He said this so brutally and so categorically that a silence reigned during which those who were present let their minds dwell on the dreadful waste of an opportunity for engaging the enemy on equal terms which this bag of wind had so recently let slip. The young Prince was faced by a more difficult problem than any the enemy could impose on him; he knew that for him there was no easy way out, so he was quite calm. Vendôme went on talking at him and telling him that the battle wasn't lost yet, and he talked of fresh action during the night and at first light.

Everyone listened to him in silence; no one wished to say anything until the Comte d'Évreux, claiming privilege as Vendôme's nephew, said straight out that the army was in a state of extreme disorder. Various others, plucking up their courage, held the same view. Vendôme at last looked round and shouted: 'Well, I know what you have all wanted all along—a withdrawal. And you, Sir'—looking straight at the Duc de Bourgogne—'have had nothing else in mind for a long time. Now you can have your own way.'

Heavily and most bitterly defeated, the French army fell back and admitted the enemy to the soil of their country. But the savage warfare between the upright, straight-laced Duc de Bourgogne and the foul-mouthed soldier, the Duc de Vendôme, had barely begun.

THE FIRST DECLINE OF THE DUC DE VENDÔME

After the disaster at Oudenarde the French forces were split. One part was driven back over its own border and the Allies successfully besieged Lille; the other still retained a foothold in Flanders awaiting the inevitable siege of Ghent.

IT was no longer fitting that the Princes should remain in Flanders and they received orders to return, but they were reluctant to do so because of the current danger to Ghent. The Duc de Bourgogne had a further reason because the Duc de Vendôme did not seem to have received the same orders and was obviously settling down on the border as though he expected to command the army in the next spring's campaign. But although he did not let on to anybody, Vendôme had in fact been recalled. For the first time he realized that he was going to have to give an account of himself and that certain things which hitherto he had treated lightly would on inspection not look so good. He went so far as to beg to be allowed to stay with the army, though he put it that this would be to oblige his King and against his own inclinations. While an exchange of letters was going on, the Princes were peremptorily ordered home and departed.

Since there was finally no way out, the Duc de Vendôme left the army; he arrived at Versailles on 15 December and went to make his bow just as the King was going in to dinner. The King embraced him

135

and they conversed pleasantly during the meal, though it was all small talk. Then the King said that he would see the Duke in Madame de Maintenon's apartments next day for a business discussion; such a postponement was unusual and did not seem to be a very good omen. The Duc de Vendôme next went to make his bow to the Duc de Bourgogne, who was extremely polite in spite of what had happened in the field. Then the Duke went to pay his respects to Monseigneur and, finding himself well received, tried to press the Prince to visit him at Anet; but to his intense surprise Monseigneur gave him a reply so evasive that it amounted to a refusal. Vendôme was most embarrassed and left as soon as he could. I met him on the steps and saw him by the light of my own links, for he was without linkmen and accompanied only by Alberoni; he seemed to be annoyed and was heading for the Duc du Maine's apartment.

On the following day he had his interview with the King in Madame de Maintenon's apartment, and it lasted less than an hour. He stayed altogether eight or ten days at Versailles and Marly, and then set off for Anet. It was obvious that he knew all was not well, for he actually had to ask people to visit him at Anet—whereas before it had been a mark of considerable distinction even to get near the place, which was always packed. Now some pleaded a previous engagement, some promised to go and did not turn up, and everyone complained about the distance which so recently they had thought nothing of.

The day after Vendôme's return, on the 16th, the Maréchal de Boufflers[1] arrived and at once asked the Captain of the duty guard to tell the King he was there. The King had just concluded his interview with Vendôme, and sent word that the Marshal was to come at once to Madame de Maintenon's room. As soon as he entered the King went to him and embraced him two or three times and expressed his gratitude and admiration. They moved into the room and the door was closed. The King then said to him that in view of the great services which he had rendered to his country, he must name his own reward. Boufflers replied that all the reward he asked for was the approval of his sovereign, and however much the King pressed him he would say no more.

Finally the King said, 'Well, Marshal, since you will not ask for anything, I will tell you what I have made up my mind to—and if

---

[1] This brave and honest soldier, who had just capitulated at Lille, spent much of his military career trying to pull other peoples' chestnuts out of the fire; few men deserved better of their country in those unhappy years.

there is anything else you want, you may ask for it. I create you a Peer.
I give the reversion of your office as Governor of Flanders to your
son. And I give you the *entrée* equal with the First Gentleman of the
Bedchamber.'

The Marshal sank to his knees, overwhelmed by a generosity
which far exceeded his expectations. These three favours were in fact
extraordinary, and that which gave its recipient the greatest pleasure
was the Peerage. The King had regretted creating fourteen Peers in
1663, and had felt himself forced into the creation of four more two
years later. After that he said he would make no more and the Duke-
doms which he subsequently bestowed did not carry with them a
Peerage but were described as "verified" Dukes. Louis XIV is
thought by some to have invented this status, but that is not so, it
goes back for centuries.

Two days before Christmas the Duke of Berwick returned to
Court, and started to speak his mind freely about the conduct of the
Duc de Vendôme in Flanders. Encouraged by his example, various
other officers who had been on the campaign began to talk. A lot of
new light was thrown on recent events and there was a growing
indignation.

During the winter Vendôme, although living at Anet, was drawing General's field allowance; this gave the impression that he was
determined to command the army again in the spring and the spirits
of his clique rose accordingly. But on 2 February, 1709, he came to
Versailles for the Candlemas ceremonies, and he was then told that
his services would no longer be required. He was directed to cease
drawing his field allowance and although it was a bitter disappointment he put as good a face upon it as he could: the only visible change
in his demeanour was that he was a little less insolent.

A SEVERE WINTER

THE appalling cold began on Twelfth Night and lasted for two
months; it was worse than anyone could remember. In four days the
rivers, including even the Seine, were frozen over, right to their
mouths, and—something which had never been seen before—the sea
even froze round the coast firmly enough to bear the weight of a horse
and cart. It was said to be as bad as severe winter weather in Denmark
or Sweden. A false thaw melted the snow which had lain all this time,
and it was followed by a sudden renewal of the frost which lasted as
severe as ever for three weeks more.

1709 The cold was so intense that at Versailles bottles of liqueurs with a high alcoholic content burst with the frost even in rooms where a fire was blazing; I saw it happen several times myself. One evening when I was having supper with the Duc de Villeroy in his small bedroom, in spite of his having put the wine on the mantelpiece to warm, lumps of ice fell out into our glasses when we poured the decanters.

The second frost finished everything. Fruit trees were killed off, there were no nuts, no olives, apples, or grapes left. Other trees died in large quantities. The crops were destroyed in the ground and the desolation and general ruin were indescribable.

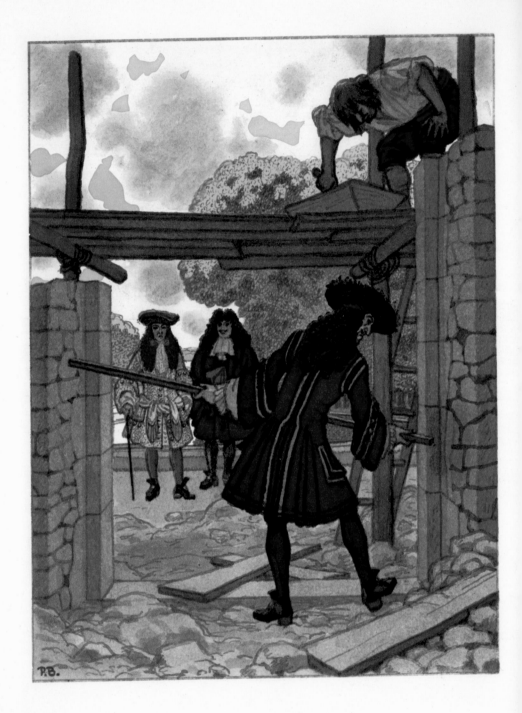

Le Nôtre does the King's bidding

1709

FINAL FALL OF THE DUC DE VENDÔME

ENDÔME's downfall was in three stages, the first of which I have described when he returned from Flanders and was told that he would not be given another command.

He had retired to Anet where so few people now came to see him that grass was beginning to sprout between the flagstones of the courtyard. He asked for permission to attend only at Marly and Meudon, and there his strident, haughty voice was as aggressive as ever so that, although few people took any notice of him, a stranger might even then have been impressed. He could still be familiar with Monseigneur, the King was still friendly, the Duc de Bourgogne was civil; only the Duchesse de Bourgogne was lying in wait for him.

She had her chance at the first visit which the King paid to Marly after Easter. Everyone was playing brelan then, and Monseigneur often sat down to play with the Duchesse de Bourgogne in the early afternoon. On one occasion they needed a fifth to make up their table and Monseigneur, seeing the Duc de Vendôme across the room, unthinkingly called him over. The Duchesse de Bourgogne then said in a quiet but penetrating voice that it was quite bad enough to have to put up with the presence of the Duke at Marly, but when it came to playing cards with him she begged to be excused. Monseigneur could not argue the point and looked round for someone else. Vendôme meanwhile came up to the table and suffered the absolute ignominy of being sent away again; he retired to his room in a fury.

While she was still playing the Duchess thought over what had occurred, and determined to turn a strategic success into complete victory. She was naturally gentle and timid, but on this occasion as soon as the hand was over she plucked up enough courage to run to Madame de Maintenon and explain how bitterly uncomfortable it was for her to have to meet the Duc de Vendôme after what had occurred between him and her husband in Flanders, and she thought it mean of him to avoid Versailles which was big enough for the two of them but to turn up constantly at Marly where she could not get away from him. She went on to say that since he had been relieved of his command because of the mistakes he had made, the only reason for his still being received at Marly must be the King's personal affection for him, which she found rather painful since it reflected upon the King's own grandson and herself. She said it all well and briefly, for the King was just coming.

Madame de Maintenon took it up with the King that evening, and she scored a complete success. The King was tired of Vendôme, and anyway he loathed having discontented people near him. He was therefore very glad to rid himself of Vendôme and please both his granddaughter and Madame de Maintenon at one and the same time. Before he went to bed he sent a message to Vendôme requesting him not to ask for invitations for Marly in future because his presence there was distasteful to the Duchesse de Bourgogne. This was an absolute thunderbolt to Vendôme; but he kept his temper and went off to stay with some friends at Clichy. There were some rather unpleasant rumours going round at that time about the gambling at Marly and it got about that this was the reason why Vendôme had taken his leave, so to save his face he had to go back two days before the King's departure; but he never crossed the threshold again.

Once he had recovered his temper, Vendôme surveyed the scene and realized that nothing had been said about Meudon. He felt sure that he would always be welcome there by Monseigneur and he boasted about it. Two days before Monseigneur went to Meudon, Vendôme would go to Versailles to pay his respects to the King and then very ostentatiously spend the rest of the time at Meudon where in his hey-day he would not have dreamed of wasting more than twenty-four hours. The Duchesse de Bourgogne always went over to see Monseigneur, and was once more offended by Vendôme's parading himself and once more bided her time.

About two months later the King and Madame de Maintenon went to Meudon for dinner and took the Duchesse de Bourgogne with them. The Duc de Vendôme was ill advised enough to present himself among the first who greeted them as they got out of their carriage. The Duchesse de Bourgogne gave him a frigid bow and walked past him looking the other way. The Duke realized he had been snubbed, but for all that went up later in the afternoon to the table where she was playing cards and she cut him dead. This miffed him considerably and he sulked in his room until the late evening. Meanwhile the Duchess complained to Monseigneur of the way Vendôme behaved, and she also expressed her views most bitterly to the King and Madame de Maintenon.

The next morning Vendôme complained to Monseigneur of the way the Duchess treated him, but he got a very dusty answer. He then enlisted what allies he could, but Monseigneur's reply was that he had better have the decency to keep out of the way of the Duchess until he had made his peace with her. Vendôme was cut to the quick, but there was more to come. The following afternoon he was playing papillon when d'Antin entered the room and asked if the game was nearly over. Vendôme asked why he was interested, and d'Antin said, 'Because I've done what you asked me to do.'

Vendôme replied, 'I haven't asked you to do anything for me,' but then realized that d'Antin wanted to speak to him; and together they went into a dressing room where they could talk privately. D'Antin told him that he had been commanded by the King to ask Monseigneur as a favour not to invite Vendôme to Meudon in future because his presence was disagreeable to the Duchesse de Bourgogne, and to convey the same message to Vendôme himself. When he heard this Vendôme said what he thought with the entire picturesque vocabulary of which he was the master. That evening he approached Monseigneur who looked at him coldly, without moving a muscle, and said that he had better not come to Meudon any more. He spent his last few days there in frustration and anger, then retired to Anet to seek what few pleasures he could find with his peculiar vices and his servants.

It was a singular victory for Madame de Maintenon, who had always resented him because he would never bow the knee to her, and everyone at Court henceforward trembled at her power.

BREAD RIOTS IN PARIS

As the War of the Spanish Succession dragged on, and the dreadful slaughter of Malplaquet was imminent, conditions in France deteriorated to an alarming degree.

DISTURBANCES were now frequent in the Paris markets, which necessitated a fifty per cent increase in the regiments of French and Swiss Guards kept on duty in the city. Even d'Argenson, the Lieutenant of Police, was the centre of an unpleasant incident at Saint-Roch where he was set upon by an angry mob after one unfortunate member of it had been trampled under foot. The Duc de la Rochefoucauld was sent a vile anonymous letter directed against the King, reminding him that there were still Ravaillacs[1] in the world and ending with an untimely eulogy of Brutus. The Duke went at once to Marly and said that he must see the King on urgent business. The arrival in such a hurry of a retired courtier who was also blind impressed the Gentlemen-in-Waiting, and the

[1] The assassin of Henri IV.

Duke was soon able to tell his story in person to the King. He was not very well received. The purpose of the Duc de la Rochefoucauld's visit became known afterwards, and people also found out that the Ducs de Bouillon and de Beauvilliers had received similar notes which they had taken to the King without making such a fuss about it. What worried the King much more was the abusive posters which were being stuck up all over Paris; there were also a good many rather unpleasant lampoons in circulation.

Monseigneur in going to and returning from the Opera had more than once been menaced by a mob, containing a preponderance of women all demanding bread, so that even surrounded by his guards he feared the worst and they for their part did not dare to treat the crowd roughly for fear of worse developing. He got away by distributing largesse and promising wonders, but as no wonders happened he did not dare go to Paris any more. From his own windows the King could hear the people of Versailles demonstrating in the streets; everywhere extremely outspoken speeches were made, urging direct action since its consequences could be no worse than dying of starvation.

As a distraction the unemployed were given work shifting a huge mound of earth between the Saint-Denis and Saint-Martin gates, and they were paid off with a small issue of poor quality bread. On 20 August it happened that there was not nearly enough bread to go round. One woman in particular was so vocal that she set all the others off. The police in charge of the disturbance were ill advised enough to threaten her, which only made her worse, and in desperation they slapped her into a nearby pillory. In a matter of minutes an unruly crowd had torn the pillory up by its roots, and set off through the streets looting every bakery and cake shop in sight. The shops put their shutters up as quickly as they could, the disorder spread and the mob marched on doing no harm to anyone but demanding bread and appropriating it wherever they could find it.

The Maréchal de Boufflers had unwittingly gone that morning to see his lawyer whose office was in the quarter which was the centre of the riots. The Duc de Grammont also had an appointment with the same lawyer, and, meeting Boufflers, tried to persuade him to turn back; but when he found the Marshal adamant he went on with him. A hundred yards from the lawyer's office they came upon the Maréchal d'Huxelles in his carriage and since he had come from the centre of the trouble spot they stopped him to ask for news. He said that it didn't amount to much really, but advised them to turn back and then hurried off himself like a man who wanted no part of it. The Marshal

and his father-in-law pushed on but the farther they went the worse
it got, and people were shouting to them from the windows to go
back before they got themselves killed.

When they reached the top of the rue Saint-Denis the Marshal
thought that it was time they abandoned their coach, and the two of
them pushed through the mob on foot. He kept remonstrating with
them and promising bread and finally they listened to him: there
were cries of 'Vive le Maréchal de Boufflers!,' and he kept on pushing
his way through and reasoning with them as best he could. The
people begged him to tell the King of their pitiful state and to get
them bread. He promised, and when he had given his word the mob
dispersed with a few last cries of 'Vive le Maréchal de Boufflers!'
This was a great public service, for at that moment d'Argenson was
marching to the scene with large reinforcements of French and Swiss
Guards and had it not been for the Marshal there would undoubtedly
have been terrible bloodshed.

As soon as he got home the Marshal had a hasty meal and went at
once to Versailles. He was thanked by the King, who offered him the
Governorship of the City of Paris, which he declined. Arrangements
were made for an immediate distribution of bread, the streets were
patrolled day and night, and the reputation of the Maréchal de Boufflers deservedly stood higher than ever.

A WINDOW IN THE TRIANON[1]

THE King loved building, the more so now that he had no mistress to
take up his time. He had pulled down the Trianon de Porcelaine,[2]
which was built for Madame de Montespan, and had it rebuilt as we see
it today. Louvois[3] was the Minister of Works. The King had a very
exact eye, and one day he noticed that one window in the new building

---

[1] Although Saint-Simon wrote this passage à propos of political events in 1709, in
fact what he is describing took place in 1688.

[2] Louis bought the village of Trianon in 1662-3. He had the village demolished and
a garden laid out in its place. Then in 1670 he had built a small palace faced with faïence
tiles of blue and white, from which it derived its name of the Trianon de Porcelaine; it
was completed in 1673. The new building, the Grand Trianon, was begun in 1687 to the
plans of Mansard and Robert Cotte. Although more or less complete by 1691, it commanded the continued attention of the King for years to come.

[3] François-Michel Le Tellier, Marquis de Louvois (1639-91). Son of the famous Chancellor Le Tellier, he himself became a great War Minister, and Louis's greatest victories
were during his term of office. He finally lost the King's confidence and died suddenly
of apoplexy just as he was about to be dismissed.

was slightly narrower that the others. He pointed the difference out to Louvois so that it could be remedied, which would have been easy at that time since the stonework between the windows had not yet been built up. Louvois said he thought the window was all right, but the King insisted. The same thing happened on the following day without making any impression on Louvois, who was very self-opinionated.

On the next day again in the Grand Gallery the King met Le Nôtre. Although Le Nôtre was really a garden designer, at which he excelled, the King often consulted him on architectural questions. The King asked him if he had been recently to the Trianon and he said no, he had not. So the King directed him to do so. On the following day: the same question, and the same answer. The King knew quite well what was going on, so he ordered him to be at the Trianon that afternoon, at the same hour when Louvois was to be in attendance. This time Le Nôtre did not dare to disobey.

At the appointed hour the King arrived and in the presence of Louvois reverted to the question of the window which the latter still said was exactly the same size as all the others. The King asked Le Nôtre to go and measure it, knowing him to be so upright that he was incapable of telling anything except the truth. Louvois lost his temper, so did the King, and Le Nôtre stood there doing nothing. Finally the King gave Le Nôtre a direct order to go and measure the window, while Louvois continued to mutter and maintain that there was nothing wrong with it.

Le Nôtre found that the King was right and the window was several inches out. Louvois still wanted to argue but the King had by now reached the end of his patience; he told Louvois to shut up and to have the window pulled down and put up again that afternoon; completely unlike his usual even temper, he really went for him. What upset Louvois most was that he had to stand there and take a dressing down not only in front of all the bricklayers and the courtiers, officers of the guard and so on who always followed the King about on his walks, but also a motley crowd of servants, because since the walls were only just being built the whole site was open and anyone could go anywhere. Talk about this went on for a long time and people wondered what would be the end of it, realizing really that the window would have spoilt the whole façade and would have had to be pulled down sooner or later. Louvois, who was not accustomed to being spoken to like that, went home raging and in despair. His few close friends were really worried and called to find out what had happened. In the end he told them; he was undone, he said, and for a mistake of a few inches the King was prepared to forget all his great

services to the crown; but, he went on, he would soon get even, for
he would start such a war that the King would soon have to stop
fiddling about with bricks and mortar and call him back into harness.
And that is exactly what he did.

Louvois had a considerable hand in engineering a situation which in the
autumn of 1688 led Louis to undertake a brutal invasion of the Palatinate.
The whole of this rich land was laid waste, every dwelling place destroyed, the
population put to the sword and the few survivors driven from their homeland.
This senseless blitzkreig *had led to general hostilities which got worse until*
France was humiliated by the Peace of Ryswyck in 1697.

MADAME DE MAINTENON'S
APARTMENTS

MADAME de Maintenon's apartments[1] were on the same level as the
hall of the King's Guards, and facing it. The first antechamber was a
narrow room; this led into a second, somewhat similar in shape, into
which only the Captain of the Guard was allowed to enter; beyond this
was the main room which was very large. Between the door by which
one entered from the second antechamber and the fire-place was the
King's arm-chair, with its back to the wall, a table before it, and two
small chairs—one for the Minister with whom the King might be
working and the other for his portfolio. On the other side of the fire-
place in a recess hung with red damask was Madame de Maintenon's
arm-chair with a small table in front of it. Beyond, in an alcove, was
her bed. Opposite the bed, up five steps, was a door which led into
another large room—a drawing-room, beyond which again was the
first antechamber of the Duc de Bourgogne's apartments.

The Duchesse de Bourgogne and ladies with the *entrée* used to
play cards every evening in the drawing-room. The Duchess used to
go next door whenever she felt like it during the evening, to see the
King and Madame de Maintenon sitting on either side of the fire.
Monseigneur used to go into the drawing-room after the theatre, but
the King never crossed the threshold and Madame de Maintenon
very seldom went in there.

Before the King's supper Madame de Maintenon was brought her

---

[1] These rooms were altered beyond recognition in the nineteenth century. Madame de
Maintenon's room as shown today is only a part of the original.

own meal,[1] which was served by her maids and a valet. The King was in the room, usually working with one of his Ministers. As soon as the short meal was over the table was cleared, and Madame de Maintenon's maids would quickly undress her and she got into bed.[2] When the King was told that his supper was ready he would disappear for a minute, then have a word with Madame de Maintenon, and ring a bell which sounded in the drawing-room. Then Monseigneur, if he was there, the Duke and Duchess, with her ladies, and the Duc de Berry would file through Madame de Maintenon's room to supper, the men preceding and the ladies following the King. Any ladies who were not attached to the Duchess then went away. There might be some guests who were dressed for the supper (one of the privileges of that drawing-room was that people might call upon the Duchess without being in full evening dress), and they would have to go round by the hall of the Guards without passing through Madame de Maintenon's room: no men except the three mentioned were allowed into the room.

THE DISMISSAL OF CHAMILLART

The more tired Chamillart became through overwork and the more the affairs of France declined, the nearer the hounds bayed at the heels of the Secretary of State—there was never a shortage of persons willing to tear down a great man from his office: though in fact Chamillart was by no means great. He was a conscientious plodder. It is hardly surprising that in the end the King lost confidence in a Minister so generally attacked by everyone, including Madame de Maintenon, and who seemed to have no interest in defending himself.

ON Sunday, 9 June, late in the morning the Maréchale de Villars, whose apartments were next to ours, looked in (as she often did) and asked us if we would have supper with her for a chat, because she thought she would have some news for us. She said that she was on her way to dine privately with Chamillart, which had once been considered a great honour, but now things had changed so much that she thought she was doing him a favour by going. She knew nothing for certain, as she assured us afterwards, but was going entirely on the rumours of the last few days, to which fuel had been added by the

---

[1] She had given up dining at the King's table some years before.

[2] It is recorded that she disliked having to undress beside the table at which the King was working.

attitude of the Papal Nuncio who had come out against Chamillart.

That same morning the King, as he went into the Council, called the Duc de Beauvilliers aside and said that he wished him to go after dinner to Chamillart and say that, for the sake of the State, he was obliged to ask for his resignation; but that at the same time he wished that they should both remain friends, and that Chamillart should remain assured of the King's esteem and of the satisfaction which his great service had given in the past. Beauvilliers was to add that the King, as a sign of respect, would continue his pension as a Minister, which was 200,000 livres per annum, and would add to it a personal allowance of an equal amount; in addition he said that he would allow Chamillart's son the same sum per annum, desiring him to buy the office of High Steward from which Cavoye had just been ejected. The King also said he would direct that the next Secretary of State should pay Chamillart 880,000 livres for the office, which was to include a fee for the office of royal secretary.[1]

The Duc de Beauvilliers, distressed by the necessity of performing so difficult a duty, begged hard to be excused. The King replied that he wished him to do it because he managed such matters so well; then he turned on his heel and followed the Duke back into the Council chamber, where the Chancellor, Torcy, Chamillart, and Desmaretz were waiting for him. No suspicion of what was about to happen was allowed to appear at the Council, and not a shadow crossed the King's face. Indeed, on one subject which was brought up for discussion, the King told Chamillart to prepare a memorandum and bring it to him in Madame de Maintenon's apartment that evening. Greatly distressed, Beauvilliers stayed on at the end of the meeting and again expressed his great distaste for the task assigned to him, and begged that, if he must do it, he might be allowed to take with him the Duc de Chevreuse, who was also a close friend of Chamillart. To this the King gave his consent.

At about four in the afternoon the two brothers-in-law were announced to Chamillart, who was working alone in his study. They went in feeling, as one can imagine, extremely uncomfortable. The unhappy Minister immediately sensed that they had come on some business of more than ordinary seriousness, and without giving them time to open their mouths said, with a quiet, serene expression: 'Well, Gentlemen, what is it? If what you have to say concerns me alone, please speak. I have been expecting it for some time.'

Such gentle firmness moved them so much that they could hardly

---

[1] Chamillart paid 300,000 livres to the daughters of his predecessor.

say what they had come for. Chamillart listened to them without any change of expression, then said:

'The King is master. I have tried to do my best, and I hope that whoever succeeds me will be happier and more successful. It is something to be able to rely on his goodness and to receive a testimony of it at such a time.' Then he asked if he might write a letter to the King and if they would be kind enough to take it for him, and when they replied in the affirmative he sat down, still quite unmoved, and wrote a letter expressing his respects and thanks, which, when he had finished, he read out to them. He had just finished the memorandum which the King in the morning had asked him to prepare; he read it over, signed and sealed it, and asked them to deliver that as well. They chatted for a few minutes; Chamillart spoke to them of his son and of what an honour it was for him to be the nephew of them both through his wife. Then the two Dukes left, and Chamillart began to pack his things. He wrote a letter to Madame de Maintenon reminding her of her past kindnesses and, without any recriminations, said goodbye. He wrote a note to La Feuillade, his son-in-law, at Meudon telling him of his disgrace; and sent a message to his wife, who was in Paris, to join him at l'Étang, without saying why. He sorted his papers, then sent for the Abbé de la Proustière (head of the Secretary of State's household), and handed them over together with the keys for his successor. All was done without any sign of emotion, regret, or reproach. Then he went downstairs and, getting into his coach with his son, drove away so quietly that it was a long time before anyone knew that he had left Versailles.

1711

THE DEATH OF MONSEIGNEUR

✠✠✠✠✠s Monseigneur was on the way to Meudon with the Duchesse
✠ 𝓐 ✠ de Bourgogne on the Wednesday after Easter they met a
✠ 𝓐 ✠ priest bearing the Host on his way back from visiting the
✠✠✠✠✠sick. They got down from their carriage and knelt. Monseigneur asked what was the matter with the sick man and was told
that he had smallpox, of which there was an epidemic at the time.

Monseigneur had had smallpox slightly as a child, but he was still
afraid of it, and that evening he said to Boudin, his doctor, that he
would not be surprised if he had caught it again. The next morning
he was going wolf-hunting, but when he got up he felt faint and fell
into a chair. Boudin sent him straight back to bed, and was worried
about his pulse all day. The King was told by Fagon that Monseigneur
was ill, but he thought little of it and went off to dine at Marly.

The Duc and Duchesse de Bourgogne had dinner at Meudon and
would not leave Monseigneur for a moment. The Duchess looked
after her father-in-law with the grace which she brought to everything she did; she could hardly feel much distress at whatever the
immediate future might bring, but she nevertheless looked after the
patient with unaffected assiduity. The Duc de Bourgogne had never
had smallpox but, although the nature of Monseigneur's illness was
increasingly obvious, he would not leave the bedside until it was time
for him and the Duchess to go to the King's supper.

When the King heard what they had to tell him he said that he
would go to Meudon and remain there throughout Monseigneur's
illness. He forbade his grandchildren to go near the place, and was
thoughtful enough to extend the ban to anyone at court who had not
had smallpox; in addition he said that those who had had it already
might visit Meudon to pay their respects if their sense of duty demanded it or stay away to allay their fears, just as they pleased. Most
of the guests staying in the house were sent away.

The following day it was known for certain that Monseigneur had
smallpox. The King held his Councils and saw his Ministers as usual.
Several times a day he visited Monseigneur and sat by his bedside.
On the Monday he and the Duchesse de Bourgogne went over to
Marly for a walk, and as they were passing the gardens of Versailles
the King saw his grandchildren, but would not allow them to come

149

near him, merely calling hello to them. The Duchess had had small-pox, though it had left few marks.

The King never enjoyed being away from his own homes, so that his visits to Meudon had always been fleeting, and then only to please Monseigneur. Madame de Maintenon was even more uncomfortable there, for wherever she was she always liked to have a private retreat which no one could enter except the Duchesse de Bourgogne: when she was at Versailles there was Saint-Cyr; she had a private house in Fontainebleau, and something similar at Marly. As it looked as if they would have to stay at Meudon for some time, the King's interior decorators were told to get Chaville ready for her: a house within Monseigneur's park which he had bought from the estate of Le Tellier, the Chancellor.

When I got to Versailles I wrote to Beauvilliers asking him to tell the King that I had returned as soon as I heard that Monseigneur was ill, and would have gone to Meudon except that I understood that I was forbidden since I had never had smallpox. Beauvilliers wrote back saying that it was a good thing I had come back, and that the King, quite understanding, had expressly forbidden either me or Madame de Saint-Simon to go near Meudon.

Versailles was very different from Meudon. Here the Duc and Duchesse de Bourgogne were openly holding court, and it seemed like the first light of a new dawn. The whole court was there, together with masses of visitors from Paris. There were even people from Meudon, and, since discretion has never been a French characteristic, they had only to say that they had not been into Monseigneur's room that day to be admitted.

The rooms were packed with people come to pay their respects to the young people—their *lever* and *coucher*, dinner and supper, and whenever they went for a walk were the favourite times. Both of them behaved with great dignity and seriousness; they spoke to everyone and were most accessible. Every quarter of an hour or so a despatch came from Meudon with the latest bulletin. The patient seemed to be as well as could be expected, and most people thought he would re-cover. Five days went by like this, with everyone sitting on the fence ready to face whichever way circumstances demanded.

The Paris fishwives, who had shown such faithful allegiance when Monseigneur had had that terrible attack of indigestion some time before, now appeared again. They came to Meudon in several hired coaches. Monseigneur had them admitted; they flung themselves on their knees at the foot of his bed, and, delighted to hear that he was getting on well, said that they would have a *Te Deum* sung when they got back to Paris. Monseigneur, who rather enjoyed such attention, told them that such celebration was somewhat premature; but he thanked them, and directed that they should be shown over the house, given dinner, and rewarded with money.

Life continued quietly at Versailles, but there was a change at Meudon. The King went several times a day to see Monseigneur, who appreciated it deeply. But in the afternoon, before the meeting of the Council of Despatches, the King was very upset by the serious swelling of Monseigneur's face; he left after a few minutes, and was weeping when he came out. Everyone there reassured him as well as they could, and when the Council was over he went for a walk in the garden. Meanwhile Monseigneur had failed to recognize the Princesse de Conti, which alarmed Boudin. About four in the afternoon he looked so bad that Boudin suggested to Fagon that they should call in another consultant, for he said that as court physicians they had little experience of infectious diseases, and another opinion would be valuable. Fagon, however, would not hear of the idea.

But, while the King was at supper, Fagon and the others in the sick-room began to lose their heads. They tried one treatment after another without giving any of them time to take effect. The priest who used to look in last thing every night found the doors wide open, which was most unusual. He went in and, sizing up the situation in a second, ran to the bedside, took Monseigneur's hand, and began to offer him consolation. Seeing the patient was conscious but unable to say a word, he got something out of him which did for a confession, and exhorted him to contrition. The poor Prince said a few words clearly, mumbled others, and pressed the priest's hand.

Fagon appeared in the supper-room, crying that all was lost; the King sprang up, and almost fainted. The disastrous change from a situation which had seemed to be completely under control struck terror into everyone. The King, almost beside himself, went at once to Monseigneur's room; some foolishly tried to stop him, but he rebuked them, saying that he insisted on seeing his son again and that there might yet be hope. As he reached the door the Princesse de Conti met him and pushed him back, saying that now all that mattered was his own preservation. The King, scarcely conscious, fell back on to a settee, and as anyone came out of the sick-room he clutched at them and asked for news. No one dared to say a word. Madame de Maintenon had arrived and sat beside him, trying to weep, and begging him to come away—for the carriages were at the door. Monseigneur had lost consciousness, but his body fought on fruitlessly for an hour more. The Duchess and the Princesse de Conti hurried to and fro from the sick-bed to the King, and the rooms were packed with a throng of courtiers elbowing one another. At last Fagon came out and announced that the end had come. The King was deeply moved, and distressed that Monseigneur's confession should have been left so late. He spoke somewhat harshly to Fagon and then went out to the front door. He found that Monseigneur's berlin had been brought round for him; with a wave of the hand he indicated that they should bring some other vehicle. Yet in spite of everything he was not completely prostrate with grief, for, catching sight of Pontchartrain, he told him to warn his father and the other Ministers to be at Marly the next morning for a Council of State, but to come a bit later than usual. Pontchartrain replied that the business was purely formal and suggested that it should be postponed for twenty-four hours. The King assented. The King then got into his carriage with some difficulty, supported on both sides, and Madame de Maintenon followed.

Monseigneur was fairly tall and stout, but not obese. He was dignified and haughty, but not outrageously so. He would have been handsome if he had not broken his nose as a child while playing with the Prince de Conti. He was fair, with a red, sunburned face. He had beautiful legs and very small feet. He walked very uncertainly, always putting the same foot down twice; he was terrified of falling, and if the ground was not perfectly level he always required someone to lean on. He had a good seat on a horse, but was not a bold rider. Out hunting he was always given a lead by Casaus, and if he lost touch with him he would stop at once. He seldom galloped, and if he lost hounds he would pull up under a tree and then, after a leisurely search, go home. At one time he was a great gourmet, but since his violent attack of indigestion (which had for a time been mistaken for apoplexy) he had only eaten one big meal a day and kept a careful check on his appetite—although, like all the Royal Family, he was by nature a big eater.

As for his character, the truth is that he had none. He had a good deal of common sense, but no ability. He appeared proud and dignified, which was partly his nature and partly his portly bearing and his habit of imitating the King, his father. He was very obstinate, and his life was tied up in protocol. His indolence and dullness gave him a superficial appearance of good nature, but underneath it he was very hard. He was kind to servants, but it was only show and seldom went beyond asking them personal questions. In spite of his apparent familiarity he was quite indifferent to other people's grief or misfortune; this, however, was more from want of thought than anything. He was extraordinarily reserved, and hence could be safely trusted with any secret. It was generally believed that he and his mistress, Mademoiselle Choin, never discussed affairs of State—possibly because such matters were beyond their comprehension. Dullness and timidity made him extraordinarily reticent, yet at the same time he had an almost exaggerated sense of his own importance (if such a thing can be said of the Dauphin) and insisted on his rights at all times and in all places. Mademoiselle Choin once remarked upon his silence; he replied that the words of people in his position carried great weight and an ill-considered remark could do irreparable harm, and for that reason he would rather say nothing at all. To someone as indolent and as indifferent to all about him as he was, silence in any case came more easily, but although his precept was excellent, he rather overdid it.

In his private affairs he was extremely business-like and kept detailed accounts in his own hand. He knew exactly what the smallest thing had cost him, in spite of the fact that his total expenditure was enormous—most of it going on building, furniture, and jewellery; Meudon and his pack of wolf-hounds also cost a lot, for he allowed himself to be persuaded that he enjoyed hunting. He used to be a great gambler, but after he got involved in so much building he would only play for low stakes. In other respects he was tight-fisted to an undignified degree; he very seldom gave any of his servants a pension, though he was fairly liberal in his gifts to the Capuchin house at Meudon. It is incredible how little he gave to his beloved Choin—a mere 400 louis a quarter, which he handed to her himself in gold coin: never more or less. And that was all she got, except an occasional present once or twice a year, which occasioned him a great deal of heartburning before he could make up his mind to it. To do her justice, no one could have cared less—partly, perhaps, because she knew that whatever she did she would never get more out of him, but chiefly because by nature she really did not seem interested in such matters. No one knows to this day whether she was married to him or not; most people in their circle swear that she was not. She was a plain woman—dark-haired and snub-nosed, but with an intelligent face; long before Monseigneur died she had got old and fat, and she stank.[1] During Monseigneur's illness she visited him several times a day, and the King, who knew of it, far from turning her out of the house in the usual way, actually reprimanded Madame de Maintenon

[1] Monseigneur is said to have taken to snuff because of the stench from her decayed teeth.

for not calling upon her. This seems to me strong evidence that a marriage had taken place.

Monseigneur had nothing to recommend him to his father except the fact of being his son and successor—and this was a good enough reason for the King to keep him at a distance. He had not the slightest influence at court—in fact if he showed a preference for anyone it was quite enough to put paid to that person's hopes for ever. Accordingly, if he was asked to obtain a favour for anyone he replied frankly that his interest in the matter would be fatal. For many years he had been kept fully informed on matters of State, but he played no part whatever—he knew what was going on, and that was the end of it. Knowing that he had no influence, and conscious perhaps of his own intellectual inferiority, he deliberately kept out of public affairs. Certainly he regularly attended the Councils of State, but he never went near the Finance meetings or the Council of Despatches, though he had the right to. And he never once sat with the King during his hours of work in his study. Generally speaking he was a punctilious son and courtier—never falling short in his duty, but never going an inch beyond it. No subject in the realm showed greater respect for the King. Consequently he enjoyed his liberty at Meudon all the more. And although he must have seen that the King did not like him going there, he made no attempt to reduce or curtail his visits. He spent little time at Versailles, and even when the court was at Marly he would break it up by going to Meudon for a few days. This suggests that he did not really like the King, but he never ceased to admire him. He did his best to copy him, and the curb that he put on his own conduct showed that he feared him to the end.

1712

THE DEATH OF
THE HEIRS TO THE THRONE

✤✤✤✤✤N 5 February, at about midday, the Duc de Noailles gave ✤the Dauphine[1] a very beautiful snuff-box, full of Spanish snuff which she tried and found excellent. Afterwards she went to her own room, which no one was allowed into, and left the box on the table. In the evening she started shivering and went to bed; she was too ill to get up to attend the King's supper. She was feverish all night, but the next morning she got up as usual and was all right during the day; but in the evening the fever returned. On Sunday the 7th the fever again seemed to abate during the day, but at about six o'clock in the evening she was seized with a terrible pain just below the temple; the area affected was quite small, but the pain was so acute that when the King came to see her she had to beg him to leave the room. The pain went on all the next day; snuff, tobacco, and opium were tried, and she was bled twice from the arm, all without success. Eventually the pain subsided a little, but the fever seemed to increase; she said the pain was worse than anything she had known in childbirth.

This violent attack set everybody talking about the snuff-box which the Duc de Noailles had given her. As she was going to bed on Friday, the day she was taken ill, she had asked Madame de Lévis to bring it from her room, saying she would find it on the table. Madame de Lévis could not find it, and although everyone searched high and low, it was never seen again. This extraordinary circumstance coupled with the Dauphine's sudden illness gave rise to the darkest suspicions—suspicions which, it is true, did not reflect on the person who had given her the box, and which were confined to a very small circle. The King did not know that she took snuff, although Madame de Maintenon did. If the King had come to hear of it he would have been very angry, and that was why suspicions about the box were rigidly suppressed.

During Monday night and all Tuesday she was very drowsy; she was in a high fever and sometimes delirious. The King came to see her frequently. Some marks which appeared on her skin gave rise

---

[1] By the death of Monseigneur, the Duc de Bourgogne became Dauphin.

to the hope that she might have measles, as there was a lot of it about both in Versailles and Paris, but that soon proved wrong. The King came to see her on Wednesday morning; she had just been given an emetic which reacted satisfactorily but produced no improvement. The Dauphin never left her bedside, until the doctors forced him out into the garden to get some fresh air; he did not stay out long, but hurried back again to his wife.

Shortly afterwards it was feared that the end was near, and her confessor was sent for. By now the Dauphin had collapsed. In order to remain at the bedside he had concealed the fact that he was himself desperately ill; he was in a high fever, and was taken away and put to bed.

The confession lasted a long time; afterwards Extreme Unction was administered, and the sacred Viaticum which the King went to meet at the foot of the grand staircase. The Dauphine was bled at seven in the evening and seemed a little easier, but for all that it was a terrible night. Early the next morning the King came in. An emetic was given at nine o'clock, but with little effect, and she grew steadily worse all day, being only conscious for a few minutes from time to time. Late in the afternoon the attendants panicked and allowed a lot of people to force their way into the room, in spite of the fact that the King was there. Just before she breathed her last the King left the room, went down the grand staircase, and drove off in his coach with Madame de Maintenon to Marly. Both were overcome by the deepest grief and could not face going to see the Dauphin.

Although the Duchess was little more than a child when she came to France, she had been well trained for the position to which she was called and there was never an apter pupil. Her amiable qualities won all hearts, and the ambitious treated her with deference for the influence which she gained over the King and Madame de Maintenon, as well as over her own husband. She was gentle and timid, with a deep dislike of hurting anyone, but she was smart. She had the ability to conceive long-term plans and the perseverance and determination to carry them out.

She was not really good-looking. Her cheeks were pendulous, her forehead too prominent, her lips too thick, and her nose of no particular shape. Her hair was dark brown, with beautifully arched eyebrows of the same colour. She had lovely eyes. She had lost many of her teeth and those which remained were so decayed that she used to make jokes about it herself. She had a wonderful skin and complexion, a long neck, and small but beautifully shaped breasts. She was tall and slim, and perfectly proportioned; she walked like a goddess floating over clouds. In fact she was as charming as anyone could be.

She went to any amount of trouble and often risked her own health to please the King and Madame de Maintenon; her long observation of them had taught her how to behave with them, when to be quiet and when to be amusing; and for them she would give up her own pleasure at any time. She got to know them better and was closer to them than anyone else—even the King's children or his Bastards. Her attitude to the King in public was one of grave deference, and she was timid and respectful to Madame de Maintenon, whom she always called 'Aunt.' But when she was alone with them she would flutter round, chattering ceaselessly; she perched on the arms of their chairs, or sat on their knees; she would throw her arms round their necks, kiss them, cuddle them, and ruffle their clothes. She turned over the papers and letters on their desk, and if they seemed in a good temper, read everything and talked about it. She had the *entrée*, even when important despatches had just arrived, and the King would see her whenever she wished, even the middle of a Council meeting. She used to say the first thing that came into her head when she was with the King and Mme de Maintenon. One evening, at the time when it was hoped to make peace with England through Queen Anne, she heard them discussing the English Government quite favourably. 'Aunty,' she said, 'England is obviously better governed under a Queen than under a King, and do you know why?'—she fluttered round the room as she spoke—'Because under a King the country is really ruled by women, while under a Queen it is controlled by men.' The odd thing is that they both laughed and agreed with her.

As the Dauphine expired the King went to Marly with Madame de Maintenon, and retired at once to her rooms. They were both plunged in the deepest sorrow—the only real sorrow the King had ever felt.

The Dauphin, prostrate, was so ill that he could not leave his room and saw no one except his brother, his confessor, and the Duc de Beauvilliers, who, ill himself, had struggled from Paris to console his erstwhile pupil. Little did they realize that they were meeting for the last time. Cheverny, d'O, and Gamaches spent the night in the Dauphin's room, but they only saw him at intervals. The following morning they begged him to go to Marly so that he would not be upset by the movement going on in the room above where the Dauphine was being laid out, and he agreed. He left at seven by a back entrance and was taken to his carriage in a chair. He got out at the chapel and heard Mass; thence he was taken round to his own apartments and carried in through one of the long windows in a chair.

1712 Madame de Maintenon came to see him immediately, but the meeting was so painful that she could not bear to stop for long.

As it was getting near time for the King's *lever*, his three *menins*[1] went in and I ventured to accompany them. When he saw me he made a sign of recognition which was most touching. But I was absolutely horrified by his appearance. His eyes were staring and there was a wild look about him; his face had changed, too, and I noticed that it was sort of blotched. His eyes were full of tears which he was trying hard to hold back.

A few minutes later a message came that the King was awake; when he heard this the Dauphin turned round but did not move. The *menins* suggested once or twice that it was time he went to the King, but he did not seem to hear. Then I went over to him and made signs, without any result, and I spoke to him softly. As he still did not move, I took his arm and, saying that the King certainly wanted to see him and since he would have to go sooner or later it would look better if he went at once, I ventured to propel him gently towards the door. He gave me a look which went right to my heart, and left the room. I followed for a while, then turned aside to try and control my feelings. I never saw him again.

When the Dauphin entered the King's room there was already a large number of people there. As soon as the King saw him he called him forward and embraced him several times; they did not say much, and their few words were broken by their tears. The King then held the Dauphin away and had a look at him, and he was horrified by the symptoms which I have mentioned. He directed his doctors to feel the Dauphin's pulse, and they said afterwards that it was extremely bad, but in public they merely remarked that they advised the patient to go to bed. The King embraced him once more and urged him to look after himself and to go to bed. He obeyed, and he never rose again.

On Thursday the 18th I was told very early in the morning that the Dauphin had heard Mass and received the Sacrament just after midnight, after which he spent two hours in prayer. Then he sank for a while into delirium. Later Madame de Saint-Simon came in and told me that he had received Extreme Unction and had passed away. I cannot describe my feelings; if these memoirs should ever see the light long after my death, my readers will, I am sure, share the feelings of my wife and myself. For several days we hardly spoke, and all I felt was that I wanted to get away from the court and everything to do with it.

[1] Young noblemen attached to the person of the Dauphin.

The Duke came into the world with a terrible nature, and when he was young everyone dreaded what would become of him. He was incredibly passionate; in his rages he would vent his feelings on everyone and everything within reach. He could not bear to be thwarted; if the weather, even, interfered with his plans he would go off into transports of fury which threatened to tear him to pieces. He was extremely obstinate, pleasure-loving, and fond of women—though curiously his tastes were heterosexual. He loved food and wine, and was almost too fond of hunting; music sent him into a trance. He adored gambling, but it was dangerous to get in a game with him because he could not bear to lose. In short, he was a slave to every sort of pleasure. He was sulky and cruel; his humour was savage and he loved egging on someone who had a personal idiosyncrasy and then mimicking it so well that his victim was left speechless. But his extreme intelligence showed in everything he said; even when he was in one of his tempers, his remarks were logical and to the point. Everything came easily to him—in fact he knew so much on so many subjects that his wide knowledge kept him from specializing in anything.

He was rather short. His complexion was dark and his face long—the upper half was flawless, but the lower half was too pointed. His chestnut hair was so luxuriant that it almost stuck up too far. He had good legs and the best feet I ever saw, except the King's. When he came out of the nursery his legs were rather long for his body, but he stood up straight; ere long it was noticed that his back was becoming rounded, and in time, in spite of every precaution, he became hunchbacked with one shoulder higher than the other. It is surprising that for all his sharp, inquiring intelligence he never seems to have realized how misshapen he appeared to other people—or perhaps he realized, but could never allow himself to admit it.

The education of a prince of such character was no easy task. But God, to whom all hearts are open and who gives grace according to His divine wish, saw fit that the character of this prince should be changed in every respect. Between the age of eighteen and twenty He changed him completely, and a most tiresome youth became a gentle, modest, and kindly man.[1]

On Sunday, 6 March, the two baby Sons of France, who had been ill for some days, suddenly got much worse with the same symptoms

---

[1] God's instrument in bringing about this transformation was Fénelon, who became the great Archbishop of Cambrai. Appointed tutor in 1698, Fénelon wrote his *Fables*, *Dialogues des Morts*, and *Télémaque* for the amusement and instruction of his pupil.

from which the Duke and Duchess had died. The two children had been sprinkled at their birth, but not formally baptized. So the King ordered Madame de Ventadour to have it done at once; she gathered as many important people together as she could find and the ceremony was performed, both little boys being christened Louis. On the following Tuesday the court physicians called in five doctors from Paris. But the serious situation did not prevent the King from holding the usual Council of Despatches; he went out shooting in the afternoon and was working on State papers with Voysin in the evening. In the case of the new little Dauphin the doctors decided on various remedies, including bleeding, but they all proved to be useless and he died the same night. He was five and a few months—a sturdy and intelligent little boy.

The Duc d'Anjou was not yet weaned. The Duchesse de Ventadour, with the gentlewomen of the bedchamber, took charge of him and would not allow him to be bled or dosed. The Comtesse de Vérue had brought back with her from Italy a counter-agent which she had been given by the Duc de Savoie when she was critically ill from poisoning in Turin, and she gave what she had to the Duchesse de Ventadour for the little Duc d'Anjou—but it could not be given to the Dauphin as well, because it was dangerous for anyone who had been bled. The Duc d'Anjou recovered and is now our King, Louis XV. The body of the little Dauphin was taken to Saint-Denis and laid beside those of his father and mother, and the Duc d'Anjou, now the only survivor, acquired the rank and title of Dauphin.

The King was determined that he would, if possible, discover the cause of such wholesale disaster so that either his suspicions might be set at rest or he would be able to take precautions against such horrible events recurring. He therefore gave the most precise instructions to the Faculty of Medicine. They conducted a post-mortem examination, and their views were not very reassuring. In the case of the Duchess they could find no natural cause of death, only some unnatural symptoms inside the head near the seat of the excruciating pain which she had suffered. Fagon and Boudin felt certain she had been poisoned and made no bones about saying so in front of Madame de Maintenon. Boulduc's gloomy silence added weight to their words. Only Maréchal[1] said that he thought the possibility of poison was very remote and that he had seen the same symptoms in other patients. The King then ordered a post-mortem on the Duke, and the results were horri-

[1] Georges Maréchal (1658–1736). First surgeon to both Louis XIV and XV, and the most celebrated medical man of his day.

fying. All the main organs had lost their proper consistency; when the Duc d'Aumont was handed the heart, in order to place it in a separate casket, it simply melted to nothing; the smell was appalling and penetrated throughout the adjoining apartments. The doctors waited upon the King that evening in Madame de Maintenon's room to make their report; Fagon and Boudin swore that in their opinion the victim had died from the administration of a particularly violent poison, but again Maréchal said that he could find no trace of poison and that he had often found the same symptoms in other patients. There was no attempt made in the King's private circle to conceal their most horrible and calumnious views. Madame de Maintenon got angry with Maréchal even in the King's presence, saying that everyone knew not only that it was poison but exactly who had done it—going so far as to mention the name of the Duc d'Orléans. Horrified, the King made a gesture which seemed to convey agreement, and everyone was angry with Maréchal because he would not toe the line. Fagon nodded sagely, and Boudin declared that no one in his right mind could doubt that the Duke had done it and merely shrugged his shoulders in an insolent way when Maréchal disagreed.

Over the bodies of these two young people a storm of intrigue broke out and the members of the intimate circle showed themselves at their worst. Madame de Maintenon's hopes were now centered entirely in the Duc du Maine.

THE PROMOTION OF THE BASTARDS

WHEN I got to my rooms at Marly at about noon on 29 July I found a message from Maisons asking me to come at once to his house in Paris. I had a dinner engagement which I could not get out of, but I ordered my carriage and slipped away as soon as I could.

When I got to Maisons's house I found him alone with the Duc de Noailles, and I never saw two men in such a state. After a few minutes they told me that the King had decided to legitimize his Bastards and their descendants for ever, not only giving them rank with Princes of the Blood, but also giving them the right of succession to the throne if the other branches of the Royal Family should become extinct. When I heard this I subsided into the nearest chair and started thinking.

I was awoken from my reverie by the other two. They stamped up and down the room, banging the furniture and shouting. I must say all this struck me as a bit suspicious—for one of them was normally very reticent and in any case was not personally affected by this development, while the other was invariably calm and self-possessed. I could not see any reason for all this fuss and came to the conclusion that it was all put on for my benefit. They said that the declaration had been drawn, signed, and sent to the *Parlement*, and the fact that nothing could be done was what made them so mad. I was angry too, but I must say that all this carry-on made me laugh. And as any argument was obviously useless, I took my leave and got back to Marly as quickly as I could.

By the time I got there it was nearly supper-time. I went straight into the salon, where I found everyone standing around in gloomy silence—drawing off into knots and whispering. I saw the King sit down to supper, and he seemed to be looking round about him in an even haughtier way than usual. It was less than an hour since the announcement had been made and everyone was still on the defensive, not knowing what to say. As soon as the King had sat down I left and went to Monsieur du Maine's apartments. Once something is a *fait accompli* and there is nothing to be done about it, a situation becomes much easier—although I had refused to acknowledge the intermediate step which had been granted to the Bastards, I had made up my mind what I would do in this case. As soon as my name was announced to the Duc du Maine, the doors were opened and, in spite of his lameness, he seemed to be borne on wings towards me. I said that I came to offer him my congratulations in all sincerity. I told him that we did not pretend to be on a par with the Princes of the Blood, and all we wanted was our proper due which was that no one should come between us and the Princes. So now that he, his brother, and his sons were really Princes of the Blood, we could all rejoice at the disappearance of that half-way status which we had all resented. The Duc du Maine's delight at being thus congratulated was quite indescribable.

A DAY IN THE KING'S LIFE

I MUST describe the daily routine in the life of Louis XIV as I saw it during the twenty-two years that I was at court.

At eight o'clock every morning the King was awoken by his First *Valet-de-Chambre*, who slept in the room with him. At the same time the First Physician and First Surgeon were admitted; and as long as she lived the King's former wet-nurse also came in and would kiss him. He would then be rubbed down, because he perspired a great

deal. At a quarter past eight the Great Chamberlain was admitted, together with those members of the court who had the *grandes entrées*.
The Great Chamberlain then opened the curtains round the bed,
which had been drawn again, and offered him holy water from a stoup
at the head of the bed. This was the chance for any courtier who wished
to ask a favour or speak to the King, and if one did so the others withdrew to a distance.

The Chamberlain then handed the King the book of the Office
of the Holy Ghost, and having done so retired to the next room with
everyone else. The King said the Office, which is very short, and then,
putting on his dressing-gown, summoned them back into the room;
meanwhile the second *entrée* was admitted and, a few minutes later,
the body of the court. By the time they came in the King was getting
into his breeches (for he put on nearly all his clothes himself), which
he accomplished with considerable grace. He was shaved every other
day, with the court watching; while it was being done he wore a short
wig, without which he never allowed himself to be seen—he even
wore it in bed when he was being dosed. While his barber was at work
he sometimes talked to those around him, about hunting or some
other light topic. He had no dressing-table at hand, only a servant
who held up a glass for him.

When he had finished dressing he knelt down at the side of his
bed and said his prayers; all clergy present knelt as well, but the others
remained standing. Next the King went into his study, followed by
those permitted to do so—which, as a number of appointments carried this privilege, amounted to quite a gathering. He then announced
his appointments for the day, so that everyone knew what he would
be doing every quarter of an hour. Then the room was cleared of
everyone except the Bastards and their former tutors Montchevreuil
and d'O, Mansard or his successor d'Antin, and the private servants—
all of whom had come up the back stairs without passing through the
bedroom. This was the time when they had a chance of talking
privately with the King; it was also the time when the King liked to
talk over the plans and progress of any work being done on his
buildings and gardens, and the interview was long or short according
to how much there was to discuss.

While these interviews were in progress the courtiers waited in
the Gallery until the King was ready to go to Mass, at which the choir
always sang a motet. The Ministers were told as soon as he had gone
to the chapel, and they then gathered in the King's study, where important persons could take the opportunity of having a word with
them. As soon as Mass was over the Council met, and that was the

last engagement for the morning. One or other of the Councils met every day except Thursdays and Fridays—Thursday was kept free, and the few private audiences which the King very occasionally granted took place then; on Friday he used to make his confession, and his confessor would often stay with him until dinner-time. Dinner was at one, but on the days when there was no Council it would be earlier if the King wanted to go hunting; if a Council sat late, dinner was kept back without the King being reminded of the time.

Dinner was always *au petit couvert*—that is to say, the King ate alone in his bedroom; a small square table was put by the middle window. The meal was substantial whether he had ordered *petit couvert* or *très-petit couvert*, for even the latter consisted of three courses, each made up of several different dishes. As soon as the table was brought in the principal courtiers entered and the First Gentleman of the Bed-chamber went to inform the King that his dinner was served. Occasionally I have seen Monseigneur and his sons standing throughout dinner without the King asking them to be seated, though it did not often happen. The Princes of the Blood and the Cardinals always stood. Monsieur often attended, and when present always handed the King his napkin and then remained standing. If the King saw that he intended to remain, he would ask him if he wished to be seated: Monsieur would bow, and the King would order a seat to be brought. After a few minutes the King would say, 'Brother, pray be seated'; Monsieur would then bow again and sit down. He would remain seated until the end of the meal, when he would again hand the King his napkin.

Sometimes if Monsieur had come over specially from Saint-Cloud, the King would ask him if he would care to dine. If Monsieur said 'Yes,' the King would order a place to be laid opposite, and Monsieur was served in exactly the same way. Monsieur was always very chatty when he dined with the King, whereas the King himself used hardly to say a word unless one of his favourites was present. Dinner was very seldom *au grand couvert* except on the principal feast-days, and occasionally at Fontainebleau if the Queen of England was there. No lady was ever allowed to be present at the *petit couvert*, except occasionally the Maréchale de la Mothe who had retained the privilege from the days when she used to be royal governess.

As soon as he had finished his dinner the King rose from the table and went into his study, where he spent some time feeding his pointers and playing with them. Then he changed, and while he did so a few privileged persons were allowed to be present, at the discretion of the First Gentleman of the Bedchamber; after which he went down to

the Marble Court by his own private staircase. Between the foot of
the stairs and his carriage, which was waiting, anyone was at liberty
to speak to him—and the same in reverse on his return. He liked
fresh air, and if he could not get it he suffered from headaches and
vapours, which had originally been caused by too much perfume—
with the consequence that for years he had not cared for anything
except orange water, and anyone who was going to approach him
had to be very careful about this.

He felt neither heat nor cold, and wet weather affected him very
little—it had to be very bad indeed to stop him from going out. At
least once a week, and more if he were at Marly or Fontainebleau,
he went stag-hunting. Once or twice a week he shot his own coverts,
usually choosing Sundays or feast-days when there were no works
for him to inspect; he was a first-class shot. Most other days he would
walk round having a look at whatever building was in progress.
Occasionally he would take ladies out and have a picnic in the forests
of Marly or Fontainebleau. No one went on his walks with him except
the holders of the most important positions. But when he strolled
round the garden at Versailles any courtier was at liberty to go with
him; the same applied to the gardens of the Trianon if he was staying
there, but if he merely went over for the day from Versailles it was not
permitted for the court to accompany him. At Marly the guests whom
he had asked might go for a walk or leave him alone, just as they
chose. In the gardens at Versailles he was the only person to wear a
hat; but at Marly there was a special privilege—when the King said
'Gentlemen, your hats,' they all put them on, and woe betide anyone
who did not do so smartly.

The privilege of riding to the King's stag-hounds was fairly wide-
spread—at Fontainebleau anyone who wished could go, elsewhere
only those who had the *justaucorps-à-brevet*. The King liked to see a
good field, but too many people bothered him and he thought that
they spoiled the sport. He appreciated people who liked hunting, but
he thought it silly for anyone to ride to hounds who did not really
enjoy it, and he never minded if anyone begged to be excused. It was
the same with cards: he liked to see high play kept going the whole
time at Marly, but there was no obligation on anyone to take part.
On wet days at Fontainebleau he liked to watch a good tennis match,
a game at which he had been very good when he was young.

If there was no Council he often went over to Marly or Trianon
for dinner with the Duchesse de Bourgogne, Madame de Maintenon,
and other ladies. After dinner one of the Ministers usually came in
with some work, and when that was done he would pass the rest of a

summer afternoon strolling with the ladies or playing cards. Sometimes he would get up a lottery in which there were no blanks, and every ticket drew a prize of plate, jewellery, or a dress length of rich material, which was a delicate way of making presents to the ladies about him. Madame de Maintenon drew a ticket like the others, but usually gave away her prize.

The King's supper was served, always *au grand couvert*, at ten o'clock, and the entire Royal Family sat down with him.[1] The meal was attended by a large number of people, both those who were entitled to be seated and those who were not. Forty-eight hours before the King went to Marly any lady who wished might attend the supper and this was regarded as presenting herself for Marly. The men presented themselves in the morning by going up to the King and simply saying 'Sir, Marly,' but towards the end of his life this fussed the King and there was a page stationed in the Gallery who took the names of those who wished to go. But the ladies continued to present themselves to the end of his life.

After supper the King would stand by the balustrade at the foot of his bed for a few minutes, with the whole court about him; then he would bow to the ladies and retire into his study, where he played for an hour or so with his children and grandchildren, both legitimate and illegitimate. He would sit in one arm-chair and Monsieur in another, for in private they were just two brothers. Monseigneur always remained standing with all the other Princes; the Princesses sat on footstools. The *Dames d'Honneur* to the Princesses used to wait in the Council chamber, next to the King's own study. But at Fontainebleau there was only one big room, so these ladies were permitted to sit in the same circle with the Princesses, and the other ladies stood behind or could, if they wished, sit on the floor.

Before he retired to bed the King went to feed his dogs; then he said good-night and, going into his room, knelt down at his bedside to say his prayers. After he had undressed he would bow, which meant 'Good-night,' and at that sign all the court retired. As they filed out he, standing by the fire-place, gave the password to the Captain of the Guard. This was the *grand coucher*; it was followed by the *petit coucher*, a short ceremony for which only those who had the *grande entrée* were allowed to stay. It was the last opportunity for the day of speaking to the King, and if anyone stepped forward the others withdrew at once and left him alone with the King.

[1] A frequent complaint was that the King was late and the meal often did not start till eleven-thirty.

166

The King invariably wore some shade of brown, and his coat had little embroidery; sometimes there were black velvet trimmings, but often the only decoration was gold buttons. He never wore rings, and the only precious stones about his person were on his shoe-buckles and his garters. His hat was edged with Spanish lace and had a white plume. Normally he wore his ribbon under his coat, but at weddings and similar festivities he wore it outside; it was very long and richly adorned with precious stones.

At least once a month the King took medicine; on those days he heard Mass in bed. After that Madame de Maintenon, the Duc du Maine, and the Comte de Toulouse came in to amuse him. Madame de Maintenon sat on an arm-chair by the head of the bed, and the Duke, who was lame, sat on a tabouret—and he always used to go out of his way to be as amusing as he could. The King stayed in bed for dinner until about three in the afternoon, then got up, and the rest of the day was normal.

1714

THE KING MAKES HIS WILL

✤✤✤✤✤T this time the King made his will, with the most extraordinary provisions for its safeguarding and for keeping its
contents secret. Old age was beginning to tell on him; so far
he had not changed his way of life, but those who saw him
in private were worried about him. His health, which had been excellent all his life, was beginning to break down under the burden
of his troubles. After years of victory and triumph he had been suddenly overwhelmed by an unending succession of appalling disasters,
together with domestic difficulties. All his family except the little
Dauphin had gone—leaving him the victim of the most gloomy reflections, for he expected to go the same way himself at any moment.
Madame de Maintenon, the Duc du Maine, helped by Fagon, Bloin,
and the main servants of the household, did all they could to foster
these ideas in the King's head—which was not difficult because everyone believed that the recent deaths had all been the result of poison.
Even Maréchal really thought the same, though to spare the King
worry he always said that he did not agree.

The Duc du Maine could not afford to give the King any rest, for
he had made up his mind to supplant the only Prince who had reached
his majority—the Duc d'Orléans. In this ambition he was abetted by
Madame de Maintenon, partly because he was the person she loved
best in the world and partly because she loathed the Duke. They
therefore continued sedulously to foster the horrible suspicions which
had become directed against the Duke, and the King's feelings can be
imagined when daily he had to see the alleged perpetrator of such
ghastly crimes eating at his own table and even at times receive him
alone in his study.

Nothing could fill the void in the King's life left by the death of
the Duchess who had not only been the life and soul of the court, but
had been the object of his entire affections and the only person with
whom he had ever been entirely at ease. He leaned more and more
on Madame de Maintenon and the Duc du Maine, whom he had come
to believe had a good head for business; interested persons, too, had
persuaded the King that the Duke was a simple soul, devoid of ambition, devoted to the King and his own family. All this pleased the
King who became more and more fond of this son and amused by his

stories—for I never met anyone who could tell a story so well. Yet no one could do more damage more subtly; he was a brilliant mimic and could cruelly hit off people's ridiculous ways to perfection—what is more, he was clever enough to know just when, without his motive being noticed, his words would drop on fertile ground to best advantage. When we think of what we know about him already, it is impossible not to feel horror at such a snake enjoying the King's most intimate confidence.

Madame de Maintenon and the Duc du Maine had to work fast while the King remained in his present state of mind. If they did not intend actually to place the crown on the Duke's head (and I don't doubt for a moment that is what they had in mind), they were determined at any rate to make him so strong that the Regent would be forced to treat him as a power to be reckoned with. No one could dispute the Duc d'Orléans's right to the Regency, but the infamous rumours about him had been so widely spread and believed that his position was seriously undermined. He was regarded with suspicion in the provinces, and at court no one would be seen speaking to him. There was nothing that the Duke could do to clear himself, for he could not approach the King, whose mind was being steadily and constantly poisoned against him.

This was the Duc du Maine's chance and he was quick to take it. With Madame de Maintenon he put his plan into execution, which was to get the King to sign a will drawn up by themselves which would secure to the Duke the position he desired. He knew perfectly well what happened to such wills as a rule, but in this case he hoped that the prestige of the testator was so great that no one would dare to set the terms aside. He hoped that the King would, for the safety of the child who would succeed him as well as for the welfare of the nation, consider it wise to circumscribe as far as possible the powers of the Regent, who since the renunciation of the Spanish branch[1] had but this one little boy between himself and the throne. He hoped also that the power shorn from the Duc d'Orléans would be transferred to the Bastards, and that he himself would be appointed sole guardian of the young King. The Duc du Maine imagined that these arrangements, so insulting to the Duc d'Orléans, would be generally well received, would confirm the sinister rumours about the poisoning, and would make him as the royal guardian idol of the country. As if that were not enough, he planned that the Regent should be such

[1] The son of Monseigneur on becoming Philip V of Spain in 1700 renounced all rights to the French throne.

in name only and that the actual government should be in the hands of a Regency Council the members of which should be nominated in the will—handpicked, of course, to ensure that he and his brother would always enjoy a majority. How well he selected the names became apparent when the will was opened: so long as the King lived its terms remained a secret.

But inducing the King to sign a will was but half the task before Madame de Maintenon and the Duc du Maine: they had to ensure the safe keeping of the document, and to so involve the *Parlement* of Paris that they and the bench throughout the country would feel bound to make themselves responsible for its proper execution. They began their campaign through Voysin,[1] the new Chancellor and Secretary of State, who dropped hints on every available occasion, while they were pleasant to the King, flattered him, amused him, and admired him.

But when Voysin seemed to be making little progress they changed their tactics. They became sad, serious, and silent; they never began a conversation, and if the King said anything they answered as shortly as possible and let the matter drop; sometimes they took no notice at all when he spoke, unless he put a direct question to them. The few ladies who were admitted took their cue from Madame de Maintenon, and if she did not speak, they dared not. Soon in the King's private rooms the only person who ever said anything was the Comte de Toulouse, who was not in the plot; no one would have described him as a scintillating conversationalist and he told endless stories about shooting and his gardens at Rambouillet. Anyone else who opened his mouth soon shut it again when he found that the Duc du Maine did not pick the subject up as he always had been wont to do. Maréchal and other medical advisers watched astonished, and became more and more worried about the King: they saw that he was unhappy and bored, and they feared that if things went on much longer in the same way his health would be affected.

No one knew what happened, but everything suddenly changed and all of a sudden Madame de Maintenon and the Duke could not do enough to make up to the King for their previous sulking. But some light was soon thrown on it. The King had already addressed words to the Duc du Maine which showed that the concession which

---

[1] Daniel-François Voysin (1655–1717). Rose to the position of Secretary of State for War in 1709, and Chancellor and Keeper of the Seals in 1714. It was he who revealed the contents of the King's will to the Duc d'Orléans who, as a reward, confirmed him in his office as Keeper of the Seals until his death.

Inside, the King lies dying

enabled a Bastard to be considered as in line for the throne had only
been extorted from him under pressure. Generally the King showed
the very greatest self-restraint and never betrayed his feelings, but he
could not keep from returning a second time to the subject of the will.
When he was in his private room with the two Bastards and d'Antin
and d'O a few days before any announcement was made, he suddenly
rounded on the Duc du Maine and in a bitter tone said: 'It is all your
doing. But don't you ever forget this: however great I may make you
during my lifetime, after I am gone I can do nothing for you. Then
it will be up to you to hold on to your new position—if you can!'
Everyone present was astonished at this outburst, because nothing
said previously had led up to it and it was so unlike the King's usual
attitude. It was a startling revelation of the secret ambitions which the
Duke was harbouring—the King seemed to be charging the Bastard
with riding roughshod and himself with weakness in yielding to such
treatment. The Duc du Maine looked overcome and everyone else
stood silent, their eyes downcast. Not until the King went off into
his dressing-room did anyone dare to breathe. This was the first clue
to the solution of the problem which had defeated us all: two days
later the mystery was unravelled.

It was at Versailles on Sunday, 2 August. Mesmes and Daguesseau,
First President and *Procureur-Général,* had been summoned to the
presence and went into the royal study immediately after the *lever*. As
soon as they were alone, the King unlocked a drawer in his desk and
took out a packet sealed with seven seals; handing it to them, he said:
'Gentlemen, this is my will; its contents are unknown to anyone but
myself. I hand it to you in order that it may be placed in the custody
of the *Parlement* of Paris, and it would not be possible for me to give
a greater sign of my esteem than entrusting the safe keeping of this
document to them. The fate of my father's will and of those of his
predecessors hardly fills me with confidence as to the ultimate fate
of this one; but be that as it may, people have been at me to make one,
so I have done it. I have been given no peace until I signed it. Now
perhaps I shall be left alone for a little. Here it is—take it away.
Whatever may come of it in the end, at least I have earned a little
peace and quiet.' With that he gave them a curt nod and walked out
of the room.

On the following day the Queen of England came over from
Chaillot to see Madame de Maintenon. While she was there the King
came in; he was obviously still boiling, and as soon as he saw her he
burst out: 'Madame, I have made my will. I have been badgered into
it, and I hope now that I have signed the thing that I shall be left in

peace. But I know just how little it is worth. While we are alive we can do as we please, but we are worse off than an ordinary citizen so far as making arrangements for the future is concerned—just look at what happened to my father's will and those of any other Kings you care to think of. I know all that, but they worked on me until I made the thing. Well, now it's done; I could not care less what happens to it, but at least I may get a little peace for a change.'

As he spoke he looked straight at Madame de Maintenon. He spoke with such bitterness that it showed what a terrible struggle he had been through before he had given in from sheer exhaustion. What he said was so remarkable that I was at some pains to check his exact words: his remarks to the First President were repeated to me by the First President himself some time afterwards, while the Queen of England told her part of the story immediately to her great friend the Duchesse de Lauzun. From the King's abrupt manner, his unusual quietness, and his haughty tone when he did say anything, it took him at least a week to get over the ordeal he had been through. It is certain that there were some very ugly scenes, but Madame de Maintenon and the Duc du Maine had got what they wanted, so they could afford to put up with a lot of bad temper in return—feeling that if they were unfailingly pleasant the King would be only too pleased eventually to sink back into the restful peace that he had bought so dearly.

1715

THE BEGINNING OF THE END

HE King's health was breaking up visibly, and his appetite, which had always been so good, was falling off. Up till now he kept to his usual routine without variation, but the small symptoms which could be noticed were not missed by those at court, and foreign countries were equally interested and well informed. In England bets were laid as to whether he would still be alive by 1 September—that is, in three months' time; and although the King liked to be told everything that was going on, it can well be imagined that no one was particularly anxious to relay these titbits from London to him.

He usually had the Dutch papers read to him by Torcy after the Council of State. Torcy never had time to run over them beforehand, and one day as he was reading he came on a quotation of the odds from London, hesitated, and quickly went on to something else. The King realized that he had skipped something and asked what it was; Torcy turned red and muttered that it was only some rude remarks not worth repeating. Torcy was forced to read out the odds from beginning to end. The King pretended not to mind, but he was really deeply hurt—so much so that when he sat down to dinner soon afterwards he could not refrain from talking about it, although he did not mention the newspaper. I happened to be present that day, and he looked straight at me and several others as if he expected us to say something. I lowered my eyes and held my tongue; but Cheverny, though usually so discreet, started to mumble about the same kind of rumours which he said he had heard in Vienna and Copenhagen when he had been Ambassador. The King let him wander on without paying the slightest attention, and looked as if he were much more annoyed than he cared to show. It was obvious that he was doing his best to eat and appear as if he had an appetite; but he did not swallow much of what little he put into his mouth. An A.D.C. to Lord Stair, the British Ambassador, who had just come back from England was said to have spread stories about the King's health which started the betting. Lord Stair was furious and had the A.D.C. sent home.

FOR more than a year the King's health had been declining; Fagon, his First Physician, was himself getting so old that he was the only person who did not notice it. Maréchal, the First Surgeon, spoke to Fagon about it but was rebuffed; at last he ventured to broach the subject with Madame de Maintenon. He told her that, after feeling the King's pulse, he was sure that the trouble was a slow fever, and that if the illness were allowed to go on unchecked the consequence would be serious. Madame de Maintenon lost her temper and said that Fagon was too experienced to make a mistake, so all Maréchal got for his pains was a snub.

The King used to suffer from terrible attacks of gout, and for these Fagon would bury him at night between feather mattresses which made him perspire so violently that in the morning he had to be rubbed down before the Great Chamberlain and the Gentlemen of the Bedchamber could be admitted. Instead of the finest champagne which at one time had been the only wine he drank, he had for some years drunk nothing but Burgundy and water—and sour Burgundy at that. He used to laugh when he thought of the expressions of visiting nobles who asked to be allowed the privilege of tasting the King's own wine! He never drank his wine neat, nor did he ever have a liqueur. He never took tea, coffee, or chocolate; at his *lever*, instead of bread and wine, for some time he had been in the habit of drinking two cups of an infusion of sage and veronica, which he used to like sometimes during the day as well. Apart from that he never took anything between meals except a few pastilles of cinnamon—he used to put a handful of them into his pocket at dessert, together with a few biscuits for his pointers.

During the last year of his life he became more and more costive, and Fagon made him eat a great deal of iced overripe fruit at the beginning of his meals. For dessert he ate a lot more fruit, with a mass of sweetmeats. He ate salads all the year round. He liked very strong soups, and they, like all the dishes set before him, contained twice as much seasoning as anyone else would have cared for. These spices and the sweetmeats were strictly against Fagon's orders, and an expression of acute pain used to pass over the doctor's face when he saw what the King was eating.

In the end so much fruit and soup spoiled his appetite and damaged his digestion. I have heard him say that he had never been hungry in his life; and even when his dinner was unavoidably delayed he never missed it until the first mouthful of soup, when he felt his appetite

revive. Indeed he always ate so enormously both at midday and in the
evening that people who watched him were amazed.[1] So much water
and fruit, without any spirits to settle it, was bad for his blood; and
this, with the debility induced by his constant perspirations at night,
killed him. For when a post-mortem was performed they could find
nothing wrong, and there was no reason why he should not have
lived to be a hundred.

On Wednesday, 21 July, the King was seen by four doctors, who
after their consultation said nothing except to agree with Fagon, who
had prescribed cassia. For some days he had been unable to eat meat
and hardly even any bread; he had never eaten much bread, and for
years had had the crusts cut off because he had no teeth left. To make
up, he was given more soup, minced meat, and eggs; but his appetite
was very small. Next day he was worse. Four doctors more were summoned, but again they merely confirmed Fagon's treatment, which
was now quinine and asses' milk last thing at night.

By now everyone realized that the King was dying. In consequence
the apartments of the Duc d'Orléans were as crowded as previously
they had been deserted. Things went on thus until late August. On
the 22nd the King at his *coucher* told the Duc de la Rochefoucauld to
bring him in the morning a selection of coats for him to choose from,
for the mourning for the son of the Duchesse de Lorraine was just
ended. He could no longer walk; he had not been dressed for some
time, and had only got out of bed to have supper in his dressing-gown.
He could swallow no solids. Doctors slept in his room every night.
But he must have thought that there was a chance he might recover,
or he would not have bothered to wish to choose a coat which he
would never wear. He kept up his Councils, all State business, and his
amusements. Men are unwilling to die, and so long as it is possible
they will always shut their eyes to the inevitable.

The King was now completely confined to his rooms. During the
day the whole Court assembled in the Gallery outside. The antechamber immediately outside the bedroom was kept free except for a
few personal servants and several medical assistants who were ready
to heat up any potions or medicines that might be required. Those
who had the *entrée* came into the private rooms from the long gallery
by a glass-covered door, which was opened only when they scratched,[2]

---

[1] A specimen meal was four plates of different kinds of soups, a whole pheasant, a
partridge, a large salad, two huge slices of ham, a plate of seasoned mutton, pastry, fruit,
and hard-boiled eggs of which he was very fond.

[2] One did not knock on the royal door, but scratched with one's fingernails very quietly,
whereupon whoever was charged with the task would open the door and close it again.

and then quickly shut again. Secretaries of State and Ministers came in that way and waited in the room by the Gallery, with the Princes of the Blood and the King's daughters, until he asked for one of them, which seldom happened.

On Saturday, the 24th, the King passed a bad night—not really much worse than usual, for he never slept well. His leg was considerably worse, and very painful. He heard Mass as usual, and dined in bed in the presence of the most important members of the court. Then there was a meeting of the Finance Council, after which he discussed business with the Chancellor. He had supper standing up in his dressing-gown, and this was the last time when courtiers were present. I noticed that he could not swallow any solids, and he seemed to dislike being watched; he could not finish, and he finally asked the courtiers to leave the room. He was then put back to bed, and when his leg was examined it was found to be covered with black blotches. He sent for Father Tellier and made his confession.

On the 25th, the Feast of St. Louis, he was much worse, and no one tried any longer to conceal that he was in serious danger. For all that, he insisted that the ceremonies customary on that day should be observed—that the drums and hautboys should play beneath his window as soon as he awoke, and the band of twenty-four violins should play in the next room during dinner. After dinner there was no one in the room except the Chancellor and Madame de Maintenon, and either then or the previous day he must have signed the codicil to his will. The Duc du Maine, who thought of no one but himself, considered that the King had not done enough for him and determined to get what more he wanted added in a codicil. It shows with what complete cynicism he and Madame de Maintenon worked on the dying King. By this codicil the King put his household, civil and military, at the disposal of the Duc du Maine immediately after his death. The Maréchal de Villeroy was put under his orders and they would thus be virtually masters of the young King. With two Regiments of Guards and two Companies of Musketeers at their disposal they would control Paris. The Regent would hardly have any authority; he could even be arrested at any moment if it pleased the Duke.

After the Chancellor had left, Madame de Maintenon sent for her ladies and at about seven the gang arrived. While the ladies were talking, the King dropped off to sleep; when he awoke his mind was wandering. His doctors were sent for, and his pulse was found to be so bad that they advised him to receive the last Sacrament at once, for he had returned momentarily to lucidity. Father Tellier heard the King's confession, while the Cardinal de Rohan went to the Chapel to fetch the Host. The ceremony lasted about fifteen minutes. After that the dozen or more people who had been present went out, and— what a time for such things!—a writing-desk was placed across the bed and the Chancellor presented the codicil; after adding a few lines, the King signed it and handed it back. He then talked privately with the Maréchal de Villeroy. After which he received the Duc d'Orléans and talked rather longer; he spoke kindly, but it is terrible to have to report that, within a few minutes of the Sacrament having passed his lips, he could bring himself to assure the Duke that he would find nothing unsatisfactory in the will; finally he commended the State and the young King to his care. Next the Duc du Maine was called in, and was joined by the Comte de Toulouse. As the doctors then wished to dress the King's leg, everyone left the room except Madame de Maintenon and the necessary attendants. While this was going on the Chancellor showed the codicil to the Duc d'Orléans. When the doctors had finished, the King heard that his daughters were in the next room, so he called them in; after a while they were weeping, so he asked them to leave as he wished to rest.

The next day he sent word to Madame de Ventadour to bring in the Dauphin. The little boy was lifted on to the bed and the King said: 'My child, you are about to become a great King. I have been too fond of building: try not to fall into the same mistake. And I have been too fond of war: try to live at peace with your neighbours. Render unto God that which is God's: remember what He has done for you, and see that your subjects do Him honour. Try to take some of the burdens off your people, which unhappily I have failed to do. Remember how much you owe to Madame de Ventadour.' Then to her he said: 'Madame, I should like to embrace you,' and, doing so, he said: 'My dear, I bless you with all my heart.' They lifted the child down then, but the King asked for him to be brought back again: he kissed him once more and blessed him for the last time. Then the Dauphin was led away to his own apartments.

During the 27th very few people were admitted. In the evening the King remarked to Madame de Maintenon that he had always been told it was difficult to compose one's mind for death, but that he did not find it so. She said that it must be hard for a man of worldly attainments, with hatred in his heart, or owing anything to anyone. 'Ah,' said the King, 'as a private individual I owe nothing to any man; if I owe anything to my Kingdom, I throw myself on the mercy of God.' He passed a very bad night, and he was seen to clasp his hands repeatedly as he said his prayers. The next morning he said something to Madame de Maintenon which was meant kindly but which she did not care for at all. He said that he was sorry to leave her but, at her age, he could expect to see her again soon. Not long after that Madame de Maintenon left the King's room with her veil down; she descended the great staircase. At the foot she stopped, raised her veil, and kissed the Maréchal de Villeroy who had escorted her. With dry eyes she said 'Good-bye, Marshal,' then she got into one of the King's carriages and drove to Saint-Cyr.

The King rallied during the 29th, but by the evening he had again relapsed. Late at night his leg was examined—it was mortified up to the knee and the thigh was very swollen; he fainted while the doctors were at work on it. He missed Madame de Maintenon and asked for her frequently; finally he was told that she had gone to Saint-Cyr (whence she had not intended to return) and he sent for her. All Friday, the 30th, he was half asleep and delirious; during his few lucid moments his mind turned to religion. On Saturday he was unconscious nearly all day, and mortification had spread up into the thigh. Late at night he was so bad that the prayers for the dying were said; the preparations penetrated to his fading mind, and he said the responses so loudly that he could be heard above all the priests. He recognized the Cardinal de Rohan and said, 'This is the last favour that the Church can do me,' and that was the last time that he spoke to anyone. Several times he was heard repeating '*Nunc, et in hora mortis.*' Then he said, 'Help, O God, help me quickly!' Those were his last words. He was unconscious throughout the night. At a quarter to eight on Sunday, 1 September 1715, he passed away—three days before the completion of his seventy-seventh year and in the seventy-second of his reign. No French monarch ever attained to so great an age, nor has Europe ever known so long a reign.

THE KING'S WILL

THE King's death found the Duc d'Orléans quite unprepared, as if it were completely unexpected. Since we had last talked things over he had apparently given no further thought to what he was going to do, nor to the appointments which he would have to make. In consequence, as I had predicted, he found himself so bogged down in detail that he had no time left for matters of real importance.

I was told of the King's death as soon as I woke up. I dressed and went at once to pay my respects to the new King. The crowd had gone by then and I was almost alone. Thence I went to the Duc d'Orléans's apartments, which were packed. I asked him to come with me into his

private study and I made one further effort to persuade him to summon the States-General, but with no avail. Then I reminded him of
the promise which he had given to myself and about a dozen peers
that he would acquiesce in our remaining covered when voting in the
Parlement, and he repeated it. I further reminded him of the decision
he had made about the King's funeral—that in order to keep down
expense and avoid the inevitable quarrels over a full-scale ceremony,
the precedent set at the death of Louis XIII should be followed and
everything be as simple as possible. In fact this was done, and no one
loved the old King enough to question it.

I next went to the apartments of the Duc de la Trémouille,[1] where
we had agreed to meet as soon as possible after the old King's death.
A number of the Dukes were already there. The Archbishop of
Reims,[2] the senior of the peers deputed to wait upon the Duc d'Orléans about the affair of the hat, reported the promise which he had
received, and I also said that it had again been repeated to me. We
agreed to stick together, and then parted.

At dinner time I went to see the Duc d'Orléans again, and found
him now free. He admitted that he had not drawn up a list of appointments, and in fact had given very little thought to the future. There
was no point in reproaching him; I just shrugged my shoulders and
asked him to be careful of those who would come to ask favours of
him, particularly the Ministers. I then turned to the question of the
will and its codicil; what, I asked him, did he intend to do at the next
day's meeting of the Paris *Parlement* when these documents would be
tabled. He was always full of fire and blood in his private study, but
unfortunately his resolution ended there; he made all sorts of promises, and I did my best to impress upon him how essential it was that
he should keep them. I spent nearly two hours with him.

While I was dining with friends I received a message that the Duke
would like to see me again, and asking me to bring with me some of
the Dukes who were with me. It was by now about eight in the evening. He spoke to us very plausibly, asking us not to create a precedent
at the next day's ceremony, although he himself had promised it. He
said that matters of great import to the state would have to be dealt
with, and it would be most awkward if consideration of them were
interfered with by what, after all, was a personal matter. We were as-

---

[1] Charles-Louis-Bretagne, Duc de la Trémouille et des Thouars, Prince de Tarente et
de Talmont (1683–1719), First Gentleman of the Bedchamber.

[2] François de Mailly (1658–1721), great-uncle of the three sisters who successively became the mistresses of Louis XV.

tounded by this complete *volte-face* from that very morning; we looked at one another, and said that we regretted that we could not possibly agree. The Duc d'Orléans seemed very much put out; he admitted that there was much in what we said so far as our rights were concerned over this question of the hat, and various other matters in which the *Parlement* was getting above itself; but he said that we ought to choose a more proper occasion for airing our grievances and not bring them up at a meeting when there was important public business to be discussed.

'But, Sir,' I said, 'when the public business is completed you will snap your fingers at us and our grievances. If we do not bring them up now you will put us off indefinitely and our sacrifices will have been in vain.'

He then gave his solemn word that as soon as the affairs of state had been settled he would take up all the points at issue between the *Parlement* and ourselves and give a decision in our favour. I begged him to think carefully and not to promise more than he could perform, because we would assuredly hold him to his word. He repeated his promise, but asked us not to introduce extraneous matters into the next day's business.

Those who had come with me were not at all pleased; but they were frightened; they grumbled, but not one of them dared to speak up. They had been accustomed to servitude so long that the shadow of the old King still lay heavy upon them and they did not dare oppose the Prince who now stood in his place. There was a good deal of muttering, but as we did not seem to be getting anywhere I took it upon myself to speak again. I pointed out that it would be very difficult to contact all the Peers who had met that morning, and practically impossible to convince them of his decision to settle the dispute in our favour. I suggested therefore that he should agree to one of our number rising at the beginning of the meeting to say that we protested against the encroachment of the *Parlement* upon our privileges, in the matter of the hat amongst others, but as we had no desire to hinder the course of public business we would waive the subject on this occasion, relying on his promise to settle the matter in our favour at the first opportunity. I asked him also to allow the Speaker to ask for confirmation of this promise and that he should then publicly repeat it.

The Duc d'Orléans was considerably relieved at this; he agreed at once and asked that I should be the spokesman, assuring us once again that he would settle everything in our favour as soon as his regency was firmly on its feet. I said I thought that the Archbishop of Reims as senior Peer should speak, particularly as I was afraid of saying too much once I started. But they all wanted me to undertake the task, and the Archbishop added that he thought that I would do it much better than he—the usual answer when people want to get out of doing something unpleasant. The Duke said that he did not mind how strongly I spoke. So it was settled, by no means to our satisfaction.

We all met the following morning between five and six o'clock at the house of the Archbishop by the Pont Royal; there was a good deal of dissatisfaction, but after I had pointed out the difficult position in which the Duc d'Orléans was placed, they seemed placated and soon after seven we got into our coaches and drove in procession to the *Parlement*. We found it already assembled. The Duc de la Rochefoucauld, the Duc d'Harcourt and two or three other Peers were already there; they had sent a message to the Archbishop to say that they would agree to any decision reached at the meeting, but unfortunately they would not be able to be present because they had to attend the reception of the Duc de la Rochefoucauld. He had refused to take his seat because he was furious at the King's decision to give me precedence over him, but he did not want to miss this meeting so he had been received that morning. I was told that the First President had suggested that the Duke should protest against the King's decision and that the *Parlement* would back him. But the Duke very properly replied that the King's decision was final and that he had no intention of appealing against it. The First President was rather set back by this; he was only trying to sow discord among us, but the Duc de la Rochefoucauld saw the trap and would have no part of it. As soon as I came in he made room for me above him, and I was half inclined to say something about what had happened; but on second thoughts I decided to give him a bit more time to get over his irritation, for he was a surly fellow and might not have appreciated my compliments.

We had been in our places about a quarter of an hour when the Bastards arrived. The Duc du Maine was absolutely bursting with pleasure—strange words perhaps, but the only way to describe him. Beneath his air of cheerful satisfaction there was evident confidence which out of politeness he tried not to show. He advanced several paces and bowed low to the First President, who returned his salutation with an equal air of pleasure. He then bowed three times to the Peers, and I noticed that the bows returned were on all sides stiff and very formal. His brother was calm and at his ease as usual. In a moment Monsieur le Duc came in, followed by the Duc d'Orléans. As soon as everyone had settled down, I saw that the First President was about to speak, so I held up my hand, uncovered and covered again, and addressed the assembly.

I said that I had been requested by the Peers to make it plain that, since there was urgent business on the agenda, they were prepared on this occasion to tolerate the *Parlement*'s unseemly innovations over the hat and other matters in order that their private grievances should not hold up affairs of State; but, I said, I was directed in their name to protest formally against all such infringements of their rights. I further declared that in abstaining from bringing up the subject of our rights, we did so confident in the solemn promise made to us by the Duc d'Orléans that he would decide these questions as soon as public affairs allowed, and, I added, he had given me permission to say this and I now—raising my hat—formally called upon him to repeat his promise. A profound silence prevailed while I was speaking, which showed how surprised everyone was. The Duc d'Orléans raised his hat and looked rather embarrassed as in a low voice he confirmed what I had said.

A brief silence followed, then the First President ordered the late King's will and codicil to be brought in.

The public was supposed to be excluded but the Great Chamber was nevertheless crowded with interested spectators of all classes. The Duc d'Orléans had persuaded himself that in case of necessity he could rely on support from England, so *he had had a place* kept for Lord Stair.[1] A rather more immediate form of help was provided by a regiment of Guards which picketted all the approaches, and picked officers and men were stationed throughout the building. The Duc de Guiche, who had resigned his dukedom to his son, was standing in an alcove. He had always said that he supported the Bastards during the late King's lifetime, but they were soon to find that they could not count on him, for the Duc d'Orléans had bought him over with a promise of 600,000 livres; he was the only beneficiary from this bargain because, although the proceedings were not entirely without incident, there was never any risk of disorder.

The deputation returned bearing the King's will and codicil; these were handed to the First President who presented them to the Duc d'Orléans. The Duke then passed them down the bench of *Présidents-à-Mortier* to Dreux, one of the Counsellors, saying that he had a good voice and was well placed so that everyone could hear him.

---

[1] John Dalrymple, Earl Stair (1673–1747). Fought with distinction under William III and Marlborough. Was sent as Ambassador to France in 1715 and became a close associate of the Duc d'Orléans. In 1743 he commanded the British forces in the victory of Dettingen, at which George II was present.

The reading of the documents was listened to eagerly in complete silence; everyone fixed his eyes on Dreux. In spite of his manifest pleasure the Duc du Maine looked somewhat ill at ease, like a man facing up to an unavoidable serious operation. The Duc d'Orléans appeared unmoved. As the reading proceeded I noticed a mingled expression of astonishment and indignation on everyone's face, and when we reached the codicil a shudder went through the assembled company. The Duc du Maine noticed it, for he was watching everyone closely; he turned pale and glanced at the Duc d'Orléans.

When the reading of the will and its codicil was finished the Duc d'Orléans rose and gazed round the assembly. He began with a reference to the late King and said a few words in praise of him. Then, raising his voice, he said that he approved of what we had just heard in so far as the superintendence of the young King's education was concerned; he also approved of the arrangements for that admirable institution at Saint-Cyr. As far as the government of the country was concerned, he said that he proposed to deal separately with the will and its codicil. He said that he found the provisions difficult to reconcile with what the late King had said towards the end of his life, or with the assurance he had frequently given that the Duke would find nothing exceptionable in the will. He thought that the King could not have realized the full implications of what he had been induced to sign—looking straight at the Duc du Maine as he spoke. A Regency Council was proposed with powers so wide that no authority was left to him, and this was not only a flagrant disregard of his birthright, but a personal slight to which he could not honourably submit. He said that he had sufficient confidence in the present assembly to expect that his authority as Regent would be confirmed as it should be—that is, complete and independent. So far as the Council was concerned, he agreed that there should be one but he felt strongly that its constitution should be left entirely to him as he could not possibly discuss affairs of state with people who did not enjoy his own confidence.

His few words seemed to make a great impression. The Duc du Maine started to say something, but the Duc d'Orléans leant across Monsieur le Duc and said, 'Wait your turn, Sir!' The whole affair was quickly settled the way the Duke wanted it. The Regency Council appointed in the royal will was annulled, and the Duke was appointed Regent with full powers. He was empowered to select a new Council, which was to be no more than a consultative body with a casting vote reserved to himself. When this was decided there was such general acclaim that the Duc du Maine did not dare to open his mouth; he reserved his strength for a defence of the codicil, and, indeed, if he got his way there he would have outpointed the Duc d'Orléans.

There was a few minutes' silence. Then the Duc d'Orléans rose again. He said he was astonished that those who had suggested the provisions of the will, not content with making themselves the real rulers of the country, had seen fit to secure control of Paris, of the Court, of the King's person, and of himself. It appeared, he added, that the *Parlement* agreed with him that the terms of the will were quite incompatible with his personal honour, and furthermore contrary to every law and custom; yet the codicil went even further, threatening his liberty and even his life, and further left the young King completely in the power of those same persons who had taken advantage of a King dying in his old age, to extort concessions which he could not possibly have understood. He concluded by saying that no regency could possibly function under such conditions and he looked to the *Parlement* in its wisdom to annul a codicil which could bring nothing but trouble to the country.

There was a sympathetic silence while he was speaking. The Duc du Maine, whose colour had changed as he listened, now rose; this time the Duc d'Orléans did not stop him. He said that since he had been entrusted with the education and hence the safety of the person of the King it followed that he should have charge of the royal household, both civil and military, otherwise he could not exercise a proper responsibility for his charge. He concluded by referring to his devotion to the late King which, he said, had been so well understood that it had been reciprocated by a complete confidence.

Here the Duc d'Orléans interrupted and said that he could not accept the last statement. The Duc du Maine tried to qualify it by referring to the Maréchal de Villeroy, in whom he said the late King had also reposed his confidence. The Duc d'Orléans replied that the late King presumably placed as much confidence in himself as anyone, and he could hardly be expected to carry out his duties on suffrance from someone who happened to command the Guards and hence controlled Paris and its vicinity.

As I saw that the ensuing argument was degenerating into an unseemly wrangle, I made a sign to the Duc d'Orléans to go into the next room and have it out in private. I was chiefly motivated by the fact that the Duc du Maine was obviously getting braver, while the Duc d'Orléans was weakening his own case by even condescending to argue. The Duke was very short-sighted and did not see my signs, so after a minute or two I went over to him and said: 'If you would go into the next room, Sir, with Monsieur du Maine, I think that you could talk more easily.' And going even closer I looked at him and

184

made a sign which this time he noticed. He nodded, and I had hardly got back to my place before I saw him leave the room. Everyone rose and so I could not see if anyone went with them, but shortly afterwards the Comte de Toulouse and Monsieur le Duc went out. After a while the Duc de la Force went in to see what was going on. He returned after a short while and as he passed whispered to me, 'For God's sake, get in there. Things are going from bad to worse; the Duke's giving in. Go in and break it up; get the Duke back and ask for an adjournment until after dinner. Then get him to summon the officers of the Crown to the Palais-Royal, and round up the borderline Peers and the reliable magistrates.'

This seemed good advice, so I got up and went at once into the next room. I found the Duc d'Orléans and the Duc du Maine standing apart by the fireplace and arguing in low tones. I approached them in the correct attitude of someone who wishes to speak. The Duke turned and said: 'Well, what's the matter now?'

'I have something urgent to tell you, Sir,' I said. He went on talking, so that I had to approach a second time. He turned to hear what I had to say, but I replied: 'No, Sir, not like that; come over here,' and I took his hand and led him away from the fireplace. The Comte de Toulouse fell back to make way for us, as did the others—even the Duc du Maine. I whispered that he had nothing to gain by letting the discussion go on any longer, since the Duc du Maine could certainly not be talked into agreeing to the suppression of the codicil; the best thing he could do would be to adjourn the meeting. 'You are right,' he said, 'I'll do it.' 'But,' I said, 'for goodness' sake do it at once and don't let them freeze you with minor details. Monsieur de la Force sent me in to give you this advice.' He said no more, but went straight up to the Duc du Maine and said it was too late to talk any more, and the session would be resumed after dinner.

As the Duke was leaving the room Monsieur le Duc went up to him, and a short and apparently amicable conversation ensued. They passed close to me on their way back to the Great Chamber, and the Duke told me that Monsieur le Duc had asked for the Chairmanship of the Regency Council, since the provisions of the will were to be set aside, and he had granted the request. I think he had previously promised this position to Monsieur le Duc but had not dared to tell me.

The Duc d'Orléans then addressed the assembly, saying that he would not detain them any longer at this late hour and business would be resumed after dinner. He then said that he had appointed Monsieur le Duc Chairman of the Regency Council. He then added that since the *Parlement* had supported his claim for what was justly due to him as his birthright, he intended to lay before them his plans for governing the country, and furthermore he intended to benefit from their accumulated wisdom and would restore to them at once their ancient right of remonstrance. This last announcement was received with general applause.

I had been asked to dine that day with the Cardinal de Noailles, but I thought it so important to make good use of the break and not let the Duc d'Orléans out of my sight that I sent a note of apology and went off in my coach to the Palais Royal. A large crowd had gathered round the door, including several who had been present at the sitting. Everyone I knew asked for news and to them all I replied that everything was going according to plan, but that the business was not yet finished. I found the Duke alone with Canillac. We talked over what was to be done next and the Duke gave his instructions. Then at two o'clock we sat down to dinner—the Duke, Canillac, Conflans, his First Gentleman of the Bedchamber, and myself; I must say that, with the exception of one occasion in the Duchess's house at Bagnolet, it is the only time that I sat down to dinner with him.

It was nearly four when we got back to the *palais*; I went in a few minutes before the Duke and found everyone assembled in their places. I thought that they all gave me a curious look, and I suppose they must have known where I had been. I was careful not to give anything away by my expression. As I passed the Duc de la Force I said that his advice had been most timely, and everything was going well.

Almost immediately after, the Duc d'Orléans came in. When the assembly was settled again, he spoke and said that he had been unable to reach any agreement with the Duc du Maine and that he must therefore formally draw attention to the most extraordinary codicil which the King had been drawn into signing on his death-bed. Its provisions, he said, were far more objectionable than those of the will which the assembly had already agreed to annul. If the Duc du Maine were given control of the entire household, civil and military, he would be left master of the King's person, the Court, Paris and the whole of France. The liberty, and even the very life of the Regent would be in his hands, for he could have him arrested whenever he willed. He added that surely the assembly could not agree to the Duc du Maine occupying such a position for which there was no precedent, and relying on the wisdom and common sense of the *Parlement*, he asked for an expression of their opinion.

The Duc du Maine appeared as wretched in public as he could be formidable in the safety of a private meeting. His face, usually ruddy, was absolutely white and he looked as if he had been sentenced to death. He muttered some sort of reply which was practically unintelligible and his air was now as subservient as in the morning it had been audacious. While he was still speaking, votes were taken and the annulment of the codicil was carried with acclamation. All this was quite irregular, as the proceedings over the will had been; they were brought about in a sudden outburst of indignation. The Law Officers of the Crown should have spoken before the votes were taken, and indeed the First President had not even asked for votes—they were given spontaneously.

After two further speeches in favour of the Duc d'Orléans, the Duc du Maine, seeing himself completely defeated, tried one last expedient. He rose and said with unexpected force that if he were to be deprived of all the authority conferred upon him by the codicil, he could no longer be held responsible for the King's safety, and he therefore demanded that he be relieved of all responsibility except superintendence of the education.

'Certainly, Sir,' replied the Duc d'Orléans, 'that is perfectly reasonable.'

The First President, who was as depressed as the Duc du Maine himself, then took a formal vote which confirmed everything which had been decided. The Duc du Maine was stripped of his power, all authority was vested in the Regent who could appoint and remove members of the Council as he chose. All important public business was to be conducted by the Regency Council, with the Regent having a casting vote; Monsieur le Duc was appointed Chairman under the Duc d'Orléans. While the votes were being taken the Duc du Maine sat motionless, his eyes downcast, his face as pale as death; but his brother and his son showed no sign of interest in what was going on. When the decisions were announced there was general applause, after which the Regent addressed the assembly again. He thanked them for the confidence placed in him and said that he would endeavour to use his authority in the best interests of the country. He said that he would now like to explain the administrative changes which he proposed to make, and he put them forward with confidence because he was merely implementing the designs of the Duc de Bourgogne found among his papers after his death. He referred briefly but eloquently to the great gifts and high principle of the Duc de Bourgogne, and then said that in addition to the Regency Council he proposed to establish five other councils to deal with various departments of State affairs and that on two of them, those for ecclesiastical and home affairs, it was his intention to include members of the *Parlement* whose particular experience would be of value. The magistrates broke into loud applause, in which the public joined; the First President thanked the Regent shortly and the meeting broke up.

> Later in the same year the question of the Peers' privileges was raised again. The Duc du Maine obviously owed them nothing, and the Duc de Noailles, trying desperately to distract attention from his own shortcomings on the finance committee, stirred up trouble and drew a group around him. These dissidents persuaded the Regent to go back on his own word solemnly given and do nothing. The Peers, thus split, were powerless until Saint-Simon was able to rally them again for the attack—but it took three years to achieve his object.

1716

QUARRELS

✤✤✤✤✤ T one of the balls at the Opera there was a quarrel between
✤ 𝒜 ✤ the Duc de Richelieu and the Comte de Gacé, the Maréchal
✤ 𝒜. ✤ de Matignon's eldest son. They called one another out into
✤✤✤✤✤ the street and both were slightly wounded. Whereupon they
were both sent to the Bastille where they remained for six months and
were at home to a multitude of visitors. The Duc and Duchesse du
Maine had stirred up a great deal of ill-feeling among the nobility and
this was still rampant. In consequence these gentlemen created an
enormous disturbance because they were asked to leave their swords
when visiting the prisoners, whereas the Dukes retained theirs. To
please them, the Regent ordered an enquiry, although he knew well
enough what the answer would be—that this practice was long-established custom. The result was that they still had to take off their swords
and we still wore ours, as the Dukes were entitled to do in the Bastille
or any other prison which they chose to visit. I remember once going
to Fort-l'Évêque in the old King's time and no one asked me to leave
my sword; indeed, I would not have countenanced such a suggestion.

About the same time two young men supping with the Prince de
Conti got into a frivolous dispute. Both of them had had too much to
drink and nothing further would have come of it if their host and some
of the guests had not maliciously tried to convince them the following
day that they had quarrelled really seriously. One of them was Jonsac,
the son of d'Aubeterre, and the other Villette, the half-brother of Madame de Caylus. Monsieur le Duc, not wishing the marshals to have
to intervene in an affair which had taken place in the Prince de Conti's
house, sent for them both and persuaded them to shake hands. But
those who had made a mountain out of this particular molehill went
on so that the two families came to the conclusion they would be dishonoured if the matter was not settled by a duel. Neither of the two
principals wanted any part of it, but, having been hounded into it, they
both fought very bravely. Both were wounded, Villette seriously.
This was all brought about because the other duel, the first fought in
broad daylight under the Regency, had been dealt with so leniently.
This time the *Parlement* took action and Villette was forced to flee the
country, dying shortly afterwards. Jonsac went to ground and did not
reappear until he felt it was safe; he got off with a stiff prison sentence.

1716 This affair drew attention once again to the first duel, and as a result the two young men, Girardin and Ferrant, were obliged to flee, were tried *in absentia* and executed in effigy. But this tardy decision did little to check the fighting.

The Duc d'Orléans was very short-sighted. One of his eyes was considerably better than the other, but he had the misfortune to hit his good eye with his racquet while playing tennis, of which he was very fond. He nearly lost the sight of this eye altogether, but it was saved, although its vision was now worse than his other bad one.

The Duchesse de Berry now took advantage of the reigning confusion to assume the honours normally reserved for the Queen, although Madame de Saint-Simon warned her that she was asking for trouble. She drove through Paris, even along the Quai des Tuileries where the King was, preceded by kettle-drums. The Maréchal complained the next day to the Duc d'Orléans who promised that so long as the King remained in Paris no kettle-drums should be heard in the streets but his own. The Duchesse de Berry did not dare to do it again, although she tried one or two equally unsuccessful experiments.

After taking and discarding various lovers she had fallen head over heels in love with Rioms, a younger son of the Aidic family who had neither wit nor good looks to recommend him. He was short and thick-set, with pale, chubby cheeks so covered with pimples that his face looked like one big sore. Though he was ready for anything, he never expected to be embroiled in an affair of this nature. But it quickly became very hectic and lasted until the death of the Duchesse, apart from a few liaisons on the side. He came of a poor family, had several brothers and sisters, and was at the time a Lieutenant in a regiment of Dragoons; Madame de Pons, Lady-in-Waiting to the Duchesse de Berry, and her husband were related to him and they brought him to Court to see if they could make anything of him. The Duchess fell in love with him as soon as he arrived, and in no time he was master of the Luxembourg. His great uncle the Duc de Lauzun was delighted; it made him think of the old days of the Grande Mademoiselle, and he gave his nephew advice on managing his mistress.[1]

Rioms was quite an honest fellow, mannerly and respectful. He was well aware that his charms could scarcely have attracted anyone but a Princess of such remarkable depravity. In consequence he was unaffected and set out to make himself generally liked, except that he treat-

---

[1] The Grande Mademoiselle was Louis XIV's cousin. She and the Duc de Lauzun were lovers for many years. At one time the King gave permission for them to marry, but withdrew it. The Duke treated his exalted mistress abominably.

ed his mistress exactly as the Duc de Lauzun had treated the Grande Mademoiselle. He soon had a splendid wardrobe, his suits liberally adorned with the most costly lace; he always had plenty of money and a mass of jewelry and precious snuff boxes. He did not make things easy for the Princess. He deliberately excited her jealousy and frequently reduced her to tears. Gradually he mastered her to such a degree that she would not do the smallest thing without his permission. Sometimes when she was dressed for the opera he would make her stay at home, and sometimes force her to go when she did not want to. She had no freedom even in what she wore. It amused him to make her alter her hair style, or change all her things just when she had finished dressing. She used to ask him over night what she should wear the next day, but as often as not he had changed his mind by the morning. If she dared to do anything without his permission he went for her as if she were a servant, and sometimes she was crying for days at a time.

This Princess, who delighted to display her imperious pride, so debased herself as to dine with him in the most obscure company—she, at whose table none might be seated but the Princes of the Blood! These parties were arranged by Madame de Mouchy; she and Rioms fixed the dates and sent out the invitations. She often acted as a peacemaker between the Princess and Rioms, who indeed preferred her to his mistress. The Princess knew perfectly well what they were up to behind her back, but she dared say nothing which might deprive her of a lover she adored and a confidante who was indispensable. This way of life went on quite openly; in the Luxembourg everyone treated Rioms as the master of the house, and he was careful to be on good terms with everybody. The only person he treated like dirt was the Princess; her eyes filled with tears sometimes at the way he spoke to her, and she was loving and submissive even in public.

The Duc d'Orléans was extremely distressed over the scandal, but he could not say a word to his daughter because she vented on him all her pent-up irritation at Riom's rudeness—with interest. Sometimes when something even more scandalous than usual had happened he would venture to remonstrate; then she would go for him as though he were a coloured slave and sulk for several days until he was at his wit's end to know how to make it up. Normally father and daughter saw one another every day, generally at the Luxembourg.

I MUST now say a word about the Regent's daily life. He devoted the whole morning to State affairs, and every department had its appointed day and hour. At the beginning of his regency he was an early riser, but later he got less and less punctual; it really depended on what time he had got to bed. He started work alone in his bedroom before he dressed. Then he held his *lever* which did not last long; next he gave audiences over which he used to waste rather a lot of time. The rest of the morning until 2 P.M. was devoted to heads of departments.

At 2.30 P.M. he took a cup of chocolate. While he drank it various courtiers were admitted and he would talk with them for a longer or shorter period as he felt inclined, but the maximum was half an hour. Then he would go to see the Duchesse d'Orléans, and on to the Regency Council if it was sitting that day. Every day he waited upon the King either in the morning or the afternoon; he always addressed himself to the Monarch with the deepest respect, which both pleased the young King and set a good example.

By five in the afternoon his work was over. Then he would go to the opera or to the Luxembourg; if it was fine he might drive over to Saint-Cloud to see Madame, his mother. He always treated her with affection and respect, and if she was in Paris would call upon her before she went to Mass.

At supper he was always surrounded by the most peculiar company: his mistresses, sometimes a couple of girls from the opera, probably the Duchesse de Berry, about a dozen men—they varied and were drawn from the circle which he called his rakes, a few odd dissolute youths, one or two society ladies of questionable virtue and a handful of nonentities who were invited for their brilliant conversation. The food and wines were exquisite, and sometimes the guests themselves would do the cooking with silver utensils. Everything was discussed with the utmost freedom; nothing and no one was spared, not even the Duke himself—although it must be admitted that all this malicious gossip seldom made any impression on him. There was a lot of hard drinking and the guests rivalled one another in their lewd and impious talk. When they had created a considerable disturbance and were all as high as kites they staggered off to bed to get ready for the next day. Once the Regent had sat down to table he was incommunicado, and no one could have access to him, even on the most urgent affairs of State, until the next morning.

The Regent's time was largely divided between his family, his amusements and his debauchery. He wasted a good deal of time over audiences which he granted too freely and was too slow in bringing to a close. I reminded him several times how critical he had been of the old King's absorption in minor detail, and he admitted that he made the same mistake, but he never did anything about it. Further, a lot of the business put before him could have been settled in no time at all, but he would drag it out partly from his inability to make up his mind and partly because he had a tiresome love of setting people against one another—*Divide et impera*, as he was so fond of saying. Consequently the most trifling matters often got so complicated that even he could not cope with them.

People liked his easy-going ways, but they took advantage of his willingness to receive them in a way which barely showed respect. Also when some people, such as Stair, the Maréchal de Villeroy, or members of the *Parlement* became importunate he had difficulty in keeping them within bounds. I used to warn him to beware and sometimes I was able to prevent something undesirable which I could see coming, but more often he would tell me I was quite right and then let his easy disposition lead him off into doing the opposite. One memorable thing was that no one—neither his mistresses, the rakes nor the Duchesse de Berry—ever succeeded in worming any political information out of him, even when he was drunk. He lived publicly with Madame de Parabère and several other women; he was on good terms with them all, and their jealousy and constant back-biting amused him. But this collection of women and the filthy and impious conversation which was known to go on round his table gave great offence to right-minded people.

1717

THE ATTACK ON THE DUKES

THE 'nobility,' as they liked to call themselves, continued their sniping at the Dukes, encouraged by the Duc and Duchesse du Maine who were always looking for a party which they could use for their own ends. Madame du Maine was ever mindful of her declaration that 'when a man has been placed in succession to the Crown, he should set the Kingdom on fire from one end to the other before he should allow that position to be taken from him.' They sent emissaries in every direction, stirring up the provincial nobility and urging them to send deputations to Paris. In the end a memorandum was drawn up in protest against the privileges and honours normally accorded to all Dukes and Duchesses. In the first place it was intended that the memorandum should be presented by the Grand Prior, and the Maltese Ambassador, as generally disliked as his brother the First President of the *Parlement*, summoned all Knights of Malta then in Paris to attend the presentation. But the Regent saw what was coming and, summoning the Ambassador, forbade any assembly of the Knights except on business solely connected with their Order. The memorandum was finally presented on 18 April by MM. de Châtillon, a Knight of the Order, de Rieux, de Laval, de Pons, de Beauffremont and de Clermont. But the Regent refused to accept it, sharply expressed his displeasure, and walked out of the room.

We were not particularly frightened by this demonstration. The instigators did not publish the memorandum, but we were able to get a sight of it; we made no reply, but treated the whole thing with silent contempt. In fact by the time these eight gentlemen appeared before the Regent, he had woken up to the potential danger and gave them a reception which was more than they had bargained for. I myself never talked to him about this, nor about the dispute between the Princes of the Blood and the Bastards which was closely linked with it. I took the same line as I did over the *Parlement*. The Regent kept mentioning it to me, but I would shrug my shoulders, saying that he knew my views and must make up his own mind. Finally he told Monsieur le Duc that he had decided to settle the matter forthwith, but that he first wanted to consult a select committee drawn from members of the Council. At once the Duc and Duchesse du Maine let it be known that the only judgement to which they would submit would be that of the King once he had reached his majority, or the States Gen-

eral. Their declaration was well founded: the King's majority was still
far distant, and so far as the States General was concerned they hoped
that their own party would soon be strong enough to influence deci-
sively any decision.

The Duc d'Orléans saw beyond any shadow of doubt that if he gave
way he might as well resign his regency, and likewise that any further
delay would set a disastrous precedent. The Duc and Duchesse du
Maine, who were kept closely informed by Éffiat and others, relied
on his good-natured weakness and lack of resolution which emboldened them to back so bold a demand; but this time they had bitten off
more than they could chew, and it was a visit of the Duchesse du
Maine to the Palais Royal which precipitated the crisis. Forty-eight
hours later the Princes of the Blood and the Bastards were directed to
lodge their respective pleadings without delay, which indicated that
the dispute was about to be settled. It was just this moment which the
'nobility' chose for presentation of their own memorandum, and the
rebuff which they received so smartly threw them completely off balance. Many declared that they had been led up the garden path and
would never have lent their names to the thing if they had not felt sure
that it had the Regent's approval, and indeed had been prepared at his
secret direction. Many offered their apologies to him and to any Dukes
whom they knew personally. The Duc and Duchesse du Maine and
those in their confidence did their best to press on and to work up a
sense of outrage that the memorandum should have been rejected.
The eight who had presented it were in the forefront, but they were
not quite so vocal as before and indeed even tried to negotiate with
the Regent. But he was at last well aware of what was going on and
would have nothing to do with them—although he was polite to them,
a habit of which he could not break himself. In fact he was now thoroughly alarmed and was determined to call a halt to all the ridiculous
pretensions of the 'nobility.'

On 14 May the Regency Council issued a proclamation that His
Majesty, on the advice of his Council, expressly forbade any nobleman
of whatsoever rank within his kingdom to sign the memorandum under threat of the severest penalties, and adding that it was his intention
to maintain the rights and privileges of his nobility as established by
his forbears and that he had no intention of making any changes.
When this subject had come up at the Council I looked round at the
other Dukes present and, as the senior, said to the Regent that as we
all belonged to the second order in the Kingdom, that is to say the
nobility, I hoped that he would permit us to withdraw during the discussion of a matter which touched us personally. Nothing had been
arranged beforehand, but when I got up to leave I was followed by all

the other Dukes. As I was leaving the Comte de Toulouse whispered to me: 'What about us? Had we better leave?' I said: 'You must suit yourself, but I think there is no doubt that we should.' We went out into the anteroom and were joined at once by the Princes of the Blood and the Bastards. There were a few of the so-called nobility skulking around in the corners, having apparently found out that something was going on in the Council; our appearance took them by surprise.

The next step was the appointment of six Commissioners to enquire into the dispute between the Princes of the Blood and the Bastards; they were directed to submit their report by 20 June at latest. This definite step completely embarrassed the Duc and Duchesse du Maine, who realized that their declared intention to submit only to the judgement of the King or the States General had been a fatal mistake. They had hoped to frighten the Regent, but the Council's proclamation made it clear that they had miscalculated and then they didn't know what to do next. In some perplexity they turned to some of the more hot-headed among the nobility and talked them into doing something equally silly and even more impertinent.

Thirty-nine persons of quality signed in the name of the nobility and presented to the *Parlement* of Paris a petition in which they demanded that the dispute between the Princes of the Blood and the Bastards should be referred to the States General on the grounds that since the succession to the throne was involved the question could only be decided by the second order formally assembled. This was an unparalleled piece of impertinence. These persons were acting entirely on their own authority, they were not even selected by the nobility whose name they were taking in vain; indeed the nobility, unless formally summoned by the King, had no corporate power nor the right to depute anyone to speak on its behalf. Such an assumption of the name and functions of the nobility alone rendered these persons liable to severe punishment; their misdeeds were in fact even worse when it is realized that the object was to destroy the Regent's authority and to wrest from him the right of decision in a matter of prime importance. However, the *Parlement* showed a greater sense of responsibility than these gentlemen did and instead of feeling flattered by the unprecedented honour of receiving a memorandum from the second order, in fact found difficulty in taking it seriously. Although the First President was usually little more than a cat's-paw of the Duc and Duchesse du Maine, on this occasion he took the memorandum straight to the Regent and asked for instructions.

The Duc d'Orléans felt that unless he made an example of the six gentlemen who had presented the memorandum he might as well give up his regency altogether. He laid the memorandum before the Council and was obviously very angry. But although it was decided to punish the offenders, those who had his ear worked upon his good nature to mitigate the sentences. He flattered them by having them arrested by officers of the Bodyguard; three of them were taken to the Bastille and three to Vincennes, where they were well treated but were not allowed to receive visitors. These arrests created a considerable stir because the Duc d'Orléans was so chronically good-natured that they had seemed unlikely; but the injudicious clemency shown to the offenders largely undid the good and made it seem like a triumph for the nobility.

While all this was going on the six commissioners were engaged in preparing their report on the dispute between the Princes of the Blood and the Bastards, which they submitted on 1 July. They found that the Bastards should not be allowed to succeed to the throne, that the rank given to their children should be withdrawn and that their own standing should be modified. This was considered much too lenient by the *Parlement* which registered it under protest; in spite of which, the Duc d'Orléans took it upon himself to so alter the terms of reference that the Bastards lost nothing except the right of succession to the throne and the right of crossing the floor at sittings of the *Parlement*. His appeasement, however, did not satisfy the Duchesse du Maine, who shrieked her head off for days. The Duchesse d'Orléans also wept for two months, receiving only her closest friends.

On 17 July the six prisoners who had presented the memorandum were released and brought before the Regent. He said that they must realize that he never used harsh measures unless they were absolutely necessary, whereupon all the lot of them just looked at him without saying a word and left the room. That they should have been set free so quickly looked like victory, and their silence when in the presence seemed to imply that they were really sparing the Regent a well-merited rebuke. Once they had left the room, the Regent realized that he had made a mistake in being so mild with them and he repented when it was too late, as so often happened. He did, however, turn Châtillon —one of the six—out of his rooms in the Palais Royal and stopped his pension of 12,000 livres. Châtillon was in fact very poor; the loss of this pension forced him to retire to a little property he had near Thouars, and nobody ever heard of him again.

The Regent had not the moral strength to grapple with this very complicated question, and, in spite of various small tactical moves, in general he left it until he was forced eventually more urgently to face it in the following year.

1718

THE LIT DE JUSTICE

✣✣✣✣✣ N the last week of August rumours began to circulate of an
✣ *ℐ* ✣ impending *lit de justice*. Not that the Regent had thought
✣   ✣ about it as yet, but the rumours were caused by the mon-
✣✣✣✣✣ strous and continual encroachments of the *Parlement* on the
royal authority. Some considered this the only way of bringing them
to a halt, but others were afraid of it; but in general the opinion was
that this was the only way to check audacity which had been nourished
by the Regent's weakness in the face of recent events in Paris and
Brittany. This weakness encouraged subversive elements in the belief
that he would never have the courage to hold a *lit de justice*.

The Abbé Dubois returned from his negotiations with the English
Government in London at this time and was alarmed by the diminution of his master's standing. Law likewise was alarmed lest he should
fall into the clutches of the *Parlement*. The Keeper of the Seals equally
had earned the hatred of the *Parlement* when he was Chief of Police.
These three joined together, and Law gained the support of Monsieur
le Duc, so keenly interested in the financial system, who smelled an
opportunity of satisfying his hatred of the Duc du Maine by over-
throwing him and taking his place about the King's person. This alliance of varying interests with a common object bore upon the Regent
and made him realize the danger he was in, the one remedy open to
him and the necessity for speedy action. They persuaded him so completely and everything was agreed so quickly that no one had the
slightest suspicion of what was going to happen.

I was in complete ignorance myself until one day after dinner, when
I was working as usual with the Duc d'Orléans, he broke off from
what we were doing and spoke most bitterly of the *Parlement* and its
actions. I replied with the coldness and disinterest which I customarily
showed on this subject and went back to our business. But he stopped
me and remarked that he saw very well that I did not want to talk
with him about the *Parlement*; I said this was so, as he must have
realized long since. He pressed me, and I told him coldly that he could
hardly have forgotten the views I had expressed to him, both before
and during the Regency, about the *Parlement*; that other counsels,
some possibly treacherous and certainly interested in setting him and
the *Parlement* off against one another to their own advantage, had pre-

vailed; and further that he had got it into his head that because of the hat business and its consequences I was incapable of any unbiased thoughts about either the *Parlement* or the Bastards: so much so that I had made up my mind to keep my mouth shut. I added that it was difficult now for me to say anything on the subject, but that I saw the fulfilment of my prophecy rapidly approaching; there was a time when he could control the *Parlement* with no more than a nod or a frown, but the easy good nature with which he had treated them had encouraged them to the point where he would now either have to reconcile himself to losing his authority as Regent entirely—and possibly even be called upon to give an account of his stewardship—or else restoring the situation by violent methods which would be very difficult and might even fail; the longer he delayed the worse it would be. One thing, I said, he must do, and that was to examine himself first and make up his mind whether he had sufficient resolution to make the effort necessary to reassert his authority, for if he began such a serious business and did not go through with it he would finish up in an infinitely worse position than he was in at present. It was a long time since he had heard me speak so forcibly; I spoke slowly, firmly and coldly and let him see by my indifference to what even he might decide how little I thought him capable of any decisive action or of carrying it through to a conclusion. He was stung, and coming on top of what, unknown to me, Dubois, Law and Argenson had said to him, my words had a remarkable effect.

The resolution passed by the *Parlement* which I have transcribed[1] had up to now not been actually published, but its contents had become known; it was followed by the commission which they gave to the King's representatives,[2] and this was the last straw which made the Regent determined to act. It was also known that the *Parlement*, in defiance of the Attorney General, had appointed special commissioners to carry out his duties in his place, that these had already secretly examined a number of witnesses, and that arrangements had already been made to send ushers to arrest Law without warning and hang him within three hours in the precincts of the Law Courts.[3]

When this became known, coming as it did on top of the pub-

---

[1] A resolution passed on 12 August which aimed at restricting the activities of the Bank, which was not to handle public moneys, and laid down that no foreigner, even if naturalized, was directly or indirectly to handle any public funds.

[2] To enquire into the whereabouts of all paper money paid into the Bank, to the monthly public lottery and the Mississippi scheme.

[3] The Law Courts were private property administered by a bailiff who was responsible solely to the *Parlement*.

lication of the resolution I have mentioned, the Duc de la Force and Fagon, Counsellor of State, went on the morning of Friday, 19 August, to see the Regent and urged him so pressingly that he directed them both to pick up Law and bring him to my house to talk over what ought to be done. This they did, and it was the first intimation I had that the Duc d'Orléans realized the predicament he was in and was determined to act.

During the conference at my house I saw the great firmness which Law had shown previously crumble away until he ended up in tears. Our discussion really did not get us very far because what was needed was a display of force, and we did not know if we could count on the Regent. The safe conduct with which Law had been provided would not stop the *Parlement* for a moment. Threatened from all sides, Law, more dead than alive, did not know what to say or what would become of him. What to do with him seemed to us the most urgent point. If he were arrested, he would be strung up long before the negotiations and proposals, which the Regent in his weakness would try first, could be succeeded by what would really be needed in the first instance: to call out the guards and break down the doors of the Law Courts; it would be appalling if they eventually arrived to find nothing but a body swinging at the end of a rope. I advised him to retreat at once to the Palais Royal, and occupy Nancré's rooms, a friend of his who was away in Spain; this cheered him up a bit, the Duc de la Force and Fagon approved, and he left at once. He would have been equally safe at the Bank, but I thought that his taking refuge in the Palais Royal would have more effect and would commit the Regent more deeply, and it would be useful as Law would be available on the premises for consultation at all times.

Once that was settled, I suggested that a *lit de justice* was the only means of quashing the *Parlement*'s resolutions, and the others agreed. While we were discussing this, I was suddenly struck by a thought which pulled us up short. It struck me that the Duc du Maine and the Maréchal de Villeroy, who were more closely bound up with the Duke than he allowed to be known, would never allow a *lit de justice* to take place, which would be so contrary to all their schemes; to get out of it they would plead the extreme heat[1] and bad effect which this and the danger of crowds and bad air might have on the health of the King—arguments which would be bound to affect the Regent; if he persisted, they might say that they regarded the danger to the King so great that they would refuse to accompany him, and the King, un-

---

[1] Paris was sweltering in a terrific three-weeks' heat wave.

der their influence, might well refuse to appear without them. If that
should happen, everything would fall to the ground and such a display of the Regent's impotence would produce far-reaching effects. These reflections brought us up short; but I thought of a way out, which was to hold the *lit de justice* at the Tuileries. This would mean that there would be no need to summon anybody until the very morning on which it was taking place, and this secrecy would take everyone by surprise; furthermore there would be no danger to the King, and if force were needed it would be more readily available if the affair took place in his own home instead of the *Palais de Justice*. We agreed upon this, and, as soon as Law had gone, I dictated a memorandum to Fagon setting out as much as was necessary for the carrying out of the business in secrecy and without meeting with any obstacles. By nine in the evening we had finished, and I told him to take the memorandum to the Abbé Dubois, who had just come back from England enjoying the renewed confidence of his master. Before the conference Law had told me the views of the Abbé and the Keeper of the Seals, and that they were resolved to press the Regent to extricate him at once from his predicament. The same day, forty-eight hours after his return, Dubois came to see me; first he gave me an account of his negotiations, and then we discussed the *Parlement*. He seemed to me to have the right idea. In the present situation we could not do without him, and we counted on him to bolster up the Regent's determination. Such was the plan on Friday, 19th of August, which was the first day on which I heard any serious talk of the Regent, alarmed at last, doing anything to extricate himself from the clutches of the cabal and the *Parlement*.

The following day, Saturday, 20th August, the Duc d'Orléans summoned me for four o'clock that afternoon. While I was still at home Fagon came to see me and said that the Abbé Dubois was vacillating, was talking of negotiating with the *Parlement* and was listening to a lot of bad advice from his close friend d'Argenson. This made me realize only too well that we had to deal with a narrow mind which boggled at the thought of positive action, with a man consumed with jealousy because the Regent had sent the Duc de la Force, Fagon and Law to seek my advice. And finally that, as one of boundless ambition who, proud of his London treaty, wished to enjoy the fruits of his success and saw that he and his treaty might both be lost in the general execration if he got caught between the Regent and the *Parlement*, he imagined that he might do himself a bit of good if he could bring about some wretched compromise of which the Regent would be the victim, and the *Parlement* would be flattered and the Jansenist party pleased by the return of the Chancellor from Fresnes. He was not interested in our plan or in getting the Regent out of his predicament. Fagon and the Duc de la Force, who joined us, were both worried about the mental attitude of the Regent whom they had just left after reporting what had gone on at my house the day before. Fagon, a capable man, had been at pains to show our memorandum to the Abbé Dubois, and when he left the Abbé was thinking of compiling another one. This he did, and produced it this morning; it was much more detailed but in parts much weaker.

I went to the Palais Royal at four. A moment later La Vrillière arrived and relieved me of the company of two rakes, de Grancy and de Broglie, whom I had run into in the big study, familiarly taking their ease with their wigs off. We had not been there long before we were told to go into the new Gallery, painted by Coypel, where we found Asfeld[1] showing a lot of maps of the Pyrenees to the Regent and the Maréchal de Villeroy. The Duc d'Orléans greeted me familiarly, which showed that he needed me; a moment later he whispered that he had a lot to talk to me about when we were all assembled, but he had to get rid of the Maréchal first. It was the first indication I had, that there was to be any kind of meeting, nor did I know with whom. La Vrillière asked me if I had business with the Regent. I said yes. He said he had been summoned for four o'clock; 'me too,' I replied.

The Marshal took me aside later and went on as usual in a kind of dull, malicious tone about the precautions he was taking for the King's person and the shower of anonymous letters he was receiving—written most probably by himself and the Duc du Maine. Finally he took his leave. The Duc d'Orléans breathed again, and took me into the studies behind the Grand Gallery, overlooking the rue de Richelieu. When we got there he took me by the arm and said that he had reached the crisis in his regency, and that everything was at stake. I said that I realized that only too well, and that everything depended on him alone. We had hardly sat down when the Abbé Dubois came in and started talking in riddles about the *Parlement*. But he was not received very well; the Regent got rid of him as soon as he could, giving orders that he was not to be disturbed except when the Keeper of the Seals arrived, and then he shut the door. I then said that before we went on I ought to tell him what Fagon had said that morning about the Abbé Dubois's attitude to the Chancellor and the Keeper of the Seals, and his extreme caution *vis-à-vis* the *Parlement*. The Regent replied that

[1] Claude-François Bidal, Chevalier and later Marquis d'Asfeld, Director General of Fortifications. The forthcoming war with Spain was already in contemplation.

Paris bread riots

this tied up with what he had noticed himself, and my thoughts appeared to him well founded. I urged him to beware of a man like this
who could change so quickly for no apparent reason. He assured me
that Dubois would never betray him, but that we would need to feel
our way carefully.

After these few words we got down to business. He said that he
had made up his mind to deliver the *Parlement* a real body blow, that
he liked the idea of a *lit de justice* at the Tuileries rather than the Palais
for the reasons I had given, that he had made sure of M. le Duc by
giving him a further allowance of 150,000 livres as Chairman of the
Regency Council, and that this morning already he had received a
promise of support from the Prince de Conti. He added that M. le
Duc wanted the King's education taken out of the hands of the Duc du
Maine, which suited him because he had no desire to see his enemy so
near a King growing older and better informed every day, and that
he had made up his mind to hold the *lit de justice* on the following
Tuesday if possible, and there remove the Duc du Maine from office.

I interrupted him and said shortly that that was not at all my view.

'Oh! And why is that not your view?' he interrupted me in turn.

'Because,' I said, 'it is too much to undertake at one time. What
is the most important problem you have, and one which will admit of
no delay? It is the *Parlement*. That is the great point: be content with
that. Striking a real blow here, and sticking to it afterwards, will immediately re-establish your authority, and there will be plenty of time
then to think about the Duc du Maine. Do not confuse the two: in
thinking of their common downfall, you ascribe to them common interests. He will make himself out to be, and indeed will be, a martyr
in the cause of the *Parlement* and hence of the public. First see how the
public take your actions against the *Parlement*. You should not get rid
of M. du Maine until you can and must and until the public and the
Parlement both expect and desire it. You have allowed both of them
to build up the Duc du Maine at their own convenience, and you are
now trying to overthrow him at the wrong moment. One more
thought—does M. le Duc really want charge of the education for himself, or is he only interested in the overthrow of the Duc du Maine?'

'He is not even thinking about it,' replied the Regent.

'That may be,' I said, 'but please try to make him see reason over
the crisis. And, Sir,' I added, 'please remember that when I speak
against the humbling of the Duc du Maine, I am going against my
own best interest. You know the strength of my own feelings on this
subject and how much I hate M. du Maine, who by the deepest and
most premeditated blackness brought about the crisis over the hats

and deliberately induced the heavy consequences. But the good of the State and of yourself is more dear to me than my ranks or my personal vengeance, and therefore I beg you to consider carefully before you act.'

The Regent was perhaps more struck by my self-control than by the force of my arguments. He embraced me, agreed quickly and said that I had spoken as a friend and not as a Duke and Peer. I took the opportunity of reproaching him gently for his suspicions on this subject. We then agreed to leave the Duc du Maine for another less complicated occasion. The Duc d'Orléans came back to the subject of the *Parlement* and suggested that the First President should be removed. I disagreed again, saying that he and the Duc du Maine were much too close for it to be possible to strike down one without the other; that nothing would be more dangerous than an attack going off half-cock against a man as unpleasant yet so strongly entrenched as the Duc du Maine; that we must wait to see off one as clearly as the other; and that once more I was speaking as a friend and against my own interests, because all I wanted myself was just to get rid of a wretch who had brought about all our present troubles at the first opportunity.

The Regent praised me, thanked me again, and seemed to think that I was right. He said that he had made up his mind to follow the memorandum which I had dictated to Fagon and not that of the Abbé Dubois. The latter wanted the *lit de justice* postponed until after Saint-Martin, to restrict the operation to rescinding the *Parlement*'s resolutions and the exiling a few of the particularly mutinous members after the House had risen; while I wished to invoke a head-on clash. After discussing broadly the difficulties and their remedies, we got down to details. I explained what I had in my mind and at the Regent's request undertook to organize the actual mechanics of the *lit de justice* with Fontanieu, head of the royal Office of Works, but keeping everyone else in ignorance—particularly the Duc d'Aumont, his immediate superior as First Gentleman of the Bedchamber on duty and a pawn of the Duc du Maine and the First President.

The Keeper of the Seals had been announced for some time. Once we had reached agreement, the Regent went into the room next to the study where we were and from the doorway summoned the Keeper, La Vrillière, and the Abbé Dubois who were waiting by themselves at the other end of the room. This was the room in which the Duc d'Orléans normally worked during the summer. He usually sat with his back to the wall, in the middle of a long desk which stretched before him. He took his usual seat, with me beside him, the Keeper of the Seals and the Abbé Dubois opposite, and La Vrillière near me at one end. After a short discussion of the agenda, the Keeper of the Seals read the draft of a resolution breaking the *Parlement*'s decisions which was to be passed by the Regency Council; we made a few small alterations. The Abbé Dubois disagreed with everything to such an extent that I thought he must have been entirely inspired by the double-crossing spirit of the Chancellor. There was an argument and we all came out against him. In the end he became embarrassed, but not to the point of taking back any of the astounding contradictions.

Just as the reading of the proposed resolution was finished M. le Duc was announced. The Duc d'Orléans put on his wig and went to meet him in the antechamber. While he was gone we walked two or three times up and down the Gallery, d'Argenson and Dubois going on with their argument the whole time. La Vrillière and I shrugged our shoulders and continued to support the Keeper of the Seals. La Vrillière also showed me a draft of the proposed declaration suppressing the *Parlement*'s new charges, which I thought was good.

Not long after I heard the door open through which His Royal Highness had gone to find M. le Duc. I went ahead of the others and saw the Regent with M. le Duc behind him. As I was a party to the understanding between them I asked the Regent laughingly what he proposed to do with M. le Duc and why he brought him in here to disturb us.

'You see him here,' he replied, taking M. le Duc's arm, 'and I hope that you will see him here often in future.'

Then, looking at the two of them, I expressed my joy at their union, and added that in this lay their best interest, not in joining with the Bastards.

'As for this man,' said the Regent to M. le Duc, and putting his hands on my shoulders, 'you can talk to him in complete confidence, for there is no one in the world more in favour of a union of the legitimate Princes and against the Bastards.'

I smiled and confirmed this emphatically. M. le Duc expressed his respects to the Regent and made some civil remarks to me.

We then all sat down again; M. le Duc sat between the Duc d'Orléans and myself. His Royal Highness, after a short reference to M. le Duc, asked the Keeper of the Seals to read the draft again. M. le Duc strongly approved of it. When it was finished the Duc d'Orléans rose and called M. le Duc over to the far end of the room; he summoned me a moment later. There he told me that they were now going to decide on ways and means, and the most pressing matter was the preparations for the *lit de justice*; he asked me to go at once to see Fontanieu for him. As I left them I raised my voice and mentioned to His Royal

Highness the draft declaration which La Vrillière had shown me in the Gallery and said how good I thought it was.

Just as I was getting into my carriage one of Law's servants, who had been waiting for me, told me that his master asked if I would at once go to see him in his apartment, which was close by. I found him alone with his wife,[1] who left the room immediately. I told him that all was going well, that M. le Duc was on our side and was with the Regent at this moment; I knew from his wife that it was Law who had been instrumental in bringing them together. I added that I had an urgent commission to perform in connection with all this, which he would hear about from the Regent or from myself in due course. At this he seemed to breathe more freely, and I went off to Fontanieu's house in the Place Vendôme.

At the time when the special taxes on financiers imposed by the *Chambre de Justice* had come before the Regency Council I had been able to do Fontanieu a good turn.[2] He had married his daughter to Castelmoron, a nephew of the Duc de Lauzun. At this time M. and Mme de Lauzun were engaged in a lawsuit over their claim to the Randan property which had belonged to the late Duc de Foix; it was being heard before a special commission and Fontanieu was appearing for them. At his house I was told that he was attending a meeting of the commissioners in the Marais, miles away. The porter, seeing my irritation, said that if I would go in and see Mme de Fontanieu, he would meanwhile find out if his master were still in the neighbourhood where he had intended to make a call before going on to the meeting. I went up to Mme de Fontanieu, who was often at the Hôtel de Lauzun, and found her alone. I passed the time talking about the Lauzuns' case and made my excuse for wanting to see her husband on an urgent point which had cropped up in this connection. Fontanieu had been found nearby and soon arrived. I was now in an embarrassing position because his wife knew as much about the case as he did and both of them begged me to discuss it then and there without bothering to go to Fontanieu's study. However, I finally got Fontanieu to move by paying his wife compliments and saying that I really had no desire to waste her time over this Randan business.

When we got to his study I chatted on for a few minutes about the Lauzuns to let the servants get out of the room. Then to his great

---

[1] Catherine Knollys, third sister of the Earl of Banbury. It is in fact very doubtful if they were ever married.

[2] Saint-Simon gives no details of this in his memoirs. In the roll of those taxed Fontanieu appears as General Treasurer of the Navy.

surprise I went outside to see that they were out of earshot and then
firmly shut the door.

I then told Fontanieu that I had not come to talk to him about the lawsuit but about something quite different which would demand all his industry and discretion, that the Duc d'Orléans had charged me to tell him of it, but before I did so I wished to know categorically whether His Royal Highness could count on his entire support. It is extraordinary what an effect the wildest rumours artfully put about can have.[1] Fontanieu's first reaction was literally to tremble from head to foot and he went as white as a sheet. He stammered that he was at the service of His Royal Highness as far as his duty would permit. I smiled and looked straight through him; this apparently made him realize that he owed me an apology for having doubts about any commission which might pass through my hands—which he did, but with the embarrassment of one who did not want to reveal what had just flashed through his mind. I reassured him as best I could, said that I had vouched for him to the Duke, and then revealed that the matter in hand concerned a *lit de justice* in the place and organization of which we needed his help. As soon as I said this the poor fellow gave several deep sighs as if a great weight had been taken off his chest, and asked if that was really all I wanted. In his relief at getting off so cheaply he promised everything, and I must say that he kept his promise both in what he did and the secrecy with which he did it. He had never seen a *lit de justice* and had not the first idea what was required. I sat down at his desk and drew a diagram; I dictated the necessary explanatory notes to him because I did not want them to exist in my own handwriting. I spent over an hour going over the whole thing, and I moved his furniture round to give him a better idea of what happened, so that he could have everything prefabricated and then erected in the Tuileries in a matter of minutes. When I thought that I had explained everything sufficiently and that he understood it all, I drove off; after a bit I redirected my coachman to the Palais Royal as if I had changed my mind, so as not to give my men any idea that there was something going on.

A *Garçon Rouge*[2] took me upstairs where Ibaguet, concierge of the Palais Royal, was waiting for me at the entrance of the Duc d'Orléans's apartment with a request from the Duke that I should write to him. This was the time of day given up to the rakes and to supper, with

***

[1] A reference to the lies deliberately put about that the Regent was attempting to poison the Princes.

[2] That is to say, a member of the personal staff in the red livery of the Duc d'Orléans.

which no business was allowed to interfere. I sat down in the winter study and wrote a letter, not without considerable indignation at the thought that he would not interrupt his pleasures even for a matter as important as this. Furthermore I was put to the disagreeable necessity of telling Ibaguet not to let him see the letter until he was in a fit state to read it, and to burn it afterwards. Then I went on to see Fagon, who was not at home, and thence to my own house where I found that he had come to see me. Soon afterwards M. de la Force also arrived to ask what had happened, and was pleased at what I told him.

The next morning, Sunday the 21st, when I got up at half-past seven I was told that a valet had come early that morning with a letter from M. le Duc to be given to me personally, but had gone off to hear mass at the Jacobin church while waiting for me to awake. I had had little to do with him and indeed of late I had treated him and the other princes with a neglect which verged on the improper.

In due course I went to my study with the valet and opened the letter which he gave me. It was written by M. le Duc in his own hand and read:

Sir,
   I think it absolutely necessary that I should have a talk with you about matters which you know of. I also think the sooner the better. So if possible I would like it to be tomorrow morning, Sunday. See when you could come to me, or I to you, and choose a time which would be least noticeable, for there is no point in giving people ideas. I shall await your answer tomorrow morning.
   Meanwhile I pray you to count upon my friendship, as I hope I may on yours.
                                                         H. de Bourbon

I thought for a few minutes after reading the letter and decided to go and see M. le Duc. After asking the valet what time the Duke's *lever* was, I thought it best for me to go there rather than for him to come to me, as he might be noticed by the President Portail who lived opposite and would more than likely be at home on Sunday morning. I did not want to put anything in writing so I simply told his valet to tell him that I would attend his *lever*.

Accordingly I went to the Hôtel de Condé where I found the Duke just finishing dressing; happily there was no one with him except his servants. He received me as one self-possessed for his age, politely but without undue eagerness. Indeed he remarked that it was something of a novelty to see me there. I replied that since the Council had nearly always met in the morning and he was seldom in Paris on the other days, I had had little opportunity, but since the time of the meetings had now changed I hoped to have the honour of seeing him more frequently. He finished dressing and suggested we go into his study, shut the door, asked me to take an arm-chair and sat down himself.

He began apologizing for the liberty he had taken, and after a few compliments got down to business. He asked me straight away if I did not agree with him that there was no point in going for the *Parlement* if at the same time one did not strike at the man behind them. From what the Regent had said the previous evening I had expected something of the sort, but without appearing stupid I was not sorry to be able to make him be the first to mention the Duc du Maine by name. I asked him how he intended to get at M. du Maine. 'By taking the King's education away from him,' he replied. I said that there was no need for this to be done at the *lit de justice*, it could be done at any time. He argued that since this appointment had been conferred on the Duke at a *lit de justice* it could only be cancelled by a *lit de justice*. I disagreed, but he cut me short, saying that this was the Regent's view also.

I realized that I could not beat about the bush any longer. I said that the more I thought about it the less confident I felt. On the other hand I had to watch my own personal feelings and it was possible that for this reason I exaggerated the dangers. I had a horror of seeing private interests, however just in themselves, leading to consequences which might be serious for the State, and the dearer such interests were to me the more determined I was to put them behind me and act throughout as a man of honour. I wasted no words, but came straight to the point. I said that there was an infinity of difference between the two points on which M. le Duc wanted my views: no sensible person who was at all impartial could deny that it would be in the best interests of the State, the King and the Regent to relieve the Duc du Maine of his responsibility for the King's education, but equally no one could deny that such a move was fraught with danger. I pointed out to him what a coup it was for M. du Maine to have captured that position, what power he enjoyed through his high appointments, what added strength would accrue to him if he and the *Parlement* were attacked on common ground, and what authority the reputation rather than the actual appointments of the Comte de Toulouse would bring to this party; in short nothing could be more undesirable than civil war and the quickest way to bring it about would be to attack the Duc du Maine.

M. le Duc listened to me carefully and replied that in his opinion to attack the Duc du Maine was the only way to avoid civil war. I asked him to explain his view which was so directly contrary to my own. He said we were all agreed that the King's education must be taken out of the hands of the Duc du Maine, so the next thing to be considered was whether it could be done with less danger at some other time. In his opinion the longer the Duke was left anywhere near the King, the more the King would get used to him and might in due course become an obstacle which at present he was too young to be. The Duc du Maine, he said, had gained so much ground since the start of the Regency by virtue of having the education in his charge that when the King came of age it was reasonable to suppose that he would be the first man in the State, that his position would be strengthened as the King grew older and the danger of attacking him would increase in the same proportion. He agreed that it was annoying that the Duc du Maine's affairs should get mixed up with those of the *Parlement*, but that would just have to be got over somehow.

He went on to say that he would speak of the Duc d'Orléans not as to a close friend but as to a man honest and reliable whom he knew he could trust. He would be happy to let the present occasion go and tackle the problem of the Duc du Maine another time if the Regent could be relied upon. Three times already the Regent had promised to remove the Duc du Maine from office and done nothing about it— at the late King's death, then the following day at the first meeting of the *Parlement*, and last when the dispute arose over the Princes of the Blood; each time it had not been a vague assurance but a definite promise, and each time he had let the thing slip through his fingers. If the Duc du Maine remained close to the King until he came of age the Regent was lost, and it would be the wildest folly not to take advantage of the present occasion.

This is no more than a précis of what he said, and when he had finished he asked me to reply precisely. I could not deny the truth of the views which he put forward, 'but,' I said, 'would this prevent civil war? It all shows what a great mistake it was to leave the Bastards in their positions after the King's death, when everyone expected their downfall. Now that people have got used to the present state of affairs, and the Bastards seem even to have been reinforced by their success in their dispute with the legitimate Princes of the Blood, to do what was not done at the King's death must surely bring about civil disorder. You say that the upright nature of the Comte de Toulouse would prevent them from starting anything: that is no more than a pious hope. Do you suppose that he would stand by and watch his brother's downfall with disinterest? And another thing, Sir, do you really think that you can stop there? How can you possibly leave the command of the artillery, the Swiss Guards and his other regiments as well as the Governorship of Guyenne and Languedoc—great and turbulent states dangerously adjacent to Spain—in the hands of a man whom you have mortally offended and from whom you have just

wrested not only the charge of the King's education but also all his
vast ambitions for the future?'

'Very well then, Sir,' the Duke interrupted, 'he must be relieved
of those commands.'

'You can't really think that, Sir,' I said. 'You can't do that without accusing him of some crime, and what crime can you allege against
him? He would be driven even more firmly into the arms of the *Parlement* by the allegations that he had been in conspiracy with them.
And at a time like this do you want to make an issue out of his trafficking with Spain, even if it could be proved? The first would be taken
as an act of public benefaction and the latter as a personal attack upon
the Regent which could be insulated from both King and State. What
will you do if, having taken the King's education out of his hands, you
get stuck at that point? That is why I tried to get them out of it when
the King died, and to have them deprived of everything except their
worldly goods and their standing as Dukes and Peers according to
their proper seniority. There is no one who would not have applauded
such action at that time and have considered it very lenient, and no
one who would not have welcomed such a brake put forever on those
whose boundless ambitions extend even to the very throne. Even the
Comte de Toulouse would hardly have felt he could oppose it, and
this is a case where his natural honesty would have allowed him to follow his own thinking.

'But now, after three years, to strip someone from his offices when
he has committed no crime is a tyranny which would alarm everyone
holding any position, who would fear he might find himself similarly
treated and would resent such an arbitrary wielding of authority. Do
not reduce them: it would give them every reason for combining together in opposition. Furthermore you have got to reckon with the
vengeance, the rage and the fury of the Duchesse du Maine, who was
not afraid to say during the late King's lifetime that if any of her husband's rank, honours and claims to the throne were ever in danger of
being set aside she would have no hesitation in stirring up civil strife
to prevent it. After what I have said, Sir,' I went on equally firmly
but with less heat, 'you can understand how strongly I feel that in
the best interests of the State M. du Maine should be left alone. You
honour me by speaking to me in confidence and with such frankness,
and I can only reply in the same spirit. I know quite well that the standing of the Bastards cannot be altered so long as the education of the
King remains in the hands of M. du Maine, just as it could not be
maintained if he were deprived of that post. No criminal charges are
necessary to achieve this; all that need be done is to put through a bill

based on the prayer which we in a body offered to the King and the Regent at the time of your suit against the Bastards. I assure you that the thing dearest to me is my dignity and rank; worldly wealth came to me later and I would joyfully give it up if I could see the dignity of my position properly restored. Nothing has more profoundly debased me than the rise of the Bastards, and nothing could affect me so favourably as once again to take precedence over them. I have said so to their faces—to Mme d'Orléans and her brothers—not once but many times both during and since the late King's lifetime. No one has brought about such horrors as M. du Maine did over the hat business, and there is no one on whom I have so exquisite a desire to revenge myself. When I subdue such feelings in myself and suggest that he be left alone it can only be because I see the potential danger to the State as both powerful and evident. I can offer no stronger argument.'

M. le Duc had listened to me with the closest attention and he remained silent for a few minutes. Then in a quiet, firm voice—which I never like to hear in a business discussion because it always means that the speaker has irrevocably made up his mind whatever the obstacles—he said:

'Sir, I appreciate all the difficulties which you have set forth, and they are considerable. But there are two points to be taken into account on the other side which appear to me incomparably more important. One is that the Duc d'Orléans and I will be lost if the education remains in the hands of M. du Maine until the King attains his majority; and the other is that there will certainly be no change if the present opportunity is allowed to pass. You can add it up any way you will, but this is what it boils down to: that I can no longer trust the word of the Duc d'Orléans, and I am not prepared to sit down idly and wait for total ruin to overtake me in four years' time.'

'What about the risk of civil war?' I asked.

'This is what I think about civil war,' he said; 'M. du Maine will either be sensible or he won't. He will be closely watched and we shall soon see which way he means to jump. If he is sensible, as I think he will be, there will be no trouble; if he is not, there is a ready-made case for stripping him ruthlessly.'

'What if his brother, whose province is already in almost open revolt,[1] should join him?'

'No, he is too honest to start anything. But we must watch him and see that he doesn't go to Brittany.'

[1] The Comte de Toulouse was Governor of Guyenne. Brittany also was in a state of open unrest.

'How? by arresting him?'

'Certainly, for, having been warned not to go, he would have asked for it.'

'But, Sir,' I said, 'do you realize where all this is leading you? You would drive into open revolt a man justly admired for his upright and patriotic character, and his disassociation of himself from his brother's lunatic views—in support of which he would be prepared to lose his honour, in the same way that he joined in his brother's suit against you, even though he disapproved of it. I assure you that the esteem which I formed for him after the King's death has grown into affection, and, something which I marvel at myself, it has even softened my views towards him over the vexed question of rank. Surely you, his nephew whom he has looked after since birth, must have some feelings of consideration for him?'

'I love the Comte de Toulouse with all my heart,' he said, 'and I would give anything to save him from all this; but when it is a matter of necessity, and my own downfall and the welfare of the State is in question, circumstances alter cases. For, my dear Sir, shall I not be liquidated in four years' time? And am I supposed to sit back and regard the prospect with tranquility? Put yourself in my position. If there is going to be trouble, there will be much less now than there will be if we go on allowing the cabal to grow in strength; and there is always the possibility, in my view, that if we act now nothing will happen at all. Well, there you are. What do you think about that, and what are you really boggling over?'

To give us both time for reflection I digressed; in any case I wanted to sound him out on the question of our own position. I told him I thought that in his suit against the Bastards he had made a great mistake in not seeking our assistance, for a concerted demonstration would have so embarrassed the Regent that he would have been forced to reduce them to their proper rank in the peerage; in this way they would have been discomforted and everyone, even the *Parlement*, would have applauded. But he had conceived a wrong idea, well known and understood by us, that it would be a good thing to have an intermediate class between the Princes of the Blood and ourselves; it was a complete fallacy because we knew our place, but the Bastards did not and were continually encroaching on their superiors.

He agreed entirely, and said that he was ready to put matters right, that his friendship with the Comte de Toulouse, of whom I had spoken, was partly the cause, but that now he was ready to agree to the whole lot of them being reduced to their proper precedence. He said that he had spoken to the Regent about it without caring very much

213

himself but in order to get something done, and, to give him the complete picture, put it to him under three headings: 1. removal of the royal education, 2. the intermediate class, and 3. the reduction of everyone to their proper precedence, that the Duc d'Orléans had asked him to reduce the whole thing to the necessary series of edicts and proclamations and he had done so. I must say that when I heard this, human nature almost got the better of me; but I pulled myself together and after a few comments asked what he intended to do about the education.

'I shall ask for it myself,' he replied with feeling.

'That I can well understand,' I said, 'but do you want it?'

'For myself, no; you can imagine that at my age one doesn't want to be made a prisoner, but it is the only way I can imagine of getting it away from the Duc du Maine.'

'If I may say so,' I replied, 'there is another way. Take it away from the Duc du Maine and don't give it to anyone. It is a sinecure anyway. Leave the Maréchal de Villeroy without anyone over him, for he will have to be left where he is in spite of all the rumours that are always running around.'

'That's all very well,' he said, 'but how do you take the education away from the Duc du Maine if no one asks for it, and no one can ask for it but me?'

'But to ask for it and to want it are two different things. Could you not ask for it in order to get it away from M. du Maine and then agree with the Duc d'Orléans that there should be no further appointment? I seem to remember His Royal Highness telling me yesterday that you weren't interested, and I think this would be the best way out.'

'It is quite true that I have never wanted the post nor should I enjoy it. But I am not inclined to ask for something and then not accept it. Since I must ask for it, then I must take it.'

I thought that it would not be a good thing to give added prominence to a Prince of the Blood, second in all the realm, by giving him charge of the King's education, and that was why I brought the subject up. When I saw him so disinterested yet so determined, I decided to try another line.

'Sir,' I said, 'this conversation must be regarded as in the strictest confidence. You have spoken to me most frankly about the Duc d'Orléans, and I must of necessity do the same. You do not know what you are talking about when you suggest taking over the King's education. It is one thing for the Duc du Maine with all his sharp practices, for he is housed next to the King, never leaves him and shares everything with him; furthermore, how could he keep up his monstrous preten-

sions without constant manœuvring. But you—what good can it do
you? You are second in the realm already. This position can neither
benefit you nor serve as a protection. It can only complicate things
between you and the Duc d'Orléans who, let's face it, is extremely suspicious and gets hold of the wrong end of the stick more easily than
anyone in the world, particularly when everyone will be only too willing to say things against you. Sir, you will be irritated to find that you
no longer enjoy any confidence, attention or consideration. There will
be plenty of people to put such ideas into your head and to tell you that
the Regent is in the same state of mind, and then you will be up against
one another. The two of you would no doubt eventually make your
peace, but such reconciliations never go more than skin deep. Your
very real and solid grandeur is based on a real and solid alliance with
the Regent. Alliance or the absence of it means to you gain or loss.
Between you two there must be an alliance without blemish, without
ripples, without faults, and which cannot be easily shaken. If you do
not have charge of the King's education, there is no grounds for disagreement; if you have, there can be a thousand. Suspicion could arise
at any moment, and you would realize it all too late.'

Since I saw that he was immovable, I tried to turn away from a
thorny subject, so that I might later return to my main object of saving
the Duc du Maine. I said to M. le Duc that I must now push his confidence to the limit, and I hoped that he would forgive me for mentioning a family matter which I felt in duty bound to bring up. After
this opening which was received with all the politeness of a man who
wished both to please and to win me over, I said:

'Sir, since you allow me, may we have a few words about Monsieur
your brother,[1] about his travels, his movements, the rumours about
him: where do we stand?'

'Sir,' replied the Duke, 'I know no more than you. My brother is
a lightweight, a child who makes up his mind what he wants to do,
does it, and tells no one. That's all there is to it.'

'I must say, Sir,' I said, 'that to know that one knows nothing is
to know a great deal. For I have not so bad an opinion of the Comte
de Charolais as to believe him capable of doing anything so important
without you and Mme la Duchesse knowing. She is the mother of
you both, and you, although young, are several years the senior and
must stand towards him in lieu of a father. Can you enlighten me on
this, which is important?'

---

[1] The Comte de Charolais, who had set out to join the army in Hungary and was
hanging about without any motive in Italy.

By way of reply Monsieur le Duc laid on the table a letter from his brother which in four lines set down his route to Genoa, and not a word more. He read it out, then asked me to look at it, and insisted that this was as much as he knew. Nevertheless when I pressed him he admitted that his brother had no position and that if he were offered one in Spain, as was under discussion, he, being no more than a younger brother with no means of subsistence, would be well advised to accept it.

'Still, Sir,' I replied, 'this younger son has an allowance of 60,000 livres, and at his age it is by no means nothing to be allowed to live with you in the Hôtel de Condé and at Chantilly in comfort and pleasure with no expense. But if he should be appointed Viceroy of Catalunya he would be in the service of the King of Spain. How would you expect the Duc d'Orléans to have confidence in you after that? You will have a foot here and a foot there; you will be—or at any rate you will very rightly be considered to be—a post office for anyone who wants to deal with Spain without admitting it. And with your brother such a thorn in the side of the Duc d'Orléans, you are asking him to throw the Bastards overboard in favour of a close alliance with yourself? If you were in his place would you light-heartedly alienate the Bastards for ever if you could not assuredly count upon the Princes of the Blood? My dear Sir, think once more'—I said as firmly as I could—'and do one thing or the other, not just fall between two stools.'

Monsieur le Duc agreed and then went back to expressing doubts as to whether there was in fact any appointment on offer, and I kept trying to get a straight answer out of him. Finally I said that a bit of straight thinking was needed, and one had to make up one's mind who was a friend and who an enemy. At last he said that if a suitable position were available his brother would return.

'Well, there's the rub,' I said, 'and I haven't been so far out in pressing you on the subject. At any rate it is no good expecting the impossible; what jobs are open to M. de Charolais?'

Monsieur le Duc started to complain about the salaries which went with these posts, which in fact were not very adequate. I finally suggested that the Governorship of the Ile-de-France should be bought back from the Duc d'Estrées, who was really not worthy of either the office or its reversionary value, and given to M. de Charolais. M. le Duc did not like the idea. So I quoted him the case of Poitou given to the Prince de Conti and reminded him that the Prince and M. de Charolais were younger brothers of equal standing.

This made M. le Duc pause for a moment. He suggested a marriage with Mlle de Valois,[1] whom his brother had always wanted. As I was engaged in very secret negotiations for her marriage to the Prince de Piémont, which was dependent upon certain exchanges between the State and Sicily and was likely to be a pretty protracted affair, I was very careful to say nothing which would encourage this idea, but I had to say something. Rather coarsely I remarked that they were both eligible and of good family, but it would be rather like Hunger marrying Thirst. M. le Duc agreed and added that in any case it was for the Duc d'Orléans to decide whether his daughter would be suitably matched with a husband who had nothing of his own. I replied that present conditions would hardly warrant a marriage which would be a charge on the State. M. le Duc tried to disagree on the grounds that they were both Princes of the Blood.

'They may command all the respect you like, Sir,' I replied, 'but look into the question a little more closely and tell me who in France, in the present state of the country, is going to be pleased at the idea of having to find four million a year to keep a Prince and Princess of the Blood in the state to which they are accustomed.' He argued over the four million, but whatever the sum, agreed that he did not know where it would come from.

He then said that there was something else about which he would like my views in the strictest confidence. He wanted to know who I thought would be Regent if anything happened to the Duc d'Orléans. Not that there was anything the matter with the Duke's health but one had to look ahead and the life he led was quite capable of killing him at any moment, which would be a disaster. I replied that I would give him a straight answer if he would promise to keep it absolutely secret. He promised and I said that without question the law must be observed whereby the regency devolved upon the King's nearest male relative of age: and that meant himself.

'That is a great relief to me,' M. le Duc replied happily, 'for I cannot disguise from you the fact that I know the Duc de Chartres[2] is being considered; the Duchesse d'Orléans has got it into her head and is working hard for it and a cabal has been formed of which I was told you were the head.'

I smiled and tried to speak but he quickly went on:

'I was very annoyed, not because I had any doubt about my rights, but there are some people whom one does not like to find in one's

---

[1] Charlotte-Aglaé d'Orléans, daughter of the Regent, who married the Duc de Modène, also known as Prince of Piedmont. *See below.*

[2] Son of the present Regent.

way; and I was not surprised that you might be one of them because I know how friendly you are with the Duchesse d'Orléans. Furthermore I also knew that you were close to the Comte de Toulouse—the two of you are always talking together at the Council meetings and having a private word either before or after—and the rumour was that the Count would be made Lieutenant General of the Kingdom, while the Duchesse d'Orléans would be her son's guardian. From this I concluded that you had allied yourself with the Bastards and were deeply involved in their plans. Everything which we have discussed has shown me, to my great pleasure, that you are not a supporter of the Bastards at all, which has encouraged me to speak so frankly on these other matters.'

I smiled again and at last interrupted him.

'Speaking frankly, Sir, I have been made out to be an enemy of yours. You can see where the truth lies and in what manner I have had the honour of speaking to you. But you should know that I had a lawsuit with the late Mme de Lussan, a cheat who had to be exposed. I did it with all possible respect which pleased Monsieur le Prince, who took no part in the proceedings. But Mme la Princesse, Monsieur your father and Madame la Duchesse would not receive me or hear a word in my favour. Nothing is more irritating than to have one's respect treated with contempt, and I was pretty outspoken on the subject. From that day forward I never entered the house of the late Duke and since then have hardly ever seen Madame la Duchesse. That, Sir, is at the bottom of my difference with the Hôtel de Condé which has caused many people to speak ill of me to you. But beware of what you are told, and judge by the facts.'

After that there followed an infinity of politeness from the Duke, a desire to deserve my friendship, excuses for the liberty which he had taken, delight at what had come out of it all—in a word, no one could have been more affable or less princely.

I replied with all the respect at my command: 'Sir, I have been around in the world for some time; I know how to form strong attachments, but no attachment has ever made me do something which I knew to be either unjust or foolish. I hope that I shall always be the same, and I must say that it would be both unjust and foolish for me to lend my support to the Duc de Chartres in his claim to the regency, in the lamentable event which we hope will never happen, when I know perfectly well that it is your due. I like the Comte de Toulouse: you will have gathered that from what I have said in this conversation. My sitting next to him at the Council meetings has created a bond between us—we discuss Council matters and rarely anything else. I never

call upon him except when it is essential, which is seldom, and I get
no pleasure from it because of the ceremonial which I cannot stand.
I wish him well, yet for all that he is one of the Bastards. He is in reality
insultingly inferior to me. Never would I consent to see a Bastard appointed Lieutenant General, certainly not to the detriment of the
Princes of the Blood. Those are my feelings which you can rely upon.
Never speak of them, I beg you again, for I do not wish to get mixed
up with the Duchesse d'Orléans over a contingency which I hope will
never arise.'

The Duke repeated that the only thing he insisted upon was the removal of the Duc du Maine from about the King's person, and he
begged me to see the Duc d'Orléans that morning and do what I
could; if it would make matters any easier he would willingly accept
whichever of the three draft projects the Regent preferred. I suggested
that he too should go to the Palais Royal that morning, so that the
Regent could be in no doubt as to his determined views; but I asked
him to go after me because I wanted time in which to prepare the Duc
d'Orléans. I promised, therefore, to be there at half-past eleven and he
said he would arrive at half-past twelve.

In taking my leave I said that I would omit nothing of the arguments which he had put forward, but that I could promise no more
since I was still acutely conscious of the danger of attacking M. du
Maine at the present time; I said that I would put both sides of the
argument without prejudice and leave it to the Regent to decide.

Monsieur le Duc expressed himself as quite satisfied with this frank
approach, and we parted with many expressions of mutual esteem. He
wanted to conduct me to my carriage but I deliberately preceded him
through the study door in order to prevent him, and we parted in his
antechamber where fortunately almost no one was waiting.

I arrived at the Palais Royal and, as things always go wrong when
one least wants them to, I found that the Duc d'Orléans was closetted
with the Maréchal d'Huxelles and Cardinals de Rohan and de Bissy
who were reading out to him some rambling documents about the
Cardinal de Noailles. There were quite a number of people in the big
study, and I waited there on tenterhooks; I was even more on edge
when I saw Monsieur le Duc arrive punctually at twelve-thirty. He
did not want the Regent told that he was there, but about a quarter of
an hour later he consented. I was furious that he would have a chance
to speak before me. But he was not in there more than fifteen minutes
and when he came out he said the Duc d'Orléans had told him that he
would be at least another hour with the Cardinals, whereupon he had
taken his leave and decided to come back later for the Council meeting.

1718 I forgot to mention that I had arranged that if I considered my talk with the Duc d'Orléans warranted it I would meet him that evening in the Tuileries gardens and that I would let him know about this at the Council. At the Palais Royal we hardly acknowledged one another and I was glad to see him go without any more being said.

Meanwhile I realized that I should be in a worse position if I could not get into the study. So I took the liberty of interrupting His Royal Highness; but instead of going in I sent the first *valet de chambre* to ask if I could have an urgent word with him. He came out at once. I took him over to the window and told him that while he was fooling about with those two Cardinals who were wasting his precious time over something which he wouldn't agree to anyway, I wanted to see him before Monsieur le Duc, who had said that he was coming back, and give him a long report on the important conversation I had had as a result of the note sent to me early that very morning. He replied that he thought so since Monsieur le Duc had mentioned that he had both written to and seen me. It was to gain time that he had told Monsieur le Duc that he would be busy for some time with the Cardinals; in fact, he did have about another hour's business with them but if I would wait he would send them away. He went into his study, told them that he was tired and in any case the business could be dealt with better in two sessions than in one, and within fifteen minutes they came out with their portfolios under their arms. I entered in their stead, the doors were closed and the Duc d'Orléans and I walked up and down the gallery talking for two good hours.

Long as my conversation with Monsieur le Duc had been I reported the whole of it to the Duc d'Orléans, commenting as I went. He was struck by the force of my arguments against attacking M. du Maine and rather alarmed at Monsieur le Duc's insistence on this point.

I reminded him rather too brusquely that he had failed to demote the Bastards when the Princes of the Blood, *Parlement* and the public were crying out for it and everyone expected it. 'Believe me,' I said, 'this business is so dangerous and you have so often and so gratuitously broken your word on the subject that if you let it slip through your fingers again there will be nothing more to be done. Monsieur le Duc has told you that he does not want charge of the King's education but that if he asks for it he must have it, and that his asking for it is the only way of removing it from M. du Maine. Do you realize, Sir, the full implications of that apparently simple statement? The second subject in the Kingdom, under cover of giving rein to his personal dislikes, is trying to strengthen his own position without offence to you by obtaining control of the education. When he has got it you

220

will be dependent on him because you cannot take it away from him
as you can from the Duc du Maine and you must realize what it is
like for the Regent to be dependent on anyone—particularly when it
is his own doing. And another thing—if the Bastards had been de-
moted at the time of the old King's death there would have been no
superintendent of the young King's education and Monsieur le Duc,
not being then of age, could not have asked for the post; the Maréchal
de Villeroy would have been left in charge as tutor and you would
have been master of everyone, however distinguished, and in consequence of the education. What a difference!'

The Regent sighed, convinced, and asked me what I thought he
ought to do. I replied that I would tell him; that I would not go behind
Monsieur le Duc's back, and that when I left him I had told him that
I would faithfully recount to His Royal Highness everything that had
been said in our conversation, but that I reserved the right to express
my own opinions as strongly as I saw fit. I then said to the Regent that
the only way I could see to avoid dismissing M. du Maine under the
present difficult circumstances would be to recall M. de Charolais,
that he should insist on this, although the Hôtel de Condé faction regarded it as impracticable because there was no steady post available
for him since the Governorship of the Ile-de-France was not acceptable to them and there would be difficulty in raising a sufficient dowry
for Mlle de Valois. I said that they could hardly fail to realize that this
was essential, because the point at issue was whether he could really
count on the support of the Princes of the Blood in dismissing M. du
Maine and it was obvious that there must remain an element of dubiety
so long as M. de Charolais remained outside France and in a position
to accept the Governorship of Catalunya under Spanish sovereignty.

The Duc d'Orléans liked the sound of this expedient which got so
near to the marrow of the affair that I hardly thought it would be
necessary to draw his attention to it. He told me that the *lit de justice*
would probably be held the day after tomorrow, or in four days at
most, which was far too soon to get the Comte de Charolais back, and,
once this opportunity had passed, there would be time enough to deal
with his affairs—for the business with the *Parlement* was so pressing
that Monsieur le Duc himself could not suggest any action except a
lit de justice. He assured me that he would be firm on this point with
Monsieur le Duc, and added that he would like me to go to the
Tuileries that evening to see what effect His Royal Highness's words
would have had.

He went on to say that he doubted if the *lit de justice* could take
place the day after tomorrow because the Keeper of the Seals was

doubtful if he could prepare the documentation in time. I took a poor view of this because I saw it as the prelude to a long series of postponements and changes. I asked him to what date he proposed to postpone the affair, because strong measures which came to nothing always leaked out with lamentable results.

'Until Friday,' he said, 'for Wednesday and Thursday are Saints' days and that is the soonest we can manage.'

'All right,' I said, 'so long as it is Friday, come what may.'

There was a little more conversation with the Regent, chiefly on the shortcomings of the Parlement, and then Saint-Simon took his leave to go home, somewhat ill-tempered, to a very late midday meal. He returned for the Council, tipped the wink to Monsieur le Duc, but eventually missed him in the gardens because he was held up by the importunity of the Abbé Dubois. So ended the Sunday of endless discussion.

The following morning there was a further meeting of the Regency Council at which it was agreed that the Parlement's decrees should be annulled. Considerable discussion followed as to whether the Duc de la Force, who had attended the Council as Vice-President of the Treasury, should be made a member of it, and this was finally agreed. But Saint-Simon pointed out that this would seriously offend the Duc de Guiche, Vice-President of the War Office, and after further discussion he too was appointed.

When the Duc de Guiche had gone, after being told of his appointment, I asked the Duc d'Orléans how he was getting on with Monsieur le Duc, and explained how we had missed one another the previous evening. We were walking up and down the Great Gallery; he stopped, turned to me and said that he had never met anyone so stubborn and it frightened him.

'And so?' I asked.

'And so,' he said, 'he wants charge of the King's education and won't let it go.'

'What about his brother?' I interrupted.

'Always the same old story. I can see perfectly well that they are as thick as thieves. Sometimes he says, as he did to you, that his brother is an irresponsible child, always doing the first thing that comes into his head, for whom he cannot answer; and then, when I talk to him about a position in France, he says in that case his brother would come back and one could absolutely rely on him. I twisted his tail a bit and pointed out the inconsistency of all this, and he was rather embarrassed. But he kept his foot down just as firmly and I got no further.'

'That is to say,' I replied, 'that you now know what was never really in doubt, that they are hand in glove and that Monsieur le Duc is the master. To be sure of his support you have got to do two things: give him the education, and give his brother a good position. How are you going to get out of that, Sir? The question of the education is the more serious, but even so I can't see a suitable position available for the other one.'

'It doesn't worry me,' said the Regent, 'so far as a position is concerned there is nothing I can do since there is none vacant, and there is no answer to that. I am not in the least afraid of his being given something in Spain; Alberoni is going to think twice before saddling himself with a penniless French Prince of the Blood who will expect both riches and authority. As for the education, I shall do nothing; there is a man on my side who will get this idea out of Monsieur le Duc's head, for he has great influence over him, and is coming to see me shortly.'

'May I ask, Sir, who this is?'

'La Faye, his secretary, whom he consults about everything; between ourselves, I grease his palm.'

'Fine,' I said, 'do what you like so long as you save the education.'

We ran over things again and then, coming back to Monsieur le Duc, he asked me to try to arrange a meeting again in the Tuileries to see what the effect of my earlier conversation had been, and then to come and report to him the next morning; I was to use the back door to avoid arousing suspicion, since it was unusual for me to see him every day.

When I got home I sent a message to the Duc de la Force to attend that afternoon's meeting of the Council of which he was now a member. He came to see me at once. I have never seen a man so delighted. I got rid of him as soon as I could. This appointment to the Council produced a discovery. The Duc de la Force wanted to tell the Maréchal de Villeroy[1] and went to see him after dinner, before the Council was due to begin. He wanted to go in through the big study where the Council was generally held when the Maréchal de Tallard saw him and, asking where he was going, said that he had just been having a private talk with the Marshal who had gone to sleep in the middle of it so he had left him. The Duc de la Force, who was afraid of being reprimanded by the Marshal, pushed on to write his name in the book. When he went into the study he found Falconet, a doctor from Lyons who was always with the Marshal, who asked where he was going; he told him, and repeated what the Maréchal de Tallard had said. This good fellow, who was always perfectly straightforward, replied: 'They may say he's asleep, but he isn't. When I was with him the Duc

---

[1] Chairman of the Finance Committee of which the Duc de la Force was President.

223

du Maine came in, then the Maréchal de Villars; they shut the doors and have been there ever since.'

This was the first thing the Duc de la Force told me when I arrived. Soon after we saw the Duc de Villars come in by the ordinary door, then after a discreet interval the Duc du Maine entered through the King's door and finally the Maréchal de Villeroy followed. This carefully arranged entry struck me and I urged the Duc de la Force to tell the Regent what he had just told me as soon as possible, which he did.

Meanwhile I was buttonholed by Monsieur le Duc who said that he had looked all over the Tuileries gardens for me. I told him I had been late and explained why, and I asked him to meet me again that evening. I cut the conversation short and moved away so that we would not be noticed, which one always feels nervously fearful of when there is a good reason for it.

After the Council the Duc d'Orléans asked the Princes, who liked to go shooting in the country during the week, to remain in town because there would be a special meeting of the Council on the following Thursday at which the *Parlement*'s edicts were to be annulled and there would also be some further business left over from this afternoon to complete.

When I got home I kept watching the clock to make sure that I did not miss Monsieur le Duc again. I asked Louville to drive me so that I could dismiss my own servants who had never before seen me go to a public garden. Louville drove through the garden and the second time round I found Monsieur le Duc in the path which we had agreed upon. I again apologized for the previous evening and explained once more how it had happened. Then I asked him how he had got on with His Royal Highness. He replied that he had not made much progress. This, I said, was hardly surprising since the problem of his brother was an obstacle which only he himself could remove. He went over the whole thing again and explained about his brother leaving France and just what he wanted. I remarked that what he had done the honour of telling me was no doubt true since he said so, but it was not very credible that a prince of that age should make his first trip, and to a foreign country at that, without saying a word to either his mother or his brother, and that he took with him old family servants—among them a gentleman most highly spoken of[1]—without even telling them where they were off to; furthermore this departure had taken place at a time when they were being obstinately refused justice in their case against the Bastards and I begged him to realize how much it had ag-

---

[1] Jean-François de Billy, mentioned by name later in the conversation.

224

gravated the situation. As far as the darkness permitted I saw Monsieur le Duc smile and he not only did not reply much but I felt that he did not even try to cope with my arguments. He simply said that it all depended on the Duc d'Orléans, and that the whole thing would be solved by giving his brother a position, adding that it could easily be done at the expense of the Duc du Maine. We then had a long conversation along the same lines as our talk at the Hôtel de Condé. I held principally to two points—the danger of civil disturbance, and the Comte de Toulouse, but I did not get anywhere. I found myself up against a man who had made up his mind not to lose an opportunity which might never come again of achieving his end, and who had little confidence in the Regent's word. He admitted that there were arguments in favour of postponing the demotion of the Duc du Maine but that he was not such a fool as to take the risk. He added that the Duc d'Orléans knew quite well what was needed to keep them together, and what happened over the King's education on Friday would decide whether they were to be allies for ever or permanently estranged. I replied that the Regent and the second subject in the realm had need of one another, one more than the other admittedly, but nevertheless a union between them was in the best interests of the State; that it was to the advantage of both of them to remove the King's education out of the hands of the Duc du Maine and consequently I thought that he should trust His Royal Highness and not make it impossible by untimely demands on behalf of M. de Charolais at the risk of provoking civil war.

'Look, Sir,' Monsieur le Duc replied heatedly, 'we are only going round in circles. I have already told you there is no danger of civil war, and if there were it would be a less serious affair now than later because the longer the Bastards go on as they are at present the stronger their party will become. You and the Regent both agree that it has got to be put a stop to by taking the education away from the Duc du Maine. If he wants to throw everything away by putting the matter off again and again and breaking every promise he has made to me ever since the old King's death, I can assure you I don't. And a civil war to defend my rights would be a hundred times worse later than it would be now. Anyway I don't think it would happen: the Comte de Toulouse is too sensible and his brother too timid. Let us not waste any more time arguing the toss about that. So far as my brother is concerned, let the Duc d'Orléans promise that he will do something and then trust me. Once the *lit de justice* is over there will be plenty of time to do whatever needs to be done about my brother, who will come back to this country as soon as it has been fixed up.'

'But, Sir,' I said, 'may I let you into a secret? You are an honest man in whom one can confide, but I beg you not to let the Duc d'Orléans know that I have told you; for I have it from him, and I think you ought to know, that we are much better informed about your brother's activities than you imagine.'

'What is it?' he said with emotion, promising to keep the secret.

I really did not care whether he kept the secret or not, but I thought it worthwhile making him promise in order to impress him the more. I then told him that we knew from intercepted letters (from Alberoni to the Duke of Parma, which I did not tell him) that in connection with the present Spanish project in Italy[1] 10,000 pistols had been earmarked for a private individual. I stressed particularly a *private* individual—not the head of a state, nor a contractor nor a banker, from which we had drawn the conclusion that the only private individual who could be worth such a considerable sum must be M. de Charolais.

Monsieur le Duc said how pleased he was that I had told him this. But he said that in his brother's suite everything passed through the hands of the Sieur de Billy, the much trusted gentleman of their household whom he had praised so highly, and that Billy was quite incapable of being party to anything of this sort without reporting back. And he then assured me on his oath, with such sincerity that I was convinced, that he had no reason to suppose that his brother was trafficking with Cardinal Alberoni or anyone else in Spain.

This was a considerable relief to me, and I said so. He then turned to the subject of Mlle de Valois, and I said as much as I could in favour of the Prince de Piémont. He did not press the matter, as he had in the Hôtel de Condé, either because he realized the difficulty of producing enough money for the two of them or because he was too taken up with his own affairs, and he passed on to the question of a governorship for his brother. He pressed me to see the Duc d'Orléans the following morning, to stress how he felt and dwell on the danger of delay; he himself would call later in the day. Then he said emphatically that on the events of Friday, and not a day later, would depend his entire devotion to the Duc d'Orléans, and that if he was let down never again would he go as far as from where we were standing to the other side of the path for him. He asked me to tell the Regent what he had said and to add that if the education were entrusted to his charge on Friday he would be moved by a depth of feeling which would last so long as he lived.

---

[1] Alberoni's projected expedition against Sicily.

I demurred so far as I could, but he finally drove me into a corner by saying that since I had reserved to myself the right of putting my own views to the Regent, the least I could do was faithfully to convey his own words when he asked me to do so. I agreed to do as he asked and took advantage of his gratification to mention the question of our standing *vis-à-vis* the Bastards, and he promised me that on the following day he would tell the Duc d'Orléans that after mature consideration he thought the reduction of the Bastards to their proper precedence in the peerage was the soundest of all the suggestions and draft edicts which he had seen.

We parted, having agreed to meet at the same place the following day; Monsieur le Duc, as we parted, apologized for all the trouble he had caused me and paid me a number of compliments which I returned. I said how sorry I was not to accompany him from the gardens and disappeared down one path while he took another; I found my coach waiting for me and went home.

The next morning, Tuesday 23 August, I went to the Palais Royal at half-past nine; Ibagnet, who was expecting me, let me in by the back door. The Regent was at Mass, but as soon as he returned he came to find me and shut the doors. We walked up and down the Great Gallery and I reported what Monsieur le Duc had said the night before. He fully approved of what I had said about the 10,000 pistols, and he was very relieved to hear that this sum had not gone to the Comte de Charolais and that he was not in the pay of Spain. We went over most of the important points, and it seemed to me as if he considered the marriage of the Comte de Charolais with his daughter as a practical proposition. I pointed out to him the very much greater advantages of a marriage with the Prince de Piémont, which would increase the standing of his regency and bring a valuable alliance with the King of Sicily; I added also that he ought to have some consideration for the Duchesse d'Orléans, since it would be turning the knife in the wound if the downfall of her brothers were immediately followed by the marriage of her daughter to the son of a sister whom she had hated all her life.[1] Finally I said as much as I thought fit to bolster up the Duke's resistance to Monsieur le Duc's arguments. But I felt that two things had made a deep impression on him—one was what I had just told him about the Comte de Charolais in Spain and the other was the strength of Monsieur le Duc's protests which I had in duty bound reported. I did not shrink from telling how often Monsieur le Duc said

[1] The Comte de Charolais was the son of Madame la Duchesse who, like the Duchesse d'Orléans, was a daughter of Louis XIV by Mme de Montespan.

that he had broken his word, and although he said it was not true I could tell by the way he answered that the cap fitted.

We then went on to talk about the practical details of the *lit de justice*. I happened to mention in passing that owing to the lack of space the high seats would only be raised one step, but I thought that this would be sufficient to distinguish them from the lower seats. Whereupon he drew himself up and said that would not do at all as the high seats in the Great Chamber had five steps. I pointed out the practical difficulties and told him that according to him no one was more jealous of his standing as a peer than I, but in the circumstances I would be satisfied. Not a bit of it. He went over all the possible ways of arranging things as he wanted without finding an answer, and finally told me to see Fontanieu and get something done about it. This drove me to desperation, because the Duc d'Orléans had never shown the slightest sense of dignity either in himself or in others. A slight change in the steps was not going to make any difference to his standing as Regent, and as for the peers he had shoved them around so much that I could not believe that he could all of a sudden start worrying about their honour and dignity. In my mind I thought that, cornered by Monsieur le Duc so that he had to agree to a formal *lit de justice*, he was looking for any way of getting out of it; the three-day postponement had made me suspicious and this new move, so completely out of character, confirmed it. This made me very unhappy; for the rest of our talk I tried to get him to say something which would throw some light on this important point, but without success. If what I suspected was in the Regent's mind, he managed to hide it from me with complete success.

'Have I told you,' he asked, 'of the talk I had last Tuesday with the Comte de Toulouse?' When I said no, he told me that after a conference with the Comte de Toulouse and the Maréchal d'Estrées, the Count had stayed behind and requested permission to ask a question. The question was whether the Regent was satisfied with him and with the way he conducted himself. After every assurance, he then asked if he might put another question concerning his brother who was worried by current rumours that the Regent intended to have him and the Maréchal de Villeroy put under arrest. The Regent laughed as though it were something not worth taking seriously. The Count pressed him and he said that he had no such idea. The Count then asked if he might give his brother a positive assurance on this point and, when the answer was in the affirmative, he then asked if the Regent were dissatisfied with his brother and how he thought the rumours could have started. The Regent said that he had no idea how such a rumour could have got about, but that he could not honestly say that he was satisfied with the Duc du Maine. The Count wanted details, whereupon the Duc d'Orléans asked if he really thought that deliberately stirring up the *Parlement* was a good thing. The Count replied frankly that it seemed to him a criminal act, and asked if there was any more against his brother beyond this. The Duc d'Orléans then said that there was positive evidence that the Duke had been in negotiation with Cardinal Alberoni.

'Worse and worse,' remarked the Count tartly, 'I regard that as nothing more or less than treason.'

Whereupon the Duc d'Orléans really told him everything about his brother's goings on. The Count replied that he could not really believe that his brother was as bad as all that and he begged the Regent to stick to the truth; then he added that as for himself he had given an oath of allegiance because he regarded the Regent and the State as one and indivisible and that he would guarantee his own loyalty to that oath but could not answer for his brother.

This conversation seemed to me to be very important. I said to the Duc d'Orléans that I had never seen anything so straightforward and so admirable as the behaviour of the Comte de Toulouse, and at the same time nothing could be more unfavourable to the Duc du Maine than that his brother, so obligated to support him, should in fact have been so critical. The Regent listened carefully. I said that this clearly showed what a mistake it had been to leave the Duc du Maine intact, but nevertheless one must not lose one's sense of proportion and I wanted to point out and invite his most serious reflection upon the dangers of attacking the Duc du Maine and the *Parlement* together and driving them into an alliance. The Regent then told me that the Maréchal de Villeroy had also brought up the subject of the rumoured impending arrest of himself and the Duc du Maine and most humbly asked if he could be reassured on the subject. I said that whatever happened he at least must be left where he was, for if he were removed and anything happened to the King all the old vile calumnies against His Royal Highness would be raked up again. He agreed and said that in any case the Marshal's age and incompetence made it a matter of indifference whether he remained in office or not.

We then went back to the subject of Monsieur le Duc, and I tried to find out how the Regent felt about the Duc du Maine and the subject of our rank. He prevaricated. I begged him to reflect once more on the consequences of taking away a position of such importance as the education from the Duc du Maine and giving it to a Prince of the Blood as obstinate as Monsieur le Duc, and I pointed out that if the

Duke had already been deprived of so important a position he could be no more furious or intractable if he were simultaneously reduced to his proper precedence in the peerage. The Regent replied that he had once wanted to do it but Monsieur le Duc had been against it because he was anxious to keep an intermediate rank between the Princes and the peerage, and he wanted me to know this straight out so that I would not be deceived by Monsieur le Duc's protestations. I then left, with some glimmerings of hope.

I realized that neither the Duc d'Orléans nor Monsieur le Duc was in the least interested in the restoring of our rank. I decided that both of them were intent on avoiding the issue—particularly the Regent who was a master of every kind of deviousness even if it landed him in trouble afterwards. I also realized that the Regent would be no more capable of resisting Monsieur le Duc's pressure on this point, once the idea were put into his head, than he was on the subject of the education; and I thought that it would not be impossible to bring Monsieur le Duc on to our side since he had need of me as a go-between and also had already shown some signs of repenting of his previous error over the intermediate rank by including in one of his three draft memoranda a clause calling for the reduction of the Bastards. I realized that the time had come to speak frankly to him. These questions ran round and round in my head all day, and I was frightened of myself lest I should allow my own interests to affect my clear vision of what was best for the State.

While I was thinking things over the Duc de Chaulnes forced his way into my house in spite of the fact that I had ordered the doors to be closed against everyone who was not already in the secret. He was the son and nephew of the Ducs de Chevreuse and de Beauvilliers, and a very close friend of mine. I had been instrumental in obtaining his elevation to the peerage, and he had never forgotten it; in addition he was as concerned as I was about the dignity of our standing. He had come because he had heard rumours of the Regent's fury with the *Parlement* and he wanted to discuss it with me to see if we could not make something out of it. I was sorry not to be able to take him into my confidence; I chatted generally and said good-bye to him as soon as I could.

I was expected at the house of the Duc de la Force, where Fagon and the Abbé Dubois were also due. As they both lived some way away I was there first. I had a chance of voicing my doubts arising from the fuss the Duc d'Orléans had made that morning over the steps up to the chairs in the Tuileries. He was as alarmed as I was, and when Fagon arrived he felt the same. Together we went over the mémoire which I had dictated to him; he had made several important and useful additions to cope with the *Parlement*'s possible refusal to attend the Tuileries, the affixing seals on various key points of the Palais de Justice and the like. The Abbé Dubois, after we had kept him waiting for some time, came in with various excellent points on the actual procedure and suggested signs which could be used if the *Parlement* showed signs of walking out of the *lit de justice* and it consequently became necessary to arrest some of them or the whole gang, lock, stock and barrel.

I did not have time to go over the whole thing with them. The business of the steps up to the chairs was worrying me, and I wanted to talk the Duc d'Orléans out of this trivial objection. I had sent a message to Fontanieu to expect me at his house. Between us we worked out a way of giving the seats three good steps. Fontanieu was worried about the three days' postponement because his workmen were dying of curiosity as to what was going on and would have all the longer in which to find out. When I left him I got into my coach and said, 'home,' but when I was passing the corner of the Tuileries gardens I pulled the cordon and said that it was such a fine evening that I would take a walk and the coach should wait for me at the Pont Royal.

It did not take me long to find Monsieur le Duc. I asked him to take off his ribbon of the Order, and he put it in his pocket. He had seen the Duc d'Orléans after me that morning and I realized that he had found things easier. This irritated me because I could see where it was leading us and I knew that I would get nowhere with so stubborn a man who had got the bit between his teeth. He told me that the Regent had spoken to him about the 10,000 pistols and his relief that it had not been sent to the Comte de Charolais, which surprised me because it had nothing to do with the matter in hand. I pressed him again about the Prince's return and the question of a position. He stuck to his point that a specific post must be found, and that this could easily be done at the expense of the Duc du Maine. I begged him once more to consider the consequences. We went on arguing but we made no progress.

'Wait a minute, Sir,' I said, 'I have just had an idea which I cannot promise that the Duc d'Orléans will accept but which I will certainly put to him if you wish, and, since I think that it is a reasonable way out, I shall urge his acceptance of it. I would like the Duc d'Orléans to write you a letter promising to give you the King's education once the *Parlement* has been dealt with. By that means you are in an impregnable position, for if he keeps his word you will have got what you want, and if he does not you have a weapon in your hand with which to rouse the Duc du Maine just as bitterly as if the education had actually been taken away from him Then you would force the Regent's hand, for so long as you held his letter he could not afford to remain at odds both with you and with the Duc du Maine.'

'Sir,' replied the Duke firmly, 'I put no more trust in letters signed by the Duc d'Orléans than I do in his word. He has deceived me too often and to fall for this one would really be too stupid.'

I argued, but it was no good; he was firmly determined to have the King's education or nothing.

The conversation continued interminably as they walked up and down the garden in the dark. Saint-Simon, unable to dissuade Monsieur le Duc, bargained with him and offered to do his best to secure the support of the peers if the Duke would press the Regent to reduce the Bastards and restore the peerage to its proper standing. On this they agreed. They also agreed that an edict should be brought in reinstating the Comte de Toulouse in his present rank. They parted very late with expressions of extreme cordiality.

Next morning, Wednesday 24 August, Millain[1] arrived punctually at half-past eight to show me the three draft edicts which he had drawn up on the instructions of Monsieur le Duc. He told me that the Duke had sent for him that morning and told him the gist of our conversation; he had asked him to tell me that he had not been able to close his eyes all night for worry, but his mind was made up and he would keep his word over the question of our rank.

Millain and I went over the edicts together. The first dealt with the education of the King; the second with the intermediate rank; and the third with the reduction of the Bastards to their proper rank in the peerage. I skipped the second and concentrated on the first and third which seemed to me very well phrased—particularly the latter which was pretty well in the form in which it was finally adopted. I told Millain to start on a new one for the reinstatement of the Comte de Toulouse, I would do the same and we would meet at the same hour the next morning when we would compare our drafts, adopt whichever was better, or hammer out a third version between us. I told him to keep Monsieur le Duc up to the mark, and we parted after a fairly long discussion.

I then went straight away to the Palais Royal to report my conversation with Monsieur le Duc to the Regent. He shut the door of his big study and we walked up and down the Great Gallery.

---

[1] Jean-François Millain was Monsieur le Duc's secretary for Council affairs and lived at the Hôtel de Condé.

From the start I could see that he had made up his mind to give the King's education to Monsieur le Duc; my objections were in vain. I represented to His Royal Highness the danger of a half-hearted attack on the Duc du Maine, the embarrassment it would cause in his own household, and the difficulty of getting the Comte de Charolais back from abroad if he did find a good governorship for him by taking one off the Duc du Maine. The Regent was convinced of all this, and in his desire to take the education away from him he regarded relieving him of all his offices as merely a necessary corollary. I saw that it was no good arguing, and I contented myself with reminding him that what he contemplated doing to the Duc du Maine was against my advice, and that, although it was contrary to my own interests and my desire for revenge, I had throughout opposed him and Monsieur le Duc in this matter because I considered it politically dangerous to attack the Duc du Maine and the *Parlement* at the same time. I then proposed the reduction of the Bastards to their proper precedence and told him what Monsieur le Duc and I had agreed on this subject. I added the old and obvious argument that this reduction could not make the Duc du Maine any more intractable than he was going to be anyway, and I stressed the justice and simplicity of this operation which merely consisted in putting into operation a resolution which had already been drawn up.

The Regent admitted the rightness of everything I had said except this last point; here he tried to persuade me that although the resolution existed through the presentation to the King and himself of our request signed by the Peers in a body at the time of the suit between the Princes of the Blood and the Bastards, the actual formula was open to discussion. The answer to that one was easy: since the King and the Regent had accepted our request as it stood and had communicated its contents to the Bastards, there could be no question of any alternative formula. This shut him up, and he fell back on saying that the Bastards had not made any reply. I said that they had had plenty of time, and if this point were to be accepted the way would be open for them to contend that the request to the King was bad in law and called for no reply, and that, since there was no way of forcing their hands, the thing could drag on indefinitely. After further argument he gave in, and I took the opportunity of pointing out once more how he had let us down over the hat question and various similar things. His excuse was that he had not wanted to rub the nobility up the wrong way. I pointed out with an indignation which I could not conceal that he had succeeded in rubbing a large number of people up the wrong way and had done nothing since to put matters right; that for themselves the nobility could not care less whether the Duc du Maine took precedence over us or we over him; that the law and precedent were on our side and it was only his own ill will towards us which, so contrary to his own interests, had dictated his actions. Finally I got him to admit that our cause at least had nothing to do with the nobility and that indeed our demands were well founded.

When I saw that I had got him in a corner, I said that Monsieur le Duc realized more clearly than he did the desirability of having us all on his side and of repairing as far as possible the harm which had been done; that he was not unaware that His Royal Highness had been so kind as to saddle him with all the responsibility after the case against the Bastards of drawing upon himself our dislike, that he wanted to put a stop to it and was prepared to admit that his idea of the intermediate rank was undesirable and impracticable and expressly to ask for the reduction of the Bastards to their proper precedence. I said that now that we had got to the point we would see how far the dislike of His Royal Highness for us could really go; I myself was astonished daily that with such fury in my heart I could go on seeing him and talking to him after the way we had been treated, and that it was only the habit of thirty years' friendship which made it possible—but, I added, he should not judge the other peers by the same standards since they had neither the same standing nor the same reasons for remaining loyal to him as I had.

Then I shut up and bothered more about watching his expression than replying to what he said. He looked downcast, a man torn between regrets and his own weakness, in whom that very weakness brought endless vacillation. I did not press him, for I wished to give him time to think without subjecting him to a further outburst.

But finally I could not resist saying: 'Well, Sir, are you still determined to ruin us, in spite of Monsieur le Duc?'

He began to smile and answered in a conciliatory tone that he had no wish to do so, that he would see if Monsieur le Duc really wanted the Bastards reduced, and if that was so he would do it.

'If you talk to Monsieur le Duc,' I said, 'I know what the answer will be. But will you really do it?'

'Yes,' he said, 'I want to do it and would have done so before if it had not been for him, and if he is now in favour I will most certainly do it.'

I thought this sounded as if he was leaving the back door open, but I did not like to press him too far. I turned to the question of the Comte de Toulouse.

234

The Lit de Justice

The conversation continued at great length. The Regent accepted the principle that, after the reduction, the Comte de Toulouse should be restored to his previous rank. The actual agenda was discussed, and the Regent expressed the hope that the two brothers would not be present. Saint-Simon pointed out how firm he would have to be if they did turn up, and the Regent promised that nothing would turn him aside. Saint-Simon harboured serious and secret doubts. The Regent asked Saint-Simon to see the Abbé Dubois and the Keeper of the Seals about possible difficulties, and again expressed his dissastisfaction about the number of steps up to the high seats.

As I was about to leave, I said one last word about the reduction of the Bastards. He gave me his promise but I didn't believe it and, raising my voice, I said, 'Sir, you will not do a thing and you will regret it for the rest of your life, just as you already regret letting the Bastards get away with it after the old King died.'

His hand was already on the handle of the door into his large study, and I slipped down the back stairs and home to dinner.

When I rose from table I received warning of a conspiracy of the Duc du Maine and various members of the *Parlement*, which was almost ripe, to declare the King's majority and appoint a Council under him made up of their cabal with the Duc du Maine in the chair. This seemed to me crazy, because all law, usage and good sense were against it. But the devious ways of these people, their detestation and distrust of the Regent's weakness, the public concern over the country's finances, the misgivings of the Duc du Maine, the wild audacity of his wife, the stark fear of the Maréchal de Villeroy, their intrigues with the Prince de Cellamare and Cardinal Alberoni, the plain speaking of the Comte de Toulouse about his brother only the day before—all these made me think that I could not afford to take the matter lightly and I sent a note to the Regent telling him what I had heard. Then I stayed at home with the Ducs d'Humières and Louville and would receive no one.

Between four and five in the afternoon I was told that Monsieur le Duc, after trying in vain to get into my house, had gone next door to the Duc de la Force. I had asked the Regent's permission that morning to tell the Duc de la Force what had been decided about the Bastards and the Comte de Toulouse, and it was quite understandable that Monsieur le Duc should have gone on there to find out what had been arranged about the *lit de justice*. I sent a message to Monsieur le Duc to say that I had not expected the honour of his visit, but I was at his service, and he came at once. I was very curious to hear what he had to say. I first apologized for the fact that my door had been closed, explaining that I only wanted to receive those few who were in the secret and one or two of my closest friends to whom my house was always open and who would smell a rat if they were turned away. Then I asked him for his news.

He told me, in the frankest way, that he had specifically requested His Royal Highness to reduce the Bastards and that he was full of hope, but that he had been charged to find out from me a bit more about the note I had sent that afternoon. I replied that he could not have come at a more opportune moment since all that I knew about it had come from the Duc d'Humières whom I had asked with Louville to step into another room. I fetched him and he told Monsieur le Duc that M. de Boulanvilliers[1] had heard several members of the *Parlement* discussing it and he had accordingly reported it. I suggested that the Duc d'Orléans should send for Boulanvilliers and get the story at first hand. With that Monsieur le Duc left and went back to the Palais Royal. I was pleased by what he had done about our rank, but not certain that he had been sufficiently insistent.

Meanwhile, a day or so before, Law had returned to his own house, and the *Parlement,* instead of haling him off to be hanged, became profoundly worried by the silence which had followed the Regency Council's decision to quash their edicts and sent several of its members to talk things over with him. They apologized on behalf of Blamont, President of one of the Courts. And this very morning the Duc d'Aumont had called, to discuss means of bringing *Parlement* and Regent together again. Law told us all the ridiculous details, which showed only too clearly that insolence had been succeeded by fear, and how easily a little firmness could have prevented all these tempests and indeed still could stop them. The Duc d'Aumont, a follower of the Duc du Maine and the First President, tried to justify the latter and to drag Law into the plot.

The Abbé Dubois told me that the Maréchal de Villeroy was terrified of being arrested, to such an extent that nothing could reassure him: he had called upon the Abbé, full of apologies and of his attachment for the late Monsieur and the like. From all these pointers I realized that these people were not yet ready for action, that we should take them by surprise, and that shrewd blows aimed at both the *Parlement* and that execrable Bastard would assure the maintenance of peace and authority for the duration of the Regency.

The Abbé Dubois, Fagon, and I spent some time discussing everything that could possibly go wrong and the remedies. Fagon pointed

[1] An economist and a great friend of the Duc de Noailles.

out to me that the postponement of the *lit de justice* from Tuesday to Friday in conjunction with the decision to quash the *Parlement*'s resolutions might make it embarrassing, if not actually dangerous, to arrest on the very morning of the *lit de justice* various members who it had been decided should be incarcerated in a variety of distant places; the *Parlement* when it heard what had happened might be too frightened to assemble and might refuse to come to the Tuileries, or having come might make some most awkward representation. We therefore agreed to postpone the arrests until Saturday morning, which would give us time to make any change of plan necessitated by the way the *lit de justice* had gone. I undertook to tell the Duc d'Orléans; I sent him a note saying that I had something to tell him the next morning and would come by the back door, which I asked should be left open. I then went to bed completely exhausted by so much thinking, hoping, and worrying about the details of what should be the lynch-pin of the whole affair, until I could think no more.

Early the next morning, Thursday 25 August, the Duc de la Force came to see me with his draft declaration in favour of the Comte de Toulouse. It was well done and precisely in accordance with my own thinking. Next Millain came in and hesitated, until I told him that M. de la Force was now a party to everything. We discussed the coming great events. Millain said that Monsieur le Duc would like me to go at eight that evening to the Palais Royal by the back door, while he would arrive at the main door, so that we could run over the final plans. Millain added that the Duc d'Orléans had asked Monsieur le Duc to tell me, and he asked if he might come with me and be smuggled in so that he might be on hand if he was needed.

But I was still not satisfied as to what was going to be done about rank, and I asked Millain unequivocally where his master stood in the matter; but he would say no more than Monsieur le Duc had said the previous evening. I started to put to Millain all the arguments with which I had convinced Monsieur le Duc, and I must say that the Duc de la Force gave me very little support, but Millain seemed to agree. I ended by saying, 'You have heard what I have to say, and I speak for all the peers of France who feel the same as I. Tell Monsieur le Duc what I have said. You cannot stress too strongly that I know from the Duc d'Orléans, and all the peers shall know it from me, that, come what may, our fate is in his hands, that tomorrow will bring us honour or ignominy and, whichever it is, we shall owe it to Monsieur le Duc. Sir, see that you tell him this: if he lets us down, I shall even find it within myself, and all the peers will agree, to take sides with the Duc du Maine against him; for at least in all the harm which Monsieur du

Maine has done us there was an object which he has achieved. But if Monsieur le Duc, who in rank has nothing to fear from us, abandons us at such a time, he will be doing us a mortal injury quite gratuitously with all the odium of *malum quia malum appetere*, a base philosophy to which the human race should never sink. Remember every word I have said, and please come back to tell us how far we may rely upon your master.'

I had hardly finished speaking and had no time to listen to Millain's protestations when a servant whom I had sent to the Palais Royal returned and said that the Duc d'Orléans was waiting for me and Millain was bidden to go and find Monsieur le Duc. I finished dressing and went at once.

Ibagnet was waiting for me and let me in by the back door as usual, but as he was opening one of the secret doors of the study for me, La Serre, Equerry-in-Ordinary to the Duchesse d'Orléans, caught sight of me with visible astonishment. This unfortunate encounter was irritating, but I was encouraged by realizing that the Duchess was at Saint-Cloud and it would take La Serre twenty-four hours to do anything about it. I found the Regent working with La Vrillière, who wanted to retire; but I stopped him and told the Regent that there was something I would like to say in front of him. I repeated what Fagon had suggested. The Duke told me that the same thing had occurred to him during the night when he had been lying awake with a touch of fever. I did not like the sound of this, for it might upset all our plans. It was agreed that the arrests would be postponed for twenty-four hours, and none too soon for La Vrillière was just about to give the necessary orders. He then left, and the Duc d'Orléans and I walked up and down the Great Gallery.

He spoke first about the plot which I had reported to him the previous evening, which he felt sure was without foundation; then he went on to the next day's events. I reminded him that he had fixed a Regency Council for today, after dinner, and he at once put it off for twenty-four hours. This was nothing more than a red herring, and served its purpose.

Two serious difficulties remained: whether the Regency Council should know about the plans, and what if the Bastards themselves came to the *lit de justice*. I suddenly thought of a solution, which was that the *lit de justice* should be held with open doors, which meant that it would be the same as an audience and votes would be given verbally, *sotto voce,* to the Keeper of the Seals who would go the rounds: an effectual way of silencing anyone not bold enough to repeat any insolence out loud, and convenient for the Keeper who could announce the verdict as desired without anyone being able to question it. We would rely upon the Keeper of the Seals; and there would be little to fear from either the timid Regency Council or the *Parlement*—for it would be a bold man indeed who would speak out loud, contrary to all precedent, in the presence of the King himself, surrounded by the King's Guards, and in the Tuileries. There remained the question of the possible presence of the Bastards. This would not be got round by Monsieur le Duc getting up and requesting them to leave with him, because before they did so they would have the right to demand that nothing should be done which in any way reflected on them unless they had previously agreed to it. The only thing for it was to rely upon the firmness of the Regent, which filled me with misgivings. He promised all sorts of wonders, and I must say that when it came to the point he did even better than he had promised.

While we were talking Monsieur le Duc arrived; all three of us continued the discussion and agreed upon the order of the main events for the next day. Then I took the liberty of saying that I called them both to witness that I had from the first been opposed to any attack on the Duc du Maine because of the danger of driving him into an alliance with the *Parlement*, and that I was still of the same opinion, but that, since the decision had gone against me, I begged them to stick together; on this, I said, depended the rise or fall of their common enemies as well as their own glory and peace of mind and the welfare of the State.

As I was leaving, they called me back to remind me not to forget our meeting for eight o'clock that evening, and Monsieur le Duc asked if I had seen Millain, who had of course come with me. We quickly ran over everything again, and I told them of the declaration in favour of the Comte de Toulouse which I had had drawn up and had left with Millain. I had forgotten to mention it until Monsieur le Duc brought up his name.

I went home then, more pleased and a great deal easier than I had been previously. Things seemed to be arranged as well as possible, every mischance foreseen and allowed for, the Regent was gathering strength and courage, none of us was deceiving himself, the secret was still well kept, the practical arrangements were completed and the moment for action was drawing near. Satisfied that I had done everything I could both with the Regent and Monsieur le Duc to save the Duc du Maine in the interest of the State, and against my own interests, I considered myself at liberty to rejoice in what had been decided against my advice and the fruits which would come from it. Nevertheless I still dared not give myself up to such happy thoughts

239

without being even more sure of the longed-for reduction of the Bastards, and I remained for two hours in a pleasurable state to which I yet could not completely abandon myself. Freed from responsibility for the major business which was now all arranged, I could give my mind entirely to the question of our rank and to the fact that to me alone had fallen the honour of achieving for the French peerage something which we had been unable to achieve by our united efforts.

While all this was going round and round in my head Millain arrived. He said that Monsieur le Duc had sent him to assure me that he had the Regent's promise that the Bastards would be reduced to their order of precedence in the peerage, that the declaration to that effect, together with that in favour of the Comte de Toulouse, had been sent to La Vrillière and the Keeper of the Seals for engrossing, and he was now in a position to give me a positive assurance that they would go through next day. No mistress was ever given so warm a kiss as that which I planted on the fat old cheek of the bearer of this pleasing message. Then from the bottom of my heart I expressed my feelings for Monsieur le Duc and for Millain himself who had served us so worthily in this affair. But in the midst of such rejoicing I did not lose my head. I reminded Millain that La Vrillière, friend of mine though he was, and the Keeper of the Seals were very much of the old Court, that the latter in particular had always been close to the Bastards, and that in our affairs both of them had put difficulties in the Regent's way, as he himself had told me the previous evening. It was necessary, I said, for Monsieur le Duc to put the seal on his good work by doing one thing more, and I begged that out of his friendship he would see both of them and impress upon them that he considered the reduction of the Bastards just as important as the King's education, and from the way they were getting on with the preparation of the declaration which had been sent to them he would be able to judge how reliable they were and how it would be necessary to handle them. Millain said that he saw no difficulty in that, and he would go with Monsieur le Duc to make sure himself that the two declarations had not been altered.

I spent the rest of the day at home with the Abbé Dubois, Fagon and the Duc de la Force, running over the arrangements once again. If the *Parlement* refused to come to the Tuileries the documents suspending them from their duties were already prepared, all lawsuits pending were to be referred to the Grand Council, *maîtres des requêtes* had been selected to make this decision known and to affix seals where necessary and officers of the bodyguard detailed to accompany them; if some came and others did not, those refusing would be punished in the same way; if the *Parlement* came but then refused to listen and tried to leave, again the same punishment would be meted out. If they all walked out the *lit de justice* would be gone through with and eight days later another would be held in the Grand Council to register what had been done. If the Bastards or any one else created a disturbance they were to be arrested as they left at the end, but if there was general uproar they would be arrested on the spot. Likewise if they attempted to leave Paris they were to be arrested. Everything had been carefully arranged.

The Abbé Dubois drew up a little list of signals such as crossing his legs, taking out his handkerchief and other simple movements; these were to be handed out on the morning to officers of the bodyguard chosen to take action if required. These officers would be stationed about the room and were to keep their eyes on the Regent, ready to obey any signal. He went further; in order to save the Duc d'Orléans as much trouble as possible, he had drawn up a time-table showing exactly at what hour during the night each person should be sent for and exactly what the Duke should say to him; by this means no one would be warned until it was absolutely necessary and the secret would be kept until the last moment.

About eight o'clock in the evening Millain arrived for our rendezvous at the Palais Royal. He told me that Monsieur le Duc had called on both La Vrillière and the Keeper of the Seals, had talked things over and had seen the two declarations already signed and sealed in their correct form. After thanking him, I sent Millain off to meet me at the back door of the Palais Royal so that my staff should not see us set out together, and a few minutes later I set out myself without linkmen. Ibagnet was waiting for us and took us upstairs in the dark so that we would not be recognized. I was alarmed to find the Duc d'Orléans in bed, saying he had a fever. I snatched up his wrist and took his pulse; he really was feverish. I told him it was only mental and bodily fatigue, and he would be all right in twenty-four hours. He replied that he would hold the *lit de justice* whatever he felt like. Monsieur le Duc came in and stood at the head of the bed; the four of us were alone in the room, lit by a single candle. Monsieur le Duc and I sat down, and we ran over the orders which had been given and those to come—not without some anxiety on my part at the sight of this untimely fever in someone who normally never suffered from anything of the sort.

It was agreed that the *Parlement* would be warned at six A.M. to be at the Tuileries for the *lit de justice* between nine and ten; the Regency Council was to be told at seven that the meeting summoned for that

241

afternoon would instead be held at eight, and members were to bring with them any urgent matters needing discussion so that the meeting could be prolonged if necessary. We also decided that His Royal Highness should depart from his usual practice and take votes in order of seniority in order to show his solidarity with the Princes of the Blood and to prevent anyone speaking out of turn. I suggested that if the Council ran out of business to discuss before the *lit de justice* was ready, the Regent should tell everyone to keep his seat and not allow anyone to leave the room on any pretext whatever.

Next Monsieur le Duc wanted to read what he intended to say on the subject of the King's education. The Regent and I both suggested a few changes. It then occurred to me that it would be a good thing to flatter the vanity of the Maréchal de Villeroy, and Monsieur le Duc wrote in a passage at my dictation, using a dog-kennel which I fetched him in the absence of a writing table.

Then came the great question of the Bastards. It was decided that nothing should be said about them at the Council, since they would be present, and that to keep them out of the *lit de justice* they should not be warned for it on the pretext that since their suit against the Princes of the Blood they did not care to attend the *Parlement*. The Duc d'Orléans, always an optimist, thought that this would keep them away, and, that in any case they would not be able to come in because, not having been warned, they would have neither bands nor mantle with them.[1] I said that was merely burying our heads in the sand. The Duc du Maine lived immediately beneath the King's apartments, and the Duc de Villeroy as Captain of the in-lying guard was also housed in the Tuileries. Sooner or later the Duke would notice all the furniture being brought in and would, if he possibly could, warn his father who would be sleeping in the King's room. As soon as the Maréchal de Villeroy found out what was going on he would warn the Duc du Maine, who would warn his brother the Comte de Toulouse. In consequence they would have from about six in the morning to get ready and dress correctly. I added that the more they were taken by surprise, the more they would be determined to turn up at the *lit de justice* and defend themselves tenaciously, and the only remedy was for the Duc d'Orléans to take what was coming with strength, showing no temper or emotion, in the firm knowledge that he was seeing justice done and was strengthening the royal authority temporarily reposing in his hands.

[1] At a *lit de justice* it was obligatory for princes and peers to wear bands of pleated linen, a plumed hat and a short mantle.

Another question which we discussed was what to do if the *Par-*
lement refused to vote. I suggested two alternatives: if the refusal were
silent and orderly, the Keeper of the Seals should continue to go round
taking votes as if nothing had happened. On the other hand, if the
refusal were expressed aloud either by some of the members or by the
First President or the bench of Presidents, it should be pointed out
that the King was not bound either to listen to or to accept the views
of the *Parlement*, which he asked for merely out of his royal goodness
and to show them some respect, but that he was the master and they the
subjects, and so hold firm. The Duc d'Orléans remarked that he had
often heard me say the opposite, that at a *lit de justice* everyone should
have the right to say his piece as well as merely to vote. I replied that
I was still of the same opinion but circumstances altered cases, and it
was only the peers, judges, and councillors, born of the crown and
descended from Kings, *laterales regis,* who should have the right to
deliberate on matters of State; to cast the net wider, officers of the
crown might be included by virtue of their position as an act of grace—
a grace of which the outward sign was that whereas peers came to a
lit de justice by right the officers could only come if summoned and
might only enter behind the King, not with or before him. But as far
as the officers of the *Parlement* were concerned, they had always been
the assistant judges to the peers and it was the presence of the peers
which alone allowed them the liberty of giving their opinion on matters of State, hence the phrase always inserted in resolutions, 'the
court having a quorum of peers.' I went on to give further reasons,
and the Duc d'Orléans was convinced that I was right and determined
to act on my suggestions.

I asked if arrangements had been made for telling the law officers
of the crown during the night. The Regent replied that they would be
warned at the same time as the *Parlement* was summoned to the *lit de
justice* and told to behave discreetly—especially Blancmesnil, the first
Advocate General, who would be told that his fortune and his future
would depend on his giving a favourable opinion without any hedging
on any question put to him.

Then the Duc d'Orléans explained to us the time-table that had
been drawn up for his actions during the night, right through until
eight the next morning when he would wait upon the King in his
mantle. I begged him to get what rest he could, and to remember that
the whole future of his regency hung upon the events of the morrow
and on the execution of them with firmness and presence of mind.
With that I wished him good night and withdrew to the foot of the
bed; I thanked Monsieur le Duc for the visits which he had made,

whereupon he thanked me and embraced me twice. Millain had remained standing throughout the conference and had made some very useful comments. Before leaving I approached the bed once more and asked permission of the Duc d'Orléans to take the Duc de Chaulnes into our confidence since he would know something was going on during the night because of the orders to the Light Horse of which he was Captain; the Duke consented. I took his pulse, not without some misgivings. I assured him that the fever would not amount to much, without feeling any too sure myself. I then took my leave at exactly ten o'clock, and left with Millain the same way as I had come.

I stopped my carriage in front of the Hôtel de Luynes, quite near my own house, and sent a message to the Duc de Chaulnes asking if he would come and speak to me. He came out without a hat and got into the carriage, whereupon my coachmen, whom I had instructed, immediately drove off to my house; the Duke was extremely surprised at being carried away like this, but I did not say a word until we were safely in my study. He was even more surprised when behind closed doors I told him of the great events prepared for the next day. We rejoiced together over this sudden and unexpected re-establishment of our status, the hope of which, however distant, had been our only consolation under the horrible tyranny of the late King.

A few days before I had found out by chance that Contades, Major of the Guards and a very trustworthy and intelligent man, proposed to go home to Anjou on leave. I ran into him at the Palais Royal just as I was getting out of my carriage. He gave me his hand, and I whispered in his ear that if I were he I would quietly postpone my leave. He promised to do so without my having to say any more and he said nothing about it to anyone. It was a good thing that I did this. At one in the morning the Duc d'Orléans summoned the Ducs de Guiche, de Villeroy and de Chaulnes, respectively Colonel of the Guards, Captain of the in-lying Bodyguard, and Captain of the Light Horse; he sent for Artagnan and Canillac, Captains of the two companies of Musketeers, and Desgranges as Master of Ceremonies in the absence of Dreux who was staying with Chamillart, his father-in-law, at Courcelles to give them their orders while La Vrillière gave what orders were necessary throughout the city. Something is always forgotten, and in this case we had quite overlooked the Swiss Guards. Contades, woken up by the Duc de Guiche and told something of what was going on, went at once to His Royal Highness, who had not said a word to him, for orders. He pointed out to the Regent that the Swiss Guards were so loyal that there was nothing to fear from them and they would be mortally offended if they were deliberately overlooked. The Regent ordered him to see to it, and at four o'clock Contades went to the Tuileries to awaken the Duc du Maine, Colonel General of the Swiss Guards. The Duke had only been in bed about an hour after returning from a fête given by the Duchesse du Maine at the Arsenal where she was still living. The Duc du Maine was undoubtedly taken by surprise, but he hid his fear and asked Contades as lightly as he could whether he was alone; reassured on this point, he opened the door. Contades explained the orders which he had been given by the Regent, and the Duc du Maine immediately sent a message ordering the Swiss Guards to stand to. In his anxiety to know what was going on I do not suppose that he slept very well after that.

At about five o'clock in the morning of Friday 26 August the roll of drums was heard, and soon after the tramp of soldiers in the streets. At six Dangeau went to the *Parlement* to present his letter de cachet. The Gentlemen, to use their own phrase, were only just arriving; they sent word to the First President, who had the chambers called together. This took about half an hour, and they eventually replied that they would obey the summons. Then they debated how they should go to the Tuileries—by carriage or on foot. They decided on the latter since it was more usual, and they also hoped that by walking through the streets they would gain sympathy and arrive surrounded by a howling mob. What actually happened I will recount in due course. At the same time horsemen went to the homes of all peers and officers of the crown, the Knights of the Order, Governors and Lieutenant Generals of provinces who were to accompany the King to advise them all of the *lit de justice*. Desgranges in this sudden situation did not even have time to attend himself. The Comte de Toulouse had been supping with the Duc de Nevers near Saint-Denis and had only just got home. The French and Swiss Guards were stood to in their quarters, the Light Horse watch and two companies of Musketeers were also under arms; there were no police, who do not mount a watch, and the only normal watch on duty was that of the French and Swiss Guard at the Tuileries.[1]

If I had had little sleep during the last week, I certainly slept even worse on this night, the eve of such important events. I got up before six and shortly after I got my warning order for the *lit de justice*, on the back of which was a note that I was not to be specially woken up, which was a special piece of civility by Desgranges; he said to me later that he thought it was unnecessary since what was going to happen was

---

[1] Dangeau in his memoirs says that the military precautions were much more considerable than Saint-Simon makes out.

no news to me. All the others were to be got out of bed specially, and astonishment was pretty general.

At about seven a gentleman usher came from the Duc d'Orléans to warn me that the Regency Council would meet at eight and that cloaks would be worn. I dressed myself in black which was the only formal costume I had except a very splendid gold affair which I did not want to put on because I feared that it might be taken as an insult to the *Parlement* and the Duc du Maine. I took two gentlemen with me in my carriage and set out to see everything. I was filled at one and the same time with misgivings, with hope, joy, reflection and concern over the weakness of the Duc d'Orléans and of all the things that could go wrong. I was also firmly determined to do everything I could to help without seeming to be in the know, and to appear attentive, circumspect, modest and moderate.

Leaving my own house, I stopped at Valincourt's gate, opposite the back entrance to the Hôtel de Toulouse. He was an intelligent and honourable man who moved in the best circles, Secretary General of the Navy, who had been since his young days with the Comte de Toulouse and enjoyed his confidence. I did not want the Count to feel that he was in any personal danger, nor to let him get mixed up with his brother. I asked Valincourt, whom I knew very well, to come and speak with me. He came out half-dressed and worried by the noise in the streets, asking at once what was going on. I leaned towards him and said quietly: 'Listen well and remember every word. Go and tell the Comte de Toulouse that he must take my word, be careful, and things will happen which may not please him but at the same time he himself will finish up all right. I don't want him to have a moment's anxiety. Now go quickly.' Valincourt pressed my hand as hard as he could and said: 'Ah, Sir, we have realized for a long time that there was bound to be an explosion: they have been asking for it, all of them except Monsieur le Comte, who will be eternally obliged to you.' He went at once to pass on my message to the Count, who knew that I had saved him from being dragged down with his brother's fall and never forgot it.

I arrived at eight o'clock in the Grand Court of the Tuileries without having noticed anything out of the ordinary on the way. The coaches of the Duc de Noailles, the Maréchaux de Villars and d'Huxelles and a few others were already there. I went up without meeting many people and entered through the double doors of the guard room which were closed. The *lit de justice* was arranged in the big anteroom where the King normally took his meals. I stayed for a minute or two, had a look round to make sure that everything was in order, and whispered a word of congratulation to Fontanieu. He told me that he had only got there with his workmen at six, that everything had been put together so quietly that the King had not heard a sound, and one of the valets, coming out of the King's bedroom at seven, had been absolutely astonished to see the carpenters at work, that even the Maréchal de Villeroy had only learned about it from him, and no one in the house had any idea what was going on. After having a good look round, I went over to the throne which was just being put in its place. I meant to go into the second antechamber but the pages told me that the door was shut. I asked where people were to wait before the Council began and where those were who had already arrived. Several of them offered to show me upstairs. Cotte's[1] son took me up a small staircase at the top of which was a various assembly including some officers of the Chancellery. He led me to a door which was opened for me by an usher as soon as I appeared. Here I found the Keeper of the Seals and La Vrillière and a few of their close friends. We were pleased to find ourselves assembled alone so that we could run over things again before the operation began. This was not actually what I had had in mind. The coaches which I had seen in the courtyard all belonged to suspect parties, and I wanted to find out where they had got to, watch their movements and break up their conversations. Arriving by chance in the Keeper's room, I felt that he might suggest coming with me, so I gave up the idea.

The Keeper of the Seals was standing eating a slice of bread, no more concerned than if he were about to attend an ordinary Council meeting, not in the least worried about the events which were shortly to revolve round him or the important things which he was going to have to say in public. His only doubt was about the firmness of the Regent and he rightly insisted that it was absolutely vital not to retract one inch from the agreed line. I reassured him, though I was none too confident myself. I asked if they had made adequate arrangements for being kept informed of what was going on in *Parlement*; they said yes, and indeed everything did work very well. I then asked to see the deeds which were to be registered; there was no time to read them, but they showed them to me in their order. I particularly wanted to look in rather more detail at those concerning the reduction of the Bastards and the ancient rights of the peers. 'Here you are,' said the Keeper of the Seals, as he showed it to me, 'this is your one.' I mentioned this particularly because the words were quoted afterwards as proof that I had been in the secret all along, and they must

---

[1] The King's first architect.

have been heard by someone listening at the keyhole, because the three of us were alone with the door shut.

We were still discussing all the possibilities when the arrival of the Duc d'Orléans was announced. We quickly ran over the last few points and then, while the Keeper was putting on his robes for the *lit de justice* so as not to have to change after the Council, I went downstairs so that we would not be seen to come in together.

During the heat wave meetings had been held in this room, which is the last one in the row, because the King, finding his own small room too stuffy, was sleeping in the Council chamber;[1] but on this important day as soon as the King got out of bed he was taken to be dressed in his own small room and then on to his study. The curtains of his bed and that of the Maréchal de Villeroy were drawn, and the Council table was set at the foot of them. When I went in I found a large number of people already present, attracted in a hurry no doubt by the first inklings of so unexpected an event; some members of the Council were among them. The Duc d'Orléans was standing in the middle of a large group at the far end of the room and, as I found out later, had just come from the King's room where he had found the Duc du Maine, wearing his mantle; the two of them had walked to the door together without exchanging a word.

After a leisurely glance round this gathering I went into the Council room. I found most of the members there scattered about the room looking grave. Almost complete silence reigned and no one was moving about: they stayed where they were standing or sitting. I did not join anyone but remained by myself to watch.

A moment later the Duc d'Orléans came in, very free and easy, showing no sign of emotion, and looking round the assembled company with a smile; this seemed a good omen. I asked him his news and he replied aloud that he was well, and then added in my ear that apart from being frequently woken up for orders he had slept well and was determined not to weaken. This pleased me, and from his bearing it did seem that he meant it; I gave him a word or two of encouragement. Next Monsieur le Duc arrived; he came straight up to me and asked me if I thought the Regent was in good form and would be firm. The Prince de Conti, morose, distrait and envious of his brother-in-law,[2] seemed occupied all about nothing. The Duc de Noailles was looking round the whole time, his eyes sparkling with rage at finding

---

[1] Rooms on the first floor of the palace overlooking the courtyard and therefore shaded from the sun.

[2] He was married to Mlle de Bourbon and Monsieur le Duc to Mlle de Conti.

248

himself amongst the general throng on such a great occasion, for he had no idea what was going to happen. Knowing how close they were to one another, I had expressly asked Monsieur le Duc to tell him nothing.

Monsieur du Maine then appeared, wearing his mantle; he came in from the small door of the King's apartment. He made a number of deep bows, of which he was never sparing, and then stood by himself, leaning on his stick,[1] by the Council table at the foot of the beds, considering everybody. It was there, face to face across the table, that with the greatest pleasure I made him the most cheerful bow I have ever made in my life; he returned it in like manner and then continued staring at everyone in turn, a worried look on his face, and muttering to himself.

Monsieur le Duc came across to me again to tell me how distressed he was to see the Duc du Maine in his mantle and urged me to brace the Duc d'Orléans; then the Keeper of the Seals came and said the same thing. A moment later the Duke himself came to tell me how put out he was at seeing Monsieur du Maine in his mantle, but he did not show any sign of weakness. I told him that I had always warned him to expect it, that any weakening would be fatal and that he had crossed the Rubicon. I added a few firm words of encouragement as quickly as I could, for I did not want to be seen talking to him too long. As soon as we parted, Monsieur le Duc came up, impatient and worried, to know what sort of mood the Regent was in; I replied in one word—'good'—and sent him off to keep the Duke busy talking.

I do not know whether these movements, which everyone was watching, scared the Duc du Maine or not, but no sooner had Monsieur le Duc left me and gone across to the Regent than he in turn went to talk to the Maréchal de Villeroy and d'Éffiat who were sitting side by side with their backs to the wall near the door of the King's apartment. They did not get up when the Duc du Maine approached them; he remained standing and the three of them had a long whispered conversation, and judging from the expression on the faces of the two who were sitting down, whom I watched carefully, they were very worried and surprised men. Eventually the Duc du Maine came back to where he had been before, across the table from me, and I noticed that he looked distracted and was muttering to himself more than ever.

Next the Comte de Toulouse arrived, just as the Regent left Mon-

[1] He always carried a stick because of his lameness.

sieur le Duc and the Keeper of the Seals with whom he had been talking. The Count was wearing his mantle; he saluted the company gravely; he appeared reserved and he spoke to nobody. The Duc d'Orléans found himself facing him, and turned towards me, although I was some distance away, as if to show his distress. I nodded my head slightly and gave him a straight look as much as to say, 'all right.' The Duc d'Orléans went up to the Comte de Toulouse and said aloud, so that those nearby could hear, that he was surprised to see him wearing his mantle, that he had not warned him for the *lit de justice* because since their last resolution he knew that he would not wish to meet the *Parlement*. The Comte de Toulouse replied that this was indeed so, but when the good of the State was concerned he put all other considerations on one side. The Duc d'Orléans turned on his heel without replying, came across to me and said, 'It cuts me to the heart to see that man there. Do you know what he has just said?' He repeated the Count's words, and I tried to comfort him by reminding him that the re-establishment of the Comte de Toulouse had already been agreed upon. He interrupted to say that he would like to explain things to him, but I replied that this would be very tricky and should only be undertaken as a last resort. I turned then so as to lead him back to the general company and cut short this private conversation which I was afraid would be noticed.

The Duc du Maine meanwhile had gone back to the Maréchal de Villeroy and d'Éffiat, they sitting and he standing in front of them as before. Then the Duke left these two and made a sign to his brother to join him at the foot of the Maréchal de Villeroy's bed, where he had again taken up his stand. He said little and seemed very agitated. The Comte de Toulouse was equally curt, and it was clear that there was some disagreement between them. The Duc du Maine became more insistent, and at last the Comte de Toulouse walked away between the feet of the two beds and the Council table, to where the Duc d'Orléans and Monsieur le Duc were talking by the fire-place, stopping at a suitable distance as one wishing to speak. After a minute or two the Duc d'Orléans noticed him and, leaving Monsieur le Duc, went over to him. The two of them turned away from everyone else for some time, with the result that it was impossible to find out what they were talking about, since one could see nothing but their backs and there was neither a gesture nor a sign of emotion between them.

The Duc du Maine remained standing alone where he had last spoken with his brother. His face seemed absolutely without any emotion, except every now and then when he cast a furtive glance in the direction of this conversation which he had promoted and then

looked round with an air which had in it something both of a condemned criminal and of a guilty culprit.

Eventually the Maréchal d'Huxelles called me over. He was standing so close to the Duc du Maine that there was only a table between
them, but he had turned his back; standing beside him, and thus forming a little group, were the Maréchaux de Tallard and d'Estrées and
the former Bishop of Troyes; as I approached them the Duc de Noailles
also walked across. Huxelles asked me at once what was going on, and
when I replied that I could just as well put the same question to him,
he asked me if any difficulty had arisen about the Princes or the children of M. du Maine in connection with the *lit de justice*. I replied that,
so far as M. du Maine and M. de Toulouse were concerned, no difficulty could arise, since the judgement delivered in the action brought
by the Princes of the Blood against them left them in full possession
of their honours; but that so far as M. du Maine's children were concerned, we should certainly not allow them to appear.

We remained thus loosely grouped for some time, and I occupied
myself in watching the Duc du Maine, with an occasional glance at
the Regent and the Comte de Toulouse who were still talking together. Eventually they separated, and I had a good chance to look at
them, for the Comte de Toulouse walked across the room towards us,
turned at the end of the table, and then, passing between it and the
two beds, went up to his brother who was still leaning upon his stick
by the foot of the Marshal de Villeroy's bed from which he had not
stirred. The Comte de Toulouse was greatly troubled, even angry,
and the Duc du Maine, seeing him in this mood, completely changed
colour.

Meanwhile I remained where I was, watching the Comte de Toulouse approach his brother, who still did not move, and trying hard
to gather what they were talking about. Suddenly I heard myself
called, and turning round, I saw that it was the Regent, who, after
walking up and down in front of the fire-place alone for a moment,
wished to speak to me. I went to him at once, and found him deeply
moved. 'I have told him everything,' he said at once, 'I could not
help it. He is the best fellow in the world and he is breaking my
heart.' 'But, sir,' said I, 'what have you said to him?'

'He came up to me,' replied the Regent, 'as an emissary from his
brother, who had begged him to see me and to tell me of the embarrassing position in which he found himself. The Comte de Toulouse said that his brother realized that the scene was set for an event
of some importance; that he could also see that he was out of favour
with me; and that he had sent him, the Comte de Toulouse, to ask me

frankly if I wished him to stay or if he would do better to leave. I must say that I thought it best to tell the Count that, since he asked, I thought his brother would be well advised to go. The Comte de Toulouse then asked for an explanation. I cut it short, however, and told him that, so far as he himself was concerned, he could safely remain since his position was to stay unaltered, but that some disagreeable things were probably going to happen to M. du Maine and that I thought that it would be as well if he were not present. The Comte de Toulouse asked me, with some insistence, how he could possibly remain what he was if his brother were attacked, when both kinship and honour demanded their complete equality. I replied that I was sorry, but that all that I could do was to distinguish merit and virtue by separating them from their opposing qualities. Then I said a few friendly words, which he received very coldly, and then he went off to tell his brother what I had said. Do you think I did wrong?'

'No,' I replied, since there was nothing to be gained by discussing the subject further, and there was no point in embarrassing a man whose resolution I was only anxious to reinforce. 'I am glad,' I added. 'Such frankness shows that you intend to be firm and are afraid of nothing. And now that things have got this far there will be an even greater need for firmness.' He seemed to me quite resolute, but at the same time most anxious that the Bastards should leave the room, and I think that that was really why he had acted as he had. Monsieur le Duc then came up to us. I stayed with them as short a time as possible and I advised them to separate too, since by now the eyes of the whole room were divided between us and the two brothers.

The Duc du Maine, pale as death, looked as though he was going to faint. Very slowly, so slowly that he hardly appeared to move at all, he crept to the foot of the table, while the Comte de Toulouse walked across, said a few words to the Regent, and then went slowly down the room. All this only took a moment. Then the Regent, who was now standing by the King's chair at the Council table, said in a loud voice: 'Gentlemen, let us be seated.'

One by one we went to our places. On reaching mine I looked back and saw the two brothers by the door through which we usually entered as though they were just about to leave. I leapt to a place between the King's chair and the Regent's so that the Prince de Conti would not hear what I was saying and whispered excitedly to the Regent, who was already in his place: 'Look, sir, they are going.' 'Yes, I know,' he answered calmly. 'Yes,' I replied, 'but do you know what they will do when they get outside?' 'Nothing. The Comte de Toulouse asked my permission for his brother and himself to leave, and he promised me that they would be prudent.' 'And if they are not?' I asked. 'They will be, and if they are not I have given orders to see that they are watched.' 'But if they do something foolish or try to leave Paris?' 'They will be arrested. My orders are quite clear, I can assure you.'

Hearing this I returned to my place in a calmer state of mind. I had scarcely reached it, however, before the Regent called me back to say, that, as the Bastards had now gone, he had changed his mind and would like to bring their affairs up before the Council. I replied that, as the only objection to doing so was now removed by their with- drawal, I thought it would be a great mistake not to do so. He re- peated the same thing in a low voice, across the King's chair, to Monsieur le Duc, and then called the Keeper of the Seals; both of them agreed, and after that we all took our places.

All this had only added to the anxiety and curiosity around us. Since all eyes had been upon the Regent, few had realized that the Bastards had left. When we turned to take our seats, therefore, every- one saw their places were vacant and remained standing, waiting for them. Seeing this, I sat down in the Comte de Toulouse's chair. The Duc de Guiche, who was on the other side of me, thereupon left a seat between us, his nose in the air, still waiting for the Bastards. He then told me to sit next to him, and that I had taken the wrong chair. I ignored him, and looked round the company, which by now was a sight worth seeing. At his second or third insistence I replied that on the contrary he should move up to me. 'What about the Comte de Toulouse?' he asked. 'Come along,' I said, and then, seeing him motionless with astonishment as he looked across the table to where the Keeper of the Seals had taken M. du Maine's place, I pulled him by the coat from where I sat and said: 'Come here and sit down.' I pulled so hard that he sat down, without understanding. 'What is all this?' he said once he had sat down, 'where have they gone to?' 'I have no idea,' I replied impatiently, 'but quite obviously they are not here.'

At the same time the Duc de Noailles sat down next to the Duc de Guiche. Furious at not having been party to the day's events and having made up his mind that I must be in the secret, he leant across the Duc de Guiche, consumed with curiosity, and said to me: 'For God's sake, my dear Duke, I wish you would be good enough to tell me the meaning of all this.' My relations with him, as we have often enough had occasion to see already, were absolutely nil, and I was even in the habit of treating him very badly. I turned to him with a cold and disdainful air, looked him up and down, and turned away again. That was my sole reply. Then the Duc de Guiche urged me to say something, swearing that I must know very well what was going on. I denied this.

Before describing what happened at this Council, I think I should show exactly how we were seated and the exact disposition of the room in which we sat, so that in this way it may be easier not only to comprehend what I have already described but also to understand what follows.

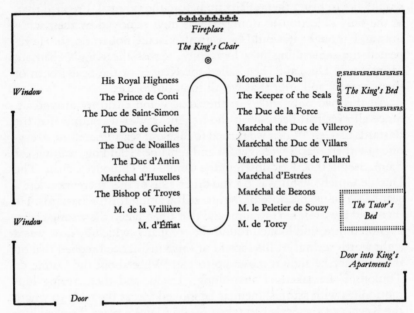

It should be noted, in regard to this plan, that the Maréchal d'Huxelles always sat on the right of the table so as to get the light when he had to read despatches and Monsieur de Troyes always sat next to him to help him. Although on this occasion there was nothing for him to read, he still followed his usual practice and in this way upset the correct order of precedence at the bottom end of the table. This however did not prevent the votes being taken in their proper order. It should also be noted that, as the Council table was not long enough to accommodate everyone comfortably down the two sides, both Éffiat and Torcy were at the end, and that Éffiat sat almost in the middle so as to leave M. de la Vrillière more room for all his writing materials. At the other end of the table the Duc d'Orléans moved round a bit towards the King's chair so that he could more easily see both sides of the table,—something he never did as a rule. But apart from being able to see his side of the table better, I think he was not sorry to let himself be seen in a prominent position.

The Keeper of the Seals had his black velvet bag, in which the seals were lying open and in which were all the necessary documents signed and sealed, ready at his feet; while his other bag, in which were arranged in their proper order all the papers he meant to read before the Council, as well as all the documents which had to be registered at the *lit de justice*, lay on the table before him. The King remained in his own room throughout, and not only did he not appear in the room in which the Council was held, but he did not even enter any of the adjoining rooms.

When everyone was finally seated, the Duc d'Orléans looked slowly around the table, with all eyes upon him. After a pause he said that he had summoned this meeting of the Regency Council to hear the final draft of what had been decided at their last meeting. Then he said that he thought that the only way of registering this decision of theirs, which they would now hear read, was to hold a *lit de justice*; that as the weather was too hot to allow them to run any risk to the King's health by holding it at the Palais de Justice, he had thought it best to follow the example of the late King, who from time to time had summoned his *Parlement* to the Tuileries; that, moreover, as it had proved necessary to hold a *lit de justice*, he thought it would be wise to take this opportunity of registering the letters appointing the Keeper of the Seals; and that he proposed to open the session by having these letters read first. Whereupon he directed the Keeper of the Seals to read them.

During the reading of these letters, which had no other purpose than to compel the *Parlement* to recognize the Keeper of the Seals, whose person and commission they detested, I spent my time observing the faces of those around me. I saw in the Duc d'Orléans an air of authority and alertness which was so new to me that I was surprised by it. Monsieur le Duc, looking gay and radiant, seemed full of confidence. The Prince de Conti, astonished, distracted, morose, seemed neither to see nor to take part in what was happening. The Keeper of the Seals, grave and pensive, seemed to have too much on his mind, indeed, he had a great deal of responsibility at his first appearance. Nevertheless, as he laid out his bag before him, he seemed clear in his own mind, decided and firm. The Duc de la Force, with lowered eyelids, was examining everyone's face. The Maréchaux de Villeroy and Villars consulted together from time to time; both seemed angry and downcast. No one seemed better composed than the Maréchal de Tallard, but even he could not quite stifle his agitation which showed from time to time. The Maréchal d'Estrées looked literally stunned. The Maréchal de Bezons, sunk more deeply than ever in his enormous wig, seemed very intent, his eyes downcast and angry. Peletier, completely at his ease, looked about with frank curiosity. Torcy, three times more pompous even than usual, was slyly watching everything. Éffiat, alert, irritated, angry, seemed ready to fly at someone's throat at every minute; his eyes were haggard, he frowned at everyone and kept glancing quickly from one side of the room to the other.

As for those on my side of the table, I could only see them occasionally when someone moved; out of curiosity I occasionally leant forward over the table and, turning my head, looked down the line from one end to the other, but I could not do it very often and then only for a few seconds. I have already mentioned the Duc de Guiche's astonishment, and the Duc de Noailles's disgust and curiosity. D'Antin, usually so easy in his ways, seemed now to be stiff and on his guard. The Maréchal d'Huxelles tried hard to seem at ease, but he could not hide the despair that was in his heart. As for old Troyes, his mouth all agape, he showed nothing but surprise and embarrassment; he hardly seemed even to know where he was.

As soon as the reading began, it was obvious to everyone after what had passed in the room before Council began sitting and from the disappearance of the Bastards, that something was brewing up against them. Curiosity about what the nature and severity of this something might be, held everyone in suspense, and this, added to the astounding fact that a *lit de justice*, obviously intended to strike at the *Parlement*, had no sooner been announced than it was on the point of being held showed such strength and foresight in a prince who was generally considered to be entirely incapable of either, that everyone was bewildered. Partisans of the *Parlement* and of the Bastards waited for what might be coming next with something akin to terror; while many others were offended at being left in ignorance and forced to share in the common surprise, besides resenting the fact that the Regent had got away from them. Never have I seen so many long faces around me, and never such universal and obvious embarrassment. In this troubled state of mind there were not many, I think, who paid any attention to what the Keeper of the Seals was reading. When he had finished the Duc d'Orléans announced that he thought it a mere waste of time to count the votes of the Council, either on the subject of what had been read or on the question of having it registered, and that he was sure everyone would agree with him that it would be as well to begin the *lit de justice* at once.

Then, after a short but significant pause, the Regent gave a brief résumé of the various reasons which had led the previous meeting to quash the various decrees of the *Parlement* they had heard read to them, and to do so in the form of an edict emanating from the Council itself. He added that, with the *Parlement* in its present mood, it would only further compromise the King's authority to send this edict to the *Parlement* for registration, seeing that it had already publicly and formally refused to register it; that, realizing that a *lit de justice* must be held, he had thought best to prepare for it secretly, so as to obviate all danger of cabals and to prevent the ill-intentioned from having time to make preparations for continuing their disobedience; that he had come to the conclusion, in agreement with the Keeper of the Seals, that the frequency as well as the form of the *Parlement*'s recent remonstrances made it necessary to remind that body of the limits of its duties, of which for some while now it seemed to have lost sight; that the Keeper of the Seals would now read to the Council its edict quashing what the *Parlement* had recently decreed, and setting forth the rules which it must in future observe. Then looking at the Keeper of the Seals, he said: 'You, sir, will explain the matter to these gentlemen better than I can; please be so good as to do so before reading the edict.'

The Keeper of the Seals then began to speak, setting out in greater detail what the Regent had already touched upon, and explaining the nature of the *Parlement*'s right to make remonstrances at all. He showed the origins of this right, its usefulness, its inconveniences, and its limits; the act of grace by which it had come into being, the abuses it had led to, and the distinction between the royal power itself and the *Parlement*'s authority, emanating from the King; the incompetence of these tribunals in matters of State or of finance, and the necessity for repressing them by the issue of a sort of code (this was the word he used) which in future would set forth the exact rules both for the matter and the form of these remonstrances. He explained all this quite shortly, as well as with grace and impartiality. Then, when he had finished, he began to read the decree in the form in which it was subsequently printed, and as all the world may read it to-day, except for a few small alterations, so small that I cannot remember what they are.

As soon as the Keeper of the Seals had finished, the Regent, contrary to his usual custom, gave his opinion first and praised in the firmest tones what had just been read. Then, with the air and manner of a regent which no one had ever seen in him before, and which succeeded in completely surprising his audience, he added: 'I intend to-day, Gentlemen, when counting your votes, to depart from my usual rule, and I think it would be as well to do so throughout the rest of the session.' He passed his eyes down both sides of the table, and as he did so one might have heard a cheese-mite walking. Then he turned towards Monsieur le Duc and asked for his opinion. Monsieur le Duc voted for the edict, giving his reasons shortly but very forcefully. The Prince de Conti followed suit. Then as the Keeper of the Seals had given his opinion after finishing his reading, it came to my turn to speak. I agreed with the others, though, as I did not wish to abuse the *Parlement* unnecessarily nor yet to seem to lend His Royal Highness my backing, as the Princes of the Blood had done, I did so in more general, though just as forceful, terms.

The Duc de la Force held forth at greater length. Everyone spoke, for the most part very shortly, and several—the Maréchaux de Villeroy, de Villars, d'Estrées, de Bezons, Monsieur de Troyes, and Éffiat, for example—were unable to hide their regret at not daring to oppose what they saw was a foregone conclusion, and one from which it was clear they could not hope to subtract anything of its force. Their faces betrayed the discouragement they felt, and it was plain to every eye that the *Parlement*'s defeat was neither what they wished for nor what they had imagined could possibly happen. Tallard was the only one who succeeded in hiding his feelings; but the suffocating monosyllable in which the Maréchal d'Huxelles replied tore the last shreds of dissimulation from his face. The Duc de Noailles contained himself with such difficulty that he said more than he intended, and with a depth of feeling worthy of Fresnes.[1] The Duc d'Orléans spoke last but with most unusual power; then he paused and looked carefully round the table.

At this moment the Maréchal de Villeroy, full of his own thoughts, asked between his teeth: 'But will they come?' One by one others began to say the same thing. The Duc d'Orléans said that they had told Desgranges they would and added that he had no doubt of it himself. Immediately afterwards he said that he would like to know the very moment the *Parlement* set out, and the Keeper of the Seals replied that he would be informed. The Duc d'Orléans said that we had better tell someone at the door to bring us the news. At this Monsieur de Troyes was on his feet. I was immediately alarmed at the thought of what he might say when gossiping at the door, and ran to it ahead of him. On my way back d'Antin, who had turned round to intercept me, begged me to tell him what was happening. Answer-

---

[1] Where the Chancellor Daguesseau was exiled in his country house.

ing that I knew nothing, I slipped away from him. 'Oh, come off it!'
he answered.

I had hardly returned to my place before the Duc d'Orléans said
something which again brought Monsieur de Troyes to his feet, and
in consequence I was again upon mine. As I passed La Vrillière I
begged him in future to go to the door whenever it was necessary
because I was afraid of what Monsieur de Troyes or someone else
might say, and that, from where I sat, I could not keep myself going
without making my action too obvious. This was a necessary precaution and La Vrillière attended to it henceforth. D'Antin was again
waiting for my return, and he begged and prayed me with clasped
hands to tell him what was going to happen. I held my ground however and merely answered: 'You will see.' On my return the Duc
de Guiche also urged me to speak, saying that it was quite evident
that I was in the secret, but I still remained silent.

When all these comings and goings were finished the Duc d'Orléans drew himself up in his chair and announced to the company, in
a tone even firmer and more masterful than on the previous occasion,
that he had another proposal to make, and one a good deal more important than that which they had just heard. This opening brought
astonishment once more to everyone's face, and we all kept perfectly
still. After a moment's silence the Regent said that he had already
given judgement in the case between the Princes of the Blood and the
'legitimized'—that was the term he used, without adding the word
'Princes.' He said moreover that, when the judgement had been
given, he had had his reasons for not going beyond it; that it was
none the less his duty to render justice to the Peers of France, who,
at the time when the Princes of the Blood had lodged their plaint,
had as a body asked for judgement in their favour in a Request, which
the King had received and which he, the Regent, had communicated
to the 'legitimized'; that the same justice should be done to so illustrious a body, composed as it was of the greatest in the land, of the
first nobility in the State, all of whom were charged with honours and
most of whom had distinguished themselves by the services they had
rendered to their country; that, if at the time of their request he had
thought it best to give no reply, he now held himself to be doubly
bound not to postpone an act of justice on a question which could
no longer be left in suspense, and upon which the hearts of all the
Peers were set; that it was with sorrow that he saw people (that was
his word) who were so near to him elevated to a rank of which they
were the first examples, and which had continually been augmented
contrary to every law; that he could not shut his eyes to the truth;

259

that the favour which several such Princes had recently enjoyed had unbalanced the standing of the Peers; that in the past the hurt thus done to their dignity had only lasted as long as the authority which had over-ridden the law; that in this way the Duc de Joyeuse and the Duc d'Epernon, as well as the two MM. de Vendôme, had been reduced to their rank in the peerage immediately after the deaths of Henri III and of Henri IV; that M. de Beaufort had held no other rank during the late King's reign, nor had M. de Verneuil, whom the late King had made a Duke and Peer in 1663 with thirteen others, and who, when being received by the *Parlement* at a *lit de justice*, had taken his seat with them after all those whose peerages were of an earlier date; that, in the interests of equity and good order, he could no longer permit a denial of justice to so many considerable persons, all belonging to the first dignity in the State; that the 'legitimized' had had plenty of time in which to make their reply, but could produce no arguments against the weight of law and precedent; that all he had to do was to give judgement in a case already pending; that, to give this judgement full force, he had drawn up the declaration which the Keeper of the Seals would now read to them in order that it might be registered at the *lit de justice* which the King was now about to hold.

A profound silence followed this speech, so unexpected and so clearly pointing to the solution of the riddle of what was going to happen to the Bastards. Many faces were clouded and sombre. On those of the Maréchaux de Villars and de Bezons, of Éffiat and even of the Maréchal d'Estrées, anger showed clearly. For a moment or two Tallard seemed to have taken leave of his senses, and the Maréchal de Villeroy's face fell. I could not see the Maréchal d'Huxelles's face, much to my regret, and it was only just occasionally that I could catch a sidelong glimpse of the Duc de Noailles. All eyes were upon me, and I had to take care to compose my own features, over which I had laid as it were an extra layer of gravity and modesty. I forced my eyes to move more slowly and never looked up. As soon as the Regent had opened his mouth, Monsieur le Duc had glanced at me in triumph, which had nearly upset my gravity, and had warned me to redouble my precautions and not to expose myself to the risk of meeting his eyes again.

Holding myself in like this, half my attention fixed on devouring the expressions on the faces of others and half on watching myself, so completely immobile as almost to be glued to my seat, my whole body under control, my mind soaked through and through with the acutest and most lively delight that joy can give birth to, and with the warmest emotions that the satisfaction of desires long held and

most perseveringly adhered to can give, I found the necessity of controlling my transports so painful that I literally sweated in my anguish, yet, even so, this anguish was the most voluptuous sensation
I have ever experienced in my life, before that day or since. How
feebly do the pleasures of the senses compare with those of the mind,
and how true it is that one can only judge one's ills by the good one
feels when they are ended!

A moment or two after the Regent had finished speaking, he told
the Keeper of the Seals to read the declaration, and the latter read it
through at once, from one end to the other, without stopping to make
comments by the way as he had done with the previous business.
While I listened to this reading, sweeter to my ears than any music,
my attention was divided between an attempt to see if it were exactly
as Millain had drawn it up and shown it to me, and my curiosity to
see what impression it made upon my fellows. It was with delight
that I saw it was unchanged. It took me but a few moments to perceive
by the change in the expressions of those around me what was passing
through their minds, and but a minute or two longer to realize that
some remedy would have to be found for the despair I saw in Villeroy,
and the fury I saw in Villars, if they were not to be carried too far
astray by the disorder of their present feelings, which I realized it was
beyond their power to master. The remedy was in my pocket and I
drew it out immediately: this was a copy of our plea against the
Bastards. I laid it on the table before me, folded open at the last page,
where all our signatures were printed in large capitals. The two Marshals glanced up and no doubt recognized the document at once, or
at least so I judged by the sullen discomfiture in their eyes, which
quickly succeeded something more threatening, especially in those of
the Maréchal de Villars. My two neighbours asked me what the paper
was; I told them and showed them the signatures. Then everyone in
turn looked at the document though no one else asked me what it was.
Indeed it was recognizable enough, and although the Prince de Conti
and the Duc de Guiche only asked because they were sitting next to
me, I have never seen two men less capable of reading what was under
their noses than they were at that moment.

Before making this demonstration, I had hesitated between the
fear of showing too clearly that I was in the secret and the risk of
allowing those two Marshals to make a scene, which I could see they
were on the point of doing, and the effect of which might well have
been dangerous. I knew that nothing could serve to hold them in
check as well as this sight of their own signatures. But to show it them
after they had spoken would have served no end but to shame them,

and would not have prevented the trouble they would have stirred up. I therefore took the safest course and have reason to believe that I acted wisely.

The reading was listened to with great attention and with the deepest emotion. When it was finished the Duc d'Orléans said that he was sorry that all this was necessary; that the men in question were his brothers-in-law; but that it was as much his duty to act justly by the Peers as by the Princes of the Blood. Then, turning to the Keeper of the Seals, he asked for his opinion. The latter's reply was short, dignified, and well-phrased, though it was clear that he was treading as delicately as a cat on hot bricks; he concluded in favour of registering the declaration. After this His Royal Highness looked round the room and said that he would continue to take the votes, starting from the top of the table. Thereupon he asked Monsieur le Duc, whose reply was very short, somewhat nervous, but very polite to the peers. The Prince de Conti agreed, but still more shortly. Then the Duc d'Orléans asked for my opinion.

Contrary to my usual custom I made him a deep bow, though without rising from my seat, and said that as I had the honour to find myself the senior Peer at the Council table, I thanked His Royal Highness most humbly, not only on my own account, but on that of the other Peers present as well as of all the Peers of France, for deciding to do us justice in a matter which we had so ardently desired and which touched our dignities and persons so closely; that I begged him to rest assured of our gratitude and to count upon our complete attachment to himself after an act of equity so long hoped for and so complete; but that in this sincere expression of our sentiments must consist our only opinion, since, as we were parties to this suit, we would not possibly act as judges of it. I ended this short speech with a deep bow from where I sat, and the Duc de la Force followed my example. He was, however, the only one to do so.

After that I was careful to see whom the Duc d'Orléans would next address, so that, if it were a Peer, I might interrupt, and in this way prevent the Bastards from having the least pretext for demanding a revision. However there was no need. The Duc d'Orléans had heard and completely understood me, and he jumped at once to the Maréchal d'Estrées. He, and nearly all the rest of the company, voted almost without speaking, professing to approve of what, for the most part, it was clear they thoroughly disliked. I had tried to pitch my voice so that it would just be heard by everyone present, even preferring not to be entirely heard by those who were furthest from me, to making the mistake of speaking too loud, and I had tried to assume an air of gravity, of modesty and of simple gratitude. Monsieur le Duc made me a malicious little sign and smiled, to show that I had spoken well; but I retained my gravity and turned to look at the others. It is impossible to give an idea of the faces around me. The atmosphere which I have already described became heavier than ever. On both sides of the table my fellow-councillors seemed to be overwhelmed with surprise; some were morose, some irritated, and all were nervous, though a few well-pleased like la Force and Guiche, who told me so quite freely.

After the votes had been given almost as soon as they were asked for, the Duc d'Orléans said: 'Well, Gentlemen, that is that: justice has been done, and the rights of the Peers are safe. Now I have an act of grace to propose to you, and I do it with all the greater confidence because I have been careful to consult the interested parties who have joined with me in this, and I have drawn the declaration in such a way as to hurt no one. What I am going to suggest regards the Comte de Toulouse alone. Everyone here knows that the Comte de Toulouse has always disapproved of what has been done in his and his brother's favour, and that he has upheld his rank during the regency only out of respect for the late King's wishes. His virtues, his merits, his application to duty, his probity and disinterestedness are generally recognized. However, I could not possibly avoid including him in the declaration you have just heard. Justice demands no exception in his favour, and I had to safeguard the rights of the Peers. But, now that those are safe, it seems to me that I may restore by an act of grace what I have taken away in justice to rights of birth, and make the Comte de Toulouse a personal exception which, in confirming the rule, will leave him, and him only, in the possession of all the honours he enjoys, to the exclusion of all others, and without any rights to his children, if he should marry and have them, and without giving any title to anyone to be treated in the same way. I am pleased to announce that the Princes of the Blood agree, and that those of the Peers whom I have been able to consult have not only agreed with me but urged me to act as I am doing. I have no doubt that the esteem which the Comte de Toulouse has acquired here will make this proposal agreeable to you all.' Then, turning to the Keeper of the Seals, he continued: 'Will you now, sir, read the declaration?' The Keeper of the Seals without a word immediately did as he was bid.

During His Royal Highness's speech my attention was once again engaged in estimating the impression it was making. The astonishment it caused was general, and so acute that, to judge by the expressions of those to whom it was addressed, it would appear that no one at first seemed able to grasp it or even to have recovered from his astonishment by the time the reading was over. Above all, those who had been particularly distressed by the first declaration seemed now to be even more upset by this panegyric in favour of the Comte de Toulouse, as well as by the distinction which it made between the two brothers. In their first involuntary reaction they showed that it was a party matter with them, since, if personal affection alone had been at work, the second announcement would have been some consolation to them, and not, as it clearly came in in this case, as an aggravation of their distress, caused not only by the fact that it seemed to cast the Duc du Maine into lower depths than ever, but also by the fact that unless the younger brother should deign from his distinguished position to stoop to his elder's aid, the elder would be deprived in future of his support.

I was delighted by the evident success of our plan, and triumphed inwardly, so much so that when the Duc de Guiche showed disapproval, I received his remarks rather curtly. Villeroy was confounded, Villars raging, Éffiat's eyes were rolling in their sockets, and Estrées shaken out of himself by surprise. These were the most obviously upset. Tallard, his head thrust forward, seemed to be taking in the Regent's words one by one as they were delivered, and his attitude remained the same when it came to the Keeper of the Seals to read the declaration. Noailles, inwardly terrified, could not completely hide his fear. Huxelles, his whole mind given over to mastering his emotion, made no sign. . . .

When the declaration had been read, the Duc d'Orléans said a word or two in its favour and then asked the Keeper of the Seals to give his opinion. The latter did so in a short speech in honour of the Comte de Toulouse. Monsieur le Duc, after paying tribute to the Count's merits, expressed himself delighted to be able to show his esteem and affection for him. The Prince de Conti hardly said a word. Then, in my turn, I told His Royal Highness what a joy it was to me to see him, not only doing the most complete justice to the rights of the Peers, but also, by this unheard-of act of grace, honouring the merits of the Comte de Toulouse, who was of all men the most deserving of such treatment, for his moderation, his loyalty, and his attachment to the good of the State: that the more clearly the latter had recognized the injustice of the rank to which he had been elevated, and the more worthy of it he thereby became, the better would it be for us Peers to yield place to his personal merits . . . that I was therefore heartily in favour of the declaration; and that, bearing in mind that I was the senior Peer present, I was not afraid to add the humble thanks of all the Peers of France for what he was now doing. As I finished I looked across the table, and it was easy to see that my praise had met with no approval there, and my thanks perhaps with even less. As each one spoke in turn he seemed to bow his head beneath the rod. Some, but they were very few, muttered a word or two between their teeth. The blow at the cabal was becoming more and more complete, and as surprise gave way to reflection the bitterness and acute regret to be seen on the faces opposite made it plain that we had only just struck in time.

When the voting was finished, Monsieur le Duc threw me an excited glance and made as if to speak. The Keeper of the Seals, who was sitting beside him, failed to notice this, and also made as if to say a few words. However, the Duc d'Orléans told him that Monsieur le Duc had something to say first, and at once, without giving the Keeper of the Seals time to answer, and sitting straight up in his chair like a true king, he said: 'Gentlemen, Monsieur le Duc has a proposal to make to you, a proposal which I consider just and reasonable, and I do not doubt that you will agree to it, as I have done.' Then, turning to Monsieur le Duc: 'Sir,' he said, 'will you please explain.'

The excitement which these few words caused in the assembly is indescribable. It seemed to me that I was looking upon men who, after being attacked now on this side and now on that, are suddenly surprised by a new enemy in the midst of the place where, in the hope of gaining breathing space, they have sought refuge. 'Sir,' said Monsieur le Duc, addressing the Regent as usual, 'since you have now done justice to the dukes I think I have the right to demand it also for myself. Our late King gave His present Majesty's education into the hands of M. du Maine. I was then a minor and, according to the late King's ideas, M. du Maine was a Prince of the Blood and capable of succeeding to the throne. I have now reached my majority, and not only is M. du Maine no longer a Prince of the Blood, but he has been reduced to his proper rank in the peerage. The Maréchal de Villeroy is to-day his senior and takes precedence over him in every respect. This being so, it is impossible for the Maréchal de Villeroy to remain the King's tutor under the superintendence of M. du Maine. I therefore ask for the post, nor do I think, considering my age, my quality, and my attachment to the King and to the State, that my request can be refused. I hope (and here he turned towards his left) that I shall profit from the instructions of the Maréchal de Villeroy, learn to acquit myself under his guidance, and deserve his friendship.'

As the Maréchal de Villeroy listened to this speech, and heard the words 'superintendence of the education,' he bowed himself almost to the ground, leaning his forehead on his stick, and remained thus for several minutes. It even seemed as if he heard no more of the speech at all. Villars, Bezons and Éffiat bent their shoulders as though this were the final blow. I could see no one on my side of the table except the Duc de Guiche, who, when he had mastered his prodigious astonishment, approved. Estrées was the first to recover his wits; he shook himself, gave an odd kind of whinny, and looked upon the company like one who has come back from the other world.

When Monsieur le Duc had finished, the Duc d'Orléans gazed slowly round the whole company, then said that Monsieur le Duc's demand was just; that he did not think it could be refused; that one had no right to ask the Maréchal de Villeroy to remain under M. du Maine, now that he preceded him; that the superintendence of the King's education could not be more worthily filled than by Monsieur le Duc; and that he was sure the proposal would be passed unanimously. After that he immediately asked the Prince de Conti for his opinion. He gave it in one or two words. Then came the Keeper of the Seals, also very short, and then myself. I merely remarked, and I looked at Monsieur le Duc as I said it, that I agreed with all my heart. All the others, except M. de la Force who said a few words, voted without uttering a syllable, nodding their heads, and the Marshals scarcely even doing that. Éffiat followed their example, and his and the Maréchal de Villars's eyes were blazing with rage. When the votes had been taken, the Duc d'Orléans turned towards Monsieur le Duc and said: 'I believe, sir, you wish to read what you mean to say before the King at the *lit de justice*?' Thereupon Monsieur le Duc read his speech just as it has been printed.

A few moments' silence, sad and deep, succeeded this reading, during which the Maréchal de Villeroy, pale and nervous, was muttering to himself. At last, like a man who had chosen his course, he turned towards the Regent, his head lowered and his eyes almost dead, his voice very quiet and said: 'I wish to say only this. All the King's dispositions have been overthrown, and I cannot look upon it without pain. M. du Maine is a very unhappy man. . . .' 'Sir,' replied the Regent impatiently, in a loud voice, 'M. du Maine is my brother-in-law, but I prefer an open enemy to a hidden one.' The reply was so strong that many bowed their heads again; Éffiat kept shaking his from side to side. The Maréchal de Villeroy was faint with terror. From across the table I could hear the sound of sighs escaping, now here, now there, but always as it were involuntarily. It was clear that the glove lay on the ground, and no one knew where the quarrel might end. To make a diversion, the Keeper of the Seals suggested

Arrival of members of the Parlement

reading the discourse he had prepared as a preliminary to our edict quashing the *Parlement*'s decrees, and which he was to read at the *lit de justice* before the proposal of the edict. As he was finishing, someone came in to tell him that he was wanted at the door.

He went, and came back a little later, going not to his seat but to the Duc d'Orléans, who drew him into a window embrasure. By now almost everyone was in a state of the greatest apprehension. The Regent went back to his place, and told the company that he had just been informed that, when all the Chambers had been assembled, the First President, in spite of his promise to Desgranges, had immediately put forward a proposal that they should refuse to come to the Tuileries, saying that it was useless to go to a place where they would have no liberty, and that the King should be informed that his *Parlement* would listen to his wishes in its ordinary place of assembly, whenever it should please him to do them the honour to come to them, or to send them word that he was coming. The Regent added that this had caused some excitement and that the matter was still under discussion.

The Council was stunned by the news, but His Royal Highness said quite gaily that he had suspected something of the sort, and ordered the Keeper of the Seals to tell them what he thought should be done if the views of the First President prevailed. The Keeper of the Seals asserted that he could not believe that the *Parlement* would go so far as to disobey, and that if they did it would be a formal disobedience contrary to right of usage. Then at some length he insisted that nothing could be more pernicious than to run the risk of allowing the royal authority to be met with a flat refusal, and concluded in favour of laying the *Parlement* under an immediate interdict if it were so far to commit itself. The Duc d'Orléans said there could be no hesitation on this point, and then asked for the opinion of Monsieur le Duc, who spoke strongly in favour of the same course. The Prince de Conti followed suit and so did I. M. de la Force and M. de Guiche replied in the same sense. The Maréchal de Villeroy, in a cracked voice, seemed to be searching for some sonorous phrases that would not come to his tongue; he deplored the extremity and did all he could to avoid being forced to give a precise opinion. Compelled at last by the Regent to make himself clear, he did not dare to oppose the motion, but said that it was with regret that he acquiesced, and wished to point out how dangerous the results might be. The Regent interrupted him again to tell him that there was no need to worry; that everything had been foreseen; and that it would be far more dangerous to allow such a refusal to pass. Then he went on to M. de Noailles, who answered shortly, and almost with an appearance of shame, that it was very sad, but that he must agree.

Villars was longing to make a speech, but he contained himself and said that he hoped the *Parlement* would obey. When pressed by the Regent, he suggested that we should wait for news before coming to any decision, but when pressed again he concluded in favour of the interdict, though his annoyance and irritation were clear. After that no one dared to oppose, but a nod of the head was all that came from most of them. As soon as the motion was passed, the Duc d'Orléans began to discuss the interdict in detail as well as the several remedies which might be needed, much as I have set them forth above, though he made no mention of private signals nor of arresting anyone. All that was discussed was what our course of action should be if the *Parlement* decided to make a protest. The Keeper of the Seals suggested that we should go at once to the King and then inform the *Parlement* that the King wished to be obeyed, and obeyed immediately. This was agreed to.

Shortly afterwards Desgranges came in, and went to the Duc d'Orléans to tell him that the *Parlement* had set out on foot and were already leaving the Palais. Everyone, not least among us the Duc d'Orléans, was greatly relieved to hear this.

As soon as Desgranges had left, with orders to inform the Regent as soon as the *Parlement* approached, the latter told the Keeper of the Seals that when, at the *lit de justice*, he brought up the subject of the Bastards, he must do it in such a way that there would not be a moment's doubt about what was going to happen to the Comte de Toulouse. . . .

After this the Regent, now quite at his ease, told the various presidents of the councils to read their reports. However, no one had been warned to bring his report with him, although orders to this effect had been issued, and everyone had come to the meeting convinced that nothing was going to be discussed except the *Parlement*'s decrees. Then the Maréchal de Villars said that he could report on one matter from memory, though he had no papers with him, and in fact he delivered the clearest and justest report that I had ever heard, for generally this kind of thing was not his strong line.

After this the Council came to an end for want of further business and everyone was preparing to rise from his seat as usual. I leant across the Prince de Conti and made a sign to the Duc d'Orléans, who understood me and begged everyone to remain seated. La Vrillière, at his orders, went out for news, but none had as yet arrived. It was just ten o'clock. We remained seated a good half hour longer, for the

most part in silence, each one talking just occasionally to his neighbour. By then anxiety was growing and people kept getting up and
going to the windows. The Duc d'Orléans restrained them as best he
could, but after Desgranges had come in again and announced that
the First President had already arrived in his carriage, and that the
Parlement were now quite near, the Council split up into groups and
it was impossible to keep them seated any longer. At last the Duc
d'Orléans got up himself, and, seeing that this was all he could do,
announced in a loud voice that no one, whoever he might be, was to
leave the room on any account whatever. He later repeated this warning two or three times.

We had hardly risen before Monsieur le Duc came up to me. He
was delighted with our success, and greatly relieved by the Bastards'
absence, which had enabled us to lay their business before the Regency
Council, and thus to avoid all possible trouble on that score at the
lit de justice. I told him briefly what I had noticed on the faces of those
around us, for I did not wish to be with him long. Soon after I had
left him, the Duc d'Orléans, his mind brimming over with the same
thoughts, came up to me and took me on one side. I gave him a more
detailed account than I had given Monsieur le Duc of the expressions
I had caught upon the faces around us. Particularly I described Éffiat
to him. He seemed to be surprised by what I told him about Bezons,
and he deplored his weakness, and the way he was governed by
Éffiat, who even before the late King's death had become for him a
sort of lode-star. I asked the Regent if he were not afraid of the
Bastards getting together with the *Parlement* and their friends, and
suggested that they might yet boycott the *lit de justice*. His usual self-
confidence, which enabled him to neglect all reflection, all fore-
thought, all precautions, prevented him having the least doubt upon
the subject. And indeed the Duc du Maine had appeared to me so
lifeless, and his friends upon the Council so disconcerted, that I was
not really afraid myself; nevertheless, I was anxious to arm the Regent
against every possible surprise.

After this I left him and noticed the Maréchaux de Villeroy and
de Villars sitting with Éffiat; they seemed less to be speaking than
thinking together out loud, like men caught by surprise, furious, yet
conscious of defeat. After a time Bezons and the Maréchal d'Estrées
joined them; then they separated; then they joined again; with the
result that, whether they were two or three or four together, they
were scarcely ever to be seen with any of the others. Tallard next
came up, not to all at once, however, but to one of them here and to
one of them there, for a short time only and, as it were, on the sly.

1718 Huxelles did the same, and so did Le Peletier. The Keeper of the Seals held himself aloof most of the time, thinking about his duties; when he joined anyone it was the Duc d'Orléans, Monsieur le Duc, myself or La Vrillière.

Meanwhile I kept walking slowly and continuously up and down the room, alone so far as I could be, for I wanted nothing to escape me, and I was keeping a careful watch upon the doors. Wandering round like this I could say a word now here, now there, just as I wished; moreover I could keep the suspects under supervision and even surprise and interrupt their councils. I noticed that d'Antin was usually alone though sometimes joined by the Duc de Noailles. The latter had gone back to his earlier habit of keeping his eyes fixed on me; he seemed utterly dismayed and greatly agitated, and, in contrast to his usually free and easy ways, he now showed every sign of embarrassment. D'Antin took me aside to tell me that, considering his relationship to the Bastards, he did not see how he could appear at the *lit de justice,* and to ask me if I thought he might venture to ask the Regent to excuse him.[1] In view of the peculiarity of his position, I thought this could be arranged. He begged me to speak to the Regent for him, but I could not do it then, because Éffiat and his friends seemed to me to have had their heads together too long. I therefore went over to them and sat down with them for a while.

Éffiat could not resist saying that we had just heard some pretty strange decisions and he did not know who was responsible for them; but he prayed God that the Duc d'Orléans would find them satisfactory. I replied that the decisions he mentioned were certainly very strong and very good ones; that that made me think that the arguments which led to them must be good ones too; and that I shared his surprise and his good wishes for their success. The Maréchal de Villeroy sighed deeply, gave voice to several empty and meaningless exclamations, and shook his wig to emphasize his feelings. Villars said a little more; his words were short and bitter; he showed his despair over the fall of the Duc du Maine, but to hide his feelings he turned the conversation onto the *Parlement.* I answered with nods and gestures; I contradicted nothing and said nothing. I was not there to argue or persuade, but to see and hear. From everything I heard I gathered that they were routed, that the cabal had been caught on the wrong foot and that they had no hopes of the *Parlement* which was as unprepared as they were.

---

[1] The Comte d'Antin was the one son whom the Marquise de Montespan bore her husband; he was therefore half-brother of the Duc du Maine and Comte de Toulouse.

After a time I left them, for I did not wish my supervision to be noticeable, and I went off to do d'Antin's commission. The Regent told me that d'Antin had already spoken; that he approved of his embarrassment and of his delicacy in this matter; that he had given him permission not to attend the *lit de justice* on condition that he did not say a word to anyone; that d'Antin had agreed to remain in the Council chamber as if going on to the *lit de justice*; and that, while it was in progress, he would remain behind in the room without going out, until the session was over. After that I went up to d'Antin who told me the same thing. He kept his word exactly. Indeed Mme de Montespan's legitimate son, close as he was to all his bastard brothers and sisters, could not decently have appeared at this *lit de justice*. . . .

La Vrillière had been watching me carefully for some time, and took me aside at the first opportunity. No doubt he had noticed that I was on a new footing with Monsieur le Duc, and indeed both before and after the actual Council this had been only too obvious. Moreover, Monsieur le Duc had been to see him the previous evening and spoken about the reduction of the Bastards to their rank in the peerage. He now asked me to tell Monsieur le Duc of his joy and satisfaction at what had just passed, and to assure him of his attachment, saying that he could not do so himself in front of all this company.

Could anything show your courtier better than this? La Vrillière had always belonged whole-heartedly to the old King's party, and in consequence to that of the Bastards, to whom moreover he was tied by his relations with their old napkin-washer, Mme de Maintenon, who, I may say in passing, fell ill and wept far more bitterly and far longer at this reversal of all her plans than she had done at the late King's death, by which her health had been unaltered. La Vrillière had been at grips with Monsieur le Duc over Burgundy and had got the worst of it, so that he needed to make his number with a prince who was obviously going up fast. I gladly delivered the message.

In the meanwhile everyone was becoming impatient at the *Parlement*'s tardiness and people kept sending for news. Several of them, longing to go out and perhaps to gossip, suggested inquiring themselves, but the Regent allowed no one out of the room but La Vrillière, and, seeing that the desire to go out was increasing, took his stand by the door himself. I had several conversations with him, with Monsieur le Duc and with the Keeper of the Seals, about various remarks I had heard. I persuaded the Regent to repeat several times his refusal to allow anyone to leave the room. During one of these short conversations with him I spoke to him about the Duchesse d'Orléans's distress upon hearing the news, of how he should take pity on her and allow her full liberty, and of how the first thing he should do was to write her an affectionate letter. I even suggested that, while he had nothing better to do, he might write it on the Council table now, but he said it was impossible in front of all these people. It was easy enough to persuade him to feel sorry for her distress, but he did not seem to me to be deeply touched. Nevertheless, he promised me to write in the course of the day as soon as he found himself free to do so. I was uneasy about what the Bastards were doing, but I did not like to emphasize my fears. He spoke to everyone around him quite easily, indeed as if nothing in particular were happening, and it must be confessed that he was the only man in the room who retained his serenity without effort and without the least affectation.

The *Parlement* finally arrived, and like so many children we all rushed to the windows. The members arrived in their scarlet robes, two by two, entering by the great gate of the courtyard, which they crossed to the Hall of the Ambassadors, where the First President, who had arrived in his coach with the President Alègre, was waiting for them. The First President had walked across the small neighbouring courtyard so as to have less ground to cover on foot.[1] While nearly everyone crowded to the windows I took care not to lose sight of the interior of the room, partly because of the little conferences which were still in progress, and partly to see that no one made his escape. Desgranges came several times to tell us how things stood, although no difficulties had in fact arisen, and all the time I kept walking up and down and looking carefully around me. Either because their need was real, or from the usual desire for the forbidden, several Councillors now asked to be allowed to leave the room for urgent purposes of nature. The Regent gave them leave but told them to keep their mouths shut and to return at once. He even ordered La Vrillière to go out with the Maréchal d'Huxelles and several other suspects, nominally to satisfy a similar need, but in reality to keep his eye on them. La Vrillière understood and performed his commission faithfully. I did the same for the Maréchaux de Villars and de Tallard, and, having noticed Éffiat on the point of opening the small door into the King's apartments for the Maréchal de Villeroy, I hurried forward, ostensibly to help, but in reality to stop him talking by the door or sending any message to the Bastards. I then remained with Éffiat to prevent anything of the sort happening when the Marshal returned; and I then shut the door carefully again.

I must confess that the mental and physical strain of what I was

---

[1] He was suffering from gout.

doing—the continuous effort of watching here, of interrupting there, and of foreseeing what might happen next, of watching the whole of the vast Council chamber, as well as the multitude of people whom I wished to keep my eye on and if possible hinder plotting without their noticing—was very considerable. The Duc d'Orléans, Monsieur le Duc and La Vrillière all played their parts excellently, but they subtracted little from mine.

Finally, with the *Parlement* in its place, the Peers arrived and all the presidents gone, in two groups, to put on their furred cloaks behind the screens arranged for them in an adjoining room, Desgranges came to tell us all was ready. There had been some question of whether or not the King should dine while waiting, and I had carried my point that he had better not, since I was afraid that if he were to eat before his usual hour and then go straight to the *lit de justice* he might possibly feel sick, which would have been extremely awkward. As soon as Desgranges had told the Regent it was time to start, His Royal Highness ordered him to tell the *Parlement* to have their deputation ready to receive the King at the far end of the Salle des Cent-Suisses, as had been arranged. Then he announced in a loud voice that it was time for us to go and call for the King.

On hearing these words I was overcome with joy and excitement at the thought of the spectacle which was so soon to meet my eyes, and this warned me to redouble my hold on myself. I had already told Villars to walk with us,[1] and Tallard to join the other Marshals of France in his proper order of seniority, because on these occasions verified Dukes have no standing. As for myself I laid in the largest store of seriousness, of gravity, and of modesty that I could possibly carry, and then I followed the Duc d'Orléans, who went in by the little door and found the King in his study. On the way, the Duc d'Albret and one or two others paid me extravagant compliments, trying to find out what was happening. I answered politely; I complained of the crowd and of the awkwardness of my cloak, and so reached the King's study.

The King was wearing neither cloak nor neck-band, but was dressed in his usual clothes. The Duc d'Orléans remained with him for a short time, and then asked him if it were his pleasure to start. Immediately a way was cleared. The few courtiers, who had returned here after failing to find a seat in the chamber where the *lit de justice* was to be held, stood aside, and I made a sign to the Maréchal de Villars, who then walked slowly towards the door. The Duc de la

---

[1] Because he was a Duke and Peer.

Force came after him, and I followed, taking care to walk immediately in front of the Prince de Conti. Monsieur le Duc followed him and the Duc d'Orléans came next. Behind him came the Ushers of the King's Chamber with their maces, then the King surrounded by the four Captains of his Bodyguard,[1] the Duc d'Albret, the Great Chamberlain, and his tutor the Maréchal de Villeroy. The Keeper of the Seals followed because his appointment had not yet been registered by the *Parlement*;[2] then came the Maréchaux d'Estrées, d'Huxelles, Tallard and Bezons, who could only attend the session as part of the King's suite and could not precede him. They were followed by the Knights of the Order, and the Governors and Lieutenant-Governors of Provinces, who had been summoned to follow in the King's train, and who would sit on the low seats,[3] uncovered and without the right to speak, on the Bailiffs' Bench.[4] In this order we went along the terrace to the Salle des Suisses, at the far end of which the deputation from the *Parlement*, composed as usual of four *Présidents à Mortier* and four Councillors, was waiting.

While they were approaching the King, I told the Duc de la Force and the Maréchal de Villars that we had better go and take our places now, and thus avoid the crush at the King's entrance. They followed me in single file, walking in full ceremony and in order of seniority. There were only three of us to make this entrance, since d'Antin did not come, the Duc de Guiche had resigned his peerage,[5] Tallard was not a Peer, and the four Captains of the Bodyguard always stood round the King with their staves in their hands at these great ceremonies. But before saying any more I think I had best draw a plan of the *lit de justice*, which at a glance will make clearer most of what follows.

I think it would serve little purpose to go into more detail about the arrangements, and this should be enough to enable everyone to understand what I am about to tell and how it all took place. In my list of the Peers I have, in accordance with the invariable custom when taking their opinions on these occasions, used the correct designation of their peerages, instead of those they usually employ, and by which they are known to the world. Monsieur de Laon was a Clermont-Chaste, and Monsieur de Noyon a Chateauneuf-Rochebonne—later

---

[1] The Ducs de Noailles, Villeroy, and Charost, and the Marquis d'Harcourt.

[2] If it had, he would have preceded the King, as the Chancellor always did.

[3] As opposed to the high seats of the Dukes and major officials of the crown.

[4] So called from the ancient offices of Bailiffs and Seneschals, now replaced by Governors.

[5] In favour of his son Louvigny.

Archbishop of Lyons with a brevet to retain his rank and honours.
The Duc de la Feuillade and the Duc de Valentinois sat on the second
bench provided for the lay peers, but they only went there after the
King's arrival.

When the *Parlement* was seated, I entered by the door through
which a few moments later the King would make his entrance. There
was not a great crowd, and the Officers of the Bodyguard cleared a
way for me, as well as for the Duc de la Force, and the Maréchal de
Villeroy, who followed me in single file. I paused for a moment at
the open space which led onto the floor of the chamber, utterly overwhelmed with joy at the sight of so magnificent a spectacle, and at the
thought of the precious moments that were approaching. Indeed I had
need to wait a moment in order to compose myself sufficiently to see
what lay before my eyes, and to put on once more my mask of gravity
and modesty. I knew that I had to face the careful scrutiny of a body
of men in whom a dislike of me had been long and carefully engendered, as well as of all the curious spectators, anxious to pierce
the mystery which was now to be revealed at a meeting of such importance so unexpectedly brought together. Moreover, if only from
the fact that I had just left the Regency Council, it was clear that I
must be prepared to answer their questions. I was not mistaken, and
as soon as I appeared all eyes were fixed upon me.

I walked slowly forward to where the Chief Clerk was sitting, then,
turning between the two rows of benches, crossed the breadth of the
hall just in front of the two Law Officers, who saluted me with many
smiles, and mounted the three steps to the high seats where we were
to sit, and where all the Peers that I have set down above were already
in their places. They rose as I approached the steps. I saluted them
respectfully from the top of the third step. Walking slowly forward
I placed my hand on La Feuillade's shoulder, though he and I were
far from being friends, and whispered in his ear that he should listen
attentively to what I was going to say, and not to betray himself by
so much as a sign; that after a declaration which only concerned the
Parlement, there would be two others which would affect us deeply;
that we were on the point of attaining the happiest and most unhoped-
for moment in our lives; that the Bastards were to be reduced to
their rank in the peerage and would henceforth take precedence only
by their seniority among us; and finally that the Comte de Toulouse
would have his rank restored to him, as an exceptional case and without benefit to his issue. For a moment La Feuillade failed to understand, and then he was so overcome with joy that he was unable to
speak. He pressed himself against me and, as I left him, said: 'But

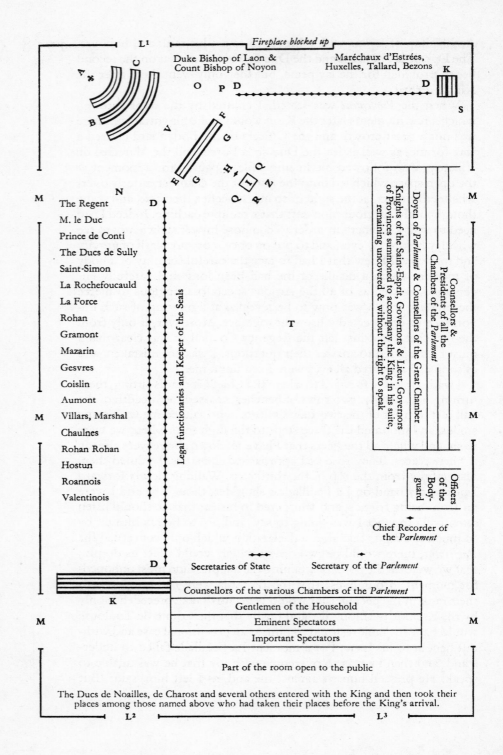

Fireplace blocked up

L¹

Duke Bishop of Laon &
Count Bishop of Noyon

Maréchaux d'Estrées,
Huxelles, Tallard, Bezons

K

A
C

O   P   D

D

S

B

F
G

E
H   Q
Z
Q   R

N
D

M

The Regent
M. le Duc
Prince de Conti
The Ducs de Sully
Saint-Simon
La Rochefoucauld
La Force
Rohan
Gramont
Mazarin
Gesvres
Coislin
Aumont

M   Villars, Marshal
Chaulnes
Rohan Rohan
Hostun
Roannois
Valentinois

Legal functionaries and Keeper of the Seals

T

Knights of the Saint-Esprit, Governors & Lieut. Governors
of Provinces summoned to accompany the King in his suite,
remaining uncovered & without the right to speak

Doyen of *Parlement* & Counsellors of the Great Chamber

Counsellors &
Presidents of all the
Chambers of the *Parlement*

M

M

Officers
of the
Body-
guard

Chief Recorder of
the *Parlement*

D

Secretaries of State   Secretary of the *Parlement*

K

Counsellors of the various Chambers of the *Parlement*

Gentlemen of the Household

Eminent Spectators

Important Spectators

M

M

Part of the room open to the public

The Ducs de Noailles, de Charost and several others entered with the King and then took their
places among those named above who had taken their places before the King's arrival.

L²   L³

how about the Comte de Toulouse?' 'You will see,' I replied and passed on.

Walking past the Duc d'Aumont, I suddenly remembered the fine meeting he had arranged with the Duc d'Orléans for that afternoon or the day after to reconcile him with the *Parlement*, and to put an end to all these sad misunderstandings; as I looked at him I could not refrain from a mocking smile. I stopped between Monsieur de Metz, who was in his own right also the Duc de Coislin, and the Duc de Tresmes, and told them the news. The first sniffed, but the second was overjoyed and so suddenly surprised and pleased that he made me say it all again. I then told Louvigny, who though not so greatly astonished was at least as much delighted. At last I arrived at my place between the Duc de Sully and the Duc de la Rochefoucauld. I saluted them and then we immediately sat down. I threw a quick glance at the spectacle before me and then, drawing the heads of my two neighbours towards mine, I announced my news. Sully was as delighted as he could possibly be; the other demanded drily: 'But why this exception in favour of the Comte de Toulouse?'

I had several reasons for treating the Duc de la Rochefoucauld with reserve, and, though it is true that since judgement had been given in my favour in our suit over precedence he had always behaved perfectly towards me, I yet felt that my victory lay heavy on his heart. I was therefore content to reply that I knew nothing about that, and then did my best to show him what an outstanding success we had gained. However, much as he disliked the fact of my precedence, he found it a still more difficult matter to forgive the Comte de Toulouse for taking the post of Grand Huntsman from him. . . .

Seated as I was above the level of the rest of the assembly, with no one in the high seats in front of me (since the extra bench which had been provided for such Peers as could not find a place upon our

---

A. The King on his throne. B. Steps to the throne, with the King's carpet and cushions. C. The Great Chamberlain, reclining on these cushions, covered, and with the right to speak. D. The high seats on the right and on the left of the throne. E. Small step up to the throne, covered by the lower end of the King's carpet, but without cushions. F. The Provost of Paris, with his baton, reclining on this step. G. Ushers of the King's Chamber, kneeling, their silver-gilt maces on their shoulders. H. The Keeper of the Seals in his chair, with arms but without a back. I. A small desk before him. K. Steps leading to the high seats. L. Doors. 1. Used only to enable Messieurs de Troyes, de Fréjus, and de Torcy to watch the proceedings. They were at the back and all standing. In front of them, and a little to one side but still within the doorway, was the Marquis d'Harcourt, standing and uncovered, with his baton as Captain of the Bodyguard, but without the right to speak. The other three Captains of the Bodyguard were all dukes and thus otherwise provided for. 2. Used only by the Peers entering and leaving. 3. Open for entry of the Public and the King. M. Windows with stands for spectators in their embrasures. N. The Maréchal de Villeroy on a stool, covered, and with the right to speak. O. The Duc de Villeroy, Captain of the Guard on Duty, seated, covered, and with the right to speak. P. Beringhen, First Equerry in place of the Grand Equerry, seated, but uncovered and without the right to speak. These two men, as well as the tutor, were so placed on account of the King's tender age. Q. Heralds in their tabards. R. Desgranges, the Master of Ceremonies, seated, but uncovered and without the right to speak. S. Entrance to the high seats on the left for the episcopal peers and the Law Officers of the Crown. T. Floor or empty space in the middle. V. Passage joining the two groups of high seats and on the same level. Y. A second bench of high seats for lay peers in case of need. Z. The chief clerk to the *Parlement*, whose duty it was to register the declarations at the end of the session.

row only reached as far as M. de la Force), I had a good view of the whole assembly. I watched them as long and as carefully as I could. There was only one constraint, which was that I did not dare to fix my gaze on any object for too long. I was afraid that the fire, the sparkle, the excitement in my eyes might betray me; and the more I realized that I was continually catching the eyes of those at whom I was looking, the more careful I was to cheat their curiosity by my reserve. Even so I could not resist throwing a scintillating glance towards the First President and the Great Bench, the view of which from where I sat was very good. Then I looked round the *Parlement*, and saw almost unbelievable expressions of amazement and stupefaction, which seemed a good omen. Moreover, the sight of the First President, still insolent in his downfall, and of the other presidents, disconcerted yet attentive, was the most agreeable sight I had ever seen. As for the curious spectators, and among them I include all those without the right to speak, they seemed equally surprised, but not so utterly bewildered; and their surprise seemed somehow calmer. In a word, everyone was on tenter-hooks and trying hard to find out what was going on from the faces of those who had just come from the Council chamber.

I had little leisure to continue my examination, for the King soon arrived. The excited whispers caused by this entry, which continued until the King and everyone who accompanied him were in their seats, were really extraordinary to listen to. The eyes of all were upon the Regent, the Keeper of the Seals, and the other principal actors in this scene, trying to discover something from their expression. The fact that the Bastards had left the Council chamber had already redoubled the excitement; but not everyone had known of this until now, when their absence was apparent to all. The consternation of the Marshals—and particularly of the senior among them, sitting in his place as tutor of the King—was evident. Not seeing his master, the Duc du Maine, the First President cast a frightened look at Monsieur de Sully and at me, who were occupying the seats in which he had expected to see the two brothers; his discouragement grew deeper than ever. In a moment the eyes of the whole assembly were upon us and I noticed that a look of concentration, as well as of expectation that something startling was now coming, was on everyone's face.

The Regent had an air of majesty, gentle yet resolute, which was new to him; his eyes were attentive and his bearing grave yet easy. Monsieur le Duc, though he too looked grave and calm, had an air of triumph about him which seemed to light up his whole person and it was clear that he was holding himself in. The Prince de Conti looked sad and morose, and as if he were miles away. During the rest of the session it was difficult for me to see their faces, as I could only glance in their direction under cover of looking round at the King, who was serious, kingly, and at the same time as pretty a sight as one could wish to see, with a charming gravity in his bearing, and an air of interested attention, without the least trace of embarrassment, which showed him at his best.

Even when everyone was seated in his place, the Keeper of the Seals remained silent and motionless in his chair for a minute or two; his eyes were half-closed as he looked round the room with a penetrating glance. The extraordinary silence of the chamber testified to the fear, the strained attention, the troubled consciences and the curiosity with which everyone was consumed. The same *Parlement*, which in the late King's reign had so often summoned the same d'Argenson before them and, as he stood uncovered at the Bar, had given him his orders as Lieutenant of Police; this *Parlement* which more recently, and even during the Regency, had shown him such ill-will that at times one did not know what might become of him; this *Parlement*, which had held back prisoners and documents in order to make things difficult for him; this First President, so haughty to him and so proud in the knowledge that his own master, the Duc du Maine, was behind him and feeling so confident of obtaining the Seals; this Lamoignon, who once boasted that he would have d'Argenson hanged in that very Chamber of Justice in which he had since dishonoured himself for all time; these men, this *Parlement*, were now to see him, wearing the envied robes of the highest office among them all, presiding over them, effacing them, and, in the exercise of his functions and on the very first occasion on which he had acted at their head, putting them in their places and reading them a public lesson upon their future behaviour. Indeed it was a pleasant thing to watch them turn their eyes away from this man who was now to curb their arrogance in the very place from which they drew its source, and to see that, for all their pride, they could not now meet his gaze.

After the Keeper of the Seals had, as it were, felt the pulse of his august audience in the manner of a preacher, he uncovered, rose from his seat, walked up the steps to the throne, sank to his knees in the middle of that step on which the Great Chamberlain was reclining, and was given his instructions. Then he came down, resumed his seat, and once again put on his hat. I may say that as each new subject was opened he went through the same ceremony, and also before and after taking the votes on each occasion. At a *lit de justice* neither the Chancellor nor the Keeper of the Seals ever addresses the King in any other manner; and on this occasion, whenever he went up to the King the Regent also rose from his seat and approached the King to listen and to suggest the instructions.

When the Keeper of the Seals had regained his seat, he waited for a moment and then opened this memorable occasion with a speech. The official report of the *lit de justice*, drawn up by the *Parlement* and printed, is in everyone's hands so there is no need for me to report the speeches of the Keeper of the Seals, the First President and the Law Officers of the Crown, or the various documents which were read and registered. I shall content myself with a few observations. The first speech; the reading of the letters appointing the Keeper of the Seals; the speech of Blancmesnil, the Advocate General, which followed; the taking of the various opinions; the Keeper of the Seals's pronouncement; the order given, and sometimes repeated, to open and then to hold open the two double doors: these were no surprise, but only served as a preface to what was coming and, as the moment drew near when everything was to be revealed, to raise the curiosity of the assembly to boiling point.

With this first act out of the way, the second was opened by a speech from the Keeper of the Seals,[1] so strong that it pierced the *Parlement* to its very heart; consternation was plainly visible on all their features. Out of all their number there was scarcely one who summoned up the courage even to whisper to his neighbour. The only thing I particularly noticed was that the Abbé Pucelle, who in spite of the fact that he was a clerical Councillor was seated on the bench opposite me, kept standing up whenever the Keeper of the Seals was speaking in order to hear him better. The face of the First President was bitter with misery, spite, shame and confusion. Those on the Bench which, in the language of the Law Courts they call the Great Bench to flatter its occupants, the *Présidents à Mortier*, simultaneously bowed their heads as if at a signal. Although the Keeper of the Seals spoke no louder than was necessary to be intelligible to all, he managed his voice so well that not a word was missed by anyone in the assembly, nor for that matter was there one word which failed to find its mark.

The reading of the declaration was grimmer still. Each sentence seemed made to augment not only the attention but the misery of those members of the *Parlement*—those haughty magistrates, whose proud remonstrances had not yet been enough to satisfy their sense

---

[1] On the subject of reducing the *Parlement* to its original functions as a purely judicial body.

of self-importance and ambition, and who now beheld themselves
reduced with ignominy to the exercise of their proper functions and
at the same time firmly and publicly chastised without a soul to pity
them but their own cabal. Fully to express what one glance revealed
to me at this extraordinary moment is impossible, and, though I have
the satisfaction of knowing that nothing escaped me, I still regret
that I cannot reproduce the scene exactly as it was for other eyes.

Blancmesnil's presence of mind amazed me. Whenever his office
required him to speak, he did so with a modesty of expression, a
sagacious air of embarrassment that was contradicted by the mastery
of his performance, and a phrasing so delicate that one would have
thought he must have prepared his speech before.

As soon as the opinions had been taken and the Keeper of the
Seals had made his pronouncement, I noticed a movement upon that
Great Bench of theirs. It was the First President who wished to speak,
and indeed to make that famous remonstrance which has since been
printed, and which is a monument of impudence towards the Regent,
of insolence towards the King, and of the most refined malice from
beginning to end. Nevertheless the villain trembled as he made it.
The breaks in his voice, the constraint in his eyes, the obvious anxiety
and nervousness of his whole bearing, showed only too clearly the
poisonous nature of the man, and the fact that he could not deny
either to himself or to his Company this malicious offering.

But now at last I was able to savour, with a delight which passes all
my powers of expression, the spectacle of these proud lawyers, proud
to the extent of daring to refuse us our salute, on their knees in
homage before the throne while we, beside it, seated upon our high
seats with our heads covered, looked down on them from above.
Could any situation, could any posture, plead more convincingly or
bring better evidence to bear upon the gulf which lies between those
who are *laterales regis* and this *vas electum*[1] of the Third Estate! My
eyes were fixed—nay, glued—upon those haughty bourgeois, watching those magistrates of the Great Bench as they knelt and rose,
watching the ample folds of their furred cloaks undulating at each
fresh genuflection that they made, watching them continue until by
the order of the King through the mouth of the Keeper of the Seals
they were told to cease, remembering that the wretched fur upon
their cloaks which pretended to be ermine was in fact only squirrel,
and revelling in the sight of all their heads uncovered and humiliated,
at our feet.

[1] 'Chosen vessel.' Cf. Acts IX, 15.

When the remonstrance was finished, the Keeper of the Seals mounted once more to the throne, returned to his place and then, without asking for a vote, looked straight at the First President and announced: 'The King wishes to be obeyed and obeyed immediately.' The words were like a thunder-clap, striking presidents and councillors to the earth, for all the world to see. They bowed their heads, and it was a long time before most of them looked up again. As for the rest of the spectators, with the exception of the Marshals of France, they seemed to be little moved by this spectacle of desolation.

However, this commonplace triumph was nothing in comparison with what was immediately to follow. As soon as the Keeper of the Seals had, by his last pronouncement, ended the Second Act, he passed straight on to the Third. I had already, as he passed to take our votes on the edict concerning the *Parlement*, warned him not to consult us when the next matter came up, and he had told me that he would not. I had done this as a precaution against any absent-mindedness on his part. After a few moments' interval between the pronouncement of the *Parlement* and what was to follow, the Keeper of the Seals once again mounted the steps to the throne and, on returning to his place, remained there a few more moments in silence. At this all saw that, although the *Parlement*'s business had been dealt with, there still remained another matter before the Assembly, and everyone was in suspense, wracking his brains as to what it might be. I learnt later that most of the members of the *Parlement* were expecting a decision in our favour on the question of saluting, and I shall shortly explain why this question was not mentioned. Others, seeing that the Bastards were absent, were nearer the mark in thinking that they would be concerned in what was coming, but not one of them guessed in what way or to what an extent they were to be affected.

At last the Keeper of the Seals began to speak, and he did so in such a way that his very first sentence announced the fall of one brother and the preservation of the other. The effect of this sentence on the faces around me cannot be described. Occupied as I was with controlling my own features, I yet succeeded in missing nothing on those of others. Astonishment was the emotion which prevailed. Many, either out of hatred for the Duc du Maine, or out of affection for the Comte de Toulouse, or perhaps again from a real respect for equity, seemed pleased; but several were dismayed. The First President completely lost countenance; his features, usually so complacent and bold, worked convulsively; only the excess of his rage prevented him from fainting. As the declaration continued his sufferings grew even worse. Every word had legal effect and each new phrase announced a fresh defeat. As the Clerk to the *Parlement* read on, the general attention became very strained; everyone remained silent, anxious not to miss a word.

When two-thirds of the reading was finished, the First President ground together the few teeth that remained to him, then placing his forehead low upon the handle of his stick which he clutched tightly with both hands, he remained in this curious and significant position until the declaration, so damning to all his hopes and so full of the promise of life for us, was ended.

In the meanwhile I was feeling almost dead with joy; my pleasure was so great that I feared I might faint, for my heart was full and it could expand no further. In my fear of betraying what I felt, I had to do myself such violence that it was terrible, and yet my pains were a delight. I compared those years of servitude, those miserable years when, a victim of the *Parlement,* I had only served as a pawn in the Bastards' triumph as they climbed step by step above us; I compared those days, I say, with this, our day of justice and of the re-establishment of our rights, this downfall for them and of compensating resurrection for us. With the most powerful delight I recalled what, even under the despotism of his father, I had dared to tell the Duc du Maine on that scandalous day when our rights against the *Parlement* had been denied us. My threats had now come true and their accomplishment lay before my eyes. I gave thanks, as if for a debt I owed to myself, that it was through me that all had been accomplished. Now, in this splendid and brilliant scene, in the presence of the King and of all this august assembly, the fruits of victory lay at my feet. I triumphed; I wallowed in revenge, and in the delight of satisfying desires which were not only the most urgent, but also the longest held, of any I had ever known. I was tempted to care no further what might happen. Nevertheless I continued to listen to this stimulating reading with my whole attention, and I noticed that the words seemed to resound upon my heartstrings as if a bow had been drawn across some instrument of music. At the same time I watched the different impressions they were making upon others.

At the very first word on this subject that the Keeper of the Seals let fall, the eyes of the two Episcopal Peers met mine. Never have I seen such surprise on any men's faces, nor such obvious transports of joy. Our places were too far apart for me to have had a chance of warning them, and they could not resist the uprush of emotion that suddenly assailed them. For a moment I allowed my eyes to feast upon their joy, then, fearing that I should succumb if I looked any longer, I turned resolutely away.

As soon as this reading was over, the Clerk to the *Parlement*, in accordance with the instructions of the Keeper of the Seals, who had indeed handed him both the declarations together, began upon that in favour of the Comte de Toulouse. By now the contrast between the two brothers had become so plainly marked that the First President and M. du Maine's other friends were completely swept off their feet, for they found this declaration more surprising even than those which had gone before; and indeed to those who did not know the reasons for it, it must have seemed unintelligible. The Comte de Toulouse's friends were naturally in ecstasy, but those who were indifferent, though pleased to see that an exception had been made in his favour, considered it unreasonable and unjust. I noticed that on this occasion opinions were much more divided, and that, though the reading was listened to attentively, men began to whisper to their neighbours as they had not done previously.

The reading of the important clauses relating to the consent of the Princes of the Blood and the request of the Peers of France revealed the intentions which lay behind the declaration, and caused the First President to raise his nose sharply from his stick on which he had been leaning. One or two of the peers, incited by Monsieur de Metz,[1] grumbled under their breath, furious as they complained to those around them that upon a matter of this importance they had not been consulted in a general assembly before being made to present it to the throne as a request. How we could possibly have run the risk of exposing a secret of this nature to an assembly of Peers, made up of men of all ages and of all sorts of differing sympathies—and still less how we could have discussed our reasons before such an assembly— was a matter which they did not stop to explain. It is true that there were not many who were shocked, but those who were gave as their reason the fact that the Peers on the Regency Council had answered for those outside it without authority, and I suspect that their motive for objecting was more petty jealousy than any genuine feelings about the Comte de Toulouse. The murmurs ceased as quickly as they had begun, and, after all, one can do nothing in this world without meeting with some disagreement.

As soon as the Advocate General had finished speaking the Keeper of the Seals mounted the steps to the throne again, and began by taking the votes of the Princes of the Blood. After that he came to the Duc de Sully and to me. Happily I had a better memory than he had,

---

[1] The Bishop of Metz was in his own right the Duc de Coislin, and it was as such that he was present on this occasion.

or perhaps than he wished to have, on this occasion. At any rate I knew my business. I took off my plumed hat with a significant sweep, and I said in intentionally loud tones: 'No, sir, we cannot act as judges. We are parties to this and all we have to do is to return thanks to the King for his graciousness in doing us this act of justice.' He smiled and begged my pardon. Then, before the Duc de Sully could open his mouth to say a word, I gave the Keeper of the Seals a little push, and, looking around me, was pleased to notice that my refusal to vote had been observed by all the spectators. The Keeper of the Seals stopped, and, without speaking to the remaining Peers on our bench, or to the two Episcopal Peers, went straight to the Marshals of France; then he went down to the First President and the *Présidents à Mortier*; and then on to the lower seats. As soon as this was accomplished he mounted the steps to the throne and, on his return to his place, announced that the decree would be registered, and thus put the finishing stroke to all my joy.

Immediately afterwards Monsieur Le Duc rose from his seat and, after bowing to the King, forgot to sit down and cover himself again before speaking as, following the uninterrupted right and usage on these occasions, all Peers of France are entitled to do. Because of this right we none of us rose. However, standing and uncovered, as I said, he made his speech, exactly as it stands printed in its place after the preceding speeches. As he had not a good voice for these purposes his reading was almost unintelligible. As soon as he had finished the Duc d'Orléans arose and committed the same fault. Standing and uncovered, he said that Monsieur le Duc's demand seemed to him to be just, and then, after a few compliments, added that, as the Duc du Maine would henceforth take precedence from the date of his peerage, it would be quite impossible for the Maréchal de Villeroy, who would now be his senior, to serve under him, and that this seemed a most powerful reason for removing him, quite apart from the other arguments which Monsieur le Duc had put forward.

With this fresh demand the astonishment of the assembly and the despair of the First President and of all those who, to their present regret, had pinned their hopes on the Duc du Maine, reached their highest point. The Maréchal de Villeroy, though he did not wince, looked sourer than ever, and the eyes of the First President filled with tears. I could not see how the Maréchal d'Huxelles, his cousin and intimate friend, received the news, for his face was completely hidden beneath the vast outlines of his enormous hat, dragged down over his eyes; but he did not stir. The First President was stricken to the earth by this final blow; he screwed his head round and downwards;

and at one moment I thought that his chin had fallen onto his knees.

In the meanwhile the Keeper of the Seals ordered the Law Officers of the Crown to speak. They replied that they had not heard Monsieur le Duc's proposal, whereupon the paper on which his speech was written was passed along to them from hand to hand, and the Keeper of the Seals repeated what the Regent had said about the Maréchal de Villeroy's seniority. Blancmesnil took one glance at Monsieur le Duc's speech and then spoke. After that the Keeper of the Seals asked for our votes. I gave mine in a clear and rather loud voice saying: 'On this matter, sir, I am whole-heartedly in favour of giving the superintendence of the King's education to Monsieur le Duc.'

After his final pronouncement, the Keeper of the Seals called for the Chief Clerk and ordered him to bring his papers and his little writing desk and place them by his own, so that everything which had been read to and decided by the assembly might be registered and signed forthwith, one after the other, in the King's presence. All this was done, in proper form, under the gaze of the Keeper of the Seals who never once took his eyes off the table. But as there were five or six things to register it all took a long time.

I watched the King most carefully when the question of his education came up, and I noticed no change whatsoever in his features, not even a moment's constraint. This had been the Last Act of the spectacle, and while the registrations were in progress he looked as fresh as he had at the beginning. However, as there were now no speeches to occupy his attention, he started to laugh and joke with those around him, pointing out various things which amused him, and even noticing that the Duc de Louvigny, who was some way away from the throne, was wearing a velvet suit and seemed too hot in it, making fun of him very charmingly. His indifference towards the subject of M. du Maine impressed everyone, and gave a public denial to the stories which M. du Maine's friends attempted to put abroad, that his eyes were red with tears although he did not dare to show his feelings either at the *lit de justice* or afterwards. The truth of the matter is that his eyes were dry and happy; that he only pronounced M. du Maine's name once, after dinner the same day, when he asked quite carelessly where M. du Maine was going; and that he never mentioned him or any of his children again. As for the latter, they had never troubled to see much of him, and even while they were still with him had held a little court apart and had played among themselves. Much the same was true of the Duc du Maine, who, either for political reasons or else because he thought him still too young, had never visited the King except in the mornings, sometimes

while he was still in bed, and never again during the day except on
duty.

While the registrations were in progress I allowed my eyes to wander slowly over all parts of the assembly, and, although for the most part I held myself in sternly, I could not resist the temptation of taking some further revenge on the First President. Even while the session was in progress I had over and over again cast long and venomous glances in his direction. A stream of contempt, disdain, scorn and revenge flowed forth from my eyes and pierced him to the marrow. Often when he met my eyes his own would drop, but once or twice he looked straight at me and then I took pleasure in shaping my mouth into a mocking and bitter smile, which forced him to look away in confusion. I was wallowing in his rage and it was with delight that I let him see it. Once or twice when he was looking I pointed him out to my neighbours with a nod of the head and thus publicly made fun of him. Indeed to put it shortly I allowed my desire to triumph over him full rein, and continued to do so as long as ever I could.

At last the registrations came to an end and the King, followed by the Regent, the two Princes of the Blood and all his suite, came down from his throne to the level of the lower seats by the steps leading to the chair of the Keeper of the Seals. At the same moment the Marshals of France came down the steps at the end of the high seats; and while the King, accompanied by the deputation which had met him on his arrival, crossed the floor, they passed between the Councillors' benches, on the far side of the chamber from where we sat, to join the King's suite at the door by which the King had entered and through which he now left. At the same time the two Episcopal Peers walked past the throne and placed themselves at our head. As they passed me they shook me warmly by the hand and kissed me with the most lively joy. Two by two in order of seniority we followed them along our bench and, descending by the steps at the far end, walked straight ahead through the door which was opposite to us. After us came the *Parlement,* who left by the door by which I had entered and by which the King had entered and left. A way was made for us between the steps and our door, but the crowds and the whole spectacle about us seemed to hem us in and to put constraint upon our words and upon our hearts. I was almost suffocated. I went straight to my carriage, which I found at once, and fortunately for me I was so quickly out of the courtyard that I suffered no hindrance, and within a quarter of an hour of leaving the *lit de justice* I was home.

I have forgotten to say that, shortly before leaving the Council chamber to attend the *lit de justice*, at a moment when the Regent,

287

1718 Monsieur le Duc and I happened to find ourselves together, the other two had made an arrangement to meet with the Keeper of the Seals at the Palais Royal as soon as the session was over. At the same time they had invited me to join them. I had tried to refuse, but they had insisted, saying that they wished to be able to discuss whatever might happen in the meantime. However, seeing that no difficulty of any sort had arisen, I thought myself free to stay at home, and was indeed well pleased not to have to add a further proof of the fact that I had been in the secret, a fact which was already giving rise to envy. I arrived home at about half-past two and found the Duc d'Humières,[1] Louville and all my family waiting for me at the foot of the stairs. . . . Even my mother, who had not previously left her room since the beginning of the winter, was now so curious to hear the news that she was there to meet me. We remained downstairs and went into my study, and while I changed my coat and shirt I did my best to reply to their excited questions.

Suddenly a footman came in to tell me that M. de Biron, who, in spite of the orders I had given to have my door shut to all the world, had succeeded in forcing his way in, was waiting to see me. I was longing for a moment or two to myself, but that was not to be. Indeed a moment later M. de Biron put his head round the door and asked to be allowed to have a word with me. Still only half dressed, I led him through to my main apartment.

He told me that the Duc d'Orléans had expected me, on leaving the Tuileries, to go straight to the Palais Royal; that I had promised to do so and that he had been surprised at not finding me there; that, nevertheless, no great harm had been done, and that he had only spent a moment or so with Monsieur le Duc and the Keeper of the Seals; but that His Royal Highness had directed him to come and find me at my house, and to tell me to go to him at once at the Palais Royal, since there was something he wished me to do for him. I asked if Biron knew what this was. He told me it was to go to Saint-Cloud to break the news to the Duchesse d'Orléans. This was a terrible blow. I argued with Biron about it. He agreed that it was a miserable commission for anyone to have to undertake, but urged me not to waste a moment in going to the Palais Royal, where my coming was awaited with impatience. He added that, though he pitied me profoundly for the confidence thus placed in me, the Duc d'Orléans had told him that there was no one else he could trust to undertake the task, and

---

[1] He was only a *duc à brevet*, or verified duke, and not a peer and had therefore not been summoned to the *lit de justice*.

had said this in such a way that there could be little hope of my being
excused. He said moreover that he thought that it would show an ill
grace on my part to resist too strongly.

When I returned to my study my face was so changed that Mme de
Saint-Simon cried out on seeing me, thinking that something terrible
had happened. I told them all that I had just heard. After Biron had
said a few words urging me to go immediately and to submit, he went
off to dinner; ours was already served. I stayed for a minute or two to
give myself a chance to get over the shock, and then, seeing that it
would be wiser not to make the Duc d'Orléans more stubborn by my
slowness in doing what he wanted, I decided to go to him, though I
was determined to do everything I could to avoid being forced to
undertake so difficult and so onerous a duty. I swallowed some soup
and an egg, and set out for the Palais Royal.

1718

MY THANKLESS TASK

✦✦✦✦✦ FOUND the Duc d'Orléans alone in his big study. He was
✦ *I* ✦ awaiting my arrival with impatience, striding up and down.
✦ ✦ As soon as I appeared he came to me and asked if I had seen
✦✦✦✦✦ Biron. I told him that I had, and that I had come to receive
my orders. He asked me if Biron had told me what it was he wanted
of me. I said that he had; that to show my obedience I had come at
once in my coach with six horses to be ready for anything he might
wish; but that I thought that he had not fully reflected upon what he
wanted me to do.

At that moment the Abbé Dubois came in to congratulate the
Regent upon the success of the morning and to exhort him to remain
firm and show himself the master. I joined in both these sentiments.
I praised His Royal Highness for his unaffected, yet serious and
kingly manner, for the clarity, the conciseness and the precision of
his speeches before the Council, and for everything else which I could
sincerely praise in his behaviour. I wished to encourage him for the
future, and also to put him into a good humour, so that we might be
at our ease together, and so that he might feel more inclined to excuse
me from delivering this detestable message. The Abbé Dubois ex-
patiated on the *Parlement*'s terror, and on the small satisfaction they
had received from the people in the streets, where no one had followed
them, and where they must from the shops and houses along their
route have heard words very different from what they had first expected. What he said was true; indeed, some members of the Company
had been so frightened that they never got as far as the Tuileries at all,
while that famous rebel Blamont, the *Président aux Enquêtes* had re-
neged on the very steps of the Tuileries and fled to the chapel, where
he had been taken ill and felt so weak that he had had to be dosed
with spirits and revived with the sacramental wine from the sacristy.

As soon as he had finished regaling us with these stories, the Abbé
Dubois left and we resumed our previous conversation. The Duc
d'Orléans told me that he could understand my dislike of being forced
to tell the Duchesse d'Orléans news which, considering her opinions,
was sure to be terribly distressing to her, but that he must confess to
me that he found it impossible to write to her; that their present
situation was such that he could not speak tenderly to her; that his

290

letter would be kept and shown to others, a risk which he dared not run; that I had always acted as a conciliator between him and his wife; that they both had the same confidence in me; that that was why I had always been so successful; and that it was this, and also my friendship with them both, that had determined him to beg me, out of the love I bore to them both, to undertake this commission for him.

After such compliments and expressions of respect as I thought to be necessary I replied that of all men in the world I was the least fitted for this commission; that I was well known to be extremely sensitive where the rights attaching to my dignity were concerned; that the Bastards' rank had always been intolerable to me; that I had continually and passionately hoped for what had now come to pass; that, both before the late King's death and since, I had said as much to the Duchesse d'Orléans a hundred times; that I had occasionally said the same thing to M. du Maine, and even once to the Duchesse du Maine, at Paris, on the only occasion on which I had spoken to her on the subject; that I had also informed the Comte de Toulouse of my feelings several times; that the Duchesse d'Orléans could not therefore possibly fail to be aware that to-day must be for me a day of triumph; that, considering all this, it would not only show a great want of respect but be a real insult for me to go and tell her what I knew would cause her pain, and what she at the same time must know would be causing me the greatest joy imaginable.

'You are wrong,' said the Duc d'Orléans, 'and your arguments are false. It is just because you have always spoken frankly on this subject, not only to the two brothers but to the Duchesse d'Orléans as well, and because you have always held your head high on these occasions, that you are fitter than anyone else to do what I ask of you. You have told the Duchesse d'Orléans exactly how you think and exactly how you feel, and she has never once resented it; on the contrary she has always respected the frankness and outspokenness of your behaviour; and, though she will be offended, and bitterly offended, by the thing itself, she will not be offended with you. She is very fond of you. She knows how you have striven for peace and union in our home. For this reason there is no one from whom she will receive the news better, and there is therefore no one who is better fitted to give it than you—you who know all our affairs, and to whom both she and I, each on our own behalf, can speak our minds about the other. Do not refuse me this proof of your affection. I know perfectly well how disagreeable this message must be to you, but in important matters like this, one really must not refuse a friend!'

I argued, I protested, and we both said a great deal, but in the end there was nothing for it but to give way. It was useless to tell him that this would be the end of my friendship with the Duchesse d'Orléans, and that the world would think it strange that I should take such an embassy upon my shoulders. He had no ears for what I said, but continued to press me so hard that I had to obey.

At last therefore I agreed to go, and asked for his instructions. He told me that all I had to do was to tell her the facts; to say that he had sent me; and to add at once that without the strongest proofs against her brother he would never have been driven to such extremes. I told him that he must expect his wife to take the news hard, and be prepared to forgive her everything during these few days; to give her leave to stay at Saint-Cloud, or to visit Bagnolet, Paris, or Montmartre, and to see him or not to see him according to her wishes; to put himself in her place and to soften the severity of the blow by every little act of kindness his tolerance and attentiveness could possibly suggest; to allow her every caprice, her every fantasy, full play; and not to be alarmed by anything she might do. He agreed with all I said, and showed that he felt a genuine compassion and affection for the Duchesse d'Orléans, but he could not help returning again and again to her strong leanings on the subject of the Bastards. However, I changed the conversation, and said that this was not the moment to blame her for that. I also begged him not to be surprised or annoyed if the Duchesse d'Orléans, knowing what I had come to tell her, refused to see me. He agreed that in that case I need not insist, and promised not to be angry with her.

After taking these precautions, and I meant to make use of the last of them if the chance to do so came my way, I begged him to tell me if, in the case of Madame's happening to be at Saint-Cloud as well, he would like me to see her. He thanked me for having thought of this, and begged me to give her a full account from him of all that had happened that morning. Then he begged me to be sure, whatever happened, to come straight back and to tell him all about it. I protested once again against this abuse of my obedience, and told him of my repugnance, of the personal and particular reasons I had for resisting him, and of the gossip to which he was exposing me. Then at last I left him, overwhelmed with expressions of his friendship for me and with regrets that he should be asking so much of mine for him.

As I left him, I found one of the Duchesse d'Orléans's pages, booted and spurred, outside. He had just arrived from Saint-Cloud. I begged him to return at the gallop and, on his arrival, to inform the Duchesse Sforza that I was coming with a message from the Duc d'Orléans, and that I begged that I might see her the moment I got down from

my carriage, and to speak with her in private before seeing the
Duchesse d'Orléans or anyone else. My plan was to see no one but
her, to charge her with my burden, and, under cover of my respect
for the Duchesse d'Orléans, not to deliver my message in person at all,
counting on the Duc d'Orléans's assurance that he would have no
objection if his wife refused to see me, and thinking that on my
return I should be able to persuade him that I had acted for the best.
However, all my poor plans were upset by the foresight of the page.
He had no desire to be the bearer of news of this kind which he had
heard as soon as he had arrived at the Palais Royal and which was
rapidly becoming public property. On his return he therefore merely
announced that I was coming, took care not to breathe a word to the
Duchesse Sforza, and smartly disappeared. I learnt this later, but as
soon as I arrived at Saint-Cloud I saw pretty clearly what must have
occurred.

In order to allow the page time to arrive before me and to warn
the Duchesse Sforza to be ready to receive me, I drove at a gentle trot,
congratulating myself upon having laid my plans so cleverly. However, I was still nervous that I might have to see the Duchesse d'Orléans after the Duchesse Sforza had given her the news, though it
certainly never crossed my mind that at Saint-Cloud they might still
be in ignorance of the more important of the morning's events.
Nevertheless my anxiety was inexpressible and it grew steadily worse
as I approached the end of my miserable journey. . . .

Filled with these mournful thoughts I saw my coach draw up in
the great courtyard at Saint-Cloud, and all the windows were filled
with people who had rushed to watch my arrival. I stepped down from
my coach and, as I did not know where the Duchesse Sforza was
lodged, I asked the first man I met to conduct me to her. At once one
or two servants ran off to warn her, and returned with the news that
she was at Benediction with the Duchesse d'Orléans, whose apartments were only separated from the chapel by a hall, at the entrance
of which I was standing. I made a dive for the Maréchale de Rochefort's apartments, which also gave onto this hall, and as soon as I
arrived I begged her servants to go and find the Duchesse Sforza
for me. They returned a moment later to say that they did not know
what had become of her, and that the Duchesse d'Orléans had just
heard of my arrival and gone straight to her apartments to wait for
me. Next moment a messenger arrived from the Princess herself, and
immediately afterwards another. I had just sent another servant in
search of the Duchesse Sforza, for I was resolved, whatever happened, to wait for her arrival, when the Maréchale de Rochefort came

in, hobbling upon her stick, to tell me that the Duchesse d'Orléans had sent her to bring me to her. A long argument followed, for I was still resolved to find the Duchesse Sforza, though I did not know how to do it. In order to gain time I asked to be taken to the Duchess's apartments, but the Maréchale seized me inexorably by the arm and asked to be told the news.

At my wit's end, I answered: 'Only what you know already.' 'What?' said she, 'we know nothing here at all, except that there has been a *lit de justice* and we are all dying to hear why, and what has happened.' I was so astonished by this that I made her repeat what she had said, and then give me her promise that it was true that no one at Saint-Cloud had heard the news. After that I told her what had happened, and it was her turn almost to fall to the ground in astonishment. I was still determined to do all I could to avoid going to the Princess, but, as six or seven messengers had arrived while this conversation was in progress, I was forced at last to accompany the Maréchale, who held me by the wrist, poured out her alarm to me, and then told me how she pitied me for the scene I was now to witness, or rather to create.

At last, shivering with apprehension, I reached those apartments of the Duchesse d'Orléans which are known as 'Les Goulettes,' where her people were ready waiting for me. When they saw my face they looked at me in terror. The Maréchale left me as I entered the bedroom; there I was told that Her Royal Highness was in a little marble drawing-room down three steps leading out of it. I turned in that direction, and the moment I caught sight of the Princess, which was at some distance, I saluted her with a respect that was quite unusual between us. She could not see my face, and as she begged me to approach her voice was gay and unforced. 'My God, sir,' she cried, 'what is the meaning of that expression; and what have you come to tell me?' Seeing that I remained where I was, without stirring and without saying a word, she repeated her question in an agitated tone. Very slowly I took a few steps towards her and at her third appeal I said: 'Do you know nothing, Madam?' 'No, sir, I know nothing whatsoever except that a *lit de justice* has been held, but of what happened there I have not heard a word.' 'Ah, Madam,' I interrupted her, turning half away from her as I did so, 'in that case I am a far more unhappy man than even I imagined myself to be.' 'What, sir?' she replied, 'tell me quickly—what is the matter?' She had been lying at full length upon a couch, but at this she rose to a sitting position. 'Come here and sit down,' she told me.

At that I went closer, and told her I was in despair. Still more and

294

more distressed, she said quickly: 'Speak. It is better to hear bad news from one's friends than from anyone else.' At this I was pierced to the heart and I could think of nothing but the pain I must give her. I walked a step or two nearer, and then I told her that the Duc d'Orléans had reduced the Duc du Maine to his rank by seniority in the peerage, and at the same time had re-established the Comte de Toulouse in all the honours he had previously enjoyed. At this point I paused for a moment. Then I added that he had given the superintendence of the King's education to Monsieur le Duc. At that her tears began to flow abundantly. She said nothing in reply; she did not cry out; but she wept most bitterly. She pointed to a chair and I sat down, my eyes lowered for a moment or so.

Then I told her that the Duc d'Orléans had rather forced me to accept than charged me with this sad commission; that he had expressly ordered me to say that he had in his hands the strongest possible proofs of the Duc du Maine's guilt; that out of consideration for her he had long done nothing; but that he had been unable to put off this moment of retribution any longer. She replied with a good deal of sweetness that her brother was very unfortunate, and a little later asked me if I knew what her brother's crime was or at least of what sort of crime he was guilty. I said that the Duc d'Orléans had told me nothing but what I had just told her and that I had not dared to question him on a matter of this kind, especially when I saw that he volunteered no more himself.

A little later I told her that the Duc d'Orléans had expressly charged me to tell her how greatly he sympathized with her in her present sorrows, to which I added all that in my distress I was able to call to mind to soften my terrible commission. Then, after an interval, I expressed my personal sympathy with her grief, as well as the repugnance I had felt and the resistance I had put up when called upon to undertake the mournful task. She answered me only by sighs, with here and there an occasional word between her sobs. I ended, as I had express permission from the Duc d'Orléans to do, by letting her see that I had done all I could to prevent this blow from falling upon her. At this she said that I must forgive her if at present she found it impossible to show more gratitude. I replied that it was only natural that she should not be able to see beyond her present trouble, and said everything I could think of to console her, adding that whatever seemed good to her would meet with the approval of the Duc d'Orléans; that she could see him now, or not until she wished to do so, whichever she preferred; that she might stay at Saint-Cloud, or go to Bagnolet or Montmartre, and stay there as long as she chose; that in a word she could please herself entirely; and that I was expressly directed to beg her to put no constraint upon herself and to do whatsoever she considered best.

At this she asked me if I knew what the Duc d'Orléans would prefer her to do in regard to her brothers, saying that she would not see them if he would prefer her not to. I replied that the fact that I had no instructions on this point showed that he would be perfectly agreeable to her seeing them; that as regarded the Comte de Toulouse, who was exactly as he always had been, there could be no possible difficulty; and that as for the Duc du Maine, I did not think there could be any either, and would even answer for it on my own responsibility if necessary. Then she spoke about the latter, saying that he must indeed be guilty of something very serious and that she was reduced almost to hoping that it were so. A fresh outburst of tears followed these words.

I remained for some while on the seat where I was, not daring to lift my eyes, and in as miserable a state as a man could be in, uncertain whether to go or stay. At last I told her of my embarrassment, saying that I thought she would like to be alone for a while before giving me her instructions, but that my respect for her was such that I could not act without knowing what she would prefer me to do. After a short time she said she would like her women. I rose, sent them to her, and told them that if Her Royal Highness wanted me I should be found either with Madame, or with the Duchesse Sforza, or else with the Maréchale de Rochefort. I could not find either of the last two ladies, and I therefore went upstairs to see Madame.

The moment I entered I saw that my coming was expected, even with some impatience. The room was not crowded, but all who were there clustered round me. I did not say a word to them. One of them then went into Madame's study, where she was writing as usual, and told her I had come. She sent for me at once. When I went in she rose and said with enthusiasm: "Well, sir, you have brought the news?" After that her ladies left, and I was alone with her. I made my excuses for not having visited her first, as indeed I ought to have done, saying that the Duc d'Orléans had assured me that she would approve of my going first to the Duchesse d'Orléans. She said that I had done quite rightly, and then asked for the news. I was enormously surprised to find that she too knew nothing except that there had been a *lit de justice,* the results of which were still unknown to her. I told her at once that the King's education had been given to Monsieur le Duc, that the Bastards were reduced to their rank in the peerage, and that the Comte de Toulouse had then been re-instated. Her whole face was suffused with joy as she replied with an expressive 'At last!' which she immediately repeated. Then she said that this was what her son ought to have done long ago, but that he was too good-natured.

I reminded her that she was standing, but she politely continued to do so. She said that it was the folly of the Duchesse du Maine that had brought her husband to this; she spoke to me of the Princes of the Blood's action against the Bastards; and then she told me of the extravagant remarks of Mme du Maine, who, after judgement had been delivered, had said straight out to the Duc d'Orléans, showing him her two sons,[1] that she meant to bring them up with the memory of this day, and the desire to avenge themselves for the wrong he had done them, graven on their hearts. After we had each of us said a few words about the hatred which the Duc and Duchesse du Maine had always borne, and the ill offices, and even worse, which they had always done to the Duc d'Orléans, Madame begged me to give her a detailed account of our morning's work from beginning to end. Once again I pointed out to her that she was standing, and that what she wished to hear would be a long story, but her excitement was so great that it was useless to urge her further.

The Duc d'Orléans had instructed me to tell her everything that had passed both at the Council and at the *lit de justice*. I therefore told her the whole story from the very beginning. After a quarter of an hour Madame sat down, but even then only with the utmost politeness. I was with her the best part of an hour, speaking nearly all the time, and often answering her questions. She was delighted to hear of the *Parlement*'s and the Bastards' humiliation, and that her son had shown himself so firm.

After this the Maréchale de Rochefort asked to be allowed to come in, and after conveying the excuses of the Duchesse d'Orléans, asked Madame's permission to take me back to her mistress, who wished to speak to me. Madame sent me off at once, but urged me strongly to return to her as soon as the Duchesse d'Orléans had finished with me. Thereupon I went downstairs with the Maréchale. On entering Her Royal Highness's apartments I was assaulted by her women and all her other servants, who immediately rushed up to me to beg me to persuade Her Royal Highness not to go to Montmartre, as she had just announced her intention of going. I assured them that my message was in itself a bad enough task for any man to undertake without adding anything to it on my own account; that Her Royal Highness was in no fit state to be contradicted or controlled; that I had foreseen

---

[1] The Prince de Dombes and the Comte d'Eu.

that she would want to go to Montmartre and had taken my precautions; that the Duc d'Orléans was perfectly agreeable to this course or to anything else that might bring Her Royal Highness some mitigation of her grief; and that I refused to say a word more. They still continued to protest, but I went on, and found the Duchesse d'Orléans lying on the sofa on which I had left her, a writing case on her knees and a pen in her hand.

As soon as she saw me she said that, as I had assured her that the Duc d'Orléans was agreeable, she meant to go to Montmartre, but that nevertheless she was writing to him for permission. Then she read me the beginning of her letter, six or seven lines of her large handwriting on a small sheet of paper. She looked at me with a sweet and affectionate air. 'My tears are too much for me,' she said, 'and I have asked you to come so that you may do me a favour. My hand will not write properly, and I beg you to finish my letter for me.' Then she handed me her writing case with the letter on top. I took it. Then she dictated what remained for her to say, and I wrote it down immediately following what she had written herself. I was amazed by the conciseness with which she expressed herself in this letter, the choice of terms, the correctness of the sentiments, and the orderliness and justness of the arrangement, which were indeed such that the best of writers in a mood of unruffled calm could scarcely have done better, while hers were the spontaneous utterings of one, not only deeply agitated, not only surprised by a sudden uprush of the most violent passions, but writing amidst her sobs in a paroxysm of tears. She finished by saying that she would go for a time to Montmartre, there to weep for her brothers' sorrows and to pray for her husband's prosperity.

All my life long I shall regret not making a copy of that letter. Everything in it was so dignified, so just, so orderly; everything was so true and yet so well within the compass of her duty. Indeed it was such a perfect example of the art of letter-writing that, although I remember well what was in it, I dare not write it down for fear of spoiling it. What a pity it is that such intelligence, such sense, such proportion, that a mind so capable of self-possession even in moments of this kind, when all restraint is difficult, should have been rendered useless, and worse than useless, by the madness of her passion for the cause of Bastardy, which ruined it completely. When the letter was written I read it to her. She preferred not to close it, and begged me to deliver it myself. I told her I was returning to Madame, and that before leaving I should call upon Her Royal Highness again to see if she had any further instructions for me.

Just as I was finishing my talk with Madame, the Duchesse Sforza came to speak with the latter about the Duchesse d'Orléans's visit to Montmartre, and to ask Madame to keep Mlle de Valois with her. Mother and daughter were not on the best of terms, and the latter detested the Bastards and the rank they had been given. Madame very kindly approved of all the Duchesse d'Orléans's plans and said how sorry she was for her. After this interruption I continued my narrative. I was just finishing when the Maréchale de Rochefort arrived to ask Madame to be so kind as to go down to the Duchesse d'Orléans, who in her present state was unable to come upstairs to see her. She told us that the Duchesse d'Orléans had changed her mind about Montmartre and now intended to stay at Saint-Cloud. When the Maréchale had left I finished my tale and followed Madame. However, as I wished them to be free to talk together alone, I declined to enter the apartment with her.

After a time the Duchesse Sforza came out and told me that the plans had once again been changed, and that the Duchesse d'Orléans would go to Paris. On hearing this I asked the Duchesse Sforza to return the letter which the Duchesse d'Orléans had given me for her husband, and to ask if she had any further instructions to give me. The Duchesse Sforza came back at once and led me into her own room and then out to take the air by that fine piece of water which lies before the steps of the Château. We sat down on the side nearest to Les Goulettes, and once again I had to tell my tale. I did not forget to avail myself of the Duc d'Orléans's permission to let it be known how I had tried to save the Duc du Maine, but I also said that, when I saw that I could not save the education, I had been in favour of reducing him to his rank in the peerage and had also been responsible for the Comte de Toulouse's re-establishment. . . .

Madame Sforza, who was a very good friend of mine and entirely reliable, who moreover had her own reasons for not loving M. and Mme du Maine, and who was only distressed by what had happened on the Duchesse d'Orléans's account, said she wished to know nothing of what I had done to bring about the reduction in rank, but that she would make use of the rest. I had long been on terms of affection with the Duchesse d'Orléans; she had shown her confidence in me repeatedly; she had various reasons for being grateful to me; I was of use as an intermediary between her and the Duc d'Orléans; and I still wished most strongly to be in a position to contribute to their union and to the interior harmony of the family. After a long talk I begged the Duchesse Sforza to tell the Duchesse d'Orléans that, as she was now coming to Paris, I would not wait until Madame came out to pay her another visit. Then I went off to the Palais Royal where I found that the Duc d'Orléans was in conference with the Duchesse de Berry. As soon as he heard of my arrival he came out to see me in his big study, and I told him of all that had passed.

He was delighted to hear of Madame's joy when I told her the news about the Duc du Maine, and he told me that the Duchesse de Lorraine's would be as great. He had just received a letter from the Duchess urging upon him the course he had just taken, and Madame had also, as she had informed me, received one from her on the same subject. But he was not so pleased to hear of the Duchesse d'Orléans's intention of returning at once to Paris, and indeed he seemed to be thoroughly put out about it. After telling him the facts, I said all that I could think of likely to touch his heart, stressing the respect, the obedience, the submission to his wishes the Princess had shown me from the first, and laying the greatest emphasis upon her letter. . . . He asked me to advise him on whether or not to see her on her arrival. I told him I thought he had better go down to his study the moment she arrived, call for Mme Sforza, and then tell her to inform the Duchesse d'Orléans that he was there and would see her or not, whichever she preferred, to ask after her, and to do exactly what she wanted of him. On the other hand, I said that if he saw her he ought to show her every possible affection, to be prepared for a cold reception, perhaps for reproaches and most certainly for tears; that it was the merest humanity, and, further, his duty as a gentleman, to suffer everything on this occasion with the utmost patience and good-temper, and, however ill she might speak or act, only to treat her the better for it.

I hammered all this into his head as best I could and, after taking a small revenge and reproaching him for the way in which he had abused my affection for him, I left him to await his wife's arrival. As for me, after such a week, and still more after a day so tiring mentally and physically to round it off, I went home to rest. When I got back it was almost night.

I learnt later that the Duchesse d'Orléans arrived at the Palais Royal half an hour after I had left. Her brothers were waiting for her in her apartments. As soon as she saw them she asked if they had permission to visit her, and with dry eyes, declared that she would never see them at all if the Duc d'Orléans should ask her not to. After that they remained behind closed doors for an hour. As soon as the brothers had gone, the Duc d'Orléans went downstairs with the Duchesse de Berry who had stayed behind to uphold him in the coming scene. Never did anyone show more self-control than the Duchesse d'Orléans on this occasion. She even told the Duc d'Orléans

that she was far too well aware of the extreme honour which he had
done her in marrying her for any other sentiment to take precedence
over that. This was the first time in all their thirty years of married life
that she had ever spoken like this. Then, more deeply moved, she
asked his pardon for regretting her brother's misfortune, saying that
she believed him guilty, and since he had been considered worthy of
such a punishment she could only hope it were true. Then came tears,
sobs, and cries, not only from the wife but from the husband and
daughter as well. This sad scene lasted more than an hour. When it
was over the Duchesse d'Orléans went to bed, and the Duc d'Orléans
and the Duchesse de Berry returned upstairs. The resulting relief for
all concerned was immense.

Next day and the following passed in sweetness, after which the
Duchesse d'Orléans, worn out with her efforts, began to think once
again of her original purpose, which was to discover her brother's
crimes, and then to arrange a meeting between him and her husband
(she seems to have staked everything on their meeting face to face)
with the ultimate intention either of announcing her brother's misdeeds or else of having him re-established. As time went on, and she
was still as far from gaining her ends as ever, there followed sulks,
tears, moods of bitterness, and outbursts of fury upon fury. She
would shut herself up in her room and refuse to see anyone, even her
son whom she passionately loved, and at times she was quite beyond
herself. She knew only too well the man she had to deal with. Anyone
else but the Duc d'Orléans, once he had reached the end of his tolerance and good-nature, would have asked her once and for all quite
firmly whom it was she preferred, himself or her brother. If she had
answered that she preferred him, he would then have pointed out
that his interests should come first, that she had better not mention
her brother or anything to do with him again, that he forbade her to
mention him or to trouble the peace and understanding between them
by referring to any subject which could only serve to destroy it. On
the other hand, if she had said her brother, he should have told her
that, in that case, she could go away to a place he had chosen for her,
with such people as he approved of, where she would hear neither
from her brothers nor from himself nor their children. With some
such wise, and indeed necessary, precaution as this, the Duc d'Orléans
could easily have avoided those scenes and have spared himself, and
her too, such torments, such bitterness, such importunities, such discomfort, and such misery. . . .

However, it was no business of mine to suggest such salutary behaviour to the Duc d'Orléans, and I was extremely careful not to allow

him to have a glimpse of what I thought. Indeed I was especially careful, now more than ever, never to mention the Duchesse d'Orléans to him; and whenever he complained to me about her, I let the subject drop, because I had begged Mme Sforza at Saint-Cloud to tell the Duchesse d'Orléans that I thought it would be more respectful to leave her quite alone during the first days of her sorrow, as I had no wish to importune her, and that I would wait for the honour of seeing her until Her Royal Highness should send me a message bidding me to come to her. Next day, therefore, I merely called upon the Princess without going in. After that, I saw Mme Sforza who said that Her Royal Highness begged me not to take it in ill part if, during these first few days, she could not see me without pain. I understood this, and appreciated how painful the contrast between what she would know to be my pleasure and her own sorrow must be. However, those first few days never ended, and from that moment I have remained in her bad books.

Home again from my visit to Saint-Cloud, I thought that I ought to go to the Hôtel de Condé where, as I heard, the whole world had been flocking with congratulations. I found Madame la Duchesse, who had chosen her day for taking medicine unfortunately on this occasion, in bed. But I was received at the Hôtel de Condé almost as I had been received at Saint-Cloud on the day when the Duchesse de Berry's engagement had been announced. So the world changes. Monsieur le Duc took me aside, and then everyone else stopped me to have a word. Even those favourites of the household with whom I was no more than acquainted overwhelmed me with their compliments, and I hardly knew whether I was on my head or on my heels. I talked for a long time in private with d'Antin, and then with Torcy, and I urged the latter to see his friend Valincour, as I meant to do myself, and advise him to urge restraint on the Comte de Toulouse.

I was urged by Mme de Laigle, on leaving, to make friends with Madame la Duchesse, but I would not hear of this, and replied frankly that I had always been on too good terms with the Duchesse d'Orléans to make this friendship possible, considering their dislike for one another. . . .

On leaving the Council, the Duc du Maine and the Comte de Toulouse had gone straight to the former's apartments and shut themselves in with a few of their closest followers, whom they selected so well that no one knows to this day what took place on that occasion. . . .

The difference in treatment between the two brothers not only redoubled the despair of the elder and the resentment of his wife, but did more than anything else to urge them to influence the Comte de

Toulouse to throw in his lot with theirs. Within his own circle he was greatly inclined to do so, but M. d'O, who still retained over his own pupil and his household something of his former influence as tutor, dissuaded him from it. It was not that M. d'O was lacking in feeling for the Duc du Maine, but he put his own interests first, and he strongly objected to seeing his master ruined and forced to live in exile in the country.

I learnt later that the Chevalier d'Hautefort also spoke to his master with a frankness that went far to persuade him to take the same course. The Chevalier d'Hautefort was the Comte de Toulouse's Equerry and a Lieutenant General by sea. He was a brother of the Duchesse de Berry's First Equerry, of Surville, who had commanded the King's Regiment and whose disgrace made such a stir, and of Hautefort, the Lieutenant General who had since died a Knight of the Order and a furiously disappointed man (and that not without some cause) at his failure to be made a Marshal of France. The Comte de Toulouse's Hautefort was a wily old fellow, who, without virtue or philosophy of any kind, put up a sort of a show of both, and succeeded in taking in many fools. His position with his master had made advancement in the navy an easy matter for him.

Hautefort advised his master quite frankly that he had been had by a lot of people who had never cared twopence for him, who had always acted without consulting him, who made a profit out of him both for themselves and for their children, and whose foolish intrigues had now led them to the point where they now found themselves; that, however touched he might be by their fall, he must admit that it in itself brought him a most flattering and indeed unheard-of distinction; that he should weigh in the balance whether or not he wished to lose this distinguished position, not to speak of the offices he occupied, in order to follow the fortunes of a woman who was round the bend and her husband who made fun of him in private, and to shut himself up at Rambouillet for the rest of his life at the age of not yet forty; that, if he did this, after being for a day or two the popular hero of one or two idiots, he would soon find himself deserted, his choice deemed ridiculous, and with nothing to look forward to as he grew older but boredom and regret; that, so far as he, Hautefort, was concerned, he could tell him frankly that all the efforts he had made to belong to him had been expended in the expectation of serving a Prince of the Blood, true or apparent, and not a private person, and of living with an admiral who was in a position to make his service a pleasant and agreeable one; that on those conditions he would be delighted to spend the rest of his life with him; but that, so far as running off to banishment at Rambouillet with him was concerned, he must beg him not to count on him; that all the Comte de Toulouse's best adherents thought the same and, one after another, would silently follow his example; but that as for himself he preferred to tell him this straight out. It is said that nothing gave the Comte de Toulouse more cause to reconsider the situation than this apposite declaration. . . . The possibilities that lay ahead made him tremble, and eventually he decided to hold firmly to his rank and position in the world. That evening he and his brother went, as I have said, to the Duchesse d'Orléans at the Palais Royal, while Mme du Maine and her children retired to the Hôtel de Toulouse, where he found them on his return. One may guess how they spent the evening. The Maréchal de Villeroy, Monsieur de Fréjus and a very few others went to see them. Next day, Saturday, the Duchesse d'Orléans called. There were fresh scenes, and Mme du Maine went to bed and lay there as still as a statue.

That same Saturday, the day after the *lit de justice*, I sent a message to Valincour asking him to come to see me. He came. I talked to him quite frankly of the choice which lay before the Comte de Toulouse. I did not hide from him what I had tried to obviate, nor, when I saw that the education was lost, that I had urged the reduction in rank. I also told him that it was I who had first thought of, proposed, and carried through, the declaration in favour of the Comte de Toulouse. I reminded him that I had never hidden my sentiments in regard to the Bastards' rank, and I begged him to speak strongly to his master and to prevent him from sacrificing himself to his brother's interests. Valincour agreed that I was right, and asked to be allowed to tell the Comte de Toulouse how deeply he was in my debt; that was what I wished. Then above all else I urged him to see that the Comte de Toulouse attended the meeting of the Council, which was to be held the very next day, Sunday, and after that to see that he got rid of his guests,[1] as soon as possible. Valincour was already bored with them.

A little later Valincour returned to convey to me the thanks of the Comte de Toulouse, and to tell me that, in spite of his personal sorrow and the way in which his family was being persecuted, he would remain in Paris and attend the Council on the following day. This was a great relief to me, for it assured me of the weakening and ultimate fall of the Duc and Duchesse du Maine's party, and of the fact that the brothers were bound henceforth to drift apart. He gave me to under-

---

[1] i.e., the Duc and Duchesse du Maine.

stand that the stay of the Duc and Duchesse du Maine at the Hôtel de Toulouse was a burden to everyone, and that next day, Sunday, they would go to Sceaux, whither, in his opinion, it was scandalous that they had not gone already.

I begged Valincour to find out from the Comte de Toulouse whether he would like me to congratulate him or to keep silent. I also asked him the same question on behalf of Monsieur le Duc, who was greatly troubled on this point, since he was longing to show his personal feelings of affection for him, and yet, not knowing what he had better do, had asked me to find out for him which course would be the most acceptable. Valincour said that he thought that at the first, silence would be best, but that he would put both our cases quite openly to the Comte de Toulouse and let me know his answer. Indeed he wrote to me that very evening saying that, as the Comte de Toulouse was more sensible of his brother's loss than of any honour done to himself, which incidentally could only serve to heighten his brother's sorrow, he would prefer that Monsieur le Duc and I said nothing to him on the subject at all. I told Monsieur le Duc this, and I also passed on what I had said to Valincour to the Duc d'Orléans, who was delighted to hear of the Comte de Toulouse's decision to attend the Council. The latter called on the Duc d'Orléans that Saturday evening. The visit was short but, the Duc d'Orléans told me, satisfactory to both of them.

Next day, Sunday, M. and Mme du Maine left for Sceaux. After their departure the Comte de Toulouse held the Navy Council as usual and, in the afternoon, attended the Regency Council. His manner was distant, grave, and distinctly chilling. There were some who were surprised and some who were annoyed to see him there. Very few spoke to him, and soon after his arrival we took our seats. As soon as I had sat down I whispered in his ear that he had been treated as he had wished, and that there was one thing that I could not resist saying, which was that this was the first day in my life it had ever been a pleasure for me to sit below him; his reply was icy. I did not say another word to him throughout the meeting. The coldness between us lasted some time. I think that apart from other reasons he thought that it was only proper to maintain this attitude for a while, and I was in no hurry to persuade him to change his mind. However, little by little, we resumed our old relations. I even heard through the Duchesse Sforza that he blamed the Duchesse d'Orléans for refusing to see me. . . .

I heard later that the Duc and Duchesse du Maine laid much of the blame for what had occurred to them upon my shoulders, though they were careful never to say so in public. I was content to have put the good of the State above all other considerations, and, satisfied with myself upon this main point, I enjoyed our triumph to the full....

After their return on foot from the Tuileries to the Palais de Justice—a return which can have given them as little satisfaction in the streets as their coming had done—the *Parlement* took some time to recover from the fright and the shame they had so recently experienced. However, they did their best to gain what clandestine revenge they could by writing on the loose leaves of their secret registers that they had neither been able nor had they wished to have any voice in the proceedings at the *lit de justice*, and that they protested against everything that had been done there. Mme du Maine had sent for the First President, and by the time he got home her messenger was waiting for him; he did not dare to disobey her and he went. He was received with a perfect torrent of abuse and reproaches and treated as if he had been the lowliest footman caught in some petty act of peculation; he could not get a word in edgeways either to excuse himself or to reply. She blamed him for not having prevented and forestalled all that had happened, she overwhelmed him with the most contemptuous and the most cruel reproaches, and, after an hour spent listening to this spate of horrors, he went away nursing this addition to his fury. We heard all this next day; you may guess whether I pitied him or not, and indeed he had sold himself so infamously and so often that he did not deserve our pity. Anyone less dishonest would have died rather than be subjected to such treatment.

On the day following the *lit de justice*, Saturday, the 27th of August,[1] twenty-seven Musketeers, in three detachments commanded by their officers, each of whom was accompanied by a *Maître des Requêtes,* called upon Blamont, the President of the Courts of Inquiry, and the two Councillors, Saint-Martin and Feydeau, got them out of bed at four in the morning and took them away. All three were in mortal terror, but they put up no resistance. Each of them was bundled into a coach which was ready waiting and transported, the first to the Îles d'Hyères, the second to Belle-Île, and the third to the Île d'Oléron. They spoke to no one on the way, nor in the places where they were imprisoned, and they were all scared to death lest the next time they were moved they should find themselves on the banks of the Mississippi. Nothing of any value was found in the houses of the two Councillors, but any amount in Blamont's houses, both in Paris and in the

[1] It was during the night of Sunday and Monday that these arrests actually took place.

Blamont is arrested

country, to the latter of which another *Maître des Requêtes* had gone at the moment of Blamont's arrest. It is an extraordinary thing that a man who, by the open way in which he conducted his campaigns, seems to have been looking for trouble, should yet have been so imprudent, or should have imagined himself so secure, as not to have taken more care to have his papers in safe keeping.

The news of these arrests, which might have been carried out less ostentatiously, was no sooner known at the Palais de Justice than the Chambers assembled and passed a resolution to send a deputation to the wives of the exiled men to commiserate with them on their husbands' detention, and furthermore to send the largest possible deputation to the King and the Regent to complain of what had been done. A deputation accordingly set out on Sunday morning to the Palais Royal, and in the afternoon to the Tuileries. The First President spoke in terms that were urgent but yet within the proper bounds of moderation and respect. In both cases the reply was almost similar, weighty but vague.

On Monday and Tuesday the Palais de Justice was shut, and one lawyer who conducted a case before the Court of Aids was almost drummed out of his Company which had agreed to go on strike. However, this decision, the object of which was to create civil disorder by completely suspending the course of justice and to give us a recurrence of that celebrated crisis which Broussel[1] had produced during the last minority, could not last long. On Wednesday the *Parlement* once again resumed its duties of its own accord, but the Law Officers were directed to go every day to the Palais Royal to demand the recall of the exiled members. This manœuvre, as ridiculous as it was unfruitful, was continued until the 7th of September. In France we love extremes, and the next move was to pass a motion that, as the suspension of justice had had no effect, *Parlement* would not rise but continue sitting until after Lady Day in September. However, the *Parlement* had not the courage to carry this through, and instead the President in charge of the Vacation Court was instructed to call upon the Regent frequently and demand the return of the absent members. However, when the President heard where the members had been sent and that they were detained incommunicado, he realized that there was little hope of getting them freed in the near future, and

---

[1] Pierre Broussel, Councillor-Clerk to the *Parlement* of Paris. In 1648 Anne of Austria, on Mazarin's advice, arrested him and other leaders of the opposition. But he was so popular that on the following day barricades were erected in the streets of Paris and an angry mob forced the Queen Regent to release the prisoners.

in consequence only called upon the Regent two or three times, thus sparing himself a useless errand. . . .[1]

On the day after the *lit de justice* Monsieur le Duc entered upon his new duties and took charge of the King's education. A few days later he moved into the apartments which M. du Maine had occupied at the Tuileries. . . .

I OBTAIN TWO FAVOURS

ABOUT this time I obtained two favours which, as I have never received any which have given me more pleasure, I can never forget. From what I have said at the beginning of these memoirs it will be remembered that the man above all others whom I have most profoundly admired and respected, and for whom I have felt the tenderest affection (an affection which happily for me was reciprocated) was the saintly and famous Abbé de la Trappe.[2] At his death Monsieur de la Trappe had left a brother, a man whom I had never seen, and with whom I had had nothing to do. This brother was by a big margin the senior officer in the Galleys; he had won the respect and affection of his corps; he was the senior squadron commander, and had been commander of the port of Marseilles for years and years; and at the age of eighty-four or five he still retained his good health and the use of all his faculties. It suddenly occurred to him to take advantage of his good fortune in this respect to make a trip to Paris, a thing which so far as I was aware of he had never done before. It was Monsieur de Troyes,[3] who was his first cousin on his father's side (they were the children of two brothers), who told me of his arrival. He was known as the Chevalier de Rancé. I made haste to call upon him and to ask him to dinner. He was so like Monsieur de la Trappe that I may say without fear of scandal I fell in love with him at first sight, and everyone laughed at the way in which I found it impossible to take my eyes off him. There was nothing in his conversation to suggest old age except his wisdom, and he had all the air and manners of one who has lived long in the great world.

---

[1] The two members were allowed to return to Paris in November 1718; Blamont remained in custody until the following January, when he was allowed to retire to his country seat.

[2] Armand-Jean Le Bouthillier de Rancé (1626–1700). A wealthy and worldly priest who was First Almoner to the Duc d'Orléans, he felt the call in 1657, distributed all his worldly wealth to the poor and retired to the Abbé de la Trappe, which order he reformed and made into one of the strictest in existence.

[3] The Bishop of Troyes, the famous preacher Bossuet.

Suddenly it occurred to me to do him a good turn, but one for which there was no precedent. Never had there been more than one Lieutenant General of the Galleys, a post which is saleable, and which was then filled by the Marquis de Roye. I decided to ask the Regent to create a second such post specially for the Chevalier de Rancé, though on condition that the post should lapse after his death, and that after that things should once again resume their natural course.

Feeling that it would not be polite to do anything without the knowledge of Monsieur de Troyes, I talked it over with him. He was delighted by my suggestion and promised to do anything to help me. At the same time I begged him to keep the secret between the two of us so as not to raise false hopes, or to create any disappointment if we met with a refusal. Friendship, when it is really strong, can be most moving: I described the services, the merits and the qualities of the Chevalier de Rancé so well to the Duc d'Orléans that, in the presence of Monsieur de Troyes who helped me a bit (he could not do more because I gave him little chance to speak), I succeeded in having a second Lieutenant General of the Galleys created, though the post was not to be filled again after the Chevalier de Rancé's death, with a salary of 10,000 livres a year in addition to what the Chevalier was receiving already.

I was transported with the most lively joy which, to my surprise, was greatly increased by that of the Chevalier de Rancé, whose amazement passed all bounds. As was to be expected I took good care that the document was most carefully worded. The Chevalier de Rancé spent two months in Paris, which was far less than I should have liked, and he lived to enjoy his promotion several years longer. Nevertheless precedents are always dangerous in France, and when the Chevalier died such a case was made out for the age, seniority, service and noble birth of the Chevalier de Roannais, the then senior squadron commander, that the post was continued for him, although it has lapsed since.

We have already in these pages seen how I came to fall out with the Duc de Mortemart when Mme de Soubise died, to such an extent that M. de Beauvilliers to the end of his life always ordered the Duke out of the room whenever I came in; and there was further trouble between us over the petition against d'Antin. I was not on speaking terms with him, although I knew all his family, including his mother, very well. . . . He had also picked a quarrel with the Maréchal de Villeroy over the carrying out of their duties, in consequence of which he had sent in his resignation. That affair cost him the Duc d'Orléans's sympathy. Shortly after I had obtained this promotion for the Chevalier de Rancé, another dispute broke out between him and the Maréchal de Villeroy; the former, knowing himself to be in the wrong, was thoroughly high-handed, while the Marshal, with right upon his side, acted most moderately. The quarrel was laid before the Regent, who promptly decided in the Marshal's favour and blamed the other all the more severely because he had already had enough of the original dispute, Mortemart's resignation, and various other frequent minor quarrels and disputes in which he had been engaged. Irritated at having lost his case after all the publicity he had given to it, and still more perhaps at having received a severer dressing-down than was usual from the Regent, Mortemart never gave the matter a second thought, but once again sent in his resignation as First Gentleman of the Bedchamber in a remarkably tactless letter.

Fortunately this happened on a day when I was due to work with the Duc d'Orléans, and I arrived just as he finished reading the letter. I found him in a fury, and after telling me all about it he said that this time Mortemart would be taken at his word, and he would be delivered once for all from his impertinences. Then, looking up, he remarked that I had arrived at an opportune moment. My horror at the suggestion that I should be given anything at the expense of M. de Beauvilliers's grandson was so great that it inspired me with feverish eloquence. I told the Duc d'Orléans that he had to consider not the Duc de Mortemart but the memory of the Duc de Beauvilliers. . . . He went on arguing and pointed out that this was an excellent and indeed an unique opportunity to get rid of Mortemart. At this my indignation burst out afresh and the result in the end was that the letter of resignation was torn up.

On leaving the Palais Royal I went to the Duchesse de Mortemart[1] to tell her of the folly her son had just committed, of the difficulty I had in saving him, and of the care she must take in future to prevent a third relapse, which would assuredly be beyond my powers to remedy, or else might easily occur without my knowledge, since even on this occasion it was the greatest good fortune that the letter should have arrived on the same day as, and only a few minutes before, I was on duty with the Duc d'Orléans.

When his temper had worn itself out, the Duc de Mortemart realized the peril into which it had thrown him, and was only too thankful not to have lost his post. Three days later I was very much surprised to see him walk into my room and offer me his deepest

---

[1] Marie-Anne Colbert, sister of the Duchesse de Beauvilliers and the Duchesse de Chevreuse.

thanks. I replied coldly that he owed me none, since I had done nothing for his sake but only out of loyal and affectionate gratitude to the Duc de Beauvilliers, whose family must always be infinitely dear to me, and for whose grandson's sake I was anxious to preserve his post. Then in a few words I exhorted him never again to run the risk of testing the Duc d'Orléans's patience so far as he had done on this occasion. My frank and curt reply cut this visit short, and it ended coldly but quite politely. I have never heard from him again from that day to this. Next morning, his wife, whom he kept almost in captivity, but whose virtue, piety, intelligence and behaviour deserved a very different husband, came to thank me from the depths of her heart for what I had done. We embraced affectionately at the end of the visit, and this was the last time I saw her, for she died soon afterwards. Her husband never knew what he had lost.

However, to finish with this matter once and for all so that I may not have to come back to it later, I was still worried over these dismal follies of the Duc de Mortemart. One could never be sure that they would not drive him into further quarrels, as ill-founded as the last had been, that he would not lose his head as he had lost it already, and that the Duc d'Orléans would not finally, his patience exhausted, get rid of him and I would be able to do nothing about it. This preyed on my mind so much that after two months I decided, without mentioning it to anyone, to ask the Duc d'Orléans to grant the reversion of the post of First Gentleman to the Duc de Mortemart's son, who was barely seven years old. In this way I should not have to worry any more about the father's pranks, he would no longer be able to sell his post, and, if once again he were foolish enough to lose his temper and send in his resignation, there would be no need to placate him, since his son would automatically become the holder of the position. Having made up my mind, I played my cards so successfully that I got the reversion for the boy.

Overwhelmed with joy at having assured this post for the Duc de Beauvilliers's grandson, on leaving the Palais Royal I went straight to the Duchesse de Beauvilliers, the Duchesse de Mortemart, and the Duchesse de Chevreuse in turn to tell them the news. Their surprise and joy were indescribable. I told the first two that it was essential to put the fact on record, and therefore to go and thank the Regent publicly. Next day, therefore, though neither had appeared in public for many years or gone anywhere except among their family and a very small circle of close friends, I accompanied them to the Palais Royal. I went in to the Duc d'Orléans's study and warned him that they were come to thank him. He came out at once. Everything went off perfectly

1718 and the reversion was drafted that very morning. These formal thanks made the matter public. Nothing in the world has given me greater pleasure than this, and the whole family have been grateful to me ever since. . . .

THE END OF THE COUNCILS

The Councils, set up by the Regent at Saint-Simon's suggestion to govern every department of national life and so decentralize power, were not a success. Their downfall was hastened by the ambitions of the Abbé Dubois who had no interest but in his own future.

IN the meanwhile the Abbé, whose influence over the Regent was now more powerful than ever, decided to lose no time in furthering his own fortunes. His position as a Councillor of State and a member of the Council for Foreign Affairs, to the considerations of which body he now left little but the most obvious and superficial matters, did not satisfy him. The fact that he had to lay anything, however unimportant, before the Council irked him. For the sake of his Cardinal's hat, which was the end he always kept in view, it was of importance that England and the Emperor should see in him the unique master of all our foreign policy, without even a phantom council around him. At the same time Law found himself similarly bored with the Council for Finance. The Council for War was already little more than a bear-garden, and, now that it was decided to allow the little that remained of our Navy to sink still further into disrepair, the Council which bore its name was utterly void and useless. Home Affairs was hanging on by a thread, largely because the Duc d'Orléans never cared twopence about what d'Antin did or did not do. As for Ecclesiastical Affairs, it could hardly carry on, as we shall see in due course.

Generally speaking, all these subsidiary councils had been very badly arranged from the outset, chiefly owing to the Duc de Noailles's desire to confound and embroil their proper functions, and to make them a ridiculous nuisance, with the object of destroying them and of making himself Prime Minister. And though he never succeeded in this end, he did succeed in weakening them and in blazing the trail for the Abbé Dubois to get rid of them and thus arrive at the position which he had vainly attempted to occupy himself. . . .

'The Constitution' was the last straw. The Council for Ecclesiastical Affairs only met once again, at the Archbishop of Bordeaux's house, and was then dismissed for ever. The downfall of this Council led to that of the others. The Regent sent a letter from the King to the heads of the various Councils, thanking them for their services, and then appointed Dubois to be Secretary for Foreign Affairs, and Le Blanc to be Secretary of State for War. . . .

There were, however, some who saved themselves from complete shipwreck. The First Equerry retained the Bridges, Lanes, Roads and Pavements of Paris, and gained much honour in their administration. The Marquis de Brancas kept the Stud Farms and succeeded in ruining them. Both of these men had been members of the Council for Home Affairs, and now retained their emoluments with some increase. Asfeld remained in charge of the Fortifications and Engineers, while everything in connection with the Cavalry was left to the Comte d'Évreux and to Coigny their Colonels General. Several Councillors retained their salaries. Canillac refused his. He hoped for something better and obtained it. He persuaded the Duc d'Orléans to ask him to enter the Regency Council, and when the invitation came he was so gracious as to accept it.

A FÊTE FOR THE DUCHESSE DE BERRY

Monsieur le Duc since the *lit de justice* had been very pleased with the Duc d'Orléans and wanted to show his pleasure; so he decided to give a fête for the Duchesse de Berry. He therefore invited her to spend some days at Chantilly. The visit lasted ten days, and each day there were fresh entertainments. The profusion, the good taste, the gallantry, the magnificence, the invention, the art, the charm displayed in the various surprises competed one against the other for supremacy. The Duchesse de Berry went with all her court about her. She did not modify one inch of her ideas of grandeur, and she should indeed have been well satisfied by the respect with which she was treated and all the honours accorded to her on this occasion. Without yielding a single claim to precedence she yet treated Monsieur le Duc and the Dowager Madame la Duchesse with great politeness, but towards Monsieur le Duc's wife she affected a haughty and disdainful manner and finally left Chantilly without having spoken a single word to her. She could never forgive her for having broken the marriage between the Prince de Conti and her sister. . . .

Lassay, who had for years occupied in the Dowager Madame la Duchesse's ménage a position similar to that of Rioms in the household of the Duchesse de Berry, had orders to do the honours of Chantilly for the latter. He kept a separate table for him; he had a calèche, with relays, always ready for him and for the Duchesse de Berry; and his attentions were so marked as to become ridiculous.

In the midst of these sumptuous pleasures a tragedy very nearly occurred. On the far side of the canal there was a fine menagerie where Monsieur le Duc kept quantities of the rarest birds and beasts. A large and handsome tiger suddenly escaped and ran loose in the gardens on that side, where musicians, comedians, and men and women of all sorts were walking. You can imagine the fright and anxiety among the assembled crowds. The tiger's master rushed to the spot, went up to him, and cleverly got him back into his cage, without anyone's having suffered any hurt beyond the fear they had experienced.

THE MARRIAGE OF THE
CHEVALIER DE SAINT-GEORGES

THE Chevalier de Saint-Georges[1] had long been urged to marry and have children in order to keep up the hopes of his party in England. His unhappy fortunes made it difficult for him to effect an alliance appropriate to the position he ought to have occupied and to which he had a right. Now, however, arrangements were concluded for a marriage with the daughter[2] of Prince James Sobieski and his wife, who was the sister of the Empress, the wife of the Emperor Leopold, and of the Duchess of Parma, the mother of the Queen of Spain and of the Elector Palatine. Prince James was the son of the famous John Sobieski, King of Poland, and of Marie Casimire de la Grange, the daughter of Cardinal d'Arquien. He was a Knight of the Golden Fleece, Governor of Styria, and he lived at Ohlau in Silesia where he had large estates. He gave as dowry 600,000 livres, and the Pope gave 900,000 livres, with a pension of 80,000 livres a year and household furniture. The wife, who had first been married by proxy, left Ohlau for Rome on the 12th of September, accompanied by her mother. However, arrived at Innsbruck, they were both suddenly arrested by order of the Emperor, who in order to curry favour with King George, in this shabby fashion cancelled the pension he had granted Prince James, ordered him to leave his estates, and forbade the Duke of Modena to go on with the marriage, the contract for which had already been signed, between his son and another of Prince James's daughters. This was carrying persecution

---

[1] Prince James Stuart, the 'Old Pretender.'
[2] Marie-Clémentine Sobieska.

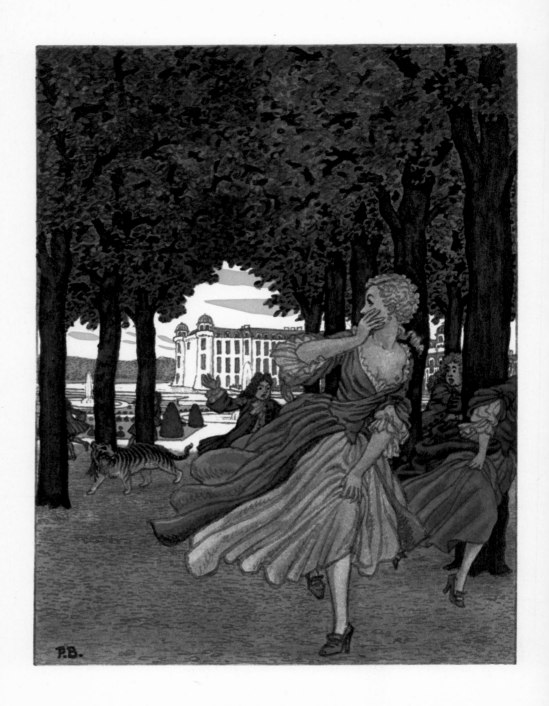

A tiger in the garden

to strange lengths—so far in fact that even in England it was held to be dishonourable to say the least of it. The Pope was very indignant.[1]

THE DEATH OF THE
MARÉCHAL D'HARCOURT

The Maréchal d'Harcourt died on the 19th of October aged only fifty-five. Continual apoplectic fits had reduced him to such a state that he could not speak a word, but was compelled to point with a stick at the letters of a large alphabet in front of him, which a secretary, continually on the watch, wrote down and translated into words—a procedure which engendered considerable impatience and irritation. For a long while the Marshal had seen no one but the closest members of his family and two or three intimate friends. Such was the terrible end of a man, destined for affairs of State and high positions as much by his intelligence and capacity as by his skill in intrigues, and fitted thereto by the subtlety, the sweetness and the charm of his mind, and the way in which he seemed to be cut out to give pleasure to everyone. He has so often been mentioned in these memoirs that I shall now say no more of him. He left very little money. He had drawn more than 60,000 livres a year from the King but there was hardly anything for his eldest son, and he had several children.

A RECALCITRANT ARCHBISHOP

I should not report the following trivial matter if it did not mark the beginning of a period of silence in the Regency Council upon the subject of 'The Constitution'[2] which lasted from this time forward. . . . I have already in another place spoken of Auvigny, that sham relation of Mme de Maintenon's, of his discovery by Godet, Bishop of Chartres, of his promotion to the bishopric of Noyon and then to the archbishopric of Rouen. Auvigny was a good, sincere and honourable man, but ignorant beyond all description, stupid, pig-headed, the very excrement

---

[1] Indignation won and the marriage took place in the following year. There were two children from it: Prince Charles Edward, the 'Young Pretender,' and Henry Cardinal of York.

[2] Of the Church. The struggle centered round the Jansenists who had been condemned by Pope Clement XI by his Bull *Unigenitus* in 1713, and continued for many years to come.

of the seminaries, and a fanatic on the subject of 'The Constitution.' With the authority of Mme de Maintenon behind him, he had long been accustomed to act in the most arbitrary fashion in his diocese and indeed had driven his subordinates almost to despair by imposing upon them the pettiest and most miserable rules of Saint-Sulpice, and by regarding any disobedience of them as an unforgivable crime.

The death of the King and the consequent fall of that authority which in the past had given him the right to do as he pleased, seemed to have rendered him no more reasonable, but had only served to bring troubles upon him without correcting his behaviour. Suddenly he made a most violent attack on certain of his parish priests, citing them before his ecclesiastical court, and having them laid under an interdict. From this court the parish priests appealed to the Vacation Court of the *Parlement* of Rouen, which annulled the interdict and returned them to their duties, reprimanding the judge and putting the Archbishop into a fury. The latter at once rushed off to Paris to have this judgement upset and the Vacation Court reprimanded in its turn. The Keeper of the Seals, true to his old party and as ardent as the archbishop himself—though being more intelligent, he was more circumspect—promised to carry through the matter for him.

I was in complete ignorance of this affair when, arriving at the Palais Royal on Tuesday, October the 23rd, to work with the Duc d'Orléans before going on to the meeting of the Council which was to be held immediately afterwards, I got down from my coach, and found the Archbishop of Rouen waiting for his. He was puffing and blowing and seemed to be greatly agitated. Indeed he was so preoccupied that he never said a word to me, though I knew him well from the days when he had been my diocesan bishop at Noyon; I had always been on good terms with him. Seeing him so distracted I saluted him to no purpose and went on, but I immediately suspected that he had been to see the Regent upon some urgent matter, and that as likely as not it had to do with some vexation over 'The Constitution.'

On reaching the Duc d'Orléans I told him of this meeting, and then asked if the Archbishop had been to see him and if he knew what was worrying him to such a degree. He told me that the Archbishop had just left; that he was in fact greatly incensed against the Vacation Court at Rouen, who had heard the appeal and proclaimed his action to be an abuse of his powers of interdiction and therefore quashed it; that the Archbishop was asking for justice; and that the matter would be brought up at the Regency Council. Though the Duc d'Orléans had put the matter so tersely I could see that he was prejudiced in favour of the Archbishop; that the Keeper of the Seals had been speaking to him; and that the judgement of the Vacation Court was to be quashed and itself reprimanded without further ado. I did not say a word, but I cut short the work I had to do and left the Palais Royal to see Monsieur le Duc at the Tuileries. I told him what I had just learnt, and that we ought not to allow this matter to go through without looking into it more closely. He agreed, and said that he would mention the matter to several members before the Council sat. I went up to his rooms to see them arrive. I spoke to the Comte de Toulouse, who also agreed, and to several others whom I persuaded to join me. The Duc de la Force, who, for political as well as party reasons was a firm adherent to 'The Constitution,' wished to resist me. I spoke to him firmly, saying that, since my only aim was to see clearly how the land lay and to prevent the matter from being hushed up, without taking sides, I had all right, justice and reason on my side when I insisted upon his agreeing with me. He was afraid of me and promised to take my side.

When the Duc d'Orléans and everyone else had taken their places, he told the company that before opening the session in the usual way, the Keeper of the Seals had a report to give them on a matter outside the agenda affecting the Archbishop of Rouen. He then made a sign to the Keeper of the Seals for him to speak. Argenson's report was made with all the skill and force of which he was a master, but was entirely on the Archbishop's side, and did not even mention the arguments of the parish priests. He concluded, as I had foreseen he would, in favour of quashing the judgement of the Vacation Court, of confirming the sentence passed by the Episcopal Court at Rouen, of censuring the parish priests, and finally of reprimanding the Chamber which had given the judgement complained of. As soon as he had finished speaking, the Duc d'Orléans called on M. de Canillac, the junior member of the Council, to speak.

I immediately interrupted and, turning to the Regent, I said that the Keeper of the Seals had given us a very able account of the Archbishop's reasoning in this affair. I spent a moment or so in praising the charm and eloquence of this report, and then I added that, though we were now perfectly acquainted with the arguments of the Archbishop, we still had no information about the case of the parish priests, and in consequence about the reasons which had led up to the judgement we were now considering, of which the Keeper of the Seals had told us not a word; that the Vacation Court of the *Parlement* at Rouen must have had some reason, be it good or bad, for delivering the judgement in question; that, knowing as we did one side of the matter and nothing at all of the other, we could not possibly come to any decision ourselves; and that for this reason what we had better now decide was not upon the correctness or incorrectness of the judgement, of the reasons for which we knew nothing, but, if His Royal Highness was agreeable and if it were convenient, as I thought it must be, to ask the Vacation Court of the *Parlement* at Rouen to pass up its reasons for the judgement it had given, so that we might then be in a position to decide with full knowledge whether to quash the judgement or allow it to stand. While I was speaking I saw all the members of the Council prick up their ears, and I noticed the Keeper of the Seals shake his head as if he were thoroughly put out.

What I said struck the Duc d'Orléans as reasonable, so much so that he said that I was right, and that the only thing to do was to vote on this fresh issue. He asked Canillac for his opinion immediately and then the others. Everyone agreed with me, even Éffiat and Monsieur de Troyes, who were afraid to reveal their true feelings, and who saw that the motion would pass in any event. The Keeper of the Seals preferred to bow his head and say nothing. When it came to the Duc d'Orléans to speak, he merely said: 'Passed unanimously.' Then turning to the Keeper of the Seals, he added: 'Please ask the Vacation Court of the Rouen *Parlement,* sir, to pass up to us the reasons which led to the judgement in question.' Instead of replying, Argenson turned round in his chair, and said in a low voice to the Duc de la Force, who repeated it to me later: 'I tell you, sir, that it is useless to mention anything to do with "The Constitution" here, and I promise you this is the last time I shall ever bring it up.' He kept his word, and from that time on we never heard another mention of 'The Constitution,' not even about this matter which had just been set in hand.

A good while later Pontcarré, First President of the Rouen *Parlement* and a friend of mine, informed me, much to my surprise, that everyone in his Company was aware that they owed it to me that their judgement had not been upset but held to be good, and that they had placed on record in their registers a note of what I had done for them at the Regency Council.

THE DUCHESSE DE BERRY'S PRESUMPTION

SEEING that the King was still very young and had many fine houses, and that she herself was a widow without children, the Duchesse de Berry now asked to be given Meudon. She obtained it from the Duc d'Orléans in exchange for the Château of Amboise, which had been given her in her marriage contract. Nevertheless the gift of Meudon caused a lot of talk. She made Rioms its governor, but du Mont, its previous governor, continued to receive exactly the same salary as he had received before. . . .

The Duchesse de Berry now attempted a thing entirely without precedent, which was so ill-received that she never dared to repeat it. When visiting the Opera, she took her seat in the stalls, from which several rows had been removed to make room for her, on a sort of dais, with all the ladies of her household, about thirty in number, around her, and this little group was separated from the rest of the stalls by a barrier. To make the whole thing more amazing the Duc and Duchesse d'Orléans were present in the theatre at the time, sitting in the large Palais Royal box, and appearing by their presence to authorize this usurpation. The fact that the King was in Paris made the whole business more outrageous than ever.

A short while later she attempted something else as bad, but this, like the other, created so much stir that she did not try it a second time. She took it into her head to give a public and ceremonial audience to the Venetian Ambassador, sitting in an arm-chair upon a dais with three steps up to it. Mme de Saint-Simon had warned her against this, but all to no purpose. The surprise occasioned among the ladies around her, among those who were standing as well as among those with a right to be seated, was extreme; indeed there were many who wished to leave the room, and who were only with difficulty restrained from doing so. The Ambassador stopped in his tracks when he saw this extraordinary spectacle and for several moments remained uncertain whether to proceed or to withdraw. However, not wishing to create a scene, he approached to receive his audience, but after his last bow and a few moments' silence he turned his back on the Duchesse de Berry and stalked out of the room without another word. As soon as he had left the Luxembourg he set to work with the result that the same evening all the Ambassadors made a formal protest against this usurpation, declaring that they would not call upon the Duchesse de Berry in future without a full assurance that the performance would never be repeated. Indeed not one of them called on her for a long while, and they were only appeased in the end, and that with the greatest difficulty, upon receiving the assurance they had asked for. I may mention in passing that no Queen of France has ever given a ceremonial audience on a dais, or even on a special carpet.

THE CELLAMARE CONSPIRACY

I was troubled to see that everything was now tending towards a rupture with Spain. The interests of the Abbé Dubois depended on it. At the time of which I am speaking we were considering no more than a secret subsidy to England if she should declare war with the Emperor against Spain. After talking over the matter casually, we decided, the Duc d'Orléans and I, to go into it more deeply. In spite of my protest he dragged me into his box at the Opera one evening, and then, giving orders that no one was to knock, he shut the door after him. We were alone together, and I need not say that our thoughts were not upon the opera. . . .

During the next week I did what I had never done before throughout the Regency: I went three or four times to the Palais Royal and (something which had never happened to me before) on each occasion I was unable to see the Regent. I was terribly worried about the threat of war, and my anxiety was only increased when I found the Regent's door so firmly closed against me, for I realized that it was Dubois who was preventing him from seeing me. I wrote asking to be allowed to see him but there was no answer. I wrote again; he sent me a verbal message, saying that as soon as he could see me he would let me know. Then I realized that the case was desperate, and I was not mistaken. The day the news was made public the Regent sent to me saying that I could see him when I wished. I went to the Palais Royal, and I found him with his head sunk low upon his breast, and in such embarrassment and shame that he could not look me in the face. My greeting was cold and was followed by a long silence.

At last he broke it to say in a low voice: 'Well, what have we got to say to one another now?' 'Nothing at all,' I answered, 'when once a thing is done it is no good talking about it. I can only hope you are satisfied. For the rest I beg you to believe that, if my reasons for seeing you had been private or personal, I should never have dreamt of beating at your door as I have done for the last week. You know it is not my custom, nor is it to my taste, to try and force my way in upon anyone. However, I thought that on this occasion my attachment to you and my duty to the State compelled me to go beyond my normal bounds. You thought it better not to see me. I can therefore wash my hands of the whole matter. Let us talk about something else.' I thereupon drew some papers out of my pocket and spread them on the desk. . . .

For some time Cellamare, the Spanish Ambassador, a man of much

intelligence and good sense, had been engaged in stirring up trouble.[1]
One can see this in the extracts from his letters that M. de Torcy made
and which I have already given. It was obvious that Cardinal Alberoni had only one object in view and that Cellamare was doing
what he could to oblige. The project was nothing less than a revolt
throughout the realm against the government of the Duc d'Orléans,
and, without exactly knowing what to do with the Duc d'Orléans
himself, to put the King of Spain at the head of affairs in France, with
a Council of ministers appointed by him and a Lieutenant of the
Regency who would wield the actual power: and this was to have been
no less a person than the Duc du Maine. They counted on the various
Parlements, with that of Paris leading the way, on the heads and principal movers of 'The Constitution,' on Brittany whole-heartedly, on
the old Court, who were used to the yoke of Mme de Maintenon and
the Bastards; and for a long while now they had been busily employed
in winning everyone they could to the Spanish cause by promises of
advancement and hopes of every kind. . . .

With things in this state, with Spain ready to strike and all those in
France who were thirsting for revenge or personal advancement
ready to join in, it now became necessary to make the exact situation
abundantly clear to Madrid. Realizing the danger of entrusting a communication of this nature to any of his own people, Cellamare asked
to be supplied with a courier from Madrid, saying that no ordinary
man would do, but that he must have someone whose position was
above that of a courier's, and whose person and quality would place
him above suspicion. The better to hide this important secret a young
ecclesiastic in Madrid, named, or at least known as, the Abbé Portocarrero, was chosen, and he was given as his assistant the son of Monte-
leon. The plan could not have been better conceived. Here were two
young men, meeting apparently by chance in Paris, one coming from
Madrid, the other from The Hague, and joining company to make their
return journey to Spain together. The name of Portocarrero is an imposing one, and ever since the days of the famous Cardinal Portocarrero it has been a sure passport to favour in France. The other was
the son of a man who had long been the Spanish Ambassador in
London, and before that Spanish Ambassador in Paris, where he had
made many friends. Moreover, the father had always been an avowed

---

[1] The Prince de Cellamare (1657–1733), Spanish Ambassador at Paris. The first advances had come to the King of Spain from the Duchesse du Maine, expressly against her
husband's wishes. In spite of what Saint-Simon says, Cellamare seems to have been an
unwilling go-between, with no belief in the possibilities of success, but was ordered to
continue by his master, Cardinal Alberoni.

friend of France, and in favour of continuing the Franco-Spanish alliance. Everyone knew this, and Dubois had seen enough in England to reassure himself on the point, and to know that this attachment to France had brought the Ambassador into disfavour with Alberoni. . . .

What could look more natural than that these two young men, both of them bearing names agreeable to the French, coming one from Spain and the other from The Hague and meeting in Paris apparently by chance, should return to Spain together; and who would ever have suspected them of being entrusted with important papers by the Ambassador, who had his own couriers as well as Spanish couriers making their return journey on whom he could rely? I even think that the two young men themselves were in ignorance of what they were charged with, since after all it must have seemed quite natural to them that, as they were going to Spain, the Ambassador should give them some casual letters to take there for him.

The young men left at the beginning of December and, on account of the coming rupture with Spain, they were supplied with special passports signed by the King himself. In their company was a Spanish banker, who had recently gone bankrupt in a big way in England, and whom the English had been given permission by the Regent to seize wherever they could find him in France.

It will be apparent that I was very ill-informed about the whole of this important business, but I cannot, nor should I wish to, tell more than I know, and for the rest I can only give my conjectures. By now the Abbé Dubois was more the Regent's master than ever before, and, for fear of meeting with opposition, or even of sharing anything with an equal, he insisted on everything being kept a secret, and the Duc d'Orléans obeyed him implicitly. Moreover, as we shall see, in this matter the Duc d'Orléans himself knew only what the Abbé Dubois wished him to know or thought it best that he should know.

Now, perhaps it was that the Abbé Portocarrero's arrival, and the shortness of his stay in Paris, seemed suspicious to Dubois and his instruments; it may be that Dubois had bribed someone of importance upon the Ambassador's staff; and perhaps it merely seemed strange that these young men should have left in such bad company as that of a bankrupt, whom Dubois had already arranged with the English to have arrested, and that Dubois then thought that it would be best to have them all three arrested together and to seize all their papers, in order to prevent the bankrupt's escaping by handing what he had over to the others. But, whatever his reason, the Abbé gave orders to have them followed, and they were all arrested at Poitiers, where their

papers were seized and immediately taken to the Abbé Dubois by the
courier who, immediately after their arrest, was sent off from Poitiers
to give him the news.

Chance is responsible for a great deal in this world. The courier
from Poitiers entered Dubois's house at the moment the Duc d'Orléans
went to the Opera. The Abbé Dubois ran quickly through the papers
in time to give the Duc d'Orléans the gist of them by the time he left
his box. But this was the rakes' hour, and the Duc d'Orléans, with a
carelessness before which everything had to yield place, would allow
nothing to keep him from his cronies; on this occasion he used the
excuse that the papers were not ready for him because the Abbé
Dubois had not yet had time to go through them thoroughly. The
early hours of the morning never saw the Duc d'Orléans at his best;
his head was still heavy with wine while his stomach was trying to
cope with the heavy supper, and it was only natural that he should
make very little sense of anything. The Secretaries of State have often
told me that at times like these they could, if they had wished, have
got him to sign anything. Yet this was the hour chosen by the Abbé
Dubois to give him a report on the papers which had arrived from
Poitiers, or at least on such of them as he desired to bring forward. He
certainly showed no more than he wished, and these papers never left
his hands for perusal by the Duc d'Orléans, or naturally by anyone
else.

The blind confidence, or rather the utter neglect of proper precaution, shown by the Duc d'Orleans on this occasion is incomprehensible, but what is stranger still is that he continued to act in the same
way throughout the business, and allowed Dubois to be in sole possession of all the circumstances which so suspiciously surrounded this
case, as well as of all the proofs, and thus to be the only man who had
the power to convict, to absolve or to punish, as he wished. The only
others admitted into the secret were the Keeper of the Seals and Le
Blanc. Not even Dubois could entirely dispense with their services,
but even then he only told them as much as he thought it necessary
that they should know. Moreover, the first was not only very intimate
with him, but completely under his influence, while the second was
only dependent and had little cause to boast of any intimacy. Both of
them were amazed by his conduct, but terrified of asking the simplest
question or of going beyond their orders by a hair's breadth, since it
was on his whim alone that their positions hung and he never allowed
them to forget it. . . .

On the day following the arrival of the courier from Poitiers, Prince
Cellamare, who had been warned of this disquieting event, but who

still retained the hope that the arrest of the young men and the seizure of their papers had only been due to the presence of the bankrupt banker, hid his anxiety under an appearance of complete calm, and at one o'clock in the afternoon he called on M. Le Blanc to ask for the return of a packet of letters which he said had been entrusted to the young men because they were on their way back to Spain and had been provided with the King's passport. Le Blanc, who was already very fully informed in more ways than one by the Abbé Dubois and by the Duc d'Orléans, who had seen him with the Abbé later, about what answers to make to the Ambassador in the various different contingencies that might arise, answered that the packet had been opened; that it contained matters of importance; and that, so far from being able to return the contents to him, he had orders to take him to his house with the Abbé Dubois, who as soon as he had heard that Cellamare was with Le Blanc, had set off to join them. The Ambassador was told to get into Le Blanc's coach, and the Abbé Dubois and Le Blanc both got in with him.

Realizing that he would not be treated in this way by anyone without good reason and feeling sure of what he was doing, Cellamare did not object to accompanying them, nor did he for one moment lose his air of tranquil *sang-froid* throughout the good three hours that they were with him, searching in all his desks and boxes, and putting upon one side whatever papers they wished. Indeed, through the whole of this affair he seems to have shown no fear and to have acted as if his conduct were completely above suspicion. He treated M. le Blanc very civilly, but in addressing the Abbé Dubois, with whom, now that the plot was discovered, he saw politeness to be so much waste of breath, he was careful to show the utmost disdain. On one occasion Le Blanc went up to a little box, and Cellamare called out: 'M. Le Blanc, M. Le Blanc, leave that; it is right up the Abbé Dubois's street.' He then looked pointedly at the Abbé Dubois and added: 'The Abbé has been a pimp all his life and that box contains letters from women.' Not daring to be angry, the Abbé Dubois passed this off with a laugh.

As a matter of fact this can have been no more than a *bon mot* which Cellamare had been waiting for a chance to let off. He was already an old man, and he looked even more than his age. He had any amount of wit, of knowledge, of capacity, which he turned to good effect; he was not in the least debauched, and, if he had an air of gallantry about him, this was purely social, to help him in finding out what he wanted to know, in maintaining supporters for the King of Spain, and, without imprudence, to sow discontent among the Regent's followers. That was his only reason for mixing as much as he did in society, for

whenever possible he preferred to stay at home to work and read at
his ease.

The moment he got home, his two acolytes beside him, a detachment of Musketeers took possession of the building and of all its entries. When everything had been examined the King's seal and that of the Ambassador were affixed at all the writing-desks and boxes that held papers. The Abbé Dubois and Le Blanc then went off together to make their report to the Regent, and left the Ambassador and his domestics in the charge of the Musketeers and of M. de Liboy, one of the Gentlemen-in-Waiting in Ordinary to the King, as the custom is with Ambassadors on difficult occasions of this kind.

M. de Liboy was a man of intelligence and understanding, and he was always being chosen for these wretched jobs.

I had already heard that morning of the capture at Poitiers, without knowing exactly who had been arrested. While I was having lunch a uniformed messenger arrived from the Duc d'Orléans to tell me to be at the Tuileries at four o'clock for a meeting of the Regency Council. As this was not a day on which we usually met I asked the messenger what had happened. He was surprised by my ignorance and he told me that the Spanish Ambassador had been arrested. As soon as I had swallowed a bite of food, I left and went off to the Palais Royal where the Duc d'Orléans immediately told me all that I have set down above. I asked him about the papers. He said that they were in the hands of the Abbé Dubois who had not yet had time to examine them or to tell him what they contained; and that he would have something to put before the Regency Council, whom he personally wished to inform of these events. With these words and others equally vague we passed some time, and then I went off to wait at the Tuileries. When I got there, I saw astonishment on the faces of many around me, and little groups of two, three, or four men together. The general effect was of men surprised by anything so startling as the arrest of the Spanish Ambassador, and generally inclined to condemn it.

The Duc d'Orléans arrived soon after. He had more than any man I have ever known a real gift for impromptu speaking. He could say what he wanted to say, no more and no less; his words were to the point; and he had a natural grace on these occasions appropriate to that air of a polished man of the world which never deserted him. He opened the meeting with an account of the men and of the papers which had been seized at Poitiers, saying that the arrest had been the means of discovering a very dangerous conspiracy against the State; that this conspiracy was on the point of coming to a head; and that the Spanish Ambassador had been found to be the prime mover. His

Royal Highness then showed that his reasons for making sure of the Ambassador's person, for searching his papers and for putting him under the guard of Liboy and the Musketeers had been most urgent. He spent some time explaining that diplomatic immunity did not extend to cases of conspiracy, and that an Ambassador proved himself to be unworthy of his position when he entered into, and still more when he was the instigator of, any plot against the state to which he was accredited. He cited several cases where an Ambassador had been arrested for less. He added that he had directed that all Ministers of foreign countries residing in Paris should be informed of what had occurred, and then he invited Dubois to tell the Council what had been done at Cellamare's house, of how Cellamare had reacted, and then to read to the Council two letters, found among the seized papers, which that Minister had written to Cardinal Alberoni.

The Abbé Dubois then stammered through a short and ill-arranged account of what had passed at the Ambassador's house, and spoke at somewhat greater length about the importance of the discovery and of the conspiracy itself, so far as it could be at present understood. The two letters he read made it perfectly clear that Cellamare was the fountain-head of the whole affair, and that Alberoni was by no means so deeply implicated as his Ambassador. Apart from this, everyone was shocked by certain expressions used in describing the Duc d'Orléans, who was not spared either in what was said about him or in the words used to say it.

After this the Duc d'Orléans spoke again to point out with the utmost moderation that he did not suspect either the King or Queen of Spain of having entered into a conspiracy of this nature; that he attributed it only to the passionate nature of Alberoni and to the fact that the Spanish Ambassador was bent on pleasing him; but that he would ask Their Catholic Majesties that justice should be done. Then he said that no efforts must be spared to get to the bottom of a matter so capital for the peace and tranquility of the realm, and he finished by adding that until he knew more he was anxious not to disclose the names of any people who had been found to be involved in the conspiracy. This speech was warmly applauded, but I think that there were some upon the Council who breathed more freely when the Regent said that he did not wish to mention names, or to give vent to any suspicion until the whole matter had been satisfactorily cleared up.

Nevertheless next morning, which was that of Saturday, the 10th of December, Pompadour was arrested at eight o'clock, just as he was getting out of bed, and taken away to the Bastille. Mme de Pompadour and Mme de Courcillon, her daughter and Dangeau's daughter-in-

law, went to the Palais Royal. The Duc d'Orléans sent out the Maréchal de Villeroy, who was with him at the time, to make his excuses
with a few meaningless compliments. During this same Saturday, the
10th of December, Saint-Geniès was also arrested and taken to the
Bastille.

On Tuesday, the 13th of December, that is to say on the day when
it was usual for the Ministers of foreign powers to go to the Palais
Royal, all the Ambassadors attended as usual, and, though this was
the first Tuesday after Cellamare's arrest, there was no complaint
from any of them. They were all presented with copies of the two letters which had been read at the Council. After dinner the Spanish
Ambassador was placed in a coach with Liboy, plus a captain of
Cavalry and a captain of Dragoons, to go to Blois, where he was to
remain until arrival of news that the Duc de Saint-Aignan[1] had arrived
in France. A few days later Sandraski, Brigadier General of Cavalry
and Colonel of the Hussars, Seret, another Colonel of Hussars, and
several less important officers were also taken to the Bastille.

On Sunday, the 25th of December, Christmas day, the Duc d'Orléans summoned me to the Palais Royal after dinner, at about four
o'clock. Monsieur le Duc, the Duc d'Antin, the Keeper of the Seals,
Torcy and the Abbé Dubois were also present. We discussed several
matters which had to do with Cellamare and his journey to Spain, the
measures to be taken to avoid having any complaint from the other
Ambassadors, who indeed had not the slightest inclination thereto,
and the best way to draft a demand to the King of Spain for justice
which we did not expect to receive, and finally how to get round the
necessity of having the Royal Bank registered by the *Parlement*[2] and
of setting it on its feet without their help. All these matters were discussed by the Regent so coolly and with such complete presence of
mind that I had no suspicions whatsoever that anything else was
afoot.

The select meeting lasted some time. When it was over we began to
leave. I was just bestirring myself to go off like the others when the
Duc d'Orléans called to me. In the meanwhile the others left the room
and I was alone with the Duc d'Orléans and Monsieur le Duc. Once
again we resumed our seats. We were in the winter study, at the end
of the small gallery. After a moment's silence the Duc d'Orléans asked
me to see if anyone had remained behind in the small gallery, and if

---

[1] The French Ambassador in Spain. It was rumoured in Paris that he had been arrested
by the Spanish Government.
[2] They had a few days earlier refused to register it.

the door at the other end, by which one entered it from his bedroom, were shut. I went to look; it was shut and there was no one in the gallery. That settled, the Duc d'Orléans told us that no doubt we would not be surprised to hear that M. and Mme du Maine were up to their necks in this business of the Spanish Ambassador; that he had proof of this in writing; and that their aims were no less than I have set them forth above. He added that he had forbidden the Keeper of the Seals, the Abbé Dubois and Le Blanc, who were the only people who knew about this, to let the matter go any further and that he hoped we should be as discreet as they. He added that before coming to any decision he wished to have a private conference with Monsieur le Duc and me upon what we were to do.

As he said this I thought to myself that, considering that those three knew all about it, it was hardly likely that he had not argued the matter out with them, and that as likely as not he had already come to some decision with the Abbé Dubois. I said to myself moreover that the idea with Monsieur le Duc was to flatter him by taking him into his confidence and so to make him share the responsibility for whatever he had already made up his mind to do, but that he wished to have a genuine discussion with me so as not to be entirely at the mercy of the other three, and also because he was accustomed, as we have seen over and over again in these pages, to tell me his more important secrets whenever he was in a fix or had a quick decision to come to. Monsieur le Duc at once took the bull by the horns and said that we must arrest the two of them and put them somewhere where we need not worry about what they might do.

I agreed with this and pointed out how dangerous it would be not to strike at once. The Duc d'Orléans said that this indeed would be the wisest course, but he stressed the standing of Mme du Maine, chiefly I think to get the reaction of her brother's son. If this was his object, he succeeded perfectly, and that not only because of Monsieur le Duc's hatred of his aunt and her husband, which it must be admitted they fully deserved, but also because this conspiracy tended to upset the order of succession and would nullify those renunciations which had removed the Spanish family out of the way of Monsieur le Duc's branch.[1]

Monsieur le Duc replied that if anyone had the right to raise an

---

[1] Philip V on ascending the throne of Spain renounced his right to succeed to that of France, and, as one of the objects of this conspiracy was to abjure these renunciations, its success would mean that not only the House of Orléans but also the House of Condé would be one step further removed from the throne than they had been previously.

objection it would be he; that so far from being deterred by this he was all the more strongly in favour of acting immediately; that it would not be the first time—nor indeed even the twentieth—that a Prince or a Princess of the Blood had been arrested; that the greater men were by their birth the more reason was there to expect them to owe their allegiance to the State, and the greater their fault if they so far forgot their duty as to start any trouble; and finally that, in his opinion, it was of the utmost urgency to strike a blow at M. and Mme du Maine's accomplices, and thus to deprive them at the source of all the various machinations and inventions which the rage and intelligence of this husband and wife might suggest. I strongly approved of the straightforward, loyal, and sensible advice of Monsieur le Duc. I said more. I insisted upon the necessity of showing firmness and courage on this critical occasion. The Duc d'Orléans looked across at Monsieur le Duc, who again spoke in support of his views and mine. The Regent then yielded and it was with pleasure that he did so.

After a word or two about this we discussed where M. and Mme du Maine had better be imprisoned. The Bastille and Vincennes scarcely seemed suitable, since to have the two principals so close would be a continual temptation to their friends in Paris, to the *Parlement* to raise difficulties, and to the First President to plot and scheme. We discussed various places in turn for each of them, since from the moment we had decided to arrest them we had also agreed that they should be imprisoned separately. The first thing to do was to decide on a place for the Duc du Maine. Among various other suggestions the Duc d'Orléans mentioned Doullens. I seized upon the name at once. I said that Charost and his son were the Governors of Doullens; that they lived at Calais which was not far off; and that Charost's son was the Lieutenant General of Picardy. I urged that theirs was a loyal family, that Charost had always been a friend of mine, and that their personal probity, virtue and attachment to the State were such that I could answer for them myself. After that it was agreed to send the Duc du Maine to Doullens and to keep him a prisoner there under a very close guard.

That done, we passed on to a place for Mme du Maine. I represented to the others that, considering the quality, the sex and the temper of the person we were considering, this was a far more delicate matter; that she would leave no stone unturned to escape and to make trouble; that she was fearless, not only by the nature and strength of her passions, but also because, considering her sex and birth, she knew that she would really have little to be afraid of, while her husband, however dangerous he might be underground, was contemptible when caught in the open and would not only fall into complete dejection in prison and not attempt to stir, but would tremble in every limb as he thought of the scaffold which might be awaiting him. After various places had been discussed the Duc d'Orléans began to smile. Then he looked at Monsieur le Duc, and said that he, Monsieur le Duc, must come to his aid, that he must throw himself into the fray, that this was an affair of State and concerned him as much as it did himself. Then straight away he suggested the Château at Dijon.

Monsieur le Duc thought this suggestion an odd one, agreed that Mme du Maine must be sent to a place of complete security, but considered that to make him his aunt's gaoler was something he could not accept. Nevertheless, as he said this he smiled, and thereby gave the Regent an excuse to insist. Monsieur le Duc resisted. I did not say a word but I opened my eyes very wide. At last Monsieur le Duc asked me if he were not right. Then I, too, began to smile, and I answered that I could not deny that he was right, no less than the Duc d'Orléans was also right, and even more basically right than he was.

I had thought very hard and very carefully during their short dispute, and I had seen what an advantage it would be for the Duc d'Orléans to make of Monsieur le Duc a sort of partner in Mme du Maine's imprisonment, and consequently of M. du Maine's imprisonment also, as well as to have Mme du Maine in a place which was surer, and offered less hope of flight, than any other, seeing that it stood in the midst of the country of which Monsieur le Duc was Governor, and was entirely dependent on him. Moreover, I cannot disguise the fact that it gave me understandable pleasure and considerable amusement to see the Duchesse du Maine, after all her bitter lawsuits against her own family over the succession of Monsieur le Prince, the rank of Prince of the Blood, and the right of succession to the crown and so forth, to see this woman, I say, who had proclaimed with such assurance that she would see the whole realm go up in flames before she would yield a single one of the advantages which her husband had acquired by such devious means, fuming within four walls under the jurisdiction of Monsieur le Duc. The latter resisted for a long while all that the Duc d'Orléans and I could say to persuade him, but I think that after all that had passed between him and his aunt, this was due rather to feelings of propriety than to any real repugnance; indeed in the end he yielded and consented to having his dear aunt strictly incarcerated in his Château at Dijon. When all this had been agreed and we had briefly discussed the procedure, we separated.

The Monday and Tuesday following, that is to say the 26th and 27th of December, were spent in making preparations and in giving

Arrest of the Duc du Maine

the necessary orders with the greatest possible secrecy. However,
M. and Mme du Maine, who had seen the Spanish Ambassador led off
to Blois, his packets seized, his papers searched, and various other
people already arrested, were not entirely without apprehension themselves, and were thus given plenty of time to dispose of their papers
as they thought fit. This precaution taken, they faced whatever might
come with greater equanimity. Now the Abbé Dubois, directly he received the papers from Poitiers, was in full possession of the case
against them, as he proved by producing these papers for examination
later, and, if he had really gone ahead, he could have shown them to
the Regent immediately and have arrested M. and Mme du Maine at
the same time as the Spanish Ambassador if not before. Thus he could
have moved faster than they did and have seized all their important
documents; however, since he never thought of anyone but himself,
it did not suit his book to serve the State quite so conscientiously.

On Wednesday, the 28th of December, I was summoned to go to
the Palais Royal after dinner, and to meet the Duc d'Orléans, Monsieur le Duc, the Abbé Dubois and Le Blanc in the small winter study.
The object of our meeting was to make our final arrangements and
to review what had already been done. While we were in conference
the Duc du Maine came from Sceaux to the Duchesse d'Orléans at the
Palais Royal, but after an hour's conversation with her he returned to
Sceaux. Mme du Maine had been staying in Paris for several days, in
quite a small house in the rue Saint-Honoré which they had rented.
This was right in the middle of Paris, so that she could watch the turn
of events and be kept informed the whole time by her party; but her
more timid husband had not had the pluck to join her there.

Our conference at the Palais Royal lasted some time. All arrangements were made and the final details settled for arresting the culprits
the next day; all eventualities were foreseen, and proper orders given
down to the smallest matters of procedure. Nevertheless the orders
issued to the Regiment of Guards and to the two Companies of Musketeers, who had been confined to barracks all day, somehow leaked
out during the evening and made it clear to those behind the scenes
that something of importance was going to happen. When I left the
study I agreed with Le Blanc that as soon as the blow had fallen he
would send a footman to give me the news.

Next morning, at about ten o'clock, La Billarderie, a Lieutenant of
the Bodyguard, quietly and unostentatiously posted his men round
Sceaux, and then went in to arrest the Duc du Maine just as the latter
was coming out from Mass. This done, he asked him politely to be so
good as to forbear entering his own apartments and at once to get

into the coach which he, La Billarderie, had with him. The Duke had taken good care that there should be nothing compromising in his house or on any of his servants, who were the only people with him at Sceaux, so he offered no resistance. He merely remarked that he had been anticipating this compliment for several days and got into the coach without delay. La Billarderie sat beside him, while on the front seat there was a non-commissioned officer of the Bodyguards and Favancourt, a squadron leader in the First Company of Musketeers, both of whom had been detailed to take charge of the Duc du Maine in prison.

Now these last two only appeared as the Duc du Maine was getting into the coach, and at the sight of Favancourt the Duc du Maine was surprised and troubled. He would have thought little of seeing the non-commissioned officer of the Bodyguards there, but the sight of the other was a blow to him.[1] He asked La Billarderie the meaning of it, and the latter could not disguise from him the fact that Favancourt was under orders to accompany him and to remain with him in the place to which they were going. Favancourt introduced himself as tactfully as he could. The Duc du Maine said little but his manner was civil and even timid. This exchange lasted until the coach had reached the end of the avenue of Sceaux, where the troops of the Bodyguard appeared. At the sight of them the Duc du Maine changed colour.

In the coach almost unbroken silence reigned. From time to time M. du Maine would say that he was quite innocent of what had been imputed against him; that he was deeply attached to the King, and no less to the Duc d'Orléans, who must soon be forced to recognize the fact; and that it was very unfortunate for him, the Duc du Maine, that His Royal Highness should put such faith in his enemies, though who these enemies were he did not specify. He did not say all this at once, but, as it were, by gasps and between deep sighs. Again and again he would cross himself and murmur, as if repeating his prayers. Whenever he passed a church, or a cross by the wayside, he would bow himself almost to the floor of the coach. During the day he ate with the others in the coach, but he took very little, and in the evening he fed alone. The greatest care was taken of him through the night. It was not until next day that he knew he was going to Doullens, and when he did he made no sign.

I learnt all this, as well as many other details concerning his imprisonment, from Favancourt whom I knew well, and who gave me a

---

[1] Because a Musketeer was usually put in charge of prisoners of State.

full account as soon as M. du Maine was set at liberty. It had been Favancourt who had taught me my military exercises in the days when he had been under Cresnay, who at that time commanded a squadron of the First Company of Musketeers. Ever since those days Favancourt had been in the habit of calling upon me. M. du Maine had two valets with him, and he was kept within sight of his guards almost all the time.

At the very same moment as the Duc du Maine was being arrested, Ancenis, who had just received the reversion of the post of Captain of the Bodyguard from the Duc de Charost, his father, went to arrest the Duchesse du Maine in her house in the rue Saint-Honoré. One lieutenant and a non-commissioned officer from the Bodyguard, on foot, appeared at the same time with a troop of their regiment to surround the house and to post sentries at all the doors. Mme du Maine wished to take some of her jewel cases with her, but Ancenis refused to allow this; she said that at least she must have her precious stones. The quarrel grew loud on the one part and remained quite modest on the other; nevertheless she was forced to give way. She complained most bitterly against such violence being done to one of her rank, though she took care not to say anything too disobliging to M. d'Ancenis or to mention anyone by name. In spite of all M. d'Ancenis's efforts she kept putting off her moment of departure until at last, holding out his arm to escort her, he told her politely but firmly that she must leave.

Two hired coaches, at the sight of which she was profoundly shocked, were at the door; yet in the end she had to get into one of them. Ancenis got in beside her, the lieutenant and the non-commissioned officer sat in front, and the two ladies' maids, whom she had chosen to accompany her, and her luggage (which had previously been searched) were placed in the other coach. On leaving the house they made straight for the city gates, taking good care to avoid the main streets. Not a person stirred to come to her rescue. At this she could not help showing her surprise and annoyance. Not one tear escaped her, but from time to time she held forth spasmodically and in general terms against the violence done to her person. Moreover, she complained continually against the roughness of the common coach and the indignity of being forced to travel in such a conveyance. Every now and then she asked where she was being taken. Ancenis was content to tell her that she would sleep that night at Essonnes, but he said no more. Her three warders kept a profound silence, and every precaution was taken when she went to bed.

Next morning, just as she was leaving, M. d'Ancenis said good-bye to her, and then handed her over to the care of the Lieutenant of the Bodyguard and the escort. Once again she asked where she was being taken and Ancenis replied: 'To Fontainebleau'; then he went off to make his report to the Regent. The further she went from Paris the greater grew her anxiety, and when at last she found herself in Burgundy and was told that she was going to Dijon she protested indignantly. However, it was far worse when the time came for her to enter the Château, and she saw herself to be a prisoner in the care of Monsieur le Duc. Her rage seemed to choke her, and she exclaimed in fury against her nephew and the horror of having chosen such a place for her to live in.

Nevertheless, once her first transports were over, she soon came to herself again, realized that she was not in a position where rage could help her, and, having swallowed her temper, affected to feel no more than indifference to her circumstances and a sort of disdainful security. The King's Lieutenant in command of the Château was a man on whom Monsieur le Duc could rely completely; he kept her very closely guarded, and both she and her two maids were under strict surveyance.

The Prince de Dombes and the Comte d'Eu were exiled to Eu, where one of the King's Gentlemen-in-Ordinary remained continually with them.[1] Mlle du Maine was sent to Maubuisson.

Cardinal de Polignac, a close friend of Mme du Maine's, and one who in popular gossip was supposed to share all her secrets, had orders the same day to leave immediately for his Abbey at Anchin. He was accompanied by one of the King's Gentlemen-in-Ordinary, who stayed with him all the time he was in Flanders. The Cardinal left late that morning. At the same time Dadvisard, the Advocate-General in the Rouen *Parlement,* who had attracted attention because of the pamphlets which he had written for the Duc du Maine against the Princes of the Blood; two famous Parisian lawyers, one of whom had worked a good deal with Dadvisard and was called Bargeton; a certain Mlle de Montauban, who was attached to the Duchesse du Maine as a sort of Lady-in-Waiting; and one of the principal chamber-maids, a confidential favourite of Mme du Maine's, who had a sort of standing in society as a wit,[2] as well as several other of M. and Mme du Maine's servants, were taken to the Bastille.

---

[1] There was some discussion as to where the sons of the Duc du Maine should be sent; the first idea was to separate them—at Moulins and Gieu.

[2] Saint-Simon is referring to Mlle Rose de Launay, who later married the Baron de Stäal, and whose delightful memoirs are well known.

Le Blanc kept his word. I was at home, my door securely shut, so anxious over the outcome that I did not dare to open my mouth, but strode up and down my study, watching the clock, when a messenger arrived from him for the ostensible purpose of asking after my health. I was terribly relieved though I still did not know the details. My coach was waiting; I immediately jumped into it and drove straight to the Duc d'Orléans. He, too, was alone when I found him, walking up and down his long gallery. It was nearly eleven o'clock, and Le Blanc and the Abbé Dubois had just left him. I found him greatly troubled about his coming interview with the Duchesse d'Orléans, and it was with relief that I realized that I was now on such bad terms with her that he could not possibly ask me to deliver this message for him. I encouraged him as best I could, and about half an hour later, on the Comte de Toulouse's being announced, I took my leave. . . .

While the Duc du Maine remained at Doullens he was, as I have said, under the guard of La Billarderie and Favancourt. . . . Now, though Favancourt came from Picardy,[1] he was a most shrewd and clear-sighted fellow, and he performed his duties so well that he succeeded not only in satisfying those who had sent him to Doullens, but also the Duc du Maine, who from that time forward became a patron and protector of all his family. On Favancourt's return, I was anxious to question him thoroughly. He told me that the Duc du Maine looked as white as death the whole of the journey from Sceaux to Doullens; that nevertheless he never complained, or held forth, or even asked any questions, but only sighed. For the first five or six hours he did not speak at all. After that he spoke occasionally, but what little he said was chiefly concerned with what was passing directly before his eyes. At each church they passed he would join his hands together, bow his head low, and cross himself not once, but many times, and now and then he would murmur a prayer under his breath, and on finishing cross himself again. He never mentioned anyone by name, not even the Duchesse du Maine, or his children, or his servants, or anyone else.

At Doullens he spent, or at least he appeared to spend, long hours in prayer, and continually bowed himself to the ground. He became so dependent on Favancourt as to be almost childish, and behaved more like a very small school-boy towards his master than a grown man. From time to time he would amuse himself with the three valets he had with him; he had a few books but no writing materials. Very occasionally he would ask for pen and paper, and when he did, he

[1] Proverbially a slow-witted province.

would hand what he had written to Favancourt to read and seal for him. At the slightest sound, at the least unexpected movement, he went pale and seemed to believe that his end was at hand. He was well aware of what were his true deserts and realized what cause he had to fear a Prince whom he might long ago have come to understand if he had wished, and who was by nature so very different from himself. Throughout the journey to Doullens he always dined alone.

The Duchesse du Maine was in the care of the younger La Billarderie, another Lieutenant of the Bodyguard, and she found him more pliable. She took advantage of this fact, and the Duc d'Orléans suffered it to go on with his usual good nature. During her journey one would have thought she was a daughter of France being treated with the worst indignities from baseless and improper spite. A romantic heroine, her head full of the plays she had been acting at Sceaux for twenty years, she talked in the language of the theatre and the most bombastic epithets were insufficient to describe what she considered to be the righteousness of her complaint. When, on the third day, she was told at last that she was going to Dijon, her outburst became more violent than ever. The unmasking and the overthrow of all her plots, the insolence with which she thought she had been arrested, all the insupportable accompaniments of captivity of which she never stopped complaining were all as nothing compared with the thought of being taken to a fortress in the seat of government of Monsieur le Duc, over which he was completely the master. She pretended to be ill, changed her carriage, stopped at Auxerre and wherever else she could in the hope that Madame la Princesse might succeed in having her destination altered, and perhaps that her transports of temper might also have some effect. Her mother's entreaties did in fact have some success, and three of Mme du Maine's maids, together with Mme de Chambonas, her Lady-in-Waiting, were given permission to join her; a short while later the same permission was given to her doctor, and to another maid. But so far as the Château at Dijon was concerned, there was no question of any change.

1719

THE DISGRACEFUL LIFE AND ILLNESS
OF THE DUCHESSE DE BERRY

✤✤✤✤✤ HE Duchesse de Berry was still living her usual life, compounded of the loftiest grandeur and the basest and most abject servility. She alternated between most austere retreats, short but frequent, with the Carmelites in the Faubourg Saint-Germain and suppers polluted by the vilest company and filthy conversation; between the most outrageous debauchery on the one hand and the most terrifying fear of death and the devil on the other. All of a sudden she fell ill in the Luxembourg. Now this is a matter which belongs to history so I must therefore go into details—all the more so because in these memoirs I do not go in for any gossip unless it is necessary to the full understanding of what is important or interesting in the course of the years with which I am dealing.

The Duchesse de Berry would suffer no constraint; she was furious that anyone should dare to talk of what she herself took no care to hide; and yet she was miserable whenever her conduct was known. At this time she was on the point of bearing a child to Rioms, though she was hiding the fact as best she could. Mme de Mouchy passed as the lovers' confidante, though what was really going on was pretty obvious. Rioms and la Mouchy were in love with one another, and had the privacy and the opportunity to indulge themselves. They laughed at the Princess behind her back; she was completely taken in by them and together they got out of her whatever they wanted. In short, they were masters of her and of all her household, and such insolent masters that even the Duc and Duchesse d'Orléans, who knew them for what they were and hated them, yet feared them and were careful not to offend them.

Mme de Saint-Simon, who held herself aloof from these intrigues, and who was so deeply loved and respected by all the household that even this precious couple, so feared and counting for so much, shared in the general feeling—Mme de Saint-Simon, I say, used at this time only to visit the Luxembourg when the Duchesse de Berry was making a public appearance, and she used to leave the moment her official duties were over. Thus she could ignore what was going on, although she knew all about it.

However, the time came at last when the Princess was brought to bed, and, since her only preparation for the event had been a succession of suppers well sprinkled with wine and the strongest liqueurs, her condition was alarming and soon became dangerous. As soon as she saw her mistress in peril, it was impossible for Mme de Saint-Simon to do otherwise than to put in a frequent appearance. Yet even now, under the pretext of preferring to go home to rest, she still refused to yield to the Duc and Duchesse d'Orleans and the whole of Mme de Berry's household when they begged her either to sleep in the rooms which were reserved for her, and into which she had never entered, or at least to spend her days in the Luxembourg.

She found the Duchesse de Berry entrenched in a little room in her apartments, which was conveniently furnished with back-stair and entrances and well tucked away. In this room there was no one but Mouchy and Rioms, and one or two of the more peculiarly trusted women of the Wardrobe. Those who might be called upon in cases of necessity could of course be brought in quickly by the back ways. Neither the Duc and Duchesse d'Orléans, nor even Madame, were to come in when they wished, still less the Lady-in-Waiting, the other Ladies, the first waiting maid, and the ordinary doctors. These were only allowed to enter from time to time and then only for a short while. On the pretext that the Princess was suffering from a severe headache, or else was in need of sleep, they were often requested not to enter the room at all or else to go away after a minute or two. Since they all knew perfectly well what was going on, it was not often that they wished to enter, and they were usually content merely to ask Mme de Mouchy for news. At such moments the latter would open the door not more than an inch or so. And this ridiculous performance was taking place in front of the usual crowd of those accustomed to visiting at the Luxembourg or at the Palais Royal, and of many others who, either out of politeness or curiosity, came to ask for news, so that it soon became the talk of the town.

When the danger grew serious, Languet, the famous curé of Saint-Sulpice, who had already come a number of times to enquire, spoke to the Duc d'Orléans about the Sacraments. One of the difficulties was to introduce him into the room in order to make the proposal to the Princess in person. However, a more serious complication arose soon afterwards, which was that the curé, sensible of his duties, refused to administer the Sacraments at all, or to allow them to be administered by anyone else, so long as Rioms and Mme de Mouchy remained not merely in the Princess's apartment, but within the Luxembourg itself. To make matters worse he purposely announced this decision to the Duc d'Orléans in a loud voice and in front of a crowd

of people, a fact which, though it did not shock the Regent, embarrassed him considerably. He took the priest aside and talked to him
for a long time in the hope of persuading him to moderate his views.
Finding him inflexible, he suggested referring the whole matter to
Cardinal de Noailles. The curé accepted this proposal at once, and
promised to defer to the decision of the Cardinal, as his Bishop, provided he was given an opportunity of explaining his own point of
view.

Meanwhile the matter grew pressing and so, while the dispute was
in progress, the Duchesse de Berry confessed to her ordinary confessor, a Franciscan. No doubt the Duc d'Orléans, knowing that the curé
and the Diocesan were at daggers' drawn over 'The Constitution,'
and also realizing how dependent the Cardinal was upon himself for
protection in the same matter, flattered himself that he would find the
latter more flexible than the former had been. If he did so he was
mistaken.

Cardinal de Noailles arrived; the Duc d'Orléans took him and the
curé on one side; and their conversation lasted more than half an hour.
Since Languet's announcement had been made in public, no doubt
the Cardinal Archbishop of Paris thought it would be wiser to make
his in public too. Thereupon all three of them walked towards the
door of the Duchesse de Berry's room, around which most of the
visitors were assembled, and Cardinal de Noailles, speaking very
clearly, told Languet that he had performed his duty worthily; that
it was what he would expect from as virtuous, well-informed, and
experienced a man as he; that he commended him for having insisted
upon his conditions before administering or allowing the Sacraments
to be administered to the Duchesse de Berry; that he exhorted him not
to depart from this decision, and not to allow himself to be got around
in such an important matter; that, if he had need of authority behind
him, he as his Diocesan and superior forbade him either to permit the
administration of, or to administer the Sacraments himself to the Duchesse de Berry, so long as M. de Rioms and Mme de Mouchy were
in her room or even in the Luxembourg, indeed so long as they had
not been dismissed from the palace altogether.

You can imagine the startling effect of this unavoidable scandal in
that room full of people, the Duc d'Orléans's embarrassment, and the
excitement it immediately created everywhere. There was no one, not
even the leaders of 'The Constitution' or Cardinal de Noailles's bitterest enemies, not even the most fashionable bishops, the smartest
women of the world, or even the libertines, who could be found to
blame the curé or the Archbishop, since everyone knew that they were

in the right and was therefore afraid to censure them, while most people were not only horrified by the Duchesse de Berry's conduct, but also detested her for her pride and haughtiness.

After this it became a question between the Regent, the Cardinal and the curé, who were standing together by the doorway, as to which of them should tell the Duchesse de Berry, who had no idea of what was happening, and who, as she had made her confession, was expecting to see the Sacraments brought in at any moment, and to receive them. After a short discussion, made all the more urgent by the patient's condition, the Cardinal and the curé withdrew a short distance, while the Duc d'Orléans ordered the door to be opened and called for Mme de Mouchy. Then, with the door ajar between them, she on the inside and he without, he told her his business. Mouchy, astonished and even more indignant, tried to carry off the matter with a high hand, telling him just what she thought of her own merits, and of the affront these bigots were offering to her and to her mistress, who would certainly never agree to what they suggested, and who, in her condition, would probably die on the spot if anyone had the impertinence or cruelty to deliver such a message. In the end, however, she agreed to tell the Duchesse de Berry the decision about the Sacraments, and one can guess what she added on her own account.

It was not long before a reply in the negative came, delivered to the Duke by Mouchy once again through the half-opened door; with her as a go-between he can hardly have hoped for anything else. A moment later he told the Cardinal and the curé. The curé, in the presence of his Archbishop and he of the same mind as himself, merely shrugged his shoulders; but the Cardinal told the Duc d'Orléans that Mme de Mouchy, as one of the two people of whom it was essential to be quit for ever, was hardly the best person to persuade the Duchesse de Berry to see reason; that it was up to him, her father, to give her the message himself and to persuade her to do her Christian duty at a time like that when she was on the point of meeting her God. It will surprise no one to hear that his eloquence was of no avail. The Prince was far too frightened of his daughter, and in any case he would have made a poor advocate.

At this, the Cardinal immediately decided to go and speak to the Duchesse de Berry himself, accompanied by the curé. Seeing that he was bent on going at once, the Duc d'Orléans, who did not dare to prevent him, but who was afraid that if he went his daughter might do herself some sudden hurt at the sight of the two pastors, especially when she heard what they had to say to her, begged him at least to wait until she could have some warning of his approach. Thereupon he went and held another conversation at the half-closed door, the success of which was the same as of that which had gone before. The Duchesse de Berry flew into a fury, railed angrily against the hypocrites who dared to take advantage of her condition and of their sacred character to dishonour her in this scandalous and unprecedented fashion, and even blamed her father for being such a fool and a weakling as to put up with it. Indeed, according to her, the Cardinal and the curé should both have been kicked downstairs. The Duc d'Orléans came back feeling very small and miserable, not knowing what to do between them. He told them that his daughter was so weak and in such pain that they must wait for a time, and so put them off as best he could.

The attention and curiosity of the large crowd of people in the room were extreme as bit by bit during the day the details of what was going on became known. Mme de Saint-Simon was sitting with several of the Duchesse de Berry's Ladies, and one or two others who had come to hear the news, upon a window-seat not far away. She could see what was happening, and besides, from time to time, she had word of what was in progress.

Cardinal de Noailles remained with the Duc d'Orléans for more than two hours, and by the end of his visit most of the more important people had approached them. At last, seeing that without some sort of violence, a thing most foreign to his nature, he would never be able to enter the bedroom, he thought it unseemly and useless to remain there any longer. Before taking his leave he repeated his orders to the curé, warning him to take good care that no one got round him in this matter of the Sacraments, and pointing out that an attempt might be made to administer them surreptitiously. This done, he went up to Mme de Saint-Simon, drew her upon one side, told her what had passed, and then said how sorry he was not only for what had occurred but for the scandal which he found it impossible to avoid.

It was with great relief that the Duc d'Orléans went in to announce the Cardinal's departure to his daughter. However, on leaving her bedroom, he was astonished to find the curé glued to a spot by the door, and still more so when the latter told him that this was his post and that nothing would move him from it because he intended to see that no Sacraments were administered. The upshot of this was that the curé remained there for four days and nights, except for short intervals when he went to his home, quite near the Luxembourg, for food and rest. On these occasions he left two priests on duty until his return. It was not until all danger was passed that he raised his siege.

The Duchesse de Berry was safely delivered of a daughter, and after that there was nothing for her to do but to get well again.[1] However, her fury against the priest and the Cardinal continued, and she never forgave them. Moreover she seemed to be more than ever under the spell of the two lovers, who mocked at her in private, and who were only attached to her for their own ends. Even when she was better, they remained closetted with her for several days, so that the Duc and Duchesse d'Orléans were only allowed to see her for short periods at a time, and the same applied to Madame, who after the first day or two hardly bothered to visit her.

Rioms was, as I have said, a younger son from Gascony, well-born and penniless. He was the grandson of a sister of the Duc de Lauzun, of whose escapade with Mademoiselle (she had wished to marry him) the whole world knows. It was the similarity between the cases of uncle and nephew that put the idea of a like marriage into both their heads. The uncle was delighted; it seemed to him as if, in the person of his nephew, he were living his own life over once again; and it was he who led the way. The young man's empire over his imperious princess was complete. Each day she had some fresh caprice of his— always a most deliberate caprice—to bear; each day her liberty of action dwindled. Moreover, his brutal humours every day made her weep, and as often as not several times. On top of this there was the dangers she had undergone in childbirth, her horror of the scandal she had provoked, when she had found herself placed between the danger of being denied the last Sacraments and a rupture with those with whom she was so wildly in love, and her fear of the devil which nearly drove her out of her mind at the slightest clap of thunder, though previously she had never feared thunder at all. Realizing her condition uncle and nephew grew bolder. Even before this date the uncle had advised his nephew to treat his princess just as he himself had treated Mademoiselle. It was a maxim of his that the Bourbons like being bullied, and that unless you 'treat them rough' there is no holding them at all.

Moreover, Rioms was the lover of Mouchy and, as she had a complete hold over the Duchesse de Berry, he had in her an instrument ready to his hand. Their interests were the same. They had been alarmed by the scandal, and realized that something of the sort might easily happen again; fear of hell or serious reflection might produce the same result. On the other hand, if Rioms were to succeed in marrying the Princess, he would have nothing to fear, and could sit back and enjoy his incredible good fortune. Mouchy, too, had everything

---

[1] Nothing is known about this daughter and it seems probable that she died at birth.

to gain from such a union in which she would play an important part, and the two of them would be certain of possessing one another without any obstacle to their secret pleasures. I am only concerned here with setting the scene for what was yet to come, but it is certain that the plot dates, at the latest, from this illness and from the scandal to which it gave rise; it is not yet time to continue the story any further.

On her recovery, the Duchesse de Berry was so upset by the way in which everyone, down even to members of the lower classes, had talked about her illness, and about all that had occurred at that time, that she decided to win back some consideration by re-opening to the public the gates of the Luxembourg Gardens, which had been closed for a long time. Everyone was pleased; everyone profited; and that was all. She also made a vow to wear nothing but white for the next six months; this caused some laughter.

DEATH OF MADAME DE MAINTENON

ON the evening of Saturday, the 15th of April, the eve of the first Sunday after Easter, the famous and deadly Mme de Maintenon died at Saint-Cyr. What a disturbance this would have caused in Europe if it had happened a few years earlier! As it was, there were people even as near as Versailles who probably never heard of it, and in Paris it was scarcely mentioned. At the time of the King's death I spoke at such length about this woman, so miserably and so undeservedly famous, that I need say nothing more about her now except as regards her life since that time. For a period of thirty-five years without a break she played so powerful and so disastrous a part that everything about her, even her final retreat, is of interest.

Mme de Maintenon retired to Saint-Cyr the moment the late King died, and from that time she had the good sense to consider herself dead to the world, and never again placed a foot outside the grounds of the house. Moreover, with the exception of the very few people I am about to mention, she refused to see anyone, to ask anything from or to give advice to anyone, or to interfere in any matter where her name might possibly have permitted her to do so. Mme de Caylus, Mme de Dangeau, Mme de Levis were admitted to her presence, though not very often, and the last two sometimes, though still more rarely, were invited to dinner. Cardinal de Rohan called every week and so did the Duc du Maine, who always spent three or four hours alone with her. Whenever he appeared the world took on a different colour for her; and she would tenderly embrace her darling, as she called him, although he used to stink like a pole-cat.

Every now and then the Duc de Noailles used to call, though she did not seem to care much for his visits, and even less for those of his wife, though she was her only niece. As a result the Duchesse de Noailles called very rarely; when she did she seemed unwilling and uncomfortable, and her reception was much the same. The Maréchal de Villeroy went whenever he could spare the time to do so, and he was always welcome. Cardinal de Bissy seldom called. Occasionally one or two obscure and fanatical bishops went to see her: Aubigny, Archbishop of Rouen, went fairly often; Blouin occasionally; and so did Merinville, the Bishop of Chartres, her Diocesan and the Superior of the House.

When the Queen of England was at Saint-Germain she went to dinner once a week, but she did not make the journey from Chaillot, where she spent a good deal of her time. Their arm-chairs were of an exact quality and always placed opposite to one another. At dinner time a table was placed between them, upon which were laid their places, their first course, and a little bell. The young ladies of the chamber were responsible for this table. It was they who poured out their drinks, who changed the plates for each succeeding course, and who answered the bell whenever they were summoned. On these occasions the Queen used always to show them some little kindness or other. When the meal was over they cleared the table, removing everything from the room, and then brought in the coffee. The Queen used to stay with Mme de Maintenon for two or three hours; after that they would embrace; Mme de Maintenon would then take three or four steps forward—she did this on the Queen's arrival as well as on her departure; and the young ladies, who were waiting in the ante-room, would then conduct the Queen to her coach. They were all very fond of her because she treated them so graciously.

However, the visitor these young women preferred above all others was Cardinal de Rohan, who never arrived empty-handed, but always brought them enough presents of cakes and sweetmeats to last them for several days. Little actions of this sort appealed to Mme de Maintenon. Although these visits were uncommon and no one came without making an appointment, except her 'darling' who was always welcomed with open arms, seldom a day passed without a caller of some kind. On the days when no one came, and during the morning when she was not otherwise occupied, she would spend her time reading and answering the many letters she received. Nearly all of these were from the Superiors of religious communities, from abbesses or

344

even from simple nuns. Her love of directing others was always her dominating passion, and, since she wrote very well and with the greatest ease, she enjoyed dictating letters.

I know these details through Mme de Thibouville, who was a Rochechouart, quite penniless, and who was placed in Saint-Cyr while still a young child. Apart from her waiting-maids (and none of her men servants were allowed within the grounds), Mme de Maintenon always kept two and sometimes three old spinsters, as well as six young girls, to bear her company in her room; and both young and old were changed from time to time. Mlle de Rochechouart was one of the young ones. Mme de Maintenon took a liking to her and, so far as her age would allow, even took her somewhat into her confidence. Moreover, finding her clever and liking her handwriting, she always dictated her letters to her. Mlle de Rochechouart did not leave Saint-Cyr until after the death of Mme de Maintenon, whom she always mourned, although she had never received anything from her.

Just as she had always done at Court, Mme de Maintenon rose early and went to bed early. Her prayers lasted a long time; she used to read pious works to herself; every now and then she made one of the young girls read history to her, and enjoyed discussing the subject matter with those who were present and so teaching them. She heard Mass, and often various other Offices, from a gallery, the door of which was next to her own room; and it was only seldom that she sat in the choir. She communicated, not, as Dangeau tells us in his memoirs, every other day at midnight, but twice a week, usually between seven and eight in the morning, after which she would return to her gallery where she would remain for some time.

Her dinner would be simple, but dainty and exquisite in its simplicity and there was always plenty of everything. The Duc de Noailles, after Mornay's day,[1] and Blouin always saw to it that she was plentifully supplied with game from Saint-Germain and Blois, and the King's Ministry of Works supplied her with fruit. When no visitor came to dine with her, she would eat alone, waited on by the young ladies of her chamber, and three or four times a year, though not oftener, she would ask one or two of them to sit at table with her. Mlle d'Aumale,[2] who at the time of which I am speaking was getting on and who had been with Mme de Maintenon for many years at Court, was generally not one of those who was chosen. Supper was served

---

[1] He replaced Mornay as Master of the Hunt at Saint-Germain in 1717.

[2] Marie-Jeanne d'Aumale, whose memoirs of Mme de Maintenon are well known; at this time she was not quite thirty-six.

separately for Mlle d'Aumale and the Ladies-in-Waiting, of whom she was in a sense in charge; Mme de Maintenon never ate in the evening. Sometimes when the days were very fine and there was no wind, Mme de Maintenon would walk for a short while in the garden.

She always chose the Superior, her subordinates, and every one else in any authority in Saint-Cyr, herself. Current matters of detail were simply reported to her; but when anything of greater importance arose the Superior would ask for her instructions. Mme de Maintenon was known to everyone simply as Madam, and she held everything and everyone in the palm of her hand; and although she was polite and kind to the older inmates and generous to the young, in fact everyone trembled before her. With the exception of the Superior and her immediate subordinates it was only on rare occasions that she saw any of the regular inmates, and when she did so it was only because she had sent for them, or, more rarely still, because one of them had asked for an audience which she had granted. The Superior was free to go and see her whenever she wished, but she did not abuse the privilege. Nevertheless she gave her full details of, and took her orders concerning, all that happened in the house. But, except for her, Mme de Maintenon saw no one regularly.

Never was an Abbess Daughter of France, when such existed, so absolutely mistress or so punctually obeyed, so feared or so respected; yet nearly everyone living within the walls of Saint-Cyr loved her. The priests who visited her from outside were just as submissive and equally dependent. In front of her young girls she never uttered a single word about the government or the Court, but she used often to speak with approbation of the late King, though even then without going deeply into details and without mentioning the intrigues, the cabals or the political affairs of his reign.

We have already seen how, when the Duc d'Orléans called upon Mme de Maintenon directly after the proclamation of his regency, she had asked him for nothing but his protection for Saint-Cyr. He promised her that the 4000 francs a month which the late King had given her would continue to be paid regularly on the first of the month, and this promise was always most punctually performed. Thus Mme de Maintenon enjoyed a pension of 48,000 livres a year from the King. I am not even sure that she did not retain her position as governess to the King's and Mme de Montespan's children, together with various other pensions which she had been granted at that time, as well as her salary as second Lady of the Wardrobe to the Dauphine of Bavaria, just as the Maréchale de Rochefort, the First Lady, retained hers, and as the Duchesse d'Arpajon, the Lady-in-Waiting, retained

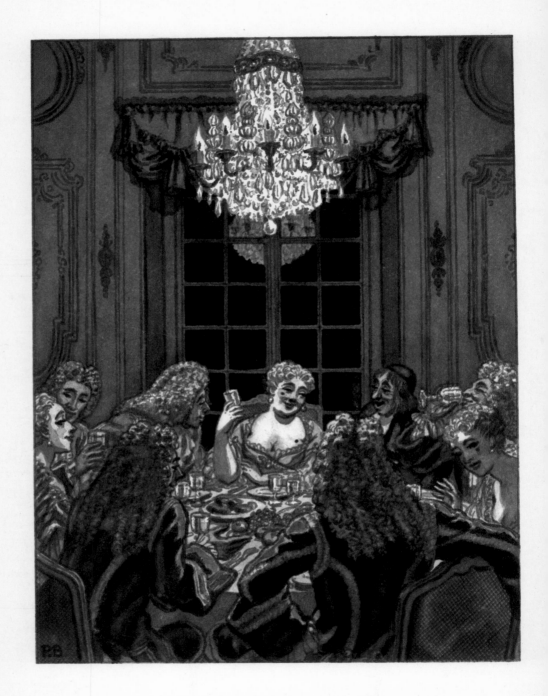

Dinner with the Duchesse de Berry

hers from the death of the Dauphine until her own death. In addition to these sums Mme de Maintenon had her estates at Maintenon, and enjoyed various other sources of income. Moreover under the terms of its original foundation Saint-Cyr was always bound, in the case of her electing to retire there, to house her, her servants and her suite, and to feed them, both servants and horses, for so long a time as she wished, free of charge. All this was most faithfully performed down even to the provision of wood and coal and lamps and candles, in a word without its costing her a single sou for herself, her servants, her horses, or indeed for anything except her clothes and her servants' liveries. Her general staff consisted of a butler, a footman, household and kitchen servants, a coach, a stable of seven or eight horses with one or two saddle horses in addition; while her personal staff consisted of Mlle d'Aumale, her maids, and the young ladies of whom I have spoken, although all of these were on the strength of Saint-Cyr; in fact she had no outgoings except charity and her servants' wages.

I have often felt astonished that the Maréchal d'Harcourt who had been so close to her, Tallard, and Villars, who owed her so much, Mme du Maine and her children for whose sake she had torn up the law both human and divine, the Prince de Rohan and so many others, never once went to see her.

The fall of the Duc du Maine at the *lit de justice* held at the Tuileries drove the first nail into her coffin. It is not, I think, too much to presume that she knew all about her darling's plots and schemes, and that her hopes for him kept her going. When she saw him arrested she gave up; a continuous fever took her, and she died at eighty-three in full possession of her intelligence and of all her mental faculties.

THE ABBESSE DE CHELLES

MME d'Orléans, who, partly from youth and partly from whim and fancy, had become a professed nun at the Abbey of Chelles, found that she could not remain in the house to which she had come under vows of obedience unless she took command. The Abbess, who was a sister of the Maréchal de Villars and a most meritorious woman, soon tired of a struggle which, although God and man were on her side, soon became intolerable to her, and troublesome to the peace and good order of her convent. She longed to resign and find a living elsewhere. She was therefore granted a pension of 12,000 livres by the King and came to live with her brother in Paris until rooms in a convent became available for her. Eventually she found a home with the Benedictines in the rue de Cherche-Midi near the Carrefour Croix Rouge, to which she retired and lived for several years, a true delight and example to the Convent, and where she finally died regretted by all.[1]

To finish with a subject which is not important enough to return to later, the end of which would take us beyond the bounds of these memoirs, the Princess who succeeded her in the post of Abbess also quickly tired of the position. Sometimes excessively austere, sometimes with nothing more about her of the nun than her garments, now a musician, now a surgeon, now a theologian, and now a director of consciences, she was everything by fits and starts and nothing for long, very intelligent, quickly bored and soon tired of her various undertakings, incapable of application, longing for a different regimen and even more for her liberty without making up her mind to renounce her vocation, she finally obtained permission to retire and to have appointed in her stead one of her closest friends in the convent. Even after this she would not stay there long herself, but went to live for the rest of her life in a fine apartment at the Benedictine Convent of La Madeleine de Traînel. Near this convent the Duchesse d'Orléans, who by that time had left Montmartre, had built a magnificent and delightful house, with a private entrance into the Convent; it was her custom to spend the chief festivals there, and she often visited it at other times.

As years went on Mme de Chelles little by little turned back to religion and to a regular way of life, and, although to the end she remained a princess at heart, her life grew more and more enlightened up till the time of her death, which occurred several years later in the convent where she had settled and which she never left again.

THE MISSISSIPPI

MEANWHILE Law still produced miracle after miracle with his Mississippi scheme. These manœuvres had produced a language of their own and one had to know this language if one wished to be in the swim. However, I shall not attempt to explain it any more than I shall attempt to explain the financial operations involved. Everyone wanted shares in the Mississippi Company, and immense fortunes were being made almost overnight. Law, besieged in his own home by suppliants and beggars, saw his door broken down, his garden invaded, his windows forced, and some even got into his study down the chimney.

---

[1] 17 September 1723.

No one talked in anything but millions. Law, who as I have said came to see me between eleven and twelve every Tuesday, often begged me to accept some shares in his Company, entirely free of charge, which he said he would look after for me without my having to bother about them, and in this way to make me the master of millions. So many people of every walk in life did make money, several of them entirely on their own account, that there is no doubt that Law would have done the same for me, and still more quickly. However, I refused to listen to him.

Soon afterwards Law approached Mme de Saint-Simon, but found her equally inflexible. If there was money going, he would rather have seen me make it than most people, since he would thereby have attached me to his interests, and my influence with the Regent was very useful to him. Indeed his next attempt was to approach the Regent himself, in the hopes that his authority might prevail over me. The Regent mentioned the matter to me more than once, but on each occasion I managed to put him off. At last a day came when he went further. He had arranged for me to come and see him at Saint-Cloud, where he had gone to work so as to take a walk round the gardens afterwards. We were sitting on the balustrade in front of the orangery, overlooking the slope of the Goulettes woods. Once again he broached the subject of the Mississippi Company and urged me more strongly than ever to accept some shares from Law. The more firmly I resisted the more urgent he grew and the more elaborate became his arguments. In the end he lost his temper and said that, considering how many men of my condition and dignity in the State were running after these shares, it showed altogether too much pride on my part obstinately to refuse what the King was anxious to give me, since it was in the King's name that all these shares were granted. I answered him that conduct of the kind he was describing would show not only pride but stupidity and impertinence; that since he was so pressing I would give him my reasons which were that never, except in the fable of King Midas, had I read of, or still less seen, anyone capable of turning all he touched to gold; that I had grave doubts about Law's possessing this attribute and suspected that his so-called knowledge consisted in little more than a cunning game, a new and clever confidence trick as it were, which could do no more than subtract what was in Peter's pockets to place it in Paul's, and so enrich some at the expense of others; that sooner or later sources would run dry and the trick would be discovered; that thousands of people would then be ruined; that I did not see how, when that time came, it would be possible to make restitution, or even to know to whom restitution should be made; and that as I hated being involved in a question of other men's goods I had no intention of dabbling in any matter which appeared to me to be so dubious.

The Duc d'Orléans did not know exactly what to reply to this. However, he was not ashamed of repeating himself, and in his discontent kept returning to his original complaint that I was refusing to accept the King's benefits. At this I fortunately lost my temper and told him that, so far from doing anything of the kind, I would make him a proposal which I should never have dreamt of laying before him if it had not been for what he had just said, and which I was so far from having thought of previously that—and what I said was perfectly true—it had only come into my head that moment.

After that I told him—and I had before told him this occasionally in casual conversation—of how my father had ruined himself in defending Blaye against the attacks of Monsieur le Prince's party; of how he had been besieged there for eighteen months, had paid the garrison himself, had provided supplies out of his own pocket, had founded cannon, had fortified the place, and had then maintained the five hundred gentlemen he had collected inside, and had been put to other expenses without ever having levied a penny upon the surrounding country, but in a word had supplied everything himself. I told him how, after the troubles were ended, my father had been granted various promises of payment by the Exchequer, amounting in all to 500,000 livres, of which he had never received a single sou, and which M. Fouquet had been on the point of settling at the time of his arrest. Then I said that if he cared to repay me that sum, and add some compensation for the loss of capital, since my father and I had had to bear the burden of having performed this valuable service to the King through all these years, together with the interest we had paid on it ever since, he would be doing me an act of justice for which I should ever be grateful to him, and I suggested that as the money was paid off I should bring him the notes promising to pay us, one by one, to be burnt before him as each fresh amount was paid. The Duc d'Orléans agreed; he spoke to Law upon the subject next day; my notes, or promises of payment, were burnt one by one in the Duc d'Orléans's study, and it was out of the money I received in this way that I was able to pay for what I did at La Ferté.[1]

---

[1] No records have survived of the work he put in hand at his country estate, but it is apparent that he did not spend all the money he received for this purpose, since at this time he also bought considerable property in Paris.

THE ABBÉ VITTEMENT

I HAVE already made some mention of the Abbé Vittement, who was made second tutor to the King on his merit, without having thought of the post for himself or any of his friends having thought of it for him—which is very rare at Court. He lived alone, without being either anti-social or peculiar, and he was generally liked and well thought of. About this time an abbey fell in with an income of some 12,000 livres a year. The Duc d'Orléans suggested to the King that he might give this to Vittement and that he should tell his tutor the news in person. The King was delighted, and at once sent for him and told him. Vittement thanked him profoundly for the gift and then begged with great modesty to be excused from accepting it. The King, the Regent, and the Maréchal de Villeroy, who was present, all begged him to take it. He answered that he had plenty to live on. The Marshal insisted and said that he could spend the gift in charity. Vittement in all humility replied that it was not worth his or anyone else's while to receive charity just for the purpose of handing it out again, held to his ground, and left the room.

It is to Vittement we owe a prophecy, as celebrated as it is amazing, and which I first heard from Bidault.[1] Alarmed by the growing power of M. de Fréjus, who had just been made a Cardinal, Bidault spoke of his fears to Vittement, who allowed him to have his say without betraying the least surprise. Astonished at finding Vittement so cool, so calm, so silent, Bidault begged him to explain his lack of emotion. 'His power,' replied Vittement, 'will last throughout his life and his reign will be limitless and untroubled. He has succeeded in binding the King with thongs so strong that the King will never be able to break them. What I tell you now is something I know. I can say no more at present. But if the Cardinal dies before me I shall then be able to explain to you what during his life-time I cannot even hint at.'

Bidault told me this soon afterwards, and I have heard since that Vittement said much the same thing to various others. Unfortunately he died before the Cardinal and carried his curious secret with him to the grave.[2] What followed showed only too clearly how right Vittement's prognostications were.

---

[1] One of the *valets de chambre* of the Duc de Bourgogne.

[2] The Bishop of Fréjus was the Cardinal Fleury, former tutor of the boy King. Louis XV dismissed Monsieur le Duc in 1726 and appointed Fleury Prime Minister at the age of 73, and the old gentleman remained in office until he died at the age of 90.

THE Duchesse de Berry's illness, of which I spoke recently, began on the 26th of March, and Easter Sunday fell on the 9th of April. She had quite recovered, but she was still refusing to see visitors. Now after what had been happening in Holy Week, it was bound to be an awkward business for her to spend Easter Week in Paris. Moreover, the Duc d'Orléans's visits were becoming rare and irksome to him, and her marriage with Rioms was causing many tears and quarrels between father and daughter. In order to avoid these quarrels and the embarrassment of the week in Paris, she decided to go to Meudon on Easter Monday. It was useless to point out to her the dangers she was running from the keen air, from the movement of the carriage, and from changing her abode at all within fifteen days of her recent illness—nothing would make her put up with Paris any longer. She therefore left for Meudon, followed by Rioms and most of the Ladies of her Household.

It was at this time that the Duc d'Orléans told me of the Duchesse de Berry's determination to make public her secret marriage with Rioms. The Duchesse d'Orléans was away at Montmartre for a day or two, and we were walking up and down the little garden in front of her apartment. Considering the Princess's passionate nature, her fear of hell, and the recent scandal, I was not greatly surprised to hear of the marriage; but I was astounded to hear that a woman so proud as the Duchesse de Berry should be so set on making a public statement.

The Duc d'Orléans told me at some length of his difficulties, of his anger, of the anger of Madame, who was all for proceeding to the last extremity, and of the extreme annoyance of the Duchesse d'Orléans. Fortunately there were at this time a number of officers leaving every day for the army on the Spanish border, and Rioms had only remained behind because of the Duchesse de Berry's illness. The Duc d'Orléans therefore decided to earn some respite by sending Rioms off, imagining that his daughter would be less anxious to declare her marriage in her husband's absence than if he were still with her. I approved this idea and next day Rioms, who was at Meudon, received an order, short and to the point, bidding him join his regiment in the Duke of Berwick's army immediately. The Duchesse de Berry was furious, all the more so because she realized the object of the order and her own powerlessness to postpone her lover's departure. Rioms did not dare to question the order; he therefore obeyed, and the Duc d'Orléans, who had not yet gone out to Meudon, postponed his visit there a day or two longer. Both he and his daughter were afraid of one another

and this departure of Rioms had not made matters easier. She had recently pointed out to him that she was now a widow, rich, mistress of
her own actions, and no longer under his control. She had repeated to
him what she heard that Mademoiselle had said when she wished to
marry Lauzun, Rioms's grand-uncle, and added a detailed list of all the
goods, the honours, the distinctions she would expect for Rioms the
moment her marriage with him was made public; she screamed at the
Duke and would brook neither argument nor opposition from him.
She was set on making her marriage public and it took the Duc d'Orléans his full resources of wit, art, cajolery, anger, menaces, and prayers
to prevail upon her to wait. According to Madame the whole thing
might well have been done with before they went to Meudon, because
if he had had his way the Duc d'Orléans would have had Rioms
thrown out of the Luxembourg windows.[1]

This premature journey to Meudon on the top of such violent
emotional scenes was hardly the best thing for the health of one so
recently at death's door. Furthermore she was anxious to hide her
condition from the public, and not to let it be known that she was at
loggerheads with her father, although the infrequency of his recent
visits to her had already caused considerable comment. She therefore
decided to give a supper for the Duc d'Orléans on the terrace at
Meudon one evening at about seven o'clock. It was in vain that the
danger she was running from the dew and the cool evening air was
pointed out to her, considering her recent recovery and how variable
her state of health still was. . . .

This supper in the open air was not a success. She fell ill that night.
This attack was aggravated by her previous weakness and by irregular
attacks of fever which had not been helped by the way in which her
desire to declare her marriage had so far met with refusal. As so often
happens with those who are sick either in mind or body, she grew tired
of Meudon and began to complain of the air and of the surroundings.
Then she was upset to find that the Duc d'Orléans's visits grew no
more frequent, and that, although she was still far from well, Madame
and the Duchesse d'Orléans hardly came to see her at all. It is true that
in this matter it was rather her pride that was hurt than her affection, for
she had never loved the two Princesses, and now, as she found them
opposing her most ardent desires, she had begun to hate them. For
that matter she had at last almost begun to hate her father, although
her empire over him was still so great that she clung to the hope of

---

[1] At one time a rumour was current that Rioms had been arrested on the way to Spain
at Madame's instigation.

being able to bring him round to her wishes. On Sunday, the 14th of May, wrapped in blankets, she had herself taken in a large coach from Meudon to La Meute. She hoped that her proximity to Paris would persuade the Duc d'Orléans to visit her more often, and that even the Duchesse d'Orléans, out of respect for the conventions would be persuaded to do so too. This journey was extremely painful and the jolting merely augmented her existing ailments so that neither the stay at La Meute nor the various remedies applied to her could reduce her violent symptoms for more than short spells at a time.

THE END OF THE MARQUIS D'ÉFFIAT

THE Marquis d'Éffiat, of whom I have spoken so often in these memoirs, at the age of eighty-one fell ill in his fine house at Chilly, near Paris, where he had gone to take a milk diet. He was brought back to Paris on the 23rd of May, but he was already so ill that there was little chance of his recovery. The Maréchal de Villeroy, who had always been his good friend and in more than one instance his dupe, at once rushed to see him, and then, hoping to gain credit for his conversion, a useful matter to one who was governor to a King, succeeded in persuading him to receive the last Sacraments. After this Éffiat took a turn for the better and he lived on for some time.

Éffiat was, as we have seen, a man much of whose life was a mystery from choice, from habit and the most sordid avarice. He always had one or two women of low birth and loose morals about him to keep him amused, and they, while they had hopes from him, cost him very little. He was Master of Monsieur's pack of hounds, a position which the Duc d'Orléans confirmed, and as First Equerry he also looked after their stables. In this way it was at their expense that every summer he used to hunt deer upon his own estates at Montrichard or in the neighbouring forests near Montargis of which he was Captain.[1] He hardly used to trouble to call upon the neighbouring nobility at all while he was there, and his hospitality was always very niggardly.

Hunting and women had been the cause of a friendship between him and du Palais, who hunted with him every summer and used to visit him regularly during the winter. This du Palais was almost his only close friend. Curiously enough du Palais was an intelligent and well-mannered fellow, and not only honourable (and known to be

---

[1] The estates at Montrichard in Touraine he inherited from his mother. Montargis was in the apanage of the Duc d'Orléans.

such), but he had served with distinction and was received in the best company in Paris. He was the only man Éffiat wanted to see during his last illness, and he looked after the dying man most attentively.

But every evening at seven o'clock Éffiat would get rid of him. His manner was perfectly polite and friendly, but it was obvious that he was firmly getting rid of him. After some days du Palais noticed the regularity of his evening dismissal, and began to wonder why. As he had been in and out of the house for so many years, he spoke to the *valets de chambre* about it. They looked at one another, and then they told him that, not only were they in exactly the same situation, but that they were just as curious to know the meaning of it as he was; that at the time he mentioned they, too, were always sent out of the room, and so firmly forbidden to re-enter, or to allow anyone else, whoever he might be or upon whatever errand he came, to enter until rung for, that they could not help wondering what might be the meaning of all these precautions. Then they added something stranger still.

They told du Palais that recently they had begun to listen at the door; that always, sometimes earlier sometimes later, they could hear their master in conversation with a voice that was certainly not his own, though they were perfectly sure that there was not, and could not possibly be, anyone but the sick man in the room; that every now and then they could distinguish an unimportant word or two, but never more than that, and then only rarely; that these conversations were seldom short and would often last an hour or more; that, on re-entering the room to answer Éffiat's bell, they could see no change whatever anywhere; and that their master seemed deep in his own thoughts, but otherwise just as they had left him.

This story only served to heighten du Palais's curiosity. Indeed he became so curious that he agreed to the servants' proposal to see if what they had told him were not true. So next day, after being dismissed as usual by Éffiat, du Palais came out of the room, and remained with the valets outside. There he listened and, just as they had done, heard Éffiat and the voice in conversation. Sometimes one voice would be raised and sometimes another, but the words he heard were few, insignificant and separated from their context. Wishing to repeat the experiment, du Palais remained behind on two or three further occasions. He discussed the matter with the valets and not one of them could offer a solution.

Du Palais knew the room as well as he knew his own, and he knew, as the servants knew, that there was no way by which anyone could possibly have got in unnoticed. He was tempted to talk to Éffiat on the subject. Although he did not quite dare to do this, he nevertheless

355

said something to him about his surprise at finding himself dismissed so regularly at the same hour. At first Éffiat took no notice; then, beating about the bush as best he could, he said something about visiting hours and the fact that he did not wish to take advantage of du Palais's friendship and kindness in coming to see him so often, and finally when the time came he said good-bye to him as usual.

This time du Palais pretended to leave the room, but really stayed inside, close by the door. A little later du Palais thinks he must have made a slight movement, for Éffiat noticed that he was still there, flew into a temper and told him severely that when he asked him to go he meant what he was saying. Then he went on to say that he could not imagine what reasons du Palais had for hiding in his room like that; that he was cruelly offended; and that, to put it shortly, if he wished to see him and to remain his friend, he must ask him to leave the room at once and never again to play a trick like that. From where he was standing du Palais answered as best he could, but Éffiat only answered: 'Go away, I say, go away.' After that du Palais left the room but stayed just outside the door. Soon he heard the conversation begin again. Neither he nor any of the valets ever found out any more.

At about nine o'clock every evening one of those women I have mentioned would come in to amuse Éffiat. Sometimes a friend looked in, sometimes du Palais returned. Éffiat never left his bed again. His mind remained perfectly clear until his death, which came on the 3rd of June. He left prodigious sums in cash, besides a great deal of other wealth and fine estates. His legacies were very handsome, and he endowed several foundations for the education of the sons of poor gentlefolk. He left Chilly to the Duc d'Orléans, who refused to accept it and returned it to the family.

THE DEATH OF
THE DUCHESSE DE BERRY

In July the state of the Duchesse de Berry's health was causing even more alarm. As the attacks became more and more frequent, she was in constant pain and running a continual fever. In fact her symptoms grew so bad that by the 14th the worst was feared. That night was so bad that a messenger was sent to awaken the Duc d'Orléans at the Palais Royal. At the same time Mme de Pons wrote off to Mme de Saint-Simon, urging her to come and to take up her quarters at La Meute. We have already noted that Mme de Saint-Simon did not see

the Duchesse de Berry except on ceremonial occasions and for the hour
in the evening when she held her court; she hardly ever stayed to supper, but merely checked over the ladies who had been chosen for
supper and to play cards. She seldom waited upon the Duchess herself
except on rare visits to the King, and although she had an apartment
at La Meute she scarcely ever went there. However, on this occasion
she accepted the advice of Mme de Pons and immediately went to La
Meute with the intention of staying there. She saw at once that things
were serious. On the 15th of July the Duchess was bled from the arm,
again from the foot later the same day, and her confessor, a Franciscan,
was then sent for.

But here I must interrupt my account of this illness, which lasted
another week, since I think that what remains to be said will be better
understood if I can first give a full-length sketch of the Princess,
though I do so at the risk of repeating here what I may have said of her
in various other parts of these memoirs.

The Duchesse de Berry in the course of her short life succeeded in
creating such a stir in the world that, although what I have to say of
her may be painful, it is none the less interesting and deserves I think
a moment or two's attention. Born with an intelligence superior to
most, she was, when she wished to be, both charming and lovable.
Her figure imposed respect and it was a pleasure to look at her, although towards the end she put on so much weight that it began to
spoil her appearance. She spoke with peculiar grace, with a natural
and spontaneous eloquence that was all her own, and a justness of
expression that surprised and charmed whoever spoke with her.
What might she not have made of these talents with the King and
Mme de Maintenon, who really wished to love her; with the Duchesse
de Bourgogne, who had not only brought about her marriage, but
had wished to adopt her almost as her own special creation; and, since
that date, with a father, Regent of the realm, who had eyes for none
but her; if only vices of the heart, the mind and the soul and a violent
temper had not turned such fine qualities into the most noxious poison. The most insensate arrogance and continuous duplicity she
looked upon as virtues on which to pride herself, while the irreligion
with which she had thought to embellish her wit completed what her
other faults had begun.

More than once in these memoirs we have noted her strange behaviour with the Duc du Maine; her horror of her mother's bastard
birth; her contempt for a father she had so easily subjugated to her
wishes; her extravagant ideas in regard to Monseigneur; her feelings
of despair whenever she thought of the rank occupied by the Du-

357

chesse de Bourgogne; and her ingratitude towards her and her husband, even though it was to them that she owed her elevation; her lack of respect for the King and Mme de Maintenon; the open hostility she always showed to those who had contributed to her marriage (and this was due to the fact that she found it unbearable to be under the least obligation to anyone); her flagrant impostures and her haughtiness; the shocking disproportion between her position in the world and her conduct—a conduct which included not only drunkenness but everything else which goes with crapulous company, with filth, and with impiety. We have seen how from the earliest days of her married life her true temperament had shown itself. We have noted how, as the days went by, there was always some fresh scandal attaching to her name. We have watched her setting out to capture this young man and that, and we have noted how these immoderate passions led her in the end to the folly of abandoning herself to La Haye and then to Rioms. We have seen how ambitious she was to have the greatest and most courageous names included in her entourage, so as to make herself an intermediary of importance between her father and Spain; how she would now take this side and now that, whichever at the moment seemed to offer the greater advantage; how, in the end, she really came to imagine that she actually held the balance of power; how more than once she usurped the rights of a queen; and on the occasion with the ambassadors dared to exceed even the Queen's prerogative.

What was even more extraordinary was the astonishing contrast between a pride by which she raised herself to the skies and habits of such debauchery that, although her rank was such that she would in public sit down to table with no one below a Prince of the Blood, in private and in the country she would not only eat with any man or woman of birth one might care to mention, but would even admit Father Riglet, the Jesuit, a man capable of saying anything, and scum of that sort who would not be allowed in any decent house in the land, and would sup with the Duc d'Orléans's rakes, whether he were present or not, and enjoy egging on their filthy remarks and impieties.

Moreover, though her depravity was common knowledge, she was always indignant that anyone dared to speak of it. She would say straight out that no one should be allowed to discuss people of her rank, not even to blame what might be deserving of censure in their most public actions, or what the speaker had actually seen, let alone whatever went on in private. It was this that put her against everyone. It was as if some sacred right of hers had been violated, as if some criminal act of ill-breeding which no one could ever forgive had been committed against her. Her death, like her life, was a strange business, and to that I must now return.

In spite of the long days and nights of pain, it was impossible to persuade her to take thought for this life, or to adopt any régime which might be suitable for her state of health. Still less could she be brought to think of the life to come. In the end her parents and doctors thought it best to speak to her in terms which are never employed with people of her rank, save in cases of necessity. Even here Chirac's impiety was an obstacle. However, as he was the only one to speak as he did, and as all the others continued to urge her to do her duty, she at last consented to make use of the proper remedies both for this world and the next. When the time came for her to receive the Sacraments, she had her doors thrown wide open, and she spoke to all those who were present about her life and present condition as if she were queen of both.

When this ceremony was finished, and she was once again with her chosen companions, she congratulated herself upon the firmness she had shown, and asked them if she had not spoken well and if she were not dying with grandeur and with courage. A little later she dismissed everyone but Mme de Mouchy, to whom she showed her keys and a safe, and told her to bring her ring-case. The case was brought and opened. Then the Duchesse de Berry, oblivious of all the presents she had already showered on Mme de Mouchy, gave her this case as well. In the past Mme de Mouchy had received many gifts, and in addition a day never seemed to pass without her filching something extra from her benefactress, sometimes money, and sometimes precious stones. Even the smallest gift would be a piece of jewelry. However, this case of rings was worth by itself at least 200,000 crowns. Greedy as Mouchy was, this stupefied even her. She went out and showed it to her husband. It was evening. The Duc and Duchesse d'Orléans had left. Both husband and wife were afraid of being accused of theft, for they knew that their reputation was none too good. Because of this they thought they had better mention the matter to some of those in the Household least bitterly opposed to them—and they were despised and detested by almost everyone.

The news got round from one to another until it reached Mme de Saint-Simon's ears. She knew the case of rings, and was so deeply astonished that she thought she ought to tell the Duc d'Orléans. She sent a message to him at once. The Duchesse de Berry was now so ill that no one at La Meute even dared to go to bed. Everyone was gathered together in the drawing-room. Seeing that this business of the rings was by now public property, and likely to go ill for her,

Mouchy grew embarrassed and went up to Mme de Saint-Simon. She told her what had happened, drew the ring-case from her pocket, and showed it to my wife. Mme de Saint-Simon called to various ladies who were standing near to come and see it too, and then in front of them (and this was her real reason for having called them) she told Mme de Mouchy that it was certainly a fine present, but so fine that she advised her to go off with it as soon as possible to the Duc d'Orléans and to tell him about it.

This advice, and the fact that it had been uttered in the presence of witnesses, embarrassed Mme de Mouchy. However, she replied that she would do so and then went off to find her husband, with whom she went to her own room. Next day they went together to the Palais Royal and asked to speak to the Duc d'Orléans, who, warned as he had been by Mme de Saint-Simon, called them in at once, and then asked the few who were in the room—for it was early in the morning—to leave. Mme de Mouchy, with her husband beside her, then paid her respects as best she could. All the Duc d'Orléans said in reply was to ask her where the ring-case was. She drew it from her pocket and gave it him. The Duc d'Orléans took it, opened it, looked to see if anything were missing (for he knew the case perfectly), shut it again, drew a key from his pocket, locked the case in a drawer of his desk, and then dismissed them with a nod of his head without a word more on either side. As indignant as they were confused, they bowed and withdrew, and were never seen again at La Meute. Soon after this the Duc d'Orléans arrived; after paying a brief visit to his daughter, he took my wife on one side, thanked her warmly for what she had done as well as for the message she had sent him, repeated to her what he had done himself, and then told her that the ring-case would not leave his custody again. He was so furious at such effrontery that he could not restrain himself from speaking his mind about Mme de Mouchy and husband in the strongest terms in the drawing-room, at which there was the warmest applause from all who were present, even the servants.

I do not know if the absence of Mouchy had a happy effect on the Duchesse de Berry, but she never spoke of her again, and soon she seemed to recover herself somewhat, and wished to receive Our Lord again. It seems that this time she received Him with real piety, and quite differently from the first occasion. It was the Abbé de Castries, her First Almoner, Bishop of Tours elect, and who afterwards was Bishop of Albi besides becoming later Commander of the Order, who administered the Sacrament. He had to go to Passy for the bread and wine, and when he returned he was accompanied by the Duc d'Orléans and the Duc de Chartres. The Abbé delivered a short, moving and most fitting exhortation, which was admired by all who heard it.

Finally, when the doctors were at their wits' end, there was some talk of an elixir invented by a man called Garus which was fashionable at the time. The secret of this elixir has since been bought by the King. Garus was summoned and arrived soon afterwards. He found the Duchesse de Berry so ill that he refused to be responsible for anything which might happen. However, the remedy was given and succeeded beyond all expectation. The obvious thing was to go on with it. Now Garus had absolutely insisted that nothing must be given to the Duchesse de Berry except by him, and the Duc and Duchesse d'Orléans had given express orders to this effect.

Meanwhile the Duchesse de Berry felt so much better that she seemed to be almost cured, and Chirac was afraid that he would be put to shame. He chose a moment when Garus was asleep upon a sofa, and then with his usual impetuosity and without saying a word of what he was doing to anyone, he gave the Duchesse de Berry a purge. The only people in the room were two nurses who had been engaged to wait upon her, and they were too much afraid of Chirac to oppose him.

The wickedness of this behaviour was only equalled by its audacity, since both the Duc and Duchesse d'Orléans were in the drawing-room at La Meute at the time. From the moment the purge was administered the Duchesse de Berry almost at once became even worse than she had been before she had first been given the elixir. Garus was summoned. As soon as he saw his patient's condition he cried out that she must have been given a purge, which, whatever it contained, was sheer poison to the Princess in her condition. He said that he would leave. Efforts were made to restrain him, and he was taken to the Duc and Duchesse d'Orléans. Uproar followed. Garus protested, while Chirac with the utmost impudence and boldness stood by what he had done. He could not deny what he had done because the two nurses had been questioned and had told the whole story.

As the debate continued the Duchesse de Berry drew nearer to her end, and neither Chirac nor Garus could now do anything for her. Nevertheless she lasted out the day and did not die till nearly midnight. When the agony grew even more severe Chirac walked across the room and, with a bow towards the foot of the bed, which in itself was an insult, he wished her a happy journey, or words to that effect, and went off to Paris. The extraordinary thing was that in spite of what had happened he remained on as good terms with the Duc d'Orléans as he had been previously.

Ever since the Duc d'Orléans's carelessness, if I may use this expression in place of a stronger word, in speaking to the Duchesse de Berry about a piece of advice which I had given him instead of profiting from it, she had conceived such a hatred for me (and this had occurred in the early days of her marriage) that I had hardly seen her except on rare occasions when it was absolutely necessary, or if such occasions did not arise, then at the outside once or twice a year in public for a minute or so at a time.

However, seeing the end was near, and also that there was no one at La Meute with whom the Duc d'Orléans could speak freely, Mme de Saint-Simon sent me word, advising me to come and be near the Duc d'Orléans at so sad a time. It seemed to me that my presence did in fact give him pleasure, and that, as he was able to relax with me, my visit was not entirely useless. Except for one or two visits to her bedroom he passed the rest of the day almost entirely with me. In the evening I was alone with him almost all the time. He told me that, on the Duchesse de Berry's death, he wished me to take complete charge; that I must see to any post-mortem examination that might be necessary; that if by any chance she happened to be with child I must be responsible for keeping the matter secret; and that he did not wish to be worried with any details, to be asked for any orders or to take any decisions in regard to her funeral and so forth.

He spoke to me very affectionately and with the utmost confidence; he said that he did not wish me to come to him for any instructions; and then he told all those of the Princess's Household who happened to be assembled there that he had given me his orders, and that it was for me, who had received his instructions, to give directions on every point which might arise. In addition to this he told me that he no longer looked upon Mme de Mouchy, with her ridiculous post of Second Lady of the Wardrobe, as forming part of the Household; that she had ruined his daughter's reputation and plundered her (and here he did not forget to mention the case of rings which he had taken from her); that he charged both me and Mme de Saint-Simon to see to it that she was not allowed to return to La Meute, supposing by any chance she attempted to do so, and still less to fulfill any functions or to drive in any of the carriages which might accompany the body to Saint-Denis or the heart to Val-de-Grâce.

I suggested to the Duc d'Orléans that it would be better if no ceremonial guard were mounted round the body; that there should be no holy water or any other ceremony; that the convoy should be decent but as simple as possible; and that above all at Saint-Denis, where the usual ceremony could not possibly be avoided, there should be no

The Duc d'Orléans is grief-stricken

funeral sermon. Very lightly I touched upon my reasons. He saw them at once, thanked me, agreed that all should be as I said, and that I had better give instructions for everything to be carried out in the way I suggested. I passed over all matters having to do with the funeral as quickly as I could, and I walked him successively through all the rooms in turn, right up to where the last one gives upon the garden, and thus so far as I was able kept him out of reach of the death-chamber.

As the evening wore on, and the Duchesse de Berry grew steadily worse, as she had done ever since Chirac had poisoned her, and lost consciousness, the Duc d'Orléans went into her room again and approached the head of her bed. The curtains were all drawn back. I only left him there for a few minutes, and then I pushed him into the study which was empty. The windows were open. He leant against the iron balustrade and wept so bitterly that I was afraid he would choke. When the first paroxysm had almost passed, he began to speak to me of the sorrows of this world and of how short a time even the most agreeable things can last. I took this opportunity to deliver the message God had given me to say, as gently, as soothingly, as tenderly as ever I could, and not only did he receive what I said very well, but he kept on prolonging the conversation.

After we had been there over an hour Mme de Saint-Simon advised me quietly that it was time for me to take the Duc d'Orléans away, as we could not leave this study except by way of the death-chamber. Mme de Saint-Simon had already taken care to send for the Duc d'Orléans's coach, and it was ready waiting for him. However, he was plunged so bitterly in sorrow that it was only with some difficulty that I succeeded at last in dragging him away. Nevertheless I succeeded in getting him to walk through the bedroom and then begged him to go to Paris. This meant another struggle, but in the end he yielded. He wished me to remain behind to see to all the orders that might be necessary, and with the greatest politeness he begged Mme de Saint-Simon to be present when the seals were fixed. After this I put him into his coach and he drove off. I told Mme de Saint-Simon exactly what the Duc d'Orléans wanted done about opening up the body, so that she might see to it, and for the rest I did what I could to prevent her staying any longer within sight of that room which now contained nothing but horror.

At last at about midnight on the 21st of July, the Duchesse de Berry died, two days after the commission of Chirac's crime. The only person to be affected by her death was the Duc d'Orléans. A few of those who lost their places were no doubt sorry, but even among them those who had nothing at all to live on seemed hardly to regret her loss. The Duchesse d'Orléans felt chiefly a great relief, though she observed all the decencies of sorrow. Madame hardly troubled to conceal her joy. Moreover, great as was the Duc d'Orléans's grief, consolation was not long in coming. The yoke under which he had placed himself so completely, but which he had often found so heavy, was broken. Above all he was relieved to find himself free from all the terrors surrounding the public declaration of the marriage between his daughter and Rioms, and from all that might have followed—an embarrassment that would have been greater even than he knew since it was discovered at the post-mortem that the poor Princess was with child. It was also found that her brain was to some extent deranged. All this promised nothing but trouble and was carefully hushed up at the time.

At about five o'clock in the morning, that is to say about five hours after the Princess's death, La Vrillière arrived at La Meute, where, in the presence of Mme de Saint-Simon, he applied the seals. As soon as this was done, she got into her coach with him beside her (those who were necessary to perform the various duties of sealing followed in La Vrillière's coach) and went off to do the same at Meudon and then at the Luxembourg. Thence they went on to the Palais Royal to report to the Duc d'Orléans what they had done. After this Mme de Saint-Simon returned to La Meute, where a still more cruel night awaited her. I mean the post-mortem, at which she was compelled by her duties to be present. After this I went off to the Duc d'Orléans to tell him what had passed and assure him that his orders had been carried out.

When the post-mortem was over, the body was laid, without a ceremonial guard, in the chapel at La Meute, where low Masses were said every morning. I went to stay at Passy with M. and Mme de Lauzun, so that, without being officially at La Meute, I might yet be near at hand. From there, even when there was no Regency Council, I went in to see the Duc d'Orléans almost every day. As there was no ceremonial, no one was obliged to wear mantles or cloaks of any kind at the Palais Royal. One went in mourning but in ordinary clothes. There was no will, and the Duchesse de Berry made no gifts to anyone, apart from those which Mme de Mouchy had succeeded in extracting from her. The Duchesse de Berry had been in receipt of 700,000 livres a year, and since the Regency she had not had to call upon the Duc d'Orléans for anything.

During the evening of Saturday, the 22nd of July, the Abbé de Castries took the heart to Val-de-Grâce, having on his left Mlle de la Roche-sur-Yon, with Mme de Saint-Simon in front and the Duchesse de Louvigny representing the King, Mme de Brassac, the Duchesse de

Berry's Lady of the Wardrobe, at one door, and, which was very strange, the Lady-in-Waiting of the Princesse de Conti, Mlle de la Roche-sur-Yon's mother, at the other. The King's mourning lasted six weeks; that at the Palais Royal, out of respect for the Duchesse de Berry's rank, three months, and Mme de Saint-Simon draped her coaches for six months, because, as we have seen earlier, out of an excess of good nature, she had always done so in the past on occasions when the Duc de Berry was draping and the King not.

On Sunday, the 23rd of July, at about ten o'clock in the evening, the body of the Duchesse de Berry was placed in a coach drawn by eight fully caparisoned horses. There were no hangings at La Meute. The Abbé de Castries and the priests followed in another coach, and the Duchesse de Berry's Ladies were in a third. There were only forty torches, and these were borne by the Princess's pages and guards. Very simply the convoy went its way through the Bois de Boulogne and the plain of Saint-Denis, and with an equal simplicity it was received in the Abbey Church.

The previous evening the Duc d'Orléans told me, without my having said a word to him about it, that the King would continue to pay Mme de Saint-Simon her full salary, that is to say 21,000 livres a year. I thanked him, and at the same time told him that he would be doing Mme de Saint-Simon and myself a great favour if he were to continue paying all the Duchesse de Berry's Ladies their salaries. He agreed to this at once. After that I asked for the same favour to be granted to the First Chambermaid, who was a most meritorious young woman, and I obtained this too.

On leaving the Palais Royal I went to La Meute to tell Mme de Saint-Simon what I had done. She at once sent a message to all the Ladies, asking them to come to her room, and saying that I was there and wished to have a word with them. In playful malice I refused to say a word until all were assembled. Then I told them what the Regent had done for them, and also that they would be allowed to retain their apartments in the Luxembourg. At this there was great and unconstrained delight, and I was heartily embraced on all sides. I advised them all to go and thank the Duc d'Orléans next day. This they did, and were very graciously received. At the same time Mme de Saint-Simon gave up her apartment in the Luxembourg with a request that it might be granted to Mlle de Langey and her brothers, to whom it had previously belonged. This was agreed to.

A request from Mme de Mouchy was sent to the Duc d'Orléans, asking for an audience, but he refused to see her, and sent her to La Vrillière. She went to see him with her husband, and promptly received orders to leave Paris within the next twenty-four hours and not to come back. Years later they returned but, whatever they did, nothing was able to re-establish them in the eyes of the world or to rescue them from the obscurity, contempt, and neglect into which they had fallen.

The state of mind of Rioms when he heard the terrible news in the army in Spain may be imagined. What an end to an adventure that had once seemed romantically to promise all that even the most fantastic ambition could conceive. More than once he was on the point of taking his life, and for a long while after this his friends who were sorry for him were careful always to keep him within sight. Soon after the end of the campaign he sold his regiment and his governorship. As he had always been well-mannered and polite to his friends they stood by him and he consoled himself by dining and wining them. But basically he remained a light-weight, and it became an obsession with him.

The memorial service for the Duchesse de Berry was held at Saint-Denis with the usual ceremony, but without a sermon, early in September.

Mme de Saint-Simon, as I have said, was forced to become Lady-in-Waiting to the Duchesse de Berry, and I had no alternative but to agree; furthermore she was never able to find an excuse for resigning this unhappy position. Everyone was very kind to her and she was given all possible freedom, but this could not make up for the necessity of holding a position she did not want; in consequence she felt nothing but pleasure and satisfaction at her unexpected deliverance from the service of a princess no more than twenty-four years old. Nevertheless the strain of the last few days of the illness and the events after the death brought on a malignant fever. For six weeks she stayed in a house which Fontanieu had lent us so that she could enjoy the air and the waters of Forges. Her condition was serious, and it was two months before she was herself again. This attack almost sent me crazy with anxiety, and I was out of everything for two months; I hardly left the house, I hardly left her room, I heard nothing of what was going on, and, except for one or two very close relations and friends, I saw no one all that time. When she began to get better I asked the Duc d'Orléans for an apartment in the new Château[1] at Meudon. He gave me what I asked for and the rooms were fully furnished. We spent the rest of the summer there, and have spent many others there since. It is a charming place, specially for excursions of all kinds. We

---

[1] Which Monsiegneur had built by the side of the old Château of Le Tellier.

had meant to see only a few friends, but being so near we were overwhelmed with visitors and the new Château was often entirely full
without counting those who were merely passing through.

THE DUC AND DUCHESSE DU MAINE

MME du Maine was now given permission to go and live in a château
near Chalons-sur-Saône[1] and went there in the charge of La Billarderie;
the Duc du Maine was given permission to go hunting round Doullens,
without leave to sleep away from his prison. At the same time the
secretary of Prince Cellamare, who had been given permission to go
back to Spain, was arrested en route at Orléans and clapped into the
Château de Saumur.

This was because the Duchesse du Maine had at last started to talk
and had admitted a great deal, perhaps in order to avoid disclosing
much more; for, as I said at the beginning of this affair, for reasons
which have never been clear to me the Duc d'Orléans never seemed
to know much about what was going on; he overlooked more than he
noticed, and the Abbé Dubois only told his master things which he
could not hope to keep to himself and he invariably kept to himself
anything which did not accord with the line he himself was taking.
Mme du Maine finally made a confession, in the form of a short
memorandum which she signed and sent to the Duc d'Orléans, that
the Spanish project had in fact been true; she named as her accomplices those whom I have already mentioned, though she assigned
them very varying degrees of responsibility. In this memorandum
she referred very contemptuously to Pompadour and various other
unimportant people who were arrested, and confirmed the Duc de
Richelieu's intention of handing over Bayonne to the Spaniards in the
hope of being given the Regiment of Guards; de Saillans, who also
commanded a regiment, was involved and Boisdavid came in for much
blame.[2] She named Laval as being more deeply involved in the plot
than anyone else; he, she said, was the chief go-between who enjoyed
the confidence of those members of the nobility who were in her party.
Finally she said that the intention had been to raise a revolt in Paris
and the provinces, to declare the King of Spain Regent and place his

---

[1] Incarceration in the fortress in Chalons itself, whence she had been moved from
Dijon, had affected her health and she asked if she might live in the country.

[2] In fact Mme du Maine made no reference in her confession to Richelieu, Saillans or
Boisdavid—actually, the last-named had never met her.

1719 nominee at the head of their troops—these moves were to have been quickly registered with the various *Parlements*; and that a large working party had been formed in Brittany—the terms were that the nobles there should have restored to them all the privileges they had enjoyed under Anne of Brittany and the two successive kings who were married to her—Charles VIII and Louis XII—in return for which they would welcome any troops the King of Spain cared to send and would place Port-Louis completely at his disposal.[1] Various Bretons were named, none of whom I knew except one or two members of the Paris and Rennes *Parlements* and I don't think that the Duc d'Orléans knew them either. If she made any charges against various members of the Court, who were in a state of obvious trepidation but were not in fact arrested, it never came to my ears.

When he was faced with this confession in the Bastille, Laval was furious with the Duchesse du Maine, calling her all sorts of names, and protesting that she was the last person in the world he would ever have suspected of such infamous conduct as to betray her friends; that for ten or twelve years, though he had seen but little of her in public, he had been with her a great deal in private; and that it was she who had first persuaded him to embark upon this business. In his anger he gave many fresh details of the conspiracy, but these details never reached my ears, or indeed the ears of anyone except the Duc d'Orléans. Only one little thing became known: that was that one night after she had dined at the Arsenal Mme du Maine went to an assignation with Cellamare without servants, without torches, with her close friends before and behind and Laval as coachman; they were run into by another coach, had the greatest difficulty in disentangling themselves and even more in hushing the affair up.

It was these confessions which earned M. and Mme du Maine some degree of liberty and put the secretary of Cellamare in Saumur. They also began the comedy between them which made one wonder who was fooling whom. These confessions were accompanied by the strongest assertions and protestations that the Duc du Maine was ignorant of every word in the business; that the conspirators were so afraid of his natural timidity that they took good care he should not even guess what was in progress—in her efforts to save him she did not spare his feelings; that if he had known he would have put a stop to the project at once, and very possibly have been so terrified that he would have given the whole thing away; that their worst embarrassment had been this necessity for keeping him in the dark; and that this

---

[1] Saint-Simon's version of this part of the confession is much exaggerated.

368

had often delayed and sometimes upset their plans for rendezvous, and had made it necessary for them to cut their meetings as short as possible. The Duc du Maine was not at all pleased when he learned of the things which the Duchess had said of him.

The Duc d'Orléans told me all this before he addressed the Regency Council. In speaking to me he made as if to despise the whole conspiracy, and to laugh at the little comedy husband and wife were playing, of the irritation of the Duc du Maine and of the use the Duchess was making of his feelings in the matter, of his sex and of his birth, in the certain knowledge that she would get what she wanted. I merely smiled and replied somewhat disdainfully that I would bet on her winning in the end because there was nothing in the world so easy to convince as a man who was set on being convinced; and with that I changed the subject. . . .

THE KING'S NEW HOUSE

THE Duc d'Orléans now offered the King a present most suitable for his age, which was to take over La Meute as a place for his amusement, and as a house to which he might invite his friends for a meal. The King was delighted. It was as if at last he had something which was really his own. He enjoyed going there, and he enjoyed the bread and milk and the fruit and the vegetables immensely. Above all he enjoyed there the amusements proper to his age. In changing its owner the house also changed its governor. The Duc d'Humières suggested Pezé to me, and I had him appointed. He knew how to manage things so that he became more and more agreeable to the King. He was also made Captain of the Bois de Boulogne, as Rioms had had both positions before him.

THE MISSISSIPPI AGAIN

LAW's bank and his Mississippi Scheme now reached the crest of the wave. Confidence in him was complete. Everyone was rushing to change real estate into paper, and the result of all this paper was inflationary prices of even the smallest commodity. Everyone had lost his head. Foreigners were envious of our good fortune, and doing all they could to get in on it. Even the English, past masters as they are in banking, commerce, and company matters, allowed themselves to be caught —and to be caught again soon after.[1] Law, though normally cool and

---

[1] The Mississippi Scheme and the South Sea Bubble both collapsed in 1720.

wise, began to lose some of his modesty. He grew tired of his subordinate position. Amid all this splendour he had set his cap at something greater,[1] and the Abbé Dubois and the Duc d'Orléans were even more in favour of the appointment.

However, this could not be done until two obstacles had been removed; he was a foreigner, and he was a heretic, and the first of these conditions could only be changed by naturalization, which would not be granted without a preliminary abjuration.[2] For the purpose of Law's conversion a man was needed who would not look too closely into matters which did not concern him, and who would be known to be safe before any compromising proposals were made to him. The Abbé Dubois had such a man already, as they say, up his sleeve. This fellow was the Abbé Tencin,[3] whom the devil has since pushed forward to such surprising fortunes. Indeed it sometimes seems as if the devil every now and then departs from his usual methods, and rewards his own, so that by one or two outstanding examples he may mislead others, and gain their souls. However this may be, the present example is so extraordinary that I propose to go into it at some length.

Well, this Abbé Tencin was a beggarly priest, the great-grandson of a goldsmith, and the son and brother of various presidents in the *Parlement* of Grenoble. Guérin was his name, and Tencin that of a small estate which served to supply names to the whole family. There were two sisters: one, who spent her life in Paris, mixing in the best company, and who married a certain Ferriol,[4] who is very little known, but who is the brother of that Ferriol who was Ambassador in Constantinople and who never married: the other sister[5] was for many years a professed nun in a convent of the Augustines at Montfleury, near Grenoble. Both were beautiful and agreeable. Mme Ferriol had more sweetness and more gallantry, the other had more intelligence and a greater capacity for intrigue and debauchery. The latter was so

---

[1] i.e., Controller General of Finance.

[2] Law did in fact take out papers in May 1716, so that the first obstacle, that of naturalization may be said to have been overcome; but he did not register at the Chambre des Comtes so that his status could have been annulled or at least challenged. In 1718 there was some talk of his conversion, but Law later denied that.

[3] Pierre Guérin de Tencin, born at Grenoble on the 22nd of August 1679. He became Cardinal and was brother of the famous Mlle de Tencin. It is typical of Saint-Simon to deny him the 'de.'

[4] Marie-Angélique Guérin de Tencin, who married Augustin de Ferriol, Comte de Pont-de-Veyle. Her relations with Vauban, Huxelles, Torcy, and Bolingbroke are well known; her literary salon was also famous and frequented by Voltaire among others. She died in 1737.

[5] Claudine-Alexandrine Guérin de Tencin, the famous Mme de Tencin, born 27 April 1682, died 4 December 1749.

lovely that very soon the best company at Grenoble used to flock out to see her at her convent, where the facility of entry and the general looseness of conduct were such that all the care of Cardinal le Camus was unable to repress them. Nothing contributed more to this state of affairs than the pleasure and convenience of arriving there after one of the loveliest drives round Grenoble, which in itself was so charming a spot; all the best families of the city always had one or two daughters living there as nuns.

In spite of all these pleasures, of which she availed herself to the full, Mlle de Tencin found the few chains she wore too heavy.[1] She had many visitors and her success was as great as it could possibly have been anywhere. But a nun's habit, a shadow of discipline (it was little more), a cloister, even though freely visited by both sexes but from which she was only occasionally allowed to stray, seemed to one who was longing to plunge into deeper waters, and who knew that she had within her a talent for intrigue which could make her a person of importance, an intolerable restraint. On top of all this came pressing reasons for hiding the results of certain pleasures from a community, which could hardly avoid being scandalized by disorders of such notoriety (or from acting in consequence), which hastened her desire to escape from the convent under whatever pretext she could, and her firm determination never to return there again.

The hearts of the Abbé Tencin and his sister, if either of them may be said to have possessed a heart, were so alike as to be really one. All her life he was her confidant as she was his. His intelligence and his gifts for intrigue served her so well that he was able for many years to uphold her in a life of fashion, of pleasure and of debauchery, in which he played his own part to the full, both in the provinces and in Paris. Indeed, under the name of 'Tencin, the Nun' she created a great stir in the world both by her intelligence and by her adventures. Brother and sister always lived together, and they managed so skilfully that it never occurred to anyone to raise an objection to the fact that it was a professed nun who was living this vagabond and libertine life, or even to the fact that she had no one's authority but her own for putting aside the veil.[2] One might write a book about this fine pair, who nevertheless, thanks to their pleasant looks and cunning ways,

---

[1] She was placed in this convent at the age of eight, and then was forced by her parents to take vows in 1698 when she was barely sixteen. The very next day she managed to see a notary and swear an affidavit that she had taken the vows under pressure, an affidavit which she swore again four years later, in 1702.

[2] She seems to have left her convent in 1708 and not to have been finally dispensed from her vows until 1712.

made many friends. Towards the end of the late King's life they had managed to obtain from Rome a dispensation to change her state, and so from being a nun she became a canoness of some place or other which she never visited. This solution of her difficulties was quite imperceptible either in her name, her clothes, or her conduct; it made no difference and it attracted no attention. Such was her status at the time of the late King's death. A short while afterwards she became the mistress of the Abbé Dubois, and soon afterwards his confidante and the directress of most of his designs and secrets. This remained a secret for some time, just so long as the Abbé Dubois still needed to take some care of his reputation. But when he became an archbishop, still more when he became a Cardinal, she was openly his mistress, ruling his household, and holding court as if she were the sole fountain of grace and fortune. It was during this time that she set to work upon the career of her beloved brother. She introduced him to her secret lover who quickly recognized him as a man perfectly suited to carry out his wishes and who indeed was extremely useful to him.

The Abbé Tencin was a bold and enterprising man, so much so that he was often considered to have a vast and masculine intelligence. He had enough patience to last for several lifetimes. Whatever the end he had in view he worked for it indefatigably, never turning to right or left and never discouraged by any difficulty. His mind was so fertile and resourceful that he falsely acquired the reputation for great ability. He was infinitely supple, infinitely discriminating, and infinitely discreet. He could be gentle or tough to suit his purpose. He was capable, without effort, of adapting any form which suited his desires; he was a past master in artifice; and he knew no restraint. He had a sovereign contempt both for honour and for religion, though he took the greatest care to respect the conventions of both. Proud or abject according to the situation or the people with whom he had to deal, he could be both with intelligence and discernment. No taste or temperament could deflect him from his course to which he held with an unbounded ambition. He loved money, not from avarice nor from any desire for spending or display, but as the only means of raising himself from his lowly origins. To good manners and pleasant abilities in conversation he added some smattering of learning, and to his singular good temper the great art of hiding what he did not wish to reveal, and a masterly judgement in choosing between the various means and courses which might help him towards his end. It was therefore no marvel if, with his sister to introduce him and to second him, a sister who was the mistress of the reigning minister, he was taken up by this minister with whom he had so much in common and whose need of him was so urgent.

372

Such was the apostle chosen by Dubois for the proselyte Law. The introductions were soon made. The sister in whose financial affairs Law had personally taken an interest from the beginning of Dubois's affair with her, had taken good care to make a friend of him. At this period in her life she was no longer much given to debauchery, except where interest and ambition were concerned, though perhaps old habits still influenced her to some extent. She was too intelligent not to see that at her age and in her condition personal ambition could not take her far. She therefore turned all her hopes upon her darling brother. She saw to it that his pockets were stuffed by Law, and as soon as they were full she took good care that he quickly changed his paper into gold.

Such was the state of affairs when it became necessary to gather to the fold of the Church this Protestant or Anglican, for Law himself did not know what he really was. As you may imagine the work was not a difficult one. However, they had the good sense to conduct the whole affair in secret, so that it was some while before it leaked out at all. In this way they saved appearances so far as the time of instruction was concerned, and at least some of the scandal and ridicule attaching to a conversion, brought about by such a converter, was avoided.

Clever as he was at hiding his tracks, the Abbé Tencin's debaucheries and adventures at the low level from which he had started had covered him with dishonour. Moreover his reputation had suffered deeply from that of his sister and of his closeness to her. It was more than he had been able to do to keep all their adventures from the public eye, and certain facts had leaked out about some traffic in benefices. Moreover it was generally known, though without any details, that he had received immense sums from Law. Try as he might, he had not quite succeeded in hiding his pernicious talents from the world, and he was held to be little better than a dangerous rogue, whose subtle intelligence and social graces had made him popular in society, where he was tolerated by those who knew him and even sought after by those who, not realizing his true character, were easily taken in by his pleasant exterior.

Chosen by the Abbé Dubois to succeed Lafitou and to go to Rome to expedite the business of his Cardinal's hat which was still highly secret, he refused to settle out of court a lawsuit brought against him by the Abbé Veissière for simony and for pocketing part of the proceeds from the sale of a priory. . . .

Anyone but the Abbé Dubois would have changed his agent after this. However, Tencin suited him so exactly and his talents were of a kind so unlikely to be found elsewhere that, in order to get him out of the way, he sent him off next day and thus avoided much of the talk which his presence might otherwise have created. No doubt Dubois was right. It was not from merit or virtue that he was hoping to receive the purple. His negotiator was the best man he knew for spending money to its best advantage, as well as for the conduct of intrigue and business negotiations, and it was on them that all the hopes of Dubois were laid.

AN IRISH MARRIAGE

THE Duc d'Orléans, untiring as ever in making new presents and in incurring fresh ingratitude, gave more than 400,000 livres to the Maréchale de Rochefort, Lady-in-Waiting to the Duchesse d'Orléans; 100,000 to her son-in-law, Blanzac; as much to her granddaughter, the Comtesse de Tonnerre; 300,000 to La Chastre; as much to the Duc de Tresmes; 200,000 to Rouillé de Coudray, Councillor of State, who had been the moving spirit in the Finances under Noailles; 150,000 to the Chevalier de Marcieu; and to so many others, whose names I have forgotten or never known, that they cannot even be numbered—all of this apart altogether from what his mistresses and his rakes extorted from him by day or extracted from his pockets by night. All these gifts were made in paper, which was at that time still worth its face value in gold, and which most people even preferred.

This thirst for money was now responsible for a curious marriage between the Prince d'Auvergne, which was the name by which the Chevalier de Bouillon had been known for some time, and a certain Mlle Trant, an Englishwoman, who professed to be of gentle birth, and to live in Paris because of her religion.[1] She had as a matter of fact long ago succeeded in worming her way into the good graces of Mme d'Alègre, whom I have mentioned more than once in these pages. In the beginning Mme d'Alègre had received her out of charity, but she had been charmed by her prattle and kept her with her for years. It was not, however, long before the young woman became

---

[1] Catherine Olive Trant, an Irishwoman whose family was of Danish origin, was the daughter of Sir Patrick Trant, Bart., of Dingle, County Kerry, who followed James II into exile in France in 1688 and lost his considerable fortune by doing so. He died at the Château de la Tour, Auvergne, in 1696, which shows that the friendship between the Trants and the Bouillons was well established. Catherine married the Prince d'Auvergne at midnight on 16 January 1720; the King signed the marriage contract. She became a widow in 1733 and died in 1738 at the age of fifty.

known for her intrigues, her supple, pliant, enterprising and bold intelligence, and above all by her practical bids for fortune. She was
one of the first to receive a large batch of Mississippi shares from Law,
and when she had them she knew how to use them to her advantage.

It was her large fortune which attracted the Prince d'Auvergne,
who had run through all his money and was bent on marrying, though
up to now he had not found a suitable match. Neither the notorious
contempt into which his debauchery and curious adventures had
brought him, nor his poverty deterred the English adventuress. The
marriage took place, to the great displeasure of the Bouillon family.
From that day on she led her husband by the nose, and with him made
an immense fortune out of Mississippi shares. In spite of this he left
little when he died, for his wife was accused of having artfully got him
to lend her all his investments and then hoarded them away. Be that
as it may, they were lost to the husband and his relations with no
means of claiming against the wife who remained on bad terms with
the whole family, and had no surviving children.[1] She tried hard both
during her husband's life and after his death to become socially
prominent but was universally rejected out of mistrust. She fell back
on devotions, philosophy and chemistry, which killed her in the end,
and brilliant conversation in her own small circle.

MY RELATIONS WITH FLEURY

I AM reminded that I ought before this to have said something about
the relations between Fleury, the Bishop of Fréjus, and myself. During
the reign of the late King our ways and the society we kept had always
been very different, and although we had plenty of friends in common
we had hardly known one another. On the other hand there was no ill-
feeling between us, and we were always polite to one another when we
met. Towards the end of his last visit to Court, shortly before the death
of the King, I used to meet him fairly often at Mme de Saint-Géran's
house. At that time he was lobbying quietly for the position of royal
tutor, and he evidently thought that I would have some weight under
the Regency which the state of the King's health made one realize
could not then be far away. I thought that he was wooing me, but he
did it subtly and I answered civilly, but our conversation did not
progress beyond pleasant generalities.

When he had resigned his bishopric and become tutor we found

[1] She bore two sons, but both died in infancy.

ourselves occupied in different ways, and his being at Vincennes was another separation; for some months after the King's return to Paris we scarcely met and then only had occasion to exchange civilities. I had reason to believe that M. de Fréjus was not satisfied with this.

We have already seen the part which Mme de Lévis played in making Fleury tutor. She was a most intelligent woman, but temperamentally so excitable that she was incapable of judging either people or things except through her emotions. At the time of which I am speaking she had a craze for Monsieur de Fréjus which amounted to a mania—but perfectly honourable, for in spite of all her transports of extreme likes and dislikes, she was fundamentally as honourable, as virtuous, as religious, and as decorous a woman as you could find. She was a daughter of the late Duc de Chevreuse, consequently a dear friend of mine, and always in the closest touch with Mme de Saint-Simon.

We were talking one evening when she got onto the subject of Monsieur de Fréjus and chid me for not liking him. I said I was surprised because really I had no reason either for liking or not liking him, that during the last days of the late King when her friendship with him was forming she was in fact almost the only person among my friends who knew him; that since the Regency we had both been very busy in different directions and had had no chance to meet. She was not satisfied, however, and returned to the charge. This made me think that she was acting in concert with Monsieur Fréjus, and that he, though keeping in the background, was busy removing all possible obstacles from his path. I said something polite about him because I had no reason to do anything else, and after that he began to make advances to me. We had a short conversation in the King's presence and then a few days later he called on me just before dinner and asked me to dine with him.

From this time on he would often come to see me, sometimes for dinner, and sometimes, too, I used to visit him in the evenings. He was, as I have said elsewhere, always good company and an excellent talker, and his whole life had been passed in good society. As we came to see more of one another we used to discuss all manner of subjects together.

Not long after he had entered upon his duties as tutor to the young King I happened to be with him rather late one evening, when a packet was brought in to him. It was, as I say, late, and he was sitting by the fire in his dressing gown with a nightcap on his head. I therefore wished to take my leave in order to leave him free to open his packet. He prevented me, saying that the packet contained nothing beyond the

young King's Latin exercises which he always sent to the Jesuits to
be done.[1] This showed common sense, as, except for his knowledge
of the great world, the gossip of the bed-chamber and the latest affaires, he was a very ignorant man. However, I took up the words
'Latin exercises' as if I disapproved of them, and asked him if he
meant to drill much Latin into the head of the young King. He said
that he did not, but only enough to make it clear that he was not
entirely ignorant of that tongue, and we had no difficulty in agreeing
that history, especially the national and international history of France,
was what it was most desirable that he should learn. At this point an
idea came into my head—an idea which I immediately passed on to
Fleury. This was a method for teaching the King a thousand little
details of our history—details which it would at all times be valuable
to him to know—in a way which he would find diverting, but which
was also the only way in which he would ever learn them. I told him
that Gaignières, a learned and enquiring man, had devoted his whole
life to historical research and had, with great care, at his own expense,
and by means of much travelling, collected a great number of portraits
of those, both men and women, who in one way or another had played
a great part in the history of our country, especially at Court, in
Government or in the army, since the time of Louis XI, and that he
had also done the same, though in a smaller degree, for foreign countries. I told him that I had often been to Gaignières's house and seen
part of his collection, for although he had a vast house in which he
lived alone just opposite the Hospital for Incurables, he had so many
pictures that he did not know where to hang them all. And then I reminded him that Gaignières on his death-bed had left this curious collection to the King.

The King's study in the Tuileries had a door which opened onto a
fine and very long gallery which was entirely unfurnished. This door
had been walled up, and some of the gallery had been partitioned off
by plain boards to make a lodging for the Maréchal de Villeroy's
valets. I therefore suggested to Monsieur de Fréjus that the valets
should take rooms somewhere in the neighbourhood—a thousand
francs would practically have covered the expense—and that the com-
municating door into the King's study should be opened and the
walls of this gallery should be covered with Gaignières's portraits
which were then, for aught I knew, lying rotting in some cupboard.

****

[1] That is to say, he sent them to be corrected by the Jesuits at the Collège Louis-le-
Grand. Several exercise books of the King's Latin verses have survived in the Biblio-
thèque Nationale.

Moreover, I suggested that he should instruct the various tutors of all the little boys who used to come and wait upon the King to run over the lives of all these people in history, and then to impart their knowledge to their pupils so that the latter might discuss them among themselves as they followed the King round the gallery and thus arouse his interest, and finally that he, Monsieur de Fréjus, should make it his business to see that the King had full instruction also.

I pointed out that in this way the King would have a continuous picture of the development of history, and so might learn a thousand details which it would be useful for a King to know, and which he could hardly come by in any other way. In this way he would be struck by the individuality of features and clothing which would help him to remember the facts and the dates of these characters; that the emulation of the children among themselves would spur him on to know more of the subject and to master it better than the others; that neither religion nor politics demanded any restraint in speaking about the birth, fortunes, actions, or conduct of those who were dead; that they and all those who had to do with them could therefore be treated quite freely; that in this way, little by little, the King might come to learn the services and disservices such men had rendered, and the various crimes and rogueries of which they had been guilty; that he might see how fortunes are made and lost, and learn the artful manœuvres whereby men have achieved their ends, have deceived, have governed, and have muzzled Kings, have made parties and creatures in their own interests, and have neglected merit, intelligence, capacity, and virtue in the process—in short that he might thus become acquainted with the ways of Courts for which the lives of all these men and women would provide him with an abundance of examples.

I suggested that this amusement might be continued right up to the time of Henry IV; that the King should then be placed upon his honour where those who came after that date were concerned and told that their discussion was for his ear alone, since their descendants and relations were still alive, although as there were also many who now had no descendants the other little boys might be allowed to hear them discussed just as they had heard their forerunners. Finally I said that to do this would be to fill the King's head with a thousand historical facts; that he would learn without even being aware that he was receiving instruction; that nevertheless, considering what part he would have to play in the future, this instruction might well be one of the most valuable he could receive; that the sight of these portraits would be a continual reminder of what he had learnt, and moreover help him to acquire a facility in the more serious, more continuous

The Abbé Tencin's sister entertains

study of history later, because wherever he looked he would always
be among men of his acquaintance, from the times of Louis XI onwards; and that this familiarity with the past would be acquired without the revolt that comes from class-room study and merely going out
and about and being amused.

Monsieur de Fréjus told me that he was charmed by this suggestion,
and that it pleased him enormously. However, he did nothing about
it, and from that time forward I began to see what would happen to
the King's education, and I spoke no more to Monsieur de Fréjus
either of the portraits or the gallery, where the Maréchal de Villeroy
remained unmoved.

Pezé was a great friend of his, and seeing that I was on good terms
with him, Pezé suggested my trying to help in securing his election to
the College of Cardinals. I do not know if this was his own idea, or if
Monsieur de Fréjus had hinted that he would be pleased if he approached me. The two men were undoubtedly made to understand
one another without the need of explanations. Pezé was anxious that
the Duc d'Orléans should be kept in ignorance of these plans, because, as the business was bound to be a slow one, the Abbé Dubois
might grow stronger while we waited, and perhaps someone else
might have also arisen to bar the way for Fréjus. After thinking the
matter over, I decided I might explore the ground a little and then see
what to do next. I had long been on close terms with the Nuncio
Gualterio. Since his promotion to the purple and immediate departure
from this country he and I had been in the habit of writing each other
a weekly letter, as often as not in cypher. I told Pezé this, and said that
I might see how the land lay through Gualterio—not that the latter
had enough standing in Rome for us to be able to make use of him
directly; but he knew what was going on, and was well fitted to give
us advice. These manœuvres lasted several months, without very
much hope of success, until Pezé gave me a message from Fréjus, asking me to give up the whole affair, and saying that it was impossible
to keep the matter from the Duc d'Orléans and that it might do him
harm. The curious point about this is that Monsieur Fréjus never
spoke to me upon the subject but once, when he told me what he had
previously told Pezé to tell me, and thanked me most warmly for the
part I had played. He never mentioned the subject to me again, nor
did I to him. Nevertheless, this business drew us together, with the
result that he used to discuss everything quite freely with me, and
indeed until the day of his death continued to speak his mind to me
about people and public affairs to a degree which often surprised me.

PROPOSALS FOR THE DISMISSAL
OF VILLEROY

ONE day late in the year I was working with the Duc d'Orléans, when after about a quarter of an hour he suddenly broke off and began complaining about the Maréchal de Villeroy. He used to do this from time to time, but today he went further than usual. From strong words he worked himself up into such a rage that he jumped up from his seat and said that the position was unbearable (those were his exact words) and that he not only wished but intended to get rid of him, and that I should be Superintendent of the King's education. I was extremely surprised, but I did not lose my head. I began to smile and replied quietly that he was not thinking of what he was saying. 'What?' said he, 'I know very well what I am saying, so well that I intend to do it and not to put off any longer something which should have been done long ago. Now what have you got to say to that?' Then he began to walk or rather to spin like a top round his small winter study.

I asked him if he had really given the matter his mature consideration, whereupon he gave me all his reasons for getting rid of the Marshal, as well as those for putting me in his place, though the latter are too flattering to be reported here. When he had finished, I spoke in my turn and refused to be interrupted. It was impossible to deny any of the complaints against the Maréchal de Villeroy, and I therefore agreed with his arguments and with the conclusions he drew from them. Nevertheless I strongly opposed the Marshal's removal. To begin with I reminded the Duc d'Orléans of the reasons I had formerly put before him in favour of taking the King's education out of the hands of M. du Maine, of how sound he had considered these arguments both at the time and since, and that he was only yielding now to force and to the constant attacks of Monsieur le Duc. I pointed out the interests which Monsieur le Duc and the *Parlement* had in common and distinguished between those and personal differences between the Duc du Maine and himself; I touched on the dangers inherent in the setting aside of the late King's will, particularly in respect of someone who had been so dear to him. Then I went on to personalities; I made abundantly clear the difference between dismissing a man who, however great and well-established he might have been, was hated, envied, and abhorred not only by the Princes of the Blood but by the great majority and was a constant danger because of his intelligence, his views and his private party—and the dismissal of one who had equally enjoyed the recommendation of the dead King, who was no danger because he possessed neither intelligence nor merit, was admired by everyone, gave the appearance of being honest, had no ambition for power or political influence, and was respected by the *Parlement* and the magistrates; in a word, except so far as the opinion of the *Parlement* was concerned, everything about the Duc du Maine and the Maréchal de Villeroy was diametrically contrary.

The Duc d'Orléans, who of all men I have ever met was the readiest with an answer and, however bad his case, the least at a loss for a reply, was so surprised, either by the strength of my argument or the firmness of my refusal, that he could not find a word to say, and continued in thought, walking the eight or so paces up and down the room which was all that the smallness of his study allowed, his head sunk upon his breast. I remained standing, without either following him or saying a word. I left him to his own reflections, and as I had said everything that needed to be said I did not trouble him with vain repetitions. The silence lasted for some time. At last he told me that there was a good deal of truth in what I said but that the Maréchal de Villeroy had lately become so unbearable and I was so perfectly fitted to the post (he elaborated this point once more) that it pained him to have to change his mind. We went over the ground again several times, and he finally said that we would think about it again another time. I replied that so far as I was concerned I had thought about it, and that I would never be Superintendent of the King's education; I added that so far as the Marshal was concerned he should think very carefully about the motives of those interested in the matter, including himself, before he took what might prove to be a most unwise step. That was as far as we got. He returned to the subject two or three times afterwards, but with diminishing confidence.

1720

RELEASE OF THE DUC AND
DUCHESSE DU MAINE

❧❧❧❧❧ HE year opened with a ridiculous comedy—a comedy ❧ *T* ❧ which took in no one, either the public or those for whom ❧ ❧ it was principally played, or even the players themselves, ❧❧❧❧❧ except perhaps Madame la Princesse who was born to be everyone's dupe. The Duc and Duchesse du Maine, who, as we have already seen, had, thanks to the perfidy of the Abbé Dubois, been given all the time that they could wish and even more in which to save their papers and to make their own arrangements—and by this I refer to the time which elapsed between the arrest of Cellamare and their own arrest—had, each in consultation with the other, from the very outset mapped out the courses which they meant henceforth individually to pursue.

Strong in the immunity she enjoyed by sex and birth, Mme du Maine, in her reply to the interrogation to which she had been subjected (only as much of it as the Abbé Dubois had been pleased to pass had been read to the Regency Council) had at once taken the whole responsibility for the plot, had accused Cellamare, Laval, and one or two others, and had done everything she could think of to shield the two Malzieux, Dadvisard and all her more intimate followers. But above all she had set out to save her husband. With this object in view she therefore made herself entirely responsible for what he had done, and said that she had not even allowed him to know what was going on, or to realize that she had any communication with Spain, or had a party, or even that she was doing anything which might tend to disrupt the State or weaken the power of the Regent. Indeed, if we are to accept her account of the affair, all that the Duc du Maine had known was that she was organizing appeals strong and numerous enough to persuade the Regent to make various reforms in his administration on points which had given rise to general complaint. It made no difference to her what she confessed. She had no fear of losing her head, or even of a long or severe term of imprisonment. Princes of the House of Condé have from generation to generation behaved far worse than she had done, and the example of what had happened to them was there to reassure her.

The Duc du Maine, on the other hand, now that he had fallen from the condition and quality of a Prince of the Blood, went in fear of his life. When he thought of all his crimes against the State, against the Blood Royal and against the Regent, whom he had so long, so cunningly, and so cruelly injured, he was somewhat alarmed to realize that reason, justice, the need to make an example, duty towards the State and the Blood Royal, even plain vengeance, all influenced the Duc d'Orléans towards punishing him. Small wonder that he took cover behind his wife's petticoats. His replies and his avowals all showed complete ignorance, and, as he and she were acting in concert, his part was not a difficult one to play. He had in point of fact seen no one but their trustiest servants, and had hardly set eyes upon Cellamare, except on one or two occasions when, unknown to all the others, he had secretly received him alone in Mme du Maine's study. Moreover, his only go-between had been his wife, and there were no papers and no depositions in existence which he need be afraid of.

Thanks to this foresight, when finally Mme du Maine was forced to speak and to confess the whole story, when Laval, in his rage at her avowal, likewise confessed, and when one or two others followed suit, the Duc du Maine was able, on hearing the story at Doullens, to break out in a fury against the folly and wickedness of his wife and to complain of his ill-fortune in being tied to a woman who was not only capable of forming such a plot, but also brazen enough to include him in her plottings without telling him a word of what was going on and to make him appear a criminal when he was nothing of the kind, and indeed was so unsuspicious of her actions that it had been beyond his power to put a stop to them, to assert his authority, or even to warn the Duc d'Orléans when he finally discovered that things had gone so far that it had become his plain duty to do so.

From that moment the Duc du Maine refused to hear his wife's name mentioned, or to have anything further to do with a woman who, without his knowledge, had thrown him and his children deep into the abyss, and when on their release from prison they were allowed to write and to visit one another, he refused even to receive a message from her or to take any notice of her very existence. As for Mme du Maine, of course, she pretended to be deeply hurt by such treatment, though at the same time she admitted how greatly she was at fault in having embroiled him without his knowledge and deceived him as she had done. Such was their position when they were given permission to return to Paris. The Duc du Maine then went to live at Clagny, a château near Versailles which had been built for Mme de Montespan, and Mme du Maine went to Sceaux. They went straight to their respective destinations without stopping in Paris, and both kept up their parts; when the Abbé Dubois thought the time had come to end their disgrace, all was well with the Regent who kept up the fiction of the Duc du Maine's innocence.

During the period of living apart, each in his or her own château, very few visitors were received, but Mme du Maine made several approaches to her husband which were studiously rebuffed. This farce continued from January, when they arrived at Clagny and Sceaux, right up to the end of July. Then they decided that it had lasted long enough.

Nevertheless the quarrel was carried to such apparent lengths that, when the Duc du Maine's two sons came back from Eu to Clagny a few days after the return of their father, they were a long time without visiting their mother, and even then saw her but rarely and then without ever spending the night at Sceaux. However, as I have said, it was decided at last to be done with the comedy, and this is how they staged the final act. On the last day of July Madame la Princesse went by arrangement to meet the Duc du Maine at a house at Vaugirard belonging to Landais, the Paymaster of the Artillery. She arrived shortly after the Duc du Maine and was accompanied by the Duchesse du Maine, whom she left outside in the coach. Then she told the Duc du Maine that she had brought a lady with her, a lady who was most anxious to see him. The meaning of this was not obscure; an agreement was reached; and the Duchesse du Maine was invited to come in. Only those three were present throughout this apparent reconciliation, and they were together for a long time. Even after this the comedy was not quite over, and they still continued to live separately for a time. However, as they saw one another often the wound healed by degrees, and in the end the Duc du Maine returned to live at Sceaux with his wife.

During these six months the Bastille was gradually emptied of all those who had been imprisoned over this business, though a few of them were given a lenient form of exile for a time. Laval was the worst or, to put it more exactly, the least well treated. He had been the moving spirit of the conspiracy and party to every secret, or so the Duchess had said in her statements—that is to say in those portions of them which were read to the Regency Council, so that no one questioned his complete complicity. That was why he left the Bastille furious with the Duchesse du Maine and never forgave her. This troubled her exactly as much as Princes and Princesses are always troubled when they have no further need of a man, for they are all convinced that others should work on their behalf while they think only of themselves. Life is always the same; and conspiracies in every century exist to prove the truth of what I say and to point the appropriate moral.

THE FINANCIAL SITUATION

THE financial disorder grew worse day by day, as did the quarrels between Law and d'Argenson, who each blamed the other for what was taking place. Access to the former was still a pleasant business. His paper money was a sort of tap which he could turn off and on at will for those who were in a position to be of use to him. Monsieur le Duc, Madame la Duchesse, Lassay, Mme de Verue had drawn millions from him—indeed they were still doing so. The Abbé Dubois could draw whatever he liked. These were strong bulwarks, apart from the fact that the Duc d'Orléans was so fond of him that he refused to be parted from him.

Moreover, the fact that audiences with the Keeper of the Seals took place more often at night than during the day was a curse to all who worked under him or had business with him. The financial difficulties and his continual quarrels with Law had affected his temper and he was becoming more and more unhelpful. Things had come to such a pass that there was nothing for it but that one should hand over to the other the complete administration which their rivalry was only driving into greater confusion. Close and even intimate as were the relations existing between d'Argenson and Dubois, and hard as the latter had tried to persuade his allies to work in harmony, his longing for the purple and the amount of money it was necessary for him to spend in furthering that project, left him no choice in this extremity. Law's conversion had been carried out with one object in view and it was time that object was achieved. Law in fact was convinced that his scheme was sound, and, when he promised marvels as soon as he was free to go his own way, he did so in complete good faith.

D'Argenson saw the storm approaching; he realized that his position was no less precarious than it was elevated; and he wished to save it. He was too intelligent, he knew the world and those with whom he had to deal too well, not to realize that if he were over-stubborn about the Finances it would cost him the Seals. He consequently gave way to Law, who was thus at last proclaimed Controller General of Finance, and who, in spite of the extraordinarily elevated position in which he now found himself, continued to come and see me every Tuesday morning, and still did all he could to convince me of the miracles which had come to pass, and of others which were to come. D'Argenson remained Keeper of the Seals, and usefully consoled himself for his sacrifice in giving up the Finances by passing to his eldest son the office of Chancellor of the Order of Saint-Louis, with reversal to his younger son. His place as a Councillor of State, which he had kept, he gave to his elder son with the Stewardship of Mauberge; his younger son he made a lieutenant of police.

The sight of a foreigner being appointed Controller General and of everything in France being put at the mercy of a system about which many were beginning to have their doubts caused considerable disturbance. However, the French get used to everything in time, and most people consoled themselves with the thought that they would no longer be compelled to put up with the absurd working hours and bad temper of d'Argenson.

Law could not take cover behind his new post of Controller General when the Prince de Conti saw fit to put a pistol to his head. This Prince de Conti was greedier than any of his family, which is saying something. He had made a fortune out of the Regent's compliance and had drawn as much again privately from Law. Not content with this, he wanted more. In the end the Duc d'Orléans grew weary; moreover he had other reasons for being displeased with him. The *Parlement* was again starting its plotting—indeed those gentlemen had even dared to show their claws—and there was evidence that the Prince de Conti was trying to play some part in these intrigues which was not only unfitting in a man of his birth and unsuited to his age, but, considering the monstrous favours which had unceasingly been showered upon him, was utterly shameless. However, rebuffed by the Regent, he had greater hopes of Law, but in this he was deceived. There followed prayers and supplications, for there was no meanness to which he would not stoop for money, and when these proved ineffectual, they were followed by an attack in force in which Law was spared neither blame nor threats of vengeance. Indeed, so determined was the Prince de Conti to put the fear of God into him that, knowing his most effective weapon against Law to be a threat to overthrow his bank, he arrived one day with three waggons demanding cash for the vast amount of paper which he possessed. To refuse would have exposed the shortage of ready money, so Law complied, but as soon as the convoy had departed, fearing a repetition of the insults and tyranny of this insatiable prince, he went and complained to the Duc d'Orléans. The Regent was extremely irritated; he realized the serious consequences which might follow from this pernicious example of bringing pressure to bear on a foreigner of no standing whom he had so lightly made Controller General. He lost his temper, sent for the Prince de Conti, and, contrary to his usual habits, gave him such a dressing-down that the latter dared not say a word and was forced to ask for pardon. The Prince, annoyed more by the sharpness of the reprimand than at the miscarriage of his plans, sought solace in women. He went on lobbying against Law, who was no longer afraid of him, and his efforts did him little honour for the reason behind them was well known as well as the fact that he had already got a fortune out of Law. But blame was general and was a serious matter for Law, who was losing public confidence so fast that the smallest mishap could invoke resentment and indignation.

THE ROYAL BALLET

THE Maréchal de Villeroy was incapable of giving the King any worthwhile instruction; his head was full of his adoring memories of Louis XIV, of happy recollections of his own youth, his long-lost grace in fêtes and ballets, his many affaires, so that in imitation of the late monarch he wished the King to dance in a ballet. It was far too soon: it was much too onerous a pleasure for the King at that age, for his shyness should have been overcome little by little and he should have been conditioned gradually to the ways of the world of which he was terrified before being made to dance in public in a theatre. The late King was brought up at a court which was brilliant, splendid, and well ordered, in which continual converse with the Ladies-in-Waiting of the Queen Mother and others had brought him out very young; he had developed a taste for fêtes and similar amusements in company with a group of young people of both sexes who enjoyed the right of being called Seigneur and Dame (this caused very little irregularity as there were only two or three people of mediocre family who were brought in purely for their good looks and dancing ability to stiffen up the ballet together with a small number of dancing masters to keep things in order and give polish). Education in those days was very different from what it is now. Then everyone was taught every kind of game or sport, graceful movements, proper respect and politeness, and a refined and decorous gallantry. Anyone can see at a glance the difference today without going into details.

Reflection was not among the Maréchal de Villeroy's virtues; he gave no thought to the difficulties either for the King himself or in the task; he merely declared that the King would dance a ballet. All that remained was to get it organized. A search was started for young people who could dance at all—there was no question of whether they danced well or badly—and one had to take what one could get, so that the result was a pretty mixed bag. Several people who should never have been allowed near the thing got in so easily that even Law, parvenu that he was, dared to ask the Duc d'Orléans if his son, who was the right age and a good dancer, might take part. M. le Duc d'Orléans, always accommodating, always favourably disposed to Law, and to tell the truth deliberately contributing to the confusion round him whenever possible, agreed at once and said that he would speak to the Maréchal de Villeroy. The Marshal, who detested Law, went red in the face with rage and said everything there was to say on the subject; but he could not stand up to the Regent, Superintendent of the education of the King, great protector of Law and lover of confusion, so that young Law was included in the ballet.[1] You can imagine the outrage which this piece of nonsense caused; everyone was offended and it was the sole topic of conversation for several days—and various other members of the ballet got spattered with some of the dirt in the process. In the end everyone was satisfied: young Law went down with smallpox, and, because of the ballet in which he should never have been included, there was general rejoicing.

The ballet was danced several times,[2] but its success did not come up to the Marshal's expectations: the King was so bored and tired by learning, rehearsing, and performing the thing that he acquired a distaste for fêtes and every kind of spectacle which lasted the rest of his life and left a void in court life. The Marshal never suggested anything of the sort again.

THE DEATH OF
CARDINAL DE LA TRÉMOÏLLE

CARDINAL de la Trémoïlle died in Rome, in disrepute and near bankruptcy. Nevertheless, he had been in receipt of various pensions from the King, a large salary as Chargé d'affaires in Rome, the rich Archbishopric of Cambrai, and five abbeys, two of which, Saint-Amand and Saint-Étienne-de-Caen, were very wealthy. Neither his name, his rank or dignity, nor even the consideration in which his famous sister, the Princesse des Ursins, was everywhere held—he had been reconciled to her after she had succeeded in procuring his promotion—were enough to cloak his ignorance, his disgraceful morals, the indecency

---

[1] What actually happened was that seven or eight of the dancers got measles at the last moment and replacements had to be found in a hurry. Young Law was among them. He was fifteen. After his father's fall he went to the Low Countries, joined the Austrian army, became an infantry colonel and was killed in action in 1734.

[2] At the Tuileries on 7, 10, 17, 21 and 24 February. It was included in a performance of L'Inconnu.

of his daily life, his extraordinary appearance, his misplaced pleasantries, or the habitual disorder of his conduct.

He was a man who, while he troubled his head about nothing, was always afraid, and he was so inconsequent that in order to be popular, or else to avoid unpopularity, he never possessed an opinion he could call his own.

Nevertheless, his death gives me an opportunity to mention an incident which up to now I have forgotten and is worth mentioning. It will perhaps be remembered that I have already said something about the blind Duc de Noirmoutier, the brother of Mme des Ursins and Cardinal de la Trémoïlle, of his intelligence, of the good company always to be found at his house, of the infinity of important affairs in which he had a hand. Although relations between them were occasionally strained, he and his sister were of necessity most intimate correspondents, and he was equally close to the Cardinal. The Bouillons had always prided themselves on being great friends of his, and all their lives had known him intimately. The Abbé d'Auvergne knew him as well as the others did, and had often made use of this fact in public.

About a year after Cardinal de la Trémoïlle had received the Archbishop of Cambrai, M. de Noirmoutier, whose house was next door to mine (we both of us had a gate which led into the gardens of the Jacobins in the rue Saint-Dominique), sent to me and asked if I would grant him a moment in which to come and see me, and further whether, considering the nature of his business, I would appoint a time in which he might speak to me alone. Now although he was used to receiving a large number of people at home, M. de Noirmoutier never liked going out or visiting people. We had just finished dinner; I asked his valet if there was anyone with him and what he was doing. He told me that he was alone with the Duchesse de Noirmoutier. The latter was an intelligent woman, sensible and meritorious, in whom the Duc de Noirmoutier put complete trust and who was his continual stand-by in his blindness. I therefore told the valet that I should not put M. de Noirmoutier to the trouble of coming to see me, that all he had to do was to open his gate into the Jacobins' garden, and that I should immediately go to him by way of mine.

M. de Noirmoutier was all the more grateful for this act of politeness because I did not know him in the least, and had never either spoken to or called upon him at his house. After our preliminary greetings were over, he paid me the compliment of saying that, although he did not know me personally, his confidence in my reputation had led him to wish to open his heart to me upon a matter which was giving him and the Cardinal de la Trémoïlle the greatest anxiety. Then he added that after giving the matter long consideration he had come to the conclusion that there was no one who could help him but myself. If this opening surprised me what followed amazed me still more.

He began by begging me to speak absolutely frankly and not to allow my answer to the question he wished to put to me to be influenced by any considerations of politeness. Then he asked me to tell him straight out how his brother stood with the Duc d'Orléans, and whether or not the latter was satisfied with his conduct. I replied that, if I were to answer him as precisely as he wished, I must admit that some time had passed since his brother's name had last come up in conversation between us, but that the Duc d'Orléans had always seemed to me to be perfectly content with his brother. At that he tried to press me, and begged me to tell him whether his brother had not been so unfortunate as to displease the Duc d'Orléans. I assured him of the contrary, but this, he told me, only succeeded in increasing his surprise.

Then he told me that the Abbé d'Auvergne, of whom as an old friend of the family and a professed intimate both of himself and the Cardinal, he saw a good deal, had proposed that the Cardinal should resign his Archbishopric in his favour, and had given him to understand that this was the Regent's wish, though he said that the Regent was anxious that his views should not become known. He added that the Cardinal had at first thought this story so extraordinary that he had not believed it, but that the Abbé d'Auvergne had become so insistent, and his warnings so grave, that he found it hard to believe that the Abbé would go to such lengths without at least some authority behind him; that the Cardinal had written to him, the Duc de Noirmoutier, to find out what the Regent wanted him to do, saying that, as he owed his post to the King and that it was due to his kindness that he had ever received it, he was prepared to hand in his resignation whenever the Regent wished; that this affair had greatly upset both of them; that he had done all he could to discover the wishes of the Regent, without being able to avail himself of a sure and certain method of approach; and that finally, not knowing to whom in the world to address themselves, he had decided on what he was now doing with the utmost confidence that I should be able to help him. He ended upon this compliment.

My surprise was so great that I insisted upon his repeating the whole story, after which the Duchesse de Noirmoutier went to find some of the Cardinal's letters, from which she read certain extracts dealing with this affair, giving the full facts and the perplexities to which they had given rise. I replied that I should repay his and his brother's confidence with another, but under the same cover of secrecy as that they had demanded from me; that on the death of the Abbé d'Estrées, at that time Archbishop-designate of Cambrai, the Duc d'Orléans had hastened to give the see to the Cardinal de la Trémoïlle, not only because of his rank, his birth, and his services at Rome, but also in order to escape the demands of the House of Lorraine in favour of the Abbé de Lorraine, to whom he particularly did not wish to give a frontier post of that importance, and also the demands that the Bouillons might put forward on behalf of the Abbé d'Auvergne, to whom he would have preferred almost anyone, seeing that his mother, his step-mother and his niece all came from the Low Countries and that all their alliances and their possessions were in those parts; that I was perfectly sure that these were the Duc d'Orléans's intentions as I had heard them at the time from his own mouth and as I had noticed nothing since that time to lead me to suppose that he had changed his mind, and because the Duc d'Orléans was a Prince so unaccustomed to act the tyrant, it was impossible to imagine his behaving in this way, especially to anyone of the condition and birth of the Cardinal de la Trémoïlle, with whom I had never known him to be dissatisfied.

M. de Noirmoutier was naturally greatly relieved to hear this opinion from anyone so intimately acquainted with the Duc d'Orléans as I was, but he wanted more, and therefore asked if it would be abusing our new acquaintance too far to ask me to speak openly to the Regent upon the subject. I said I would, but I warned M. de Noirmoutier that I could not do this unless I were free to tell the Duc d'Orléans the whole story. He answered that that was what he meant me to do, that I should ask for the matter to be kept a secret, and that I might offer the Cardinal's resignation as far as it was in his power to dispose of it, if that was what the Regent wanted.

I answered that I was sorry I had not heard of all this two hours earlier, since I had but recently left the Prince (he had sent for me towards the end of the morning) and that I could have mentioned the matter then. M. de Noirmoutier was sorry to hear this too, because the Rome courier left that night.[1] I wanted to do him a real favour, so I went straight back to the Palais Royal.

Surprised to see me again so soon, the Regent asked me the cause

[1] The courier left every Monday evening, taking twelve to fifteen days over the journey to Rome.

of my return. I told him, and he immediately burst out laughing at the incredible roguery and insolence of the trick. Then he charged me to tell M. de Noirmoutier from him that this was the first he had ever heard of the suggestion; that the thought of it had never crossed his mind; that he was well content with Cardinal de la Trémoïlle, and very far from repenting of having given him Cambrai; that he begged him to be without the least anxiety; and moreover that he would have them both know that even if the idea of resigning ever came into the Cardinal's head, and if he, the Regent, should fail to persuade him to change his mind, the last man in France, whether bishop or abbé, to whom he would give Cambrai would be the Abbé d'Auvergne.

As the time for the evening's amusements was drawing near, I did not prolong the conversation but hurried off to deliver M. and Mme de Noirmoutier from their anxiety. On hearing my account they were overjoyed. You can imagine what the three of us said about their relation and good friend the Abbé d'Auvergne; they decided that the Cardinal de Trémoïlle should write him a refusal so dry and so sharp that he would not only not dare to return to the charge but would realize as well that he had been found out. The Abbé did indeed realize this, but he did not stop calling upon M. de Noirmoutier with really incredible effrontery as if the whole thing had never happened.

THE PRESIDENT DE MESMES

I WAS at this point in my memoirs when I heard from M. Joly de Fleury, the Procurator General, an anecdote so curious and so extremely interesting that, though it is out of its place, I must include it. Had I known of it earlier I should have placed it a few days after my account of the arrest of the Duc and Duchesse du Maine.

M. Joly de Fleury and I were talking together about old times when he informed me that Mlle de Chausserais told him that shortly after the arrest of the Duc and Duchesse du Maine, the First President, de Mesmes, had come to her in a panic and asked her to get him a secret audience with the Duc d'Orléans, which he confessed he was too frightened to ask for himself; she added that she had accordingly asked for the audience but had obtained it only with the greatest difficulty.

On the day and time appointed she went to the Palais Royal, taking care to have with her her footman du Plessis, with whom the Duc d'Orléans and many other people of that day were well acquainted. To this fellow, du Plessis, the Regent then handed the key of one of

the secret doors, of which there were several, all leading from the
streets surrounding the Palais Royal straight and secretly to the Regent's apartments. Du Plessis opened the door of the First President
(for greater security he was wearing a short cloak instead of his usual
robes) and led him to the Duc d'Orléans, who was waiting for him
alone with Mlle de Chausserais.

The First President was a fine speaker, and words came easily to
him. He began by referring to what had so recently occurred and most
strongly protested his fidelity and attachment. With a mind as agile
as his tongue was eloquent he then set himself to discover from the
cold and serious manner of the Duc d'Orléans if the latter had anything against him. In this he was not successful. The Regent had himself well in hand and did not let the least sign escape him. Indeed he
went further and encouraged the First President to repeat his protestations and to make another fine speech. At last, however, he had
enough. He drew a letter from his pocket and, in a voice which showed
his displeasure, suddenly said to the First President: 'Read this, Sir.
Do you recognize it?'

The First President fell down on both knees, and, embracing not
merely the legs but the feet of the Regent, began to pray for pardon
amid a stream of regrets and self-reproaches which showed that he
had received the fright of his life. The Duc d'Orléans then took back
the letter, disengaged his feet from the President's embrace, and without a word went off to his other study. This letter which had been produced was one written in the First President's own hand, and in it he
had assured the Spanish government that he could personally answer
for the *Parlement* and had then gone on to speak without the least disguise of the conspiracy itself, as well as of the best methods for bringing it to a successful issue.

Stunned and speechless, the First President found great difficulty
in recovering his senses and in raising himself from where he knelt.
Mlle de Chausserais was almost as bewildered as he was, but in her
case it was with astonishment. She reproached him for his folly in
engaging her to get him this interview when he knew himself to be so
guilty. His only reply was to conjure her to save him and to go at once
to the Duc d'Orléans. She accordingly went and found the Regent
alone. However, he was so indignant at the First President's audacity
and impertinence in asking for an interview, and his wicked deceitfulness in daring to protest so fervently at a time when he knew of the
existence of such a letter in his own handwriting, that he told her he
meant to have the man arrested. La Chausserais knew well enough
with whom she had to deal, and she began to smile. 'Very well,' she

told him, 'have him arrested. He deserves that and worse. Nevertheless with this piece of paper in your hands, and the confession you have just forced from him, you have the man at your mercy now and can do with him what you wish. Indeed nothing better from your own point of view could possibly have happened, since he is now in your power and cannot say a word or be anything but subservient to your wishes from now on.'

Although nothing could have been more to the taste of M. le Duc d'Orléans who always favoured indirect methods and disliked head-on collisions, such as the arrest of the First President would be (even though he was such a rogue), and although the arrest would be open to question and the evidence produced would embarrass not only the Duc and Duchesse du Maine but also many others in high places, she had great difficulty in finally gaining her point. Meanwhile the First President waited in a state of suspense between life and death, for he was only too well aware from long practice of the meaning of dishonour and infamy. Mlle de Chausserais eventually went back to him and, after telling him enough of what had been said to put strength into his legs so that he was capable of using them, sent for du Plessis to take him back the way he had come. He remained in a death-like trance for a long time and had great difficulty in appearing normal when carrying out the functions of his office and meeting people publicly—particularly the Duc d'Orléans, who rightly considered that the affair had been brought to a very successful end.

It was Chausserais herself who told the Procurator General this story,[1] just as I have set it down here, which is immediately after hearing it, and many years after the death of the Duc d'Orléans.

THE PRINCESS OF MODENA

THE Duchesse de Villars[2] was appointed to conduct Mlle de Valois,[3] and three other ladies of quality, Mme de Simiane, Mme de Goyon, and Mme de Bacqueville, were ordered to accompany her. I shall have a word or two to say about the last three ladies in a moment.

[1] For her part in which she appears to have been suitably rewarded, for it is noticeable that in this year, 1720, she bought the Hôtel de Noailles in the rue Saint-Honoré for 150,000 livres and the Hôtel d'Orval in the rue Plâtrière for 120,000 livres.

[2] Marie-Angélique Fremin de Moras, Duchesse de Villars-Brancas. She was the wife not of the Marshal but of his son.

[3] Charlotte-Aglaé, the Regent's daughter, famous for her intrigue with the young Duc de Richelieu. She had just been married by proxy to the Prince of Modena, and was now setting out from Paris to join him.

Now, as every day saw some well-established and unquestioned precedent upset, Mme de Villars was most anxious not to expose herself to the possibility of any difficulties in matters of etiquette. She therefore had the lines for all conduct laid down beforehand, even in matters for which no decision should have been necessary. Among other things it was decided that she herself, except in the matter of kissing hands, should receive exactly the same treatment as Mlle de Valois, that is to say that she should have a right to an arm-chair, a cadenas at table, a salver, a covered glass, a knife, fork, and spoon of silver gilt, and plates of the same material. These were to be made like those of the Princess in every detail, as the latter had hers already. Moreover the Duchess was to have the same staff of servants to wait on her at table, and none of the other ladies of quality, who ate with Mlle de Valois, were to have anything of the kind. These arrangements naturally displeased the other ladies, so, unable to prevent them, they persuaded Mlle de Valois, who was stopping at every place she could and prolonging her journey to such inordinate lengths that complaints were sent from Modena to the Duc d'Orléans, to take her meals by herself in public whenever possible.

The Duchesse de Villars could see that this was being done on purpose, but she did not like to assume her cadenas and other distinctions when feeding alone with the other ladies—that is when the Princess elected to dine by herself—although as a fact, right up to the middle of the late King's reign, a Duchess had always been accustomed to these privileges when eating in ordinary company. She therefore contented herself with reporting what was happening. At this the Duc d'Orléans sent orders that his daughter was always to take her meals with the Duchesse de Villars and her ladies, and so it afterwards continued. I am saying all this in advance in order not to be forced to return to this subject, or to that of the marriage, later.

The betrothal ceremony was held as usual in the King's study, at about six o'clock in the afternoon on Sunday, the 11th of February. Cardinal de Rohan officiated. Mlle de Valois's train was carried by her sister, Mlle de Montpensier, who was later Queen of Spain, and the Duc de Chartres acted as proxy for the Prince of Modena.

Hardly a soul from the Court attended this ceremony, because there is nothing like the curious whims and the ups and downs of the French. There is no doubt that Princes and Princesses of the Blood have always sent out invitations to betrothals, and there is even less doubt that the Sons of France have never done so for the betrothals of their children. The Duc d'Orléans was the first Grandson of France to marry off one of his children. No precedent could be found in the marriage of the Duchesse de Berry to a Son of France, and this was in fact the first occasion on which such a position had arisen. The Duc d'Orléans, superior to the Princes of the Blood and Regent, never thought for a moment of sending out invitations. The result was that the ceremony was very ill-attended, and the crowd of men and women of all descriptions, even to the highest, who would normally commit any act of degradation to obtain his favour, for once remained at home because they had not been invited. The Duchesse d'Orléans was hurt by this but the Regent only laughed.

The King's present to Mlle de Valois was a fine necklace of diamonds and pearls,[1] and, an hour after her betrothal, he drove to the Palais Royal to say good-bye to her and to call upon her parents. The marriage was celebrated next day at the King's Mass, at which the same number of people and no more attended. When Mass was over the King held out his hand to the bride and conducted her to her coach (it was in fact one of the King's coaches) and according to the usual custom said to the coachman: 'to Modena.' Her whole company was around her, just as if she had really been setting out. She returned to the Palais Royal, a short time later caught measles, neither before nor after her illness received a single ceremonial visit, put off her departure as long as she could, and when she did go she made her travelling days as short as she dared, stopped at every place she could, and lengthened her stay in every town to the utmost. She received several scoldings from the Duc d'Orléans but to no effect, until there were so many complaints from the Duke of Modena that the Duc d'Orléans sent her orders so absolute that she had to hurry. She embarked at Antibes, and there the Duchesse de Villars and her ladies took their leave of her and set out for home again.[2]

Madame la Grande Duchesse[3] kissed the Princess of Modena good-bye and said to her: 'Go, my child, and remember to do what I did. Have a child or two and then see to it that you return to France. That is the only thing to do in your position.' This was an odd lesson, but the Princess of Modena knew how to profit by it.

---

[1] In addition to this necklace, valued at 200,000 livres, the King gave her 300,000 écus. Her father gave her 200,000 livres in cash and 200,000 worth of jewels. She also possessed a further 290,000 worth of jewelry.

[2] In fact they accompanied her to Genoa, where she went ashore for a few hours the day after leaving Antibes, and was joined by her Italian ladies-in-waiting. Mme de Bacqueville wanted to go on to Modena and stay a few months but was ordered not to. Mme de Villars was back on duty in Paris by 12 July.

[3] Marguerite-Louise d'Orléans, Grand Duchess of Tuscany, who had returned to France in 1675, and remained there ever since. She died in 1721.

LAW'S System was breaking up. If only we had been satisfied with his original idea of a bank, a bank exactly and wisely kept within its proper limits, we should have doubled the amount of money in the realm and thereby enormously facilitated its commerce as well as that of private individuals. If the bank had been in a position to meet its demands, its notes, continually exchangeable at their face value, would have been as good as ready money, and even in many cases preferable since they would have been more easily portable. Nevertheless it must be admitted, as I maintained against the Duc d'Orléans in his study and as I said straight out to the whole of the Regency Council when the motion for the bank was originally passed, however good an institution of this kind might be in itself, it could never have succeeded except in a republic or a monarchy like that of England, where the finances are entirely governed by those who provide the funds, and who, moreover, are free to vote as much or as little as they like. In a state like that of France, unstable, changing, worse than absolute, there is no solidarity, and in consequence no confidence, since the King, and in his name a mistress, a minister, or a few favourites—not to mention more serious exigencies like those which arose in the years 1707–10, or a hundred other causes—may unbalance the bank. The attraction is too great and jiggery-pokery too easy.

But what hastened the fall both of the System and of the bank itself was the inconceivable prodigality of the Duc d'Orléans, who without moderation, and, what is possibly worse, without the least discrimination immediately became a victim of the importunity of those whom he knew perfectly well to have always been his enemies, and at the same time threw money about and more often than not allowed it to be filched off him by people who laughed at his folly and felt no affection for anything but their own effrontery.

It is difficult to believe what my own eyes have seen, and posterity will consider as a myth what we ourselves can only look back on as a dream. The end of it was that our wealth was squandered on a greedy and a prodigal generation, a generation hungry and necessitous through love of luxury, through disorder, through general confusion, so that finally even paper money was short because the presses could not print it fast enough. From what I have already said the extent of some of the abuses may be gathered. The bank had been established as a resource in times of need, but its only chance of success was by balancing the accounts and, above all, by keeping in hand sufficient money always to meet all demands. This is what I used to tell Law every Tuesday morning when he came to see me. He amused me for a long time before he finally summoned up the courage to confess his embarrassment but at last he complained to me with modesty and timidity that the Duc d'Orléans was throwing everything to the winds.

From outside sources I knew more than he realized, and it was this which made me press him for a statement of accounts. When at last he confessed what he could no longer hide—and he minimized it as best he could—he assured me that he still had resources if only the Regent would allow him a free hand. I was not convinced. Then the notes began to fall in value, people began to lose confidence in them and this distrust spread to the public. The result of this was an attempt to peg them by force instead of by sound business, and as soon as it was seen that force was being used everyone saw ruin staring him in the face. The time came when an edict was published, rendering it illegal to make use of gold, or silver (and by that I mean silver money), or even precious stones as a means of exchange, and thus attempting to persuade us that, ever since the time when Abraham paid money for Sara's burial to our own times, all the civilized nations of the globe had been under a delusion and in the grossest error about the value of money and of the metals of which it is made; that paper was the only useful and necessary currency; that the greatest injury we could do our neighbours, so jealous of our grandeur and superiority, was to let our gold and our valuables pass into their hands. This was completely unrestricted, and the Mississippi Company had power to enter anyone's house, even of royalty, and seize all the gold louis and crowns they found there, with orders to leave no coins above the value of five francs; even in small change not more than two hundred francs, enough to make up even money on a note of payment or to buy the cheapest household necessities, could be kept. Moreover, one had to take all one had to the bank for fear of one's footman laying information against one. However, orders of this kind were so excessive and in every way so intolerable that no one believed in them and they could not last. There was nothing for it but a new issue of notes, in other words fresh feats of financial jugglery. One knew it to be that; one could feel it in one's bones; nevertheless, one put up with it rather than go penniless, and an even greater tyranny reconciled one to that which had gone before.

Such were the financial operations which occupied the remainder of the Regent's life and government; which sent Law flying from the country; which raised prices even of the lowest articles to six times what they had been before, and therefore raised salaries to a disastrous pitch; which ruined all business, public as well as private; which at the expense of the public made fortunes for a few of the nobility, who quickly squandered their profits and were then as poor as they had been before; but which also enormously enriched all manner of employees, and made millions for men from the very scum of our population, agents and employees of the financiers who watched the market and knew exactly when to get out. The last straw was the eminent figures, Princes and Princesses of the Blood not least among them, who with no thought for the Mississippi but interested only in saving themselves by all the considerable means within their power, recouped themselves by forming the Western Company, which was conducted in the same style of financial jugglery and did irreparable harm to the official Company for the private profit of a small number of individuals of such eminence that the Government did not dare to incite their hatred and vengeance by taking action against them.

There were one or two startling arrests at this time and several considerable sums found in houses which were searched. A man named Adine, an employee of the bank, had ten thousand écus confiscated, was fined ten thousand francs and lost his job. Many people hid their money so secretly at this time that they died without telling anyone where it had been placed, and it was lost to their heirs for ever.

The four brothers Paris were dismissed and sent away from Paris on suspicion of plotting with the financiers against Law. These brothers were the sons of an innkeeper, whose inn, at the foot of the Alps, stood all alone and without a village round about it. Its sign was 'À la Montagne.'[1] They had originally all been in their father's service, waiting on the visitors at meals, grooming their horses, and cleaning out their rooms. All four were large and well-built men. One of them became a soldier in the Guards, and remained in that Regiment for a long while. The story of their rise is a curious one.

Bouchu, the Intendant at Grenoble, was also Intendant to the army in Italy at the time when, after the Maréchal de Villeroy's capture at Cremona, Vendôme had succeeded to the command of his army. Now Bouchu, who in his youth had been a handsome, well-made fellow, was by this time a gouty old man. But he had not lost his taste for gallantry. It so happened that the chief supply clerk, responsible for the contract and supply of all stores for the army in Italy, had tastes of a similar kind, and not only had made so bold as to pay his addresses to the lady the Intendant was in love with, but also, being a younger and a more attractive man, had succeeded in cutting the ground from

---

[1] At Moirans, in the Dauphiné; he was mayor of the district, and died in 1697.

under the Intendant's feet. This had made Bouchu furious and he had sworn to get his own back. He therefore raised so many difficulties and so successfully delayed the transport of stores that, in spite of all the clerk could do to urge them forward, Vendôme, on taking up his command, or rather when he wished to advance, found nothing ready.

The clerk, who saw he was lost and had no doubt as to the cause, went tearing up and down the Alps trying to move all the stores he could while waiting for the balance to come forward. Happily for him and for the army, he happened to pass by this inn, 'A la Montagne,' and was making enquiries there as everywhere else. The innkeeper seemed to him to be a man of some brains, and he held out hopes that, when his sons, who happened to be working in the fields, returned, they would be able to find some way through for him. He kept his word, and the clerk was so pleased with the obvious intelligence and resourcefulness of the family that he put himself into their hands and they organized the transport he needed.

The clerk then sent post-haste for his mule train, and, under the guidance of the brothers who led him by paths which only they and a few villagers knew and which though difficult were direct, he managed without the loss of a single load to reach the Duc de Vendôme who was grounded for lack of bread, and was cursing and swearing at the contractors on whom Bouchu had laid all the blame. When he got over his first transports, he was so delighted to have his supplies and to be able at last to advance and put his plans into operation that he became more amenable, and agreed to listen to what the clerk had to say for himself. The latter told him with some pride of his diligence and care for the troops, and of how he had crossed the Alps by an unknown and most dangerous route. Then he showed him various letters which he had received from M. Bouchu, and which he happened to have with him. These letters proved beyond doubt that he had done everything he could to urge Bouchu to send forward the supplies. He made it clear that the distress in which Vendôme had found the army was the fault of the Intendant, and at the same time he told the Duc de Vendôme of the Intendant's hatred for him, of the causes of this hatred, and of how it had led Bouchu to endanger the whole army for the sake of ruining him personally. After this he turned to praising the intelligence and goodwill of the innkeeper and his family, to whom he said he was indebted for the formation and successful conduct of his convoy through the passage in the Alps.

At this the Duc de Vendôme's anger turned against Bouchu. He sent for him, reproached him publicly for the conduct of which he had just heard, and concluded by telling him that he had half a mind to

400

hang him there and then for having endangered the King's army. This was the beginning of Bouchu's disgrace. He kept his position a short while longer because of his servility, but within two years he was forced to resign.

This was also the beginning of the brothers' rise to fortune. The army contractors rewarded them most handsomely, and gave them fresh employment, in which they acquitted themselves so well that they quickly gained advancement, were taken into the confidence of their masters, and made large profits. In the end they became army contractors themselves, grew rich, and then came to Paris in the hopes of making a still bigger fortune. In this hope they succeeded. Indeed, their success was so great that under Monsieur le Duc they openly and without opposition were the real governors of the country, and, after a short eclipse, were once again the masters of our finances and Controllers General. Their fortune is enormous, they have made and unmade Ministers and other financiers, and they have seen the Court, the town and the provinces of France at their feet.

THE KING ATTENDS A COUNCIL

On Sunday the 18th of February the King attended his first Regency Council. He did not say a word on entering the room, nor during the Council, nor yet again on leaving, except that when the Duc d'Orléans, who was anxious that he should not be bored, suggested his leaving in the middle, he said that he would like to stay until the end. Subsequently he did not attend all our Councils, but he came fairly often, and when he did he always remained to the end without fidgetting and without uttering a word.

His presence made no difference to the order in which we sat, because his arm-chair in any case always stood at the head of the table, and the Duc d'Orléans was only provided with a tabouret like the rest of us, whether the King was present or not. The Maréchal de Villeroy still kept his usual seat.

A few days later the Duc de Berwick also joined the Council. The fact that he was a foreigner caused some murmuring. However, he was an exile from his own country and a naturalized Frenchman, having lived in this country for thirty-two years. He had served in our army all that time; he was a duke and a Peer of France, a Marshal of our army, Grandee of Spain, and General Officer commanding the armies of the two crowns; and he was of more than proved fidelity. Moreover, considering what business was now conducted at these

Councils, it hardly mattered who was a member and who was not. We were already fifteen and he made the sixteenth.

On one occasion when the King was present a kitten of his came in after him. A few minutes later it jumped up onto the table and started to walk around it. At this the Duc de Noailles, who was afraid of cats, objected. The Duc d'Orléans thereupon jumped up to remove it. I smiled and said: 'Oh, Sir, leave the kitten, he will make the seventeenth.' The Duc d'Orléans burst out laughing, and when he looked around him everyone else was laughing too, among them the King, who, next morning, at his small *lever* mentioned it to me—shortly it is true, but yet so that I could see that he had seen the joke. It went the round of Paris at once.

DUBOIS ARCHBISHOP OF CAMBRAI

As we have only recently seen, owing to the death at Rome of Cardinal de la Trémoïlle, a vacancy had occurred at Cambrai, which is the richest of our Archbishoprics and one of the finest positions in our whole church. The Abbé Dubois was at this time no more than tonsured. However, 150,000 livres make a tempting sum, and perhaps he thought that this would be a useful step towards his cardinal's hat. Yet insolent and all-powerful with his master as he was, he found this an embarrassing request to make, and he decided to mask his effrontery by a trick. He therefore began by telling the Duc d'Orléans that on the previous night he had had a pleasant dream, in which he had found himself to be the Archbishop of Cambrai. The Regent, who saw where this was leading, turned on his heel without a word. Dubois became more and more embarrassed. He stammered and began to paraphrase his dream. Then, mastering himself with an effort, he asked the Regent curtly why he should not have the post, when by a single act of will His Royal Highness could thus make his fortune for him.

The Duc d'Orléans was indignant and even alarmed, though he was not as a rule over-scrupulous in his choice of bishops. He therefore answered in a contemptuous tone: 'What? You, Archbishop of Cambrai!' and thus made it clear what he thought of Dubois's low birth, and even more what he thought of his dissolute and scandalous life. Dubois, who had gone too far to stop, cited examples. Unfortunately, there were only too many of them. . . .

But the Duc d'Orléans, less closely affected by these arguments, than embarrassed at having to resist a man who was pursuing him so hotly and whom he had long since forgotten how to contradict, tried

402

At the King's Council

to avoid the point, and said to him: 'But you are a rogue, and I don't know where you think you are going to find another rogue to consecrate you.'[1] 'Oh, if that is all that is troubling you,' said the Abbé hurriedly, 'the matter is settled. I know the very man to consecrate me, and he is just outside.' 'Who the devil would dare to consecrate you?' the Regent answered. 'Do you want to know?' said the Abbé, 'and is that really all that is troubling you?' 'Well, who is he?' said the Regent. 'He is your First Almoner,' replied Dubois, 'and he is just outside. I am sure he would ask nothing better. Indeed I shall go and ask him.' Thereupon Dubois embraced the Regent round the knees—the latter was taken so aback that he had no more to say—left the room, took the Bishop of Nantes upon one side, told him he had been given Cambrai, asked whether he would consecrate him, and received his instant promise to do so. Then he returned, twirled twice round the room, told the Duc d'Orléans that he had just had a word with the First Almoner, who had given him his promise to consecrate him, protested his thanks in his usual high-flown way, and half by assuming the truth of what he wished, half by persuasion, succeeded in sealing the bargain, without the Regent's daring once to put in a single word of protest. And that is how Dubois became Archbishop of Cambrai.

The choice was so scandalous that it caused a good deal of talk. Even Dubois, for all his insolence, was embarrassed, and the Duc d'Orléans was clearly so much ashamed of what he had done that everyone saw that he had better not mention the subject to him. But it still remained for the Abbé Dubois to receive Holy Orders. Realizing how greatly Cardinal de Noailles stood in need of his backing in the wretched squabbles which surrounded the 'Constitution,' Dubois hoped that he might be willing to ordain him. In this, however, he was mistaken, for that kind of human weakness had small part in the character of the Cardinal. Indeed, so well was the Cardinal aware of the mental and moral obliquity of Dubois, to say nothing of his public conduct, that the thought of doing anything to help him to take Orders shocked him profoundly. It was not that he did not realize the heavy burden which this refusal would henceforth lay upon his shoulders; he knew what Dubois's influence with his master was; he knew that his refusal would be taken as a serious affront; and he knew that he would have to suffer for it so long as he lived. But such things had no influence with him. When he received the *Letters Dimissory* sent to him

---

[1] An untranslatable pun; the Duke said, 'Mais tu es un sacre, et qui est l'autre sacre qui voudra te sacrer?'

for the ordination, he sadly, modestly, but very firmly refused to accept them, and, when that was done, he never spoke another word about the matter, but contented himself with having done his duty and showed that modesty, simplicity, and charity were as much a part of his nature as was his firmness. Dubois's fury may be imagined, and he never forgave the Cardinal de Noailles. Nevertheless, the latter received universal praise and admiration, which were only increased when it was seen how hard he tried to avoid them.

There was now nothing for Dubois to do but to turn to someone else. Bezons had recently been transferred from the Archbishopric of Bordeaux to that of Rouen. This Bezons was a brother of the Marshal, and, like the latter, he was not only one of the Duc d'Orléans's closest followers, but had also been very handsomely rewarded for his services. Beneath their clumsy, heavy exteriors they were both of them perfect courtiers. Now Pontoise is within the diocese of Rouen, and a few miles away from Pontoise the diocese of Paris begins. The Abbé Dubois was anxious not to waste any time or to give a handle to his enemies by making an obvious journey. He had reason to think that the Bezons were likely to prove more amenable than Cardinal de Noailles, and in this he was right. The Archbishop of Rouen granted the *Letters Dimissory*.

Then Dubois, giving as his pretext the fact that he was very busy, asked for and obtained a brief to receive all the necessary Orders on the same day, and, as for the necessity of going into retreat to make his preparation, he dispensed with that himself. One fine morning, therefore, he set out from Paris and went to a little village[1] about fifteen miles away where in the parish church which was within the diocese of Rouen and the Grand Vicariate of Pontoise, Tressan, Bishop of Nantes and the Duc d'Orléans's First Almoner, consecrated him at one and the same Mass, *extra tempora,* sub-deacon, deacon, and priest. On Bezon's death, for which he did not have long to wait, Tressan received the Archbishopric and Stewardship of Rouen as a reward for his services.

It happened that on this day when Dubois was receiving these various Orders a Regency Council was held at the Louvre. There was a great deal of measles about at the time, it had even entered the Palais Royal, and that was why we were not meeting in the Tuileries. It seemed strange to be holding a council without the Abbé Dubois, as it was his duty to keep us all informed of foreign affairs, and he told us just as much as seemed to him convenient and no more. But it was

---

[1] Chanteloup, less than a mile outside the diocese of Paris.

stranger when he appeared. He can certainly not have wasted much time in giving thanks to God for the Orders he had just received. Indeed his appearance at that moment was so disgraceful that it heightened the scandal of the original choice. The Duc de Mazarin said of him pleasantly enough on this occasion that he was returning from making his first communion.

Everyone else, including the Duc d'Orléans, had already arrived, and we were standing in groups about the room. I was in a corner at the far end, talking to the Prince de Conti, the Maréchal de Tallard, and a third whom I cannot now remember, when I saw the Abbé come in, dressed in a short coat and looking just as usual. No one expected him that day and, not unnaturally, there was an outcry. At this he looked around and, seeing the Prince de Conti, he walked in our direction. The Prince de Conti, who, though certainly without his father's charm—he was on the contrary a cynical fellow—yet had his father's laugh, took two steps forward, and all at once began to speak of the Orders the Abbé had received that morning, of the fact that, although the ceremony had been held outside Paris, the Abbé had succeeded in arriving in time to attend the Council, and of the episcopal consecration which was so soon to follow. He told Dubois of the surprise with which not only he, but others, regarded his behaviour and then, with an admirable imitation of a sermon which was as witty as it was malicious, he made the whole thing sound pathetic.

All this while the Abbé Dubois was unable to get in a single word. He let the other have his say and then replied coldly that, if only the Prince de Conti had been a little better informed in history, he would have found that what had caused him so much astonishment was not in reality very strange, since he, the Abbé, had merely followed an example set by St. Ambrose, and he told the story of St. Ambrose's ordination at some length. I did not hear the whole recital. The moment I heard the name of St. Ambrose mentioned, I fled as fast as my legs would carry me to the far end of the room, for I was horrified by the comparison, and terrified lest I should find myself ordering Dubois to have done. Indeed I felt this impulse seize me by the throat. Moreover, I was longing to point out how little St. Ambrose was responsible for his sudden ordination, what a resistance to pressure he had made, how opposed to it and how frightened he had been, and how in the end it had only been accomplished by the unanimous wish of the people, and even by a degree of force. This impious citation of St. Ambrose was the talk of the day. The nomination and ordination took place at the end of February.

In order to keep the whole of this story together, and so that I may not have to come back to it again, I shall make an end of it here and now. It will give us a curious example of the Abbé Dubois's influence upon his master, and show how dangerous it was to awaken his displeasure. The Abbé Dubois received his Bulls at the beginning of May, and was consecrated on Sunday, the 9th of June. All Paris and everyone at Court was invited except me. I was in Dubois's bad books because I did not choose my words with care when speaking to the Duc d'Orléans about his hankerings after the purple, nor about the way in which, in the hopes of attaining his ambition, he played into the hands of the English or the Emperor.

The consecration was, however, to be a magnificent affair, and I shall have a word or two to say about it. What matters for the moment is that the Duc d'Orléans had agreed to attend the ceremony. Although from the horror and scandal with which Dubois's nomination and ordination had already been received I judged that the indignation against the Duc d'Orléans was very strong, I was convinced that these superb preparations for the consecration would materially increase them. I therefore went to see him the day before this extraordinary ceremony was due to take place and I told him why I had come.

I told him that I had never once mentioned the subject of Dubois's nomination to Cambrai to him, because, as he well knew, I made it my practice never to speak to him upon any matter once it was settled; that I should not speak about it now if I had not learnt that he was intending to be present at the ceremony the next day; that I should say nothing about the scandalous nature of the appointment, although as a matter of fact, he could have done nothing to show his approbation of the man more emphatically if it had been the custom to make a Prince of the Blood a bishop, and if he were thinking of finding a post for his own second son,[1] because, as I said, I considered the matter to be over and done with. But, I insisted that my attachment to him was such that I could no longer disguise from him the terrible effect this scandalous nomination, this sacrilegious ordination and these unheard-of preparations for the consecration of a man whose origins, condition, morals, and way of life were such as those of the Abbé Dubois, were having upon the public; that I said this not to reproach him for what was already done, but that he might realize to what extent the indignation against him had grown and might see that by attending the ceremony on the morrow he would be adding enormously to it.

[1] The Duke had only one son; Saint-Simon means if he had a second who would have, as the younger, been destined for the Church.

I begged him to realize how contrary to all precedent such an attendance would be. I pointed out that not only Sons of France, but
also the Princes of the Blood, had always made a habit of avoiding all
consecrations, unless it might be for one occasion in their lives when
they had gone out of interest, as several Kings and other royal persons
had done in the past. I added that, considering how his own life and
words were continually leading people to suppose him godless, there
could be no doubt that it would be said—and not only said but assiduously spread abroad—that his only object in going to the consecration was to make a mock of God and to insult the Church; that the
effect of this would be horrible and dangerous; that, not without
reason, people would say that he was being sacrificed to the pride of
Dubois, and that such a public exhibition of his dependence as this
extraordinary behaviour would seem, would call down upon him a
hatred, a contempt and contumely that he would do well to avoid;
that in saying this I was no more than a disinterested servant of his;
that his presence or absence at this ceremony of consecration could
make no possible difference to the affairs of the Abbé Dubois, who
would be neither more nor less the Archbishop of Cambrai in either
case, and would not even diminish the splendour of the service, seeing
that, whether he went or not, it was going to be of such a kind that
even if a Son of France were on the point of being consecrated it could
not be more magnificent; that I thought such grandeur enough for a
Dubois; and, finally, that I could not see why the latter should need to
prostitute his master in the eyes of France, and then of all Europe, by
forcing him to abase himself in this unheard-of fashion, and to wear
his chains in public.

In the end I begged him not to go. I told him that he knew quite
well on what terms I now was with the Abbé Dubois; that I was the
only man of repute who had not been invited to the ceremony; that
nevertheless, if he would give me his promise, and keep his word, to
abstain from attending the consecration, I should give him my promise to go myself, and to stay there throughout the whole ceremony,
however much I might detest going, and however much it might hurt
me to think that it would afterwards be said of me, as it assuredly
would, that I had gone there as a courtier in order to rehabilitate myself in the good graces of Dubois, when such behaviour was so unlike
my natural self that I might boast that up to that day I had never lost
my virginity in matters of this kind but preserved it lovingly all my life.

This conclusion, which I uttered in an eager voice, was more
elaborated than I have set it down here, but the Duc d'Orléans listened
to it from start to finish. I was nevertheless surprised when I heard

him say that I was right, and that I had opened his eyes for him, and still more astonished when he embraced me and told me that I was a true friend of his. Immediately after that he gave me his word that he would not go, and promised me that he would keep it. Upon that we parted, I still encouraging him and promising to go myself, and he thanking me for doing so. He was not even anxious to see me take my leave. I knew him well and I looked deep into his soul. Rather was it I who left him, well content with having turned him against a course of action which seemed to me extraordinarily disgraceful. After this I wonder who could have expected him to break his word. As we shall see he fully meant to keep it. This, however, is what happened.

Although I thought myself sure of him, I was so well accustomed to his weakness and his easy manner, and to the influence which the pride of Dubois might exercise over him that I decided to make certain before I set out for the consecration myself. Next morning, therefore, I sent to the Palais Royal for news, in the meanwhile giving orders to prepare my coach, as I meant to keep my word. Used as I was to the Duc d'Orléans's wretched shiftiness, I was, however, very much upset when the man I had sent for news returned to tell me that he had just seen him getting into his carriage, surrounded with all that pomp of outriders he so seldom used except on occasions of great ceremony, to go to the consecration. I at once ordered my horses to be unharnessed, and shut myself up in my study.

Next day I heard through one of Mme de Parabère's lovers—she was at that time the Regent's reigning favourite, though it must be admitted she was not a very faithful one—that on the night before the consecration, as she lay in bed with the Duc d'Orléans at the Palais Royal (this never occurred in the bed and bedroom of the Duc d'Orléans but usually in hers), he had begun to sing my praises to her in terms that are too warm for me to quote, and to speak with feeling of my friendship for him. Moreover, he told her that he had been so deeply moved by what I had said that he had decided not to attend the consecration, and was very grateful to me for what I had done to influence him.

Parabère praised me too, and agreed that I was quite right, but her conclusion was that nevertheless he would go. Astonished by her answer, the Duc d'Orléans said that she was mad. 'Mad, if you like,' was her reply, 'but you will go.' 'And I,' said he, 'say that I shall not.' 'Yes, you will,' said she. 'But,' he replied, 'this is all very well. You say that M. de Saint-Simon is right so why in the world should I go?' 'Because I wish it,' she answered. 'Good,' said he, 'but why do you want me to go? And what new folly is this?' 'Why,' said she,

408

'because—.' 'What,' said he, 'whatever do you mean? Give me a reason if you have one.' There followed a short dispute, and then she said: 'Well, if you really want to know my reason, it is this. You know that four days ago the Abbé and I had words, and that the quarrel is not yet finished. He is the sort of devil who ferrets out everything. He will know that we slept together tonight, and if to-morrow you don't go to his consecration, he will certainly think that it is I who have stopped you. Once he has got that idea into his head it will stay there and he will never forgive me. He will do me a hundred bad turns, he will blacken me to you in a thousand different ways, and the end of it will be that we shall quarrel. Well, that is what I do not wish to happen, and that is why I want you to go to his consecration, although the Duc de Saint-Simon is perfectly right.' There followed a short debate, and then he gave her his promise to go to the consecration, which promise he faithfully kept.

Next night Parabère slept with her lover and told him the whole story, as she thought it was extremely funny. For the same reason the favourite passed it on to Biron, who that very evening told it to me. Together we deplored the bonds which held the Regent. I never mentioned the subject of the consecration again to the Regent, and he never mentioned it to me, but afterwards he was embarrassed and shamefaced in my presence. I do not know if he was so weak as to tell Dubois what, in my efforts to persuade him against attending the consecration, I had said, or if Dubois was told it by Parabère with the object of gaining credit for having changed the mind of the Duc d'Orléans, but he was certainly told by some one, and he never forgave me. I heard later from M. de Belle-Isle that Dubois told M. Blanc that, in spite of all the various obstacles I had put in his way, and the real dangers I had forced him to run, nothing had so profoundly hurt him, and that to the heart, as when I had tried to persuade the Duc d'Orléans not to go to his consecration.

Val-de-Grâce was chosen for the ceremony. Apart from being a Royal institution, it is the finest monastery in Paris and its church is the most curious that we have to show. Cardinal de Rohan, always delighted to oppose Cardinal de Noailles in all he did, was overjoyed to profit by the latter's refusal to allow Dubois to be ordained in his diocese, and took this opportunity of paying his court to the Regent and of currying favour with his Minister in offering to perform the ceremony. And it must be admitted that a Cardinal of Rohan's birth, a Bishop of Strasbourg, and the possessor of so many claims to distinction was far above anything the Abbé Dubois can ever have hoped for.

With regard to the two assistants, Nantes, by daring to ordain

Dubois, had already staked out such a claim that it would have been impossible to pass him over. And, as for the other, Dubois considered it wise to find someone whose life and conduct would somehow counter-balance his own. Massillon, the celebrated priest of the Oratory, who had risen to be Bishop of Clermont on account of his virtue, his learning, and his talents as a preacher—for even at that date among the many bad appointments a few good ones managed to slip through—was the man he wanted. Massillon, his back to the wall and with no one to turn to, realized the indignity of what was being put to him, stammered, and did not dare refuse. After all, what could such a helpless man have done in such a century, when faced with the Regent, his Minister, and Cardinal de Rohan? Nevertheless he was blamed, and very severely blamed, by the world, particularly by the good men of all parties, who for once had been joined together in the face of this enormous scandal.

The church was magnificently decorated; all France was invited; and everyone took care to be in evidence throughout the ceremony. Booths with trellis work in front of them had been erected for the Ambassadors and Ministers of Protestant countries. Another, still more magnificent, had been made for the Duc d'Orléans and the Duc de Chartres, who accompanied his father; and there was yet another for the ladies. The Duc d'Orléans entered through the monastery, and his booth, which was open to all comers, was at the far end. Both inside and without, refreshments of all sorts were being liberally dispensed by the officers of his household. Profusion of this kind continued throughout the day, and within and without the monastery there were tables for the underlings, and for anyone else who was willing to attend. The Duc d'Orléans's First Gentleman of the Bedchamber and his First Officers were in charge of these entertainments; they received the more important people, led them to their places, and finally ushered them out again; and other officers attended to the less important in the same way. At the same time the Watch and the police were busy meeting, placing, and helping to disengage the innumerable coaches which arrived as conveniently as was possible. During the progress of the ceremony—it was conducted with little decency on the part of either the new bishop or the spectators—the Duc d'Orléans was careful to express to all the more important people waiting upon him his pleasure in seeing them there, and when that was over he went off to dine with Mme de Parabère at Asnières.[1]

---

[1] A country house bought by Mme de Parabère in 1719, probably with the Regent's money.

All the bishops, the more distinguished Abbés and a quantity of important laymen were invited during the course of the service by the Duc d'Orléans's officers to dinner at the Palais Royal. The same officers acted as hosts at the dinner itself, and it was a marvel of abundance and delicacy. It was served by the Duc d'Orléans's servants and at his expense.

There were two tables, each of them laid for thirty, set out in a large room in the great apartments and filled with all that was most considerable in Paris, while several other tables, equally well served, were arranged in the neighbouring rooms for those of less consequence. The Duc d'Orléans gave the new Archbishop a very expensive diamond to put in his archiepiscopal ring. In this way the whole day was given over to the triumph of Dubois, a triumph which earned assuredly neither the approbation of man nor the benediction of God. I saw nothing of it, and the subject was never mentioned between the Duc d'Orleans and myself.

At the time when Dubois was made Archbishop of Cambrai, an ordinance was published by the town crier, to the sound of the trumpet, ordering all foreign rebels to leave such parts of France as were subject to the King's obedience within the next eight days, and after that these rebels were hunted down and punished with the utmost rigour. By these words 'foreign rebels' were meant no others than the English, and the ordinance was one of the effects of Lord Stanhope's recent visits to Paris. In point of fact this was merely to put into force an infamous clause in the treaty which Dubois had made with England, and which up to now had been tacitly in abeyance. By this clause England stood to gain everything and France nothing but ignominy of the most dangerous kind. The French refugees, who had been in England since the revocation of the Edict of Nantes, could not possibly cause us the least anxiety, since no one in our country had a right to the throne but its actual holder, and the reciprocity called for by this treaty could not apply to the French, none of whom was a rebel or opposed to the ruling house. This reciprocity was nothing more than a veil, or rather a spider's web, to promote the interests not of the English people but of the King and his ministers who were frightened even of the shadow of the legitimate and rightful King, although he was settled in Rome, and those English who followed him or were so discontented with the régime as to favour his cause without actually belonging to his party. The proximity of France to England was a continual anxiety to the house of Hanover because of the Jacobites who had sought refuge here.

DEATHS OF MME DE LILLEBONNE AND MME LA DUCHESSE

VARIOUS people died about this time. Among them was the Comtesse de Lillebonne, who for several years now had taken to calling herself the Princesse de Lillebonne. She was the bastard daughter of Charles IV, Duc de Lorraine, so famous in history for his treachery, and of the Comtesse de Cantecroix. She was the widow of the younger brother of the Duc d'Elbeuf. I have often had occasion to speak of her, and I have said enough about her character to make it unnecessary to enlarge upon it here. With all her virtue, her sense of dignity, her correctness of behaviour, she yielded nothing to the other Guises in ambition, or in those qualities of the mind which her family have made their own. Indeed, she would have made a useful addition to their number in the innermost counsel of the League.[1] Mlle de Guise, the Chevalier de Lorraine and she formed a sort of alliance together. Mme de Remirement,[2] her elder daughter, and Mme d'Espinoy, her younger, took after her completely. Her death was a severe loss to both daughters, as well as to Vaudémont, her brother by the same liaison, who was, if possible, a more dangerous *Guisard* than herself. They used all to live together in Paris, in the Hôtel de Mayenne, that temple of the League, where they still maintain a room, known as the 'Cabinet de la Ligue,' exactly as it always used to be, out of veneration or rather out of a sort of religious cult they have, for a spot where all the most secret and intimate counsels of the League were held. No doubt it serves to keep alive their regrets and their ambitions.

Madame la Duchesse, the sister of the Prince de Conti and of Mlle de la Roche-sur-Yon, died on the 21st of March, in Paris, at the Hôtel de Condé, after a long illness. She was thirty-one years old; she had been married about seven years, during which time she made little effort to control herself.[3] She was mourned but not regretted. Since the Princes of the Blood had been refused their request to be allowed to stand guard over the coffins of princesses of this standing, the usual rapid burial took place. Two days after her death, with no ceremony at the Hôtel de Condé except the barest necessity, she was taken to

---

[1] The confederation formed by French Catholics under the inspiration of the Guise family in 1576 originally to oppose the Protestants; subsequently waged civil war against Henry III and Henry IV until the Treaty of Angers in 1598.

[2] We have met her more frequently under the name of Mlle de Lillebonne. She became abbess of Remirement in 1711.

[3] She ate and drank too much, but the real reason for her bad reputation is not clear.

the Carmelites in the rue Saint-Jacques and buried there. The cortège was most magnificent. Mlle de Clermont[1] accompanied the body with the Duchesses de Sully and de Tallard, at the request of M. le Duc and Mme her mother. A few days later Monsieur le Duc received everyone, and his ante-room was like a second-hand cloak shop with all the impropriety which has marked this new-fangled custom ever since it started.[2] Mme la Duchesse, who left no children, had made a will and Mlle de la Roche-sur-Yon was the beneficiary. There was a good deal in the estate including a mass of jewelry, because the Prince de Conti had been very generous to this princess who was his eldest daughter. Mlle de la Roche-sur-Yon did not come off very well and M. le Duc quickly took the whole thing into his hands; but a few years before his death he made restitution to Mlle de la Roche-sur-Yon who had never complained officially and had by then put the matter out of her mind. The King went into mourning for five days for Madame la Duchesse.

The Comte de Horn[3] had been in Paris about two months, mixing in low society, and spending his time in gambling and debauchery. He was a man twenty-two years old, tall and well-built, and a member of that old and famous House of Horn, known since the eleventh century as one of the smaller dynasties reigning in the Low Countries which produced a long succession of illustrious descendants. The small town or manor of Horn in Brabant, which is near Roehrmond, is the birthplace of and has given its name to the family. It is within the territory of Liége, and once formed part of the ancient county of Loos.

This young Comte de Horn came to the rue Quincampoix[4] on Good Friday, the 22nd of March, with the object, as he said, of buying shares to the value of a hundred thousand crowns. For this purpose he had arranged to meet a broker in a public house there. The broker arrived with his bag and his shares, and the Comte de Horn, as he explained, with two of his friends. However, next moment the three of them had fallen upon the wretched broker. The Comte de Horn stabbed the broker several times with his dagger and then took his bag from him. One of the two so-called friends was a Piedmontese,

---

[1] Marie-Anne de Bourbon-Condé, sister-in-law of the deceased.

[2] The Duke received his visitors wearing a formal cloak and the ante-room contained a pile of spare cloaks for those who had come without. Saint-Simon strongly disapproved of this slipshod practice and commented most unfavourably when it began in 1710.

[3] Antoine-Joseph, Count de Horn, captain of Protestant cavalry in the Austrian service, son of Count and Prince de Horn and born in 1698.

[4] In which Law's bank was situated.

named Mille, and it was he who, seeing that the broker was not dead, killed him.

By this time the people of the public house, who had heard a noise, ran up to see what was happening. Though they were not in time to prevent the murder, they captured the assassins and arrested them. In the middle of the scrimmage one of the cut-throats escaped, but the Comte de Horn and Mille were unable to follow his example. The people of the public house then sent for the officers of justice, and handed over their captives to them; they were then taken to the Conciergerie.

This horrible crime—it had been committed in broad daylight—made a great stir, and immediately several influential people, related to the illustrious House of Horn, went to beg the Duc d'Orléans to have mercy on the culprit. However, the Duc d'Orléans tried to avoid seeing them, and quite rightly gave orders that the wheels of justice should be set in motion at once. In the end the relations managed to see the Regent. They attempted to argue that the Comte de Horn was mad, and even went so far as to allege that he had an uncle in a mad house, and they begged that he should be sent to the *Petites Maisons*[1] or to the Fathers of Charity at Charenton who also take charge of lunatics. The Regent's reply was that the sooner people who carried their madness to such a pitch of fury were put out of the way the better. Failing in their demand, they next pointed out how infamous it would be if a member of so illustrious a House were to be brought before a criminal court, and they proved that they were related to many of the noblest Houses in Europe as well as to nearly all its reigning sovereigns. The Duc d'Orléans replied that the infamy consisted in the crime and not in the punishment. They urged that their House had the honour to be related to his. 'Very well, my good Sirs,' he answered, 'I shall share your shame.'

The trial was neither long nor difficult. Law and the Abbé Dubois, who were naturally interested in the safety of their brokers, without whom their paper would immediately fall in value and become useless, made common cause and saw to it that the Duc d'Orléans remained inexorable, while he, to finish with the persecution he was undergoing from those who were begging him continually for pardon, and Dubois and Law for fear that in the end he might yield, did their utmost to force the *Parlement* to hurry the trial forward.

---

[1] An asylum founded in 1557 in the rue de Sèvres. Its name came from the fact that it was almost entirely composed of small houses built around the various central courtyards.

In the meanwhile the prosecution went ahead, and in the end the prisoner was condemned to the wheel.[1] At this the relations lost all hope of saving the criminal, and turned all their thoughts to having the sentence commuted. Some of them even came to see me to beg my help, although I am in no way related to the House of Horn. They told me that the sentence was a desperate tragedy for them and for all their relations in the Low Countries and in Germany; that in those countries there was an important distinction drawn between the various penalties inflicted on criminals of quality; that if a man's head were cut off it made no difference to his family, but that the wheel inflicted such infamy on them that the uncles, the aunts, the brothers and sisters, and all the three following generations were excluded from entering any noble monastery or convent, which apart from the ignominy entailed was a very serious hurt, since it put an end to all hopes of establishing the various members of the family or giving them any chance of rising to be Canonesses or Sovereign bishops. This argument touched me, and I promised to do my best to state their case to the Duc d'Orléans, but without holding out any hope that I would speak in favour of a pardon.

It was Holy Week and I was just on the point of setting out for La Ferté. I therefore went straight to the Duc d'Orléans and told him what I had just heard. Then I said that whoever were to ask him to spare the Comte de Horn's life, after the commission of what was in every way so detestable a crime, would show that the only interests he had at heart were those of the Horn family, and that he was no true servant of his; that nevertheless I also thought that it was hardly acting in his best interests to insist on the wheel, to which it was certain that the Comte de Horn would then be condemned; that I was of the opinion that we could find a compromise, and I knew how he usually liked to find a way through, which would be an ample fulfilment of justice and the reasonable expectations of the public and at the same time avoid the prejudicial effects of the wheel upon a family which was so illustrious and had such fine alliances as that of Horn. Then I showed him quite simply how this could be done, by allowing the sentence of death on the wheel to be passed, by having a commutation

---

[1] In this form of execution the criminal's arms and legs were attached to two pieces of wood in the form of a cross. The executioner then broke the four limbs and the breast, after which the body was attached to a wheel suspended from a stake, the broken arms and legs were tied behind the back and the man's face turned uppermost, in which condition he was left to die a lingering death. By this time it had become, however, a usual practice for the judges to order the man to be strangled before he was attached to the wheel.

of the penalty already signed and sealed beside him with nothing but the date to fill in when the sentence was eventually passed, by then sending this immediately to the necessary authorities, and by having the Comte de Horn's head cut off the same day. In this way justice would be accomplished, the sentence of death upon the wheel would be properly pronounced, the public would be satisfied by the fact that the Comte de Horn had been put to death; and the family would be grateful to him for having saved their honour. The Duc d'Orléans agreed that I was right, approved of my suggestion, and saw that it was in his own interest not to set so many important people against him, if at the same time it were possible to act with justice and to do his duty by the public. He therefore promised me to follow my advice.

After that I told him that I was leaving the next day, and that Law and the Abbé Dubois were so set on the wheel that if they could they would drag his consent from him by force. He promised me once again to stand by his decision to commute the sentence, and then went on to say as much in favour of that course as I could have done myself. I told him that I was not related to the Horns, that I did not even know them, and that I was not in any way in touch with those who were agitating in their favour, but that my only reason for urging him to take this course was my attachment to his person and his interests, and then I conjured him to remain firm in the resolution he had taken. He promised me again, and knowing him well I could see that he meant what he said. I therefore took my leave of him, and the next morning I set off for the country.

However, what I had foreseen happened. Dubois and Law immediately set upon him and succeeded so well that the first news I heard at La Ferté was that the Comte de Horn and his fellow scoundrel, Mille, had been broken alive and died upon the wheel at the place of execution in Paris on the Tuesday after Easter, the 26th of March, at about four o'clock in the afternoon, both of them on the same scaffold, and after having been put to the question. The results were just what I had foretold they would be. The Horn family, and all the great nobility of the Low Countries and even of Germany, were horrified, and did not mince their words in speech or letters. There were even the strangest plots of vengeance, and years after the death of the Duc d'Orléans I used to meet men who even then could not resist talking to me about it, and releasing all the venom which they had stored up in their hearts for so long.

A FLOOD OF PENSIONS

In spite of the financial situation the Duc d'Orléans now let loose another flood of pensions. He gave one of 6000 livres and another of 4000 livres to all those who held the ranks of Lieutenant General or Major General respectively, but with this limitation: that no one who held a Governorship or was in receipt of another pension could apply for this, unless the other pension was for a less amount, in which case that pension would be made up to the amount in question. As the number of recipients was very large this was not only a great expense, but it pleased no one. Old Mme de Montauban, whom I have occasionally mentioned here, received a pension of 20,000 livres, and M. de Montauban, the Prince de Guémené's younger brother, another for 6000 livres. The Duchesse de Brissac, who was very poor, and who lived with and at the expense of her brother, Verthamon, the First President of the Grand Council, had one of 6000. Mme de Coëtquen, M. du Puy Vauban, M. de Polastron, and the late M. de Puyzieulx's daughter, who was the widow of Blanchefort the gambler, and her son, all received pensions of 4000 livres. In addition to these, eight or ten others, varying between three and four thousand livres, were also granted.

I obtained one of 8000 for the Maréchale de Lorges, and one for 6000 for the Maréchale de Chamilly, whose affairs were in a bad way as a result of her dealings in Mississippi shares. M. de Soubise and the Marquis de Noailles each received a present of 200,000 livres down. Even Saint-Geniès, on leaving the Bastille and being sent into exile at Beauvais, instead of further off as had originally been intended, received a pension of a thousand livres.

The fact of the matter was that everyone wanted a larger income because of the height to which the price of the smallest commodity had risen. Other prices went up in proportion, and although things had fallen since, they have always remained far above what they were before the Mississippi affair.

The Marquis de Châtillon, who since those days has risen to such heights of fortune, had a pension of 6000 livres on quitting his post of Inspector of Cavalry, and, finally, Payronie, the King's First Surgeon on the retirement of Maréchal, received one of 8000 livres.

AN UNPOPULAR MARRIAGE

ONE day, towards the end of April, I was working with the Duc d'Orléans when he told me of a marriage that was being arranged between the Duc de Lorges and Mlle de Mesmes, and said that the First President had asked for his consent to the match. I had not heard a word of this match, and, to tell the truth, the news made me furious. It will have been noticed more than once in these pages how much I had done to help this brother-in-law of mine. Indeed, I could have had him appointed Captain of the Guards if only he had been prepared to sell his little house at Livry, in order to raise the 500,000 livres which the Maréchal d'Harcourt wanted for the post. It will be remembered, however, that he preferred to keep his house.

It was now more than I could tolerate to see him marrying the daughter of a man whom I so obviously hated, and whom, when I ran into him at the Palais Royal I never met without showing my dislike, sometimes in the most pointed way. I returned to Meudon, where we had already taken up our quarters, and told Mme de Saint-Simon of the horrible behaviour of her brother, at which she was as much surprised and hurt as I was. I told her that, never so long as I lived, would I meet either him or his wife, that I should also refuse to see the Maréchal de Lorges and M. and Mme de Lauzun, if any of them were to sign the marriage contract or attend the wedding.

Moreover, I made my intention generally known, and in doing so allowed my tongue full liberty in public when expressing my opinion of the father and his prospective son-in-law. This outbreak of temper, and it was as strong as I could make it, caused a good deal of disorder in our family, which up to this time had been most closely united and lived almost continually in each other's company. For a time it stopped the marriage completely. In spite of this, however, I saw nothing of the Duc de Lorges, who hoped that his sisters would be able to bring me round, and between his hopes for this fine marriage and his fear of me was far too much embarrassed to dare to visit me.

A RATE OF INTEREST

THE Duc d'Orléans, under the influence of his most trusted financial advisers, determined to reduce the interest payable on 'the funds' to two per cent. This was a great relief to the debtors, but also a great reduction in the revenue of the creditors, who, trusting in the good faith of the government, the common custom in these matters, and the laws

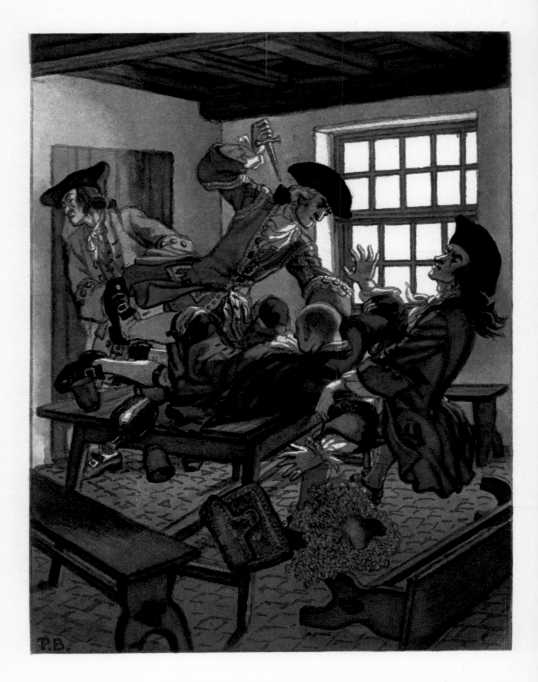

The Comte de Horn's treachery

of borrowing, had lent their money at five per cent, and always been in peaceful enjoyment of that amount. However, the Duc d'Orléans called a meeting of the various government advisers on financial matters, and with their help determined to issue an edict to this effect.

Then the *Parlement* protested strongly and passed a remonstrance. Aligre was presiding on the day when this occurred, as the First President had, according to his own account, gone off to his country seat to take a cure. It is true that he had had a slight attack of apoplexy, for which he had been treated the previous year at Vichy. But there is no doubt that he was delighted to be able to avoid the necessity of committing himself with the Duc d'Orléans, after the cruel dressing-down he had recently received from him, without losing his grip upon the *Parlement*. He knew, like everyone else, the low opinion in which Aligre was held, and he realized that it would be perfectly safe to let him have his head. Moreover, he was no doubt delighted to see a fresh quarrel arise between the Regent and the *Parlement*; he wished it to come to a head in his absence; and he hoped to be able to come back later and to play his usual part of umpire between party and the Regent, and in this way, while keeping the embers secretly alight, to draw money from the Regent, whose complaisance he no doubt considered to be limitless.

Eight days after the resolution in favour of a remonstrance was passed, Aligre, with a deputation from the *Parlement* behind him, brought it in writing to the King, and, after making a feeble speech, left it with him. This was on the 17th of April. When it was seen that the remonstrance met with no success, the *Parlement* assembled on the 22nd and resolved not to register the edict and to make a fresh remonstrance. On leaving the sitting, the King's Officers came to the Palais Royal to make their report. The Duc d'Orléans replied curtly and drily that the decision he had come to would not be changed, and immediately left them.

THE RETURN OF RIOMS

RIOMS, who, while serving with the Maréchal de Berwick's army in Spain, had received instructions, at the time of the Duchesse de Berry's death, to keep away from Paris, was now permitted by the Duc d'Orléans to come back. There can be no doubt that if he had returned from his campaign immediately after her death his presence would have caused talk. However, it was now thought that sufficient time had elapsed for all to be forgotten.

Nevertheless, he had the sense to see that, after what had passed, his presence at the Palais Royal was likely to prove as embarrassing to him as it would be to the Duc d'Orléans, and he did no more than pay a formal call. Indeed, he went out little anywhere, but contented himself with the sort of life which pleased him best, a life of pleasure among his friends, and sank into something which was very near obscurity. Although the Mississippi Scheme had arrived a little late for him, he was very comfortably off, and he now resigned from his regiment and gave up all thoughts of further service.

PRESS GANGS FOR THE MISSISSIPPI

AFTER juggling with the question of the Mississippi as a mountebank juggles with his cups and balls, its directors at last decided, as the English had done, to turn their vast dominions into a going concern. With the object of finding the country a population, press gangs were set to work arresting all the sturdy beggars and men of no standing that they could find, to which they added a quantity of women off the streets. If this measure had been wisely and intelligently carried out, with all the precautions that are necessary in cases of this kind, it might not only have attained the object in view, but also have relieved Paris and the provinces of a heavy, valueless, and sometimes dangerous burden. Instead of this it was administered, in Paris and elsewhere, with so much violence—not to speak of the roguery of those who, by influencing the authorities, succeeded in having their private enemies arrested —that it excited the widest indignation. Moreover, no care whatever had been taken to provide for these unfortunate people while on the road or at their ports of embarkation. They were shut up at night in barns without being given any food. Sometimes they were even forced to lie in ditches by the roadside, wherever they happened to be when evening fell, and from which they were not allowed to emerge for a moment. Their cries for help excited the pity and indignation of all who heard them, but, as neither the alms of the merciful nor the little that was given them by their guards were enough, a terrible number of them died.

Such inhumanity, joined to the barbarity of the guards, and to the shocking fact, until this time without precedent, that many of those who were being carried off were not of the quality prescribed, but merely people whom others desired to put out of the way and had therefore bribed the authorities to get rid of, raised such an insistent and imperious outcry that the measure had to be given up. But some of these wretched people had by this time been embarked, and their treatment on the voyage seems to have been as bad as what had gone before. Those who had not been embarked were now released, and allowed to go to the devil in their own way, and no further arrests were made. Law, who was regarded as the author of these measures, became very unpopular and the Duc d'Orléans had reason to repent of having given his consent.

RETURN OF THE COMTE DE CHAROLAIS

THE Comte de Charolais returned at last from his long travels abroad. Monsieur le Duc, satisfied with what he had done for him, ordered his return, and met him at Chantilly with all his family and friends around him. Turményes was among the latter. He had served with credit as a Master of Requests and as the Intendant of a province. He could if he wished have made his way in the world, and done so to everyone's satisfaction. However, on the death of his father, who was Keeper of the Royal Treasure, he preferred the solid abundance of that post to all the hopes of advancement his profession could hold out to him. He was a very intelligent fellow, well-read and well-informed, by nature gay and free-spoken, though only within reason, and with plenty of tact and consideration for the company and occasion in which he found himself. He mixed with the best people at Court and in the town. He was clever, capable, upright and obliging in his profession, and without the least boastfulness; he was esteemed and trusted by the Ministers; he got on excellently with the Regent; and he was on terms of great familiarity with Monsieur le Duc and the Prince de Conti (both fathers and sons), so much so that they would accept anything from him, though they would have been furious with anyone else who dared to speak to them as he did. It was the fact that he lived at l'Isle Adam, added to his love of hunting and of the table, that had first formed this friendship with the fathers, and he had succeeded in continuing the same relationship with the sons.

Now Turményes was a man who knew very well what he was saying, but who found it difficult to resist a joke. His liberty in language, which was in any case no more than a decent freedom and entirely without insolence or personal offensiveness to his superiors, had grown with the impunity he enjoyed. He was small and fat, with a very short neck, a head right down on his shoulders, and he wore his fair hair very long. This gave him an awkward, clumsy look, and earned for him the nick-name of 'Court-Collet.'

Hearing that his brother was just on the point of arriving, Monsieur le Duc went out with all his company to welcome and embrace him as he stepped down from his coach. The company, anxious to pay its respects to the young Prince, pressed closely round. As soon as the meeting between the two brothers was over, Monsieur le Duc presented the Comte de Charolais to his guests. However, the Comte de Charolais contented himself with a careless glance at those around him, and remained where he had got down from his coach for a considerable time without addressing a word to anyone.

Seeing what was happening, and irritated by it, Turményes turned to the company and coolly, but quite clearly, said: 'My dear Sirs, I advise you all to send your children travelling and to spend a lot of money on them.' This remark had a great success and was repeated everywhere. Turményes did not deny that he had said it, and Monsieur le Duc and the Comte de Charolais only laughed.

However, Monsieur le Duc must have been used to this sort of thing. When Law's shares were just appearing on the market, Monsieur le Duc happened, in front of a crowd of people, to boast a little too complacently of the amount of them he held. This was followed by a silence and then 'Court-Collet' was heard to say in impatient tones: 'For shame, Sir, your great-grandfather only prided himself upon five or six actions[1] in his life, but they were worth a good deal more than yours are.' At this everyone looked down, and Monsieur le Duc merely burst out laughing, and never bore Turményes the least resentment. He let off a number of good remarks against the Ministers of the late King and, since the Regency, against M. the Duc d'Orléans himself, who also only laughed. Although comparatively young, he only lived a year or two longer, and his death was generally regretted.

A QUEER MARRIAGE CONTRACT

As a result of abject folly on the one hand and of the most horrible cupidity on the other, there was signed at this time a contract of marriage which was perhaps the oddest that has ever been entered into between two parties. Incidentally it is a good example of what Law's system did for France, and deserves a mention here. . . . The contract in question was one drawn up and executed by the Marquis d'Oise, aged thirty-three, the son and the younger brother of the two Ducs de

---

[1] A pun; 'actions' means not only what it does in English, but also 'shares,' in the sense of stocks and shares. The great-grandfather was, of course, the Grand Condé.

Villars-Brancas, of the one part, and the daughter of André, the famous Mississippi speculator, of the other. André had made a pile of money in Mississippi shares, but his daughter was still only three years old, and it was therefore agreed that the marriage should not be celebrated until she was twelve. The conditions were: 100,000 crowns down, 20,000 livres a year until the day of marriage, and further millions on the marriage being consummated. In the meanwhile the Ducs de Villars-Brancas, father and son, were both to receive a large sum for their consent.

There was of course a great deal of talk about this marriage, but what will not *auri sacra fames* accomplish? Law's fall eventually put an end to the bargain before the marriage could take place, but by that time the two Brancas, father and son, who had expected something of the sort, had taken good care to receive their payment in advance. The limit was reached when fifteen years later actions to recover some of this money were brought against them, and when, without the least shame, an emotion to which the Brancas are not in any case much addicted, they fought them in the courts.

DEATH OF THE MARQUISE D'ALLUYES

THE Marquise d'Alluyes died in the Palais Royal at about this time. The name of her family was Meaux du Fouilloux, and she had been Lady-in-Waiting to Madame, Monsieur's first wife. In 1667, being no longer young but still very beautiful, she had married the Marquis d'Alluyes, the son and brother of Charles and François d'Escoubleau, both of them Marquis de Sourdis, and Knights of the Order, the one in 1633 and the other in 1688. Alluyes, the elder brother, received the Governorship of Orléanais from his father, and he and his wife, though he the more seriously, were both involved in the Voisin affair,[1] and were exiled for some time. The husband died in 1690, without children; though allowed to return to Paris, he had never received permission to see the King again.

The Marquise, who was an intimate friend not only of the Comtesse de Soissons, but also of the Duchesses de Bouillon and de Mazarin, spent her whole life in the intricate conduct of affairs of the heart. When age at last excluded her from having any of her own she became all the busier in aiding and abetting those of others. The Marquis

---

[1] Catherine des Hayes, widow of Monvoisin, was a famous seer who was burnt alive at Paris, 22 February 1680.

d'Éffiat, who has so often been mentioned in these pages, married one of her husband's sisters. She bore him no children and he lost her early in his career. However, he always protected Mme d'Alluyes at Monsieur's Court and she was a friend of both Monsieur and Madame until death came to separate them.

Mme d'Alluyes was not a wicked woman, and she engaged in no intrigues but those of gallantry. However, these last interested her so deeply that, right up to the time of her death, she acted as a sort of rendezvous and confidante for all the love affairs of Paris. Every morning there would be a crowd of lovers round her, telling her of the progress of their various affairs. She loved the world and was passionately fond of gambling though she had but little money and spent it all in play. In the morning she would, as I have said, have long talks with the lovers all around her; they would give her all the latest news of the town, and tell her how their own affairs were progressing. When that was done, she would send out for a slice of pâté or of ham, sometimes perhaps for some salt meat or a little pastry, and she would eat it while she talked. In the evening she would go out to sup and to gamble wherever she could get an invitation, and return at about four o'clock in the morning and go to bed. This life suited her so well that she remained plump and fresh, without the least infirmity, until she was well over eighty, when she died after a short illness, and a long life spent in nothing but the search for pleasure, and that without the least constraint and without a care in the world. She had never worried her head about anyone's opinion of her, though she took a pride in being a sure and secret friend; the whole world loved her; but no women ever visited her.

A QUARREL BETWEEN THE KING OF ENGLAND AND THE PRINCE OF WALES

FOR many a long day now a kind of open warfare existed between the King of England and the Prince of Wales. There had been scandalous outbreaks of temper; the whole Court had taken sides; and the matter had even been mentioned in Parliament. On more than one occasion King George's attacks upon his son had been most unbecoming. He had long ago dismissed him from his palace and refused to see him anywhere. Moreover, he had cut down his allowances so that it was difficult for him to live. The result of all this was that Parliament began to put difficulties in King George's way, some of them quite serious ones.

As a matter of fact, the reason why the father could never tolerate the son was because he did not believe that he was his. He suspected, indeed he believed that he knew, that the Duchess, his wife, daughter of the Duke of Wolfenbüttel, had been guilty of misconduct with the Count of Königsmark, whom he had surprised coming out of her room one day, and there and then had had thrown into a burning oven, after which he had shut his wife up in a country house where she was forced to spend the remainder of her days under a strict guard.

The Prince of Wales, who considered himself ill-treated for a cause of which he personally was innocent, had always resented his mother's imprisonment and the effects of his father's hatred upon himself. However, the Princess of Wales, who was a sensible, intelligent, well-mannered and gracious woman, had done what she could to soften her father-in-law and the King had been unable to refuse her his respect, or even to desist from being fond of her. In the same way she had conciliated all the English; and in time the Court about her, which had always been large, included all the best and most distinguished men of the day. In course of time the Prince of Wales began to take greater and greater liberties, to disregard his father, and to address the Ministers in such haughty terms that finally they became alarmed. They feared at once the Princess of Wales's credit and the fact that they might be attacked in Parliament, a body which has always enjoyed the sport of baiting Ministers. All these considerations were redoubled when it was discovered how strong the opposition was likely to be, and especially when it was realized that the fruits of such opposition must necessarily fall upon the King.

The Ministers therefore told him of their fears, which he shared to the extent of agreeing to be reconciled with his son upon certain conditions and through the mediation of the Princess of Wales, who on her side realized the difficulty of creating and maintaining a party in opposition to the King and who had always sincerely wished for peace within the bosom of the Royal Family. She therefore seized this chance, and, trusting in the ascendancy she had over her husband, brought about a reconciliation.

The King gave the Prince of Wales a large sum of money and received him; the Ministers saved their skins; and everything seemed to have been forgotten. The extreme to which affairs had gone between them had led the British people to expect an open rupture at any moment, and had caused just as much talk throughout Europe, where each power tried to egg on or to heal the breach according to its own interests. This reconciliation gave Europe a new topic of conversation and a subject for speculation.

Mme de Coëtquen died in Brittany where she had long lived in retirement on her estates. She was a Chabot, a daughter of the Rohan heiress, and a sister of the Duc de Rohan, of the beautiful and clever Mme de Soubise, and of Mme d'Espinoy. One of these sisters was older than she was and the other younger. Mme de Soubise's beauty had made her husband a Prince (what else did it not do for her?) and Mme d'Espinoy was in possession of an honorary *tabouret*, which old Charost's credit had procured her at the time of her marriage to the Prince d'Espinoy, so Mme de Coëtquen used to say of herself, pleasantly enough, that she had fallen between two *tabourets*.

She was an intelligent, dignified woman, as well as beautiful, and in her time she had made her mark in the world. She was haughty and imperious and she and her sisters were always in close alliance. She is famous for the passion she inspired in M. de Turenne, and for having learnt from him the secret plans of the siege of Ghent, when no one but he and Louvois had been told by the King. Longing to show her power over M. de Turenne, she had been guilty of a breach of security to someone else. Fortunately this person was discreet, and realizing the importance of the information allowed it to go no further. But the King came to hear of it, and he questioned Louvois, who protested his innocence. The King then sent for M. de Turenne, who at that time was at daggers drawn with Louvois, but Turenne's honesty was more powerful than his hatred. He blushed and confessed his weakness. Then he begged to be forgiven. The King, not ignorant of love's empire, just laughed, but he could not resist amusing himself a little at M. de Turenne's expense, and he rallied him with still being so susceptible to the powers of love at his age. Finally he told him to see to it that Mme de Coëtquen was more discreet in future, and to take good care that the person to whom she had so indiscreetly prattled should keep his or her mouth shut too.

Until M. de Turenne's confession the King had not known that it was Mme de Coëtquen who had first learnt and then been guilty of revealing the secret. Fortunately it went no further, and the execution of that great siege was in no way prejudiced. The late King always treated Mme de Coëtquen with great respect; she was in his sister's confidence, and she knew a good deal of what was going on behind the scenes. She was well suited to Court life and to play a part in the great world, and this she did for a very long time.[1]

---

[1] Among her lovers she numbered the Chevalier de Lorraine and the Great Condé.

Return of the Comte de Charolais

DEATH OF CHAULIEU

A FEW days later the Abbé de Chaulieu died. He was an agreeable rake who kept very good company, had a gift for pretty verses, moved in the best circles, and had but small respect for religion. That he had no more respect for honour either came out in spite of himself. For many years he lived with the two Vendômes, running their house and looking after all their business affairs for them. Indeed the Duc de Vendôme had always relied upon his brother, the Grand Prior, and on Chaulieu under him. We have already seen how the Duc de Vendôme found his fortune had gone, how the Grand Prior and Chaulieu had joined together to fleece him, how he had dismissed Chaulieu and quarrelled with the Grand Prior, taking the management of his household and of all his other affairs out of their hands, and going to the King for help, and how the King had instructed the elder Crozat, who was later the Comte d'Évreux's brother-in-law, to administer M. de Vendôme's household and estates.

All this made little difference to Chaulieu. His tone in the world was just as high, his relations with the Grand Prior seemed to grow even closer, and he laughed at whatever might be said with all his customary insolence. Nevertheless, he did not dare to come to Court, although no one had taken him seriously enough to warn him to keep away. He was only tonsured; he professed to be a gentleman; and he managed to get one of his nephews a place in the Gendarmerie, of which the young man made nothing. His right to call himself of noble birth was, to say the least of it, obscure, and his family was certainly not wealthy. The discovery of his rogueries cut him off from a large portion of society.[1]

THE DECREES OF MAY TWENTY-SECOND AND THEIR RESULTS

THE 22nd of May, this year, has become famous for the publication of a decree issued by the Council of State and regulating the shares in the Company of the Indies, or what was formerly known as the Mississippi Company, and also the bank notes. The object of this decree was, month by month, to effect the diminution in the value of these notes and shares

---

[1] With the aid of the Grand Prior he obtained abbeys and benefices yielding 30,000 livres which enabled him to keep up his house in the Temple, which was a centre for men of letters, including the young Voltaire.

so that, by the end of the year, they should neither of them be worth more than half what they were at the beginning. Now this is what in the language of bankruptcy lawyers and financiers is known as 'showing one's behind,' and the decree showed it so effectually and so plainly that at once everyone began to imagine the finances to be in an even worse state than they really were, seeing that the decree did not even suggest a remedy for recent ills.

Argenson, who had been given the Treasury and attained to the Seals through Law, who, during his administration of the Treasury had done all he could to impede the latter and who in the end had been forced to give them up, was strongly suspected of issuing this decree out of sheer malice, and of having clearly foreseen the evils which it must bring in its train. The excitement was universal and terrible. There was not a rich man who did not see himself hopelessly ruined, nor a poor one who did not fancy himself beggared. Then the *Parlement*, whose own system was so opposed to that of Law, seized the opportunity to put itself forward as the public's champion by refusing to register the decree, and making the strongest protest. The result of this was that when at last the decree was withdrawn the public gave all its gratitude to the *Parlement*, although actually the cause was no more than the general distress and the tardy realization that a mistake had been made in the first place. However, this withdrawal did little more than reveal the fact that the government regretted having disclosed the true condition of Law's operations, and certainly produced no remedy. The result was that confidence was now radically destroyed and there remained no hope of restoring it.

In these straits there was nothing for it but to make a scape-goat of Law. That, of course, was what the Keeper of the Seals had meant to happen all along. However, he had the good sense to remain contented with his cunning revenge, and showed no intention of coming out into the open or of again taking over what he had once been forced to give up. Nevertheless, though he was too clever to want to have control of the finances in the state in which they then were (since after holding them for a month or two Law would have been forgotten and he would have become the culprit), he knew too much to be able to tolerate a new Controller General, who, so long as he remained in power, would have had the upper hand of him. He therefore divided the work into five departments[1] and was careful to choose the holders

---

[1] Argenson himself took over the Crown property, M. Amelot took Commerce, M. de la Houssaye took the farming of the taxes, M. des Forts the Compagnie des Indes and the Mint, and M. Fagon took the Bank.

of these offices himself. In this way he actually resumed his control
over the Treasury and was able to treat his four colleagues rather as
dependents than as veritable equals.

Law's meeting with the Regent was another comedy. With the
Duc de la Force to accompany him, he went up to the ordinary entrance of the Palais Royal, where, either for the sake of secrecy, or
else perhaps because the Keeper of the Seals, who hated them both,
merely wished to mortify them, he was refused admittance. However,
next day Sassenage brought him in by the back way and this time he
was received. Monsieur le Duc, his mother and all their followers were
far too deeply involved in Law's affairs to abandon him. They therefore all rushed over from Chantilly, and there was another scene for
the Duc d'Orléans to put up with.

The Abbé Dubois was at this time so deeply occupied with the
question of his ecclesiastical advancement, which was now moving
fast, that at first he was taken in by the decree I have mentioned.
After that he did not dare to stand up for Law in the face of the whole
world. He was therefore content to remain a neutral, and thus a useless
friend, though as yet Law did not dare to complain of his behaviour.
On the other hand Dubois was afraid of breaking with a man from
whom he had drawn such enormous sums of money, who in desperation might be tempted to tell all, just as he did not dare to protect a
man for whose blood the public was howling. For some time Law
remained in this position, hanging, as it were, by a thread, and without
a foot on solid ground. In the end, as we shall soon see, he was forced
to yield and once again to change his native land.

The decree of which I have been speaking was issued and withdrawn during the time when the Regency Council was having a short
vacation, and I myself was staying at La Ferté. On the day before my
departure I went to take my leave of the Duc d'Orléans, and found
him in the small gallery, almost alone. He drew the Maréchal d'Estrées, someone else whom I no longer now remember, and myself,
upon one side and told us of this decree, upon which he said his mind
was now made up. I told him that, although I professed to know
nothing about financial matters, this decree seemed to me most dangerous; that the public were not likely readily to accept a forfeiture of
half their wealth, especially at a time when they had every reason to be
in terror about the other half; and that the worst palliative that I could
think of seemed to me better than the one he was suggesting, and of
which he would surely repent.

It will have been noticed over and over again in these memoirs how
often I have given wise advice without being listened to, and that

though the events which I foretold proved me right, they never succeeded in teaching the lessons which ought to have been drawn from them. The Duc d'Orléans's manner in replying to me was perfectly serene, and he seemed certain of success. The two others seemed to agree with me, but they said little. Next day I left for the country, and everything happened as I have told.

From the moment the Duc d'Orléans saw Law in the way I have set forth above he took to working with him once again. He even, on Saturday, the 25th, sat with him in his small box at the Opera, with every appearance of being calm and quite untroubled. Nevertheless, seditious writings and pamphlets, some biased and some well argued, poured out, and there was general consternation.

The *Parlement* assembled on Monday, the 27th of May, in the morning, and the First President, the Presidents Aligre and Portail, the two Abbés Pucelle and Menguy were chosen to make the remonstrances. At noon on the same day the Duc d'Orléans sent La Vrillière to inform the *Parlement* that the decree of Wednesday the 22nd of May was withdrawn, and that the shares and bank notes would retain their original value. Finding that the session had risen, La Vrillière went to the First President's house to deliver his message. During the afternoon the deputation of five visited the Palais Royal and were well received. The Duc d'Orléans confirmed the message he had sent by La Vrillière and added that he was anxious to restore the interest payable on the loans issued on the Hôtel de Ville to two and a half per cent. The deputies appealed to his clemency and sense of justice to make it at least three per cent. The Duc d'Orléans replied that he would like to make it not merely three but four or even five per cent, but that the present conditions would not allow of his going beyond two and a half. Next day, the 28th of May, the decree restoring the bank notes to the value they had before the decree of the 22nd of May was made public. Nevertheless that decree, though it had remained in force for only six days, had had a great effect.

On Wednesday, the 29th, La Houssaye and Fagon, Councillors of State and Intendants of the Treasury, visited the bank in company with Trudaine, the Merchants' Provost. At the same time Le Blanc, Secretary of State, called on Law to inform him that the Duc d'Orléans had dismissed him from his post of Controller General of the Treasury; that he thanked him for the pains he had taken; and that, as he seemed to be unpopular in Paris, he thought it his duty to place an officer of merit and good reputation beside him to prevent any harm befalling him. At the same time Besenval, a major in the Swiss Guards, who had been warned for duty, arrived with fifteen men of his regiment to remain day and night in Law's house until further notice.

Law had expected neither the loss of his office nor the arrival of this guard, yet he took both very calmly, and his habitual coolness did not leave him for an instant. It was on the following day that the Duc de la Force took Law to call upon the Duc d'Orléans by the ordinary door when the Duke did not wish to see him, but received him the following day when he was brought in at the back by Sassenage. On Sunday, the 2nd of June, Besenval and the fifteen Swiss were withdrawn from Law's house. The jobbing of stocks and shares, which had formerly been carried on in the Rue Quincampoix was now removed to the Place Vendôme, where the space was larger and where the jobbers would not hold up the traffic so much, but those who lived there did not find the change so convenient. The King surrendered to the bank the hundred million shares in it he personally held.

In the midst of all this fuss the Duc d'Orléans, who was incensed with Argenson for his decree of the 22nd of May which was the origin of these troubles, and by the fact that His Royal Highness had been forced against his will to get rid of Law, wished to relieve him of the Seals. He spoke to me about it one day when I had come over from Meudon to work with him. He gave me his reasons as a man does when his mind is made up, and then all at once he suggested giving them to me. I burst out laughing. He told me that there was nothing to laugh at, and that he could see no one else but me for the post. I expressed my surprise at what seemed to me so extraordinary a proposal, saying that surely among all the magistrates he must be able to put his hands on someone capable of upholding the dignity of the position; that if not he had better turn to the bishops; but that to have recourse to a gentleman who neither knew nor could know a word about the law or the forms and precedents necessary for administering that office, seemed to me most peculiar. He replied that nothing could be simpler or easier, and that the administration was a matter of pure routine that I could learn in less than an hour, and which would come automatically once I was in office.

I insisted on his making a proper search for someone suitable. He took up an *Almanach Royal,* and patiently read through the names of all the principal magistrates, giving me a sketch of their posts and reputations, and then added one by one his reasons for their exclusion. From them he went on to consider the Regency Council, and again gave me his objections to every one in turn. Finally he took the bishops, though he dealt with them more carelessly, because in truth there was no one there who was worth a moment's thought. I argued against his exclusion of several magistrates, especially in the case of the Chancellor. I even spoke in favour of several members of the *Parlement*, particularly Gilbert de Voisins, but neither of us could convince the other. I told him that I could well understand why a magistrate should wish to be given the Seals, since the authority, the rank, and the family prestige they brought must be for him a real temptation; that I on the other hand could not be tempted in this way, since nothing of the sort could possibly appeal to me; that the Seals could bring no honour to my family, nor alter my rank, my habits, or my way of life; that on the other hand they would expose me to the laughter of everyone who would see me bursting my brains in an attempt to learn a calling which I would give up long before I had done more than scratch the surface of it; that moreover I had no wish to endanger my conscience, my honour, or his friendship for me which was precious, by rightly or wrongly sealing or refusing to seal decrees and declarations which he should send me, or to attach my signature to decrees of the Council which had been passed in secret.

The Regent would accept none of my arguments. He did his best to excite me by pointing out the unusualness of what he proposed, and by citing the examples of the first Maréchal de Biron and the Constable de Luynes. The discussion lasted a good three hours, but he could not shake me. At last, worn out by my resistance, he allowed me to take my leave, but only on condition that on the morrow he should send two emissaries to me at Meudon (he did not tell me their names), who might perhaps succeed in overcoming my resistance, and whom he begged me to receive and to hear so long as they should wish to speak. To this I had to yield, and it was only after I had done so that he could bring himself to let me go.

Next morning came and went without my seeing anything of these spokesmen. But half way through dinner the Duc de la Force and Canillac came in. I was amazed to see the latter. I had no acquaintance with him at all beyond occasional meetings in public. I had seen him in my house or his perhaps four or five times during the first fortnight of the Regency. We had never seen one another again except, since he too had become a member, across the table of the Regency Council. We had made no approaches to one another there and we had never met elsewhere. He was, as I have said, a man entirely given over to the Abbé Dubois, to the Duc de Noailles, and to Lord Stair; but his character has already been sketched.

Their arrival did not prolong our meal. They ate like men who are in a hurry to have done, and they had hardly swallowed their coffee before they begged me to take them to my study. They had come well briefed, and I felt sure that the Duc d'Orléans had given them

full details of the long conversation I had had with him about the
Seals upon the previous afternoon. The Duc de la Force was the first
to begin what I shall not call the conference but the pleadings, and
they were not short. After him came Canillac. He was a man who enjoyed speaking, who did it very well, and who on this occasion allowed
his talent full play. Their great argument was the necessity for getting
rid entirely of the Keeper of the Seals, whose disloyalty, arising out
of his dislike for Law, had been responsible for that fatal decree of
the 22nd of May, which he had introduced in order to ruin Law, and
which, by revealing what should have remained hidden, showed that
he had taken no thought for the perils into which he was throwing
the Duc d'Orléans. Moreover, they pointed out that the disorder in
the Treasury had been partly brought about by the obstacles he had
thrown in Law's path, in his administration of the Treasury and in all
his other operations. Other arguments were: that the *Parlement*'s
hatred for the Duc d'Orléans was growing daily worse; that not only
were they becoming better organized, cleverer and more cautious in
their attacks, but also, ever since the lesson he had given them at the
lit de justice—one which they would never forget—more bitterly en-
venomed; that this fact made it impossible to choose any one of them
for the post of Keeper of the Seals; that this argument applied equally
to the Chancellor, who was exclusively and irrevocably a member of
that body, from which he issued and which he seemed to think divine;
and that at the present juncture it was of the first necessity to have a
Keeper of the Seals whose loyalty to the Duc d'Orléans was such
that it could never be doubted, never be shaken, and was so well
known to be utterly beyond their reach, that the cabal would tremble
and be confounded by it.

Of course this did me great honour, but words come easily when
one is anxious to persuade. They continued in the same strain. What
they needed was a man of brains, of intelligence, of courage; a man
whose reputation for honour, for truth, and for disinterestedness was
quite unsullied; who was well known to have refused all shares in the
company or the bank; whose name had never been connected with
finance and who had always refused to have anything to do with it;
who had dignity and knew it; who was jealous for the royal authority;
who, finally, had the gift of words and would be fearless in the face of
all remonstrances and attacks by the *Parlement*, able to contain them
by his replies, and thus preserve the Regent from all weakness suggested to him from without, and to which he was only too naturally inclined, at a time when any weakness would be his certain ruin.

Then they said that it was absurd to hope to find in the ranks of the magistracy a man of this weight who did not belong body and soul to his own order; who did not either love or fear the *Parlement*; who would not be inclined to weaken in the present financial situation; who would be above finding pleasure in the fact that we had fallen into grave embarrassment through having wilfully left the beaten track; who would be strong in the face of all the troubles which the *Parlement* and its underlings were fomenting and fanning against us; who, above all, would not continually be thinking of his own safety, and terrified by what he was told might come to pass when the Regency was over; and who again would not be frightened by what was happening even while the Regency lasted. They added that it was equally useless to hope for anything from those who composed the Regency Council, almost all of whom were weak, incapable, timid, or easily led astray, while the rest were ignorant or tarnished in such a way that it would be most dangerous to make use of them. After this M. de la Force again began to speak, but I proposed that we should go and finish our conversation, which had already lasted nearly three hours, in the fresh air, on the terrace leading to the Monastery of the Capuchins.

On our way there M. de la Force did his best to tempt me in undertones with the pleasant prospect of being in a position to humiliate the *Parlement* and its First President, and to have my revenge for what had passed during our affair with them over the question of our hats. He pointed out that, under the severe exterior of the Keeper of the Seals, I should in fact be their superior and hardly be able to help enjoying the chance of treating them as such, while at the same time doing good service to the State and to the Duc d'Orléans. In the meanwhile Canillac had gradually drawn out of earshot but whether this was by chance or by design I do not know. However, towards the end of our conversation he rejoined us, with all the easy manners of a man of the world who, without sacrificing his prejudices, is perfectly willing to take what comes so long as it favours the end he has in view. The weather was lovely and the view from the terrace very fine, and for a few moments there was a truce to the serious matters we were discussing. In this way we reached the end of the terrace and arrived at what is known as the Capuchins' bastion. There we sat down and, although the view was even lovelier than before, we went back to our conversation.

As may be imagined my visitors had not done all the talking. From time to time I had put in a word or two, although, while Canillac was talking, it was easier to let him have his way. It was at this point that they laid before me in greater detail the dangers threatening the Duc

434

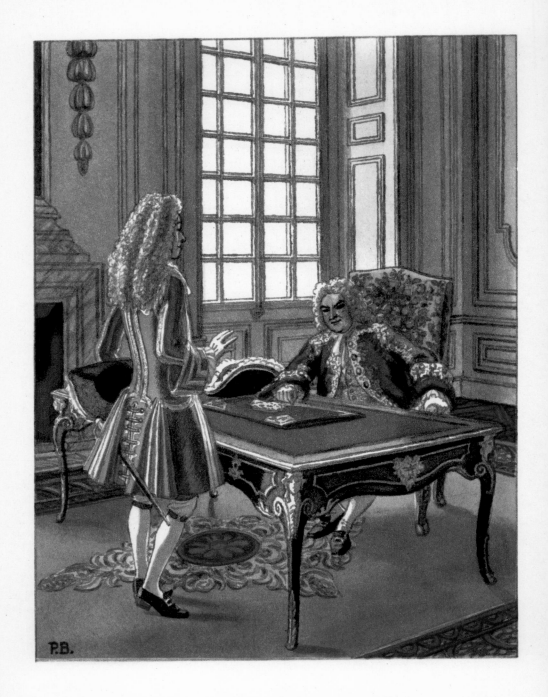

The Duc de Saint-Simon declines the Seals

d'Orléans, the various ambitions and schemes of the *Parlement*, the fact that these were backed by many people of importance, the public discontents, the disorder in public affairs, and the prospects of the King's majority, which was now a little less than three years off. This all took some time, and it was vividly put. The names of the people who were most under suspicion, their intrigues, their ambitions, and their personal interests, were cited. I was constantly surprised by the way in which Canillac agreed to all that M. de la Force said, and that he, who was the public champion of the *Parlement* and the First President, who was a friend of the Maréchal de Villeroy (the latter, after courting him assiduously, had completely won him over) and who was so friendly with the Duc du Maine, should have painted their characters in such colours. I could not resist saying at intervals that if only I had been listened to, and if only I had not had to fight against such powerful opponents and men who had such influence over the Duc d'Orléans, neither the *Parlement* nor a single one of the people he had mentioned, and whose names he had not hidden from me, would now be in a position to be considered at all or to cause us the least anxiety. At that I looked at Canillac and he dropped his eyes.

It is true that the *Parlement* and all those who, with M. and Mme du Maine, had recently been so thoroughly disconcerted and alarmed, now seeing the weakness of the treatment meted out to them and despising it, had quickly recovered their courage and set to work again. However, I did not see in what way my possession of the Seals could remedy a situation which was due in the first place to the ill conduct of public affairs and the fact that this had become known, and in the second to the carelessness and innate weakness of the Duc d'Orléans. This was really the gravamen of my defence.

However, if I wished to report in detail all that was said and discussed on one side and the other, I should never have done. I shall therefore be content to say that I was urged by these two men with all the arguments they could muster, and as if upon my acceptance or refusal of the Seals hung the whole fortunes, the salvation, nay the very life of the Duc d'Orléans. I was not to be persuaded and I stood my ground. Night was coming on—I should explain that we were now at the end of May and the weather was more beautiful than words can possibly express—and I suggested a return to the house. During the walk back my colleagues adopted a pathetic tone; they told me of their regrets; and they said that I, too, would repent of what I had done when I saw what events were in store for us. It was clear that they had expected to succeed and were greatly disappointed. On arriving at the new Château I took care not to go in but led them to where there was still company outside.[1] This company I joined, for I wanted to be rid of my two men. I had been with them nearly seven hours, and I was very tired. Their coaches had been waiting for them goodness knows how long. They stood about talking for a short while, then they said good-bye to me and took their leave.

I have never understood this fancy of the Duc d'Orléans—still less Canillac's fevered anxiety to persuade me. I have always been convinced that the Duc d'Orléans was perfectly sincere in his efforts to secure a Keeper of the Seals who would be firm and loyal, who would help him to deal with the various intrigues and operations of the *Parlement*, and who yet, as I had proved by my behaviour in the case of the Duc du Maine and the First President de Mesmes at the time of the *lit de justice* at the Tuileries, would not encourage him to go too far. I am sure too that the Duc de la Force was genuine. He was always delighted to be given a commission of any sort, it would have pleased him to see the Seals taken from the hands of the lawyers, and he would have been overjoyed at the thought of a duke, whom he knew to detest the *Parlement* and the First President, in a position to hold them in check and to mortify their pride. I was never on good terms with Dubois, I had enraged him by my behaviour over his consecration, and, as nothing happened without his knowledge, I suppose that it would have delighted him to see me committing some stupidity, getting myself involved with the *Parlement*, and then to be able to reconcile them with the Regent at my expense, so that in the end I might become annoyed and retire from politics altogether.

On the other hand Law, who had always courted me, and knew that I had cost him nothing however hard he pressed me or got the Regent to press me, and that I would have nothing to do with finance, no doubt wished to see me in possession of the Seals, as a man whom he could trust to be entirely sure and firm; who would not stand in his way or do anything to injure him behind his back; who would hold in check the hostility of the various departments of finance whenever I saw that right was on his side, a thing which he would have every chance of showing me; whom he need have no cause to fear on the score of hatred, jealousy or envy where the Duc d'Orléans was concerned; and who would give courage and dignity to the Prince and uphold him in the face of the *Parlement* and of the cabal which always sided with it.

These reflections did not occur to me until after the long conversa-

---

[1] The Château which Monseigneur had built near to Le Tellier's old château, and which the Regent had lent to Saint-Simon for a summer residence the year before.

tion which I had at Meudon, when what I had gone through gave birth
to them on the following day. Canillac was jealous of the Duc d'Orléans's confidence in me, he was also a friend of the Duc de Noailles,
of the First President, and of all their gang, and he hated me. His acceptance of this commission and all his eloquence can therefore only
have come from a hope that I should commit some folly while I held
the Seals, and that from this folly he and his friends might draw some
advantage.

Thoughts, however, of this kind had nothing to do with my refusal; indeed they only came to me long afterwards. What influenced
me at first, and influenced me so strongly that I never doubted my
decision, was the prospect of undertaking a post, which was not only
important but in the limelight, about which I did not know the first
thing, and which would expose me to the necessity either of issuing
edicts, declarations, and decrees, which might be bad, wicked, or for
all I knew pernicious, without realizing their possibly dangerous effects, or of refusing point-black to have anything to do with them.
Another reason, though one which would have yielded to superior
arguments, was my dislike of a post which could give me only passing
fame, which would set people grumbling once again at a fresh precedent, which would give me no rank or glory, or anything which was
of the least value to me, but which, considering my ignorance of the
subject, could only involve me in months of useless and of thankless
toil.

My refusal, and the fact that it was clearly definite, were reported to
the Duc d'Orléans at a time when events were so critical that there
was not a moment for him to lose, and the result was a sudden conference, to which I was not called, and which indeed was attended by
no one but the Abbé Dubois, Law and the Regent himself. At this
conference it was decided that Law should pay a visit to the Chancellor, whom they knew to be sick to death of his exile at Fresnes; that
the Chevalier de Conflans who was a cousin of the Chancellor, a friend
of his, and an excellent witty fellow at an argument, should accompany
him, as the representative of the Duc d'Orléans whose First Gentleman of the Bedchamber he was; and that Law should then explain to
the Chancellor the present turn of affairs, and find out if there was any
chance of his coming to terms, whether he was likely to seal what he
was told, whether he was prepared to work with him, Law himself,
and finally whether he was to be trusted in his attitude towards the
Parlement, not in the matter of his honesty which was never in question, but merely to find out if he still retained his old weakness and
liking for that company. Conflans's part was different. He was, first,

437

to threaten the Chancellor with an indefinite continuation of his exile, lasting even beyond the termination of the Regency, with a loss of all credit with the Duc d'Orléans, and then to dangle before his eyes the prospect of a return to favour and to confidence, and the re-possession of the Seals, if only he were honestly prepared to do what was wanted of him.

Three and a half years of exile at Fresnes had already done much to soften the severity of a Chancellor who was now fifty years of age, and who, after reaching the top of his profession so young, had counted on long years of enjoyment of the Seals on which to advance his family in the world. All these hopes had been ruined by his exile, and he was further away from being able to settle his family's affairs than he would have been if he had remained Procurator General. Conflans was well aware of how the Chancellor felt about these matters and of how his disappointment was augmented by the loneliness of exile. He therefore made good use of his opportunity with the result that Law found all his speeches most favourably received, the Chancellor agreed to everything, and the public when it heard the news, received it very coldly and proclaimed: '*Et homo factus est.*'

Strong in the knowledge of the success of this embassy, the Duc d'Orléans, on Friday the 7th of June, sent the Abbé Dubois to ask Argenson to deliver up the Seals. The latter then brought them to the Duc d'Orléans in the afternoon of the same day, and, as he had received them, not as is usual, in commission, but under a special charge registered at the *lit de justice* in the Tuileries, he at the same time handed in his resignation. The Chancellor arrived during the evening of the same day; at twelve next day he went to the Palais Royal; and then he accompanied the Duc d'Orléans to the Tuileries, where the King once again delivered him the Seals. However, as he owed them to Law who had brought him out of exile, his return to power marked the first breach in a reputation which up to that time had been a high one, but which ever since that day has slowly decreased, until at last, by degrees, and through the succession of events it has fallen very low.

Argenson had not wasted his time. Born poor, he retired a rich man; his children, who were still quite young, were well provided for; and his brother was laden with benefices. He took his defeat with great tranquility, but, as so often happens to those who outlive their importance, he died soon afterwards. His place of retirement was very odd. He went to live in a women's convent in the Faubourg Saint-Antoine known as the Madeleine de Trainel, on the outskirts of which he had long ago furnished himself rooms, which were very fine and comfortable and as spacious as a good-sized house. There he had lived

for many years whenever he was free to do so. The convent had received many favours through his influence, and he had even endowed
it handsomely himself, for the sake of its Superior, a certain Mme de
Veyny, who claimed to be a relation of his and of whom he was certainly very fond. She was a most attractive and witty woman, and it never
occurred to anyone to speak ill of her.[1] All the Argenson family paid
court to her. Nevertheless, it is a curious fact that, when he was only
Lieutenant of Police and on one occasion fell ill, she not only left her
convent to look after him, but actually came and lived in his house for
a while.

Argenson retained the rank, the dress, and all the outward trap-
pings of a Keeper of the Seals, not that this mattered, as from now
onwards he kept closely to his rooms. Once or twice he visited the
Duc d'Orléans, who continued to treat him with every consideration,
by the back way. He called, too, upon the Abbé Dubois who also
visited him occasionally. Once he called on the Chancellor. Except for
two or three particular friends he showed no signs of wishing to see a
soul outside his family and he grew terribly bored. This same Mme de
Veyny and her convent, after Argenson's death, became the Duchesse
d'Orléans's chief pleasure in life.

During the afternoon of the day on which the Seals were returned
to Chancellor Daguesseau, he attended a very curious conference, summoned by the Duc d'Orléans, at which were present the Maréchal de
Villeroy, as sole representative of the Regency Council, Des Forts,
Ormesson, the Chancellor's brother-in-law, and Gaumont, all three
of whom were Councillors of State, and at the head of the various departments of the Ministry of Finance left open by Law's removal from
office. The five deputies appointed by the *Parlement* to make the remonstrance, that is to say the First President, Presidents Aligre and
Portail, and the two Clerical Councillors to the Grand Chamber, the
Abbé Purcelle and the Abbé Menguy, were also present, as was La
Vrillière, who was there as secretary to the Council in case any orders
might have to be given. The result of this conference was that the
edict issuing a loan on the Hôtel de Ville at two and a half per cent
was registered by the *Parlement* next day, that is to say on Monday,
the 10th of June, and published on the day after that. After Argenson's
retirement Des Forts, though he had no official title and though his
functions were not precisely the same, became in fact Controller
General. However, I shall not continue to burden these memoirs with

[1] A surprising statement, as all other contemporaries concur in being shocked by this
liaison.

the multitude of decrees, the continual changes in the personnel of the departments, and all the other financial manœuvres of this time. All I shall say now is that the four brothers Paris, of whom I have spoken elsewhere, were sent into exile in Dauphiné.

Attempts to restore the confidence of the public had been in progress for some time, and it was thought that one of the best hopes for bringing this about would be to destroy such paper money as had been honoured in so public a fashion that no suspicions of its being possible to put it into commerce and exploit it a second time could arise. With this object in view it was decided to deliver over all such paper to the Merchants' Provost, week by week, and that he should then burn it in the town hall in front of all the town officials and whoever else, whether bourgeois or common people, might wish to attend. Trudaine, the Councillor of State, was Merchants' Provost at this time. He was a hard man, exact in all his dealings, but without tact or polish and not very well educated. He had small interest in politics, but was a stickler for honour and justice, and universally recognized to be an honest man. He owed all that he had become to the late Chancellor Voysin, his sister's husband, and the company he had always kept had taught him neither esteem nor affection for the Duc d'Orléans or his government. Moreover, he had never disguised the fact that he held the 'system' and all its fruits in detestation.

Well, when the first occasion for burning this paper arose, he expressed himself so crudely about the whole business, as well as upon the subject of certain mistakes which had been made by those whose duty it was to hand it over to him, that those gentlemen were offended and turned the Duc d'Orléans against Trudaine, saying that, in the difficult times they were all undergoing, and when public confidence was so important, the post of Merchants' Provost could not be in more dangerous hands. To make matters worse, Trudaine then imprudently allowed himself to show surprise when some of the notes were being publicly burnt in front of him, and in such a way as to suggest that they had passed through his hands before. The Duc d'Orléans was immediately informed of this, and it is true that Trudaine's remarks had given rise to comment, and that their effect, so far as confidence was concerned, was bad.

A day or two later I left Meudon, as my habit was, to go and work with the Duc d'Orléans. When I arrived I found the First President alone in one of the large rooms belonging to the Great Apartments, the one in fact which leads into the Small Apartments. The Regent immediately came up to me and said: 'I am most anxious to see you, as I have something of great importance to tell you.' Then he made a

dive for the other large room, the one which has the platform and the
dais, and, with me at his side, he began to walk up and down and to
tell me about what had happened at the Town Hall, exactly as it had
been told to him. He immediately added that all this was conspiracy
between the Maréchal de Villeroy and the Merchants' Provost and
that he was resolved to be rid of both of them.

I allowed him to exhaust his spleen; then I did my best to remove
this idea of a conspiracy from his mind, and attempted to draw him a
sketch of Trudaine's character. I condemned his lack of polish; above
all I blamed his imprudence; but I insisted that it deserved neither the
scandal nor the insult to his pride which the fact of relieving him of
his post of Provost before his time would make of it. All that was
necessary, I said, was to give him a firm warning to be more guarded
in what he said in the future. To give more weight to my words I
told him that it was not out of any friendliness for Trudaine that I
was speaking in this way; that he might remember that not so long
ago he had been so good as to grant me a place, as Alderman of Paris,
for Boulduc, the King's Apothecary, a man very distinguished in his
profession, and for whom I had an affection of many years' standing;
and that thereupon I had asked Trudaine to put this business through for
me, and he had most boorishly refused my request. The Regent remembered the incident clearly but continued to urge his point as I did mine.

We turned to the subject of the Maréchal de Villeroy, and the argument became still livelier. I pointed out to him the double danger he
would be running if, at a most critical time, and after taking the King's
education out of the hands of the Duc du Maine, he were now to interfere with it again. I told him of the horrible rumours which would
again be going the rounds among a public made desperate by the
money it had lost, and a populace which his enemies were doing their
best to stir into revolt. Then, in regard to the Merchants' Provost, I
made it clear to him that what he suggested doing would only serve to
confirm his enemies in the suspicion to which Trudaine's imprudence
had given rise; that by removing a man of Trudaine's reputation for
honourable dealing, for probity, for justice, and for love of right, he
would at once destroy all chance of credit and confidence among the
public; that the conclusion which would universally be drawn was
that once again he, the Duc d'Orléans, was playing the mountebank,
and burning false paper in order to re-issue the genuine among the
public. Finally I pointed out that it was an unexampled act of tyranny
to remove a Merchants' Provost from his post before the expiration
of his term of office, merely because he refused to make himself a
party to what was nothing more or less than trickery.

The Duc d'Orléans was so deeply persuaded of the greater danger to which he would be exposed if he were to leave the two men in their posts, that he told me his mind was made up, and that he meant to appoint me King's Tutor, and Châteauneuf, the Merchants' Provost. I loudly proclaimed my determination not to be King's Tutor, saying that the more closely I was attached to him, the Regent, the less suitable I was for the post; that he must remember what had been agreed between us when we had discussed this matter before the late King's death; and that he could not again have forgotten what I had said to him, not so very long ago, upon a subject which he was now bringing up all over again to-day.

Coming next to the second point, I begged him to call to mind that Châteauneuf was a member of a family that lived in Savoy; that he had been born in that country and had become President of the High Court at Chambéry; that he was consequently a foreigner; and that, although he had since been naturalized and become our Ambassador at Constantinople, in Portugal, and in Holland, a Councillor of the *Parlement,* and now Councillor of State, he was excluded from holding this post by the municipal regulations of the City; that, however justly and honourably he might have performed his duties as Head Commissioner of the Council at Nantes, that post was after all a poor sort of jumping-off ground for the right to displace a magistrate, popular for his virtues, especially when the appointment would offend the Parisians by putting at their head, in the place of their own man, one who was a stranger, and thus ineligible for the post, both by the laws of the City and by every precedent.

In spite of what I said the Duc d'Orléans remained firm on all points. Indeed his attitude was so determined that I became afraid, and, throwing myself at his feet, I embraced him round the knees with my two arms, and begged him, in the most moving words I could muster, to change his mind. He fidgetted with embarrassment, and did everything he could to make me loose my hold. I protested that I should not let go until he had given me his word not to interfere with either the Maréchal de Villeroy or Trudaine, but to leave them in their posts. In the end he allowed himself to be either touched or overcome, and he gave me the promise, which before rising I insisted upon receiving not once but several times. Although I have very much shortened my account of this scene I have reported all the essential facts. When it was over we worked together for some time and then I went back to Meudon, where at this time I was spending my summer months in the midst of good company, only coming to Paris on business and never stopping there for the night.

442

The very next day the Prince de Tingry, among others, came to dine with us at Meudon. Upon his arrival he told us a piece of news which, he said, had just come out before his leaving Paris. This was that Trudaine had been dismissed and Châteauneuf appointed in his place. I hid my surprise and my anxiety about what was happening to the Maréchal de Villeroy as best I could. I realized that, as his name had not been mentioned, nothing could so far have happened. Nevertheless, the fact that the Regent's promise under this head had been so quickly broken made me suspicious about the other case, and that not from any affection or esteem I had for the Marshal, nor on my own account, since I was perfectly determined to refuse the post of King's Tutor and to stand by my refusal, but purely for the sake of the Duc d'Orléans, and because of what I thought would be the results of removing the Maréchal de Villeroy from his post. Happily, at the moment, there was no more question of this. I do not know if the promise, which I had rather compelled the Regent to give than obtained from him, was merely granted to get rid of me, or if those who had previously forced him to come to his decision had resumed their influence over him on my departure. I am inclined to believe that my first supposition is the right one, and that, if the Duc d'Orléans had had a successor ready to take the place of the Maréchal de Villeroy, as he had one for Trudaine, the Marshal would have fallen at the same time as the latter.

The Abbé Dubois had always had a fondness for Châteauneuf ever since the days when he had dealt with him in Holland, and that in spite of the fact that the latter had not been popular with the English. Châteauneuf was poor and extravagant; his various embassies, even though at one time he had been at Constantinople,[1] had cost him a great deal; he was now in want; this post as Merchants' Provost would supply his needs; and the Duc d'Orléans had always had a liking for him.

Four days later there was a meeting of the Regency Council. As it happened to be my month on duty for receiving petitions, I went to the Tuileries shortly before the meeting and took up my post in the room immediately preceding the Council Chamber, just behind the King's arm-chair and the table where petitions were laid. I was standing between the two Masters of Requests, ready to receive the petitions, or rather to see them thrown upon the table and then taken up by the two Masters whose duty it was to report on them to me. After

---

[1] Which was supposed to be a lucrative post. Dangeau says that it was worth 80,000 livres a year to its ambassador.

that the three of us would take them to the Duc d'Orléans, though only after making a rough précis of what they all contained. One of the two Masters happened to be Bignon, who died young after being made a Councillor of State. He was the son of another Councillor of State, who was Intendant of Paris, and an intimate friend of Mlle Choin, of whom I spoke when telling the story of the Duchesse de Berry's marriage. It was on that occasion that I referred to my relations with the Bignon family, and to its original cause.[1] This Bignon in question was also a nephew of that Bignon, who also was a Councillor of State, and who had once been Merchants' Provost.

Bignon now told me that, although his uncle was far from well, he would already have paid me a visit at Meudon if he could possibly have done so; that he had something to tell me; that, indeed, he was anxious to see me without delay; and that he had asked his nephew to ask me if he might call upon me in Paris, and if so when it would suit me to receive him. I begged him to tell his uncle that I should call upon him immediately after this meeting of the Council and before returning to Meudon. Accordingly, I went to see him. As soon as he saw me he told me that, if Trudaine had dared to go to Meudon, he would already have been there to express his gratitude and that, unable to contain his desire to do so, he had charged Bignon to give me his assurance that I had acquired in him a servant to all eternity. After this there followed a perfect torrent of thanks and praise. I had never had anything to do with Trudaine, and I could not think what Bignon meant. Indeed I remained completely bewildered. He told me that I ought not to show him such reserve; that they knew everything; and thereupon he recounted the whole of the private conversation I had had with the Duc d'Orléans, the gist of which I have reported above, word for word.

My astonishment was extreme. For as long as I could I denied the whole story. But it was all to no purpose. His account was exact. The arrangement of my arguments, even most of my phrases, and above all my peroration, were repeated to me by Bignon with such curious fidelity that, in spite of myself, I could not disavow what I had said and was reduced to begging both him and Trudaine, if they really wished to show me their gratitude, to promise me their secrecy. So far as the Maréchal de Villeroy was concerned they realized the importance of the secret, and they kept their word, but they were unable to submit on the other point and Trudaine's debt to me was published

---

[1] Saint-Simon did not refer to the origin of this friendship on that occasion. It actually was that one of the Bignons had acted as his tutor after the death of the Duchesse de Brissac.

444

to the world. After a while Trudaine came to see me, and for the rest of his life he cultivated my acquaintance. I must say too, in honour of his son, that even to this day he has not forgotten what I did for his father. What seems to me curious is how the matter ever came to leak out. Whether it was some valet, hiding between the doors, or the Duc d'Orléans himself, who repeated this conversation in all its length and so exactly, is a thing I have never been able to unravel. I did not like to mention the matter to the Duc d'Orléans, and in spite of many attempts I could never drag out of Bignon or Trudaine how it was that they had come by their knowledge.

Seeing that the news reached them, it is not in the least surprising that it also came to the ears of the Maréchal de Villeroy. Perhaps it may seem curious that my reward was his ill-will. He could not bring himself to forgive me for having been in a position to replace him, even though I had refused to do so, and had even been the cause of his retaining his post. It is true that once before he had had his reasons for fearing me in the same way, and that this last case was rather in the nature of a relapse, but on the previous occasion he had had no more than his suspicions, and not the certainty which had now come to him. The result was this ignoble sentiment, this offspring of pride and insolence, so utterly the opposite to all that a gentleman ought to feel. At a later date we shall see this feeling re-appear.

It had never, as we have already seen in many parts of these memoirs, been without cause that the Duc d'Orléans had found the Maréchal de Villeroy, in his place as Tutor to the King, a burden almost too heavy for him to bear. There was now, however, a more recent reason. From the very beginning of the Regency the Marshal had done all that was in his power to make himself agreeable to the *Parlement* and the populace. The example of M. de Beaufort had turned his head. Remembering the confidence which, towards the end of his life, the late King had always placed in him, realizing how much he had to hope from the troops he had for so long commanded, considering that he was Senior Marshal of France, that the King was in his hands, that he was Governor of Lyons and for many years past its absolute lord and master, and that his son, who was entirely dependent on him, was Captain of the Bodyguard, he seriously believed himself to be possessed of powers which could act as a counter-balance to those of the Regent, and might yet make him the first man in all France. It was for this reason that he had made a point of opposing each new fiscal edict, the dominance of Law and all his financial arrangements, indeed of opposing everything which the *Parlement* disliked being forced to register. So far as he was able, he had made the Duc de Noailles's life a

445

misery during the whole time that the latter was at the head of the Treasury, and that although the Duc de Noailles was even more indecently the *Parlement*'s humble servant than he was himself, and although his interference was never able to be anything more than superficial in this as in all other cases.

We have noted his attachment to the Duc du Maine, his despair when the King's education was taken out of the latter's hands, his personal concern and his terror when the Bastard was arrested, how basely and with what a show of solicitation for the King he performed his duties towards him, how he would present him to the Magistrates at whatever hour they came to see him, what care he took to distinguish them above all others, no matter what their reputations might be, the affected way in which he would show the young King to the people, who now had begun to love him as passionately as they had recently detested the late one. We have noted also how busily the Duc d'Orléans's enemies were engaged in discrediting him in the eyes of the populace.

It was in regard to this last point that the Marshal was becoming a real danger. It was his habit at all times to carry with him the keys of a certain cupboard, where the bread and the butter from La Meute, which the King always ate, were kept with as much care as, and far more pomp than, that with which the Keeper of the Seals will keep the keys of the case in which the Seals are lodged. The Maréchal de Villeroy one day made a scene because the King had eaten some bread and butter which came from a different source—as if all the food which day by day the young King had to eat, the meat, the soup, the fish, the seasoning, the vegetables, everything upon the table at dessert, the water, and the wine, were not just as likely to be objects of suspicion as the bread and butter. On another occasion there was an outburst about the King's handkerchiefs, which the Marshal also used to guard himself, as if the King's shirts, his linen, and in a word all his clothing, as well as his gloves, were not equally dangerous, even though it would have been absurd to keep them all under lock and key and to dole them out himself. There were thus a host of superfluous and senseless precautions, all of them tending to suggest the blackest suspicions, at which decent men and women were indignant, at which others laughed, but which impressed the common folk and fools, and which had the double effect of continually renewing the horrible rumours about the Duc d'Orléans, which his enemies had taken the trouble to put abroad, and of making people believe that it was only owing to the care and vigilance of the faithful tutor that the King had been preserved to the nation alive.

446

This was exactly what the Marshal wished to instil into the minds of *Parlement* and people, and little by little into that of the King as well. And this was what he very nearly succeeded in doing. Moreover this was why the people were so strongly attached to him. It happened at this time he had just been having an attack of gout, which, although his attacks were always very short, had given rise to a great deal of public excitement; and the fishwives now sent a deputation from among all their number to visit him. You may imagine how these ambassadors were received. The Marshal overwhelmed them with compliments and presents. His heart was filled with joy and fresh courage, and this was the reason that the Duc d'Orléans was once again determined to remove him from his post beside the King.

Argenson's elder son, who, while still very young, had been made a Councillor of State, was at this time Intendant at Maubeuge, though he did not stay there long. The younger was Lieutenant of Police. He was now dismissed from this post which was given to Baudry. Shortly afterwards he was appointed Intendant of Tours, but he too did not stay there long. Both these brothers have since that time become Ministers and Secretaries of State.

On the 15th of July, the Council passed a decree against precious stones, forbidding one either to keep them in one's possession at home or to sell them to anyone but foreigners. The outcry this produced may be imagined. The decree, coming as it did upon the top of many others, tended, as it was only too evident it must, to drive everyone to exchange his debased paper money, in which it was no longer possible to have the least confidence, for any money he could lay his hands on. It was in vain that the Duc d'Orléans, Monsieur le Duc and his mother did all they could to persuade the world that they were willing to be the first to set a good example by sending all their precious stones abroad; in vain, too, that they actually sent them, though it is true that this was only for the voyage. There was no one who believed them, nor, among those who possessed some, anyone who did not take good care to hide his jewels away, a thing which on account of the small amount of space they occupied, was easier to accomplish than was the case with gold or silver. This eclipse of precious stones did not last for long.

After reigning among us a tyrant unabashed so long, Stair now took his leave of us. It was many years before the commerce or the navies of France and Spain recovered from his influence over our politics, which in the end did even England harm, since it enabled the King, owing to the enormous subsidies he drew from us, to make himself master of Parliament and thus to overcome the barrier which stood between him and his wishes. And to think that what we really have to thank for this state of affairs is the ambition of Dubois, the blindness of Canillac, the personal perfidy of the Duc de Noailles and the mad enthusiasm of the Duc d'Orléans! Stair, who was anxious to see the King of England before the latter set out upon a visit to his estates in Germany, crossed the Channel the moment his successor, Sir Robert Sutton, arrived in this country. Never had audacity, insolence and impudence been carried in any country to such a pitch, or with such a startling success, as they were by the late ambassador. It was our misfortune that he knew the characters of the men he had to deal with so intimately. However, once again, what can one expect when universal power is given into the hands of one man, still worse when that one man is like Dubois, and worst of all when he is a First Minister who hankers after such a Cardinal?

The new Merchants' Provost continued the task of burning share certificates and bank notes at the Town Hall, until such a time as the reduction which had already been agreed upon should be accomplished.

While deputies from the *Parlement* still continued their fruitless meetings with the Chancellor, an edict was suggested with the object of turning the Company of the Indies into a commercial company, with the obligation of repaying within a year six hundred millions' worth of bank notes at fifty millions a month. This was Law's final resource as well as the last resource of his famous System. For the mountebank performances of the Mississippi Company it had at last become necessary to substitute something solid, especially after the famous decree of the 22nd of May last which had had such a disastrous effect on paper money. It was therefore proposed that in the place of the old daydreams we should have a real Company of the Indies, and it was this Company and this name which now succeeded to, and took the place of, what up to this time had been known as the Mississippi Company. However, although it was all very well giving this Company rights over the sale of tobacco as well as over quantities of other immensely lucrative sources of revenue, all this was as nothing compared with the amount of paper now spread among the populace, whatever care was taken to reduce it and however dangerous, however ruinous, however desperate a remedy this reduction might be. Other expedients were necessary, and the only one which seemed possible was to turn this Company into a 'commercial company' under which softer-sounding, though obscure and simple, title, it was intended to give the Company not merely trading but exclusive rights.

You may imagine how this suggestion was received by a public driven almost to the limits of its endurance by ordinances forbidding

448

it, under the severest penalties, to have more than five hundred livres in the house, by the continual threat of being visited and searched by Government agents, and by the necessity of paying for the smallest household necessities day by day in large bank notes. The results were twofold. First, people became so exasperated by the difficulties they experienced in getting hold of enough of their own money to pay for their daily expenses, that it was a miracle that they were ever calmed down at all, and that a general revolt did not break out in Paris; and second, the *Parlement,* strong in the knowledge that popular feeling was behind it, held firmly to its refusal to register the edict.

On the 15th of July, the Chancellor, at his own house, presented the suggested edict to the deputies of the *Parlement,* who remained with him until nine o'clock that evening, but who refused to be persuaded. Next day, the 16th, it was presented to the Regency Council. The Duc d'Orléans, who could not speak badly, however ill-founded his subject, spoke well, and Monsieur le Duc supported him. No one else said a word. We just bowed beneath the yoke. It was therefore resolved to send the edict to the *Parlement* on the following day which was the 17th of July.

During the morning of this same 17th of July, the crowds of people round the Bank and in the adjoining streets, all of them wishing to raise enough money to be able to go to market, grew so great that about a dozen people were suffocated. Three of the dead bodies were immediately borne off in an uproar and laid before the door of the Palais Royal. There was a great deal of shouting and an attempt on the part of the crowd to enter the Palace. A detachment from the various Companies of the King's Guards was immediately sent over from the Tuileries. La Vrillière and Le Blanc each separately harangued the people. The Lieutenant of the Police rushed to the scene, and a brigade of the Watch was summoned. After this the dead bodies were taken away, and, with soft words and gentle persuasion, the people were at last successfully dispersed, and the detachment of King's Guards returned to the Tuileries.

At about ten o'clock that morning, just when these disturbances were coming to an end, Law decided to go to the Palais Royal. He was greeted with curses in the streets. The Duc d'Orléans thereupon decided that it would be unwise to allow him to leave, and two days later he was given rooms within the Palace. However, he sent his coach home, and its windows were broken with stones. His house was also attacked and many of the windows broken. News of what had been happening reached us in our quarters in the rue Saint-Dominique so late that I did not reach the Palais Royal until all signs of the

449

disturbance had disappeared. The Duc d'Orléans's company was very small, but he was perfectly calm and made it clear that he was not best pleased with those who did not feel the same. Having nothing to do or say, I did not stay long.

During the morning the edict was laid before the *Parlement*, who at once refused to register it and sent the King's Officers to the Duc d'Orléans with the reasons for their refusal. He received them with considerable irritation. Next day an ordinance was published in the King's name making it an offence to assemble, under heavy penalties for disobedience, and ordering that, on account of what had happened at the Bank on the previous day, payments would cease and the Bank remain shut until further notice. These orders were attended by more good fortune than wisdom, for what were people to live on in the meantime? In fact there was no revolt, which only goes to show how good and obedient the French are, even in the face of extraordinary provocation.[1]

Nevertheless, certain troops, which had been at work on the Montargis Canal, were posted to Charenton, some regiments of cavalry and dragoons to Saint-Denis, and the King's Regiment deployed on the heights of Chaillot. Money was also sent to Gonese, to encourage the bakers to bring in their bread as usual. It was feared that they, like so many others among the merchants and work people who were now refusing paper money, would refuse to accept payment in notes. The Regiment of Guards had orders to hold themselves in readiness, and the Musketeers were confined to quarters with their horses saddled and bridled.

On the day of the *Parlement*'s refusal to register the edict I was summoned to the Palais Royal at about five o'clock in the afternoon. The Duc d'Orléans gave me an account of most of the measures which he had either taken or was resolved upon taking, and which I have just set forth above. He complained to me about the Chancellor's weakness in dealing with the *Parlement* and in conference with the deputies of that body. Then he bitterly reproached me for the embarrassment my refusal to accept the Seals had brought him. I replied that, if he would allow me to do so, I completely disagreed with him. 'What,' he interrupted excitedly, 'do you expect me to believe that you have no more spirit than the Chancellor, and that you would have refused to have put the fear of God into them?'

'It is not that,' I answered, 'but you know well enough how I

---

[1] Law is reported to have said on this occasion that the English do not bark but bite, while the French, though they bark a great deal, never really bite.

stand with the First President, and that, ever since our quarrel with
the *Parlement* over that business with our hats, I am on no better terms
with them. Moreover in the hat affair it was you, with your weakness
and your fear of the *Parlement* with which you are so quick to reproach
others to-day, who at that time not only left us up the creek, but got
yourself into the same mess as well. From that moment, right at the
beginning of your Regency, the *Parlement*, the First President, and the
whole cabal, saw what sort of a man it was with whom they would
have to deal in future, grasped how best to manage him, and at once
became bold and hardy in their line of conduct. I shall not deny that
they have given their talents full play. At the *lit de justice* you had them
at your feet, but you did not keep them there. At the sight of your
weakness their spirits revived, and with its fears so quickly at an end
the cabal resumed its strength and vigour once again. This short re-
capitulation would not be fruitless if at last you could learn to profit
from your lessons.

'Let us, however, come back to me and my acceptance of the Seals.
Believe me, Sir, if those fellows show themselves so intractable to a
magistrate they have nourished in their own bosoms, a man who is
their own chief and their natural superior, whom they love and by
whom they know themselves to be loved—believe me—they would
be impossible to a man above them whom they would know to be
holding the position temporarily, whom they held to be imposed
upon them by force, who was quite unqualified for the post, who held
a rank they hate and persecute with the last word in audacity as well
as with complete impunity, who belongs to the aristocracy which
they at once envy and despise, and who moreover is a man whom
personally they detest and by whom they think themselves likewise
detested. Sir, they would have taken it as an insult to have to treat
with me at all; their cabal would have put abroad a hundred wicked
rumours about me; their deputies would purposely, and by the very
words they used, have tempted me into answering them back; and
everyone would have condemned you for your extraordinary choice
of a Keeper of the Seals belonging to the aristocracy, and for what
they would consider your definitely bad choice of an enemy to carry
out the work of conciliation. That is what really would have happened, in other words a worse embarrassment for you and a very disagreeable one for me. There is therefore nothing to regret in my
refusal.

'On the contrary, believe me it is a good thing, which the present
occasion only serves to make more obvious. The only regrettable
factor is that you cannot produce some magistrate worthy of respect,

at the same time a royalist and an opponent of the *Parlement*'s pretensions, whom you could make Keeper of the Seals. Since there is no such man and since, for different reasons, you were determined to take the Seals away from the man who held them, who was in fact loyal to you and was, considering the pace the *Parlement* was setting and intends to set in future, the one man cut out by nature to hold them during a regency, you have done the only sensible thing possible in recalling the Chancellor and returning them to one, who, after all, is a magistrate of merit and of high reputation. However, we must start from a basis of fact; have you formed any plan for escaping from the mess in which you find yourself at present? Let us forget about the past, and see what is now to be done.'

The Duc d'Orléans then left the subject of the Seals and returned to his complaint about the Chancellor. He said that the only thing to do as far as he could see was to exile the *Parlement* to Blois. I said that in the absence of any better plan that would have to do. I said this, not because I could think of anything better myself, but because I saw with regret that, while this exile would inflict a sort of punishment on the *Parlement*, it would neither overawe them nor win them back to their allegiance. The Regent agreed, but he hoped that the magistrates, accustomed as they were to living in the bosom of their own families in Paris, with all their friends around them, would soon grow tired of the separation, be disgusted at finding their only friends among each other, and still more dislike the expense the establishments would entail, especially when this forced transplanting of necessity diminished the receipts and profits which their briefs brought them in Paris. This was true enough and, as there was nothing else to be done, we had to be content with it.

Next I mentioned the necessity for considering most carefully every eventuality which might arise, as well as the best and most prompt remedies in each case, saying that it would be far better to do nothing at all than to find oneself at a loss, or be successfully withstood in anything one attempted, a situation which would be the end of all authority. He told me that he had already thought of this; that he would do so again; that it was his intention to hold a small council at the Palais Royal next day at which he wished me to be present; and that everything could be discussed then. After this he turned to discussing the Maréchaux de Villeroy, de Villars and d'Huxelles, and several other less important people, and that was the end of our conversation.

Next day, which was Thursday the 18th of July, I accordingly went to the Palais Royal at about four o'clock in the afternoon. The council was held in the Great Apartments, in the room next to the great drawing-room. Monsieur le Duc, the Duc de la Force, the Chancellor, the Abbé Dubois, Canillac, La Vrillière and Le Blanc were all present. We sat facing one of the windows, in no particular order. The Duc d'Orléans was on a *tabouret* like the rest of us, and there was no table. Just as we were taking our seats, the Duc d'Orléans said that he wished to see if one whose presence he would rather like were waiting in the room outside, and he went out to look for him. The man in question was Silly, of whose final downfall I have spoken in advance some time ago. He was on intimate terms with Law, with Lassay and with Madame la Duchesse, who later succeeded in having him made a Knight of the Order, and he was deeply interested in all their financial dealings. The Duc d'Orléans had left him in the little room he always used in the winter, and he now followed the Duc d'Orléans into the larger room, and came up to where we were sitting. I do not know, and I have never bothered to find out, what it was he had against Le Blanc. However, no sooner had he set eyes on him than he raised his voice and, looking at Le Blanc, said to the Duc d'Orléans: 'Sir, there is a man here before whom it is impossible for me to speak, and in whose presence I beg Your Royal Highness not to compel me to remain. Indeed, Your Royal Highness was so good as to tell me I should not find him here.'

Our surprise was great, and Le Blanc was completely taken aback. 'Well, well,' replied the Duc d'Orléans, 'what does it matter? Sit down, sit down.' 'I should prefer not to, Sir,' replied Silly, and off he went. At this piece of impertinence we all looked at one another in astonishment. The Abbé Dubois ran after him, and taking him by the arm, did his best to drag him back to us. The room was a very large one, and we saw Silly shake off Dubois and again go on his way. He reached the door, and Dubois went through it after him. 'This is madness,' said the Duc d'Orléans, looking embarrassed. No one else said a word, except Le Blanc, who offered to leave the room. This the Duc d'Orléans refused. In the end he went after Silly himself. His absence lasted for nearly a quarter of an hour, during which time he was, I suppose, arguing with Silly, who deserved to be thrown (as years later he threw himself[1]) out of the window for his insolence. At last the Duc d'Orléans came back, followed by Silly and the Abbé Dubois.

During their absence no one had uttered a word except perhaps to

[1] After the fall of Monsieur le Duc, Silly, who had risen considerably in the world by that time, tried for a while to win the good graces of Fleury, but failing in his attempt, he retired to his country house and committed suicide by throwing himself out of his bedroom window.

show surprise at Silly's outbreak and the good-natured way in which the Duc d'Orléans had taken it. Monsieur le Duc said nothing whatever. Silly took his place among us as far from Le Blanc as he could and, as he sat down, he surpassed himself in impertinence by saying that he was there solely as an act of obedience, but that he would say nothing as it was impossible for him to speak in front of Monsieur Le Blanc. The Duc d'Orléans made no answer to this, and he immediately opened the conference by explaining his reasons for calling us together, and by giving us a clear statement of how things stood at the moment. Then he said it was necessary to come to a prompt decision, and that, as for him, he felt that he knew exactly what this decision ought to be. He ended by telling the Chancellor to give the meeting an account of what had passed at his house during his last interview with the deputies of the *Parlement*. The Chancellor, showing all the signs of embarrassment one might expect from one who had just returned from exile and did not wish to be banished once again, but who yet was a secret though passionate defender of the *Parlement* and in despair of being able to save them, gave us a rather long report. His discourse ended in a stammering statement to the effect that in the present circumstances which had been forced upon us, he found himself of necessity so sadly placed that all he could do was to defer to the prudence and wisdom of His Royal Highness. Then everyone voted for the Duc d'Orléans's suggestion to send the *Parlement* to Blois. Monsieur le Duc, the Duc de la Force and the Abbé Dubois spoke strongly. The others, though of the same opinion, were more measured in their terms and shorter. I thought that, considering that this matter concerned the *Parlement* and had been already settled, I ought to say very little. Silly kept his word, and did no more than make a profound bow when his turn came to speak. This done, we discussed rather shortly the precautions we should take to see that the order was obeyed, and then we rose.

The Chancellor went up to the Duc d'Orléans and spoke with him for some time alone. Towards the end the Abbé Dubois joined them. Meanwhile our numbers gradually dispersed. Monsieur le Duc was called into consultation. At last I learnt that it was now proposed to substitute Pontoise for Blois, and next morning this was carried into effect. In this way the punishment became ridiculous, and only succeeded in showing up the weakness of the government and in encouraging the *Parlement* who naturally laughed at such futility. Nevertheless, what passed at this Council was kept so strictly secret that the *Parlement* never had the slightest suspicions of our resolution until it was put into execution.

454

On Sunday, the 21st of July small detachments of the Regiment of Guards, with their officers at their heads, went at four o'clock in the morning and took possession of all the doors of the Palais de Justice. Musketeers from the two Companies, with their officers, at the same time mounted a guard on the doors of the Great Chamber, while others surrounded the house of the First President, who, for an hour or so, was in a terrible fright. In the meanwhile other Musketeers from the two Companies went separately, four by four, to all the members of the *Parlement*, and gave them the King's order to leave for Pontoise within forty-eight hours. All this was done with the greatest politeness on all sides, with the result that there were no complaints. Fairly late that evening the Duc d'Orléans sent 100,000 francs in cash and as much again in bank notes of a hundred and ten livres to the Procurator General, so that he might supply anyone who was in need of money for the journey. This, however, was not a gift.

The First President was at once more fortunate and more shameless than the Procurator General. He made so many promises, he abased himself so low, he employed so many rogues and tricksters who had it in their power to abuse the Regent's weakness and facility, both of which he regarded quite cynically, that, in the end, his exile earned him more than 100,000 crowns, counted out to him on the side by the poor Prince's agents. Moreover, the Duc d'Orléans permitted the Duc de Bouillon to lend the First President his house at Pontoise. This house was furnished and its immense and admirable garden, which lies along the river bank, is in its way a masterpiece. It had once been the apple of Cardinal de Bouillon's eye, and was perhaps the only thing in France that he regretted. With such delights to help him, the First President, who had for some time now been on bad terms with, and even openly despised by, his Company, easily recovered his position. He kept open house for all the members of the *Parlement*, whom he soon won over to visit him every day in large numbers. At these receptions there were always several tables most delicately and magnificently served. Moreover, to all who cared to ask he sent gifts of wine and liqueurs of every sort and kind. Refreshments and fruit of every kind were to be found in the garden every afternoon, and there were numerous little carriages, with one or two horses to draw them, at the service of all the ladies and older gentlemen who wished to take a drive, and card tables in the chief apartments until supper time. Mesmes with his sisters and daughter to help him did the honours.

The exile of the *Parlement* was followed by various financial operations as well as by several changes in the personnel of the various departments. Des Forts received the best post, since he was now, without being called Controller General, given full authority over all the others. I shall not, since such is not my custom, enter into details about those financial matters. Great as the disorder was, it had as yet produced no change in the extraordinary liberality and facility of the Duc d'Orléans towards men who had no merits or any needs, and for whom he did not even care. He increased Madame la Grande Duchesse's pension by another 40,000 livres; he gave a pension of 8000 livres to Trudaine, one of 9000 livres to Châteauneuf, whom he had just made Merchants' Provost, one of 8000 livres to Bontemps, the King's first valet, one of 6000 to the wife of the Maréchal de Montesquiou, one of 3000 to Foucaud, President of the Toulouse *Parlement*; and he also gave a pension of 9000 livres to the widow of the Duke of Albemarle.

Public stock-jobbing still continued in the Place Vendôme to which it had been removed from the Rue Quincampoix. This Mississippi business had tempted everyone, and, thanks to Law and the Duc d'Orléans, the scramble to stuff one's pockets with the millions that were going had been general. The Princes and Princesses of the Blood had set a truly wonderful example. The only men who were in a position to take as much as they wanted, and yet who did not do so, were the Chancellor, the Maréchal de Villeroy, Maréchal de Villars, the Duc de Villeroy, the Duc de la Rochefoucauld, and myself, who all refused to touch a single penny. The two Marshals were, in intention and in fact 'Frondeurs,' and the Duc de Villeroy naturally followed suit. With their *Fronde*[1] in mind, and with the object of becoming more and more the kind of people of whom the government would one day be forced to take notice, they had formed a strong alliance. It was not that La Rochefoucauld had, either in his own personality or in the position which he occupied, the least hopes of reaching the same heights himself, but he was immensely rich, he was proud of the part his grandfather had played in the late minority, he was not only Villeroy's brother-in-law, but had always been so closely attached to him and followed him in everything he did. This affectation of disinterestedness, and this separation between them and the Regent, although in his presence they were always among the meekest of the meek, succeeded so well with the *Parlement* and among the people that they had by now conceived the greatest hopes.

Villars was one day driving through the Place Vendôme, with his pages and his footmen about him, and the crowd of jobbers was so

---

[1] Saint-Simon is continually comparing the opposition party, with Villeroy at its head, with the Fronde which had arisen during the minority of Louis XIV.

thick that they could scarcely make way for him. From the coach door, he there and then began to inveigh against speculation, and with that braggart air of his, to harangue the crowd upon their shameful behaviour. Up to this point they let him have his say, but when he went on to add that, as for him his hands were clean, and he had never wished to have anything to do with the business, a voice from the crowd shouted: 'And what about the safeguards?'[1] The crowd took up the cry, and in spite of his usual audacity the Marshal, on this occasion shame-faced and confused, sat back in his coach, which, as it slowly forced its way through the Place Vendôme, was accompanied by jeers. Even after he had left the Place they followed him, and Paris amused itself for several days at his expense without there being a soul to pity him.

In the end it was found that the traffic through the Place Vendôme was so much upset by this business that the jobbers were removed to the enormous gardens belonging to the Hôtel de Soissons. That indeed was a fitting place for them. M. and Mme de Carignan, who lived in the Hôtel de Soissons and to whom it belonged, were now raking in the money on every side. Difficult as it would be to believe it if it were not so well known, even profits of a hundred francs were not beneath them, I do not say beneath their servants, but beneath themselves, and the millions they drew from the Mississippi, not to speak of what they made elsewhere, no doubt seemed to them a fitting reward for talents which, in so far as they consisted in the science of making money by the lowest, the vilest, and the most debased means, they had indeed brought to a pitch of perfection, which has seldom been equalled. Out of this they made an enormous profit, not to speak of the fresh facilities for gain and for tribute which also opened to them. Their great friend Law, who had been living for several days at the Palais Royal, now returned to his home, where thousands came to call on him.

The Abbé Dubois, who thought only of his promotion to the rank of Cardinal and who was willing to sacrifice the State, the Regent and everything else in the world to that one end, now took a fresh step forward. At a meeting of the Regency Council, held during the afternoon of Sunday the 4th of August, the Chancellor surprised us all by taking from his pocket letters patent for the acceptance of the Constitution *Unigenitus*, and then by reading them through to us. This was

[1] The enormous sums of money which Villars drew from enemy towns and provinces, as a sort of ransom, during his campaign across the Rhine in 1707 were well known to all the world.

done by order of the Duc d'Orléans and no vote was taken, at which I was as much surprised as I was pleased. Everyone was struck by this new expedient of failing to put the matter to a vote, which showed quite clearly what the result of doing so would have been, and how it was intended to trick and force us into the position of appearing to approve of the measure, which it was obvious no one would have the pluck to protest against. Dubois by this manœuvre gained great credit with the Jesuits and other upholders of 'The Constitution.'

As the *Parlement* refused to register the King's declaration ordering the acceptance of the Constitution *Unigenitus,* and, since Dubois, with his eyes forever on his cardinal's hat, was anxious to give some signal proof of his devotion to Rome and to the Jesuits, he not only persuaded the Duc d'Orléans to have it registered by the Grand Council, but, in order to overcome the obstacles he was likely to meet with there, to go to the Council himself accompanied by all the Princes of the Blood, the Peers and the Marshals of France upon whom he could lay his hands. It should be noted that there is a difference between these councils and ordinary meetings of the *Parlement* which is that at meetings of the Grand Council all Officers of the Crown may on all occasions sit and have the right of voting, while in the *Parlement* they may only do so when the King attends and they are in his suite. When I arrived at the Palais Royal from Meudon in order to work with the Duc d'Orléans, I found him in the Great Apartments alone, giving orders to various messengers to warn and summon all people concerned for the following morning. I was in complete ignorance of what was happening. Dubois was alarmed lest I might upset his plan, and persuade the Duc d'Orléans that there were no precedents for such solemn and useless proceedings, and that to call a Grand Council would be an expedient as weak as it was unfitting. I therefore asked the Duc d'Orléans what was happening. He told me, and then, holding out his arms towards me and smiling, he begged me not to be present at the Council. At this I began to laugh, too, and I told him that he could not give me an order more after my own heart, or which I would obey more willingly, since I should thus be spared the pain of opposing his wishes, and of expressing myself with all the force that I could bring to bear upon the question. He said that he was sure of it, and that that was why he had begged me not to come. I did what I had come to do with the Duc d'Orléans and then I returned to Meudon, angry with what he was being made to do, but greatly relieved to find myself spared, without even asking for it, from attending the Grand Council.

On the following day, the 23rd of September, the Regent went to the Grand Council in state, and there found the Princes of the Blood, the other Peers, and the Marshals of France, or at least as many of them as were in Paris. Several magistrates belonging to the Grand Council spoke against the declaration with intelligence, with thought, and at some length, nor were they in the least put out of their stride by the Regent's interruptions but answered him, respectfully it is true, but with plenty of courage and many fresh arguments. When the votes came to be taken it was found that, without the Peers and Marshals, the declaration would never have been carried, and that it was they, with only a smattering of the magistrates of the Grand Council, who constituted the majority. I learnt that my absence caused much comment, and that there were many who either went or sent their servants to look at the mass of coaches to discover if mine were among them. I dare not say that the world applauded my absence. The Abbé Dubois, though he did not mention the matter to me, was extremely annoyed by it, and also extremely surprised when he heard from the Duc d'Orléans that it was he who had told me about the meeting beforehand and had begged me not to attend.

DEATH OF DANGEAU

PHILIPPE de Courcillon, known as the Marquis de Dangeau, died in Paris on the 9th of September at the age of eighty-four. He was a sort of imitation of a great man, and his curious memoirs are interesting enough to make it worth our while to consider his character at some length. His family which had certainly not been very noble very long, came from the country round Chartres and was originally Huguenot. Dangeau himself became a Catholic early in life, and having done that he at once set out to make a name and fortune for himself in the world. Among the many injuries which this country suffered, and for that matter still continues to suffer, from the ministry of Cardinal Mazarin, high play, with all the knavery that accompanies it, was perhaps the worst. Great and small alike were soon its willing victims. However, Mazarin's affection for it was understandable enough, since it not only provided him with an immense source of income for himself, but it enabled him to strike a blow at the nobility, whom he hated (as for that matter he hated the whole French nation), and among whom he was anxious to abase every man of any greatness or distinction. Alas, the lesson which he taught us then has since his death been learnt so well that I think we can foretell at no very distant date the end and dissolution of the present monarchy.

However that may be, when Dangeau first appeared upon the scene, gambling was in the height of fashion at Court, in town, and indeed everywhere. Now Dangeau was a tall, finely built fellow, though he grew stout with age, and his face, though always agreeable, promised what it fulfilled only too exactly, an insipidity that made one sick. He was penniless or as nearly so as makes no matter. However, he set himself to learn all that there was to be known about all the games of chance that were then in vogue: picquet, la bête, ombre, grand and little prime, hoc, reversi, and brelan, and to master all the combinations of the games and cards he could. In this he succeeded so well that, even at lansquenet and basset, he was rarely at fault, but weighed up the odds, and put his money on the cards he knew by calculation ought to win. This knowledge was worth a lot to him, and his winnings soon put him in a position to be welcomed in good houses in Paris.

A little later he found his way to Court, and in a very short while he was mixing with the best society. He was sweet-natured, tolerant, sure in his conduct, very gentlemanly, obliging and honourable; but, beyond that, so dull, so insipid, such a fervent admirer of every little thing, provided it belonged to the King or those near to the throne, so much the humble servant of all the mighty, and, after his rise, so puffed up with pride and foolishness, without ever forgetting his respect for all the world or being any less snivelling, and so eternally occupied with showing his pretensions to distinction, that one could not but laugh at him.[1]

---

[1] Saint-Simon wrote this passage in 1747. Moreover it cannot be denied that the fall of the old nobility and the gradual elevation of a race of financiers, having no attachment to the soil, were among the causes of the Revolution.

1721

THE SPANISH MARRIAGE AND A CARDINAL'S HAT

⁜⁜⁜⁜⁜ o r some time the Abbé Dubois had prevented his master ⁜ 𝓕 ⁜ from telling me anything of what was going on in foreign ⁜ ⁜ affairs. But this did not keep the Duke from giving me ⁜⁜⁜⁜⁜ tit-bits from time to time, though in little detail, and I for my part displayed no curiosity. One day early in June I went to work with the Duc d'Orléans and found him walking up and down alone in his large room. As soon as he saw me he took my hand and said, 'Aha! I must let you into a secret—something which I have wanted most in the world and which I am sure will give you equal pleasure; but you mustn't tell a soul.' Then, laughing, he said, 'If M. de Cambrai knew I had told you he would never forgive me.' Then he said that he had made his peace with the King and Queen of Spain, and that a double marriage had been arranged—the King with the Infanta,[1] as soon as she was old enough, and the Prince of the Asturias with Mlle de Chartres.

If my pleasure was great, my surprise was even greater. The Duc d'Orléans embraced me, and after my first reflections on the personal advantages which would accrue to him from such a grand affair and the great expediency of the King's marriage, I asked him how he had managed to bring it about—especially the arrangements for his daughter. He said that the whole thing had been fixed in a trice, and that the Abbé Dubois was a hell of a fellow when he had set his mind on something. The King of Spain, he said, had been delighted that the King, his nephew, had asked for the hand of the Infanta, and the other marriage was made a *sine qua non* which brought the King of Spain up to scratch.[2] After we had expressed our mutual pleasure over these arrangements, I said that his daughter's engagement ought to be kept secret until the very moment of her departure, and that of the King until its consummation in order not to excite the enmity of the whole

---

[1] Louis XV's first cousin, and three years old at the time. The engagement was broken off subsequently since the French succession was in too uncertain a state to wait a minimum of eleven years for the birth of an heir.

[2] Published documents indicate that the initiative came from the King of Spain, but there is evidence that he was forced into proposing the double marriage by the Abbé Dubois's implanting in his mind the idea that the Regent had other plans for Louis XV.

of Europe which had always dreaded a union of these two great branches of the royal family, and towards the prevention of which all their political machinations were directed. Since the Infanta was only three years old, having been born in Madrid on the 30th of March 1718, there would be some years in which the fears aroused by the marriage of his daughter with the Prince of the Asturias might be allayed—for she was already twelve and the Prince fourteen.

'I think you are quite right,' replied the Duke, 'but it is not on, because the Spaniards want an immediate announcement and intend to send the Infanta here as soon as the formal proposal has been made and the marriage contract signed.'

'That's crazy!' I cried, 'what useful purpose will it serve to set the alarm bells ringing all over Europe?'

'Quite true,' the Duke said, 'and I feel the same, but the Spaniards are a stubborn lot; that is the way they want it, and it's all agreed. The arrangement means so much to me that it is no good your asking me to jeopardize the whole thing for the sake of this single risk.'

I gave it up and shrugged my shoulders in impatience. After discussing the matter a bit longer, I asked him what he intended to do with this child when she arrived. He said that he intended to put her in the Louvre. I disagreed, and said that the extensive suite and rich table which would have to be kept up at the Louvre would be very costly and quite unnecessary, that the expenses would constantly grow and the child would meet people from whom it would be desirable to keep her away as long as possible. Worse still, the King would have to pay her some attention and thus would see her childish ways, while she would see him as she was growing up; there would be between them either too much familiarity or too much restraint, which in either case would probably end in mutual antipathy; the King would be unhappy, and the Princess could hardly fail to be spoiled. Since the die was cast, I thought that it would be better to put her in the beautiful apartments of the Queen Mother at the Convent of Val-de-Grâce, where the air was good and the gardens lovely, in the charge of the Duchesse de Beauvilliers, a childless widow whose husband had been Governor of the King of Spain. The Duchess was a woman of virtue, piety and intelligence; she knew the ways of the Court at which she had spent her life in high estate and much respected, all of which singled her out as the one person for the appointment. I added that I thought she would refuse the position but would be forced to yield to the King of Spain, who should make the representations to her; there should be no Ladies of Honour or officials, but just the Duchess who should engage a small staff of personal servants and have sole charge of the child's education and household. No vast equipage of horses, carriages or guards. Once or twice a year the King should visit her for a quarter of an hour, and in the same way she should go to him, on which occasions the royal carriages and guards should be sent for her and she should be taken round Paris and to Court. As she grew up and the time came for her to meet various ladies, it should be in the discretion of the Duchesse de Beauvilliers to choose both the individuals and the occasion for their presentation. She should not leave Val-de-Grâce until the day before her marriage, when she would find her household all prepared for her under the supervision of the Duchess.

The Duc d'Orléans listened quietly, and replied that there was much in what I said, but that the position could not be taken away from the Duchesse de Ventadour, Governess of the Children of France.

'But,' I said sharply, 'this is not a Child of France!'

'No, but she was the King's Governess,' replied the Duke, 'and the Infanta who is to be brought up to marry the King should not be placed in the hands of anyone else, and the Duchesse de Ventadour is not the kind of woman to see herself mewed up in Val-de-Grâce.'

'Isn't that just fine!' I said. 'The Infanta and all that could be arranged for her are to be sacrificed to Mme de Ventadour who, with her tastes, will completely spoil her and let the child and the women who will flock round her do just as they like. Mme de Ventadour and her set, allied as they are to the Maréchal de Villeroy, are your enemies who, you and I and everyone know, have done and will continue to do you all the harm they can as long as they have the chance.' I went on further, but it was a waste of time; finally I shut up, realizing that the choice had in fact been made by the Abbé Dubois in order to curry favour with the Rohans, expecting, as he did, support from the Cardinal de Rohan for his hat which was already under consideration in Rome.

During all this discussion I did not forget to think of myself and of so golden an opportunity of making the fortunes of my second son. I said to the Duke that since everything was already arranged as he had said, it would be necessary to send someone at once to make the formal demand for the Infanta's hand and to sign the marriage contract; whoever went would have to be someone of title and standing and I begged him to appoint me the Ambassador in this instance, with his recommendation to the King of Spain to make my son, the Marquis de Ruffec, a Grandee. I reminded him that simply to please his friend Canillac, to the mortification of everyone, he had made a Peer of

La Feuillade, whom he disliked so much that he had once even got to the point of having him beaten up, which as he must well remember I had had great trouble in preventing, and yet on top of all that had given him a lot of money ostensibly to pay for his mission to Rome on which there was never any intention of sending him. I gave further instances of honours and rewards which he had heaped on unworthy recipients, and added that I had never asked for my second son to be made a Duke although he had been slighted over and over again by the promotion of La Feuillade, Brancas, de Nevers and people of that kidney. 'But,' I said, 'I do ask for one thing for him: that he shall now be given the rank and honours of a Duke which is the natural outcome of an embassy sent to arrange the marriage of the King and which as the result of his being made a Grandee will meet with general approval.'

The Duc d'Orléans hardly let me finish, but agreed at once to all that I had asked, promising to do all that he could in the matter of my son's elevation: he spoke in a most friendly tone, only asking that I keep the whole matter a close secret and not compromise it by any obvious preparations for my mission.

I understood quite well that apart from the necessary secrecy of the mission he needed time in which to bring the Abbé Dubois round to his point of view. I expressed my thanks and asked for two favours. The first was that I should not have an ambassador's normal emoluments, but a lump sum so that I could meet my expenses without ruining myself; the second that he would not give me any further tasks to undertake in Spain, as I did not wish to be away from him too long, and wished only to stay long enough for my son to be made a Grandee and then return. I was afraid of what Dubois would get up to in my absence, finding himself unable to prevent the embassy, and in the event my fears were well founded. The Duc d'Orléans readily granted both my requests on the grounds that he wanted me to return quickly. I thought that I had struck a great blow for my family and I took my leave well contented. But, dear God, what little things are men's plans and triumphs!

As time passed following the elevation of the new Pope and he was pressed more and more to keep the word which he had given to the Abbé Dubois in the event of his election,[1] the Abbe's impatience increased to such a degree that he could not rest. He nearly went mad

****

[1] Cardinal Conti was elected Pope Innocent XIII in April; at some point during the deliberations of the Sacred College he gave an undertaking to Cardinal Rohan regarding the Abbé Dubois.

when he heard that the Pope had made one solitary appointment to the Sacred College on the 16th of June in the person of his own brother, the Bishop of Terracini, who for ten years had been a monk in Monte Cassino. However, he did not have to wait much longer: one month later, on the 16th of July, the Pope made him a Cardinal together with Don Alessandro Albane, nephew of the late Pope. He received the news and the compliments with extreme pleasure, but he kept his display of emotion within decent bounds and attributed his success to the protection of the Duc d'Orléans, who in fact had little or no part in it. But he had no hesitation in letting it be known that what really gratified him was not so much his elevation to the purple as the unanimity of all the powerful men who had brought pressure to bear upon the Pope without any thought for their own advancement.

Although there was no love lost between us, I thought that it would set the Duke's mind at rest if I paid my compliments to Dubois, particularly as I would have a good deal to do with him in connection with my mission. So I called upon him; he overwhelmed me with compliments, protestations and recognitions of the honour which I had done him, without any reference to the past. In view of the reason for my calling, the occasion was formal; there were a lot of people there, and he used his red skull-cap, which he had just received from the King, as though it were black;[1] he made a great play of placing me on his right hand and when I left accompanied me to the door of his apartment and out into the little court adjoining. The Duc d'Orléans was very pleased at what I had done, and I never met the new Cardinal without his coming up to me, accompanying me to the door and showing every conceivable respect, which I treated just about for what it was worth.

When Dubois received his scarlet skull-cap from the hands of the King, he took his episcopal cross from around his neck and gave it to the Bishop of Fréjus, saying that it was lucky and for this reason he would like him to have it. Fréjus blushed and received it with the greatest embarrassment. Although this cross was made in the conventional form, it was unmistakable, and in consequence Fréjus was forced to wear it because in the King's presence he was always running into Dubois. A few days later Fréjus was dining with the Duchesse de Lude, with this cross about his neck; among the company were M. and Mme de Torcy. Mme de Torcy did not like Dubois and at the same time deeply disapproved of the aura of Jansenism which hung

---

[1] The Cardinals claimed equality with the Princes of the Blood, and hence superiority over the Peers.

around Fréjus; at the dinner table she started making the bitterest remarks about this cross to such an extent that Fréjus didn't know whether he was coming or going, and the rest of the company had to change the subject. Fréjus never forgave Mme de Torcy, nor her husband although he had nothing to do with it—he was much too prudent to get himself into that sort of compromising situation, and in fact it was a blunder on the part of his wife.

Not long after this the Duc d'Orléans told the new Cardinal that he had promised the Spanish mission to me and had promised to help me to obtain the standing of Grandee for my son. There is no remedy for a *fait accompli*, which the Cardinal Dubois recognized. He was very put out and made up his mind to get back at me when he could. To achieve this he had to cover his tracks, hide his annoyance from the Duc d'Orléans, and smother me with compliments in order to draw me in deeper.

THE SPANISH MARRIAGE

The Cardinal Dubois was not at all pleased at the Duc d'Orléans's selection of Saint-Simon as Ambassador to Spain, but he minutely supervised every detail down to demanding to see samples of the clothes that the Duke and his son proposed to wear. He made endless difficulties. Finally Saint-Simon set out on the 23rd of October for Madrid, where he arrived on the 21st of November. He was received in audience on the following morning.

WE arrived at the palace as the King was about to return from Mass, and we awaited him in the small salon between the salon of the Grandees and the Hall of Mirrors in which no one is allowed unless summoned. A few minutes later the King entered from the salon of the Grandees. Grimaldo[1] told him I was there as he was entering the room, and he came straight across to me, preceded and followed by a number of courtiers, but it seemed to me not nearly such a gathering as we were accustomed to at our Court. I made a profound bow; he expressed his pleasure at my arrival and asked after the King, the Duc d'Orléans, what my journey had been like, and how my elder son was getting on, who he knew was laid up ill in Burgos; then he went into the Hall of Mirrors. At once I was surrounded by the whole Court and overwhelmed with compliments and expressions of pleasure at the proposed marriages and the union of the two crowns. Grimaldo and

---

[1] Josepe Guttierez, Marqués de Grimaldo, Philip's favourite and Minister for Foreign Affairs.

466

The Abbé Dubois a Cardinal!

the Duque de Liria told me who everyone was; almost all of them spoke French and we exchanged endless civilities.

A quarter of an hour after the King's return I was sent for. I went alone into the Hall of Mirrors which is vast, much longer than it is wide. The King with the Queen on his left were standing side by side almost at the far end of the room. I approached, making three deep bows. I may mention here that the King never wears a hat except at public audiences or when going to or returning from Mass in the Chapel. The audience lasted half an hour, for one cannot bring it to an end until one is dismissed.

At the end of the conversation, in which the Queen talked more than the King, Their Majesties did me the honour of saying that they would like to show me their children and commanded me to follow them. I went alone with them through the Queen's study and an interior gallery where there were several Ladies- and Gentlemen-in-Waiting, who had evidently been warned, and with this small suite in train we reached the apartments of the Infantas. I have never seen prettier children than Don Ferdinand and Don Carlos nor a sweeter baby than Don Felipe. The King and Queen seemed pleased to show them off to me. Then we passed on to see the Infanta, to whom I showed the greatest gallantry I could. In fact she was enchanting. . . . On Tuesday the 25th of November I had my formal audience. Maulévrier, who had not been put to any particular expense in his position as Ambassador, came early to my house and was soon followed by Don Gaspard Girón and a magnificent carriage from the royal stable drawn by eight handsome greys, into which the three of us climbed at the appointed hour. Two grooms held each fourth off-side horse on a leading rein. There were no postillions, and the royal coachman drove with his hat under his arm. Five of my coaches filled with all those who had come with me followed, then about twenty more filled with gentlemen of the Court who had been sent by the Duques de Liria and de Sartine to do me honour. The royal carriage was flanked by my servants in livery and the officers of my household—that is to say valets, cellarmen, etc. Maulévrier's coaches—there were only two of them—followed behind the last of mine. Arriving in the forecourt of the palace, I might have thought myself at the Tuileries. The regiments of Spanish Guards, officers and men in uniforms similar to the French Guards, and the Walloon Guards uniformed in the same colours as the Swiss Guards[1] were on parade with colours flying and drums beating. There

---

[1] The uniform of the French Guard was blue with red facings and silver lace, red waistcoat, breeches and stockings; the Swiss Guards wore the same colours reversed.

were crowds in the streets and the shops were decorated with their windows full of spectators. There was joy everywhere.

Dismounting from the carriage we found the Duque de Liria and the Prince de Chalais, Grandees of Spain, and Valouse, First Equerry, who said that they had come to offer their duty as Frenchmen. Caylus might well have been present as a fourth. The staircase was lined with halberdiers uniformed as our Cent-Suisse, but in the correct livery,[1] halberds in their hands. We were conducted to the room next to the audience chamber, the door of which was closed; all the Grandees and persons of quality were present, and the room was less crowded than at our own Court but showed a greater sense of discretion.

I remained with this crowd for a time while the King came from his own apartments to the audience chamber by a door opposite to that used by the Grandees who were awaiting him. I must admit frankly that what I had seen of the King of Spain had impressed me so little that I had given small thought to what I ought to say on this occasion.

I was summoned, and all the persons of quality went in a crowd before me, leaving me alone to be accompanied by Don Gaspard Girón on my right and beyond Maulévrier, who was the other side of me, the Marshal of the Diplomatic Corps. As I neared the door La Roche came up to me and said in a low tone that the King had asked him to say I must not be surprised if he uncovered only at my first and third bow and not at my second, that he would do more for an Ambassador of France than for anyone else, but this was a custom from time immemorial which he could not vary. I begged La Roche to offer my humble duty to His Majesty and my sensible appreciation of this gracious gesture. Then I walked through the door. As I crossed the threshold the two others fell back, and I must say that the spectacle before me and the thought of what I was to say drove any thought of them from my mind.

In the centre of the wall opposite to me in this vast room was a canopy with no dais beneath which the King was standing; a short distance immediately behind him was the Grandee of Spain, Captain of the Duty Guards, who was the Duc de Bournonville; on the same side, standing alone against the wall, was the Royal Majordomo; the wall opposite and the end of the room were lined with Grandees. The rest of the room was lined with persons of distinction. The door

---

[1] The Cent-Suisse of the French King on ceremonial occasions wore black velvet slashed with white and pink satin. Saint-Simon means that the design of the uniforms was similar, but they were in the Spanish colours, red and gold.

468

through which the King had entered was filled with senior officials who were not Grandees. The King and the Grandees were covered; no one else was. There were no Ambassadors present.

I paused for an instant on the threshold and considered this majestic spectacle, over which a profound silence reigned. I slowly took a few paces forward and made a deep bow which the King at once acknowledged by uncovering and sweeping his hat to his waist. In the middle of the room I made my second bow, in which I inclined myself slightly to the right so that my eyes fell upon the Grandees, who all uncovered but not with so large a gesture as on the first occasion when they had followed the King. I then advanced equally slowly up to the King and made my third bow, whereupon he uncovered at once, as did all the Grandees. They then all replaced their hats.

I then began my speech, and covered after the first few words without being told to by the King. I paid the King compliments and spoke about the union of the royal house and the two thrones, the joy and affection shown in both countries as I had found on my journey from Paris to Madrid, the personal attachment of our King to his uncle; then I said that the request for the Infanta's hand would draw even more closely together the ties of blood and mutual interest. Next I expressed the thanks of the King and of the Duc d'Orléans for his choice of Mlle de Montpensier as a bride for the Prince of the Asturias. His Royal Highness, I said, was deeply touched by so great an expression of His Majesty's kindness, and offered his most profound respects and an assurance that he would do everything in his power as Regent to further the interests of His Catholic Majesty with the same zeal as if they were those of France herself. I concluded by saying how much joy I felt at having the honour of appearing before His Catholic Majesty charged by the King with putting the final touches to so desirable a negotiation; and that I myself felt the liveliest satisfaction, apart from that shared by all France and Spain, because I could never forget His Catholic Majesty's birth and in consequence I had always felt for him the most profound respect and attachment.

If I had been surprised by my first sight of the King of Spain and if I had been little impressed by the previous audiences which I had had of him, I must say that his reply on this occasion completely astonished me. He replied to each point of my speech in the same order with such dignity, grace and majesty, and often with a choice of words remarkable for its appositeness, that I thought that I was listening to our late King, who was unrivalled as a speaker on this sort of occasion. While making clear his equality, Philip V at the same time seemed able subtly to imply his deference to the King his nephew as head of his house, and to express his affection for the son of a brother whom he had loved so well and still mourned so tenderly. He showed that he was a Frenchman at heart without for one moment forgetting that he was King of Spain. He made it plain that his joy sprang less from the interests of his throne than from the forthcoming union of the two branches of his own family. . . .

When the King had finished I thought it proper to make a few comments and as the particular servant of the Duc d'Orléans to express once again my master's thanks. Instead of replying directly, the King of Spain did me the great honour of complimenting me and saying how pleased he was that I had been chosen for this task. Then, uncovering, I presented to him the officers who had come with me, and he then withdrew, doing me the honour of exchanging a last friendly word as he did so.

I was again surrounded by everyone present who complimented me, and then all the Grandees went off to the Queen's apartments, except those few who stayed to accompany me to the next audience. We moved into the next room where we were awaited and were told that all was ready.

The doors opened and we were summoned. The audience chamber was the counterpart of the small gallery through which, on the day of my first audience, I had followed Their Majesties to see their children. This room was not quite so long but equally as wide as the other, with which it was connected by big open arches which were its sole source of light. The far end of the room where we and a host of others found ourselves was rather dark; a few paces forward there was a barrier with a gate in it which was opened for me only when I was ready, so that I went forward entirely by myself. At the other end of this long room the Queen was seated on a kind of throne, a very large and decorative arm-chair, with her feet on a huge footstool which I saw, when she rose to leave, concealed several small steps. The length of the wall, leaning against it and covered, were the Grandees. Opposite, in front of the arches, were a number of square cushions of velvet, red satin and damask and all decorated with gold lace. The velvet cushions were occupied by the wives of the Grandees and those of satin and damask by the wives of their eldest sons, all cross-legged or squatting on their heels.

I stood in the doorway for a few moments taking in this imposing spectacle, while the Duques de Veragua and Liria and the Prince de Masseran, who had done me the honour of accompanying me, slipped away to their places among the Grandees.

After I had looked around me, I advanced slowly until I was level with the second cushion, where I stopped and bowed low. Then I advanced further to the middle of the room and bowed again, turning slightly towards the cushions as I did so and slightly towards the Grandees as I rose again; the ladies inclined slightly and the Grandees uncovered. Then I walked to the foot of the throne where I bowed again, and the Queen acknowledged me with a marked inclination. Then I said, 'Madam,' and having said it, covered, immediately removing my hat again and remaining uncovered for the rest of the audience. The Grandees remained uncovered following my second bow.

My speech followed the same lines as that which I had made to the King, suitably adjusted.

Her Majesty was simply dressed but wearing magnificent jewels, and wore a grace and dignity which accorded well with a great Queen. She was so overcome with joy as to feel positively embarrassed, as she told me herself afterwards. Nevertheless she replied in the most well-chosen terms. If I had come before her first I must say I should have been enchanted by what she said; but I admit that for all her intelligence and naturalness she could not match the rightness, the precision of the King, nor the inherent tone of authority which bespeaks a descent from generations of Kings and brings with it a natural majesty which has no equal.

When she finished I made a deep bow and withdrew as hastily as decency permitted in order to get to the farthest velvet cushion. My duty was to bend my knee slightly before each cushion and say, 'A los pies á Vuestra Excelencia,' whereupon each lady smiled and inclined slightly, and I had to get back to the top by the time the Queen had descended from her throne and was ready to leave the room.

I had not yet completed this task when I saw that the Queen was already at the door leading into her own apartments. She had been so graciously friendly towards me that I thought I might presume a little on such a happy occasion. So I ran across to her, saying that she seemed to be in a great hurry. I saw her stop and turn, so I said that I did not wish to miss a moment and an honour so precious; she laughed and extended to me her ungloved hand, which I took, sinking upon one knee. I thanked her profoundly, and we remained in the doorway chatting for a few moments while her Ladies-in-Waiting gathered about her.

Maulévrier, the French Ambassador in Madrid who so resented Saint-Simon's special mission, disgraced himself during these audiences by deliberately omitting to put his hat on, although he said he had forgotten. He was out to discountenance Saint-Simon whenever he could, and Cardinal Dubois had also sent embarrassing instructions. For the formal signing of the marriage contract it was agreed that Maulévrier would have in his hand a copy of the Spanish version to make sure, as it was read out, that nothing had been omitted, while Saint-Simon would follow clause by clause in a French copy.

Still worrying about what would happen over the documents, I set out with Don Gaspard Girón in the royal carriage, followed by the same cortège as on the occasion of my first audience. I sat alone on the back seat with Don Gaspard opposite. There were crowds in the streets and every window was filled. I found everyone of any consequence already at the palace; the Grandees had been summoned, the Papal Nuncio, the Archbishop of Toledo, the Grand Inquisitor, and the Secretaries of State. Following the plan I had made, I slipped through, talking here and there as I went, until I got to the door of the Hall of Mirrors where I remained, apparently in casual conversation. We had to wait nearly three quarters of an hour, and with so much on my mind I was very worried. But finally the door opened and the King and Queen entered with their children.

From my place beside the door I was able to speak to the King, and walk along beside him.

When we got to the salon of the Grandees there was a table set across the room, covered with a cloth and writing materials upon it. Six arm-chairs were ranged along it, arm to arm. The manner in which the Royal Family seated itself was unlike anything I have seen in any other country; the King took the chair on the extreme right, with the Queen on his left, the Infanta next, then the Prince of the Asturias, etc., and this same arrangement was followed in all public functions such as Court balls and the theatre.

The Majordomo-major and the Papal Nuncio, who followed the last Infanta, were extremely surprised to see me standing beside the King's chair where I had placed myself under cover of the conversation which I had diligently pursued. Continually to right and left of me I heard expressions of *Signore* and *Señor,* because neither of them spoke French, so I bowed happily to both of them with the air of a man who was thoroughly enjoying an occasion which was made for rejoicing, turning again to the King whenever I could. It was then that I noticed Maulévrier; he was trying to shove in between the Papal Nuncio and myself, but the Nuncio, with a slight bow, stood firm. I dared not make room for him because this would have shown that I had not taken up my position by any means by accident.

When everyone was seated and the crowd had quietened down, Don Josepe Rodrigo, opposite to the Queen, was directed to read out the contract. As soon as he began I turned to Maulévrier and asked him in a whisper, as best I could, if he had the Spanish copy to collate and the French copy for me. He replied that when he had left his home they had not been ready, but he would go and fetch them. 'There's time enough,' I said, turning back and engaging the King in conversation whenever I could without offending my neighbours too obviously. The reading went on for a long time; Rodrigo read loudly and very distinctly the contract between the King and the Infanta and the separate act in which the achievements of the ten witnesses and the presence of the Grandees of Spain were duly set out. I did not know what to say any longer to hold the King's attention, so I asked him if I might have an audience for the following morning which he readily granted me, and I spun this out until the reading was pretty well finished.

The reading of the contract so bored the Queen that she asked straight out how long it was going on for. She seemed to expect that the whole thing would subsequently be read in French, so I suggested that we should skip the preamble which contained nothing of importance. I was anxious to hide the fact that we hadn't a clue as to what was in this preamble, since Maulévrier had not brought a copy with him; he had been working over the final text with Grimaldo, and I had only the first draft which Dubois had given me in Paris.

When Don Rodrigo had finished reading the contract in Spanish he walked to the table and handed a pen to the King who, instead of taking it, asked what other documents had to be read. I remarked modestly in a low voice that there should surely be a contract in French. Don Rodrigo, to whom the King repeated my remark in Spanish, replied that he thought not, and in any case it would serve no useful purpose. At this point Maulévrier, who so far had not uttered a word, said that he would go and get it and left the room at once. In the pause which inevitably followed, the King remarked to me that the French version of the contract was evidently not essential since it had not been tabled. By way of reply I suggested that he should summon Grimaldo, who was standing behind the circle of Grandees. The King summoned him to speak; he approached between the Majordomo-major and myself and said that he did not think the French version was essential. I replied that the preliminary heads had been signed in both languages by the Marquis de Bedmar and himself, to which he said that that was quite different. I did not understand what he said too well because the King, who graciously consented to interpret between us, did not explain the whole thing very well. I replied with great restraint that it seemed to me proper that each Monarch should have a copy of the contract signed and witnessed in his own language, and as I was saying this Maulévrier reappeared. Grimaldo replied most politely that he did not think that this presented any difficulty since he had seen a letter to Maulévrier from Cardinal Dubois expressly stating that the two deeds were not necessary. I turned round and stared at Maulévrier in astonishment; and he with great embarrassment muttered that there had been something about it in one letter which the Cardinal had written him. I quickly made up my mind. I said to the King and Queen that of course I would do whatever they wished without question, and if it eventually appeared desirable that a deed in French should be signed I trusted that they would sign it privately at a later date. At the same time I put out my hand as though to place the deed before the King, but without touching, which would have been an infringement of the duties of the Secretary of State Rodrigo. It seemed from the expression of the King and Queen that this little passage pleased them very much.

Rodrigo at once approached the Nuncio, and then placed the deed before the King, gave him the pen, and withdrew. The King, having signed, pushed the deed along to the Queen and gave her the pen. She signed in turn and then held the hand of the Infanta while she wrote her name very prettily. Next the Prince of the Asturias and his two brothers signed. I cannot describe the joy which greeted the completion of this document. A moment later the King and Queen rose, and Rodrigo conducted Maulévrier and myself to a small table in the window; Their Majesties stood by while we both signed the deed. It goes without saying that there were no chairs and we had to sign our names standing up. I then expressed to Their Catholic Majesties my grateful thanks for the privilege of signing in their presence.

I accompanied the King and Queen to the door of the Hall of Mirrors, being careful to show proper deference to the Majordomo-major and the Nuncio so that they could not take exception to the place which I had taken up. . . .

I went back to my house after the ceremony which had lasted a long time because so much had to be read out and because of the discussion over the French version of the deed. As I was writing a letter Don Gaspard Girón arrived to ask if I would like to go with him to see the illuminations in the Plaza Mayor. I sealed up my letter at once and we got into his carriage, and the chief members of my suite followed. We were driven by a back way to avoid seeing the illuminations prematurely, and we found ourselves taken to a splendid house which

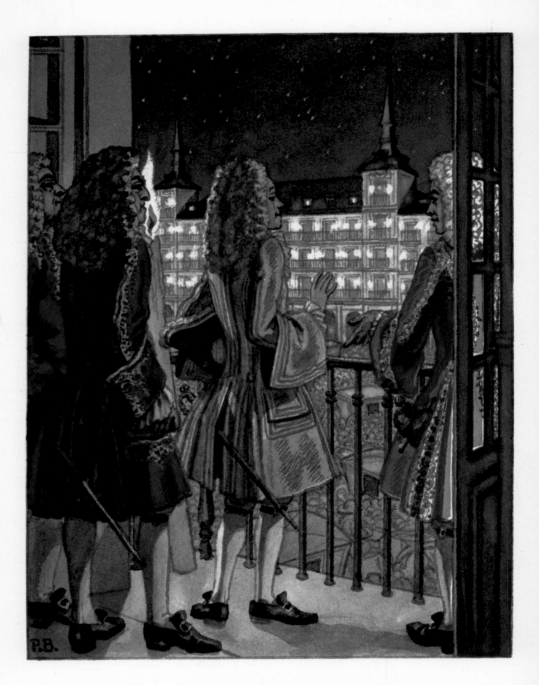

Illuminations for a marriage contract

the King and Queen always use when they go to the square to watch a fête. We saw nothing as we alighted and went up the stairs, for all the windows had been shuttered, but when we got to a room over-looking the square we were overcome, and when we stepped out onto the balcony I was quite speechless for seven or eight minutes.

This square is bigger than anything I have seen in Paris or else-where, and is longer than it is broad. The houses round it are all uni-form: five stories high with regular windows giving on to wrought-iron balconies which are all alike. On each of these balconies[1] were two great torches of white wax, fixed to the sides and tilted forward so that they appeared to be balanced in thin air. The light which they gave was incredible, and the whole scene was magnificent. You could read the smallest print anywhere in the square.

As soon as I appeared on the balcony the populace in the square crowded round and shouted, 'Señor, toro, toro!' They wanted me to obtain permission for a bull fight which is the thing they love most in life and which the King for some years had forbidden because it was against his conscience. I contented myself with just mentioning to the King the next day what had happened, and remarked on how over-whelmed I had been by the splendour of the illuminations.

I had scarcely time to go home and have supper before I had to go to the palace for the ball which the King had had arranged in the salon of the Grandees and which lasted until two in the morning.

Two days after the signing of the marriage deed Saint-Simon learned that Mlle Montpensier had left Paris, and he hastened to tell the King and Queen the good news. He had the unusual experience of being received by them when they were still in bed, both wearing night caps and the Queen sitting up doing a piece of needlework. Not long afterwards Saint-Simon caught smallpox and was in quarantine for six weeks, but he recovered with no ill effects. On the 9th of January 1722 there was an exchange of the two Princesses on the Île des Faisans in the Bidassoa river, between France and Spain, and on the 22nd the Prince of the Asturias and Mlle de Montpensier were married. There was general celebration, and a week later Saint-Simon's younger son, now fully re-covered from his illness, was created a Grandee of Spain. The next eight weeks Saint-Simon spent in sight-seeing, then on the 21st of March he took his formal leave of Their Catholic Majesties and three days later set out once more for France. His embassy was over, but he had made many friends in Spain with whom he corresponded regularly for years to come.

---

[1] There were 680 round the square in all.

1722

RETURN OF THE COURT TO VERSAILLES

✣✣✣✣✣ T was finally decided that the King should give up living in
✣ *G* ✣ Paris for good, and that the Court should move to Ver-
✣ ✣ sailles. The King proceeded there in state on the 15th of June,
✣✣✣✣✣ and the Infanta on the following day. They occupied the
apartments of the late King and Queen respectively;[1] the Maréchal
de Villeroy was lodged in the rooms next to the King's study. The
Cardinal Dubois had the entire apartments of the office of works to
himself, as Colbert and Louvois had had before him; he busied himself with his project of becoming Prime Minister, and to this end he
intended to isolate the Duc d'Orléans as far as he could. Life in Paris
made it easy for the Regent to see people for whom there was no room
at Versailles and indeed could not even be received there, and the
move would also interrupt the suppers with the rakes and the women
who hung around them. The Cardinal knew quite well that the Duc
d'Orléans would slip away to Paris as often as possible and that the
intrusion of state affairs would be a constant inconvenience; this interference with his pleasures would soon bore him and incline him
towards buying his liberty by the simple expedient of appointing the
Cardinal Prime Minister. Once he was in office he knew that he had
nothing more to fear from his master's departure to Paris, where the
Duke would drown himself once more in the opera and his disgraceful
suppers to the exclusion of all thought of duty. The Duc d'Orléans
occupied the rooms of the late Monseigneur on the ground floor, and
the Duchess went back to those she had always had above, next to the
Duke's old rooms which were unoccupied.

ARREST OF THE MARÉCHAL DE VILLEROY

*Cardinal Dubois was busily engaged in removing his enemies who stood as
obstacles between himself and the position of Prime Minister which he intended
to have. He procured the exile of the Duc de Noailles, and next turned his attention to the Maréchal de Villeroy.*

---

[1] Those of the King were immediately above the main entrance in the Cour de Marbre,
those of the Queen immediately to their left as one faces the entrance.

CARDINAL Dubois soon decided that he would never be able to persuade the Duc d'Orléans to dispense with the Maréchal de Villeroy. He was so well aware of the difficulties and dangers that he had really given up the idea. Every day which passed without his being appointed Prime Minister seemed like a year, yet he knew that he could not press for the appointment in the face of the terrific opposition which would come from the Maréchal de Villeroy and his supporters. Worrying over this problem made the Cardinal even more impossible than usual and led to his complete neglecting of even the most important state business. He finally made up his mind to have one more go at the Marshal. But as he did not dare to do anything on his own, he decided to enlist Cardinal de Bissy who was very much on his side because his attitude over the Constitution and the King's confessional had so endeared him to the Jesuits. Dubois explained all his difficulties and what he had had to put up with from the Marshal; he dwelt upon the benefits which would ensue from his being able to get on with his work instead of being constantly sniped at by Villeroy, and he represented that nothing would give him greater pleasure than to be reconciled with the Marshal.

The close friendship which had existed between the Marshal, the Cardinal and Mme de Maintenon, the intrigues over the Constitution as well as their mutual dislike of Cardinal de Noailles had led to a close friendship between Villeroy and Bissy. The ambitious prelate was not slow in seizing on a straightforward and respectable mission on which he could do himself a bit of good. Having come up the hard way, Bissy looked upon his eminence as a stepping stone to greater things; he wanted to do something for his nephew[1] and now that cardinals were admitted to the Council he wanted to be one of the chosen few. He thought that if he could help to draw this tiresome thorn from the Cardinal's flesh and at the same time do a service to the Maréchal de Villeroy, who was so near to the Regent, he had nothing to lose.

He therefore went to work on the Marshal, who as a result asked for an interview with the Cardinal. The two cardinals were in the seventh heaven. Dubois asked Bissy to tell the Marshal that he was very moved and would be delighted to call upon the Marshal at any time. Bissy was delighted to convey this message, and as a result the Marshal invited Bissy to accompany him on a visit to Dubois. This visit took place on a Tuesday morning when I normally stayed at home at Meudon, but it happened that on that particular day I had something to talk to the Regent about at Versailles. Bissy and Villeroy

[1] The Marquis de Bissy, at that time a humble Brigadier.

found the Cardinal's anteroom full of diplomats, for this was the day when he received foreign ambassadors.[1] By long-established custom they were received in the order in which they arrived, and not by precedence. When Bissy and Villeroy arrived they found that Dubois was closetted with the Russian ambassador. They wanted to send a message in that the Maréchal de Villeroy had arrived, but he would not have it and sat down to wait on a settee with Cardinal Bissy.

When the audience was over Dubois emerged from his study to see the Russian Ambassador out, and noticed at once these two sitting quietly together. He ran over and there was a flurry of compliments. He made his apologies to the waiting Ambassadors, explaining that the Marshal's time away from the King was limited, and invited them both inside.

When they had entered the study there was a further exchange of compliments, but as they progressed the Maréchal de Villeroy became enamoured of the sound of his own voice and began to let fly a few home truths. Dubois was so surprised that he did not even seem to grasp what was being said to him. But as the Marshal got into his stride Bissy interrupted and tried to remind him of what they were there for. But the Marshal by now was in full flood and it went to his head: from criticism he progressed to the wildest insults. The absolute impropriety of insulting someone in his own house, particularly when the object of the exercise was to achieve a reconciliation, made Bissy wonder what on earth was going on and drove Villeroy himself on deeper and deeper. Having got all his complaints off his chest he went on to threats and a torrent of scorn. 'You are all-powerful,' he said. 'Everyone bows to you, nothing can stand up to you; compared with you who has any stature in the country? Believe me, there is just one thing that you haven't done yet, and you had better get around to it quickly so that you can have a bit of peace and quiet: have me arrested —if you dare. What are you waiting for? Have me arrested, I tell you, that is one thing you haven't done!' And so he went on abusing and insulting the man who quite sincerely thought to have him arrested would open for himself the gates of heaven. You can imagine that all this did not go on without frequent remonstrances from Bissy, but he had no chance of stopping the torrent. Finally, beside himself with rage, he seized the Marshal by the arm and shoulder and propelled him out of the room. Dubois more dead than alive followed as best he could. All three of them composed themselves as best they could,

[1] The Secretary of State has always been at home to foreign ambassadors on Tuesday mornings, a custom which has continued into the present.

but even so it was obvious to all the ministers in the anteroom that there had been a violent quarrel and the news quickly flashed round Versailles—augmented by the public derision and boasting of Villeroy himself.

Meanwhile I had been working with the Duc d'Orléans and we went on talking for some time afterwards. He had gone into his dressing room and I stayed behind in the study collecting up my papers when the Cardinal Dubois came in like a tornado, his eyes popping out of his head; seeing that I was alone, he demanded to know where the Duc d'Orléans was. I said that he was in his drawing room and asked what on earth was the matter. 'I am undone, I am undone!' he cried and made off for the dressing room. His voice was so loud that the Duke had heard him and came running out; they met in the doorway, and the Duke came back into the middle of the room asking what was going on. The Cardinal's reply took a long time, for his normal stammer was made much worse by his absolute rage, and he ended up by saying that after such a premeditated insult the Duc d'Orléans would have to choose between him and the Maréchal de Villeroy, for after what had happened there was no room at court or in public affairs for the two of them.

I cannot describe the astonishment which the Duc d'Orléans and I felt; we could not believe our ears. The Duc d'Orléans asked a few questions, and I did too, trying to get things straight. Livid as he was, there was no ambiguity or contradiction in what Dubois said; he was quite ready to send for Bissy to bear him out. The Cardinal absolutely insisted, and the Duc d'Orléans, most embarrassed, asked me my opinion, as someone who had always been opposed to the dismissal of the Marshal. I replied that I was so shaken by what we had just been told that I would need time to collect my thoughts.

The Cardinal didn't look at me, but concentrated on the Duc d'Orléans who he saw was in an awkward position; he insisted that he must make up his mind; the Duke turned to me again. I finally said that I had always regarded the dismissal of the Maréchal de Villeroy as extremely dangerous, for reasons which I had explained often enough, and I still felt the same now that the King was older and had nearly reached his majority, but I had to admit that after the appalling scene which we had had described to us it seemed even more dangerous to leave such a man close to the King; his action was tantamount to drawing his sword on the Duc d'Orléans, and his ironic demand for arrest indicated that he knew well enough he deserved it but felt secure in the knowledge that it would never happen. I added that the Marshal had never ceased to lobby against the Duc d'Orléans from the first day of the Regency, and it now seemed that he intended to throw off his mask and come out in open opposition; since His Royal Highness asked my opinion, I would say, without having had time for mature consideration, that the Marshal should be relieved of his office, but in due time in order to make sure that nothing went wrong.

While I was speaking the Cardinal was all eyes and ears, drinking in my words like someone listening to his own sentence. My views pleased him, so far as his fury would permit. The Duc d'Orléans approved of what I had said, and the Cardinal, darting me a look of gratitude, urged haste as things could not be left as they were for long. It was finally agreed to spend the rest of the day working out ways and means, and I was to come back at half-past three the following afternoon.

When I arrived the next day I found Cardinal Dubois already with the Regent. Monsieur le Duc came in a moment later; he knew all about it, but the Cardinal, now rather more composed than he had been the day before, insisted on giving him a short version of what had happened. After some further discussion Cardinal Dubois left. The Duc d'Orléans sat down at his desk and Monsieur le Duc and I sat opposite. The Duc d'Orléans summed up the pros and cons of the matter very well without any marked bias one way or the other, but he seemed embarrassed and consequently very undecided. He went over the relations between himself and the Maréchal de Villeroy from the very day of the late King's death, but he kept it short because he was addressing two people who really knew as much about it as he did. The real point for discussion was which presented the lesser danger—to leave him where he was or dismiss him. After a short résumé the Duc d'Orléans asked me to express my views. I replied that I still felt as I did the evening before, and the more I thought about it the more certain I became that after what had happened the danger of leaving the Maréchal de Villeroy about the King's person infinitely outweighed the dangers of dismissing him, great as those might be. I said that the Marshal had always seemed to me to be possessed of a rather ineffectual ill-will, to be mixed up in a lot of intrigue badly conceived and incompetently pursued, and to spend his time with a timid lot who dissolved into pitiful excuses and protestations at the slightest frown from the Regent; so long as he did no more than that I had thought that he was doing no harm in strutting about theatrically. But this recent scene put a new complexion on things; here was a man who had been treated with every respect by Cardinal Dubois and who had gone to the interview, with Cardinal de Bissy as intermediary, intending to make the peace, yet had been so completely carried away by the sound of his own voice as to lose his head completely, and after starting by showing great wisdom had ended up like a lunatic, ranting like a drunkard beating his head against a wall or taking on an army single-handed. Puffed up with his own importance and delighted that Cardinal Dubois had made overtures to him, he had persuaded himself that he was indispensable and could say and do what he liked. I added that it was possible that he had deliberately deceived Cardinal de Bissy and had gone with the intention of insulting an unpopular minister and so raising himself in public esteem. But whatever he had had in his mind, the result was the same. He had taken sides against the Regent and had crossed the Rubicon in no uncertain manner. To put up with him would be to show an unbearable weakness and encourage all the malcontents and those who had expectations from the King's majority to unite. It would strengthen the *Parlement* and undermine the Government's authority both at home and abroad. Thus I finished my short speech, to which the Regent had listened most attentively although he looked very uncomfortable.

When I had done he asked Monsieur le Duc for his views. Monsieur le Duc said that he agreed with me and said that if the Marshal were left in office the Regent might as well pack up—those were his words. He added that there was not a moment to lose.

The Duc d'Orléans then asked my views as to how it should be done. I said that it divided itself under two headings: the pretext and the actual execution. The pretext had to appear impartial, something to which the Marshal's friends could not take exception; above all there should be no suspicion that his disgrace was in any way connected with his insulting the Cardinal, for if this were so the punishment would obscure the hurt which had been done and there would be a public outcry. There must be no hasty action following on the heels of and inevitably connected with these terrible insults, and happily the Regent had just the right excuse ready to hand—an excuse known to everyone, an excuse to which there was no answer. I reminded the Duc d'Orléans that he had complained to me several times that it was impossible for him to talk to the King alone in his study, and if he wanted to discuss really private matters the Maréchal de Villeroy was always listening in on the grounds that by virtue of his position he could not let anyone, not even His Royal Highness, speak in such a way to his charge: and this to the Regent, a Grandson of France, was an unparalleled and insufferable insult. Affairs of State involved many matters which were for no one else's ears, not even those of the Maréchal de Villeroy, and to claim that nobody could speak to the

481

King on any subject without his being party to the conversation was the last word in insolence. The Regent, I said, should utterly reject this, speak to the Marshal as he had not been spoken to before, and make it clear that he himself by the authority and in the name of the King was master of the realm. This to the public would be reason enough for action, but, I said, once it had been arranged it must be done properly.

'You have taken the words out of my mouth,' the Regent said, 'that is what I was going to suggest. What do you think, Monsieur?'

Monsieur agreed with what I had suggested and said that he saw no alternative to carrying out the plan as soon as possible.

It was then agreed that the Marshal should be arrested on these grounds and sent at once to Villeroy where, because of his age, he should be allowed to rest for a couple of days before being sent on to Lyons or somewhere. I added that the question of a new tutor to take his place must not be forgotten, and it must be someone who was certain to be loyal to the Duc d'Orléans. The Duke asked me to go and work out the details with Cardinal Dubois whom I would find waiting for me. I had not seen the Cardinal or any of his minions for some time, except for the few minutes recently in the Regent's presence. But the way the Duc d'Orléans spoke made me think that he and the Cardinal had agreed on the arrest of the Marshal before this conference, which was only held to give Monsieur le Duc and me the opportunity of coming to the same conclusion without the Cardinal being present.

I went at once to see Cardinal Dubois, and was extremely surprised at the company which I found there, all of whom he told me were in the secret. There was the Maréchal de Berwick, who had just arrived from Guyenne, the Cardinal and Prince de Rohan, Le Blanc and Belle-Isle. Le Blanc's presence was essential because he would be responsible for the arrangements; he was a resourceful man, full of ideas, and had long been party to all the Regent's secret operations. As for Belle-Isle, he saw so little of the Regent, who did not like him, that I thought him rather out of place. I was astonished to see the Maréchal de Berwick there because in the old King's time he had been rather a protégé of the Maréchal de Villeroy who, knowing his master's predilection for bastards of blue blood, had been largely responsible for his rapid promotion in the service, and the two of them had always been very friendly. Cardinal Dubois always treated the Rohan brothers with the greatest respect and he had brought them in as a mark of distinction. I have never seen such scandalously ill-concealed pleasure and bitterness as they displayed; all the spleen came pouring out

Arrest of the Maréchal de Villeroy

which had built up over the breaking of the engagement between their lame daughter and the Duc de Retz[1] and had been further increased by his immediately marrying the elder daughter of the Duc de Luxembourg.

I will not go over all that was discussed and agreed at this little meeting, because it all went off according to plan. I will only say that as soon as I sat down Cardinal Dubois told me that everyone present was in the secret, that I could speak without reserve, and that they were longing to hear what the Duc d'Orléans had decided—as if he didn't know. I told him very shortly. The discussion on ways and means which followed was very long, and I took little part in it; most of the talking was done by Cardinal Dubois and Le Blanc. The Maréchal de Berwick was not so guarded as I would have expected; I think that he had got rather tired of the patronizing air which the Maréchal de Villeroy affected towards him, and which he had decided he could well do without. I arranged with Le Blanc that as soon as the deed had been done he would send a messenger to Meudon to enquire after my health, and I would know from this meaningless compliment that the Marshal was in the bag.

I went back to Meudon that evening, where we always had a number of guests for dinner or supper. The sole topic of conversation was the scene which the Maréchal had created; he was universally blamed for his behaviour, but in the ten days which followed before his arrest I do not think any one suspected that the matter was to be taken any further. I was delighted at the general tranquility, which helped to reassure the Maréchal de Villeroy and made matters easier.

Three or four days later I saw the Duc d'Orléans again and he told me that in the absence of anyone better, and bearing in mind my advice, he had decided to appoint the Duc de Charost tutor to the King; he had seen the Duke who had been delighted to accept and had gone off to shut himself in his rooms at Versailles so that he would not get involved and would be ready to assume his duties at the crucial moment.

On Sunday the 12th of August after dinner the Duc d'Orléans went to work with the King as he always did on so many days each week, and as it was summer he went after he had had his walk. The business in hand was to run over a number of vacant appointments and to make recommendations for the filling of them, together with a few foreign despatches. At the end of this, at which it was customary for the

---

[1] The Marquis de Villeroy, son of the Marshal, who became Duc de Retz after he married Mlle de Luxembourg.

Maréchal de Villeroy and sometimes the Bishop of Fréjus to be present, the Regent asked the King if he would be pleased to step into the small study as he had something private to say. The Maréchal de Villeroy at once objected, and the Duc d'Orléans could not have been more pleased as he saw him walk into the trap. With great politeness he pointed out to the Marshal that the King was so nearly of age that it was time he should begin to assume some authority by having laid before him confidential matters which could be for his ear alone. In fact, the Regent added, he probably ought to have begun this policy earlier, and the fact that he had not was entirely out of deference to the Marshal. The Marshal puffed and blew and shook his wig; he thought he knew, he said, the respect owed to the Regent, but that he was by virtue of his office responsible for the King's person and therefore could not allow His Royal Highness to speak to the King in private because he himself must know whatever was said; much less could he allow them to speak together in another room, for his duty forbade him to let the King out of his sight for a moment.

At this the Regent looked straight at him and said that he was not only under a misapprehension but was also forgetting himself, that he would do well to ponder the weight of his own words, and that only the respect due to the royal presence prevented him from being told baldly what he deserved; then the Regent said that he would say no more, bowed low to the King, and abruptly left the room.

The Marshal, furious, trotted along for a few paces muttering and gesticulating without the Duc d'Orléans showing any sign that he either heard or saw him. The King looked astonished and the Bishop of Fréjus sniggered. Although he had swallowed the bait, it seemed unlikely that the Marshal would fail to detect the difference between insulting the Cardinal Dubois, whom everyone disliked, and flouting the authority of the Regent himself in the very presence of the King. This was indeed so. Less than two hours later the Marshal, while boasting of what he had done, was adding that he would consider himself unfortunate if the Duc d'Orléans thought him lacking in respect when he was only trying to do his duty, and he would call the following morning to clear matters up and he was sure that the Duke would be satisfied with his explanation.

All arrangements had been made in preparation for the day when the trap was to be set for the Marshal. It was only necessary to add the final touches when it became known that evening that the Marshal proposed to walk into the trap of his own accord. Beyond the bedroom of the Duc d'Orléans was a large and handsome study with four big French windows opening on the garden. This study formed a corner where members of the Court waited, and next to it was a small study where the Duc d'Orléans worked and called in anyone distinguished or favoured to whom he wished to speak.

The word was given. Artagnan, Captain of the Grey Musketeers, was in this room and knew exactly what he had to do; he had gathered a group of reliable officers and men who knew from these preparations that something was up but did not know what. Outside the windows he had posted a detachment of Light Horse. Many members of the Duc d'Orléans's household were assembled in the bedroom and the big study.

At midday the Maréchal de Villeroy arrived with his usual fuss and bustle; he was alone, for he had left his chair and attendants beyond the guardroom. He strutted in, stopped, looked round, and walked on a few paces; out of politeness those present followed in his wake. He asked in an authoritative tone whether the Duc d'Orléans was free; he was told that his door was closed and he was working. The Marshal raised his voice and said that he had to see him and was going in; as he started forward La Fare, Captain of the Duc d'Orléans's Guards, stepped in front of him, told him he was under arrest and asked for his sword. The Marshal flew into a rage, and there was a general disturbance. At that moment Le Blanc entered. A chair, which had been kept hidden, was planted in front of Villeroy, he shouted in protest, but, as his legs could no longer support him, he was picked up and bundled into it. In a flash he was carried out into the garden, La Fare and another officer on either side, and the Musketeers and Light Horse fell in behind. They hurried down the steps of the orangery, the great gate was open and a carriage was waiting; the raging Marshal was tossed into it. Artagnan rode beside the carriage, a Musketeer officer in front with du Libois, one of the Gentlemen-in-Ordinary to the King, beside him; twenty Musketeers with mounted officers surrounded the coach, and off they went.

That side of the garden was deserted in the noonday sun; but considering the number of people who were in the Regent's apartments at the time, although they quickly dispersed, it is extraordinary that the arrest did not become generally known at Versailles for some two hours. The Maréchal de Villeroy's servants, to whom no one had dared to say a word, were still waiting by the guardroom with their Master's chair; and those of his household who were waiting for him in his own rooms behind the King's study were in complete ignorance until the Duc d'Orléans sent them word that the Marshal had gone to Villeroy and that they had better take him whatever he would need. At Meudon I received the prearranged message just as I had sat down to dinner, but it was not until nearly supper time that people arrived from Versailles to tell us what had happened. There was considerable surprise and consternation.

CORONATION OF LOUIS XV

THE time for the Coronation was rapidly approaching. From the way things had gone under the Regency I realized that the Coronation, the one occasion on which the rank and standing of the peers has always been most evident, would on this occasion bring them nothing but ignominy. The main blow had been struck by the edict of 1711 which laid down that the Princes of the Blood, and failing them the Royal Bastards and their descendants, should represent the hereditary peerage in preference to any other peers at a coronation. The ignorance, bad faith and proved ill-will of the Grand Master of Ceremonies, the pride of Cardinal Dubois whose sole interest was to exalt the position of the cardinals, and the Duc d'Orléans's taste for mixing up ranks on principle did nothing to reassure me. Nevertheless I decided to speak to the Regent about it; I made representations and was met with nothing but embarrassment, muttering and a mind obviously made up.

Cardinal Dubois evidently knew that I had spoken to the Duc d'Orléans and was not satisfied, for he approached me and tried to get me to expect marvels. He was afraid of what did in fact happen. He wanted to flatter me and then leave the dukes standing in the crowd. He pressed me further, and in the end I told him what I thought; he backed and filled, talked in general terms about dignity and the necessity for the peers being present and promised that they would be treated properly. I told him that all he had said added up to nothing, and that it was not my idea to go to the Coronation merely to be insulted; if the Duc d'Orléans wanted the dukes to be present he should summon them properly and sign a proper declaration in duplicate in the presence of witnesses, and furthermore he should give precise instructions to the Grand Master of Ceremonies.

Dubois had no intention of being committed in this way because he wanted to trap the dukes and then laugh at them, and he said that a promise would be just as good as the written word. I replied shortly that what had happened over the hats and a few similar incidents had made it abundantly clear how much one could rely on solemn promises, and he could either get matters put down in writing or else do without the presence of people whom he seemed to regard as useless passengers. The Cardinal then turned on his most persuasive tone,

486

but it made no impression on me. The Duc d'Orléans also asked me if
I were not coming and, without daring or wishing to importune me,
did his best to persuade me. When both of them realized that I could
not be moved, the Cardinal tried to get me to promise that I would
not prevent the other dukes from attending, bearing in mind what a
serious effect their absence would have. I replied that it was he and
the Regent who were preventing the dukes from attending by neglecting the due solemnities; furthermore I said that I had no control
over the other dukes, but I knew their duty and nothing would make
me change my views.

I had already discovered, more easily than I ever hoped, that not
one of them would go to Reims or to any of the other churches or to
any festivity unless he held a specific office which made it impossible
for him to absent himself. Once I was certain of this I went to take my
leave of the Duc d'Orléans and to say good-bye to the Cardinal Dubois
four or five days before the King left for Reims; I said that I was going
to La Ferté, and I left the following day. Both of them tried hard to
persuade me to go to Reims; and when they found that they could
not, they asked me if I would go to Villers-Cotterêts where the Duc
d'Orléans was giving a series of magnificent fêtes. I replied modestly
that since it was impossible for me to attend the Coronation I should
be very out of place at the festivities. I had agreed with all the dukes
that no one other than those on duty would go either to Reims or
Paris, and they all faithfully carried out this undertaking. I went off to
La Ferté about a week before the King's departure and did not come
back until about ten days after his return.

The Coronation was a shambles, and contrary to every precedent.
It struck one at once that every effort had been made to keep out those
who had the right to be present; the preference had been given to the
judiciary and only those nobles had been summoned whose presence
was essential by virtue of their offices. The same lack of any sort of
order marked the ceremonies at Reims from the first vespers to the
final service on the following day, the royal festivities and the state
procession. I do not know what was in the Bastards' minds but neither
the Duc du Maine, his two sons, nor the Comte de Toulouse was
present. The Comte de Toulouse was begged to go, but he flatly refused and stayed at Rambouillet. Of the six cardinals present in Paris
only Noailles was not invited; this was a gesture from Dubois to the
Cardinal de Rohan and the Constitution *Unigenitus* which had helped
him towards his hat. Rohan thus found himself the senior of the four
cardinals present.

The ecclesiastical peers had two claims to the senior position on their side. Without question they, with the lay peers, played the principal part throughout the ceremony, and since the Archbishop of Reims was the officiating priest in his own cathedral the five others sat in line with him. Coronation precedent was a third reason. Cardinal Dubois wished to draw attention to his elevation to the Sacred College and to shine among his colleagues. He did not wish to seat the cardinals behind the ecclesiastical peers nor did he dare put them in front as that would interfere with the ceremony. So he compromised by having a bench set up for them behind the ecclesiastical peers but raised so that there would be nothing between them and the high altar and the last cardinal—Polignac—would not be hidden by the Archbishop of Reims and his attendants. Behind the cardinals were seated the archbishops and bishops with their attendant clergy.

Opposite to the ecclesiastical peers the lay peers were seated; there was no one corresponding to the cardinals. Behind the lay peers were the three marshals chosen to carry the honours; the Maréchal d'Estrées, as the senior, carried the crown. Below and slightly behind them sat the Secretaries of State with nothing in front of them except the extreme end of the bench on which the lay peers were seated. There was one short minute during the ceremony when a stool was placed between them and the peers for the Duc de Charost, but the seniority of their seating was not actually diminished because the Duke only sat there for a matter of minutes as the King's tutor, a position which did not normally exist at the time of a coronation.

The first four seats in the choir were occupied on one side by the four Knights of the Saint-Esprit bearing the four pieces of the offering and on the other by the four barons charged with guarding the holy ampulla. This was a new piece of nonsense purely to indulge their desire to see the ceremony, and on top of it their four equerries were placed in four low seats just below them and bearing their banners embroidered with their arms on one side and those of France on the other, while the Princes of the Blood representing the peers had neither equerries nor banners. The function of the four barons is to fetch the sacred ampulla from the abbey church of Saint-Remi and return it there immediately after the ceremony; their four equerries carrying banners embroidered with their own armorial bearings (not those of France) should precede them and this gives no offence because they form a little procession of their own. The banners are laid up in the abbey church in memory of the honour done to the four barons in charging them with this duty.

Here is another example of the departures from precedent on this occasion. The common people, who comprise the Third Order, have always come into and filled the nave of the cathedral at the moment when the King is led in. Their function, as it used to be in olden times in the Champs de Mars, is to agree to what has been resolved by the other two Orders, the clergy and nobility. As soon as the King takes his place the Archbishop of Reims should turn to all those seated in the choir to ask for the permission of the nation, and all those present in the nave are presumed to give their tacit support to the assent given by those in the choir; contrary both to precedent and to symbolic meaning, on this occasion the public was not admitted until the King was enthroned.

Two crowns are used in the ceremony: the great Crown of Charle-magne and a second, jewel-encrusted, made to fit the King. The great Crown is too big to wear and is only used symbolically during the ceremony. At one point the Archbishop of Reims places it over the King's head and the twelve peers in waiting support it each with one hand, and the King is led thus to his throne. When the King is enthroned each of the peers in turn kisses him on the cheek in full view of the assembled multitude and then, turning towards the nave, cries 'Long live King Louis XV!' and the crowd replies, 'Long live King Louis XV!' As each shout goes up a twelfth of the doves brought in cages for the purpose are released and a twelfth of the allotted sum of money is thrown to the people.

These proclamations of the peers to the people, the release of the birds and the distribution of money were all omitted; the reasons are obvious and I will not go into them. Nor will I speak of the fanfares and the artillery salute which should have accompanied each proclamation so that with each shout from the assembly doubling and redoubling, the nave should have rung with a mounting splendour of sound; there was none of this.

As soon as the King is enthroned the great crown is laid aside by whoever is charged with the honour of carrying it. Then the King himself takes the small crown and places it on his own head; he takes it off and lays it aside as occasion demands, such as when he goes to the altar to make the offering and to receive the sacrament.

Mistakes were also made at the royal banquet which followed the Coronation, or if they were not mistakes they were innovations which had not occurred at any previous coronation. When the King returned to his apartments from the cathedral his gloves had to be burned because with them he had touched the sacrament, and his shirt also for the same reason; in fact he changed his clothes completely, then assumed his royal mantle and retained the small crown. The gloves were taken off and burned, it is true; so was the shirt, but according to precedent the King should not have taken this off until after the banquet when, retiring to his own rooms, he should remove the coronation robes and never wear them again. Some Kings have been known to change their shirts before the banquet, but they still dressed again in the robes which they wore in the cathedral in order to attend the banquet. So this was an unfortunate precedent.

There was one more blunder which sprang from the habit of letting everyone do as he liked. The room always used for the royal banquet was enormous and L-shaped; so that those dining round the corner could not see what was going on at the top table. The long leg of the 'L' was plenty big enough and normally contained the tables allocated to foreign ambassadors and the Great Chamberlain. But Le Tellier when he was Archbishop of Reims used the palace a great deal and, since he found the shape of this immense baroque room uncomfortable, he had it divided into two without thinking of the purposes for which it might be needed. The question now arose as to where the ambassadors were to be seated; they could not be in the same room as the King without being crowded together right under his nose, nor could they be removed to a respectful distance without finding themselves in the next room. In the end they were put in the same room as the King's table in line with, but below, the two tables of the peers temporal and spiritual, which led to a further nonsense because the suffragan bishops of Reims who for the first time were seated with the peers spiritual thus found themselves placed higher than their superiors, the ambassadors and the Great Chamberlain, and, what was even more ridiculous, higher than the Chancellor. Furthermore it was quite ridiculous to seat the two marshals of the diplomatic corps in full view of the King on an occasion like this, both because their office is comparatively unimportant and because they should have been with the ambassadors.

I will not go on about the infinite number of other mistakes which were made; nor will I say anything about the superb fêtes which the Duc d'Orléans and Monsieur le Duc gave for the King at Villers-Cotterêts and Chantilly on their return from Reims.

1723

DECLINING HEALTH OF THE
DUC D'ORLÉANS

✤✤✤✤✤ HEN the court returned to Versailles I was given the new
✤ W ✤ Château at Meudon, fully furnished. The Duc and Du-
✤ W ✤ chesse d'Humières were staying with us, and they were
✤✤✤✤✤ very good company. He wanted me to take him over one
morning to Versailles to thank the Regent, who had just bestowed
upon him at my request the governorship of Boulogne which had
fallen vacant through the death of the Duc d'Aumont.

We found the Regent in his dressing room at stool surrounded by
his servants and two or three senior officials. I was horrified by his
appearance. His head was sunk on his chest, his complexion purple
and a besotted expression on his face which I had not seen before.
When he was told I was there he slowly turned his head without raising
it and asked thickly what I wanted. I told him. I had come in to ask
him if he would go to his living room so as not to keep the Duc
d'Humières waiting, but I was so astounded that I stopped short. I
took Simiane, First Gentleman of the Bedchamber, across to the window and expressed my surprise and fear for the Duke's health. Simiane
replied that for a long time he had been like this in the morning, to-day
was no worse than usual, and that he would be all right when he had
pulled himself together and got dressed.

He did not seem much better, though, when he was finally dressed
and came out. He received the thanks of the Duc d'Humières in a
heavy, dazed way and scarcely answered—he who had always been
the most polite man in the world, never at a loss for the perfect and
gracious reply. A moment later we withdrew. We dined with the Duc
de Gesvres who was to take the Duc d'Humières to offer his thanks to
the King.

The Regent's condition made me think very seriously. For some
time the Secretaries of State had been telling me that in the morning
they could get him to sign anything even if it were against his own
interest. It was entirely the result of his suppers. He himself had told
me more than a year before, when we were working together and he
had to keep getting up and leaving the room, that Chirac purged him
constantly because his stomach was so overloaded that otherwise he

had no appetite when he sat down to table—and this in spite of the fact that he ate nothing in the morning and took nothing at all during the day except a cup of chocolate between one and two o'clock. I had remonstrated with him then, but it was quite useless. I know Chirac had told him that continuing with these suppers could only end in one of two ways—apoplexy or dropsy of the chest (for his breathing was already becoming affected). He merely said that he hoped it would not be dropsy which led to a slow, suffocating death, but that he would prefer apoplexy which killed suddenly before one had time to think.

Anyone else, instead of being choosy about the way he was going to die, would have taken himself in hand and led a sober and decent life, in which case his constitution was so strong that he would probably have recovered and have lived happily for years to come. But he was blind to his own welfare.

SUDDEN DEATH OF THE DUC D'ORLÉANS

WE know that the Duc d'Orléans dreaded a lingering death which was known to be inevitable—although a long illness can be a blessing to those who can take advantage of it—and he always wanted to die suddenly. Alas! His wish was granted and his end was quicker even than that of Monsieur.

I went from Meudon to see him at Versailles on the 2nd of December immediately after dinner; I had three quarters of an hour alone with him in his study. We walked up and down talking over political affairs on which he had to report to the King later that day. I found him heavy and dull as he had been recently, but otherwise unchanged, and his mind was as clear as ever. After that I went straight back to Meudon. I talked with my wife for a while; we were alone, for the weather was against inviting visitors; then she went to her study and I to mine.

About an hour later I heard voices raised and a sudden commotion. I went out and found my wife in a state of alarm with one of the Marquis de Ruffec's grooms who had just come from Versailles to tell me that the Duc d'Orléans had apoplexy. I was very upset but hardly surprised: we had expected it for some time. I sent for my carriage, flung myself in it and set off as fast as I could. At the gates of the park I was stopped by another messenger from the Marquis de Ruffec who told me that all was over. I stayed there for more than half an hour sunk in sadness and reflection. Then I made up my mind to go to Versailles, where I shut myself up in my room. Nangis, who wanted to be first equerry, had succeeded me in the Regent's entourage, and he had a short conversation, being followed by Mme Falari, a pretty adventuress who had married another adventurer, brother of the Duchesse de Bethune; she was one of the mistresses of the late prince. His briefcase was filled with the business which he had to discuss with the King, and he sat talking with her for nearly an hour while waiting for his appointment. As they were sitting close to one another in two arm-chairs, he suddenly slumped beside her and never regained consciousness.

Falari, understandably scared out of her wits, screamed louder and louder for help. As no one heard her, she did what she could for the poor prince and then ran out through the big study, the ante-rooms, without finding anyone, and finally out into the court and the lower galleries. It was the time when the Regent normally worked with the King and no one was on duty because they knew there would be no callers and he mounted alone by the small staircase to the last ante-room, where his briefcase was brought to him. Falari finally found someone, but no one responsible, and she sent messages in all directions by anyone she could. By chance this unhappy event took place at an hour when everyone had gone about his own affairs or was visiting, so that it was fully half an hour before a doctor or surgeon could be found, and almost as long before any of the Duke's servants put in an appearance.

The doctors, as soon as they came, realized that the case was hopeless. They laid him out on the floor and bled him, but he showed no sign of consciousness. As soon as the news became known, every one hurried there and soon the large and small studies were packed. In less than two hours it was all over, and soon the rooms were as silent and deserted as they had so recently been crowded. Once help came, Falari left and got back to Paris as soon as she could.

La Vrillière was one of the first to learn of the disaster. As a courtier who knew how to turn any crisis to his advantage, he hurried off at once to tell the King, the Bishop of Fréjus, and then Monsieur le Duc. Thinking that Monsieur le Duc might well be appointed Prime Minister, he then hurried home to draw up the documents. As soon as he heard finally that the Regent was dead he sent a message to Monsieur le Duc and then went himself to the King, into whose rooms the crisis had brought a huge crowd of people.

As soon as Fréjus heard of the apoplexy he arranged with the King for Monsieur le Duc to be appointed in office, which he must have been thinking about beforehand—especially in view of what I had told him about the Regent's health. Monsieur le Duc arrived as soon as he heard of the death and was admitted to the King's room with a

493

few of the most distinguished of those assembled outside the study. The King was deeply grieved and his eyes red with tears. As soon as they had gone in and the door was shut Fréjus addressed the King and said that in view of the great loss they had suffered in the death of the Duc d'Orléans, in whose praise he said a few words, His Majesty could not do better than to ask Monsieur le Duc to assume the responsibility for public affairs and to accept the office of Prime Minister. The King did not say a word but just looked at Fréjus and nodded; then Monsieur le Duc expressed his thanks. La Vrillière had arrived armed with a copy of the Prime Minister's oath and Monsieur le Duc was sworn in on the spot. Shortly after that Monsieur le Duc and the others present in the study all left, the crowd in the next rooms joined in his train and his name was henceforth on everyone's lips.

The Duc de Chartres, at that time a debauched young puppy, was in Paris with a girl from the Opéra whom he was keeping. A message informing him of his father's apoplexy was sent to him there, and another messenger met him on the road to tell him that his father was dead. When he arrived at Versailles there was no crowd round his carriage, but only the Ducs de Noailles and de Guiche who eagerly offered their services in anything they could do for him. He treated their offer as importunate and, getting away as quickly as he could, he went up to his mother's rooms where he said that he had just met two men who had set a trap for him but he had not fallen for it. This manifestation of intelligence and political judgement was a promise of this prince's future conduct. With great difficulty it was pointed out to him that he had blundered, but he has never changed.

After this terrible night I went to the King's *lever,* not so much to put in an appearance as to make sure of having a word with Monsieur le Duc, with whom I had remained in constant touch since the *lit de justice* at the Tuileries in spite of my displeasure at the promise for the re-establishment of the Bastards which he had allowed to be extracted from him. He always stood in the embrasure of the middle window, opposite to which the King dressed, and as he was tall it was easy to see him over the crowd which packed the *lever,* which that day was prodigious. I made a sign to him to come and talk to me and at once he pushed through the crowd and came over to me. I drew him aside into another window and said that I could not conceal the fact that I was deeply grieved, but at the same time I hoped he would believe that if I had been consulted on the choice of Prime Minister he would indeed have been my recommendation, whereupon he said some kind words. I went on to say that in the briefcase which the Duc d'Orléans should have taken to the King when he was struck down was some-

494

thing on which I would like to consult him, and I begged him to send for me when he had a moment to spare and to have me admitted by the small door of his study opening on the gallery so as to avoid the crowd that would be hanging about in his rooms. He promised to see me that day but said that he was sure I would understand that in the pressure of his first day in office he could not say yet exactly when he would be free. I knew his study and that particular door because his rooms had belonged to the Duchesse de Berry when she was married; they were in the upper gallery of the new wing, opposite the staircase and quite near to my own.

From there I went to find the Duchesse de Sforza, who had always been a friend of mine and with whom I had a lot to do since I no longer saw the Duchesse d'Orléans. I told her that out of respect for the late Duke I thought it only right that I should go to see the Duchess and express my sympathy, that she knew how I felt about the lady—feelings which had not changed—but that on this occasion I felt that I should pay to the Duchess in her widowhood the proper respect, and I asked her to find out if the Duchess would receive me; I said it was a matter of indifference to me personally whether the answer was 'yes' or 'no.' The Duchesse de Sforza said she was sure that the Duchesse d'Orléans would be pleased to receive me and that she would go and ask her. As their rooms were close together, she went straight away and I waited. She came back saying that the Duchesse d'Orléans would be pleased to see me and to receive me in a manner which I would find acceptable. I went at once.

I found the Duchess in bed surrounded by a few of her ladies and senior officials and the Duc de Chartres. As soon as I drew near she spoke of our common loss, but she did not say a word about our personal relations, which was as I had stipulated. The Duc de Chartres soon left and went to his own rooms. I cut my conversation with the Duchess as short as I could, and then went to call on the Duc de Chartres who had the rooms which his father occupied before he became Regent. I was told that he was engaged. I came back three times during the morning. On the last occasion his senior valet, who felt most embarrassed, insisted on going in and telling his master who I was. The Duc de Chartres came to the door of his study, where he was closetted with the sort of common friends he preferred. He seemed stiff and embarrassed and not at all distressed. I expressed my condolence clearly, succinctly and in a firm tone. He apparently bracketed me with the Ducs de Noailles and de Guiche, for he did not do me the honour of replying one single word. I waited a few moments and then, seeing that he was not going to utter, I bowed and withdrew; he did not take one step to accompany me to the door of his apartments as he should have done, but scuttled back into his study. As I went out I looked round and everyone there seemed very surprised. I went back to my own rooms thoroughly bored with chasing round and round the château.

Just as I was finishing dinner a valet came with a message to say that Monsieur le Duc was ready for me, and I was taken in by the back door straight to his study. He came to the door to meet me, shut it, pulled up an arm-chair for me and sat in one himself. I talked over the business which I had mentioned to him that morning, and we then went on to discuss the events of the day. He told me that when he left the King's *lever* he had gone to call upon the Duc de Chartres and, after suitable expressions of condolence, had offered to do everything in his power to deserve his friendship and said that for the sake of his father's memory he felt a real attachment for him. The Duc de Chartres said not a word. He then once more expressed his wish to help in any way possible, to which the Duke merely replied with a monosyllabic 'thanks' and such an air of finality that Monsieur le Duc left at once. I told him what had happened to me in the same way. Monsieur le Duc was extremely amiable and asked me if I would not come to see him frequently. I replied that I did not wish to importune him when he would be weighed down with affairs of State and I would content myself with coming to see him when I had something to say, but I added that I was not very good at waiting in anterooms so I would be grateful if he would instruct his servants to usher me in at the first possible moment after my arrival. Further pleasantries, lasting three quarters of an hour in all, and then I fled to Meudon.

The following day Mme de Saint-Simon went to Versailles to pay her respects to the King, and to see the Duchesse d'Orléans and her son. The Bishop of Fréjus went to see Mme de Saint-Simon as soon as he knew she was at Versailles, where she never passed the night. Through all the nice things which he said about me she got the impression that he would be happier to see me in Paris than Versailles. La Vrillière joined in, and he, being much more frightened of me than was Fréjus, was a good deal more outspoken; he infuriated my wife by his complete lack of any gratitude for all that I had done for him. The wretched creature thought that he had wormed his way into Monsieur le Duc's good books by his willingness to be of service and hence hoped that he had speeded up the dukedom which he expected. Whenever he had raised this subject with me in the days of the Duc d'Orléans my vague replies had always rubbed him up the wrong way. He thought he could pull the wool over Monsieur le Duc's eyes by producing a whole lot of false arguments which he was frightened I could explode in a moment if I wanted to.

A few hints of this kind strengthened the resolution which I had formed as soon as I saw that the health of the Duc d'Orléans was failing. I retired to Paris, determined that I would not serve these new masters except in so far as it was my bounden duty in accordance with all the dignity of my standing. Fortunately for me I had never lost sight of the fact that my position might radically change, and indeed after the death of the Duc de Bourgogne, when I saw the way things were run, I did not care much either way. I saw this beloved prince die at the same relative age as that at which my father had lost Louis XIII : my father was thirty-six when the King died at forty-one, whilst I at twenty-seven saw a prince of rising thirty die when he was ripe to succeed to the throne. Events had prepared me for the time when I might outlive my usefulness, and I always hoped that I would know what to do when it came.

CONCLUSION

AND so I have reached the point at which I intended to end these memoirs. No memoirs are of any use unless they tell the truth, and they cannot be true unless they are written by one who himself has taken part in the events which he describes. And the author must be prepared to sacrifice everything to veracity. On this last point I must say a word for myself, and I do not think that anyone would disagree. It was this very love of truth which was my downfall in life; I often realized it, but I could not temporize—I had to say what I felt, even if it were to my own disadvantage. It is obvious that I was at times taken in and misled, sometimes by friendship and sometimes out of loyalty to the State which I put above all else; there were many other instances of this which I have not bothered to record because they only concerned myself and did not throw any light on the interesting events of the period I have been describing.

As far as impartiality is concerned, a virtue so essential yet so difficult of attainment, I will only say that it is an impossibility if one is describing events in which one has oneself been involved. Everyone likes a man who is upright and straightforward; everyone is irritated by the twisters who exist at every court; and no one can resist bearing a certain malice towards those who have done him wrong. Stoicism is a noble and attractive fantasy. For all that, I have tried to write a straightforward account of what I have seen and I have tried to hold my own emotions and my own prejudices in check.

May I say one last word about my style? Is it careless and repetitious, overloaded with synonyms and involutions? I realize its faults, but, concerned as I have been more with the matter than the manner, I could not help it. I am not a scholar, and I have never got out of the habit of writing fast. To correct and smooth my style would have meant rewriting the whole work, and that is beyond my powers. The ability to correct postulates an ability to write well, and that is something on which I cannot pride myself. The best that I can claim for my memoirs is that they have some sense of rightness and some sensibility, and I hope that for this reason their style may claim the reader's indulgence.